P9-AQJ-156

DISCARDED

READINGS IN
HUMAN LEARNING

[

DISCARDED

READINGS IN
HUMAN LEARNING

Edited by

LESTER D. CROW, Ph.D.

Professor of Education
Brooklyn College

and

ALICE CROW, Ph.D.

Formerly Associate Professor of Education
Brooklyn College

CARL A. RUDISILL LIBRARY
LENOIR RHYNE COLLEGE

DAVID McKAY COMPANY, INC.

New York

154.4
C88r

READINGS IN HUMAN LEARNING

COPYRIGHT © 1963 BY DAVID MCKAY COMPANY, INC.

ALL RIGHTS RESERVED, INCLUDING THE RIGHT TO REPRODUCE
THIS BOOK, OR PARTS THEREOF, IN ANY FORM, EXCEPT FOR
THE INCLUSION OF BRIEF QUOTATIONS IN A REVIEW.

44 742
March, 1963

LIBRARY OF CONGRESS CATALOG CARD NUMBER: 62–18708

MANUFACTURED IN THE UNITED STATES OF AMERICA

Preface

THE LEARNING PROCESS is becoming an increasingly significant area of psychological study. Psychologists recognize the importance of discovering, through observation and experimentation, the *how, why* and *what* of learning in the individual's developing pattern of growth and development. The editors, believing that a need exists for an assemblage of pertinent material on *human learning* deliberately excluded most experimental reports in the area of animal learning. We hope, therefore, that this *Readings* will supplement those that have been prepared on animal learning.

In preparing the *Readings in Human Learning* the editors attempted to select material that would provide sequential steps in the learning process. Attention has been given not only to the kind of material to be included, but also to its authoritative value based on the standing of the men and women whose contributions have been chosen for your study. We hope thereby to be able to help students gain insight into the psychology of learning as garnered from the ideas of these thinkers and writers in psychology.

The *Readings* begins with an explanation of what learning is, and moves quickly to a presentation of the (1) importance of general background in learning, (2) principles and conditions of learning, (3) various theories of learning, and (4) developmental aspects of learning. Careful consideration is given to the impact on learning of intelligence and aptitudes. The effects of interests, attitudes, and motivation are presented in proper perspective. Included also are excerpts from authorities in such other areas of learning as motor learning, thinking and conceptual learning, and creativity in learning. Finally, attention is directed to the significance of evaluation in learning.

The "References" associated with these reading selections are included so that anyone who wishes to do so may continue his research in any given field which is of interest to him.

Readings in Human Learning can be a valuable supplement to a course in General Psychology or can serve as a textbook for a course on the Psychology of Learning.

The editors wish to thank the authors and the publishers who cooperated in granting permission to reprint the material included in this *Readings in Human Learning*.

LESTER D. CROW
ALICE CROW

Contents

READINGS IN
HUMAN LEARNING

1. Meaning and Scope of Learning

LESTER D. CROW AND ALICE CROW,
Brooklyn College

L EARNING is an active process which takes place within the individual and is helped greatly by the stimulating and guiding influences of adults. It is essential to the achievement of an education. For learning to occur, the learner must be so aroused that he will not only initiate the learning activity but will persist in it as well. In the final analysis, all learning is self-initiated. Hence any forces that can induce the learner to utilize and synthesize appropriate stimuli from his environment will be valuable aids to continued learning. In school learning, the teacher has and continues to exert considerable influence upon the nature and extent of an individual's learning.

Learning defined. Learning involves change. It is concerned with the acquisition of habits, knowledge, and attitudes. It enables the individual to make both personal and social adjustments. Since the concept of change is inherent in the concept of learning, any change in behavior implies that learning is taking place or has taken place. Learning that occurs during the process of change can be referred to as the *learning process*.

Learning that occurs as the individual observes or talks with others, reads, reacts mentally, or attempts to solve a problem is viewed as *process*. However, if the focus is on the actual changes that are produced as a result of learning experiences, learning can be viewed as *product*. In other words, learning considered as product refers to the total of changes that result from the summation of interactions between the individual and environmental stimuli.

Learning involves making new associations and developing new ways of doing things. It enables the individual to satisfy interests and to attain worthy goals. It represents behavioral changes as he adapts his behavior effectively to whatever demands are made upon him at any one moment.

The changes that are taking place during learning may be expected to be evidenced in the learner's behavior and to become a part of his total personality. These changes may include the acquisition of items of information, the mastery of simple skills, the mastery of more complicated mechanical performance or of difficult abstract material, and improved emotional or social adjustments.

Aspects of learning. The individual consciously engages in much mental activity and strives for definite learning outcomes. However, as he engages in his daily activities, he often unconsciously acquires new attitudes, modes of thought, and forms of behavior. Many of these experiences are steeped in attitude qualities and may exercise a powerful influence upon his thinking, conduct, and relations with others.

Various aspects of learning are included in the acquisition of motor skill and factual information, and in the formation of attitudinal and behavioral habits. These represent complex interactions as the learner attempts to satisfy his interests or to attain set goals. Something is learned through every experience. The readiness of the learner, the kind and nature of his responses, and his reaction to success or failure determine, in part, the nature and extent of the learning that occurs.

Among the various types of abstract learning can be included (1) the memorization of learning material with little or no understanding of the ideas involved, (2) the formation of simple concepts, and (3) the discovery and understanding of relationships in more complex situations. Learning is demonstrated when the individual can repeat verbatim any learning content or when he can demonstrate understanding by reporting in his own words the ideas contained in the material studied. The former is referred to as *rote learning;* the latter is known as *logical learning.*

The kind of learning that takes place depends upon the approach and purpose of the learning. As the individual attends to new or novel factors in a situation, relates them to past experiences, and evaluates them he gives meaning and understanding to them. Much learning deals with the mastery of subject matter. Reading skill and verbal reproduction are essential to learning to deal effectively with ideas. In order to engage adequately in abstract thinking the learner gradually acquires basic knowledge as a background for the more complex learning situations.

Factors inherent in learning. A change in behavior that results from responses to motivating stimuli implies that the individual is different after having had those experiences. Learning as commonly conceived means not only change but improvement. However, instances can be cited to demonstrate that bad habits rather than good habits can result from improper learning.

Learning situations may be either informal or formal. During informal learning an individual's habit patterns result directly from responses in day-by-day situations. Much of this learning emanates from imitation of others. A child tends to imitate speech patterns, mannerisms, social behavior, or group standards. He tends so to adapt his behavior as to experience satisfaction in his everyday relationships with the people with whom he comes into contact. Informal learning takes place as an individual interacts daily within his home and community environments.

The learning situation which is considered more formal is that of the school. Here the learner can also involve himself in many informal experiences as he shares activities with his schoolmates and enjoys satisfactory relationships with teachers and classmates. The teacher is the key person in the formal learning situation. It is his responsibility (1) to provide the experiences that will facilitate learning, (2) to motivate individual learning, and (3) to provide a learning situation which will enable an individual to develop his learning capacity to the fullest.

Some of the factors that contribute to the amount and kind of learning that is achieved are inherent in the individual's activities; others are embedded in the environment in which the learning occurs. The learner usually is interested in achieving either an immediate or a long-range goal. Individuals constantly are learning new skills or improving those already developed, adding new knowledge, and acquiring new interests, attitudes, or habits of thinking. Interests, attitudes, social sensitivity, health status, and degree of emotional tension are influences that affect the nature and extent of learning in any situation. Hence when these factors are favorable the individual has the greatest chance for learning success. For example, the introduction of the success factor can arouse interest in learning and promote positive attitudes that encourage the learner in his pursuit of an education.

Learning starts with the learner. Any motivation within the individual which makes him receptive to stimulation is essential to goal attainment. This goal may not be reached at once if barriers of one kind or another interfere. When tension arises within the individual, energy is released and he is mentally set or ready to respond. If, however, a barrier prevents an appropriate discharge of energy, tension and sometimes frustration are experienced.

A learner pursues an acceptable line of action to attain his desired learning goal. He utilizes one or more of several possible avenues which are available to him in his striving toward a solution of a problem. Each approach involves an element of chance. Finally, action that proves to be appropriate involves factors such as (1) an element of success in terms of the goal and (2) a feeling of satisfaction and a reduction of tension if or when the motive is satisfied.

2. The Concept of Learning *

JOHN A. McGEOCH, *Late of the State University
of Iowa,* AND
ARTHUR L. IRION, *Tulane University*

The Problem of Definition

In science, as in logic, definition of concepts is of fundamental importance. However, whereas in logic definitions may be arbitrarily constructed according to formal properties, the only form of definition which has proven to be consistently useful in science is the *operational definition.* To be sure, the scientist is allowed a certain amount of arbitrariness in his definition of terms. He is allowed infinite latitude in the varieties, numbers, and complications of the operations he employs in definition. But this is his limit. He may not, without danger, go beyond the defining operations which he performs. Even when he defines the same concept by two different sets of operations, he is bound to construct transformation equations which must inevitably face the criterion of empirical validation. In the psychology of learning the definition of concepts has not always been accomplished with proper care, and defined concepts have not always retained their proper meanings. It is instructive to take the concept of learning, itself, as an example. Most definitions of learning make mention of the fact that learning consists of a change in performance. This change is definable in terms of two separate measurements of the behavior in question, the precautions and controls involved in making such measurements being of small concern to us here. The difficulty arises from the fact that most psychologists do not wish to classify all changes of behavior as learned. The student will immediately think of changes in behavior which he would prefer to designate as negative adaptation, motivational changes, fatigue effects, degenerative changes, changes produced by the maturation of the individual or by environmental variations, and so on. At this point, it is possible to define learning in either of two ways. On the one hand, we can define all changes in behavior which are *not* learned and define learning as the residual variability of behavior. On the other hand, we may take the more direct course and attempt to delimit precisely those behavioral changes which we desire to call learned. In practice, neither course has proven to be entirely satisfactory for the reasons that are outlined below.

An attempt to delimit those changes in behavior which are learned

* From John A. McGeoch and Arthur L. Irion, *The Psychology of Human Learning* (2nd ed.; New York: David McKay Company, Inc., 1952), pp. 4–7.

inevitably involves a statement of the conditions under which those changes occur, there being no other adequate science of delimiting criteria. This places the learning psychologist in a somewhat embarrassing position. On the one hand, he desires to study the conditions under which learning occurs and to estabilsh functional relationships between these conditions and the learning process. On the other hand, he may not study the learning process at all (strictly speaking) unless he makes a preliminary statement of the conditions of learning for definitional purposes. Thus, in a certain sense, he has defined away a large portion of his area of study. Furthermore, it must be noted that, by defining learning in terms of the conditions under which it occurs, the psychologist commits himself to a certain theoretical and systematic position. Thus, learning defined from the standpoint of the reinforcement theorist is a somewhat different concept from learning as defined by the contiguity theorist. If the reinforcement theorist defines learning in terms of a change in behavior which occurs under certain conditions, one of those conditions being the occurrence of reward, he has forever settled the problem (for himself) of whether *learning* can occur in the absence of reward. It is true that changes in *behavior* may take place as a result of sheer contiguity, but these changes are not, under his definition, learned changes. It is apparent that, under these circumstances, there is a considerable opportunity for dispute among psychologists. Many of these disputes may be disguised as being concerned with factual aspects of the learning process. More often than not, however, these arguments actually concern definitions.

In view of these considerations, it is probably not worth-while so early in this work to limit discussion by a rigid definition of the learning process. Probably, also, it is futile to discuss critically the various definitions which have been proposed. Instead, a general statement will be made which will include the phenomena discussed. *Learning, as we measure it, is a change in performance which occurs under the conditions of practice.* What these conditions of practice may be, it is our purpose to explore.

Learning and Retention

It has long been customary to divide the field into two main parts, "learning" or fixation, and "retention." At the level of logical analysis, this division is clear because an act must be fixated before it can be retained. In the learning of complex acts by continued practice, however, our measurements do not often separate fixation from retention, and the two are intermingled in each practice trial after the first. For the sake of convenience, the distinction between learning and retention has been given a different meaning than the logically analytic one, *learning* being used to designate the acquisition of changes in behavior during a specified time or up to a certain level, and *retention* being used to mean any measured persistence of these changes after practice ceases. Any failure of such persistence is called *forgetting*.

The way in which retention pervades learning, as these words are commonly used by psychologists, can be seen in any learning activity requiring more than a single trial, such as the learning of a series of words. The changes in behavior (verbal responses) acquired during the first trial are retained, at least in part, until the second trial. There, new ones are added to those retained; some or all of the results of the first and second trial are retained until the third trial, when more responses are added, and so on, until practice stops. If the results of the practice were not carried over from trial to trial, if they did not accumulate progressively, many trials would yield no more learning than would one trial, alone.

Not all of the acquisitions at each successive trial are carried over to the next; some are forgotten and must be refixated. A curve of learning represents a progressively greater balance in favor of retention, so that it is, in part, a retention curve. In addition to the initial modifications of behavior, which do not involve retention in the sense meant here, the retained modifications are further changed as they are repeated on later trials. Fixation and retention thus mutually interact in the course of what we call learning. It may also be stated briefly here, to be elaborated much later, that learning pervades retention in the sense that one of the conditions of forgetting is the learning of other responses. That is, one forgets by learning other things.

Usage has fixed certain names upon clusters of conditions. These names cannot mislead if one understands clearly what they mean. When studying the acquisition of behavior changes up to some arbitrary criterion, such as two perfect trials in succession, it is customary to speak of "learning" and to disregard in the naming the fact that retention has pervaded the process. Similarly, when performance is measured after an interval of no practice, it is customary to call the results measures of "retention," disregarding the fact that there would have been no learning to be retained had there been no cumulative retention of behavior changes during practice, and disregarding the fact that further learning has been one condition of loss, if any, in retention.

3. Basic Principles in a Good Teaching-Learning Situation *

WILLIAM H. BURTON, *Harvard University*

Differences among Theorists

A simple definition will be adequate for the summary here presented: Learning is a change in the individual, due to the interaction of that individual, and his environment, which fills a need and makes him more capable of dealing adequately with his environment. A technical definition satisfactory to leading theorists in the field would be more difficult to state and is not necessary for our purposes.

The effort to summarize principles of learning which underlie desirable teaching situations is seriously complicated by the fact that there are approximately a dozen learning theories available. No one has yet formulated a systematic theory satisfactory in all respects. But many facts about learning are known and accepted. There is also agreement on the place of experimental procedures for the demonstration of facts and principles. Serious differences between the various theories remain regarding the nature of certain facts, the primacy of other facts, and the interpretation of facts. These differences must, of course, affect any statement of basic theory and principle.

The differences between theorists are due in part to differences in basic viewpoint and accepted premises. Sometimes two or more theories deal with different types of learning problems, different motivations, or other factors, without sufficient attention to, or development of, a systematic theory to cover more ground. Sometimes, even, disagreements will cut across

* From William H. Burton, "Basic Principles in a Good Teaching-Learning Situation," *Phi Delta Kappan* (March, 1958), pp. 242–48. Reprinted by permission.

the groupings of theorists so that some in one camp are in agreement with some in the rival camp and in disagreement with their colleagues. These differences cannot, in the present state of knowledge, be shrugged off when we are dealing with efforts at systematic theory. We can, however, get on with a more limited job of setting up a reasonably consistent statement of principles useful in everyday teaching.

Hilgard [1] has reduced the confusion considerably by classifying the ten or a dozen theories into two basic groups which he labels *stimulus-response* (connectionism, conditioning, behaviorism) and *cognitive* (Gestalt, organismic, sign-significate). Some theories do not fit clearly within either group. He goes on to point out that although no single systematic inclusive theory is as yet available, the situation is not as bad as it seems. He avoids premature systematization on the one hand, and naive eclecticism on the other, showing that something can be learned from the serious efforts of each group of theorists. In any practical situation, as contrasted with efforts to build a systematic theory, this is a sensible view. Pure theory, an absolute necessity for full understanding, is not available. We therefore accept any facts and principles which have been carefully demonstrated and which aid us in understanding and promoting learning.

The succeeding chapters in this symposium will undoubtedly reflect some of the differences in basic theory. The present chapter, assigned as an over-all summary, will follow Hilgard's view and include principles which promise to be useful, regardless of theoretic origin. Every effort will be made, however, to maintain internal consistency in the statement.

Agreements among Theorists

Textbooks on learning and on teaching carry, among them, a considerable list of principles of learning basic to good teaching. It may come as something of a shock to the so-called practical schoolman to discover that learning theorists agree on only a limited number of these principles. Two excellent summaries [2] of agreement among theorists are available. The fifteen or so agreed-upon principles are not reproduced here, since they will be included within the various summaries to follow.

I. THE GENERAL PURPOSES OF LEARNING

The over-all purposes of learning are relevant to the social order within which they operate. We believe in the democratic way of life with its

[1] Ernest R. Hilgard. *Theories of Learning,* revised edition. New York: Appleton-Century-Crofts, 1955. Chapter 1.

[2] Ernest R. Hilgard, *ibid.,* pp. 485–487, and T. R. McConnel, "Reconciliation of Learning Theories," Chapter 7 in *The Psychology of Learning* (Forty-First Yearbook, Part II, National Society for the Study of Education). Bloomington, Ill.: Public School Publishing Co., 1942.

emphasis on (a) opportunity for the fullest development of the unique capacities of the individual, and (b) a socially oriented group within which the individual may realize his destiny. This means that one goal of learning will be the development of creativity, individual initiative and responsibility, and leadership. The other will be the development of social skills and good human relations. The use of experts and of experimentation will be learned within the democratic social process. An extended list of democratic values could be made. The following brief list may be taken as guides for learning, and particularly for teaching:

1. The dignity and worth of the individual is a primary tenet of Judeo-Christian democracy. Respect for the individual is a corollary.

2. The common good of the group is a social aim of democracy. A proper balance should be maintained between the development of the independent individual and the social individual.

3. Obligations as well as rights are inherent in a democracy. The development of a "democratic conscience" in the individual is necessary to such a society.

4. A flexible functioning of the group with freedom for all to contribute is essential to democracy, and hence to the democratic learning process.

5. The process of group discussion, deliberation, and decision on common problems is the process of democracy. Decisions are based on consensus preferably, or on tentative majority decisions when consensus cannot be achieved. (Detailed principles governing group process are summarized separately later.)

II. GENERAL PRINCIPLES OF LEARNING [3]

The principles of learning are worded differently by various psychologists. Readers may substitute any wording or listing they prefer for the composite one given here.

1. The learning process is experiencing, doing, reacting, undergoing. The actual pattern to be learned is the chief aim, but a multitude of varied learning activities and outcomes also occur. Active participation by a learner is preferable to the kind of passive reception usually involved in listening to a lecture or watching a motion picture.

2. Responses during the learning process are modified by their consequences.

---

[3] It is not possible in a short article to cite research background for each principle listed. The two research summaries already noted (Hilgard, and the Forty-First Yearbook, Part II, N.S.S.E.), together with several dozen individual research studies, were consulted. Texts in psychology and in principles of teaching were checked, though these are secondary sources. The two summaries contain bibliographies, Hilgard's alone covering over thirty pages.

3. The learning situation is dominated by a purpose or goal set by the learner, or accepted by him, and should lead to socially desirable results. The purposes and goals arise in the life of the learner.

4. The learning situation, to be of maximum value, must be realistic to the learner, meaningful, and take place within a rich and satisfying environment.

5. The learning process occurs through a wide variety of experiences and subject matters which are unified around a core of purpose.

6. The learning experience, initiated by need and purpose, is likely to be motivated by its own incompleteness, though extrinsic motives may sometimes be necessary. (See later summary on motivation.)

7. The learner will persist through difficulties, obstacles, and unpleasant situations to the extent that he deems the objectives worth-while.

8. The learning process and achievement are materially affected by the level of aspiration set by the learner. Individuals need practice in setting realistic goals for themselves, goals neither so low as to elicit little effort, nor so high as to foreordain failure. Realistic goal-setting leads to more satisfactory improvement than unrealistic goal-setting.

9. The learning process and the achievement of results is materially related to individual differences among the learners. The capacity of the learner is a critical factor in deciding what is to be learned and by whom. Brighter pupils can learn things that less bright ones cannot learn; older children can, in general, learn more rapidly than younger ones. (Any decline in adult years depends upon what is being learned.)

10. The learning process proceeds most effectively when the experiences, materials, and desired results are carefully adjusted to the maturity and background of experience of the learner. (See later summary on readiness.)

11. The learning process proceeds best when the learner can see results, has knowledge of his status and progress, when he achieves insight and understanding. That is, information about the nature of a good performance, knowledge of his own mistakes, and knowledge of successful results, aid the learner.

12. The personal history of the learner—for example, his reaction to authority (many other factors might be cited)—may hamper or enhance his ability to learn from a given teacher.

13. Tolerance for failure is best taught through providing a backlog of success that compensates for experienced failure.

14. The learning process proceeds most effectively under that type of instructional guidance which stimulates without dominating or coercing; which provides for successes rather than too many failures; which encourages rather than discourages.

15. The learning process in operation is a functioning unity of several procedures which may be separated arbitrarily for discussion.

16. The learning products are socially useful patterns of action, values, meanings, attitudes, appreciations, abilities, skills. The products are inter-related functionally but may be discussed separately.

17. The learning products accepted by the learners are those which satisfy a need, which are useful and meaningful to the learner.

18. The learning products are incorporated into the learner's personality slowly and gradually in some instances, and with relative rapidity in others. The realness of the conditions under which the learning takes place and the readiness of the learner contribute to integration.

19. The learning products when properly achieved and integrated are complex and adaptable, not simple and static.

20. Transfer to new tasks will be better if, in learning, the learner can discover relationships for himself, and if he has experience during learning of applying the principles within a variety of tasks.

21. There is no substitute for repetitive practice in the overlearning of skills (for instance, the performance of a concert pianist) or in the memorization of unrelated facts that must be automatized.

22. Spaced or distributed recalls are more advantageous in fixing material that is to be long retained.

III. GENERAL PRINCIPLES OF RELEARNING [4]

The learning of new social values and behavior is often a matter of relearning, complicated by the presence of undesirable values and patterns of action.

1. The processes and principles governing the acquisition of socially acceptable learning and of learning detrimental to society are basically alike.

2. Re-education is the achievement of changes in the learner's knowledge, belief, and values.

3. Re-education affects the cognitive structure of the individual, his perception of the physical and social worlds, that is, it changes his knowledge, beliefs, and expectations.

4. Re-education modifies the learner's personal values with respect to group and interpersonal relations.

[4] Kurt Lewin and Paul Grabbe, "Conduct, Knowledge, and Acceptance of New Values," *The Journal of Social Issues,* August, 1954, pp. 56–64. Available also in Kenneth Benne and Bozidar Muntyan, *Human Relations in Curriculum Change.* New York: Dryden, 1951, pp. 24–33. See also Kurt Lewin, "Field Theory and Learning," in *The Psychology of Learning,* Forty-First Yearbook, Part II, National Society for the Study of Education, pp. 215–242. The principles here are reworded and rearranged from the original statement.

5. Re-education influences the learner's behavior in social situations.

6. First-hand experience does not guarantee correct concepts; the total learning situation must be conducive to a change in cognition.

7. An individual's perception of the facts and values of a situation affects his behavior.

8. The possession of correct facts in the face of false perceptions does not assure change in inadequate social stereotypes.

9. Inadequate stereotypes are as difficult to obliterate as are incorrect concepts stemming from ignorance and misinformation.

10. Changes in emotional reaction do not necessarily follow acquisition of correct factual information.

11. A change in the "culture of the individual" is equivalent to a change in values, a change in the perception of social relationships, a change in "action-ideology."

    a. Hostility to re-education may stem from loyalty to old values.

    b. The new set of values must be freely chosen and accepted if re-education is to be successful.

12. Emotional acceptance of the new set of values must be a gradual process.

13. The new set of values necessary to change behavior is acquired frequently with belongingness to the group subscribing to the new values. A strong "we feeling" aids in changing values.

(At this point a few other principles might be listed, but they would be repetitions of, or obvious inferences from, general principles of learning.)

IV. GROUP PROCESS AND LEARNING

The use of group process obviously facilitates the learning of skills of communication, or participation and cooperation, of discussing evidence and conclusions. Recent research shows that, contrary to some common beliefs, pupils working in pairs or small groups do better in other areas also than when working individually. Results were superior in paragraph writing, solving algebra problems, improving reading ability, as well as in some of the tasks usually thought of as individual.[5]

1. Group process, properly applied, establishes communication and promotes interaction within a group of learners and between groups.

    a. The psycho-physical setting for group activities should enhance effectiveness in sharing information and ideas.

        (1) Books, audio-visual materials, and all other aids to learning should be assembled for the convenience of the learners.

[5] David H. Russell, *Children's Thinking*. New York: Ginn & Co., 1956, pp. 266–267.

(2) The meeting places for large and small groups should be arranged to promote freedom of discussion.

(3) Experts and consultants—resource persons—may be called in for various purposes.

(4) Direct training in group process helps to facilitate its use.

(5) Accurate records should be kept of process and results.

b. Group process should create a social system of channels of communication between any group of learners and other groups, and with the community within which the school is located.

2. Group process should deal with the problems of the learner within the group, problems common to small groups within the class, and with problems of interest to the whole class.

a. The readiness of the group should determine what type and level of problem and of learning experiences are to be used.

b. Clarification and definition of purposes and problems, the selection of activities and materials, provision for evaluating progress, should be accomplished through free participatory discussion.

c. Experts and consultants may aid in clarifying problems, in opening up new ways of solving them.

d. Experimentation and simple tryout should be utilized.

e. Evaluation of the process and its achievements, and of the degree of participation should be continuous. This often aids in clarifying or extending purposes, or in discovering new ones.

3. Leadership in group process should foster initiative and interaction as widely as possible for members of the group. Group process provides for wide sharing and changing of leadership in place of fixing authority in one person.

a. Individuals who participate in a functioning and productive group are likely to develop desirable attitudes, social skills, and understandings.

b. Leadership is substituted for authority in effective group process.

c. Authority, when used, is derived from the group and is the authority of the group over itself. Democratic authority may be delegated to any individual or committee to be exercised for the good of the group; it may be revoked when not so used.

4. Group process used for a sufficient time should modify the thinking and behavior of all participating learners.

a. The individual learns both as an individual and as a group member when he reorganizes his thinking and behavior toward problems which are of group concern.

b. The individual will learn the value of group activity as he participates in extensive continuing opportunity to make decisions.

c. The individual should be accorded respect and will learn many individual behaviors when he presents sincere arguments in disagreement with the majority of the group.

5. Group process used for a sufficient time should develop desirable social skills and human relations, with accompanying ability to effect changes of social value.

    a. The learner will see the value of uncoerced consensus and action based on group decision.

    b. Changes in persons, with resultant changes in institutions or procedures, may be affected.

V. PRESERVING THE LEARNER'S SECURITY

Distrust, fear, and insecurity are quite normal reactions to change. The abandonment of old and trusted knowledges and values with the acceptance of new values and behavior patterns is a serious matter for learners at all levels. The older the learner the more he has identified with his knowledges and values and the more necessary it is to conduct learning enterprises so that security and mental health are preserved. The need for security, being normal, must be respected by teachers and not sneered at, as we sometimes unhappily see. The general strategy is to begin with the known and to proceed with challenges likely to beget success; to proceed slowly enough that the learner may develop insight and understanding and may achieve appropriate skills for operating new knowledge and values. The discussion here is related to the more remote principles of re-learning set forth in summary No. (III) earlier.

1. Begin with problems real to the learners involved, but which contain challenge. Dealing with the familiar and with a challenge which is not overwhelming reduces tension.

2. Begin with problems which will likely yield success. Failure on a self-selected problem is not so devastating as is failure on an imposed task.

3. Allow time for development of understanding and for achievement of new skills and behaviors.

4. Develop a strong group feeling, but with full respect for the individuals within the group. (See earlier discussion of group process.)

5. Provide an atmosphere of freedom and spontaneity. An emotional climate free from tensions contributes to confidence and security.

6. Provide support in the form of recognition for contributions, praise for results.

7. Provide assurance that individual learners may contribute freely, may differ with the majority, may suggest new leads. Creative activities when accepted not only aid the learner in achieving results, but contribute to security.

8. Recognize and build upon differences in interests and special abilities

within the group. A favorable effect results from aid given to learners in understanding themselves, both their capabilities and limitations, and in understanding their relationship with others and with the group.

9. Adjust the pace carefully to the individuals and the group. Slow acceptance and development are natural.

VI. THE MOTIVATION OF LEARNING

1. A motivated learner learns more readily than one who is not motivated. Motives may be general or specific, intrinsic or extrinsic.

2. Motivations which are too intense (especially pain, fear, anxiety) may be accompanied by distracting emotional states and by undesirable learning products.

3. Excessive motivation may be less effective than moderate motivation, especially for certain kinds of tasks.

4. Learning under intrinsic motivation is preferable to learning under extrinsic motivation.

5. Purposes and goals which make sense to a learner, which meet a need, which restore the natural equilibrium of the learner, are effective.

6. Purposes and goals should be geared to the interests, activities, and maturities of the learners.

7. Extrinsic motivations operate as follows: [6]

a. Motivation by reward is generally preferable to motivation by punishment, motivation by success preferable to motivation by failure. Marks, rewards, punishments operate as follows:

(1) Marks, rewards, and punishments not functionally related to the learning situation will beget learning, but it is learning soon lost and accompanied by detrimental concomitant learnings.

(2) The more closely the mark, reward, or punishment used as motive is a natural outcome of the learning process, the better effect it has. Learning is stimulated and undesirable concomitants are at a minimum.

(3) The more clearly the learner sees that the mark, reward, or punishment is an inherent aspect of the learning situation, not artificial and imposed, the better the learning which results.

b. Social motives of competition and rivalry operate as follows:

(1) Routine skills and factual information are readily acquired under these motives without immediate detrimental results.

---

[6] Learning theorists differ considerably among themselves on these points. The summary here is an effort to give such guidance as is possible lacking a final systematic theory.

(2) Certain conversational skills and more general types of thinking may be encouraged, but may have detrimental concomitants.

(3) Creative work—imaginative work generally—is not affected favorably.

(4) Individual mental hygiene and social welfare generally can suffer severely under motives of rivalry and competition. Unhappiness, frustration, and cheating may result with the individual; exploitation, social injustice, and waste may result with the group.

c. The newer social motives of cooperation, recognition by one's fellows, opportunity for participation in planning and decision making, seem to have very beneficial effects upon immediate and later learning. (A considerable revolution in human thinking concerning competition and cooperation, both in world affairs and in individual concerns, is underway. Data are appearing from time to time which should be noted.)

d. Commendation and praise for work well done are excellent incentives. Indiscriminate or undeserved praise has a detrimental effect. Praise is better than condemnation, but the latter is preferable to ignoring the learner's efforts.

e. Success achieved by the learner in adjusting his levels of aspiration to possible achievements is valuable.

f. Goals and levels of aspiration set by the learner's family or social class may be effective, but may also have serious ill effects.

g. Liking for the teacher seems to be a safe incentive with very young learners. With older learners liking must be combined with respect. The teacher's personality should be used sparingly as an incentive, since this type of motivation can invite detrimental concomitants.

h. Sarcasm and ridicule secure only the most undesirable and detrimental learning outcomes. (Continued use of sarcasm can only result from stupidity on the part of the teacher, or as an outlet for a frustrated personality.)

8. Learning without purpose and learning to do difficult, unpleasant, distasteful tasks under compulsion and coercion does not train the learner to persist with unpleasant learnings in real life. This does not mean that difficulty is to be eliminated from learning experience. Learners will persist through serious difficulties if the objective is deemed worth-while. That is, learning under purpose is the best guarantee of persistence in learning to overcome difficulties.

9. The maintenance of interest (or motivation) is important in learning. This can be done by several means, of which the following are illustrations:

a. Use a variety of learning activities or experiences.

b. Adapt closely to individual differences, especially in group work.

    c. Make use of success and recognition by the group.

    d. Adapt to levels of maturity and experimental background.

    e. As the teacher, manifest sincere enthusiasm.

    f. Take stock and replan from time to time.

VII. THE PRINCIPLE OF READINESS

1. Readiness is the stage in a learner's development when he can learn easily, effectively, and without emotional disturbance. Readiness is one of the most important factors in adjusting learning opportunities and experiences to the learner.

2. Readiness is not a separate and disparate trait; it is a condition brought about by many factors: the individual's rate of growth or maturing, background of experience, mental capacity, attitudes and interests, oral language development, emotional and social adjustments, health, kinesthetic coordination, and others.

3. Readiness for various types of learning and learning experience appears at different times. There is a succession of readinesses.

4. Readiness cannot be forced in advance of natural growth, but programs of experience which compensate for limited experience, which make up deficiencies in certain of the items listed in (2) above, are useful.

5. Readiness or the lack of it should not be assumed without investigation or tryout of certain activities. Observation of the learner's reaction to opportunities to learn is the safe guide to determining whether readiness is present or not.

*   *   *

Because of space limitations, we have omitted summaries of:

The learning of problem-solving skills.

The acquisition of meanings, generalizations, concepts.

The achievement of attitudes and appreciations.

The development of skills and abilities.

*   *   *

VIII. PRINCIPLES OF TEACHING

A list of principles of teaching would consist of a list of inferences drawn from the principle of learning set forth in the preceding pages. Any reader can derive these principles for himself through inspection of the summaries on learning. Instead of presenting a semirepetition, there is substituted a listing of the characteristics of the learner himself, paralleled by a listing of the characteristics of a setting for learning which would fit the learner. The statements under "Setting for Learning" are directives for teaching.

The Learner	*The Setting for Learning*
1. The learner, like all living organisms, is a unitary, integrating whole.	1. The desirable setting for functional learning experiences will provide for natural integration of feeling-doing-thinking.
2. The learner, like any other living organism, seeks always to maintain equilibrium or balance.	2. Desirable learning experiences will provide opportunity for success in meeting needs and solving problems, but will also give constant challenge to go beyond immediate situations.
3. The learner is a goal-seeking organism, pursuing aims to satisfy needs, thus to maintain equilibrium.	3. The desirable setting for learning will be dominated by purposes and goals set up by the learner or learners, either by themselves or with appropriate guidance from the total group, including consultants.
4. The learner is an active, behaving, exploratory individual.	4. The setting must provide freedom to explore, to construct, to question, to differ, to make mistakes: freedom to develop creative contributions. The limits of freedom are democratic controls, rights of others, and good taste.
5. The learner has a pattern and rhythm of growth peculiar to the individual. Notable differences exist between individuals, in speed of learning, energy output, depth of feeling, facility of insight.	5. Widely varied types of learning experiences should be provided, adaptable to levels of maturity, to different rates, interests, abilities, and so forth.
6. The learner brings with him a personality, a set of aims, values, social habits.	6. The purposes and experiences established should arise out of and be continuous with the life of the learner. The family background, and social-class status, as well as the individuality of the learner, must be taken into account.
7. A learner may be quite immature in relation to one set of standards	7. Learners need sympathetic guidance while building an awareness

and experiences, and quite mature in relation to another.

and personality within their own experiences. They need protection from situations in which they can not yet act intelligently; protection from fears and anxieties; protection sufficient to insure security and status on various levels; plus challenge to grow to conquer problems, to develop self-reliance. The learner needs guidance from consultants who know and understand the problems of a growing personality; who see learning as a developmental process. Guidance must be free from domination or coercion.

8. The learner is a social animal, if normal, and naturally seeks activities involving other persons.

8. The setting must provide many varied opportunities to work in "we" relationships, developing eventually into self-directed group activity. The whole range of interactive human relationships, the cooperative group process, is essential to the development of mature socialized personality.

4. *Learning: A Process of Change* *

ERNEST A. HAGGARD, *University of Chicago*

LEARNING is the heart of the educational enterprise. This fact is entirely obvious—but even so it is sometimes forgotten. Learning is more important than attractive school buildings, administrative policies and programs, integrated curricula, or even a happy and enthusiastic teaching staff. The school may provide facilities, but after all, it is the pupils who must do the learning. Unless they learn, the plant, program and personnel of the

* From Ernest A. Haggard, "Learning: A Process of Change," *Educational Leadership* (December, 1955), pp. 149–56. Reprinted by permission.

educational system have failed, and amount only to "sounding brass, or a tinkling cymbal."

To say that the essential purpose of the school is to maximize learning does not belittle its many other functions. Many educators take the position that it is more important for the school to help develop stable, mature and well-adjusted citizens rather than "grinds" who sparkle with facts. This issue can arise, however, only if we define learning in terms of the "three R's," as some are wont to do. But from what we know about these matters, each individual's personality structure, his social effectiveness, his ability to behave responsibly and maturely, and even his neurotic conflicts, are largely learned—almost as much as are his ability to spell or repeat parts of the multiplication table. Each adult is molded by the society in which he has lived, and the school, as an agent of society, relies on learning in its efforts to shape our future citizens as well as to pass on any necessary knowledges, skills and cultural values.

Granting that learning is central to the educative process, it is nonetheless difficult (if not impossible) to say just what learning is. The best we can do is to rely on definitions which indicate whether learning has occurred, and to speculate on the conditions under which learning occurs best. There is remarkable agreement upon the definition of learning as being reflected in a change in behavior as the result of experience. There is much less agreement among psychologists and educators today on the nature of the learning process, on the conditions under which it occurs, or on the means of maximizing learning according to the school's objectives.

In a very real sense, it does us little good just to say that learning results from experience. But we do need to know the conditions under which learning occurs, and the best means for maximizing desirable learnings. This is especially true today. The crisis which now faces American education requires that we take time to think seriously about some of the premises upon which our school systems have operated, and to inquire whether they can measure up to the task of educating our youth.

Two Views of Learning

The points I wish to discuss next can be grouped under two questions: first, "If we wish to produce behavior change (i.e., learning), *what* should we try to change?" and second, "*How* should we try to bring about such behavior changes—directly or indirectly?"

These two questions are obviously related. In fact, they are really two aspects of one more general question—which boils down to our view of the nature of man, of his behavior, and of how it changes. If the question is stated in these terms, it becomes clear that divergent schools of thought exist in these matters; with the result that divergent recommendations are being made for the proper conduct of our educational enterprise. It will be sufficient here to contrast two major points of view, and their likely consequences when they are put into action in an educational setting.

STIMULUS-RESPONSE THEORY

If for no other reason than sheer priority, one point of view has dominated educational practice in America during the present century. Let us consider just two of the central assumptions of this view, namely that the learner is (or should be) passive, and that his behavior and any changes in it can be controlled by outside forces. Today, most educators would deny these assumptions, and probably would doubt whether anyone ever took them seriously. Since these assertions seem to be unrealistic, let us go back and examine briefly the origins of the above propositions before discussing their impact on classroom practice.

About fifty years ago, when the educational psychologists were eager to study learning and related processes "scientifically," they had before them a clear picture of what science, scientists, and the scientific method were like. Their model was the world of the physical scientists, and the educational psychologists tried to be like them, to use similar methods, and to develop similar theories or laws. They also seem to have thought of man in much the same terms that the physical scientists then pictured their world (e.g., that all matter is inert, unless acted upon by an outside force, or that reaction follows action, etc.). And, as one might expect, the psychologists, on the basis of similar assumptions and methods, developed laws similar to the ones then held by the physical scientists.[1]

More specifically, what form did the psychologists' "laws of learning" take? Although a variety of such laws were proposed, there are two which still receive credence in some quarters. One is the Law of Effect, which states that an act which is followed by a pleasant or rewarding consequence will be learned, whereas an act which is followed by an unpleasant or punishing consequence will be unlearned. The other proposition is the Law of Frequency, which states that the more often an act is repeated, the better it will be learned.

In the case of the Law of Effect, it almost seems as if the learner can be

[1] There are several other parallels between classical physics and this type of psychological theory. Another example is the once popular assumption that all matter is made up of various discrete (marble-like) particles. In psychology these "particles" took the form of simple learned responses, and the most complex of human behaviors were said to be made up of elementary conditioned responses wired together by neural connections. The field theories in physics and similar organizing principles in psychology have, needless to say, replaced these earlier views.

likened to a piece of litmus paper—if alkali is applied it turns blue but if acid is applied it turns red. Similarly in the case of the Law of Frequency, it almost seems as if the learner can be likened to a piece of metal—the more it is pounded the more "impression" is made on it. These analogies would sound ridiculous were it not for the fact that many of the students in our teacher education institutions are still taught that these "laws" should be taken at face value and so applied in the classroom.

Both of these "laws of learning" have been disproved innumerable times in careful research and in everyday experience. Why, then, do they continue to be taught and used? The reason for their persistence lies partly in their simplicity, and partly in the fact that they fit neatly into a more general Stimulus-Response theory of behavior and learning. According to this theory it is assumed that the subject (the learner) is passive, and his behavior and behavior change (learning) can be controlled by manipulating external forces (stimuli). (Now, it must be admitted that most Stimulus-Response theorists today would not quite admit such assumptions—although some come remarkably close to it. The important thing is that they and their followers *think and act as though* this and related assumptions were true.)

How is learning thought of in terms of this theory? Very simply: if stimuli cause responses, learning involves building up new stimulus-response connections. The only trick is to get the desired response to follow or be associated with a particular stimulus. From this point on, the experimenter (or in practice, the teacher) has the say-so in determining which stimuli are presented and which responses are to be associated with them—hence can control which learnings will take place.

The application of the Stimulus-Response theory to classroom learning sounds deceptively easy. The essential requirements are that the teacher presents the materials to be learned, and then sees to it that the pupils make the desired responses to it. In other words, if a teacher were to follow the Stimulus-Response theory to the letter, he would have the pupils sit quietly at their desks, he would determine what is to be learned, and he would then "present" it (probably by the lecture method). He would also make full use of the Law of Effect (by use of frequent rewards such as praise, gold stars and special privileges, and frequent punishments such as threats or deprivations) and the Law of Frequency (by use of ample drill—out of desperation when normal learning bogs down).

In terms of the questions raised earlier, the teacher who applies this theory tries to change *directly* the behavior patterns of the pupils. Note that nothing has been said about such things as the pupil's personality, prejudices, or value systems, whether he is interested in learning, or how he might feel about the teacher or who sits next to him. Indeed, strictly speaking, nothing need be said about such matters, if one is interested only in changing responses to stimuli by using this theory of learning.

A good deal of space has been given here to the Stimulus-Response theory of learning—more than it deserves in terms of its intrinsic merit. This was done, however, because of the great impact this theory has had on educational practice in American schools. Before concluding this section, some note should be taken of the major shortcomings of this point of view on both theoretical and practical grounds. These are:

First, the basic implicit working assumptions of this theory are untenable. To suppose that the learner is or can be passive is ridiculous, as any parent or teacher of children well knows. It is likewise unthinkable that man's behavior is determined by external forces alone. Much of what a person does or learns is determined by inner forces, such as how he views the situation he is in, and his motivations, expectations and purposes at the time.

Second, this theory does not help us to answer certain important questions. It is true that research based on this theory does help us to answer the question, "When stimulus x is presented, to what extent will response y occur?" But the more important question is, "In the *absence* of stimulus x, will response y occur?" We need to know how children come to internalize the necessary knowledges, skills and value systems so that they can manage their lives in the absence of parents, teachers, policemen and psychiatrists. In the final analysis, we require of our citizens that they learn to behave intelligently, maturely and responsibly *on their own*.

Third, this theory, when put into practice, is appallingly ineffective. This fact is best seen by watching children outside of school, and seeing just how much they effortlessly learn *and* remember. This fact is also apparent if we look back on our own "school learning" (especially if we went to a school which practiced this theory) and try to recall the academic materials that we presumably learned in the 4th, 7th or 10th grade, or sophomore year in college, or even the foreign language that we "learned" for the doctorate. In view of how easily people are able to learn and remember things outside of school, one is struck with how little of academic learning is retained for use by most adults.

MOTIVATIONAL THEORY

A Motivational theory of behavior and learning differs in many respects from the Stimulus-Response theory. Some of the major assumptions of a Motivational theory are that, although the individual is responsive to environmental stimuli, his behavior (including learning) is determined in large measure by other factors, such as his prior experiences, how he perceives the situation, and his current interests and motivations. Rather than thinking primarily of the external stimuli and responses to them, attention is focused on the individual-in-the-environment context, with emphasis on how his relations to his environment change with time.

In describing the "individual," we may, for our purposes here, speak briefly of both the perceptual and the motivational aspects of his behavior. On the perceptual side, it is assumed that the individual learns to view his world in characteristic ways which determine in part what he sees and its meaning to him, which in turn influence how he will relate to and deal with what he sees. The individual's "ways of seeing" act like flexible sieves through which the environment must pass. Also, these change with time, so that any given stimulus does not always stay the same; as the individual comes to see it differently, it ceases to be the same stimulus—even though its physical properties have not changed. Thus, suppose a child first sees his teacher as being an awesome, all-knowing authority figure, and later sees her as a warm, helpful friend. Although the teacher actually may have changed little if at all during the time, she has changed a great deal as far as the pupil is concerned. It is important to note in such cases that the child's seeing his teacher differently will influence what and how well he will learn other things in her class.

Of more direct interest, however, is the individual's "motivational structure" which develops as he is educated to be a member of society. Here, "motivation" is used to denote the forces which lie behind behavior and "structure" refers to the individual's organized, characteristic and relatively stable set of motivations. Each person's motivational structure develops with time, and it is shaped in large part by his total education, in the broadest sense of the word. Thus, the infant is motivated primarily by his biological needs, but by the time he has become an adult, his behavior is also directed toward gaining social acceptance, fun, status, money, power, knowledge or prestige—as much as in just trying to keep body and soul together. The individual's motivational structure is important also because it influences how he sees his world, or more simply, he tends to see what he wants or needs or is able to see.

If, according to this theory, the motivational structure plays such an important role in determining behavior and learning, how does it change or develop? First of all, we can assume that each person comes to every situation (school included) "equipped" with some sort of motivational structure. If he is interested in what the situation has to offer, and if parts of the environment are congruent with (or "fit") his motivational structure, both aspects interact and both are changed. The environment is changed because the person acts and, if learning occurs, the person's motivational structure is modified as a result of his changed way of relating to his environment.

"Learning" occurs when the situation requires new adjustments on the part of the person, so that his motivational structure has become modified somewhat in order to carry out the appropriate action. In such cases, the new learnings become "grafted into," and hence change, the previous motivational structure. It is clear that, in terms of this theory, learning occurs when a person actively relates to a new situation and makes new adjustments to it. This involves a change in his motivational structure—and when it changes, it follows that his behavior will change also.

Thus, both the Stimulus-Response and Motivational theories are interested in "explaining" behavior changes, but they go about it differently. There is also another difference, which relates to "predicting" behavior and behavior changes. The Stimulus-Response theory would predict that the person will do what he has learned to do in terms of the stimulus situation; a Motivational theory would predict that the person's present motivational structure, as modified by previous learnings, will determine his behavior. This difference is obvious in all those cases where the person has learned "what to do"—and then does something else.

What implications does a Motivational theory have for educational practice? Before answering this question, it would help if we recalled a frequent observation of teachers, namely that "the students who are interested in what I teach are no problem (unless it's trying to keep ahead of them)— it is the rest of the class that is making my hair turn gray." A teacher would be fortunate indeed if all of his pupils were eager to learn. But how should he try to teach those who are uninterested?

Let us begin with a teacher who has just one pupil. On the basis of a Motivational theory, he should first find out the child's present motivational structure (and especially his central and enduring interests or motivations), and then he should present the material-to-be-learned so that it "fits" the child's motivations. He should, for example, work in terms of the child's desire for a feeling of competence and of his striving toward some goal important to him, rather than just the getting of a high grade on a test. The former motivations are more durable; furthermore, if the child's only wish is to get good grades, the primary thing he may learn is how to get them more easily by cramming or cheating on examinations rather than by really mastering the material. The importance of using a central motivation to facilitate learning was illustrated with illiterates in the Army during the last war—the men learned to read in a phenomenally short time when the instructors presented the matter in terms of their being able to read the "letters from home."

Usually, however, the teacher has twenty or thirty pupils to deal with. What then? By and large, the same principles would apply, with some compromises, because the motivational structures of each child will differ, at least to some degree. This obviously makes the teacher's task difficult, and requires him to make use of motivations which are more or less common to the group as well as those which characterize various individuals. This is only saying what we all know—that the successful teacher is able to interest his whole class, and he also appeals to the special interests of each child.

But regardless of the validity of the theoretical bases of a Motivational theory of learning, or the promise of increased practical results that come from following it, there are certain conditions which may tend to interfere with its widespread application. For one thing, the current crisis in American education, which involves very great social and population pressures for the expansion of our present school system—along with economic restrictions and the lack of available facilities—make this point of view sound like a luxury which cannot be afforded the average child, at least not right now. This theory cannot be put into practice if teachers are forced to present the subject matter in a rule-of-thumb manner to overcrowded classrooms—but can we afford *this?*

Another hindrance to the application of this theory lies in the many large gaps in our present knowledge of children and how they develop. For example, we know relatively little of the mental development of children (apart from their performance on academic tests), of how they see their world and what questions they ask about it, of what subject matters, knowledges and skills excite them at what ages, and so on, and so on. We consequently know too little of how various subject matters should best be presented, in what form, at what pace, and at what age levels, in order to provide materials which "fit" the interests and abilities of the children in school—and not just conform to some outmoded or arbitrary curriculum.

To illustrate only a few of these points, let us look briefly at the "problem" of teaching mathematics. Why is it that so many of our children find it difficult? Why do so many otherwise intelligent students, even in college, say that they "just can't do mathematics or statistics" when every day of their lives they use the number system and think in terms which are essentially mathematical? Why is it that the children of a number of other cultures do not have such difficulties in this area? Part of the answer to these questions may lie in our having asked, "What mathematics should we teach fifth-grade children?" rather than "What type of mathematical questions does the typical child in the fifth grade begin to ask?"—and then gear our teaching accordingly. One series of studies which investigated the development of mathematical concepts in children found that the concepts developed, their type and order, are almost the reverse of those "taught" in most of our schools! We need to know more of what children are like in order to be able to teach them more effectively. But although there is a great deal that we do not know about child development and the learning process, we should not take refuge in our past and present ignorances, and hence continue to perpetuate the educational errors of a generation or two ago. Enough has been learned during this period that can be used to improve the current educational practices in our public schools.

A Process of Change

The fundamental consideration discussed in this paper has to do with learning as a process of change. We have examined briefly two rather different views of the learning process and some of their implications for educational practice, especially as they apply to classroom teaching and learning. It is clear that our educational leaders have some choice in determining how they will plan for the educational experiences of our children, and that what is achieved in this respect will be partly a result of their planning. The issue which faces those who will make and carry out our educational policy and programming centers around the kind of changes they wish to bring about, on both the individual and the societal levels.

There is no question but that the school is becoming an increasingly important agent for the shaping of our future citizens. Under our past and present procedures, however, the educational enterprise has too often been ineffective in what is required of it—or worse, has resulted in children's becoming uninterested in learning or using the classroom as a battleground, with the teacher on one side and themselves on the other. There is absolutely no justification for the waste that is involved when such conditions exist.

On the societal level these issues take a somewhat different form. Here, the role of the school is to help train our youth to become mature adults who can and will act intelligently and responsibly in a highly complex and unstable world. Our society can ill afford to waste a large proportion of the talent or other human resources inherent in our population by holding on to ineffective educational procedures. The pressures involved in the inevitable expansion of our educational system to teach larger numbers of pupils may lead some to think that we only need more of what we already have. But, actually, the present crisis also holds the opportunity for our educational leaders to plan those changes in our school system which will result in a *better* education for our youth.

5. The Science of Learning and the Art of Teaching *[1]

B. F. SKINNER, *Harvard University*

SOME PROMISING advances have recently been made in the field of learning. Special techniques have been designed to arrange what are called "contingencies of reinforcement"—the relations which prevail between behavior on the one hand and the consequences of that behavior on the other —with the result that a much more effective control of behavior has been achieved. It has long been argued that an organism learns mainly by producing changes in its environment, but it is only recently that these changes have been carefully manipulated. In traditional devices for the study of learning—in the serial maze, for example, or in the T-maze, the problem box, or the familiar discrimination apparatus—the effects produced by the organism's behavior are left to many fluctuating circumstances. There is many a slip between the turn-to-the-right and the food-cup at the end of the alley. It is not surprising that techniques of this sort have yielded only very rough data from which the uniformities demanded by an experimental science can be extracted only by averaging many cases. In none of this work has the behavior of the individual organism been predicted in more than a statistical sense. The learning processes which are the presumed object of such research are reached only through a series of inferences. Current preoccupation with deductive systems reflects this state of the science.

Recent improvements in the conditions which control behavior in the field of learning are of two principal sorts. The Law of Effect has been taken seriously; we have made sure that effects *do* occur and that they occur under conditions which are optimal for producing the changes called learning. Once we have arranged the particular type of consequence called a reinforcement, our techniques permit us to shape up the behavior of an organism almost at will. It has become a routine exercise to demonstrate this in classes in elementary psychology by conditioning such an organism as a pigeon. Simply by presenting food to a hungry pigeon at the right time, it is possible to shape up three or four well-defined responses in a single demonstration period—such responses as turning around, pacing the floor

---

* From B. F. Skinner, "The Science of Learning and the Art of Teaching," *Harvard Educational Review,* 24 (Spring, 1954), 86–97. Reprinted by permission.
[1] Paper presented at a conference on Current Trends in Psychology and the Behavioral Sciences at the University of Pittsburgh, March 12, 1954.

in the pattern of a figure-8, standing still in a corner of the demonstration apparatus, stretching the neck, or stamping the foot. Extremely complex performances may be reached through successive stages in the shaping process, the contingencies of reinforcement being changed progressively in the direction of the required behavior. The results are often quite dramatic. In such a demonstration one can *see* learning take place. A significant change in behavior is often obvious as the result of a single reinforcement.

A second important advance in technique permits us to maintain behavior in given states of strength for long periods of time. Reinforcements continue to be important, of course, long after an organism has learned *how* to do something, long after it has acquired behavior. They are necessary to maintain the behavior in strength. Of special interest is the effect of various schedules of intermittent reinforcement. Charles B. Ferster and the author are currently preparing an extensive report of a five-year research program, sponsored by the Office of Naval Research, in which most of the important types of schedules have been investigated and in which the effects of schedules in general have been reduced to a few principles. On the theoretical side we now have a fairly good idea of why a given schedule produces its appropriate performance. On the practical side we have learned how to maintain any given level of activity for daily periods limited only by the physical exhaustion of the organism and from day to day without substantial change throughout its life. Many of these effects would be traditionally assigned to the field of motivation, although the principal operation is simply the arrangement of contingencies of reinforcement.[2]

These new methods of shaping behavior and of maintaining it in strength are a great improvement over the traditional practices of professional animal trainers, and it is not surprising that our laboratory results are already being applied to the production of performing animals for commercial purposes. In a more academic environment they have been used for demonstration purposes which extend far beyond an interest in learning as such. For example, it is not too difficult to arrange the complex contingencies which produce many types of social behavior. Competition is exemplified by two pigeons playing a modified game of ping-pong. The pigeons drive the ball back and forth across a small table by pecking at it. When the ball gets by one pigeon, the other is reinforced. The task of constructing such a "social relation" is probably completely out of reach of the traditional animal trainer. It requires a carefully designed program of gradually changing contingencies and the skillful use of schedules to maintain the behavior in strength. Each pigeon is separately prepared for

[2] The reader may wish to review Dr. Skinner's article, "Some Contributions of an Experimental Analysis of Behavior to Psychology as a Whole," *The American Psychologist,* 1953, 8, 69–78. Ed.

its part in the total performance, and the "social relation" is then arbitrarily constructed. The sequence of events leading up to this stable state are excellent material for the study of the factors important in nonsynthetic social behavior. It is instructive to consider how a similar series of contingencies could arise in the case of the human organism through the evolution of cultural patterns.

Cooperation can also be set up perhaps more easily than competition. We have trained two pigeons to coordinate their behavior in a cooperative endeavor with a precision which equals that of the most skillful human dancers. In a more serious vein these techniques have permitted us to explore the complexities of the individual organism and to analyze some of the serial or coordinate behaviors involved in attention, problem solving, various types of self-control, and the subsidiary systems of responses within a single organism called "personalities." Some of these are exemplified in what we call multiple schedules of reinforcement. In general a given schedule has an effect upon the rate at which a response is emitted. Changes in the rate from moment to moment show a pattern typical of the schedule. The pattern may be as simple as a constant rate of responding at a given value, it may be a gradually accelerating rate between certain extremes, it may be an abrupt change from not responding at all to a given stable high rate, and so on. It has been shown that the performance characteristic of a given schedule can be brought under the control of a particular stimulus and that different performances can be brought under the control of different stimuli in the same organism. At a recent meeting of the American Psychological Association, Dr. Ferster and the author demonstrated a pigeon whose behavior showed the pattern typical of "fixed-interval" reinforcement in the presence of one stimulus and, alternately, the pattern typical of the very different schedule called "fixed ratio" in the presence of a second stimulus. In the laboratory we have been able to obtain performances appropriate to *nine* different schedules in the presence of appropriate stimuli in random alternation. When Stimulus one is present, the pigeon executes the performance appropriate to Schedule one. When Stimulus two is present, the pigeon executes the performance appropriate to Schedule two. And so on. This result is important because it makes the extrapolation of our laboratory results to daily life much more plausible. We are all constantly shifting from schedule to schedule as our immediate environment changes, but the dynamics of the control exercised by reinforcement remain essentially unchanged.

It is also possible to construct very complex *sequences* of schedules. It is not easy to describe these in a few words, but two or three examples may be mentioned. In one experiment the pigeon generates a performance appropriate to Schedule A where the reinforcement is simply the production of the stimulus characteristic of Schedule B, to which the pigeon then responds appropriately. Under a third stimulus, the bird yields a performance appropriate to Schedule C where the reinforcement in this case is simply the production of the stimulus characteristic of Schedule D, to which the bird then responds appropriately. In a special case, first investigated by L. B. Wyckoff, Jr., the organism responds to one stimulus where the reinforcement consists of the *clarification* of the stimulus controlling another response. The first response becomes, so to speak, an objective form of "paying attention" to the second stimulus. In one important version of this experiment, as yet unpublished, we could say that the pigeon is telling us whether it is "paying attention" to the *shape* of a spot of light or to its *color*.

One of the most dramatic applications of these techniques has recently been made in the Harvard Psychological Laboratories by Floyd Ratliff and Donald S. Blough, who have skillfully used multiple and serial schedules of reinforcement to study complex perceptual processes in the infrahuman organism. They have achieved a sort of psycho-physics without verbal instruction. In a recent experiment by Blough, for example, a pigeon draws a detailed dark-adaptation curve showing the characteristic breaks of rod and cone vision. The curve is recorded continuously in a single experimental period and is quite comparable with the curves of human subjects. The pigeon behaves in a way which, in the human case, we would not hesitate to describe by saying that it adjusts a very faint patch of light until it can just be seen.

In all this work, the species of the organism has made surprisingly little difference. It is true that the organisms studied have all been vertebrates, but they still cover a wide range. Comparable results have been obtained with pigeons, rats, dogs, monkeys, human children, and most recently, by the author in collaboration with Ogden R. Lindsley, human psychotic subjects. In spite of great phylogenetic differences, all these organisms show amazingly similar properties of the learning process. It should be emphasized that this has been achieved by analyzing the effects of reinforcement and by designing techniques which manipulate reinforcement with considerable precision. Only in this way can the behavior of the individual organism be brought under such precise control. It is also important to note that through a gradual advance to complex interrelations among responses, the same degree of rigor is being extended to behavior which would usually be assigned to such fields as perception, thinking, and personality dynamics.

From this exciting prospect of an advancing science of learning, it is a great shock to turn to that branch of technology which is most directly concerned with the learning process—education. Let us consider, for example, the teaching of arithmetic in the lower grades. The school is concerned with imparting to the child a large number of responses of a special sort. The responses are all verbal. They consist of speaking and writing certain words, figures, and signs which, to put it roughly, refer to numbers and to arithmetic operations. The first task is to shape up these responses—to get the child to pronounce and to write responses correctly, but the principal task is to bring this behavior under many sorts of stimulus control. This is what happens when the child learns to count, to recite tables, to count while ticking off the items in an assemblage of objects, to respond to spoken or written numbers by saying "odd," "even," "prime," and so on. Over and above this elaborate repertoire of numerical behavior, most of which is often dismissed as the product of rote learning, the teaching of arithmetic looks forward to those complex serial arrangements of responses involved in original mathematical thinking. The child must acquire responses of transposing, clearing fractions, and so on, which modify the order or pattern of the original material so that the response called a solution is eventually made possible.

Now, how is this extremely complicated verbal repertoire set up? In the first place, what reinforcements are used? Fifty years ago the answer would have been clear. At that time educational control was still frankly aversive. The child read numbers, copied numbers, memorized tables, and performed operations upon numbers to escape the threat of the birch rod or cane. Some positive reinforcements were perhaps eventually derived from the increased efficiency of the child in the field of arithmetic and in rare cases some automatic reinforcement may have resulted from the sheer manipulation of the medium—from the solution of problems or the discovery of the intricacies of the number system. But for the immediate purposes of education the child acted to avoid or escape punishment. It was part of the reform movement known as progressive education to make the positive consequences more immediately effective, but any one who visits the lower grades of the average school today will observe that a change has been made, not from aversive to positive control, but from one form of aversive stimulation to another. The child at his desk, filling in his workbook, is behaving primarily to escape from the threat of a series of minor aversive events—the teacher's displeasure, the criticism or ridicule of his classmates, an ignominious showing in a competition, low marks, a trip to the office "to be talked to" by the principal, or a word to the parent who may still resort to the birch rod. In this welter of aversive consequences, getting the right answer is in itself an insignificant event, any effect of which is lost amid the anxieties, the boredom, and the aggressions which are the inevitable by-products of aversive control.[3]

[3] Skinner, B. F. *Science and Human Behavior*. New York: Macmillan, 1953.

Secondly, we have to ask how the contingencies of reinforcement are arranged. When is a numerical operation reinforced as "right"? Eventually, of course, the pupil may be able to check his own answers and achieve some sort of automatic reinforcement, but in the early stages the reinforcement of being right is usually accorded by the teacher. The contingencies she provides are far from optimal. It can easily be demonstrated that, unless explicit mediating behavior has been set up, the lapse of only a few seconds between response and reinforcement destroys most of the effect. In a typical classroom, nevertheless, long periods of time customarily elapse. The teacher may walk up and down the aisle, for example, while the class is working on a sheet of problems, pausing here and there to say right or wrong. Many seconds or minutes intervene between the child's response and the teacher's reinforcement. In many cases—for example, when papers are taken home to be corrected—as much as 24 hours may intervene. It is surprising that this system has any effect whatsoever.

A third notable shortcoming is the lack of a skillful program which moves forward through a series of progressive approximations to the final complex behavior desired. A long series of contingencies is necessary to bring the organism into the possession of mathematical behavior most efficiently. But the teacher is seldom able to reinforce at each step in such a series because she cannot deal with the pupil's responses one at a time. It is usually necessary to reinforce the behavior in blocks of responses—as in correcting a work sheet or page from a workbook. The responses within such a block must not be interrelated. The answer to one problem must not depend upon the answer to another. The number of stages through which one may progressively approach a complex pattern of behavior is therefore small, and the task so much the more difficult. Even the most modern workbook in beginning arithmetic is far from exemplifying an efficient program for shaping up mathematical behavior.

Perhaps the most serious criticism of the current classroom is the relative infrequency of reinforcement. Since the pupil is usually dependent upon the teacher for being right, and since many pupils are usually dependent upon the same teacher, the total number of contingencies which may be arranged during, say, the first four years, is of the order of only a few thousand. But a very rough estimate suggests that efficient mathematical behavior at this level requires something of the order of 25,000 contingencies. We may suppose that even in the brighter student a given contingency must be arranged several times to place the behavior well in hand. The responses to be set up are not simply the various items in tables of addition, subtraction, multiplication, and division; we have also to consider the alternative forms in which each item may be stated. To the learning of such material we should add hundreds of responses concerned with factoring, identifying primes, memorizing series, using short-cut techniques of calculation, constructing and using geometric representations or number forms, and so on. Over and above all this, the whole mathematical repertoire must be brought under the control of concrete problems of considerable variety. Perhaps 50,000 contingencies is a more conservative estimate. In this frame of reference the daily assignment in arithmetic seems pitifully meagre.

The result of all this is, of course, well known. Even our best schools are under criticism for their inefficiency in the teaching of drill subjects such as arithmetic. The condition in the average school is a matter of widespread national concern. Modern children simply do not learn arithmetic quickly or well. Nor is the result simply incompetence. The very subjects in which modern techniques are weakest are those in which failure is most conspicuous, and in the wake of an ever-growing incompetence come the anxieties, uncertainties, and aggressions which in their turn present other problems to the school. Most pupils soon claim the asylum of not being "ready" for arithmetic at a given level or, eventually, of not having a mathematical mind. Such explanations are readily seized upon by defensive teachers and parents. Few pupils ever reach the stage at which automatic reinforcements follow as the natural consequences of mathematical behavior. On the contrary, the figures and symbols of mathematics have become standard emotional stimuli. The glimpse of a column of figures, not to say an algebraic symbol or an integral sign, is likely to set off—not mathematical behavior—but a reaction of anxiety, guilt, or fear.

The teacher is usually no happier about this than the pupil. Denied the opportunity to control via the birch rod, quite at sea as to the mode of operation of the few techniques at her disposal, she spends as little time as possible on drill subjects and eagerly subscribes to philosophies of education which emphasize material of greater inherent interest. A confession of weakness is her extraordinary concern lest the child be taught something unnecessary. The repertoire to be imparted is carefully reduced to an essential minimum. In the field of spelling, for example, a great deal of time and energy has gone into discovering just those words which the young child is going to use, as if it were a crime to waste one's educational power in teaching an unnecessary word. Eventually, weakness of technique emerges in the disguise of a reformulation of the aims of education. Skills are minimized in favor of vague achievements—educating for democracy, educating the whole child, educating for life, and so on. And there the matter ends; for, unfortunately, these philosophies do not in turn suggest improvements in techniques. They offer little or no help in the design of better classroom practices.

There would be no point in urging these objections if improvement were impossible. But the advances which have recently been made in our control of the learning process suggest a thorough revision of classroom practices and, fortunately, they tell us how the revision can be brought about. This is not, of course, the first time that the results of an experimental science have been brought to bear upon the practical problems of education. The modern classroom does not, however, offer much evidence that research in the field of learning has been respected or used. This condition is no doubt partly due to the limitations of earlier research. But it has been encouraged by a too-hasty conclusion that the laboratory study of learning is inherently limited because it cannot take into account the realities of the classroom. In the light of our increasing knowledge of the learning process we should, instead, insist upon dealing with those realities and forcing a substantial change in them. Education is perhaps the most important branch of scientific technology. It deeply affects the lives of all of us. We can no longer allow the exigencies of a practical situation to suppress the tremendous improvements which are within reach. The practical situation must be changed.

There are certain questions which have to be answered in turning to the study of any new organism. What behavior is to be set up? What reinforcers are at hand? What responses are available in embarking upon a program of progressive approximation which will lead to the final form of the behavior? How can reinforcements be most efficiently scheduled to maintain the behavior in strength? These questions are all relevant in considering the problem of the child in the lower grades.

In the first place, what reinforcements are available? What does the school have in its possession which will reinforce a child? We may look first to the material to be learned, for it is possible that this will provide considerable automatic reinforcement. Children play for hours with mechanical toys, paints, scissors and paper, noise-makers, puzzles—in short, with almost anything which feeds back significant changes in the environment and is reasonably free of aversive properties. The sheer control of nature is itself reinforcing. This effect is not evident in the modern school because it is masked by the emotional responses generated by aversive control. It is true that automatic reinforcement from the manipulation of the environment is probably only a mild reinforcer and may need to be carefully husbanded, but one of the most striking principles to emerge from recent research is that the *net* amount of reinforcement is of little significance. A very slight reinforcement may be tremendously effective in controlling behavior if it is wisely used.

If the natural reinforcement inherent in the subject matter is not enough, other reinforcers must be employed. Even in school the child is occasionally permitted to do "what he wants to do," and access to reinforcements of many sorts may be made contingent upon the more immediate consequences of the behavior to be established. Those who advocate competition as a useful social motive may wish to use the reinforcements which follow from excelling others, although there is the difficulty that in this case the reinforcement of one child is necessarily aversive to another. Next in order we might place the good will and affection of the teacher, and only when that has failed need we turn to the use of aversive stimulation.

In the second place, how are these reinforcements to be made contingent upon the desired behavior? There are two considerations here—the gradual elaboration of extremely complex patterns of behavior and the maintenance of the behavior in strength at each stage. The whole process of becoming competent in any field must be divided into a very large number of very small steps, and reinforcement must be contingent upon the accomplishment of each step. This solution to the problem of creating a complex repertoire of behavior also solves the problem of maintaining the behavior in strength. We could, of course, resort to the techniques of scheduling already developed in the study of other organisms but in the present state of our knowledge of educational practices, scheduling appears to be most effectively arranged through the design of the material to be learned. By making each successive step as small as possible, the frequency of reinforcement can be raised to a maximum, while the possibly aversive consequences of being wrong are reduced to a minimum. Other ways of designing material would yield other programs of reinforcement. Any supplementary reinforcement would probably have to be scheduled in the more traditional way.

These requirements are not excessive, but they are probably incompatible with the current realities of the classroom. In the experimental study of learning it has been found that the contingencies of reinforcement which are most efficient in controlling the organism cannot be arranged through the personal mediation of the experimenter. An organism is affected by subtle details of contingencies which are beyond the capacity of the human organism to arrange. Mechanical and electrical devices must be used. Mechanical help is also demanded by the sheer number of contingencies which may be used efficiently in a single experimental session. We have recorded many millions of responses from a single organism during thousands of experimental hours. Personal arrangement of the contingencies and personal observation of the results are quite unthinkable. Now, the human organism is, if anything, more sensitive to precise contingencies than the other organisms we have studied. We have every reason to expect, therefore, that the most effective control of human learning will require instrumental aid. The simple fact is that, as a mere reinforcing mechanism, the teacher is out of date. This would be true even if a single teacher devoted all her time to a single child, but her inadequacy is multiplied manyfold when she must serve as a reinforcing device to many children at once. If the teacher is to take advantage of recent advances in the study of learning, she must have the help of mechanical devices.

The technical problem of providing the necessary instrumental aid is not particularly difficult. There are many ways in which the necessary contingencies may be arranged, either mechanically or electrically. An inexpensive device which solves most of the principal problems has already been constructed. It is still in the experimental stage, but a description will suggest the kind of instrument which seems to be required. The device consists of a small box about the size of a small record player. On the top surface is a window through which a question or problem printed on a paper tape may be seen. The child answers the question by moving one or more sliders upon which the digits 0 through 9 are printed. The answer appears in square holes punched in the paper upon which the question is printed. When the answer has been set, the child turns a knob. The operation is as simple as adjusting a television set. If the answer is right, the knob turns freely and can be made to ring a bell or provide some other conditioned reinforcement. If the answer is wrong, the knob will not turn. A counter may be added to tally wrong answers. The knob must then be reversed slightly and a second attempt at a right answer made. (Unlike the flash-card, the device reports a wrong answer without giving the right answer.) When the answer is right, a further turn of the knob engages a clutch which moves the next problem into place in the window. This movement cannot be completed, however, until the sliders have been returned to zero.

The important features of the device are these: Reinforcement for the right answer is immediate. The mere manipulation of the device will probably be reinforcing enough to keep the average pupil at work for a suitable period each day, provided traces of earlier aversive control can be wiped out. A teacher may supervise an entire class at work on such devices at the same time, yet each child may progress at his own rate, completing as many problems as possible within the class period. If forced to be away from school, he may return to pick up where he left off. The gifted child will advance rapidly, but can be kept from getting too far ahead either by being excused from arithmetic for a time or by being given special sets of problems which take him into some of the interesting bypaths of mathematics.

The device makes it possible to present carefully designed material in which one problem can depend upon the answer to the preceding and where, therefore, the most efficient progress to an eventually complex repertoire can be made. Provision has been made for recording the commonest mistakes so that the tapes can be modified as experience dictates.

Additional steps can be inserted where pupils tend to have trouble, and ultimately the material will reach a point at which the answers of the average child will almost always be right.

If the material itself proves not to be sufficiently reinforcing, other reinforcers in the possession of the teacher or school may be made contingent upon the operation of the device or upon progress through a series of problems. Supplemental reinforcement would not sacrifice the advantages gained from immediate reinforcement and from the possibility of constructing an optimal series of steps which approach the complex repertoire of mathematical behavior most efficiently.

A similar device in which the sliders carry the letters of the alphabet has been designed to teach spelling. In addition to the advantages which can be gained from precise reinforcement and careful programming, the device will teach reading at the same time. It can also be used to establish the large and important repertoire of verbal relationships encountered in logic and science. In short, it can teach verbal thinking. As to content instruction, the device can be operated as a multiple-choice self-rater.

Some objections to the use of such devices in the classroom can easily be foreseen. The cry will be raised that the child is being treated as a mere animal and that an essentially human intellectual achievement is being analyzed in unduly mechanistic terms. Mathematical behavior is usually regarded, not as a repertoire of responses involving numbers and numerical operations, but as evidences of mathematical ability or the exercise of the power of reason. It is true that the techniques which are emerging from the experimental study of learning are not designed to "develop the mind" or to further some vague "understanding" of mathematical relationships. They are designed, on the contrary, to establish the very behaviors which are taken to be the evidences of such mental states or processes. This is only a special case of the general change which is under way in the interpretation of human affairs. An advancing science continues to offer more and more convincing alternatives to traditional formulations. The behavior in terms of which human thinking must eventually be defined is worth treating in its own right as the substantial goal of education.

Of course the teacher has a more important function than to say right or wrong. The changes proposed would free her for the effective exercise of that function. Marking a set of papers in arithmetic—"Yes, nine and six *are* fifteen; no, nine and seven *are not* eighteen"—is beneath the dignity of any intelligent individual. There is more important work to be done—in which the teacher's relations to the pupil cannot be duplicated by a mechanical device. Instrumental help would merely improve these relations. One might say that the main trouble with education in the lower grades today is that the child is obviously not competent and *knows it* and that the teacher is unable to do anything about it and *knows that too*. If the advances which have recently been made in our control of behavior can give the child a genuine competence in reading, writing, spelling, and arithmetic, then the teacher may begin to function, not in lieu of a cheap machine, but through intellectual, cultural, and emotional contacts of that distinctive sort which testify to her status as a human being.

Another possible objection is that mechanized instruction will mean technological unemployment. We need not worry about this until there are enough teachers to go around and until the hours and energy demanded of the teacher are comparable to those in other fields of employment. Mechanical devices will eliminate the more tiresome labors of the teacher but they will not necessarily shorten the time during which she remains in contact with the pupil.

A more practical objection: Can we afford to mechanize our schools? The answer is clearly *yes*. The device I have just described could be produced as cheaply as a small radio or phonograph. There would need to be far fewer devices than pupils, for they could be used in rotation. But even if we suppose that the instrument eventually found to be most effective would cost several hundred dollars and that large numbers of them would be required, our economy should be able to stand the strain. Once we have accepted the possibility and the necessity of mechanical help in the classroom, the economic problem can easily be surmounted. There is no reason why the school room should be any less mechanized than, for example, the kitchen. A country which annually produces millions of refrigerators, dishwashers, automatic washing-machines, automatic clothes driers, and automatic garbage disposers can certainly afford the equipment necessary to educate its citizens to high standards of competence in the most effective way.

There is a simple job to be done. The task can be stated in concrete terms. The necessary techniques are known. The equipment needed can easily be provided. Nothing stands in the way but cultural inertia. But what is more characteristic of America than an unwillingness to accept the traditional as inevitable? We are on the threshold of an exciting and revolutionary period, in which the scientific study of man will be put to work in man's best interests. Education must play its part. It must accept the fact that a sweeping revision of educational practices is possible and inevitable. When it has done this, we may look forward with confidence to a school system which is aware of the nature of its tasks, secure in its methods, and generously supported by the informed and effective citizens whom education itself will create.

6. Viewpoints from Related Disciplines: Learning Theory *

EDWARD JOSEPH SHOBEN, Jr.,

Professor of Education, Teachers College

THE PSYCHOLOGIST concerned with learning theory, at least as long as he keeps his professional cloak wrapped tightly about him, is likely to be embarrassed by the question, What should the schools teach? His specialty is oriented toward the discovery of *how* organisms learn rather than *what* they learn. When his functions are applied to the urgent practicalities of the school, they are usually much more like those of the technician or consulting engineer than like those of the normative or goal-setting philosopher. Issues involving "should" or "ought" are unfamiliar to him, and his methods, aimed at the achievement of generalized description rather than discrimination among values, are more assertedly than admittedly irrelevant to the task of structuring an ideal curriculum.

Nevertheless, if this apologia is kept firmly in mind, there may be some justification in permitting a learning theorist to think aloud about the character of the ideal curriculum. After all, it is impossible to observe the learning process without also observing the learning of some content. Moreover, a point often overlooked in considerations of formal learning theory is that its basic contentions and the experimental work done in its name are consistently devoted to behavior of a generally "adjustive" sort. That is, they are concerned with the individual's acquisition and modification of problem sensitivities and problem solutions—how he learns to define the conditions of his life (including those within himself) with which he must cope and to develop behavioral mechanisms for dealing with them. These topics may not be entirely foreign to curricular issues. Finally, if the learning theorist allows his professional observations and cerebrations to penetrate his life as citizen, as father, and as person, he is likely to generate some reflections that may win brief attention from the curriculum expert and the educational philosopher. It must be remembered, however, that in discussing normative questions of the curriculum, a learning psychologist may be levying on his field of expertness; he is not practicing within it.

* From Edward Joseph Shoben, Jr., "Viewpoints from Related Disciplines: Learning Theory," *Teachers College Record* (February, 1959), pp. 272–82. Reprinted by permission.

Subject Matter, Models, and Motives

Psychologically, it seems sound to argue that the essential curriculum for each school child at any given time is not what is on paper in the curriculum supervisor's office. It is much more likely to be the way he perceives his teacher. The curriculum, after all, is only a statement of what the pupil is to learn. His learning proceeds through the vital and basic mediation of the teacher. What he learns, therefore, is in significant degree a function of how he reacts to and interprets the mediating adult. The implications of this basic observation are not entirely obvious, nor are they free from complexity. It may be advantageous to unravel some of them.

The unravelling process may be assisted by looking at a somewhat different problem, that of juvenile delinquency. In a general way, delinquency represents a failure of socialization; the juvenile either fails to learn the social rules or—more frequently—he learns actively to rebel against them. One of the conditions of this unhappy and antisocial learning seems to be a particular pattern of parent–child relationships. It has been demonstrated,[1] for example, that the parents of delinquents are more overprotective, more indifferent, more hostile and rejecting, and less warm than those of nondelinquents. Parental control in the homes of delinquents tends to be either more lax or stricter and much more erratic than in the homes of nondelinquents. Finally, the parents of delinquents tend to enforce discipline much more frequently through physical punishment or threats and much less often through reasoning and explaining the nature of rules than do the parents of nondelinquents.

In other words, the behavior of the parents of delinquent children is such as to alienate their offspring rather than to draw them closer. The social tragedy of this state of affairs lies in the fact that the parents are not only distinctive persons; they are the representatives of society to the developing youngster. In learning that their parents are unfair, unencouraging, and unloving, delinquents act as if they had also learned that the world in general is unfair, unencouraging, and unloving.[2] It can accurately be said that these children have learned to want to be *unlike* their parents. More technically, they have learned motives that are at variance both with their community

---

[1] S. Glueck and Eleanor Glueck, *Unravelling Juvenile Delinquency* (New York: The Commonwealth Fund, 1950).

[2] A good discussion of this process of generalization may be found in J. Dollard and N. E. Miller, *Personality and Psychotherapy* (New York: McGraw-Hill Book Co., 1950), pp. 51–53, 98–106. For a startlingly instructive experiment on generalization, see N. E. Miller, "Theory and Experiment Relating Psychoanalytic Displacement to Stimulus Generalization," *Journal of Abnormal and Social Psychology*, 1948, Vol. 43, pp. 155–178.

and with their own long-term happiness. This unfortunate motivational learning has occurred through the mediation of undesirable models, the parents, who have inadequately represented society at large to their growing children. The "home curriculum" may not have been planned, but it is startlingly effective.

Against this instance of social learning it may be asked what the teacher represents. Of what is she a model? Whatever else she may be asked to embody, it seems clear that the teacher functions basically, either well or ill, as the model of an educated person. The school remains one of the community's agents of socialization, and if it serves at its best to advance and to change the culture as well as to preserve and to transmit it, such is the purpose of socialization agencies in dynamic and democratic societies. But what makes the school distinctive from the home, the church, the police and court system, or the Boy Scouts is its special stress on the acquisition of knowledge and the enlargement of one's capacity to reflect upon it. To make this point is neither to deny the advantage or even the necessity of being vocationally well equipped or socially adept nor to argue that the school has nothing to do with vocational training or social grace. It is, however, to declare that the school's distinctive and primary mission is to *educate,* to make available a wide stock of ideas and information and to cultivate the methods by which it can be increased, applied, and formed into new combinations. And it is, of course, merely to restate Dewey's aim of education as the informed and logically trained adult.[3]

The teacher, then, if she is to facilitate attainment of this educational goal, must be a model of the informed and thoughtful adult. But there are two other conditions imposed upon her. First, the children must learn to *want to be like her.* It is here that the lessons of the delinquency studies come home. The affection, the concern for the individual child, the reasonableness, and the consistency of the parents of nondelinquents seem important as ways of encouraging a healthy identification with society generally. Children who perceive their parents as fair and loving seem rather more inclined to emulate them in their law-abiding ways. One would expect that similar behavior in a teacher would generate more of a desire in the child to emulate her in her mastery of skills and information and her logical ways of thinking about them. But there is a second condition. Children come to school from a variety of backgrounds, and in one sense this diversity is increased through their school years in spite of whatever learnings they acquire in common. Thus, the teacher as an effective model of the informed and logically trained adult must be prepared to demonstrate her information and her cognitive skills over a wide range of subject matter, making herself perceptible as a kind of ideal to all children, regardless of the in-

[3] John Dewey, *How We Think* (New York: D. C. Heath, 1910).

terests they bring to her. The teacher is not a specialist or an intellectual virtuoso; she is a student of eagerness and breadth, visible as such to her charges. And if the inevitability of specialization reduces her range in the upper reaches of the school years, the reduction need never be complete. It cannot be if she is to remain a model of the educated person.

What is being discussed here is, of course, the basic curriculum problem vital in the lower elementary grades but important throughout the secondary school: How do children learn to like to learn? The question has nothing to do with specific subjects to the exclusion of others. Rather, it is concerned with establishing relationships of identification between children and an adult who prizes and exemplifies the intellectual accomplishments of acquiring new information and actively thinking about it. The outcome sought is the learning of a positive motivation for becoming educated. It is possible that there are few objectives in the ideal curriculum that merit a higher place.

Method vs. Substance

But a positive motivation for education, fundamental as it is, will hardly bring order into the curricular chaos that seems to threaten American schools in the mid-twentieth century. If each group and virtually each articulate person has distinctive ideas about what the school should teach, it is obvious that some of them must be disappointed. Similarly, if such anarchy prevails among the influential, it may suggest that disappointment is a not improper fate for many of the would-be legislators of the curriculum.

From the standpoint of a learning theorist, more concerned with the development of the learning process than with specific subject matters, it is natural to attack the question first, given the basic motivation, by emphasizing the importance of methods common to intellectual tasks rather than specific realms of subject matter. There is a widespread tendency to regard methodological issues as musty epiphenomena on the substantive structure of knowledge; but in science, or government, and in law it is the methods and procedures that endure and add a virtually endless stream of modification and correction as well as novelty to human experience and wisdom. It may well be that the creative insight that leads to genuinely new discovery is a function of the attributes of an unusual man, just as the novel creation in the arts is probably an outcome of some little-understood combination of events and abilities in the artist. But most of the work of the world is done by people who have simply mastered in one degree or another the techniques of disciplined thought.

For the elementary school curriculum, the implication of this point of

view is that a great deal of attention might profitably be given to such matters as sources of evidence, the processes of inference, and the interrelationships of fields of knowledge. Obviously, there is no advocacy here of formal
logic in the first grade. There is a suspicion, however, that children are
sensitive to a wide range of problems on which, according to their level of
development and ability, they can readily bring to bear the processes of
definition, collection of evidence, and logical arrangement. If the utility of
the processes can be made explicit for them through the mediation of the
teacher, the likelihood of their generality to other contexts is increased.[4]

Among other things, this focus on the identification of problems, the
gathering of evidence, and the developing of a logical order suggests that
the first exercises in formal communication in the elementary grades might
better be concerned with argument rather than narration. It seems safe to
say that not all children enjoy hearing stories; fewer enjoy telling them; but
most have opinions about something and find zest and relevance in both
witnessing and attempting the persuasion of others to their own points of
view. The debater's skill may yet be embryonic, but one may hear remarkably cogent reasoning, reinforced by a wealth of well-mastered information,
in the conversations of boys of nine about which team is a better bet in a
World Series. Is it possible that curriculum planning has overlooked the fact
that youngsters have points of view which they are eager to advance and to
defend by the time they come to school? At any rate, it may be important
to remember that to argue successfully one must know something, must
order what he knows in a logical manner, and must present his ordered
evidence in a communicative manner. The specific subject matter can perhaps range from baseball to astronomy *if* the teacher can help the child to
move toward greater degrees of subtlety and comprehensiveness in applying
these methods and toward a greater awareness of both what he is doing
and the usefulness of doing it.

More specifically, it follows from the vision of potentiality offered here
that simple laboratory demonstrations, the use of encyclopedias and other
reference volumes, and a great deal of explicit practice in making inferences
from the facts one learns and deductions from the principles one encounters
could happily be introduced at the earliest possible point and maintained as
instruction necessarily becomes more and more concerned with subject
matter. The degree of difficulty and complexity could steadily increase,
but the emphasis could be on the same basic methods of identifying and
defining problems, finding evidence relevant to their solutions, and arrang-

[4] For a review of this problem and an experimental exploration of it with adult
subjects, Robert C. Craig, *The Transfer Value of Guided Learning* (New York:
Bureau of Publications, Teachers College, Columbia University, 1953).

ing the evidence in a logical way. Analyzing a story in a reading primer, solving the problem of why ships float or whether a container of ice will overflow when the ice melts, or settling the question of what kind of class party to have all provide opportunities for guided learning in the *methods* of information-gathering and thinking. Oddly enough, most curricula say little about the explicit cultivation of these skills; yet their fundamental character is unarguable, and the fact that they begin to develop for good or ill even before the school years is known to every teacher and to every parent. Further, the multiplication of studies and subject fields can end only in distraction and superficiality unless some unifying and centralizing factor can be found. The learning theorist is likely to find it in the express and inventive attention of curriculum experts and teachers to ways of developing in all children the methods of learning common to all fields of knowledge. The curiosity, imagination, and experimental turn of mind so evident in youngsters would seem to be a natural resource for this kind of curriculum building that has yet to be effectively capitalized upon.

Content as Skills of Learning

The position sketched so far holds that the basic curriculum consists in the development of a positive motivation for learning—the elicitation of a serious and zestful enjoyment in acquiring new information and reflecting upon it—and a growing command of the techniques of orderly and sequential thought. Two assumptions underlie this argument: first, that these dynamic objectives can be attained without an *initial* focus on common subject matter for all children; second, that while these two aims retain their primacy through the school years, they gradually assume the form of a concentration on particular contents, depending mainly on the developing interests and aptitudes of particular youngsters.

But a love of learning demands exposure to something that is learned, and reinforced practice in thinking requires that one think about something. How are these "somethings" to be profitably organized? From the standpoint of a learning theorist, concerned with the progressive steps in the acquisition of knowledge, skills, and attitudes, the chronologically first and consistently important subjects are the symbolic skills—listening, reading, writing, and manipulating numbers. It is not so much the clear, practical value of these talents that gives them their curricular vitality, although their practicality provides many opportunities for pedagogical implementation and reinforcement. Rather, it is their character as a basis for all other learning, even the mastery in a technological age of functions associated with mechanics, radio, and electronics. Symbolic skills, then, are essential to education; and in a real but special sense, one may be considered educated to the extent that he has a functional power over the symbolic capacity that is so distinctively human.

Ordinarily, this unfolding of symbolic capacity in reading, spelling, or arithmetic has been assessed against some age-related norm of actual achievement. Thus, children are traditionally characterized (and graded) as "good" or "poor" in these accomplishments in terms of where they stand in relation to the average attainment of others of their own age or grade placement. Such norms have an influence on curriculum planning in providing the presumably realistic objectives for each school year.

But there is a different conception of these symbol-using functions that leads to different curricular implications. It is here that the recent work of Skinner [5] on "teaching machines" becomes most relevant for present purposes. Although Skinner places his major emphasis on the way in which his machines handle the subtle contingencies of reinforcement in the learning process, his major and revolutionary contribution may lie in two other features of his approach. First, he conceives of competence in any subject, including the symbolic skills, as approximations to total mastery, not as a point on a distribution curve for an age or a grade in achievement. Thus, the significant dimension of assessment becomes that of how far a pupil has gone toward full competence, not how he stands generally in relation to his fellows. Second, to insure steady progress at the student's own pace toward whatever degree of competence he can attain, the material to be learned is "programmed" in such a fashion that any given point is basic to the next point to be studied and that it is thoroughly understood before that next point is tackled. The important thing here is that the material to be learned is so programmed that the pupil never moves on to a new topic until he has acquired a repertoire of responses that enable him to deal correctly with the topic fundamental to it. He never, therefore, carries with him any errors learned in earlier sequences into later ones.

A general example may help to make the point clear. In arithmetic, Skinner's method first generates the numbers 0 through 9 in relation to objects, quantities, and scales. The operations of addition, subtraction, multiplication, and division are fully developed before the number 10 is introduced. Meanwhile, the child actively composes a variety of equations and arithmetic expressions. He learns to deal easily, for example, not only with $5 + 4 = ?$, but with $? + 4 = 9$, and $5 ? 4 = 9$, usually aided by illustrative materials of many kinds. There is no appeal to rote memory, even in the later learning of the multiplication tables. The youngster learns $9 \times 8 = 72$, not by memorizing it like a line of verse, but by applying such earlier acquired principles as nine times a number is the same as ten times the

[5] B. F. Skinner, "Teaching Machines," *Science,* 1958, Vol. 128, pp. 969–979.

number minus the number, that the digits in a multiple of nine add to nine, that in composing successive multiples of nine one counts backwards (*nine, eight*een, twenty-*seven,* thirty-*six*), that nine times a single digit is a number beginning with one less than the digit (nine times eight is *seven*ty-something), and even that the product of two numbers separated by only one number is equal to the square of the separating number minus one (as in 9×7 is one less than the square of 8).

The curricular problem posed as a challenge by this kind of method and the conception on which it rests is that of programming complex learning sequences such that each later step is dependent on the mastery of an earlier step, with all steps explicit and articulate. The pedagogical question of the machines can be left to research and debate in another context. The curricular issue engendered is immediately relevant.

Nowhere is this issue more pressing than in the field of symbol management. Curricular objectives in reading, spelling, grammar, clarity in speaking and writing, and mathematics have been consistently pared down in the light of "realistic" achievement data. At their upper levels of accomplishment, such talents have been conceived as primarily the intellectual property of the bright and advantaged. This tendency has been abetted to a degree by the widely shared and plausible rationalization that the acquisition of such skills is too much removed from the common sources of motivation that can be mobilized to promote children's learning. It is quite possible that this state of affairs has contributed much to the current educational crisis that is so heatedly discussed in both professional circles and the public press. More important, it may have deprived the nation and the world of a general level of cognitive power that is by no means entirely out of reach.

It seems tenable to argue that the difficulty in planning a curriculum in symbolic skills lies not so much in either the motivational or the intellectual limitations of pupils as in the stringencies of programming. This task requires that a field of performance be carefully analyzed and that its units be arranged in some developmental order. While the order follows the proposition that earlier steps be fully comprehended as a propaedeutic to later ones, it also means that the student is presented with just that material for which he is ready and on which his chances of success are maximized. As a result, each step is "easy," given mastery of the preceding series. Since success can be truly said to provide its own motivation, it is highly probable that a stronger and more general interest in language and arithmetic, as well as more accurate and fully developed skills, would result from this kind of programming.

Central to the argument here is the contention, illustrated by the example from programming in number skills, that youngsters would be learning to think, to apply general principles to a consistent flow of new problems and new information. By extending the programming concept from the basic symbolic techniques to the more substantive fields, one may generate a curricular structure that has continuity and system in it, preserving the orderliness and opportunities for sequential mastery that characterize the analyses of such particular fields as spelling or arithmetic.

For example, from the earliest cultivation of number skills, it is quite possible to move in a linear progression to algebra, geometry, and book-keeping and accounting. By combining arithmetical learnings with vocabulary and some common experiences with lights, flames, and thrown balls, one can make physics consecutive with a steady stream of previous training. Similarly, reading can be geared directly into descriptive civics, moving from there along branching lines of development into history, tied to the issues identified in this field, and literature, analyzed as outstanding expressions of the values implicit in these issues. Such programming would leave ample room for pupils to prepare written discussions, to engage in debates and make oral reports, and to spend time on dramatic presentations of aspects of the problems they study as they move into the more substantive areas of knowledge.

It must be repeated that concern here is not with teaching techniques. Rather, it is with the potentialities for the curriculum that may lie in a careful analysis of what men know, beginning with the fundamental skills by means of which knowledge is acquired. From such an analysis, more assertedly than admittedly an arduous and difficult task, it might be possible to derive a curricular structure that would promote more in the amount of information learned and in the habits of reflective thought acquired than has heretofore been considered possible. Should such a state come to pass, individual differences, will, of course, remain in learning outcomes. But these differences are more likely to be in how far various children go in completing a twelve-year course of study or in the branching directions they choose to follow in it. This is a very different thing from individual differences at a particular point within it. Parenthetically it may be noted that such an arrangement would have a decided implication for the meaning of grades. Ordinarily, a C, for example, currently implies that a pupil has less knowledge of a piecemeal sort in a whole segment of the curriculum (tenth-grade social studies, for example) than a pupil with an A, more than a youngster receiving a D. Under the system envisioned here, the student with a C would have finished less work than his confrere with an A, but he would have achieved the same degree of competence at the point he has reached as his quicker colleague when he was at that point. Motivational differences would be small because the motivation is supplied primarily by the constant string of successes that must be enjoyed at each point in the program before one advances to the next point. And at each point the pupil, within the limits of his relevant personal attributes, is learning to think and, through the successes, to enjoy the process of learning.

Curriculum and Extracognitive Development

So far the burden of this discussion has been on intellectual development through curriculum planning. The psychologist, however, whether concerned with learning theory or some other subspecialty of his discipline, is interested in other aspects of growth. A few comments may be appropriate therefore, on the physical, aesthetic, and social-emotional dimensions of child development as they relate to school experience.

To a lay eye, at least, physical education in the elementary grades rather often seems to be a matter of free play with a little peripheral instruction in games. In the secondary years, it often has the appearance of the same sort of thing, swollen occasionally by the wen of competitive athletics for a select few.[6] Psychologically there is ample room for doubt that the opportunities for important learnings are being capitalized on in such an approach to physical development. With respect to values it is explicitly assumed here that health, physical robustness, and the capacity to enjoy the functioning of one's own body are desirable things. The progressive enlargement of the child's endurance, strength, grace of movement, and sports skills then becomes a matter of curricular attention.

Again the concept of programming seems relevant. What sequence of exercises and games can be formulated which, begun in the primary grades, will permit each child to emerge from high school with confidence in his own physical prowess, a repertoire of active skills which he can enjoy through much of his life, and a background of sufficient success in them to motivate his continuance of them? The analysis called for here is not only of the skills and bodily attributes that enter into performance in tennis, golf, swimming, and other life-time sports; it also has to do with the kinds of activities that progressively develop the neuromuscular system, coordination, and stamina. With each step so planned that it involves a masterable exercise preliminary to the next step, the proportion of successes, particularly in the early years, is likely to be high, and the continuing motivation to build one's body systematically is thus built in. The motivation for play need hardly be called upon.

[6] Corrective and remedial work is not considered here. One may wonder, however, if this kind of enterprise does not represent more a service furnished through the schools as a matter of social convenience than an integral part of developmental education. To raise this problem is by no means to condemn a beneficial practice. It is, however, to suggest a different perspective in evaluating it.

But the sheer cultivation of one's physical capacities, important as it is, does not tell the whole story. Psychologists are not likely to regard competition as in itself harmful, and competitive situations make possible the acquisition of a number of useful traits that can, if properly taught, be widely generalized. Athletic competition, at least for boys, seems to offer this opportunity with special richness. Courage, persistence, the ability to lose gracefully and to win with modesty, and a zest for doing one's best are traits that it seems quite possible to cultivate on playing fields as well as in classrooms. Team games, most of which are seldom played after school years, are also valuable sources for developing attitudes about cooperation and the submergence of oneself in common goals. But they must be taught with such objectives in mind, and they must be played by everybody. The influential role often achieved by coaches underscores the importance of the adult models available to children in these contexts and the peculiar vitality of the kinds of relationships developed. Were physical development systematically conceived as a part of educational experience—the acquisition of information and skills deeply reflected upon—the nation might become enriched by more characterful as well as healthier persons.

What has been said about the social by-products of physical training can be applied, of course, to virtually any school activity that requires or permits interaction among children. Oddly enough, psychologists have made few analyses of social behavior that would permit an explicit programming of this side of human experience, but research of this sort is urgently called for. Its implications for school practice might be considerable. Until the necessary knowledge is available, however, it is doubtful if much curricular effort should be expended on the encouragement of social adeptness. Other socialization agencies, notably the home, share heavy responsibility here and they are likely to exercise a more on-going and stronger influence. As by-products, however, these character traits are important for teachers to be aware of, and their trained skills and sensitivities may be better relied on than an explicit curriculum based on as yet inadequate information.

Finally, there is the question of the arts and the development of both the aesthetic response and the performing skills. Psychological ignorance is abundant in this area, but two points may be made. Running all through these considerations of the curriculum has been the notion of education as a contribution to self-fulfillment. One of the basic reasons for curriculum planning and even a drastic revision of the concepts involved in it is that the school is an agency charged with the search for ever more effective ways of helping the individual child to realize his potentialities as fully as possible. Aesthetic potentialities of the appreciative as well as the performing minds are included in this idea of self-realization. Second, self-expression through active play and through vicarious forms of entertainment seems to be closely related to aesthetic development. The child's drawing with vivid colors, the imaginative story he creates while playing with toy soldiers, and his excited identification with the hero of a Western movie—all of which have their direct adult counterparts—are representations of the basic aesthetic potentialities. On the one hand, impulses, wishes, or personal attributes are expressed in the relative safety of the play situation; on the other hand, they are expressed for the individual in the equally safe circumstance of the medium, whether it be film or stage, music or sculpture.

It is at least possible that the difference between a child's listening to a tapped-out rhythm and an adult's listening to rhythms, or a child's crayon drawing and an adult work like Curry's "Tornado for Kansas," lies more in the complexity of conception and, consequently, in the aptitude for personal expression of either the active or the vicarious sort than in other considerations of technique. Technique is, however, the means by which the greater richness of expression is found, and both the performer and the appreciator are likely to be enlarged by understanding something of it. A problem of a unique kind is encountered here, however. The language of art, in contrast to that of all other fields of knowledge, has a private character that probably cannot be transcended. What one person reads in either Edgar Rice Burroughs or Shakespeare is likely to be different from what another finds there; one amateur pianist may find great satisfaction in interpreting so simple a piece as "Träumerei" in a fashion that another regards as thoroughly unexpressive. Similarly, on the creative side, the painter who is hurt and disappointed at the public "misunderstanding" of his work may have nevertheless experienced genuine joy and met an important need of his own in the making of his picture.

Some of this difficulty may be met by considering the arts as a form of communication. Still more can perhaps be overcome by the study of technique; as in law and the sciences, the methods seem to have enduring value even when the substance has been modified. But in the aethetic disciplines, as much seems to depend on the attributes of the consumer as on the characteristics of the product, and it is precisely this kind of private transaction between creator, interpreter, or appreciator and the individual work of art that is important. Any piece of music, literature, painting, or architecture has done at least a vital part of its work if it provides individual men on their own terms with stimulation, comfort, or an enlarged sense of self-fulfillment.

Consequently, the curriculum in the arts may require attention to two major enterprises. One is the programming of artistic materials so that the pupil becomes informed about the major techniques employed in literature, music, and the plastic and graphic arts. The performance factor may well be developed in this connection. Familiarity with rhyme, meter, diction, assonance, alliteration, and so forth, in poetry, for example, might well involve verse composition, thus permitting a dovetailing of instruction in the arts with that in symbol management. Similarly, knowledge of music, in progressing from familiarity with simple tunes to the recognition of contrapuntal techniques, could involve a progression in performance from singing melodies to part-singing and a preliminary mastery of some instrument, including the recorder, mouth harp, or harmonica. It is doubtful if a high degree of performance accomplishment is the particular business of the school, although identification of that talent certainly is.

The other side of the aesthetic experience the school can properly and effectively furnish is that of insuring within the elementary and secondary grades a reasonably full contact with a wide range of specific works of art. The objective here is to provide a basis on which the pupil can select those kinds of artistic expressions that *for him* facilitate self-realization. Whether his tastes are for Grant Wood or Michelangelo, for Raymond Chandler or Dostoevski, probably matters far less than whether he can find in the arts as amateur creator, interpreter, or appreciator the clarification of his own feelings and the understanding of his own and historical ideals that mark the cultivated man. It is doubtful that this kind of sensibility can be programmed. It depends primarily on a wide exposure to art in the context of a relationship with a sensitive and skilled teacher who more embodies the kind of actualization as a person that the arts can bring than the concept of taste as something that can be defined apart from the feelings, longings, and thoughts of the individual pupil.

Summary

This discussion has attempted to sketch briefly a conception of the school curriculum through the elementary and secondary years from the standpoint of one learning psychologist. It rests essentially on three propositions. First, a primary objective is more the development of strong motivation for on-going learning throughout life than the mastery of particular subject matters. Second, a major degree of attention must be focused on the methods of learning—defining problems, gathering evidence, making inferences, and applying previously acquired generalizations. To this end, heavy emphasis must be laid throughout the school years on such symbolic skills as language and mathematics. Finally, curricular content can be generated from an analysis of the fields of human knowledge into sequences in which each student must master prior steps before proceeding at his own pace to later ones.

These sequences can be formulated from a consideration of the basic symbols, the management of which constitutes the basis of education.

Arithmetic, for example, can lead to more advanced mathematics, physical sciences, and bookkeeping and accounting skills. Language training can move into a stepwise consideration of the way men conceive their relationships to each other and the ways by which these relationships are affected by communication. This means the social studies and behavioral sciences and, in part, the literary arts. In addition, the curriculum, conceived as an over-all plan for the socialization of the child through facilitating his self-realization, must provide for the youngster's physical development, the growth of his character in his relationships to others, and his cultivation as a person of aesthetic sensitivity.

7. Seven Principles of Learning *

STANLEY L. CLEMENT, *Associate Professor,*
State College,
Bridgewater,
Massachusetts

HAVE YOU ever refinished a piece of furniture? If so, you know that one swipe of the sander across the grain may mean hours of work removing the resulting scratches. The refinishing expert knows how necessary it is to work with the grain of the wood. Yet many teachers fail to realize the importance of working with, not against, the grain of the pupils. Too often the scratches drastically interfere with the learning process. Teachers need to know the characteristics of young people—their needs, interests, motivations, drives—what makes them act and feel as they do. Every effort should be made to capitalize upon such knowledge in planning and creating a classroom atmosphere conducive to learning.

What is learning? Is it a passive filling with facts? repeating them orally in class? or on test papers? Is it something done for teachers? for marks? for credits?

Grades too often reflect an ability to memorize and parrot back what the teacher has said or what the textbook contains. Memorization has its place, but it should not dominate the learning process. It isn't what we know (memorize) that is important but what we do with what we know. How much do we remember about a subject a short time after having taken the final test and discarded our notes? It is unfortunate that rank cards must be issued immediately at the end of a course. Life's rank card will grade on how our learning is put to use.

For real learning to take place, something must happen to the individual.

* From Stanley L. Clement, "Seven Principles of Learning," *The Clearing House* (September, 1961), pp. 23–26. Reprinted by permission.

There must be a change of behavior. Unless he thinks and acts differently as a result of the course, no education has taken place.

Too often there may be a change, but it is a negative one. Instead of learning what one is supposed to, concomitant learnings may include a dislike for a subject, for the teacher, for the school, and maybe how to cheat or get by with a minimum of effort.

How may we provide the learning situation that will bring about desirable change? How may we efficiently choose the textbook? the supplementary reading material and visual symbols? the films and other audio-visual aids? How may our lectures, class discussions, demonstrations, and group reports be more effective? How may the key to the learning process—the assignment—be made most vital? How may we evaluate any procedure or material that has been used? The seven principles of learning emphasized in this article may serve as criteria that will help us answer these questions. For each principle the *why* justifies its importance and the *how* illustrates how it may be carried out. (Only a few samples are cited of the many activities possible.)

I. Learning Should Be an Active Process

Why: Students must participate in order to react. We cannot simply pour in knowledge, but we must draw it out. It would be interesting to know what goes on in the minds of students sitting passively in class with their books closed. Young people like action; they want to be doing something. It is better to make outlines, to simulate meetings, and to demonstrate processes than merely to describe them. We learn through actual living rather than just reading about it in books. Teachers are not needed mainly to give answers but to help students find the answers.

How:

(1) Greater care in making assignments—indicating a problem to be solved, definite questions to answer, people to find out about, something definite to do besides just read so many pages

(2) Discussion, role playing, demonstration (by students), laboratory work in all subjects

(3) Film evaluation, tape-recorder use (language laboratory), teaching machines, field trips

(4) Notebooks, scrapbooks, diagrams, charts, graphs, projects

(5) Group work, debates, pupil-teacher planning

II. Learning Should Be Meaningful

Why: Understanding precedes mastery. Learning and understanding are reciprocal. Students learn only what they understand. While essential facts need to be memorized for automatic recall, the students' concern for re-membering will be minimized by the tendency to retain what they under-stand. Memorizing the steps of a geometry proof or a chemistry process will have little value unless the student understands what he is doing.

How:

(1) Teaching the new in terms of the old—connecting it to previous learning and past experience both within and outside the course

(2) Application to life situations

(3) Emphasis on assignment making

(4) Pictures, graphs, charts, maps, models, specimens

(5) Demonstration, laboratory work, films, field trips

III. Learning Should Be Useful

Why: A goal provides a motivating force. If class work seems important to the student—if it will make a difference and bring success—he will have a greater desire for achievement. And he should gain satisfaction here and now, not just entertain a promise for the future. Will it help him to get the most out of school? Will it aid in getting into and succeeding in college? Will it help in earning a living? Will it aid him in the ability to express him-self? to get along with people? Will it help avoid embarrassment because of ignorance? Whatever we do should have as its basis the meeting of the needs of the individual and the welfare of society.

How:

(1) Establishing aims for subjects, units, and daily lessons which relate to needs, drives, motives, and desires of young people—aims which seem worth while and are accepted by them—which relate to problems arising in life with which they can identify themselves

(2) Planning and evaluating work in terms of these aims

(3) Making students conscious of these aims—starting and ending each course, each unit, and each daily lesson with emphasis on the aims

(4) Pupil-teacher planning

(5) Determining from school alumni what learning they found most useful in school and what they thought was neglected

IV. Learning Should Be Interesting

Why: Interest precedes effort. Students learn more rapidly when they are highly motivated. Curiosity can be a driving force. Learning does not have to be painful. It does not lose prestige because it is interesting. This does not mean a lowering of standards. Work may only appear to be less difficult because it is pleasant and purposeful.

How:

(1) Planning stimulating assignments

(2) Using a variety of methods and materials, such as films and demonstrations

(3) Increasing pupil participation in class through discussion and debates

(4) Capitalizing on desire for social approval—having group activity

(5) Appealing to rivalry and pride through competition

V. Learning Should Be Individualized

Why: An opportunity should be provided for each pupil to realize his potential. The school used to put all students in the same mold—fitting the child to the school. Emphasis was on teaching subjects, not children; the same curriculum and methods were used for all. Teaching was beamed at the average student while the bright student became bored and the slow became frustrated. With almost everyone going to secondary school now, the ability of the average student is considerably below what it used to be.

In any grade, a large number of students are below the average of the grade below and approximately the same number are above the average of the grade above. There is often a spread of six years in any grade above the fourth and this spread becomes greater as teaching becomes better.

Adolescence is a period of rapid growth. Not only do students mature at different rates, but different aspects of the same individual vary as well. Even with ability grouping there is no such thing as a homogeneous class, only one that is relatively more so.

How:

(1) Knowing strengths and weaknesses of pupils—using grouping within a class and adapting content to the various levels

(2) Using a variety of methods and materials

(3) Having differentiated assignments—-minimum and maximum, standard and optional

(4) Basing group work on student interests

(5) Capitalizing on supervised study and help sessions to aid slow students and challenge bright ones

VI. Learning Should Be Satisfying

Why: Students will repeat satisfying experiences and shun unpleasant ones. Satisfaction may be both extrinsic and intrinsic. Because of their lack of adult maturity, young people often do not have a true sense of values. Outside motivations can be justified as long as they do not become ends in themselves and there is a chance for all to be rewarded.

How:

(1) Having the amount of praise handed out to students at least balance the amount of criticism which is leveled at them

(2) Offering incentives—honors, awards, privileges

(3) Providing opportunity for all to succeed, to hold status in the group

(4) Keeping pupils aware of their progress in relation to their ability

(5) Using negative approaches as a last resort for some cases—detention, scolding, failures

VII. Learning Should Be Unified

Why: The total learning situation is important. The student does not learn merely with his mind but physically, socially, and emotionally. All of the senses must be used. The environment or setting for learning is vital. Improper physical conditions, uninspiring teachers, and unplanned lessons are still too much in evidence.

Whole learning is more effective than part learning. We tend to divide school up into too many isolated subjects and each subject into individual doses, with resulting lack of emphasis on perspective or relationships.

How:

(1) Good room atmosphere—light, heat, ventilation, bulletin boards, etc.

(2) Being aware of the importance of teacher appearance, enthusiasm, voice, posture, and attitude

(3) Consideration of pupil health and home situations

(4) Long-range planning and long-range assignments—the unit method

(5) Setting stage, reviewing, and summarizing each day and for each unit

As we select and as we judge each of our procedures and materials, let us ask ourselves: Is it useful? Does it promote a desirable goal? Is it meaningful? Will the student understand it? Is it interesting? Will it arouse curiosity? Does it involve action? Will student participation be high? Is it individualized? Is it adapted to interests and abilities? Is it satisfying? Will it be a pleasant experience? Is it unified? Is there a clear relationship to the whole unit? If we can answer these questions in the affirmative, not only will we be teaching but the students will really learn.

8. The Multidimensional Contexts of Learning *

NATHANIEL CANTOR

THE RECENT STUDY by Dr. Philip E. Jacob for the Edward W. Hazen Foundation will prove disconcerting to many college teachers.[1] The study showed no significant changes in student values resulting from the character of the curriculum or from the basic courses in social science which students take as part of their general education. The quality of teaching had relatively little effect upon the value-outcomes of general education.

Some students have a set of mind so rigid, an outlook on human relations so stereotyped, and a reliance on authority so compulsive that they are intellectually and emotionally incapable of understanding new ideas, and seeing much less accepting, educational implications which run counter to their preconceptions. This particularly limits their responsiveness in the social sciences and the humanities whenever controversial issues arise. Such students quail in the presence of conflict and uncertainty. They crave "right answers." They distrust speculative thought, their own or their fellow students'. They recoil from "creative discussion."

One does not need elaborate statistical studies to risk the conclusion that most professionals, along with the graduates of schools of business administration, the teachers' colleges, and the colleges of arts and sciences, do not continue to learn in significant, vital ways, to "grow," or even to engage in much serious reading which is related to their professional work.

I confess after thirty-five years, during which time I have tried to discover what effective teaching and learning are, that I remain puzzled and challenged. The advertising copy, the statement of objectives and purposes found in the bulletins of the schools, are, of course, not to be taken too seriously. Faculty members of the colleges and professional schools of this country are aware of the lack of clarity and even disagreement regarding goals. If the objectives of higher education are not clearly stated, agreed upon, and striven for, it is difficult to ascertain what "effective" teaching means.

For the purposes of developing the thesis of this paper I assume that a

* Nathaniel Cantor, "The Multidimensional Contexts of Learning," March, 1958, *The Educational Forum*. © *The Educational Forum*. Used by permission of Kappa Delta Pi.
[1] *Changing Values in College:* An Exploratory Study of the Impact of General Education in Social Sciences on the Values of American Students.

college education should help a person to become aware of the nature of the world in which he lives, of the people with whom he associates, and of his responsibilities and obligations to others. A college education should help one to appreciate his own traditions, to heighten his appreciation of the different forms of beauty, and to learn how to make satisfactory sense out of his living.

I recognize my own biases in these value judgments but I fail to see how I can remain acceptably sane and avoid ethical commitments.

The spiritual roots of American teachers extended more or less deeply into the soil of American democracy. We have to live by some values. Historically, we are democratically oriented. That is the given. Our democratic postulates are not derived from science but from our society, more directly from our parents and teachers. They are not derived from science, but their implications and consequences can be rationally examined by science. In the light of our limited, but best, knowledge, what consequences are likely to follow from moral direction A, B, or C, and how can they be realized? The desirability of the consequences is judged in accord with our given democratic beliefs. There is no more need to ground our given values on ultimate moral "principles" than scientific judgments of facts need to be based upon first truths or the final logical proof for induction.

Our teachers alone cannot rebuild society, but they can prepare future leaders by helping them to assimilate ideas and to develop attitudes which can make some difference in meeting the concrete critical issues they now face and will face. The temptation of the fleshpots may be modified by the visions of Plato —and their own.[2]

Learning which might modify the accepted norms of "success" in American society would be, in my opinion, effective learning. It would present opportunities for many young people to become more sensitized to the meaning and implications of the data to which they are exposed and to make somewhat different choices in their life experiences. The question is, can this be accomplished in the colleges? I do not know whether it is possible for any large number of students. I am certain, however, that failure to do this is due in part to the traditional "knowledge approach" on the part of a majority of teachers to the teaching-learning process.[3] The "ideas" one is exposed to in the colleges do not seem to make any vital difference in the life of the students.

What actually takes place in the teaching-learning situation? How many teachers are aware of the tangled web of interpersonal relations which

[2] N. Cantor, "The Teacher in a General Education Program," *Journal of General Education* (April, 1952).

[3] I am concerned here with the colleges of arts and sciences. The graduate and professional schools present other problems.

entrap both teacher and learner? How many of us sense the vital interests of our students? Are *they* concerned with the abstractions we fool around with? Who does most of the kidding, the "profs" or the students? How much honest, meaningful communication takes place between teacher and learners? How deeply and truly concerned are we, the teachers, with what is happening to our students because of our performance? Do we fret about our lack of skill in the classroom, or is that no problem? Just what is each one of us doing in the classroom besides dealing with our specialized field of interest?

These are only a few questions regarding the realities of the learning situation. More formally I should like to discuss four different levels (there are many more) which operate in a teaching-learning group experience, namely, the social, ethical, professional, and scientific.

Social Norms

When two or more people meet there can be no communication between them unless they share certain values. Social relations as opposed to chance physical contact imply that individuals possess expectations regarding one another's behavior. A perceptive teacher will become aware of the expectations of the group he leads, and of what he expects as he leads them. I speak now of his awareness, not of his judging the desirability of the expectations. It is normal, for example, for a teacher to be aware of his status and position. He is inclined to be a bit of a prima donna. He is expected to possess superior knowledge and wants to display it. It is also generally understood that the teacher controls the class. He is in charge. He leads, students follow.

The student "learns" how to meet the regulations and requirements of the course and the professor. Over the years, both in primary and secondary schools, the pupils have learned what to expect and how to meet the demands of the classroom and instructor. They quickly learn, through the help of the experienced fellow students, the techniques to be used for the several instructors, which teachers demand deference.

The experienced teacher is aware of these folkways. He realizes how much of the classroom experience is an on-going contest of wills between the traditional authority of the teacher and the resistance of the student. He understands that it requires many weeks to modify student expectations and his own traditional teacher attitudes. New classroom norms can be established but only after periods of confusion. Students do not easily surrender their lifelong distrust of the inquisitorial instructor. They sense the mumbo-jumbo of required assignments, passing grades, and the lifelessness of texts and teachers. The skilled teacher, in time, can lessen their fears and defensiveness. Through his own genuine, spontaneous involvement in helping them learn he challenges and excites the creative effort of students. New expectations on the part of teacher and learner become the pattern. The teacher expects to help, that is his function. The student's responsibility is to learn.

Ethical Assumptions

Our culture teaches us to conform to a series of religious and ethical beliefs. These are the absolutes of our society. Our ideals of Justice, Truth, and Goodness are so taken for granted in our literature, official utterances, secular schooling, and, of course, religious instruction that it requires considerable cultural sophistication to recognize the arbitrary character of these usually unexamined premises. These sacred and taken-for-granted beliefs and ideals must be recognized by the teacher, how they have come about, how they function, how they help or hinder the objectives of learner development.

There is a growing acceptance of a goal in modern life, which, some of us think, threatens the development of individuals. I refer to the idea of teaching students "to adjust." The "life-adjustment courses" in many of the secondary schools of the country rest squarely on the idea of conformity. In fact a new social ethic in contradiction to the Protestant ethic is developing in this country. This is the central thesis of a recent study, *The Organization Man,* by William H. Whyte. Candidates for executive positions are expected to conform to the group, to adjust to group norms. It is not merely the conformity which is dangerous, it is the fact that leaders in industry and many teachers believe that it is *morally imperative* that the individual should learn or be taught to conform for his own good. Getting along with everybody and being "well-rounded" are, it is taught, much-needed goals of modern life.

A teacher who becomes aware of this basic ethic of conformity which is rapidly creeping up on us in many segments of our life (industrial relations, moral, socioeconomic, political, and educational beliefs) will be shocked to discover the degree to which he, too, has been manipulated toward or has unwittingly succumbed to conformity. He cannot, therefore, be expected to help the learner develop creatively, or to be understanding, when the student tries out his differences with the instructor, or the packaged classroom programs. The instructor needs to accept his own differences before he can easily permit the expression of student differences.

No premium is being offered for the encouragement of ill-mannered, hostile, cantankerous, neurotic misfits. Conformity to some group standards, loyalty to organization, respect for tradition, cooperation, these are all valuable and necessary qualities of organized social activity. The problems relate to the degree of conformity, to what standards, what organization, respect for what traditions, cooperation with whom under what conditions, *and at what cost to the integrity of the individual?* In brief, we are concerned with the shifting balance between the social and individual aspects of the learner. The development of maturity requires that the learner accept a deal of the responsibility for the judgments *he* makes and the risks *he* undergoes.

A skillful teacher is aware of this dilemma, the need for the preservation of traditional values and the need for maturing individuals to determine the nature of a changing order, and the roles he chooses to play.

The Science of Human Relations

If skilled teaching has a sense of direction, a purpose, and a structure, one should be able *to describe* it. This does not mean the description will adequately cover all of the dimensions. It does mean that one should be able to state the assumptions upon which one is carrying out the process, the results which follow, whether one can predict general uniformities, and whether certain principles of helping others can be communicated and further tested. There is little precise knowledge about how people learn, how groups operate, and how one teaches. People do differ in teaching skills and in learning potential. Except in the rare case skills are developed, and learning is facilitated. There have been some great "natural" teachers and some insatiable learners. The majority of teachers, however, must acquire ability, and the majority of learners must be helped to develop. It is a serious mistake to believe that any one is qualified to teach others (in the area of development of potential) without the available understanding of what is involved in learning.

The various methods and contents of educational programs are based upon certain assumptions, expressed or implied, regarding how people learn. No one method or content or combination is objectionable in itself. What is troublesome and misleading is dogmatic insistence on clichés and rules and verbal principles. Many teachers, unsure of themselves, and of what they are doing, that is, possessing little skill, seek security through the *Word*.

It is important that inquiry and research into how people learn and develop be supported. Without this knowledge the exercise of skill becomes personal idiosyncrasy. The teacher who seems to be consistently helpful will be exercising great skill, that is, he will possess the best available knowledge, and will understand how inadequate it is. Furthermore, the skilled teacher understands that even if our knowledge of human relations and learnings were more reliable and valid the logic of ideas rarely parallels the lust for living. The teacher discovers what is "wrong" with the learner. The teacher knows what "should" be done. It's a wise teacher who keeps that knowledge to himself until such time as the student wants to or is helped to become ready to avail himself of the teacher's wisdom.

Professional Level

This dimension is little understood by teachers. In every learning experience the helper must become sensitized to his own feelings toward the learners. What use does he make of himself for the benefit of the learner? What needs of his own are being fulfilled or frustrated? What are his biases which color his interpretations and distort his perceptions? The teacher is hard put to discover what the feelings of the members are toward him, toward each other and in relation to the data. What do they really want in their classes? Are they communicating or engaging in the usual folderol of pleasant intellectual amenities where no one is in danger of getting or being really hurt?

Most of us, leaders and students, fear to examine these pretty pictures of ourselves which we carry around and the pretty language with which we so clearly and simply describe our opinions, judgments, and excellent reasons for acting as we do. The individual who examines himself and others is embarking on a dangerous journey. It is hard to predict where this examination will lead one.

Skills in teaching require the development of a professional self.

By professional level I mean the teacher's understanding of how to use himself in the learning situation for the sake of the learner. The teacher's function is to assist in the development of others. Ideally the teacher's personal needs for satisfaction, approval, or control are irrelevant in the teaching-learning situation. The teacher is not being paid to use the classroom as a clinic for the expression of personal tensions. The teacher is engaged to help the learner.

No teacher, however professional in outlook, can avoid personal involvement at times. Each of us feels the need to win, to control, to dominate, to be right, that is, to make the other over in our image. If our "help" is rejected we become hostile or resentful. Or, if sometimes we succeed in dominating, we experience guilt.

The more sensitive the awareness, the more disciplined will a teacher become in dealing with personal involvement. Indeed the re-creation of the professional core of a teacher rests upon the discovery that one is using the student for one's personal needs. The teacher gains satisfaction not in becoming popular with students but in redirecting and disciplining personal feeling. This continuous intrapersonal struggle can lead to more skilled, professional use of one's self.

This is, in the final analysis, the soundest test for a teacher's performance. A teacher's competence is not formed through what the learner learns but through the skill with which the teacher encourages the student to want to learn. Everyone learns only what *he wants to learn.* No one can be motivated by another. The teacher helps by creating the most favorable circumstances in which learning can occur, if the student wants to learn. For one reason or another beyond the control of the teacher he may not want to learn. The teacher's task is to encourage, to help, to put himself at the disposal of the learner. In brief the teacher's job is to perform skillfully as a teacher. The learner's responsibility is to learn. The chances are favorable that if one performs skillfully as a teacher the learner is more likely to want to learn. Nevertheless, skillful teaching need not necessarily lead to genuine learning. Poor teaching, sometimes, cannot block learning, and excellent teaching often fails to challenge those who do not want to learn.

Verbal Magic

Most college students do not comfortably understand the physical and mathematical foundations of the universe. They do not understand the meaning of scientific methods. Their social science understanding is undigested claptrap. The college of arts and sciences graduates, and professionally trained adults outside of their area of competence, are frightfully ignorant.

I do not mean to recriminate or to scold or to appear righteous. I am presenting my considered opinion of what the colleges of arts and sciences accomplish. The study of Dr. Jacob supports what many of us suspected. Part of the failure of education, it seems to me, is the confusion between knowledge and understanding. Understanding is not to be confused with specious verbal magic, hollow concepts. All of us have attended innumerable faculty meetings characterized by the dull amenities where no one risks anything or learns anything significant. What is true of faculty meetings is true of classroom meetings. The same conspiracy of silence continues. Teachers pretend to know more than they do; they talk a great deal repeating the talk of the texts. The students repeat the talk of the talk of the text talkers. Mark Twain opens his autobiography:

. . . His (a person's) acts and his words are merely the visible, thin crust of his world, with its scattered snow summits and its vacant wastes of water—and they are so trifling a part of his bulk, a mere skin enveloping it. The mass of him is hidden—and its volcanic fires that toss and boil, and never rest, night or day. These are his life, and they are not written, and cannot be written.

Understanding, genuine learning, is made up of much more than knowledge. Compassion, tragic futility, illusory hope, humility, confusion, worry, hope, love, creativity, wisdom—all of these operate in the classroom. These multidimensional factors are the matrix of vital learning. Ideas are the spark. They should enter not as vacuums but as hot filaments illuminating the dark recesses of our being. Teachers need to understand what learning involves.

9. Conditions for Effective Learning *

RALPH W. TYLER, *Director of the Center for Advanced Study in the Behavioral Sciences, Stanford, California.*

IN THE last fifteen years, our economy has been moving more rapidly than at any previous period in history, and every one of the changes is in the direction of demanding people with more education. Persons who are able to learn only unskilled tasks will have less and less favorable opportunities for employment.

Failures and dropouts from the school will be more clearly recognized as losses to society as well as to the individual. With increasing concentration of population, with rapidly changing industrial, social, economic, and political conditions, the ability to learn new skills, to acquire new knowledge, and to deal with new problems will become even more essential.

The development of these abilities calls primarily for improvement in the quality of learning rather than in the quantity. There will be less need for the kind of learning that calls for rote memorization and greater need for the kind of learning that probes for understanding and meanings.

Upgrading the quality of learning will not be easy for the schools in the face of a continuing increase of young people and a shortage of teachers.

I do not think this task can be done by saying, "This is precisely the way teaching must go on." Rather I believe that we must set forth the conditions under which learning takes place and then encourage each teacher to use imagination and skill in providing those conditions.

* Ralph W. Tyler, "Conditions for Effective Learning," *NEA Journal* (September, 1959), pp. 47–49. Reprinted by permission.

Teachers need to realize that the heart of education is learning—that what the student is doing is essential, and the teacher's role is to make that learning possible.

With this brief preamble, I will now discuss what conditions bring about effective learning.

The first condition for learning is one we're all conscious of—***motivation.*** There needs to be some kind of drive, some kind of motive in order to keep action going on.

The social needs are sometimes strong sources of motivation in schools because every human being needs to feel that he belongs to the social group and to have some way of receiving and giving affection. A youngster's desire to be a part of a social group, a peer group, is a very important source of motivation and yet we often fail to capitalize on it.

Another source of motivation is the great satisfaction that human beings derive from their own activity, especially activity that is meaningful and that helps satisfy their curiosity by giving them some understanding of the world. The range of possible sources of motivation is great and these examples are merely to suggest the gamut.

A second condition for learning is that the learner find his ***previous ways of reacting unsatisfactory.*** Several recent studies have emphasized that just motivating someone will not produce new behavior unless that person discovers that his present patterns of behavior are unsatisfactory and need replacing by different, better ones.

A third condition for effective learning is some kind of ***guidance*** of the learner's efforts when the behavior he is trying to learn is not so simply acquired. If a person is left to discover some complex kind of behavior by trial and error, he will probably give up long before success, and so a good deal of our effort as teachers is concerned with trying to guide efforts to achieve more adequate behavior.

We may do this by demonstration: We may show the student how to use the library or how to use a piece of equipment in the laboratory or how to solve a kind of mathematical problem.

In other situations, we may provide this guidance by having the student's efforts reproduced. This is done in teaching a foreign language, for example, by recording the student's effort to speak the language and then playing the tape back so he can hear for himself where his pronunciation is going astray.

There are many other ways of guiding efforts, but guidance of some sort is essential for any kind of complex learning situation where trial and error would prove to be so inefficient that most efforts would be lost.

A fourth condition for effective learning is adequate and appropriate provision of ***materials*** for the student to use in his efforts to learn. For example, in the case of reading, it may mean having enough interesting books at the student's level in reading ability to keep him practicing and improving his skill in reading and interpretation. In the case of arithmetic, it may be having enough problems that are meaningful to him and that involve the kinds of quantitative thinking we are concerned with at that age level.

In some schools, much of the difficulty in learning lies in the fact that teachers depend almost entirely upon a textbook even though there's a wealth of life outside that might be used to help the student carry on the sort of thinking or feeling or acting that we are helping him acquire.

This is closely related to a fifth condition of learning—the provision of enough *time* to carry on the desired behavior.

The notion that all learning takes place in school is obviously a mistaken one. Long ago William James pointed out that one learns to swim in winter and skate in summer. This sounds paradoxical, and yet a good many recent psychological experiments show that after the presentation and some initial efforts there is a gestation period of thinking about it and imagining oneself doing it that makes a good deal of difference. An important aspect of learning, therefore, is to have time to carry on the desired behavior, and this involves time to react to it, to reflect upon it, to feel it, as well as to experience it overtly.

A sixth condition is that the learner get *satisfaction* from his behavior. Behavior that is satisfying to the person carrying it on tends to remain with him, become part of him, and in that sense is learned, while that which is dissatisfying or painful tends to be blotted out.

The important question is: How do we get satisfaction from the desired behavior? In some respects it is the other side of the coin to motivation—thinking of ourselves as learners motivates us largely by the anticipation of the satisfaction we are going to get.

Of course, there is the kind of satisfaction that can come in the inherent nature of the thing itself as in singing and dancing, or swimming, where you get the immediate physical satisfaction of the release of energy. Or there is the pleasure inherent in satisfying curiosity—in beginning to understand things that had seemed quite puzzling.

The satisfactions mentioned above come from the very activity. There's another kind of satisfaction which is a rather complex one—the so-called achievement satisfaction that an individual gets just from feeling he's done a thing well.

McClellan and others point out that a good many young people are brought up in families where they have not learned to forego immediate gratifications and to discover the satisfaction of postponing a reward until they really accomplish something. This is what he refers to as "achievement motivation."

A recent study made in the Detroit area revealed that in the working-class families observed, only a rather small proportion of the young people had been taught in their early childhood to postpone some gratifications and to find satisfaction in waiting a bit—even if it meant sacrifice of immediate rewards—until they could do something well. A somewhat larger percentage of middle-class children have been trained to accept and value postponed rewards.

The teaching approach to individual children must vary depending on whether they expect immediate reward or whether they are willing to postpone their gratifications.

There are other rewards, of course—the satisfaction, for example, of getting respect from peers, or of winning the approval of teachers, parents, or other valued adults. There is, too, the satisfaction of getting the job finished—of being able to say, "Well, at least that's over with."

Sequential *practice* is the seventh condition necessary to learning. To state the reason simply: Unless there is some variation in method or approach each time some behavior is practiced, the organism soon gets bored and little learning results.

That is why each new time a quantitative concept comes into arithmetic, the good teacher finds a new way of using it so that the pupils will give attention to it.

An eighth condition for effective learning is for the teacher to encourage pupils to keep *setting their sights higher* and to show them how they can improve their present standard of accomplishment. This is a particularly important task for the schools because they have students for a considerable number of years and because they focus upon those kinds of accomplishment that require a long time to achieve and that demand a high level of performance.

For example, really effective reading in the modern world requires much more than sheer literacy. And as time goes on, we find increasing demands for the interpretation of language, which makes higher and higher standards important. The same could be said of quantitative thinking, or of human relations in any of the fields we are interested in. The school is seeking to bring about a level of achievement quite beyond the average of 100 years ago. This requires that the learner stretch himself to the highest standard of performance of which he is capable.

If this is not done, a good many learners are satisfied with a relatively low standard of performance. They reach a plateau within a relatively short period of time, and then no further learning takes place. Studies, such as those made at the Harvard Human Relations Laboratory, indicate that the learner achieves better if he is helped to work toward a standard always beyond where he now is, but one which he can attain.

This is tied to a ninth condition of learning: to help the learner get some means of *judging his own performance.*

If the learner is to continue to learn—particularly after formal schooling is over—he will have to become self-directive and self-evaluative. This means that teachers must help him to devise some means of judging his achievement and of telling how close he is coming to worthy standards of performance.

The quality and efficiency of learning, both in school and out, must be sharply increased to meet the demands made upon us by the rapid changes in technology and in the wider society. Children, youth, and adults are all required to learn at several levels, from simple conditioning to the complexities of the search for meaning.

The teacher's task is to facilitate learning at all levels. This high requirement cannot be met by following set rules of teaching or by acquiring some specific techniques of instruction. To do the job well demands teaching which is adaptable to differences in students and in situations. It demands teachers who are guided by a clear idea of what is to be learned by the student and by an understanding of the conditions which must be provided in order for learning to be effective.

In this sense, the teacher is an artist conscious of his purpose, aware of the conditions with which he works, and able with creative ingenuity to work in many ways to stimulate his students and guide them toward their goals.

10. *Group Forces Affecting Learning* *

LELAND P. BRADFORD

FORCES affecting group behavior are many and dynamic. Group morale and efficiency are easily disturbed. Relationships shift in the group. Understanding of the major forces present in most groups and diagnostic sensitivity to their interplay is necessary if group forces are to increase individual learning. Of the many group forces which may affect learning, a few are singled out for elaboration.

* From Leland P. Bradford, "Group Forces Affecting Learning," *Journal of National Association of Women Deans and Counselors* (April, 1960), pp. 116–22. Reprinted by permission.

1. Group cohesiveness. The desirability of the group largely determines the degree of influence it has upon the individual member. If the group is prevented from consciously forming as a group; if individual relations are set between teacher and pupil and not among pupils; and if no group goal or product is possible, forces of group belongingness and pride leading toward cohesiveness are inhibited. If present, they have arisen because the group coalesced in a resistance to teacher and learning activities, and in this case group cohesive forces, serve to inhibit learning.

Sometimes teachers, seeking to develop group cohesive forces, inject group tasks periodically and sporadically, frequently of an extracurricular nature. This may develop a temporary group cohesiveness, depending upon whether the task is competitive or cooperative, upon the group climate, and upon the interrelationships among members and with the teacher. It will not, however, bring the steady group strength which will ultimately result if the group is encouraged to deal with its own basic group problems. Working with others on the serious and personal task of improving one's own learning will bring forth greater group cohesiveness and will increase the influence potential of group on member.

2. Standard setting. All groups set standards affecting the behavior of their members. Too frequently standards about learning are set from community, gang or playground forces, or from the anxiety and withdrawal of certain students. A few students having power and prestige with other students can very rapidly develop class standards of mediocre production. Efforts of the teacher to set standards for the group and support them with extrinsic reward and punishment systems are only partially successful and at best result in the continued clash between teacher standards and class standards.

Group standards can and should cover a variety of class situations. For example, standards may be set regarding expected levels of production, differentiation in contributions and learning production, mutual concern for the difficulties of all, role differentiations among teacher and students (what should the teacher do to give most help to the class and where are the boundaries of her power), degree of concern for class procedures, appropriate time to inject personal problems into sessions dealing with group problems, ways of showing caring and helping behavior to others, freedom to disagree with the teacher, extent to which information and experimental evidence is sought in problem-solving.

3. Group climate. A group climate which reduces individual defensiveness and anxiety about exposure of one's inadequacy and gives acceptance and emotional support to all students, will do a great deal to prevent or repair feelings of rejection, of inadequate self-image, of failure. Such a climate is paramount in creating readiness for learning, and in being able to face and solve difficulties inhibiting individual and group growth and development.

4. Involvement and participation. Research and experience indicate the much larger degree of learning, and of retention and utilization of learning, that occur when the individual is involved and participates in the activity in which learning takes place. This is obvious and well known. What is not so well known, at least in regard to general classroom practice, is that such involvement and participation are necessary in all parts of the learning process.

Generally teachers attempt to involve students in participation in classroom activities set by the teacher. This, at best, is still only *partial* involvement. The student is being prevented from fuller involvement in and responsibility for his learning. If he, with his peers, could be invited to supply data from their own feelings and learning experiences concerning the effectiveness of the procedures and activities, could jointly test the accuracy of their perceptions, could diagnostically explore individual emotional problems affecting learning, and could join in experimenting with different procedures for learning, involvement would be much deeper.

Such involvement of the class group would, in addition, serve the teacher as a good diagnostic instrument to determine motivational, perceptual, and actual difficulties in learning and would thus enable him to encourage group help to student members.

5. Effective group and interpersonal relationships. The teaching-learning process is generally a transaction among people. The transactional relationships lie between teacher and individual learner and among learners. These relationships are delicate and subject to drastic change. The process of learning, if it is at all central to the individual, can rapidly mobilize defensive reactions.

Increasingly the importance of the meaning, value and strength of relations between and among individuals is seen as crucial in fields of therapy, industrial production, even brain washing, as it is erroneously named. Equally the quality of the intragroup relations have meaning for all in the group. If there are strong subgroups that continue to operate within the class or if there is such partiality in relationships that uncertainty of position and acceptance is created for others, learning will be inhibited for some.

6. Increased member participation. Two of the difficulties facing any group are freeing members to participate, and integrating and regulating their participation. One initial block to participation in most groups is the concept that all participation should be similar in function. Only as groups explore the many different member functions which need to be performed for effective group operation is the myth of similar and equal participation buried. As a wider range of necessary participation is recognized (group maintenance functions of encouraging, harmonizing, bridging, gate-keeping for others, etc., as compared with the customary task functions of supplying ideas, opinions, and facts), wider student participation in class activities can be secured.[1] Successful participation, in time, may free some anxious students from inhibiting learning.

7. *Solving emotional problems.* Individual problems of anxiety and uncertainty loom larger when hidden. As the class group works on its problems of individual learning and brings to the surface individual fears and uncertainties, then support, reassurance, and assistance can aid each student in increasing his learning. As such emotional problems blocking learning are brought out in the group, other students feel freer to talk about their problems. Many students in such an atmosphere find their anxieties reduced and come to solve many of their own problems without recourse to group concern.

8. *Motivation for learning.* Teachers frequently have failed to utilize some of the most important motivations for learning possible to them. Motivation for learning doesn't lie only in the subject-matter value to classroom procedures, extrinsic rewards and punishment systems within the classroom system, or external pressures from family and community.

Opportunities for acceptance rather than rejection by peers, for belonging to a desirable group, for participation in joint membership ventures, for occasional leadership, provide powerful motivation for learning the subject-matter of the class.

In the fourth-grade class the children faced a class problem. They asked the teacher's help. She said she was occupied during the lunch period and suggested that after lunch they return and work out the problem themselves.

During the luncheon period she returned and looked through the window in the door. The children had formed two groups to work on the problem more effectively. Most of the stronger leaders in the class were clustered in one group. Typically, rather than face the struggle as to which of them would emerge as leader, they chose one of the more timid members of their group as leader and supported him in his leadership efforts. Their group was the most successful of the two in working on the problem. The timid member emerged with a flushed and happy face.

The next day he confided to the teacher that he couldn't get to school early enough that day and that he had never known a time when he liked school so much.

These group forces enhancing learning will be realized only as attention

[1] Benne, K. and Sheats, P. "Functional Roles of Group Members," *The Journal of Social Issues,* IV, No. 2, Spring 1948.

is given to group building and maintenance as well as to subject matter teaching. Fundamentally, the first serves the second as well as widens the areas of learning.

Given the educational purpose of helping children and youth learn and grow, a basic mechanism for learning needs to be developed which most effectively releases the student from his anxieties and inhibition concerning learning, encourages him to enter fully into the learning situation, supports him during the process of learning, and facilitates the utilization of systematic subject knowledge and experimental evidence.

Such a mechanism is the learning group, in which the efforts of all involved, both teacher and students, are directed toward eliminating blocks to learning. Just as other fields have found that attention to the development of effective groups increases productivity in that field, so can this be true of learning.

If the teacher succeeds in developing a class group, he has gained twenty to thirty partners, rather than an equal number of potential antagonists.

Group Building and Maintenance

If group forces are to be generated or released to serve educational purposes, then an effectively functioning group must be developed and maintained. Group development is not easy. Effective groups do not grow without guidance. Natural groups all too frequently serve the ends of a few, are destructive of others, and spend a large proportion of energy in malfunctioning behavior.

Group members need to be involved in group building and maintenance activities. With this point in mind, some of the major requirements for cooperative group building and maintenance can be listed:

1. Shared decision making about group goals and behavior whenever possible
2. Shared diagnosis of group difficulties and shared analysis of group successes
3. Shared analysis of required teacher and student roles and functions
4. Acceptance of all individuals as members of the group
5. An accepted standard of working on individual and group problems holding up the group task of developing a learning group
6. An accepted standard of willingness to be experimental in procedures, clarifying or changing goals and modifying group behavior
7. Efforts to utilize member resources

Requirements for the Teacher

Learner-centered and group-centered educational leadership calls for additional and different requirements than traditionally expected. However, when successful in developing a learning group, the roles required for teaching-leading-involving are more satisfying and successful than is normally true.

What, then, are the requirements upon the teacher?

He must be sincerely committed to the concept of a class group and convinced that group forces can increase individual learning. He must have diagnostic sensitivity to the emotional factors present in the group, as well as to the consequences of behavior on both task and building levels. He must be able to hear the music as well as the words in group behavior.

He must be able to help develop a structure within the class group by which learning goals can be established and accepted, learning tasks can be accomplished, learning difficulties in individual or group analyzed.

He can then be able to relinquish carefully and deliberately to the group much of his traditional control. This, perhaps, is one of the most difficult barriers to overcome. If he has sought gratification through maintaining a central, controlling, dominating, distant teacher role, he may too easily seek evidence that the class cannot take responsibility for improving learning climate and approaches, and quickly take back control he has relinquished.

He needs to be able to recognize the even greater gratification of class success even though the credit is spread throughout the class.

It needs to be clearly seen that there is nothing soft in working with a group. The path to group development and continued group maintenance can be studded with difficulties. The generation and release of human forces through involvement and participation do not result in easy agreements or an even flow of action. Yet the results in increased learning and growth usually far exceed any difficulties encountered.

At the same time that he must relinquish some controls, he needs to be clear as to which controls to maintain for a while and what his various functions should be.

He needs to be able to mix the roles of class builder with subject-matter teacher. To do this, he needs to be comfortable as a group member. For the process of group formation to be successful, he must assume a member role, although a special one.

Perhaps the most difficult problem for the teacher is to be willing to accept spoken, and not covert, criticism for past behavior and suggestions for future action. If the teacher has strong personal needs to control other people and to maintain distance from them, he will have difficulty in group formation. On the other hand, if interest in professional development and improving himself as a person is paramount to him, he will find the experience of special membership in the class group a rewarding one.

Finally, he needs to be in sufficient control of his own need systems that his needs to punish, to control, or to secure love, do not obtrude on the class.

Teacher Preparation

Where can the teacher develop the insights and skills to work effectively with the class as a group? Little, if any, of his previous experience fits him for this task. Teacher-training institutions are only beginning to recognize the importance of group forces in individual learning. Even when recognized, such insights and skills cannot be learned cognitively alone.

Teachers in preparation need experience in taking membership in a group so that they can learn at first hand some of the individual problems in becoming a member of a group, rewarding as this may be. They need an opportunity to understand their own needs and the consequences of their behavior on others. They need experience in group leadership, where the emphasis is upon group development and not upon leadership domination.

With these experiences, knowledge about individual and group behavior can expand the understandings and skills of the teacher as can information about various procedures for working with groups.

Such a combination of experience and cognitive learning does not fit readily into the present typical teacher-training or in-service program. However, experience is now present indicating how this aspect of teacher training could be carried out.

For the past fifteen years, the National Training Laboratories of the NEA has been experimenting with and developing for many occupational fields a process of unstructured group training for the development of more effective leadership and membership understandings and skills. Interestingly, this approach to learning is finding application from the first grade through the university level.

The formation and development of a group, and its continued maintenance, are basically experiences in the creation of society. A new group must develop a power structure, a common task or goal, patterns of effective communication, varying procedures for working—in short, a culture, a set of laws, procedures for dealing with task and human problems, differentiation of functioning, a process of evaluation and change.

In a structured group, these ingredients are already present. In an unstructured training group situation, usually meeting intensively for a number of hours a day over a period of two to three weeks, the group members must create and develop the structure and process of the group. From this experience they can learn not only about group development and functioning but also about their own ability to work effectively with others on a membership basis.

Imagine, if you will, twelve to fifteen teachers (actual or potential) entering a group situation in which they will work intensively for some days. The group trainer begins by indicating that the group task, as he sees it, is to work on the development of the group and that he hopes they will continuously analyze whatever they do. He says further that he will *not* serve as the group leader. He doesn't say who will or even whether there should be a leader. He says nothing about procedures or about expectations of member behavior.

Then he becomes silent. Essentially, he has blurred or made ambiguous important ingredients of any group—leadership, task, procedures, norms, expectations of behavior. After a prolonged, and sometimes painful, silence, the members rush in to fill the vacuum the trainer has created.

As they rush in, each with a desire to develop a situation most comfortable to him, every person brings out on the table his own way of responding to social situations.

In the beginning there are pulls and hauls in the group as status symbols are exchanged and various pressures for leadership and for acceptance of personal goals are made. The trainer aids the group in examining periodically its problems and difficulties. Gradually the group comes to realize that a common goal and task must be fashioned out of the desires, wishes, purposes of all. Gradually people begin to listen more intently to others. The decibels decrease as people stop shouting at one another and begin to listen. Gradually a set of norms or standards develop and become accepted—that all should have a chance to participate, that no one should manipulate the group, that no one should overdominate the situation.

Each member has a chance to learn about his own difficulties, as well as the difficulties of others, in becoming an effective member of the group. Each person has a chance to understand better his own need systems and the consequences of his behavior on others.

Out of the slow and somewhat difficult creation of a group usually comes far greater sensitivity to others, improved diagnostic awareness of the many complexities of group behavior, increased skills in working effectively with others in group situations.

With this experience, people are able to understand and utilize cognitive information from research about group and individual behavior.

If, prior to or along with their regular preparation, teachers could include intensive experience in such an unstructured group situation, then later preparation could include systematic courses in individual and group behavior. In addition, teachers in preparation should have opportunities to observe clinically class situation from the standpoint of group behavior, as well as opportunities to practice leadership skills on both task and maintenance levels.

Then teachers would be better able to help mobilize group forces to increase individual learning, no matter what the subject area.

11. Significant Learning: In Therapy and in Education *

CARL R. ROGERS, *University of Wisconsin*

PRESENTED here is a thesis, a point of view, regarding the implications which psychotherapy has for education. It is a stand which I take tentatively, and with some hesitation. I have many unanswered questions about this thesis. But it has, I think, some clarity in it, and hence it may provide a starting point from which clear differences can emerge.

Significant Learning in Psychotherapy

Let me begin by saying that my long experience as a therapist convinces me that significant learning is facilitated in psychotherapy, and occurs in that relationship. By significant learning I mean learning which is more than an accumulation of facts. It is learning which makes a difference—in the individual's behavior, in the course of action he chooses in the future, in his attitudes and in his personality. It is a pervasive learning which is not just an accretion of knowledge, but which interpenetrates with every portion of his existence.

Now it is not only my subjective feeling that such learning takes place. This feeling is substantiated by research. In client-centered therapy, the orientation with which I am most familiar, and in which the most research

* From Carl R. Rogers, "Significant Learning: In Therapy and in Education," *Educational Leadership* (January, 1959), pp. 232–42. Reprinted by permission. (This article also is reprinted in *On Becoming a Person,* published by Houghton Mifflin Company, Boston, 1961.)

has been done, we know that exposure to such therapy produces learnings, or changes, of these sorts:

The person comes to see himself differently.

He accepts himself and his feelings more fully.

He becomes more self-confident and self-directing.

He becomes more the person he would like to be.

He becomes more flexible, less rigid, in his perceptions.

He adopts more realistic goals for himself.

He behaves in a more mature fashion.

He changes his maladjustive behaviors, even such a long-established one as chronic alcoholism.

He becomes more acceptant of others.

He becomes more open to the evidence, both to what is going on outside of himself, and to what is going on inside of himself.

He changes in his basic personality characteristics, in constructive ways.[1]

I think perhaps this is sufficient to indicate that these are learnings which are significant, which do make a difference.

Significant Learning in Education

I believe I am accurate in saying that educators too are interested in learnings which make a difference. Simple knowledge of facts has its value. To know who won the battle of Poltava, or when the umpteenth opus of Mozart was first performed, may win $64,000 or some other sum for the possessor of this information, but I believe educators in general are a little embarrassed by the assumption that the acquisition of such knowledge constitutes education. Speaking of this reminds me of a forceful statement made by a professor of agronomy in my freshman year in college. Whatever knowledge I gained in his course has departed completely, but I remember how, with World War I as his background, he was comparing factual knowledge with ammunition. He wound up his little discourse with the exhortation, "Don't be a damned ammunition wagon; be a rifle!" I believe most educators would share this sentiment that knowledge exists primarily for use.

To the extent then that educators are interested in learnings which are functional, which make a difference, which pervade the person and his actions, then they might well look to the field of psychotherapy for leads or ideas. Some adaptation for education of the learning process which takes place in psychotherapy seems like a promising possibility.

[1] For evidence supporting these statements see references (6) and (8).

The Conditions of Learning in Psychotherapy

Let us then see what is involved, essentially, in making possible the learning which occurs in therapy. I would like to spell out, as clearly as I can, the conditions which seem to be present when this phenomenon occurs.

FACING A PROBLEM

The client is, first of all, up against a situation which he perceives as a serious and meaningful problem. It may be that he finds himself behaving in ways which he cannot control, or he is overwhelmed by confusions and conflicts, or his marriage is going on the rocks, or he finds himself unhappy in his work. He is, in short, faced with a problem with which he has tried to cope, and found himself unsuccessful. He is therefore eager to learn, even though at the same time he is frightened that what he discovers in himself may be disturbing. Thus one of the conditions nearly always present is an uncertain and ambivalent desire to learn or to change, growing out of a perceived difficulty in meeting life.

What are the conditions which this individual meets when he comes to a therapist? I have recently formulated a theoretical picture of the necessary and sufficient conditions which the therapist provides, if constructive change or significant learning is to occur (7). This theory is currently being tested in several of its aspects by empirical research, but it must still be regarded as theory based upon clinical experience rather than proven fact. Let me describe briefly the conditions which it seems essential that the therapist should provide.

CONGRUENCE

If therapy is to occur, it seems necessary that the therapist be, in the relationship, a unified, or integrated, or congruent person. What I mean is that within the relationship he is exactly what he *is*—not a façade, or a role, or a pretense. I have used the term congruence to refer to this accurate matching of experience with awareness. It is when the therapist is fully and accurately aware of what he is experiencing at this moment in the relationship that he is fully congruent. Unless this congruence is present to a considerable degree it is unlikely that significant learning can occur.

Though this concept of congruence is actually a complex one, I believe all of us recognize it in an intuitive and common-sense way in individuals with whom we deal. With one individual we recognize that he not only means exactly what he says, but that his deepest feelings also match what he is expressing. Thus whether he is angry or affectionate or ashamed or enthusiastic, we sense that he is the same at all levels—in what he is experiencing at an organismic level, in his awareness at the conscious level, and in his words and communications. We furthermore recognize that he is acceptant of his immediate feelings. We say of such a person that we know "exactly where he stands." We tend to feel comfortable and secure in such a relationship. With another person we recognize that what he is saying is almost certainly a front or a façade. We wonder what he *really* feels, what he is really experiencing, behind this façade. We may also wonder if *he* knows what he really feels, recognizing that he may be quite unaware of the feelings he is actually experiencing. With such a person we tend to be cautious and wary. It is not the kind of relationship in which defenses can be dropped or in which significant learning and change can occur.

Thus this second condition for therapy is that the therapist is characterized by a considerable degree of congruence in the relationship. He is freely, deeply, and acceptantly himself, with his actual experience of his feelings and reactions matched by an accurate awareness of these feelings and reactions as they occur and as they change.

UNCONDITIONAL POSITIVE REGARD

A third condition is that the therapist experiences a warm caring for the client—a caring which is not possessive, which demands no personal gratification. It is an atmosphere which simply demonstrates "I care"; not "I care for you *if* you behave thus and so." Standal (10) has termed this attitude "unconditional positive regard," since it has no conditions of worth attached to it. I have often used the term acceptance to describe this aspect of the therapeutic climate. It involves as much feeling of acceptance for the client's expression of negative, "bad," painful, fearful, and abnormal feelings, as for his expression of "good," positive, mature, confident and social feelings. It involves an acceptance of and a caring for the client as a *separate* person, with permission for him to have his own feelings and experiences, and to find his own meanings in them. To the degree that the therapist can provide this safety-creating climate of unconditional positive regard, significant learning is likely to take place.

AN EMPATHIC UNDERSTANDING

The fourth condition for therapy is that the therapist is experiencing an accurate, empathic understanding of the client's world as seen from the inside. To sense the client's private world as if it were your own, but without ever losing the "as if" quality—this is empathy, and this seems essential to therapy. To sense the client's anger, fear, or confusion as if it were your own, yet without your own anger, fear, or confusion getting bound up in it, is the condition we are endeavoring to describe. When the client's world is this clear to the therapist, and he moves about in it freely, then he can both communicate his understanding of what is clearly known to the client and can also voice meanings in the client's experience of which the client is scarcely aware. That such penetrating empathy is important for therapy is indicated by Fiedler's research in which items such as the following placed high in the description of relationships created by experienced therapists:

The therapist is well able to understand the patient's feelings.

The therapist is never in any doubt about what the patient means.

The therapist's remarks fit in just right with the patient's mood and content.

The therapist's tone of voice conveys the complete ability to share the patient's feelings. (2a)

FIFTH CONDITION

A fifth condition for significant learning in therapy is that the client should experience or perceive something of the therapist's congruence, acceptance, and empathy. It is not enough that these conditions exist in the therapist. They must, to some degree, have been successfully communicated to the client.

The Process of Learning in Therapy

It has been our experience that when these five conditions exist, a process of change inevitably occurs. The client's rigid perceptions of himself and of others loosen and become open to reality. The rigid ways in which he has construed the meaning of his experience are looked at, and he finds himself questioning many of the "facts" of his life, discovering that they are only "facts" because he has regarded them so. He discovers feelings of which he has been unaware, and experiences them, often vividly, in the therapeutic relationship. Thus he learns to be more open to all of his experience —the evidence within himself as well as the evidence without. He learns to *be* more of his experience—to be the feelings of which he has been frightened as well as the feelings he has regarded as more acceptable. He becomes a more fluid, changing, learning person.

THE MAINSPRING OF CHANGE

In this process it is not necessary for the therapist to "motivate" the client or to supply the energy which brings about the change. Nor, in some sense, is the motivation supplied by the client, at least in any conscious way. Let us say rather that the motivation for learning and change springs from the self-actualizing tendency of life itself, the tendency for the organism to flow into all the differentiated channels of potential development, insofar as these are experienced as enhancing.

I could go on at very considerable length on this, but it is not my purpose to focus on the process of therapy and the learnings which take place, nor on the motivation for these learnings, but rather on the conditions which make them possible. So I will simply conclude this description of therapy by saying that it is a type of significant learning which takes place when five conditions are met:

When the client perceives himself as faced by a serious and meaningful problem

When the therapist is a congruent person in the relationship, able to *be* the person he *is*

When the therapist feels an unconditional positive regard for the client

When the therapist experiences an accurate empathic understanding of the client's private world, and communicates this

When the client to some degree experiences the therapist's congruence, acceptance, and empathy.

Implications for Education

What do these conditions mean if applied to education? Undoubtedly the reader will be able to give a better answer than I out of his own experience, but I will at least suggest some of the implications.

CONTACT WITH PROBLEMS

In the first place it means that significant learning occurs more readily in relation to situations perceived as problems. I believe I have observed evidence to support this. In my own varying attempts to conduct courses and groups in ways consistent with my therapeutic experience, I have found such an approach more effective, I believe, in workshops than in regular courses, in extension courses than in campus courses. Individuals who come to workshops or extension courses are those who are in contact with problems which they recognize as problems. The student in the regular university course, and particularly in the required course, is apt to view the course as an experience in which he expects to remain passive or resentful or both, an experience which he certainly does not often see as relevant to his own problems.

Yet it has also been my experience that when a regular university class does perceive the course as an experience they can use to resolve problems which *are* of concern to them, the sense of release, and the thrust of forward movement is astonishing. And this is true of courses as diverse as Mathematics and Personality.

I believe the current situation in Russian education also supplies evidence on this point. When a whole nation perceives itself as being faced with the urgent problem of being behind—in agriculture, in industrial production, in scientific development, in weapons development—then an astonishing amount of significant learning takes place, of which the Sputniks are but one observable example.

So the first implication for education might well be that we permit the student, at any level, to be in real contact with the relevant problems of his existence, so that he perceives problems and issues which he wishes to resolve. I am quite aware that this implication, like the others I shall mention, runs sharply contrary to the current trends in our culture, but I shall comment on that later.

I believe it would be quite clear from my description of therapy that an over-all implication for education would be that the task of the teacher is to create a facilitating classroom climate in which significant learning can take place. This general implication can be broken down into several subsections.

THE TEACHER'S REAL-NESS

Learning will be facilitated, it would seem, if the teacher is congruent. This involves the teacher's being the person that he is, and being openly aware of the attitudes he holds. It means that he feels acceptant toward his own real feelings. Thus he becomes a real person in the relationship with his students. He can be enthusiastic about subjects he likes, and bored by topics he does not like. He can be angry, but he can also be sensitive or sympathetic. Because he accepts his feeling as *his* feelings, he has no need to impose them on his students, or to insist that they feel the same way. He is a *person,* not a faceless embodiment of a curricular requirement, or a sterile pipe through which knowledge is passed from one generation to the next.

I can suggest only one bit of evidence which might support this view. As I think back over a number of teachers who have facilitated my own learning, it seems to me each one has this quality of being a real person. I wonder if your memory is the same. If so, perhaps it is less important that a teacher cover the allotted amount of the curriculum, or use the most approved audio-visual devices, than that he be congruent, real, in his relation to his students.

ACCEPTANCE AND UNDERSTANDING

Another implication for the teacher is that significant learning may take place if the teacher can accept the student as he is, and can understand the feelings he possesses. Taking the third and fourth conditions of therapy as specified above, the teacher who can warmly accept, who can provide an unconditional positive regard, and who can empathize with the feelings of fear, anticipation, and discouragement which are involved in meeting new material, will have done a great deal toward setting the conditions for learning. Clark Moustakas, in his book, *The Teacher and the Child* (5), has given many excellent examples of individual and group situations from kindergarten to high school, in which the teacher has worked toward just this type of goal. It will perhaps disturb some that when the teacher holds such attitudes, when he is willing to be acceptant of feelings, it is not only attitudes toward school work itself which are expressed, but feelings about parents, feelings of hatred for brother or sister, feelings of concern about self—the whole gamut of attitudes. Do such feelings have a right to exist openly in a school setting? It is my thesis that they do. They are related to the person's becoming, to his effective learning and effective functioning, and to deal understandingly and acceptantly with such feelings has a definite relationship to the learning of long division or the geography of Pakistan.

PROVISION OF RESOURCES

This brings me to another implication which therapy holds for education. In therapy the resources for learning one's self lie within. There is very little data which the therapist can supply which will be of help since the data to be dealt with exist within the person. In education this is not true. There are many resources of knowledge, of techniques, of theory, which constitute raw material for use. It seems to me that what I have said about therapy suggests that these materials, these resources, be made available to the students, not forced upon them. Here a wide range of ingenuity and sensitivity is an asset.

I do not need to list the usual resources which come to mind—books, maps, workbooks, materials, recordings, work space, tools, and the like. Let me focus for a moment on the way the teacher uses himself and his knowledge and experience as a resource. If the teacher holds the point of view I have been expressing then he would probably want to make himself available to his class in at least the following ways:

He would want to let them know of special experience and knowledge he has in the field, and to let them know they could call on this knowledge. Yet he would not want them to feel that they must use him in this way.

He would want them to know that his own way of thinking about the field, and of organizing it, was available to them, even in lecture form, if they wished. Yet again he would want this to be perceived as an offer, which could as readily be refused as accepted.

He would want to make himself known as a resource-finder. Whatever might be seriously wanted by an individual or by the whole group to promote their learning, he would be very willing to consider the possibilities of obtaining such a resource.

He would want the quality of his relationship to the group to be such that his feelings could be freely available to them, without being imposed on them or becoming a restrictive influence on them. He thus could share the excitements and enthusiasms of his own learnings, without insisting that the students follow in his footsteps; the feelings of disinterest, satisfactions, bafflement, or pleasure which he feels toward individual or group activities, without this becoming either a carrot or a stick for the student. His hope would be that he could say, simply for himself, "I don't like that," and that the student with equal freedom could say, "But I do."

Thus whatever the resource he supplies—a book, space to work, a new tool, an opportunity for observation of an industrial process, a lecture based on his own study, a picture, graph or map, his own emotional reactions—he would feel that these were, and would hope they would be perceived as, offerings to be used if they were useful to the student. He would not feel them to be guides, or expectations, or commands, or impositions or requirements. He would offer himself, and all the other resources he could discover, for use.

THE BASIC MOTIVE

It should be clear from this that his basic reliance would be upon the self-actualizing tendency in his students. The hypothesis upon which he would build is that students who are in real contact with life problems wish to learn, want to grow, seek to find out, hope to master, desire to create. He would see his function as that of developing such a personal relationship with his students, and such a climate in his classroom, that these natural tendencies could come to their fruition.

SOME OMISSIONS

These I see as some of the things which are implied by a therapeutic viewpoint for the educational process. To make them a bit sharper, let me point out some of the things which are not implied.

I have not included lectures, talks, or expositions of subject matter which are imposed on the students. All of these procedures might be a part of the experience if they were desired, explicitly or implicitly, by the students. Yet even here, a teacher whose work was following through a hypothesis based on therapy would be quick to sense a shift in that desire. He might have been requested to lecture to the group (and to give a *requested* lecture is *very* different from the usual classroom experience), but if he detected a growing disinterest and boredom, he would respond to that, trying to understand the feeling which had arisen in the group, since his response to their feelings and attitudes would take precedence over his interest in expounding material.

I have not included any program of evaluation of the student's learnings in terms of external criteria. I have not, in other words, included examinations. I believe that the testing of the student's achievements in order to see if he meets some criterion held by the teacher, is directly contrary to the implications of therapy for significant learning. In therapy, the examinations are set by *life*. The client meets them, sometimes passing, sometimes failing. He finds that he can use the resources of the therapeutic relationship and his experience in it to organize himself so that he can meet life's tests more satisfyingly next time. I see this as the paradigm for education also. Let me try to spell out a fantasy of what it would mean.

In such an education, the requirements for many life situations would be a part of the resources the teacher provides. The student would have available the knowledge that he cannot enter engineering school without so much math; that he cannot get a job in X corporation unless he has a college diploma; that he cannot become a psychologist without doing an independent doctoral research; that he cannot be a doctor without knowledge of chemistry; that he cannot even drive a car without passing an examination on rules of the road. These are requirements set, not by the teacher, but by life. The teacher is there to provide the resources which the student can use to learn so as to be able to meet these tests. There would be other in-school evaluations of similar sort. The student might well be faced with the fact that he cannot join the Math Club until he makes a certain score on a standardized mathematics test; that he cannot develop his camera film until he has shown an adequate knowledge of chemistry and lab techniques; that he cannot join the special literature section until he has shown evidence of both wide reading and creative writing. The natural place of evaluation in life is as a ticket of entrance, not as a club over the recalcitrant. Our experience in therapy would suggest that it should be the same way in the school. It would leave the student as a self-respecting, self-motivated person, free to choose whether he wished to put forth the effort to gain these tickets of entrance. It would thus refrain from forcing him into conformity, from sacrificing his creativity, and from causing him to live his life in terms of the standards of others.

I am quite aware that the two elements of which I have just been speaking—the lectures and expositions imposed by the teacher on the group, and the evaluation of the individual by the teacher, constitute the two major ingredients of current education. So when I say that experience in psychotherapy would suggest that they both be omitted, it should be quite clear that the implications of psychotherapy for education are startling indeed.

PROBABLE OUTCOMES

If we are to consider such drastic changes as I have outlined, what would be the results which would justify them? There have been some research investigations of the outcomes of a student-centered type of teaching (1, 2, 3), though these studies are far from adequate. For one thing, the situations studied vary greatly in the extent to which they meet the conditions I have described. Most of them have extended only over a period of a few months, though one recent study with lower class children extended over a full year (3). Some involve the use of adequate controls, some do not.

I think we may say that these studies indicate that in classroom situations which at least attempt to approximate the climate I have described, the findings are as follows: Factual and curricular learning is roughly equal to the learning in conventional classes. Some studies report slightly more, some slightly less. The student-centered group shows gains significantly greater than the conventional class in personal adjustment, in self-initiated extra-curricular learning in creativity, in self-responsibility.

I have come to realize, as I have considered these studies, and puzzled over the design of better studies which should be more informative and conclusive, that findings from such research will never answer our questions. For all such findings must be evaluated in terms of the goals we have for education. If we value primarily the learning of knowledge, then we may discard the conditions I have described as useless, since there is no evidence that they lead to a greater rate or amount of factual knowledge. We may then favor such measures as the one which I understand is advocated by a number of members of Congress—the setting up of a training school for scientists, modeled upon the military academies. But if we value creativity, if we deplore the fact that all of our germinal ideas in atomic physics, in psychology, and in other sciences have been borrowed from Europe, then we may wish to give a trial to ways of facilitating learning which give more promise of freeing the mind. If we value independence, if we are disturbed by the growing conformity of knowledge, of values, of attitudes, which our present system induces, then we may wish to set up conditions of learning which make for uniqueness, for self-direction, and for self-initiated learning.

Some Concluding Issues

I have tried to sketch the kind of education which would be implied by what we have learned in the field of psychotherapy. I have endeavored to suggest very briefly what it would mean if the central focus of the teacher's effort were to develop a relationship, an atmosphere, which was conducive to self-motivated, self-actualizing, significant learning. But this is a direction which leads sharply away from current educational practices and educational trends. Let me mention a few of the very diverse issues and questions which need to be faced if we are to think constructively about such an approach.

In the first place, how do we conceive the goals of education? The approach I have outlined has, I believe, advantages for achieving certain goals, but not for achieving others. We need to be clear as to the way we see the purposes of education.

What are the actual outcomes of the kind of education I have described? We need a great deal more of rigorous, hardheaded research to know the actual results of this kind of education as compared with conventional education. Then we can choose on the basis of the facts.

Even if we were to try such an approach to the facilitation of learning, there are many difficult issues. Could we possibly permit students to come in contact with real issues? Our whole culture—through custom, through the law, through the efforts of labor unions and management, through the attitudes of parents and teachers—is deeply committed to keeping young people away from any touch with real problems. They are not to work, they should not carry responsibility, they have no business in civic or political problems, they have no place in international concerns, they simply should be guarded from any direct contact with the real problems of individual and group living. They are not expected to help about the home, to earn a living, to contribute to science, to deal with moral issues. This is a deep-seated trend which has lasted for more than a generation. Could it possibly be reversed?

Another issue is whether we could permit knowledge to be organized in and by the individual, or whether it is to be organized *for* the individual. Here teachers and educators line up with parents and national leaders to insist that the pupil must be guided. He must be inducted into knowledge we have organized for him. He cannot be trusted to organize knowledge in functional terms for himself. As Herbert Hoover says of high school students, "You simply cannot expect kids of those ages to determine the sort of education they need unless they have some guidance." [2] This seems so obvious to most people that even to question it is to seem somewhat unbalanced. Even a chancellor of a university questions whether freedom is really necessary in education, saying that perhaps we have overestimated its value. He says the Russians have advanced mightily in science without it, and implies that we should learn from them.

Still another issue is whether we would wish to oppose the strong current trend toward education as drill in factual knowledge. All must learn the

[2] *Time,* December 2, 1957.

same facts in the same way. Admiral Rickover states it as his belief that "in some fashion we must devise a way to introduce uniform standards into American education. . . . For the first time, parents would have a real yardstick to measure their schools. If the local school continued to teach such pleasant subjects as 'life adjustment'. . . instead of French and physics, its diploma would be, for all the world to see, inferior." [3] This is a statement of a very prevalent view. Even such a friend of forward-looking views in education as Max Lerner says at one point, "All that a school can ever hope to do is to equip the student with tools which he can later use to become an educated man" (4, p. 741). It is quite clear that he despairs of significant learning taking place in our school system, and feels that it must take place outside. All the school can do is to pound in the tools.

One of the most painless ways of inculcating such factual tool knowledge is the "teaching machine" being devised by B. F. Skinner and his associates (9). This group is demonstrating that the teacher is an outmoded and ineffective instrument for teaching arithmetic, trigonometry, French, literary appreciation, geography, or other factual subjects. There is simply no doubt in my mind that these teaching machines, providing immediate rewards for "right" answers, will be further developed, and will come into wide use. Here is a new contribution from the field of the behavioral sciences with which we must come to terms. Does it take the place of the approach I have described, or is it supplemental to it? Here is one of the problems we must consider as we face toward the future.

I hope that by posing these issues, I have made it clear that the double-barreled question of what constitutes significant learning, and how it is to be achieved, poses deep and serious problems for all of us. It is not a time when timid answers will suffice. I have tried to give a definition of significant learning as it appears in psychotherapy, and a description of the conditions which facilitate such learning. I have tried to indicate some implications of these conditions for education. I have, in other words, proposed one answer to these questions. Perhaps we can use what I have said, against the twin backdrops of current public opinion and current knowledge in the behavioral sciences, as a start for discovering some fresh answers of our own.

References

1. FAW, VOLNEY. "A Psychotherapeutic Method of Teaching Psychology." *American Psychologist* 4: 104–09, 1949.
2. ———. "Evaluation of Student-Centered Teaching." Unpublished manuscript, 1954.

[3] *Ibid.*

2a. FIEDLER, F. E. "A Comparison of Therapeutic Relationships in Psychoanalytic, Non-directive and Adlerian Therapy." *Journal of Consulting Psychology* 14: 436–45, 1950.

3. JACKSON, JOHN H. "The Relationship Between Psychological Climate and the Quality of Learning Outcomes among Lower-status Pupils." Unpublished Ph.D. thesis, University of Chicago, 1957.

4. LERNER, MAX. *America as a Civilization.* New York: Simon & Schuster, 1957.

5. MOUSTAKAS, CLARK. *The Teacher and the Child.* New York: McGraw-Hill Book Company, 1956.

6. ROGERS, C. R. *Client-centered Therapy.* New York: Houghton Mifflin Company, 1951.

7. ———. "The Necessary and Sufficient Conditions of Therapeutic Personality Change." *Journal of Consulting Psychology* 21: 95–103, 1957.

8. ROGERS, C. R., and R. DYMOND, editors. *Psychotherapy and Personality Change.* Chicago: University of Chicago Press, 1954.

9. SKINNER, B. F. "The Science of Learning and the Art of Teaching." *Harvard Educational Review* 24: 86–97, 1954.

10. STANDAL, STANLEY. "The Need for Positive Regard: A Contribution to Client-centered Theory." Unpublished Ph.D. thesis, University of Chicago, 1954.

12. *Learning: I. Understanding, Transfer, and Retention* *

ROBERT C. CRAIG, *Marquette University*

A N ATTEMPT has been made in this chapter to select those studies of the past three years which have a bearing on the practical understanding and control of learning. The writer's orientation was similar to that of Hilgard (33:486) and Burton (15) in their efforts to find and list practically important empirical relations, even though students of learning disagree about the interpretation of these facts. References consistent with

* From Robert C. Craig, "Learning: I. Understanding, Transfer, and Retention," *Review of Educational Research* (December, 1958), pp. 445–55. Reprinted by permission.

this orientation were examined for methodological adequacy, probable interest, and general availability. Since not all studies meeting these criteria reasonably well could be included, a somewhat arbitrary choice was made among similar studies in the same area of investigation. Finally, areas of marginal interest represented by isolated studies were dropped altogether, as were areas treated more intensively in other sections of this issue.

Scope of Learning Studies

The reviews of Estes (24), Walker (84), and Lawrence (47) provided year-by-year coverage of theory and research in the psychology of learning. Attempts to extend the concepts and methods of the animal laboratory to simple perceptual, verbal, and motor learning in humans were pursued with vigor. Within a sharply limited range of human behavior these studies contributed to the development of principles which may become educational hypotheses. They were not prepared nor did they often attempt to deal with complex skills, attitudes, and problem solving, or with the processes of group learning.

Research in the applied psychology of learning featured efforts to validate or qualify laboratory principles and procedures in a setting more characteristic of the educational enterprise. The influence of clinical and social psychology was manifested frequently in the concern for individual differences; fairly often in the choice of controls; and occasionally in the choice of problems, the use of comprehensive criteria, and naturalistic settings.

The investigators of classroom learning seldom found their issues or methods within any identifiable model of learning. As a result, the significance and generality of their results were often limited to the specific areas investigated. The best of the method studies were concerned with the relative effectiveness of instructional approaches which varied but nevertheless were similar in that they could be recommended by informed opinion or a history of successful use. Of definitely lesser value was the host of studies demonstrating that if you teach a skill or concept to one group and not to another, you can predict with some certainty the group which will excel on "appropriate" measures.

Goals and Motivation

Educational interpretations of the learning process assign a dominant role to the goals of the individual learner. Sears (70) described the initial phase of a research program in which attention was to be centered on factors in the achievement of goals for each child, considering both the child's self-perception of need for change and systematic observation of his daily successes and failures. This approach was exceptional. The rule was more nearly represented by studies of a learner's level of aspiration (20, 44) with respect to simple and contrived tasks in a nonsocial setting. Sivertsen (73) sharply criticized the artificial settings of these studies and presented an illustration of a type of study of probably greater value.

Some evidence (10, 29) of a positive relationship between student interest and achievement was reported. In a controlled experiment, however, Savignano (67) found that enriching the grade-school curriculum with activities based on existing hobbies and special interests did not effect academic gains or produce broader interests.

Differences in a rather general and stable achievement need, inferred from the content of stories given in connection with pictures like those of the *Thematic Apperception Test,* were found to be related to verbal learning and arithmetic performance (35, 38) but not to improvement in study skills (86), and were rather less important than nonacademic motives in overachievement (4). A children's form of a questionnaire measure of a hypothesized general energizing factor or drive, the *Manifest Anxiety Scale,* was used in a series of investigations by Castaneda, Palermo, and McCandless (17, 64). Comparisons of extreme groups selected by test scores indicated that "anxious" children tended to make more errors in the presence of competing incorrect responses. They were inferior to less anxious children on the difficult components of a learning task but tended to be superior on less difficult components.

Not all energizing and goal-directing factors are "brought to school." Some, like marks, are built into the program. One school system changed to a five-point quality scale after 17 years of experience with individual progress reports. Baker and Doyle (8) found no difference in language arts achievement in the eighth grade before and after the change.

Several investigators concluded that Hurlock's widely quoted findings (36) on the effects of praise and reproof have been overgeneralized. Siegel's analysis of variance design (71) enabled her to explore and control the effects of sex, level of ability, and spacing of trials as well as the incentive conditions used by Hurlock. No one condition was best for all the grade-school pupils with whom she worked. Boys and bright pupils, for example, did better when praised or reproved than when ignored; but girls and dull pupils did not. Silberman (72) computed multiple correlations between pupil reading growth and the independent variables of teacher praise, reproof, praise by reproof, verbal output, and time devoted to reading skills. He attributed his failure to find significant relationships to the influence of other individual or contextual variables. Brackbill and Jack (14) noted the variability among children's performances under a single incentive condition. Their experiment demonstrated that when kindergarten children were permitted some choice in the incentive for which they would strive, variability of performance on a discriminative task was markedly reduced.

The schedule or pattern of incentives has an important influence on behavior, Kapos, Mech, and Fox (42, 43, 54) conducted an extensive series of studies in which various patterns of verbal reward or reinforcement, such as praise for good work, were associated with routine arithmetical performance. A given number of reinforcements was described as more effective in a periodic than in a random schedule, and when administered to 75 per cent of the trials rather than in either a smaller percentage of trials or in all trials. Ferster and Sapon's experiment (25) in the teaching of college German was notable because it was undoubtedly the forerunner of many attempts to schedule classroom reinforcement according to principles developed in the animal laboratory by B. F. Skinner, a psychologist who has demonstrated remarkable control of the behavior of rats and pigeons. Self-checking materials were designed so that a student progressed in such small steps that very few failures occurred and knowledge of results was immediate. This possibility of "self-teaching" in some phases of the educational process was perhaps the chief advantage demonstrated in this experiment, for the number of subjects and modest controls did not permit the presentation of convincing evidence of the superiority of the experimental method over more conventional instruction.

The systematic scheduling of unobtrusive social stimuli, such as a murmured "good," "mmm-hmm," or a simple rephrasing of the subject's response, has been shown to be effective in modifying verbal or motor behavior. McNair (52), for example, used reinforcers of this type to encourage subjects to keep talking about projected slides. Hildum and Brown (32) showed that their use could increase the frequency of either pro- or anti-attitudes during an interview on a social issue. Such demonstrations suggested that subtle effects of teacher-pupil and pupil-pupil interaction might be at least as important as "announced" incentives.

Several general treatments of research on motivation appeared. The papers of the annual Nebraska Symposium (39, 40, 41) provided an overview of current theory and research on diverse topics that ranged from physiological processes to social theories. Symonds (77, 78) analyzed the evidence pertaining to the use of reward and punishment as the second and third articles in his series, "What Education Has to Learn from Psychology." Tyler's review (79) of studies on the motivation and identification of gifted pupils was timely. Finally, Hilgard's revised *Theories of Learning* (33:427-33) contained an excellent analysis of the accumulating evidence which suggests the inadequacy of the popular need-reduction or drive-reduction concept of motivation.

Concepts, Understandings, and Principles

Cognitive outcomes of broad utility were emphasized in a large number of comparative methods studies. Those which merely demonstrated that such outcomes can be taught are literally too numerous to mention. Ojemann and his associates (62) prepared special units in social studies and health in order to develop an understanding of the complex causes of human behavior. The materials were more effective with grade-school children when their teachers were "causally oriented" through in-service training. Several other classroom experiments, employing superior designs and evaluation instruments of demonstrated reliability, found different approaches to be about equally effective when each was fully exploited. The comparisons included (a) demonstrations vs. reading in ninth-grade science (13), (b) group methods vs. teacher instruction in algebra (37) and college physical science (87), and (c) "student-centered" vs. "teacher-centered" techniques in college biological science (63).

The variable of learner activity which was apparent in the foregoing studies was studied more directly in several experiments. Della Piana (2) found that learners who were led to keep trying until they discovered i.e., chose the "right" concept name for each of a series of designs, later recognized and recalled more concept definitions than learners who were told each answer after one try. Carpenter (16) and Forgus and Schwartz (26) reported that "functional" learning was more efficient than rote learning when the criterion was retention, ability to verbalize the meaning of concepts, or success with related tasks.

A further issue was the amount of information to give the learner when "discovery" rather than rote learning was expected. The results of Underwood and Richardson (82) with adults and the paired-associates technique indicated that the more information given the learner concerning the nature of concepts relating groups of words, the more rapid the acquisition. Craig (19) found that college groups, given verbal statements of relations which they then used to find the answers to verbal multiple-choice items illustrating these relations, recalled and recognized more relations in new items, immediately and 31 days after learning, than groups who induced principles by working sets of examples. In a study of similar design extending over an initial learning period of five weeks Kittell (45) obtained similar results with sixth-grade pupils. A third group, given the answers to individual examples, was also generally inferior to the group given statements of principles. Since these information conditions approximated the inductive and deductive situations, the findings appear to conflict with the results of some previous classroom studies. Classroom conditions may make it difficult to insure that the student apply dictated principles until they are thoroughly understood and can be used independently. On the other hand, the present experiments did not equate the degree of initial learning under all treatments. But they did equate instructional time, an important variable in education.

The learning of a concept for a class of words, drawings, pictures, or objects was studied with laboratory methods and adult subjects. Some findings may be briefly indicated. When items were presented one at a time in a series, grouping the items according to class facilitated the learning of class concepts (61). Similarly among examples of a class that was not relevant to the concept slowed learning (22, 81). Massed and distributed practice were equally effective (81). Whether or not concepts were learned better from drawings or models or when viewed simultaneously rather than serially, depended upon the concept and the measure of learning (57). There was no regular order of difficulty for concepts based on object, form, number, or color, that was independent of the class or the measure of learning (57, 93).

The most intriguing recent account of the early development of concepts was a case study by Navarra (58). The data were stenographic records of overt activities and verbalizations with respect to natural phenomena of a boy from age three to age six. The insights and hypotheses provided constituted a strong endorsement of the value of research in naturalistic settings.

Skill

Comprehensive reviews of recent research appeared in two curricular areas which aim at the learning of particularly essential skills, i.e., language arts (1, 30, 31) and arithmetic (89, 90). The "meaning" method of teaching arithmetic and readiness activities may be regarded as an important educational application of theory, emphasizing the influence of previously developed concepts and understandings upon the acquisition of skills. This is a form of transfer of training, and several investigations pertinent to the function of transfer in the learning of skills are reviewed in the section of that title.

Additional studies relevant to the learning of skills were reported under the topic, "Goals and Motivation." In related investigations documenting the value of knowledge of results, Howell (34) found that the use of force-time graphs for the analysis of spring starts of experienced runners clearly aided their progress toward the ideal pattern. For the learning of simple skills Bilodeau and Bilodeau (11) stated that learning was positively related to absolute frequency of knowledge of results but independent of relative frequency. In a complex target-tracking task studied by Archer, Kent, and Mote (5) a signal confirming on-target time did not significantly influence the acquisition of skill over a 66-day practice period. Stockbridge and Chambers (75) in a study of rifle aiming concluded that for practical purposes there is no advantage in providing knowledge of results in learning if it will not be available when the skill is performed.

Several studies documented the effects of systematic practice and review upon a particular skill or phase of a skill. Meddleton (55) demonstrated experimentally that carefully compiled and graded number combinations would lead to better progress than less carefully considered programs of presentation and practice, and Mason (53) reported similar findings with respect to learning word discriminations. When equally systematic, different methods often appeared about equally effective. Word recognition, a skill or skills of some current interest, can be improved by visual, phonetic, or kinesthetic approaches, or various combinations of these approaches. The finding of Mills's study (56) in grades 2, 3, and 4 was that bright children learned readily regardless of the method used, and in the same study, methods differences for children of low intelligence were not statistically significant. Wilson and Leavell (92) reported reading gains as a result of each of six types of improvement programs. The comparative standings among six groups of tenth-grade students taught by different methods depended upon the reading tests used.

In studies of practice conditions by Knapp, Dixon, and Lazier (46) five minutes of daily practice in juggling led to more rapid learning than 15 minutes every second day; there were no significant differences between high-school freshmen and college groups in this respect. Levin (48) investigated individual differences and reported extreme stability of individual performance order regardless of the spacing of practice. McGuigan and MacCaslin (51) found that the whole method was superior to the part method in learning rifle marksmanship, but in tumbling and gymnastics Wickstrom (91) found no differences in stunt learning which were significantly related to practice on the whole stunt vs. practice on the first half, then the whole.

Transfer of Training

The learning of greatest significance for education is that which can be transferred to new situations. Transfer was a major concern of several of the investigations reported in the section, "Concepts, Understandings, and Principles." The studies relating transfer to activity (16, 21, 26, 28) and to increases in the amount of information given the learner (19, 45, 82) are especially relevant. Vris (83) found principles training superior to specific training in promoting transfer of the ability to thread one type of motion-picture projector to threading another type. Initial training with three-dimensional aids or equipment was more effective than training with two-dimensional aids.

Using the criterion of general academic performance, two well-controlled studies of remedial reading on the college level provided contrasting results which can be related to differences in the type of improvement initially achieved. McDonald (49) described a reading improvement program at Cornell which emphasized vocabulary development through a study of word context and derivation. A semester of this training led to improved comprehension, as well as speed, and to improvement in general grade-point average that was still evident three semesters later. On the other hand, an intensive 27-hour program at Wayne University, described by Reed (65), led to gains in reading speed, but to no improvement in vocabulary or comprehension and no gains in honor-point ratio. Schwartz (68) reported a surprising 104-per cent gain in reading speed for technical material as a result of only seven hours of accelerator training on nontechnical material. There was a slight decline in comprehension for the technical material.

Teaching for transfer was not effective in one study. Nelson's analysis of variance (59) revealed that a deliberate emphasis on transfer possibilities was of no advantage in the initial stages of separate learning of related gross motor skills, but such emphasis did prove helpful in teaching the subsequent skill. Learning one of two related skills and then the other was more effective than alternation in practice. Transfer was a direct function of the amount of variability in practice in Duncan's study (23) of practice with multiple vs. single perceptual-motor tasks. With code-substitution learning, however, Warren (88) reported that practicing the same task for 16 days was as effective in promoting transfer as practicing a different task each day. He attributed his results to the effects of adjustment to the learning situation.

One of the most ambitious transfer studies in applied settings was that of Stolurow, Hodgson, and Silva (76) to determine transfer effects associated with different patterns of technical-school training and work experience in the Air Force. When the work-training sequence caused trainees to learn associations among causes and symptoms first in one direction and then in the reverse, small or moderate negative transfer was found. An important exception occurred. When the initial associations were learned to a rather high degree, as with long work experience, the transfer was positive. The authors suggested that their results might hold for other diagnostic tasks of a similar nature, mentioning medical diagnosis. Educational diagnosis also comes readily to mind. Might there be a negative transfer from a cause-symptom approach in the teacher-training classroom to the symptom-cause problems of schoolroom diagnosis?

The effects of pretraining on learning and performance of a variety of simple tasks were studied intensively by Spiker and his associates at the Iowa Child Welfare Research Station. Results of particular interest, as reviewed by Sears (69), included finding that learning a common name for a set of stimuli increased the tendency to generalize other responses among them, that the concept of "middle-sized" enabled children to learn a related discrimination more quickly, and that attaching labels to objects enabled discriminations to be learned more rapidly. On the other hand, verbal pretraining was not effective with a more complex finger positioning task (9), and the prior learning of related mechanical principles was of little value in learning motor skills, such as those taught in physical education, involving body movement and large muscle activity (18).

Retention and Forgetting

The results of several studies indicated that course outcomes were retained for appreciable periods. The reading improvement programs reviewed under the topics, "Skills" and "Transfer of Training," reported retention of proficiency gains over several semesters. In high-school chemistry Smeltz (74) found that the students of five public high schools retained 68 per cent of their pre-to-post-course gains on standardized tests when retested one year later.

One of the few studies which attempted to measure differential retention of course outcomes was reported by McDougall (50). Items patterned after examples in Bloom's *Taxonomy of Educational Objectives* (12) were constructed to measure four different outcomes of a unit in tests and measurements. About 79 per cent of the gains in interpolation and extrapolation abilities were retained after four months. Gains in knowledge and in the ability to translate knowledge from one form to another were retained to a significantly lesser degree, approximately 73 per cent. The exercises used to measure interpretation and extrapolation appeared to differ quite markedly from the conventional items used to measure knowledge, however. Future studies should probably control for interaction between item type and gain or loss from test to retest.

Several other studies utilized materials typical of everyday or school learning. Gilbert (27) controlled intratask generalization in the overlearning of prose passages by dropping out facts when a preselected criterion for learning was achieved. Retention was an increasing function of the degree of overlearning, and retention curves indicated that intratask generalization was not responsible for the initial rapid decrement following learning. Yuker (94) found that group recall of prose material was superior to the recall by individuals in the group and that co-operative groups excelled competitive groups in recall. Another study of groups by Anderson (3) demonstrated that the recall of case studies in an educational psychology class was improved by group discussion of similar cases, whereas recall following individual analyses of these cases was inferior to that of a control group with no intervening activity. Ausubel, Schpoont, and Cukier (7) considered the influence of intent to remember in the retention of school learnings. When intent was introduced following learning rather than before, no influence of intent was evident in retention scores.

Progress in defining the effects of such factors as similar learnings, degree of learning, and type of material on the forgetting of nonsense syllables or word lists was summarized by Underwood (80) and Lawrence (47). Underwood's review assigned a much more prominent role to interference from previously learned materials, i.e., proactive inhibition, than has been customary in or out of the laboratory. Ausubel, Robbins, and Blake (6) accounted for inhibition in typical school learning in terms of proactive inhibition through a failure to disassociate new concepts from old. They predicted that interpolated learning designed to facilitate disassociation would also improve recall. Their experimental results were consistent with their theory and prediction.

Motor learning has been regarded as particularly resistant to forgetting, probably as a result of overlearning. Neumann and Ammons (60) reported almost complete loss of learned skill on a single perceptual-motor task after one year although relearning was rapid. Ammons and his coworkers (2) also studied retention of a procedural task (object arrangement) and an airplane control tracking task learned to a moderate or high level of initial skill over periods up to two years. Absolute loss in level of proficiency increased with the length of the no-practice period. Because the differences associated with greater degrees of learning were overcome in the first few minutes of retraining, they concluded that overlearning was not particularly helpful.

Although stimulus-response analyses of quantitative changes in retention clearly dominated the study of memory, a few studies were concerned with qualitative changes. In an analysis of individual differences in the reproduction of prose passages, Gomulicki (29) plotted a bimodal distribution of subjects with respect to preference for omitting or changing details when verbatim recall was impossible. Subjects were normally distributed on all other measures which were based on a word count of reproduced materials. Walker and Veroff (85) found some support for Gestalt hypotheses of reconstruction in recall although individual differences were large. Saul (66), however, could find no evidence of progressive changes, such as

CARL A. RUDISILL LIBRARY
LENOIR RHYNE COLLEGE

trends toward closure, symmetry, and the like, when a recognition measure was used.

Terminal Comments

The customary criticisms might be leveled at the research of the period reviewed. The practical contributions of the experimental psychologists were sharply limited by the boundary conditions of their directing theories, while the efforts of classroom researchers often seemed to lack direction. There were reasons for optimism, however.

There were indications, not reviewed here, that the facts contributed by other disciplines were beginning to broaden learning theories, despite some attempts to "hold the line" until simple phenomena are thoroughly understood. Some experimental psychologists worked intensively with human subjects and with distinctively human motives and responses. Educational psychologists raised questions about the generality of commonly accepted principles for the control of learning and, in so doing, emphasized differences among learners.

During this period, a greater proportion of classroom experiments employed reasonably adequate statistical techniques and designs. The results of these experiments raised doubts about the importance of methods differences which are defined in terms of broad intent or specific teacher activities rather than what the learner experiences.

The present period was a time of questioning and of developing sophistication in research. The climate was favorable for further progress in the understanding and control of the practically important features of the situations in which individuals learn.

Bibliography

1. AMERICAN EDUCATIONAL RESEARCH ASSOCIATION. "Language Arts and Fine Arts." *Review of Educational Research* 28: 79–179; April, 1958.
2. AMMONS, ROBERT B., and OTHERS. "Long-Term Retention of Perceptual Motor Skills." *Journal of Experimental Psychology* 55: 318–27; April, 1958.
3. ANDERSON, JOHN E., JR. *Small Group Discussion Without Knowledge of Results as an Inhibitor of Retroactive Interference in Case Studies*. Doctor's thesis. Columbus: Ohio State University, 1957. 71 p. Abstract: *Dissertation Abstracts* 18: 2059; No. 6, 1958.
4. APPLEZWEIG, MORTIMER H.; MOELLER, GEORGE; and BURDICK, HARVEY. "Multimotive Prediction of Academic Success." *Psychological Reports* 2: 489–96; December, 1956.
5. ARCHER, E. JAMES; KENT, GEORGE W.; and MOTE, FREDERICK A. "Effect of Long-Term Practice and Time-on-Target Information Feedback on a Com-

CARL A. RUDISILL LIBRARY
LENOIR RHYNE COLLEGE

plex Tracking Task." *Journal of Experimental Psychology* 51: 103–12; February, 1956.

6. AUSUBEL, DAVID P.; ROBBINS, LILLIAN C.; and BLAKE, ELIAS, JR. "Retroactive Inhibition and Facilitation in the Learning of School Materials." *Journal of Educational Psychology* 48: 334–43; October, 1957.

7. AUSUBEL, DAVID P.; SCHPOONT, SEYMOUR H.; and CUKIER, LILLIAN. "Influence of Intention on the Retention of School Materials." *Journal of Educational Psychology* 48: 87–92; February, 1957.

8. BAKER, ROBERT L., and DOYLE, ROY. "A Change in Marking Procedure and Scholastic Achievement." *Educational Administration and Supervision* 43: 223–32; April, 1957.

9. BATTIG, WILLIAM F., and OTHERS. "Supplementary Report: Effect of Verbal Pretraining on the Acquisition of a Complex Motor Skill." *Journal of Experimental Psychology* 54: 375–76; November, 1957.

10. BERNSTEIN, MARGERY R. "Relationship Between Interest and Reading Comprehension." *Journal of Educational Research* 49: 283–88; December, 1955.

11. BILODEAU, EDWARD A., and BILODEAU, INA McD. "Variable Frequency of Knowledge of Results and the Learning of a Simple Skill." *Journal of Experimental Psychology* 55: 379–83; April, 1958.

12. BLOOM, BENJAMIN S., editor. *Taxonomy of Educational Objectives. Handbook I: Cognitive Domain.* New York: Longmans, Green and Co., 1956. 102 p.

13. BOECK, CLARENCE H. "Relative Efficiency of Reading and Demonstration Methods of Instruction in Developing Scientific Understandings." *Science Education* 40: 92–97; March, 1956.

14. BRACKBILL, YVONNE, and JACK, DONALD. "Discrimination Learning in Children as a Function of Reinforcement Value." *Child Development* 29: 185–90; June, 1958.

15. BURTON, WILLIAM H. "Basic Principles in a Good Teaching-Learning Situation." *Phi Delta Kappan* 39: 242–48; March, 1958.

16. CARPENTER, FINLEY. "Effect of Different Learning Methods on Concept Formation." *Science Education* 40: 282–85; October, 1956.

17. CASTANEDA, ALFRED; PALERMO, DAVID S.; and McCANDLESS, BOYD R. "Complex Learning as a Function of Anxiety in Children and Task Difficulty." *Child Development* 27:327–32; September, 1956.

18. COLVILLE, FRANCES M. "The Learning of Motor Skills as Influenced by Knowledge of Mechanical Principles." *Journal of Educational Psychology* 48: 321–27; October, 1957.

19. CRAIG, ROBERT C. "Directed Versus Independent Discovery of Established Relations." *Journal of Educational Psychology* 47: 223–34; April, 1956.

20. DAVIDS, ANTHONY, and WHITE, AUGUSTUS A. "Effects of Success, Failure, and Social Facilitation on Level of Aspiration in Emotionally Disturbed and Normal Children." *Journal of Personality* 26: 77–93; March, 1958.

21. DELLA PIANA, GABRIEL M. "Searching Orientation and Concept Learning." *Journal of Educational Psychology* 48: 245–53; April, 1957.

22. DETAMBEL, MARVIN H., and STOLUROW, LAWRENCE M. "Stimulus Sequence and Concept Learning." *Journal of Experimental Psychology* 51: 34–40; January, 1956.

23. DUNCAN, CARL P. "Transfer After Training with Single Versus Multiple Tasks." *Journal of Experimental Psychology* 55: 63–72; January, 1958.

24. ESTES, WILLIAM K. "Learning." *Annual Review of Psychology.* (Edited by Paul R. Farnsworth.) Stanford, Calif.: Annual Reviews, 1956. p. 1–38.

25. FERSTER, CHARLES B., and SAPON, STANLEY M. "An Application of Recent Developments in Psychology to the Teaching of German." *Harvard Educational Review* 28: 58–59; Winter, 1958.

26. FORGUS, RONALD H., and SCHWARTZ, RUDOLPH J. "Efficient Retention and Transfer as Affected by Learning Methods." *Journal of Psychology* 43: 135–39; January, 1957.

27. GILBERT, THOMAS E. "Overlapping and the Retention of Meaningful Prose." *Journal of General Psychology* 56: 281–89; April, 1957.

28. GOCHMAN, STANLEY IRWIN. *Personality Dynamics and Learnings: A Study of Individual Differences in Learning, Retention, Transfer of Training, and Speed of Reaction as Functions of Personality.* Doctor's thesis. New York: New York University, 1956. 178 p. Abstract: *Dissertation Abstracts* 16: 1503; No. 8, 1956.

29. GOMULICKI, B. R. "Individual Differences in Recall." *Journal of Personality* 24: 387–400; June, 1956.

30. GRAY, WILLIAM S. "Summary of Reading Investigations July 1, 1955 to June 30, 1956." *Journal of Educational Research* 50: 401–41; February, 1957.

31. ———. "Summary of Reading Investigations July 1, 1956 to June 29, 1957." *Journal of Educational Research* 51: 401–35; February, 1958.

32. HILDUM, DONALD C., and BROWN, ROGER W. "Verbal Reinforcement and Interviewer Bias." *Journal of Abnormal and Social Psychology* 53: 108–11; July, 1956.

33. HILGARD, ERNEST R. *Theories of Learning.* Second edition. New York: Appleton-Century-Crofts, 1956. 563 p.

34. HOWELL, MAXWELL L. "Use of Force-Time Graphs for Performance Analysis in Facilitating Motor Learning." *Research Quarterly* 27: 12–22; March, 1956.

35. HURLEY, JOHN R. "Achievement Imagery and Motivational Instructions as Determinants of Verbal Learning." *Journal of Personality* 25: 274–82; March, 1957.

36. HURLOCK, ELIZABETH B. "An Evaluation of Certain Incentives Used in School Work." *Journal of Educational Psychology* 16: 145–59; March, 1925.

37. JOHNSON, DONOVAN A. "Study of the Relative Effectiveness of Group Instruction." *School Science and Mathematics* 56: 609–16; November, 1956.

38. JOHNSTON, ROBERT A. "A Methodological Analysis of Several Revised Forms of the Iowa Picture Interpretation Test." *Journal of Personality* 25: 283–93; March, 1957.

39. JONES, MARSHALL R., editor. *Nebraska Symposium on Motivation: 1955.* Current Theory and Research in Motivation, Vol. 3. Lincoln: University of Nebraska Press, 1955. 274 p.

40. ———, editor. *Nebraska Symposium on Motivation: 1956.* Currey Theory and Research in Motivation, Vol. 4. Lincoln: University of Nebraska Press, 1956. 311 p.

41. ———, editor. *Nebraska Symposium on Motivation: 1957.* Currey Theory and Research in Motivation, Vol. 5. Lincoln: University of Nebraska Press, 1957. 430 p.

42. KAPOS, ERVIN; MECH, EDMUND V.; and FOX, WILLIAM H. *Schoolroom Motivation: I. Two Studies of Quantity and Pattern of Verbal Reinforcement as Related to Performance on a Routine Task.* Bulletin of the School of Education Vol. 33. No. 1. Bloomington: Indiana University, January, 1957. 43 p.

43. ———; ———; and ———. *Schoolroom Motivation: II. Two Studies of Quantity and Pattern of Verbal Reinforcement as Related to a Measure of Drive on a Routine Task.* Bulletin of the School of Education, Vol. 33, No. 2. Bloomington: Indiana University, March, 1957. 40 p.

44. KAUSLER, DONALD H., and TRAPP, E. PHILIP. "Achievement Motivation and Goal Setting Behavior on a Learning Task." *Journal of Experimental Psychology* 57: 575–77; June, 1958.

45. KITTELL, JACK E. "An Experimental Study of the Effect of External Direction During Learning on Transfer and Retention of Principles." *Journal of Educational Psychology* 48: 391–405; November, 1957.

46. KNAPP, CLYDE G.; DIXON, W. ROBERT; and LAZIER, MURNEY. "Learning to Juggle: III. A Study of Performance by Two Different Age Groups." *Research Quarterly* 29: 32–36; March, 1958.

47. LAWRENCE, DOUGLAS H. "Learning." *Annual Review of Psychology.* (Edited by Paul R. Farnsworth.) Stanford, Calif.: Annual Reviews, 1958. p. 157–88.

48. LEVIN, GERALD R. *Extraversion and Benefits from Spaced Practice.* Doctor's thesis. New York: Columbia University, 1958. 39 p. Abstract: *Dissertation Abstracts* 18: 1865; No. 5, 1958.

49. McDONALD, ARTHUR S. "Influence of a College Reading Improvement Program on Academic Performance." *Journal of Educational Psychology* 48: 171–81 March, 1957.

50. McDOUGALL, WILLIAM P. "Differential Retention of Course Outcome in Educational Psychology." *Journal of Educational Psychology* 49: 53–60; April, 1958.

51. McGUIGAN, FRANK J., and MacCASLIN, EUGENE F. "Whole and Part Methods in Learning a Perceptual Motor Skill." *American Journal of Psychology* 65: 658–61; December, 1955.

52. McNAIR, DOUGLAS M. "Reinforcement of Verbal Behavior." *Journal of Experimental Psychology* 53: 40–46; January, 1957.

53. MASON, GEOFFREY P. "Work Discrimination and Spelling." *Journal of Educational Research* 50: 617–21; April, 1957.

54. MECH, EDMUND V.; KAPOS, ERVIN; and FOX, WILLIAM H. "Schoolroom Motivation: Quantity and Pattern of Verbal 'Reinforcement' as Variables Related to Routine Performance Under Massed Training." *American Psychologist* 10: 35; August, 1955.

55. MEDDLETON, IVOR G. "An Experimental Investigation into the Systematic Teaching of Number Combinations in Arithmetic." *British Journal of Educational Psychology* 26: 117–27; June, 1956.

56. MILLS, ROBERT E. "An Evaluation of Techniques for Teaching Word Recognition." *Elementary School Journal* 41: 221–25; January, 1956.

57. NADELMAN, LORRAINE. "Influence of Concreteness and Accessibility on Concept Thinking." *Psychological Reports* 3: 189–212; June, 1957.

58. NAVARRA, JOHN G. *Development of Scientific Concepts in a Young Child, a Case Study.* New York: Teachers College, Columbia University, 1955. 147 p.

59. NELSON, DALE O. "Studies of Transfer of Learning in Gross Motor Skills." *Research Quarterly* 28: 364–73; December, 1957.

60. NEUMANN, EVA, and AMMONS, ROBERT B. "Acquisition and Long-Term Retention of a Simple Serial Perceptual-Motor Skill." *Journal of Experimental Psychology* 53: 159–61; March, 1957.

61. NEWMAN, SLATER E. "Effects of Contiguity and Similarity on the Learning of Concepts." *Journal of Experimental Psychology* 52: 349–53; December, 1956.

62. OJEMANN, RALPH H., and OTHERS. "The Effects of a 'Causal' Teacher-Training Program and Certain Curricular Changes on Grade School Children." *Journal of Experimental Education* 24: 95–114; December, 1955.

63. OLSON, KENNETH V. *An Experimental Evaluation of a Student-Centered Method and a Teacher-Centered Method of Biological Science Instruction for General Education of College Students.* Doctor's thesis. Minneapolis: University of Minnesota, 1957. 325 p. (Typewritten)

64. PALERMO, DAVID S.; CASTANEDA, ALFRED; and McCANDLESS, BOYD R. "The Relationship of Anxiety in Children to Performance in a Complex Learning Task." *Child Development* 27: 333–37; September, 1956.

65. REED, JAMES C. "Some Effects of Short-Term Training in Reading Under Conditions of Controlled Motivation." *Journal of Educational Psychology* 47: 257–64; May, 1956.

66. SAUL, EZRA V. "Immediate and Delayed Recognition of Geometric Form." *Journal of General Psychology* 55: 163–71; October, 1956.

67. SAVIAGNANO, LEONARD J. *An Evaluation of the Effect of Children's Specialties on Classroom Enrichment in Grades Four, Five, and Six.* Doctor's thesis. Boston: Boston University, 1956. 261 p. Abstract: *Dissertation Abstracts* 16: 2409; No. 12, 1956.

68. SCHWARTZ, MARVIN. "Transfer of Reading Training from Nontechnical to Technical Material." *Journal of Educational Psychology* 48: 498–504; December, 1957.

69. SEARS, PAULINE S. "Developmental Psychology." *Annual Review of Psy-*

chology. (Edited by Paul R. Farnsworth.) Stanford, Calif.: Annual Reviews, 1958. p. 119–56.

70. ———. "Problems in the Investigation of Achievement and Self-Esteem Motivation." *Nebraska Symposium on Motivation: 1957*. (Edited by Marshall R. Jones.) Current Theory and Research on Motivation, Vol. 5. Lincoln: University of Nebraska Press, 1957. p. 265–339.

71. SIEGEL, LILA C. *The Effects of Various Motivational Conditions upon Learning and Retention*. Doctor's thesis. Pullman: State College of Washington, 1955. 178 p. Abstract: *Dissertation Abstracts* 16: 995; No. 5, 1956.

72. SILBERMAN, HARRY F. "Effects of Praise and Reproof on Reading Growth in a Non-Laboratory Classroom Setting." *Journal of Educational Psychology* 48: 199–206; April, 1957.

73. SIVERTSEN, DAGFINN. "Goal Setting: The Level of Aspiration and Social Norms." *Acta Psychologica* 13: 54–60; No. 1, 1957.

74. SMELTZ, JOHN R. "Retention of Learnings in High School Chemistry." *Science Teacher* 23: 285; October, 1956.

75. STOCKBRIDGE, H. C. W., and CHAMBERS, B. "Aiming, Transfer of Training and Knowledge of Results." *Journal of Applied Psychology* 42: 148–53; June, 1958.

76. STOLUROW, LAWRENCE M.; HODGSON, THOMAS F.; and SILVA, JOHN. *Transfer and Retroaction Effects of "Association Reversal" and "Familiarization" Training in Trouble Shooting*. Psychological Monographs, No. 419. Washington, D.C.: American Psychological Association, 1956. 23 p.

77. SYMONDS, PERCIVAL M. "What Education Has To Learn from Psychology: II. Reward." *Teachers College Record* 57: 15–25; October, 1955.

78. ———. "What Education Has To Learn from Psychology: III. Punishment." *Teachers College Record* 57: 449–62; April, 1956.

79. TYLER, LEONA E. "Studies on Motivation and Identification of Gifted Pupils." *Review of Educational Research* 27: 391–99; October, 1957.

80. UNDERWOOD, BENTON J. "Interference and Forgetting." *Psychological Review* 64: 49–60; January, 1957.

81. ———. "Studies of Distributed Practice: XV. Verbal Concept Learning as a Function of Intralist Interference." *Journal of Experimental Psychology* 54: 33–40; July, 1957.

82. ———, and RICHARDSON, JACK. "Verbal Concept Learning as a Function of Instructions and Dominance Level." *Journal of Experimental Psychology* 51: 229–38; April, 1956.

83. VRIS, THOMAS. *A Comparison of Principles Training and Specific Training Using Several Types of Training Devices*. Technical Report SDC 269–7–102, Instructional Film Research Program, Pennsylvania State University. Port Washington, Long Island, N.Y.: Special Devices Center, July, 1955. 28 p.

84. ———. "Learning." *Annual Review of Psychology*. (Edited by P. R. Farnsworth.) Stanford, Calif.: Annual Reviews, 1957. p. 113–38.

85. ———, and VEROFF, JOSEPH P. "Changes in the Memory-Trace for

Perceived Forms for Successive Reproduction." *American Journal of Psychology* 69: 395–402; September, 1956.

86. WALTER, VERNE A. *The Effect of Need for Achievement on the Performance of College Students in Learning Certain Study Skills.* Doctor's thesis. Columbus, Ohio State University, 1956. 176 p. Abstract: *Dissertation Abstracts* 17: 1384 No. 6, 1957.

87. WARD, JOHN N. "Group-Study Versus Lecture-Demonstration Method in Physical Science Instruction for General Education College Students." *Journal of Experimental Education* 24: 197–210; March, 1956.

88. WARREN, JOHN M. "Intertask Transfer in Code Substitution Learning." *Journal of Genetic Psychology* 89: 65–70; September, 1956.

89. WEAVER, J. FRED. "Research on Arithmetic Instruction—1957." *Arithmetic Teacher* 5: 109–18; April, 1958.

90. ———. "Six Years of Research on Arithmetic Instruction: 1951–54." *Arithmetic Teacher* 4: 89–99; April, 1957.

91. WICKSTROM, RALPH L. "Comparative Study of Methodologies for Teaching Gymnastics and Tumbling Stunts." *Research Quarterly* 29: 109–15; March, 1935.

92. WILSON, GRACE E., and LEAVELL, ULLIN W. "An Experiment with Acceleration Training." *Peabody Journal of Education* 34: 9-18; July, 1956.

93. WOHLWILL, JOACHIM F. "The Abstraction and Conceptualization of Form, Code and Number." *Journal of Experimental Psychology* 53: 304–309; May, 1957.

94. YUKER, HAROLD E. "Group Atmosphere and Memory." *Journal of Abnormal and Social Psychology* 51: 17–23; July, 1955.

13. A Biochemical Approach
to Learning and Memory *

JOHN GAITO,[1] *Lake Forest College*

THE PROBLEM of learning and memory has been one of the most important areas of investigation for the psychologist for many years. Recently there have been a number of attempts to specify the neurological structure which is modified during learning and which provides the basis for memory.

* From John Gaito, "A Biochemical Approach to Learning and Memory," *The Psychological Review,* 68 (July, 1961), 288–92. Reprinted by permission.
[1] Now at Kansas State University.

It appears that the site which has been emphasized most frequently by theorists is the synapse. Hebb (1949) maintained that reverberatory circuits may provide the basis for short-term memory whereas long-term memory requires neural growth at synaptic junctions; his cell assemblies and phase sequences furnish the basis for all simple and complex functions. Somewhat similar ideas (stripped of cell assemblies and phase sequences) were expressed by a number of individuals at the Hixon Symposium (Jeffress, 1951) and at the Laurentian Symposium (Delayfresnaye, 1954). Gerard (1953) mentioned a number of events which he believed might provide the synaptic changes which facilitate learning and maintain memory, viz., swelling of synaptic nerve fiber end-bulbs while conducting impulses, alterations of potential, actual neural growth at synapse, and changes in nerve proteins. Eccles (1958) presented a somewhat similar view. Krech and his collaborators at the University of California have conducted a series of experiments combining the biochemical and psychological approaches and have emphasized that experience and training may significantly alter the concentration of brain cholinesterase (Bennett, Krech, Rosenzweig, Karlsson, Dye, and Ohlander, 1958; Bennett, Rosenzweig, Krech, Karlsson, Dye, and Ohlander, 1958; Krech, Rosenzweig, and Bennett, 1956, 1959; Krech, Rosenzweig, Bennett, and Longueil, 1959; Rosenzweig, Krech, and Bennett, 1956). These individuals have hypothesized that transmission of neural impulses is accomplished by the discharge of actylcholine from presynaptic neurons. Inactivation of acetylcholine by cholinesterase (as soon as the former stimulates the postsynaptic neuron) preserves discrete transmission of impulses. Their experimental work lends credence to this hypothesis. Overton (1958, 1959a, 1959b) stated that calcium displacement at the synapse, during acetylcholine-cholinesterase activity, forms the basis for memory. Likewise, he reported research which favors his hypothesis.

That some synaptic change is important for learning and memory is generally accepted. However, it is possible that these synaptic changes *facilitate or set off reactions* which allow changes to occur elsewhere in the nerve cell. Recently Halstead (1951) favored the hypothesis that nucleoproteins are the substances which have the ability to act as templates on which replica molecules are formed, both genetically and as a result of individual experience. He believed that templates exist in the brain nerve cells which are like those of the germ cells in representing native endowment but differ from the latter in having templates arising from external stimulation. He stated that the ordering of the protein templates could take place in various components of the cell and its processes. The present arguments are in general similar to those of Halstead but emphasize recent biochemical developments. We suggest that *learning and memory depend on changes in genic material (or the by-products of genic activity) either in the nucleus or cytoplasm of the nerve cell soma.*

It is obvious to psychologists that both heredity and environment contribute to behavior. Thus we can say, in very general fashion, that behavior is a function of genetic potential (heredity) as it is modified by intra- and extraorganismic environmental stimulation. Inasmuch as we are concerned only with learning (and resulting memory), let us substitute the word "learning" for the second part of the above statement. We now have: behavior is a function of genetic potential as it is modified by learning. Also we shall take this statement literally.

First, let us indicate the physical basis for genetic potential. Biochemists (e.g., Butler, 1959; Crick, 1954, 1957; Lederberg, 1960) have identified desoxyribonucleic acid (DNA), a giant molecule found in the chromosomes, as the primary hereditary material. DNA is a large double strand molecule which is wound in a helix. Each strand is a mirror image of the other and has recurring patterns of constituents throughout its length, called nucleotides. A nucleotide consists of a phosphate attached to a sugar-base linkage. Figure 1 shows a portion of the DNA molecule as it would appear if it were unwound. The sugar-base portion (a nucleoside) is considered to be the most important part of the molecule. The nucleoside of one strand is attached to its corersponding part of the other strand by a hydrogen atom. The bases consist of two types: purines and pyrimidines. Furthermore, there are two purines (adenine and guanine) and two pyrimidines (thymine and cytosine). The purines are larger molecules than are the pyrimidines. At the sugar-base points of the strands, a purine of one strand is always attached (by the hydrogen atom) to a pyrimidine. Two purines are too big to bridge the gap between the two strands and two pyrimidines are too small. Furthermore, the amounts of adenine and thymine are always equal and the amounts of guanine and cytosine are equal also, because adenine is always paired with thymine and guanine with cytosine. Thus there are two basic types. However, if we consider the order of the bases in the attachment of one nucleoside to another, this number doubles. (For example, adenine linked to thymine is different than thymine linked to adenine.) Thus there are four basic types of nucleotides.

Biochemists believe that the sequence of the bases furnish the basis for the "codes" of genetic potential (Butler, 1959; Crick, 1954, 1957; Lederberg, 1960). Even though there are only four possible nucleotides, the strands of the molecule are extremely long and allow for infinite possibilities, if the sequence of the purines and pyrimidines is considered. Thus, these sugar-base attachments may be the "language" of the genes. Crick (1954) has likened the bases to the dots and dashes of the Morse Code.

Thus he states that there is enough DNA in a single cell of the human body to encode about 1,000 large textbooks.

Now let us see how learning might modify these codes of the DNA molecule. DNA is a relatively stable molecule. However, changes of one or several nucleosides should be easier to effect. Thus electrochemical changes

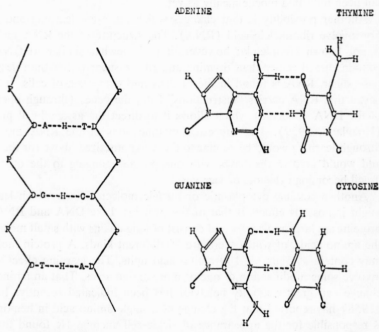

Figure 1. The DNA molecule as it would appear if unwound from its helical formation. (P. is phosphate; D. desoxyribose, a sugar; A, adenine; T, thymine; C, cytosine; G, guanine; and H, hydrogen.)

Figure 2. The bases present in DNA. (RNA is similar except that uracil replaces thymine. The point of bonding is indicated by dashed lines. C is carbon; N, nitrogen; H, hydrogen; and O, oxygen.)

at the synapse might spread to the soma and lead to the dislocation or changing of nucleosides at one or more loci. A change at one locus would modify the code.

Figure 2 indicates the structure of the purines and pyrimidines. Note that the basic structure of the purines is the same, as is also that of the pyrimidines. Adenine differs from guanine and thymine from cytosine only in the side bonds. It appears that the easiest and most logical change would be of adenine to guanine or the reverse. An NH_2 side bond must change position from top to bottom and a hydrogen atom must be replaced by an oxygen atom for adenine to become guanine. For guanine to change to adenine, the reverse events are required.

However, if a change were to occur in one purine, the attached pyrimidine would have to change likewise. Thus for thymine to become cytosine a CH_3 side chain must be replaced by a hydrogen atom and an oxygen atom replaced by an NH_2 molecule. Such events appear feasible but have not been indicated biochemically as yet.

Another possibility is that changes which represent learning and memory involve ribonucleic acid (RNA). The structure of the RNA molecule is not known completely; however, it is somewhat similar to DNA but contains uracil rather than thymine and ribose sugar rather than desoxyribose sugar. RNA is found in the nucleus and cytoplasm of cells. It is believed that RNA carries "instructions" from the genes (through operation of the DNA molecule) which allows it to direct the assembly of proteins (Hoagland, 1959). The suggested modifications of the RNA molecules through learning would be similar to those hypothesized above for the DNA and would involve the bases with one purine changing to the other and uracil becoming cytosine, or vice versa.

Another possible cytoplasmic or nucleic molecule upon which learning might impose its effects is that of the proteins. Like DNA and RNA, the proteins are large molecules and consist of long chains with small molecules, the amino acids, of which there are 20 different kinds. A protein molecule may contain as many as 100 amino acid units. The learning effect would involve some modification of one or more amino acids. That an amino acid change can greatly modify behavior has been indicated recently. Ingram (1958) has reported that the change of a single amino acid in hemoglobin is responsible for the appearance of sickle-cell anemia. He found that the normal hemoglobin cell and the sickle-form hemoglobin are the same except that in the latter one peptide was displaced slightly from the position it occupies in the normal cell. The normal peptide had two glutamic acid units and one valine unit; the abnormal cell had one glutamic acid unit and two valines. This defect is due to heredity or to mutations. However, changes in amino acids might occur through stimulation.

Thus we believe that changes in the DNA, RNA, or protein molecules may be the basis for learning and memory. These three are intimately involved in cellular activity in the nucleus and cytoplasm with the DNA commanding the process. It is believed that chromosomes consist of these three, with the DNA being the backbone of the chromosome and housing the genes. If changes occur in the DNA molecules, these changes would automatically affect RNA and protein synthesis. Likewise, changes in RNA would be transmitted to some protein molecules. However, changes might occur to protein molecules, which would have no effect on DNA or RNA.

Only the changes of the DNA molecule would be of a genic modification nature. Changes of DNA, RNA, or protein molecules might occur in the nucleus or in the cytoplasm. Gay (1960) has described the passage of minute "blebs," or blisters, containing chromosomal material, from the nucleus to the cytoplasm in the salivary glands of the larval fruit fly. These events are considered of importance in protein synthesis. It is possible that such transfer could occur also in nerve cells. Thus "recodification" of the DNA, RNA, or protein molecules might occur in the cytoplasm following such transfer. However, it should be possible for electrochemical events to permeate the nuclear membrane and bring about the changes in the nucleus.

Superficially there appears to be conflict between the synaptic hypothesis and the ideas presented here. However, this need not be the case. The synaptic hypothesis allows for changes to occur elsewhere in nerve cells but concentrates on the synaptic changes in effecting learning and memory. On the other hand the present viewpoint agrees that changes occur at the synapse but stresses the modification in the genic, or by-products of the genic, material; the synaptic changes are preliminary in nature. Furthermore, it is probable that both mechanisms are involved in learning and memory. In recent years there has been a tendency to consider memory as of two types, transient and permanent (e.g., Hebb, 1949; Jeffress, 1951), with the former maintained by reverberatory circuits but the latter, by permanent neural changes. It is possible that the two types of memory may depend upon different neurological sites. For example, a reverberatory circuit would depend upon synaptic transmission for reverberation to occur. Thus effecting short term memory may involve mainly the synapse. However, the neural change which makes for relatively permanent memory may involve changes elsewhere in the cell, e.g., in the DNA, RNA, or amino acids in the nucleus or in the cytoplasm. But permanent changes could, and apparently do, occur at the synapse. However, we believe that the synaptic changes serve the function of making the genic materials more accessible to stimulation.

The major advantage that this nucleic or cytoplasmic recodification hypothesis has over the synaptic hypothesis is that the former allows learning to directly modify genetic potential (or the by-products of genic activity) whereas the latter is faced with the problem of relating learning and memory changes to the genetic potential. Thus the synaptic hypothesis must explain the means by which learning and genetic potential affect one another, for it is obvious that genetic potential affects learning and that learning modifies genetic potential. Furthermore, the recodification hypothesis attempts to indicate the molecular basis for memory; however, the exact chemical mechanism involved in the learning process is still a major problem.

One might criticize portions of the above hypothesis on the ground that it is arguing for the inheritance of acquired characteristics. However, this is not so. The suggested changes in genic material would occur only in nervous tissue which is not passed on to the next generation. The genes in the nuclear chromosomes of the gonads (which provide the physical material for heredity) would be unaffected.

The validity of these hypotheses have not been demonstrated as yet. To evaluate such ideas (or similar ones) requires the use of the precise molecular techniques of the biochemist, cytologist, and geneticist coupled with the less molecular procedures of the neurophysiologist and the molar learning methods of the psychologist in collaborative research programs. However, the hypothesis can serve as an interesting framework for descriptive formulations and appears more logical than does the synaptic hypothesis.

References

BENNETT, E. L., KRECH, D., ROSENZWEIG, M. R., KARLSSON, H., DYE, N., and OHLANDER A. Cholinesterase and lactic dehydrogenase activity in the rat brain. *J. Neurochem.*, 1958, **3**, 153–160.

BENNETT, E. L., ROSENZWEIG, M. R., KRECH, D. R., KARLSSON, H., DYE, N., and OHLANDER, A. Individual strain, and age differences in cholinesterase activity of the rat brain. *J. Neurochem.*, 1958, **3**, 144–152.

BUTLER, J. A. V. *Inside the living cell.* New York: Basic Books, 1959.

CRICK, F. H. C. The structure of the hereditary material. *Scient. Amer.*, 1954, **191**, 54–61.

———. Nucleic acids. *Scient. Amer.*, 1957, **197**, 188–200.

DELAYFRESNAYE, J. F. (Ed.) *Brain mechanisms and consciousness.* Oxford: Blackwell, 1954.

ECCLES, J. C. The physiology of imagination. *Scient. Amer.*, 1958, **199**, 135–146.

GAY, H. Nuclear control of the cell. *Scient. Amer.*, 1960, **202**, 126–136.

GERARD, R. W. What is memory? *Scient. Amer.*, 1953, **189**, 118–126.

HALSTEAD W. C. Brain and intelligence. In L. A. Jeffress (Ed.), *Cerebral mechanisms in behavior.* New York: Wiley, 1951.

HEBB, D. O. *The organization of behavior.* New York: Wiley, 1949.

HOAGLAND, M. B. Nucleic acids and proteins. *Scient. Amer.*, 1959, **201**, 55–61.

INGRAM, V. M. How do genes act? *Scient. Amer.*, 1958, **198**, 68–74.

JEFFRESS, L. A. (Ed.) *Cerebral mechanisms in behavior.* New York: Wiley, 1951.

KRECH, D., ROSENZWEIG, M. R. and BENNETT, E. L. Dimensions of discrimination and level of cholinesterase activity in the cerebral cortex of the rat. *J. comp. physiol. Psychol.*, 1956, **49**, 261–268.

———., ———., and ———. Correlation between brain cholinesterase and brain weight within two strains of rats. *Amer. J. Physiol.*, 1959, **196**, 31–32.

———., ———., ———., and LONGUEIL, C. L. Changes in brain chemistry of the rat following experience. Paper presented at American Psychological Association, Cincinnati, September 1959.

LEDERBERG, J. A view of genetics. *Science,* 1960, **131,** 269–276.

OVERTON, R. K. An effect of high- and low-calcium diets on the maze performance of rats. *J. comp. physiol. Psychol.,* 1958, **51,** 697–699.

———. The calcium displacement hypothesis: A review. *Psychol. Rep.,* 1959, **5,** 721–724. (a)

———. *Thought and action: A physiological approach.* New York: Random House, 1959. (b)

ROSENZWEIG, M. R., KRECH, D., and BENNETT, E. L. Effects of pentobarbital sodium on adaptive behavior patterns in the rat. *Science,* 1956, **123,** 371–372.

14. Educational Theory and the Psychology of Learning * 1

GUY T. BUSWELL, *University of California at Berkeley*

A S BACKGROUND for this paper I should like to quote an illustration given by Guthrie (*1*) on the first page of this chapter in the National Society Yearbook on "The Psychology of Learning." It consists of a description of a day in school as told by a boy in the elementary grades. His account is as follows:

We have a man teacher. He doesn't get mad much. We talk a lot. If somebody throws a pen or stuff like that, he puts you out in the hall. We have 20 words for spelling. We write them on Monday and Wednesday and Friday, but it only counts on Wednesday and Friday. Then we have social science. It's really history, but he likes fancy names for things. Then we study geography and then mathematics—really arithmetic, you know. He gives us some fancy doo-jigs to work with. About two boys get their seats changed if they've been poking somebody. Then the teacher gives us exams and stuff and we have recess—ten min-

* From Guy T. Buswell, "Educational Theory and the Psychology of Learning," *The Journal of Educational Psychology* (March, 1956), pp. 175–84. Reprinted by permission.

1 Presidential address read at the meeting of the Educational Psychology Division of the American Psychological Association at the Annual Convention in San Francisco, September 10, 1955.

utes—not much time for doing things. We mostly play marbles. Then the bell
rings and we go in and the teacher talks a lot about notices. Then the music
class. The music teacher talks a lot. We don't sing much. Sometimes we sing a
review song, but mostly the teacher talks. Then we have reading. The teacher is
nuts about ancient literature. Then we check our books at the book table. They
have about 200 books. Some of them are good and some are corny. We have
shop, too; make things. There's a jig saw and a lathe and a sander and a printing
press. We use all those things. I made a record case and a broom holder and a
box.

From the point of view of a boy, school consists of a summation of days
and years of experiences such as those described. Certainly his account
seems trivial and unimpressive as a sample of this multibillion-dollar enterprise we call Education. From the point of view of the psychologist and the
educator, the behaviors described by the boy are likely to be evaluated in
terms of the pattern of changes they produce in the boy as a human organism, in terms of the particular knowledge and skills that are developed,
and in terms of the general intellectual and emotional habits that result.
The educator will be concerned with the question of whether such behaviors as those described by the boy will produce the kind of outcomes
expected by society, and, if so, with the theoretical explanation of such
outcomes. The psychologist will be concerned with a theory of learning that
will explain the changes produced in the boy, although he will probably
be less concerned about what outcomes are expected by society. The main
concern of this paper is how a theory of education as expressed by the
educator is related to a theory of learning as formulated by the psychologist.
In general, theories of education have been formulated quite independently of theories of learning and, likewise, learning theories have been set
up by psychologists who are often quite innocent of an intimate knowledge
of what goes on within schools. One of the main concerns of the Educational Psychology Division of the American Psychological Association, so
it seems to me, should be to bring together the learning theory of the
psychologists and the educational theory of the school.
At one of the section meetings of the American Association for the
Advancement of Science, a competent educational psychologist made the
statement that learning theory had no value for teachers in the classroom.
Yet, since teaching implies learning, how can it be that a serious study of
the theory of how one learns can have no value for the teacher? One is
tempted to explain this opinion as due to the failure of the theorist to illustrate and to verify his theory in terms of the kinds of learning that are
carried on in schools. For example, the classical experiment in conditioning
is simple and clear in showing how substitute stimuli will produce the flow
of saliva in the dog. One can illustrate the process of conditioning quite

easily with young children by stimulating a fear response of running away from an assortment of stimuli. Here we have a constant, original response of secreting saliva, or of running, as a result of a variety of stimulations. However, the school is not overly interested in original responses. How shall the teacher use the process of conditioning to elicit all the varied kinds of responses that are the desired outcomes of education? When close to the level of native response, the conditioning theory is easily illustrated. But how shall we tell the algebra teacher to use it in teaching a ninth-grade pupil to square the binomial "x + y"? Guthrie, in his text on the "Psychology of Learning" (2) asks the question, "What does the principle of conditioning mean in the form of practical advice?" He answers with an illustration on the same page as follows: "If we wish to teach a dog to come when he is called, our method will be to get him to come by hook or crook. There are no rules for this except what we know of dogs in general." Is the teacher of algebra to be offered nothing better than a "by hook or crook" method? Or is an unvarying production of a correct response all that is expected from the study of algebra? Further on, Guthrie states ". . . the student officer is cautioned never to give a command that he is not confident will be obeyed. If the command is followed by acts other than those commanded, the command becomes merely a cue for disobedience and the officer loses his authority." Is the teacher then never to ask a question until he is confident it will be answered correctly? And by what occult power will he know when the time is ripe? One may at least have some sympathy for the teacher who fails to find learning theory helpful. But in all truth, there is an obligation on the part of someone to make it helpful. It makes no sense when a serious study of learning and a serious attempt to teach find no common ground.

Any educational situation involves a purpose or objective, a content to be learned (a curriculum), and a process of learning. The over-all purpose or objective, what we are trying to do, is expressed as theory of education. The *process* of changing behavior in accordance with educational theory is expressed as the psychology of learning. Between these two is the content to be learned, whether substantive subject-matter or behavior traits. The thesis of this paper is that if the psychology of learning is to be effective in the schools, it must focus its interests and design its experiments with awareness of the theory of education that is currently accepted by the society in which the schools operate. As theory of education is modified, the direction of psychological study must be changed if its results are to influence educational practice. This is no different in the areas of education and psychology than in other areas. The current interest in nuclear physics has for a decade produced a new focus of attention for scientists of many fields. The movement from old issues to new characterizes a live science.

Research in the field of educational psychology should reflect the movement of educational theory. In the 1920's, research on drill in arithmetic was in harmony with educational theory; in 1955, such studies would have far less significance because the purpose and theory of teaching arithmetic have undergone marked change. The ultimate objective, of course, is not merely to relate research to currently accepted educational theory, but rather, to do the kind of research that will help to formulate an educational theory that is *valid*.

I should like to illustrate this relationship between educational theory and the psychology of learning by reference to only two of the several theories of education which might be described. During the last century, and in some places still, education was considered as basically the acquisition of knowledge. The inscription, "Knowledge is Power," was found on many school buildings. Passing on the intellectual heritage of the race was considered the primary purpose of the school. Acquirement of knowledge, with some attendant skills, was the basic aim. Prior to the Civil War, the accumulation of knowledge was not so great as to constitute any considerable burden to the learner. Then the situation changed. Particularly in the field of science, a great expansion began. This increase in subject-matter to be learned was met by devising the elective system. This gave rise to the problem of what knowledge is of most worth and resulted in a fight for time among the different branches of the curriculum. By the twentieth century the situation began to be serious, particularly in the secondary school and junior college. Pupil programs, which at first were made up of a large common group of required subjects plus a few electives, began to show a progressively smaller group of required subjects and an increase in the electives. By the 1920's it became clear that any attempt to cover the field of essential knowledge was hopeless by the required and elective system. A new venture into general education, by means of survey courses, was tried, and now such courses are a part of the program at the junior college level in many institutions. Back of all these changes was the basic question, "What is an education?" As long as it is defined as mastery of the body of knowledge, it must necessarily expand, although the individual learner's capacity to learn has undergone no corresponding change. The elective program was characterized as a specialization in depth in a few areas, with chasms of ignorance between. After thirty years of experimenting with survey courses, they are often subject to the charge of specialization in another axis; namely, specialization in superficialities. But if in theory a good education is defined in terms of knowledge and skill, what other alternatives are there, particularly in the face of a certain increase in the rate of accumulation of knowledge.

If some modification of the foregoing picture is accepted as a theory of education, then what type of psychological research in learning will likely follow? With so much to be learned, one would expect emphasis on the psychology of memory and retention. Problems of length and distribution of practice periods, whole and part methods of memorizing, prerequisites affecting the order in which different subject-matters should be learned would seem important. Major concern would be centered on subject-matter to be learned, rather than changes in the learner. One can find many specifics to illustrate both this theory of education and the kinds of learning studies mentioned.

However, one might conceive of a second very different theory of education. Rather than define a good education in terms of the knowledge and skills possessed, one might think of it in terms of certain changes brought about in the learner, by means of which he would develop abilities enabling him to respond successfully to the diverse and unpredictable situations that life will bring. Advocates of such a view would readily admit the necessity of a fairly large amount of basic knowledge and skill. Certainly they would not make a virtue of ignorance. But rather than conceive of education as an encyclopedic coverage of knowledge, they would deal with the heritage of knowledge in a highly selective way. They would probably agree on the necessity of certain knowledge and skill, for example, ability to read, knowing how to spell, knowing number facts and relations, and the skill of writing, plus other less well agreed upon additions. However, they would stress such general outcomes as learning how to think, learning how to use a library; how to design and carry out an experiment; how to meet people; how to control the emotions; how to adjust to frustrations. In the literature, the outcomes just enumerated are often dealt with in a very nebulous manner. However, if a person holding some such theory of education were asked to epitomize it, he might answer somewhat as follows: The expanding body of knowledge has already reached such proportions that an attempt by an individual to cover it is hopeless. Therefore, a better procedure might be to select carefully and coherently from racial experience a basic body of knowledge and skills which would serve as tools and background for whatever kinds of learning one might need to acquire. Using this carefully selected body of facts, concepts, skills, experiences, which would probably constitute the main load of early education, the learner would then test and enlarge his abilities through a rather thorough learning of some sample fields. The essence of such a theory of education is that it is the function of the school to help the pupil learn how to learn; that, beyond the acquiring of basic knowledge and concepts, the purpose of the school is to provide some excellent samples of learning experience in a number of fields and extending over the usual number of years devoted to general education. On completion of such a period of education, the graduate might say, "There are many things I do not know and many skills I do not have, but I know how to get them, I know how to learn what needs to be learned." This concept is the opposite from blueprinting and stereotyping the education of a child. It aims at giving him versatility and independence.

Now, supposing one held some such theory of education as has just been described, in what kind of a psychology of learning would he be most interested? Obviously, the crucial psychological problem for such a theory is that of transfer. How can the learning attained carry over and spread to other situations as they are encountered? How can the outcomes of education be generalized so as to be broad in scope? Certainly the early types of experiments on transfer, such as Thorndike's study of the effect of practice in judging the size of circles upon ability to judge the size of squares, would contribute little. The problem could not be met by studying the carry-over of one academic subject to another subject. Rather, the studies that have significance are those that deal with transfer at the general rather than the specific level; with the development of intellectual habits that may spread widely, rather than with narrow intellectual functions. Studies such as Harlow's experiments with chimpanzees in learning how to learn have high significance for such a theory of education, and they would have still higher significance if carried on with human subjects where the possession of language enhances the possibilities of transferring training.

The concept of transfer in learning how to learn applies both to subject-matter and to method and technique. The understanding embodied in the arithmetical generalization that "when both the numerator and denominator of a fraction are multiplied by the same number, the value of the fraction is not changed" is more transferable than the specific fact that two-thirds and four-sixths have equivalent value. Likewise, the acquisition of general techniques, such as how to use a library card catalogue, is of more general value than to learn the location on the shelves of a specific reference. The essential test of any theory of education is its transfer value, yet the design of most of our learning experiments dealing with transfer is feeble compared to the size of the problem to be studied.

The crux of my contention is that educational psychologists have been loath to strike out independently in solving problems in their own field. In the main, our problems deal with education in schools, with human subjects, and with higher mental processes involving language. Without the slightest criticism of experiments in general psychology, we cannot continue to be satisfied with implications for education from results of experiments with simple mental processes, with animals, and at the sublanguage level. This past summer, parents of children from coast to coast were aroused by a recent book denouncing current methods of learning how to read and proposing that the schools go back to an earlier phonetic method as the sole way of learning to read. The answer to the place of phonics in learning to read will never come from animal experiments nor from the use of nonsense syllables. Nor will it come from half of the educational experiments on phonics which measure only the effect on the ability to pronounce words. If by reading one means the ability to get meaning from a printed page, there is little experimental evidence one way or the other at the present time regarding the value of phonics. The field of reading has without doubt been subjected to more careful research than any other area of learning in the school, yet here in the case of phonics is a prime example of an opportunity passed by to do research on an important transferable function.

I am proposing that educational psychologists take their cues for research from problems of learning in schools, where the processes are complex and where the learnings carried on are at the language level. May I try to indicate what, to me, seem to be three very fruitful fields for research.

I would suggest, first, research on the success, or lack of it, in teaching students how to think. For some years our schools, particularly at the high school and college level, have proclaimed this as one of their main objectives. Yet, a critical appraisal of available research on this problem gives little evidence that schools are accomplishing their objective. When allowance is made for constantly increasing mental maturity, and when pertinent variables are controlled, it is difficult to find evidence of any marked gains in ability to think due to the work of the schools. Our claims far outrun the evidence. Is it possible to learn how to think more effectively, or are the methods of the school wrong? There is plenty of evidence that students can learn to think within the area of the subject-matter being taught, but the real issue is whether or not they can transfer the ability to other areas. For example, in a study of problem-solving last year, we found that in one group of sixty-one college students, all of whom had had a course in algebra, only twenty of the sixty-one attempted to use algebra in solving a problem where the algebraic method was the most economical way to solution, and, of the twenty who attempted to use algebra, only one succeeded in getting the correct answer. Algebra had apparently failed to contribute a method of thinking to these students. Or, to illustrate further, it is probably true that most students, and some teachers, fail to sense that the high school course in geometry is in essence a course in deductive logical thinking, using space figures as the medium of operation. Rather, geometry is usually taught as a body of content, the learning of which is a sufficient outcome in itself. Here is a major problem in learning at the abstract language level, yet the bulk of the experimentation on it is with animals and at the sublanguage level. Why do we so generally avoid experimenting on problem-solving with human subjects and in school situations where the real issues are?

I would suggest that a second area of research intimately related to current educational theory is in the learning of personality characteristics. The school expects its pupils to learn to be accurate, to carry responsibility, to be critical, to have good personal relations with others, and many more such traits. Here, clearly, is a problem in transfer of learning. Most schools deal with this problem of personal-social education in a loose, incidental manner. Whereas the school has a definite and coherent methodology, supported by a considerable body of research, for learning to read and to do arithmetic, there is little experimental evidence to guide the school in its program of personal-social education. In a widely used book on the subject, there is a bibliography of more than eleven hundred references dealing with personality; but less than a dozen of them report studies of learning personal-social traits in the schools. Admittedly, experimentation in schools is difficult, but can we not design studies with sufficient controls to take account of the difficulties?

Last, I would suggest the problem of motivation in school as of high importance for educational psychologists. Here, clearly, we are in difficulty if we rely on implications from studies of animal learning. In most animal studies, the motivation for behavior is hunger or punishment. Such incentives, obviously, are not applicable in the schools. In fact, the whole concept of tissue needs has little force for school learning. Most of the interests and motives that operate in the schools are learned, and it may well be that one of the main contributions of the school is to modify, through learning, the motivation that operates within the learner. If, for example, the school could succeed in making students intellectually curious, the operation of such a motive might have a broader effect than the mastery of any specific segment of subject-matter. The problem is, how and why do some students learn to be intellectually curious while others do not.

The three problems for research just suggested, namely, learning how to think, learning personal-social traits, and learning motivations, are not matters of great concern to a "Knowledge is Power" type of educational theory. However, to a theory of education based on the concept that the essence of education is learning how to learn, such problems are at the heart of the matter. With such a theory, the main concern is to find what curricular content and what intellectual tools are essential to carry on the kind of learning desired, and then, in turn, to what scope of subject-matter and to what depth and thoroughness should the school go in order to be sure that the student will be independent and versatile, and will feel confident that he knows how to learn as new occasions may require.

Educational psychologists must first of all be psychologists; there is no substitute for competence in the basic subject. But their field of operation is education and, in the main, is concerned with the schools which are society's principal agent for providing education. The main business of the school is learning, and psychologists should have something to say about learning. Whether what they say is understood and is useful to the school depends a great deal on whether or not the psychologist understands theories of education as well as theories of learning, and whether his research deals with problems which are important to the educational theory of the time or whether it deals with yesterday's issues. This dual role of the educational psychologist is not easy, but it is necessary.

The proposal of this paper in no sense suggests that educational psychologists do only applied research and leave basic research to the general psychologist. But basic research need not be restricted to simple mental processes, nor to subjects at the sublanguage level. Basic study of motivation can deal with learned motives as well as physiological needs. Studies of transfer can deal with situations that operate through generalizations that are expressed in language symbols as well as with mazes and puzzle boxes. The designs of research will have to be more complex, but they can be made so. If educational psychologists can play their role at this higher level of research, they will be able to contribute significantly to the validation of educational theory.

1) E. R. GUTHRIE, "The Psychology of Learning," in *National Society for the Study of Education* Forty-first Yearbook, Part II, 1952.
2) ———, *The Psychology of Learning,* Revised Edition, pp. 310. New York, Harper & Brothers, 1952.

15. Are Theories of Learning Necessary? * [1]

B. F. SKINNER, Harvard University

CERTAIN BASIC assumptions, essential to any scientific activity, are sometimes called theories. That nature is orderly rather than capricious is an example. Certain statements are also theories simply to the extent that they are not yet facts. A scientist may guess at the result of an experiment before the experiment is carried out. The prediction and the later statement of result may be composed of the same terms in the same syntactic arrangement, the difference being in the degree of confidence. No empirical statement is wholly nontheoretical in this sense, because evidence is never complete, nor is any prediction probably ever made wholly without evidence. The term "theory" will not refer here to statements of these sorts but rather to any explanation of an observed fact which appeals to events taking place somewhere else, at some other level of observation, described in different terms, and measured, if at all, in different dimensions.

Three types of theory in the field of learning satisfy this definition. The most characteristic is to be found in the field of physiological psychology. We are all familiar with the changes that are supposed to take place in the nervous system when an organism learns. Synaptic connections are made or broken, electrical fields are disrupted or reorganized, concentrations of ions are built up or allowed to diffuse away, and so on. In the science of neurophysiology statements of this sort are not necessarily theories in the present sense. But in a science of behavior, where we are concerned with whether

---

* From B .F. Skinner, "Are Theories of Learning Necessary?" *The Psychological Review,* 57 (July, 1950), 193–216. Reprinted by permission.

[1] Address of the president, Midwestern Psychological Association, Chicago, Illinois, May, 1949.

or not an organism secretes saliva when a bell rings, or jumps toward a gray triangle, or says *bik* when a card reads *tuz,* or loves someone who resembles his mother, all statements about the nervous system are theories in the sense that they are not expressed in the same terms and could not be confirmed with the same methods of observation as the facts for which they are said to account.

A second type of learning theory is in practice not far from the physiological, although there is less agreement about the method of direct observation. Theories of this type have always dominated the field of human behavior. They consist of references to "mental" events, as in saying that an organism learns to behave in a certain way because it "finds something pleasant" or because it "expects something to happen." To the mentalistic psychologist these explanatory events are no more theoretical than synaptic connections to the neurophysiologist, but in a science of behavior they are theories because the methods and terms appropriate to the events to be explained differ from the methods and terms appropriate to the explaining events.

In a third type of learning theory the explanatory events are not directly observed. The writer's suggestion that the letters CNS be regarded as representing, not the Central Nervous System, but the Conceptual Nervous System (2, page 421), seems to have been taken seriously. Many theorists point out that they are not talking about the nervous system as an actual structure undergoing physiological or biochemical changes but only as a system with a certain dynamic output. Theories of this sort are multiplying fast, and so are parallel operational versions of mental events. A purely behavioral definition of expectancy has the advantage that the problem of mental observation is avoided and with it the problem of how a mental event can cause a physical one. But such theories do not go so far as to assert that the explanatory events are identical with the behavioral facts which they purport to explain. A statement about behavior may support such a theory but will never resemble it in terms of syntax. Postulates are good examples. True postulates cannot become facts. Theorems may be deduced from them which, as tentative statements about behavior, may or may not be confirmed, but theorems are not theories in the present sense. Postulates remain theories until the end.

It is not the purpose of this paper to show that any of these theories cannot be put in good scientific order, or that the events to which they refer may not actually occur or be studied by appropriate sciences. It would be foolhardy to deny the achievements of theories of this sort in the history of science. The question of whether they are necessary, however, has other implications and is worth asking. If the answer is no, then it may be possible to argue effectively against theory in the field of learning. A science of behavior must eventually deal with behavior in its relation to certain manipulable variables. Theories—whether neural, mental, or conceptual—talk about intervening steps in these relationships. But instead of prompting us to search for and explore relevant variables, they frequently have quite the opposite effect. When we attribute behavior to a neural or mental event, real or conceptual, we are likely to forget that we still have the task of accounting for the neural or mental event. When we assert that an animal acts in a given way because it expects to receive food, then what began as the task of accounting for learned behavior becomes the task of accounting for expectancy. The problem is at least equally complex and probably more difficult. We are likely to close our eyes to it and to use the theory to give us answers in place of the answers we might find through further study. It might be argued that the principal function of learning theory to date has been, not to suggest appropriate research, but to create a false sense of security, an unwarranted satisfaction with the *status quo*.

Research designed with respect to theory is also likely to be wasteful. That a theory generates research does not prove its value unless the research is valuable. Much useless experimentation results from theories, and much energy and skill are absorbed by them. Most theories are eventually overthrown, and the greater part of the associated research is discarded. This could be justified if it were true that productive research requires a theory, as is, of course, often claimed. It is argued that research would be aimless and disorganized without a theory to guide it. The view is supported by psychological texts that take their cue from the logicians rather than empirical science and describe thinking as necessarily involving stages of hypothesis, deduction, experimental test, and confirmation. But this is not the way most scientists actually work. It is possible to design significant experiments for other reasons and the possibility to be examined is that such research will lead more directly to the kind of information that a science usually accumulates.

The alternatives are at least worth considering. How much can be done without theory? What other sorts of scientific activity are possible? And what light do alternative practices throw upon our present preoccupation with theory?

It would be inconsistent to try to answer these questions at a theoretical level. Let us therefore turn to some experimental material in three areas in which theories of learning now flourish and raise the question of the function of theory in a more concrete fashion.[2]

[2] Some of the material that follows was obtained in 1941–42 in a cooperative study on the behavior of the pigeon in which Keller Breland, Norman Guttman, and W. K. Estes collaborated. Some of it is selected from subsequent, as yet unpublished, work on the pigeon conducted by the author at Indiana University and Harvard University. Limitations of space make it impossible to report full details here.

The Basic Datum in Learning

What actually happens when an organism learns is not an easy question. Those who are interested in a science of behavior will insist that learning is a change in behavior, but they tend to avoid explicit references to responses or acts as such. "Learning is adjustment, or adaptation to a situation." But of what stuff are adjustments and adaptations made? Are they data, or inferences from data? "Learning is improvement." But improvement in what? And from whose point of view? "Learning is restoration of equilibrium." But what is in equilibrium and how is it put there? "Learning is problem solving." But what are the physical dimensions of a problem—or of a solution? Definitions of this sort show an unwillingness to take what appears before the eyes in a learning experiment as a basic datum. Particular observations seem too trivial. An error score falls; but we are not ready to say that this is learning rather than merely the result of learning. An organism meets a criterion of ten successful trials; but an arbitrary criterion is at variance with our conception of the generality of the learning process.

This is where theory steps in. If it is not the time required to get out of a puzzle box that changes in learning, but rather the strength of a bond, or the conductivity of a neural pathway, or the excitatory potential of a habit, then problems seem to vanish. Getting out of a box faster and faster is not learning; it is merely performance. The learning goes on somewhere else, in a different dimensional system. And although the time required depends upon arbitrary conditions, often varies discontinuously, and is subject to reversals of magnitude, we feel sure that the learning process itself is continuous, orderly, and beyond the accidents of measurement. Nothing could better illustrate the use of theory as a refuge from the data.

But we must eventually get back to an observable datum. If learning is the process we suppose it to be, then it must appear so in the situations in which we study it. Even if the basic process belongs to some other dimensional system, our measures must have relevant and comparable properties. But productive experimental situations are hard to find, particularly if we accept certain plausible restrictions. To show an orderly change in the behavior of the *average* rat or ape or child is not enough, since learning is a process in the behavior of the individual. To record the beginning and end of learning or a few discrete steps will not suffice, since a series of cross-sections will not give complete coverage of a continuous process. The dimensions of the change must spring from the behavior itself; they must not be imposed by an external judgment of success or failure or an external criterion of completeness. But when we review the literature with these requirements in mind, we find little justification for the theoretical process in which we take so much comfort.

The energy level or work-output of behavior, for example, does not change in appropriate ways. In the sort of behavior adapted to the Pavlovian experiment (respondent behavior) there may be a progressive increase in the magnitude of response during learning. But we do not shout our responses louder and louder as we learn verbal material, nor does a rat press a lever harder and harder as conditioning proceeds. In operant behavior the energy or magnitude of response changes significantly only when some arbitrary value is differentially reinforced—when such a change is what is learned.

The emergence of a right response in competition with wrong responses is another datum frequently used in the study of learning. The maze and the discrimination box yield results which may be reduced to these terms. But a behavior-ratio of right vs. wrong cannot yield a continuously changing measure in a single experiment on a single organism. The point at which one response takes precedence over another cannot give us the whole history of the change in either response. Averaging curves for groups of trials of organisms will not solve this problem.

Increasing attention has recently been given to latency, the relevance of which, like that of energy level, is suggested by the properties of conditioned and unconditioned reflexes. But in operant behavior the relation to a stimulus is different. A measure of latency involves other considerations, as inspection of any case will show. Most operant responses may be emitted in the absence of what is regarded as a relevant stimulus. In such a case the response is likely to appear before the stimulus is presented. It is no solution to escape this embarrassment by locking a lever so that an organism cannot press it until the stimulus is presented, since we can scarcely be content with temporal relations that have been forced into compliance with our expectations. Runway latencies are subject to this objection. In a typical experiment the door of a starting box is opened and the time that elapses before a rat leaves the box is measured. Opening the door is not only a stimulus, it is a change in the situation that makes the response possible for the first time. The time measured is by no means as simple as a latency and requires another formulation. A great deal depends upon what the rat is doing at the moment the stimulus is presented. Some experimenters wait until the rat is facing the door, but to do so is to tamper with the measurement being taken. If, on the other hand, the door is opened without reference to what the rat is doing, the first major effect is the conditioning of favorable waiting behavior. The rat eventually stays near and facing the door. The resulting shorter starting time is not due to a reduction in the latency of a response, but to the conditioning of favorable preliminary behavior.

Latencies in a single organism do not follow a simple learning process.

Relevant data on this point were obtained as part of an extensive study of reaction time. A pigeon, enclosed in a box, is conditioned to peck at a recessed disc in one wall. Food is presented as reinforcement by exposing a hopper through a hole below the disc. If responses are reinforced only after a stimulus has been presented, responses at other times disappear. Very short reaction times are obtained by differentially reinforcing responses which occur very soon after the stimulus (4). But responses also come to be made very quickly without differential reinforcement. Inspection shows that this is due to the development of effective waiting. The bird comes to stand before the disc with its head in good striking position. Under optimal conditions, without differential reinforcement, the mean time between stimulus and response will be of the order of one-third of a second. This is not a true reflex latency, since the stimulus is discriminative rather than eliciting, but it is a fair example of the latency used in the study of learning. The point is that this measure does not vary continuously or in an orderly fashion. By giving the bird more food, for example, we induce a condition in which it does not always respond. But the responses that occur show approximately

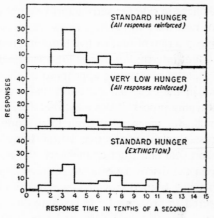

Figure 1.

the same temporal relation to the stimulus (Figure 1, middle curve). In extinction, of special interest here, there is a scattering of latencies because lack of reinforcement generates an emotional condition. Some responses occur sooner and others are delayed, but the commonest value remains unchanged (bottom curve in Figure 1). The longer latencies are easily explained by inspection. Emotional behavior, of which examples will be mentioned later, is likely to be in progress when the ready signal is presented. It is often not discontinued before the "go" signal is presented, and the result is a long starting time. Cases also begin to appear in which the bird simply does not respond at all during a specified time. If we average a large number of readings, either from one bird or many, we may create what looks like a progressive lengthening of latency. But the data for an individual organism do not show a continuous process.

Another datum to be examined is the rate at which a response is emitted. Fortunately the story here is different. We study this rate by designing a situation in which a response may be freely repeated, choosing a response (for example, touching or pressing a small lever or key) that may be easily observed and counted. The responses may be recorded on a polygraph, but a more convenient form is a cumulative curve from which rate of responding is immediately read as slope. The rate at which a response is emitted in such a situation comes close to our preconception of the learning process. As the organism learns, the rate rises. As it unlearns (for example, in extinction) the rate falls. Various sorts of discriminative stimuli may be brought into control of the response with corresponding modifications of the rate. Motivational changes alter the rate in a sensitive way. So do those events which we speak of as generating emotion. The range through which the rate varies significantly may be as great as of the order of 1000:1. Changes in rate are satisfactorily smooth in the individual case, so that it is not necessary to average cases. A given value is often quite stable: in the pigeon a rate of four or five thousand responses per hour may be maintained without interruption for as long as fifteen hours.

Rate of responding appears to be the only datum that varies significantly and in the expected direction under conditions which are relevant to the "learning process." We may, therefore, be tempted to accept it as our long-sought-for measure of strength of bond, excitatory potential, etc. Once in possession of an effective datum, however, we may feel little need for any theoretical construct of this sort. Progress in a scientific field usually waits upon the discovery of a satisfactory dependent variable. Until such a variable has been discovered, we resort to theory. The entities which have figured so prominently in learning theory have served mainly as substitutes for a directly observable and productive datum. They have little reason to survive when such a datum has been found.

It is no accident that rate of responding is successful as a datum, because it is particularly appropriate to the fundamental task of a science of behavior. If we are to predict behavior (and possibly to control it), we must deal with *probability of response*. The business of a science of behavior is to evaluate this probability and explore the conditions that determine it. Strength of bond, expectancy, excitatory potential, and so on, carry the notion of probability in an easily imagined form, but the additional properties suggested by these terms have hindered the search for suitable measures. Rate of responding is not a "measure" of probability but it is the only appropriate datum in a formulation in these terms.

As other scientific disciplines can attest, probabilities are not easy to handle. We wish to make statements about the likelihood of occurrence of a single future response, but our data are in the form of frequencies of responses that have already occurred. These responses were presumably similar to each other and to the response to be predicted. But this raises the troublesome problem of response-instance vs. response-class. Precisely

SKINNER: *Are Theories of Learning Necessary?* 131

what responses are we to take into account in predicting a future instance? Certainly not the responses made by a population of different organisms, for such a statistical datum raises more problems than it solves. To consider the frequency of repeated responses in an individual demands something like the experimental situation just described.

This solution of the problem of a basic datum is based upon the view that operant behavior is essentially an emissive phenomenon. Latency and magnitude of response fail as measures because they do not take this into account. They are concepts appropriate to the field of the reflex, where the all but invariable control exercised by the eliciting stimulus makes the notion of probability of response trivial. Consider, for example, the case of latency. Because of our acquaintance with simple reflexes we infer that a response that is more likely to be emitted will be emitted more quickly. But is this true? What can the word "quickly" mean? Probability of response, as well as prediction of response, is concerned with the moment of emission. This is a point in time, but it does not have the temporal dimension of a latency. The execution may take time after the response has been initiated, but the moment of occurrence has no duration.[3] In recognizing the emissive character of operant behavior and the central position of probability of response as a datum, latency is seen to be irrelevant to our present task.

Various objections have been made to the use of rate of responding as a basic datum. For example, such a program may seem to bar us from dealing with many events which are unique occurrences in the life of the individual. A man does not decide upon a career, get married, make a million dollars, or get killed in an accident often enough to make a rate of response meaningful. But these activities are not responses. They are not simple unitary events lending themselves to prediction as such. If we are to predict marriage, success, accidents, and so on, in anything more than statistical terms,

[3] It cannot, in fact, be shortened or lengthened. Where a latency appears to be forced toward a minimal value by differential reinforcement, another interpretation is called for. Although we may differentially reinforce more energetic behavior or the faster execution of behavior after it begins, it is meaningless to speak of differentially reinforcing responses with short or long latencies. What we actually reinforce differentially are (a) favorable waiting behavior and (b) more vigorous responses. When we ask a subject to respond "as soon as possible" in the human reaction-time experiment, we essentially ask him (a) to carry out as much of the response as possible without actually reaching the criterion of emission, (b) to do as little else as possible, and (c) to respond energetically after the stimulus has been given. This may yield a minimal measurable time between stimulus and response, but this time is not necessarily a basic datum nor have our instructions altered it as such. A parallel interpretation of the differential reinforcement of long "latencies" is required. This is easily established by inspection. In the experiments with pigeons previously cited, preliminary behavior is conditioned that postpones the response to the key until the proper time. Behavior that "marks time" is usually conspicuous.

we must deal with the smaller units of behavior which lead to and compose these unitary episodes. If the units appear in repeatable form, the present analysis may be applied. In the field of learning a similar objection takes the form of asking how the present analysis may be extended to experimental situations in which it is impossible to observe frequencies. It does not follow that learning is not taking place in such situations. The notion of probability is usually extrapolated to cases in which a frequency analysis cannot be carried out. In the field of behavior we arrange a situation in which frequencies are available as data, but we use the notion of probability in analyzing and formulating instances or even types of behavior which are not susceptible to this analysis.

Another common objection is that a rate of response is just a set of latencies and hence not a new datum at all. This is easily shown to be wrong. When we measure the time elapsing between two responses, we are in no doubt as to what the organism was doing when we started our clock. We know that it was just executing a response. This is a natural zero—quite unlike the arbitrary point from which latencies are measured. The free repetition of a response yields a rhythmic or periodic datum very different from latency. Many periodic physical processes suggest parallels.

We do not choose rate of responding as a basic datum merely from an analysis of the fundamental task of a science of behavior. The ultimate appeal is to its success in an experimental science. The material which follows is offered as a sample of what can be done. It is not intended as a complete demonstration, but it should confirm the fact that when we are in possession of a datum which varies in a significant fashion, we are less likely to resort to theoretical entities carrying the notion of probability of response.

Why Learning Occurs

We may define learning as a change in probability of response but we must also specify the conditions under which it comes about. To do this we must survey some of the independent variables of which probability of response is a function. Here we meet another kind of learning theory.

An effective classroom demonstration of the Law of Effect may be arranged in the following way. A pigeon, reduced to 80 per cent of its *ad lib* weight, is habituated to a small, semicircular amphitheater and is fed there for several days from a food hopper, which the experimenter presents by closing a hand switch. The demonstration consists of establishing a selected response by suitable reinforcement with food. For example, by sighting across the amphitheater at a scale on the opposite wall, it is possible to present the hopper whenever the top of the pigeon's head rises above a given mark. Higher and higher marks are chosen until, within a few minutes, the pigeon is walking about the cage with its head held as high as possible. In another demonstration the bird is conditioned to strike a marble placed on the floor of the amphitheater. This may be done in a few minutes by reinforcing successive steps. Food is presented first when the bird is merely moving near the marble, later when it looks down in the direction of the marble, later still when it moves its head toward the marble, and finally when it pecks it. Anyone who has seen such a demonstration knows that the Law of Effect is no theory. It simply specifies a procedure for altering the probability of a chosen response.

But when we try to say *why* reinforcement has this effect, theories arise. Learning is said to take place because the reinforcement is pleasant, satisfying, tension reducing, and so on. The converse process of extinction is explained with comparable theories. If the rate of responding is first raised to a high point by reinforcement and reinforcement then withheld, the response is observed to occur less and less frequently thereafter. One common theory explains this by asserting that a state is built up which suppresses the behavior. This "experimental inhibition" or "reaction inhibition" must be assigned to a different dimensional system, since nothing at the level of behavior corresponds to opposed processes of excitation and inhibition. Rate of responding is simply increased by one operation and decreased by another. Certain effects commonly interpreted as showing release from a suppressing force may be interpreted in other ways. Disinhibition, for example, is not necessarily the uncovering of suppressed strength; it may be a sign of supplementary strength from an extraneous variable. The process of spontaneous recovery, often cited to support the notion of suppression, has an alternative explanation, to be noted in a moment.

Let us evaluate the question of why learning takes place by turning again to some data. Since conditioning is usually too rapid to be easily followed, the process of extinction will provide us with a more useful case. A number of different types of curves have been consistently obtained from rats and pigeons using various schedules of prior reinforcement. By considering some of the relevant conditions we may see what room is left for theoretical processes.

The mere passage of time between conditioning and extinction is a variable that has surprisingly little effect. The rat is too short-lived to make an extended experiment feasible, but the pigeon, which may live ten or fifteen years, is an ideal subject. More than five years ago, twenty pigeons were conditioned to strike a large translucent key upon which a complex visual pattern was projected. Reinforcement was contingent upon the maintenance of a high and steady rate of responding and upon striking a particular feature of the visual pattern. These birds were set aside in order to study retention. They were transferred to the usual living quarters, where they served as breeders. Small groups were tested for extinction at the end of six months, one year, two years, and four years. Before the test each bird was transferred to a separate living cage. A controlled feeding schedule was used to reduce the weight to approximately 80 per cent of the *ad lib* weight. The bird was then fed in the dimly lighted experimental apparatus in the absence of the key for several days, during which emotional responses to the apparatus disappeared. On the day of the test the bird was placed in the darkened box. The translucent key was present but not lighted. No responses were made. When the pattern was projected upon the key, all four birds responded quickly and extensively. Figure 2 shows the largest curve

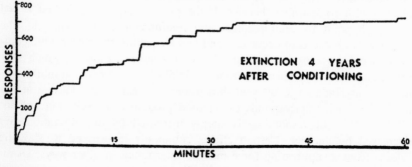

Figure 2.

obtained. This bird struck the key within two seconds after presentation of a visual pattern that it had not seen for four years, and at the precise spot upon which differential reinforcement had previously been based. It continued to respond for the next hour, emitting about 700 responses. This is of the order of one-half to one-quarter of the responses it would have emitted if extinction had not been delayed four years, but otherwise, the curve is fairly typical.

Level of motivation is another variable to be taken into account. An example of the effect of hunger has been reported elsewhere (3). The response of pressing a lever was established in eight rats with a schedule of periodic reinforcement. They were fed the main part of their ration on alternate days so that the rates of responding on successive days were alternately high and low. Two subgroups of four rats each were matched on the basis of the rate maintained under periodic reinforcement under these conditions. The response was then extinguished—in one group on alternate days when the hunger was high, in the other group on alternate days when the hunger was low. (The same amount of food was eaten on the nonexperimental days as before.) The result is shown in Figure 3. The upper graph gives the raw data. The levels of hunger are indicated by the points at P on the abscissa, the rates prevailing under periodic reinforcement. The subsequent points show the decline in extinction. If we multiply the lower curve through by a factor chosen to superimpose the points at P, the curves are reasonably closely superimposed, as shown in the lower graph. Several other experiments on both rats and pigeons have confirmed this general principle. If a given ratio of responding prevails under periodic reinforcement, the slopes of later extinction curves show the same ratio. Level of hunger determines the slope of the extinction curve but not its curvature.

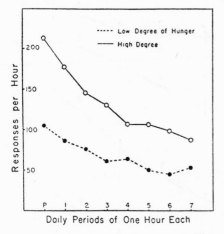
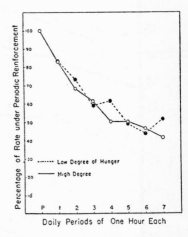

Figure 3.

Another variable, difficulty of response, is especially relevant because it has been used to test the theory of reaction inhibition (1), on the assumption that a response requiring considerable energy will build up more reaction inhibition than an easy response and lead, therefore, to faster extinction. The theory requires that the curvature of the extinction curve be altered, not merely its slope. Yet there is evidence that difficulty of response acts like level of hunger simply to alter the slope. Some data have been reported but not published (5). A pigeon is suspended in a jacket which confines its wings and legs but leaves its head and neck free to respond to a key and a food magazine. Its behavior in this situation is quantitatively much like that of a bird moving freely in an experimental box. But the use of the jacket has the advantage that the response to the key may be made easy or difficult by changing the distance the bird must reach. In one experiment these distances were expressed in seven equal but arbitrary units. At distance 7 the bird could barely reach the key, at 3 it could strike without appreciably extending its neck. Periodic reinforcement gave a straight base line upon which it was possible to observe the effect of difficulty by quickly changing position during the experimental period. Each of the five records in Figure 4 covers a fifteen minute experimental period under

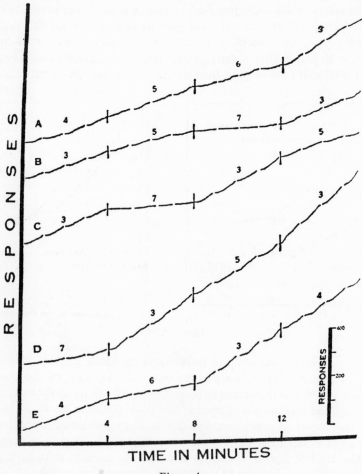

Figure 4.

periodic reinforcement. Distances of the bird from the key are indicated by numerals above the records. It will be observed that the rate of responding at distance 7 is generally quite low while that at distance 3 is high. Intermediate distances produce intermediate slopes. It should also be noted that the change from one position to another is felt immediately. If repeated responding in a difficult position were to build a considerable amount of reaction inhibition, we should expect the rate to be low for some little time after returning to an easy response. Contrariwise, if an easy response were to build little reaction inhibition, we should expect a fairly high rate of responding for some time after a difficult position is assumed. Nothing like this occurs. The "more rapid extinction" of a difficult response is an ambiguous expression. The slope constant is affected and with it the number of responses in extinction to a criterion, but there may be no effect upon curvature.

One way of considering the question of why extinction curves are curved is to regard extinction as a process of exhaustion comparable to the loss of heat from source to sink or the fall in the level of a reservoir when an outlet is opened. Conditioning builds up a predisposition to respond—a "reserve" —which extinction exhausts. This is perhaps a defensible description at the level of behavior. The reserve is not necessarily a theory in the present sense, since it is not assigned to a different dimensional system. It could be operationally defined as a predicted extinction curve, even though, linguistically, it makes a statement about the momentary condition of a response. But it is not a particularly useful concept, nor does the view that extinction is a process of exhaustion add much to the observed fact that extinction curves are curved in a certain way.

There are, however, two variables that affect the rate, both of which operate during extinction to alter the curvature. One of these falls within the field of emotion. When we fail to reinforce a response that has previously been reinforced, we not only initiate a process of extinction, we set up an emotional response—perhaps what is often meant by frustration. The pigeon coos in an identifiable pattern, moves rapidly about the cage, defecates, or flaps its wings rapidly in a squatting position that suggests treading (mating) behavior. This competes with the response of striking a key and is perhaps enough to account for the decline in rate in early extinction. It is also possible that the probability of a response based upon food deprivation is directly reduced as part of such an emotional reaction. Whatever its nature, the effect of this variable is eliminated through adaptation. Repeated extinction curves become smoother, and in some of the schedules to be described shortly there is little or no evidence of an emotional modification of rate.

A second variable has a much more serious effect. Maximal responding during extinction is obtained only when the conditions under which the response was reinforced are precisely reproduced. A rat conditioned in the presence of a light will not extinguish fully in the absence of the light. It will begin to respond more rapidly when the light is again introduced. This is true for other kinds of stimuli, as the following classroom experiment illustrates. Nine pigeons were conditioned to strike a yellow triangle under intermittent reinforcement. In the session represented by Figure 5 the birds were first reinforced on this schedule for thirty minutes. The combined cumulative curve is essentially a straight line, showing more than 1100 responses per bird during this period. A red triangle was then substituted for the yellow and no responses were reinforced thereafter. The effect was a sharp drop in responding, with only a slight recovery during the next fifteen minutes. When the yellow triangle was replaced, rapid responding began immediately and the usual extinction curve followed. Similar experi-

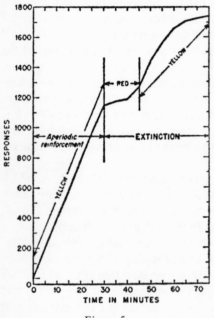

Figure 5.

ments have shown that the pitch of an incidental tone, the shape of a pattern being struck, or the size of a pattern, if present during conditioning, will to some extent control the rate of responding during extinction. Some properties are more effective than others, and a quantitative evaluation is possible. By changing to several values of a stimulus in random order repeatedly during the extinction process, the gradient for stimulus generalization may be read directly in the rates of responding under each value.

Something very much like this must go on during extinction. Let us suppose that all responses to a key have been reinforced and that each has been followed by a short period of eating. When we extinguish the behavior, we create a situation in which responses are not reinforced, in which no eating takes place, and in which there are probably new emotional responses. The situation could easily be as novel as a red triangle after a yellow. If so, it could explain the decline in rate during extinction. We might have obtained a smooth curve, *shaped like an extinction curve,* between the vertical lines in Figure 5 by *gradually* changing the color of the triangle from yellow to red. This might have happened even though no other sort of extinction were taking place. The very conditions of extinction seem to presuppose a growing novelty in the experimental situation. Is this why the extinction curve is curved?

Some evidence comes from the data of "spontaneous recovery." Even after prolonged extinction an organism will often respond at a higher rate for at least a few moments at the beginning of another session. One theory contends that this shows spontaneous recovery from some sort of inhibition, but another explanation is possible. No matter how carefully an animal is handled, the stimulation coincident with the beginning of an experiment must be extensive and unlike anything occurring in the later part of an experimental period. Responses have been reinforced in the presence of, or shortly following, the organism is again placed in the experimental situation, the stimulation is this stimulation. In extinction it is present for only a few moments. When restored; further responses are emitted as in the case of the yellow triangle. The only way to achieve full extinction in the presence of the stimulation of starting an experiment is to start the experiment repeatedly.

Other evidence of the effect of novelty comes from the study of periodic reinforcement. The fact that intermittent reinforcement produces bigger extinction curves than continuous reinforcement is a troublesome difficulty for those who expect a simple relation between number of reinforcements and number of responses in extinction. But this relation is actually quite complex. One result of periodic reinforcement is that emotional changes adapt out. This may be responsible for the smoothness of subsequent extinction curves but probably not for their greater extent. The latter may be attributed to the lack of novelty in the extinction situation. Under periodic reinforcement many responses are made without reinforcement and when no eating has recently taken place. The situation in extinction is therefore not wholly novel.

Periodic reinforcement is not, however, a simple solution. If we reinforce on a regular schedule—say, every minute—the organism soon forms a discrimination. Little or no responding occurs just after reinforcement, since stimulation from eating is correlated with absence of subsequent reinforcement. How rapidly the discrimination may develop is shown in Figure 6, which reproduces the first five curves obtained from a pigeon under periodic reinforcement in experimental periods of fifteen minutes each. In the fifth period (or after about one hour of periodic reinforcement) the discrimination yields a pause after each reinforcement, resulting in a markedly stepwise curve. As a result of this discrimination the bird is almost always responding rapidly when reinforced. This is the basis for another discrimination. Rapid responding becomes a favorable stimulating condition. A good example of the effect upon the subsequent extinction curve is shown in Figure 7. This pigeon had been reinforced once every minute during daily experimental periods of fifteen minutes each for several weeks. In the extinction curve shown, the bird begins to respond at the rate prevailing under the preceding schedule. A quick positive acceleration at the start is lost in the reduction of the record. The pigeon quickly reaches and sustains a rate that is higher than the overall rate during periodic reinforcement. During this period the pigeon creates a stimulating condition previously optimally correlated with reinforcement. Eventually, as some sort of exhaus-

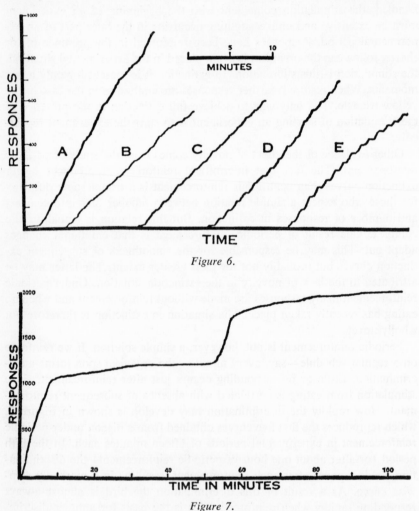

Figure 6.

Figure 7.

tion intervenes, the rate falls off rapidly to a much lower but fairly stable value and then to practically zero. A condition then prevails under which a response is not normally reinforced. The bird is therefore not likely to begin to respond again. When it does respond, however, the situation is slightly improved and, if it continues to respond, the conditions rapidly become similar to those under which reinforcement has been received. Under this "autocatalysis" a high rate is quickly reached, and more than 500 responses are emitted in a second burst. The rate then declines quickly and fairly smoothly, again to nearly zero. This curve is not by any means disorderly. Most of the curvature is smooth. But the burst of responding at forty-five minutes shows a considerable residual strength which, if extinction were merely exhaustion, should have appeared earlier in the curve. The curve may be reasonably accounted for by assuming that the bird is largely controlled by the preceding spurious correlation between reinforcement and rapid responding.

This assumption may be checked by constructing a schedule of reinforcement in which a differential contingency between rate of responding and

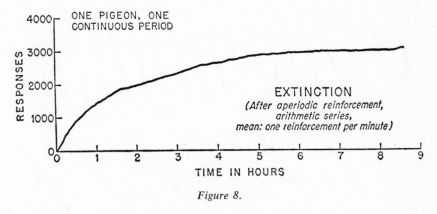

Figure 8.

reinforcement is impossible. In one such schedule of what may be called "aperiodic reinforcement" one interval between successive reinforced responses is so short that no unreinforced responses intervene while the longest interval is about two minutes. Other intervals are distributed arithmetically between these values, the average remaining one minute. The intervals are roughly randomized to compose a program of reinforcement. Under this program the probability of reinforcement does not change with respect to previous reinforcements, and the curves never acquire the stepwise character of curve E in Figure 6. (Figure 9 shows curves from a similar program.) As a result no correlation between different rates of responding and different probabilities of reinforcement can develop.

An extinction curve following a brief exposure to aperiodic reinforcement is shown in Figure 8. It begins characteristically at the rate prevailing under aperiodic reinforcement and, unlike the curve following regular periodic reinforcement, does not accelerate to a higher overall rate. There is no evidence of the "autocatalytic" production of an optimal stimulating condition. Also characteristically, there are no significant discontinuities or sudden changes in rate in either direction. The curve extends over a period of eight hours, as against not quite two hours in Figure 7, and seems to represent a single orderly process. The total number of responses is higher, perhaps because of the greater time allowed for emission. All of this can be explained by the single fact that we have made it impossible for the pigeon to form a pair of discriminations based, first, upon stimulation from eating and, second, upon stimulation from rapid responding.

Since the longest interval between reinforcement was only two minutes, a certain novelty must still have been introduced as time passed. Whether this explains the curvature in Figure 8 may be tested to some extent with other programs of reinforcement containing much longer intervals. A geometric

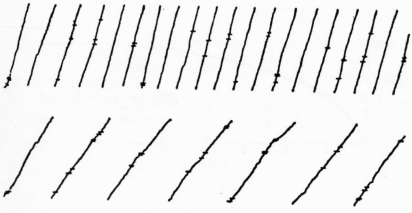

Figure 9.

progression was constructed by beginning with 10 seconds as the shortest interval and repeatedly multiplying through by a ratio of 1.54. This yielded a set of intervals averaging 5 minutes, the longest of which was more than 21 minutes. Such a set was randomized in a program of reinforcement repeated every hour. In changing to this program from the arithmetic series, the rates first declined during the longer intervals, but the pigeons were soon able to sustain a constant rate of responding under it. Two records in the form in which they were recorded are shown in Figure 9. (The pen resets to zero after every thousand responses. In order to obtain a single cumulative curve it would be necessary to cut the record and to piece the sections together to yield a continuous line. The raw form may be reproduced with less reduction.) Each reinforcement is represented by a horizontal dash. The time covered is about 3 hours. Records are shown for two pigeons that maintained different overall rates under this program of reinforcement.

Under such a schedule a constant rate of responding is sustained for at least 21 minutes without reinforcement, after which a reinforcement is received. Less novelty should therefore develop during succeeding extinction. In Curve 1 of Figure 10 the pigeon had been exposed to several sessions of several hours each with this geometric set of intervals. The number of responses emitted in extinction is about twice that of the curve in Figure 8 after the arithmetic set of intervals averaging one minute, but the curves

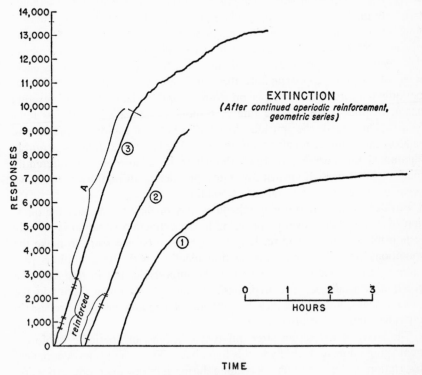

Figure 10.

are otherwise much alike. Further exposure to the geometric schedule builds up longer runs during which the rate does not change significantly. Curve 2 followed Curve 1 after two and one-half hours of further aperiodic reinforcement. On the day shown in Curve 2 a few aperiodic reinforcements were first given, as marked at the beginning of the curve. When reinforcement was discontinued, a fairly constant rate of responding prevailed for several thousand responses. After another experimental session of two and one-half hours with the geometric series, Curve 3 was recorded. This session also began with a short series of aperiodic reinforcements, followed by a sustained run of more than 6000 unreinforced responses with little change in rate (A). There seems to be no reason why other series averaging perhaps more than five minutes per interval and containing much longer exceptional intervals would not carry such a straight line much further.

In this attack upon the problem of extinction we create a schedule of reinforcement which is so much like the conditions that will prevail during extinction that no decline in rate takes place for a long time. In other words we generate extinction with no curvature. Eventually some kind of exhaustion sets in, but it is not approached gradually. The last part of Curve 3 (unfortunately much reduced in the figure) may possibly suggest exhaustion in the slight overall curvature, but it is a small part of the whole process. The record is composed mainly of runs of a few hundred responses each, most of them at approximately the same rate as that maintained under periodic reinforcement. The pigeon stops abruptly; when it starts to respond again, it quickly reaches the rate of responding under which it was reinforced. This recalls the spurious correlation between rapid responding and reinforcement under regular reinforcement. We have not, of course, entirely eliminated this correlation. Even though there is no longer a differential reinforcement of high against low rates, practically all reinforcements have occurred under a constant rate of responding.

Further study of reinforcing schedules may or may not answer the question of whether the novelty appearing in the extinction situation is entirely responsible for the curvature. It would appear to be necessary to make the conditions prevailing during extinction identical with the conditions prevailing during conditioning. This may be impossible, but in that case the question is academic. The hypothesis, meanwhile, is not a theory in the present sense, since it makes no statements about a parallel process in any other universe of discourse.[4]

The study of extinction after different schedules of aperiodic reinforcement is not addressed wholly to this hypothesis. The object is an economical description of the conditions prevailing during reinforcement and extinction and of the relations between them. In using rate of responding as a basic datum we may appeal to conditions that are observable and manipulable and we may express the relations between them in objective terms. To the extent that our datum makes this possible, it reduces the need for theory. When we observe a pigeon emitting 7000 responses at a constant rate without reinforcement, we are not likely to explain an extinction curve containing perhaps a few hundred responses by appeal to the piling up of

---

[4] It is true that it appeals to stimulation generated in part by the pigeon's own behavior. This may be difficult to specify or manipulate, but it is not theoretical in the present sense. So long as we are willing to assume a one-to-one correspondence between action and stimulation, a physical specification is possible.

reaction inhibition or any other fatigue product. Research which is conducted without commitment to theory is more likely to carry the study of extinction into new areas and new orders of magnitude. By hastening the accumulation of data, we speed the departure of theories. If the theories have played no part in the design of our experiments, we need not be sorry to see them go.

Complex Learning

A third type of learning theory is illustrated by terms like *preferring, choosing, discriminating,* and *matching.* An effort may be made to define these solely in terms of behavior, but in traditional practice they refer to processes in another dimensional system. A response to one of two available stimuli may be called choice, but it is commoner to say that it is the result of choice, meaning by the latter a theoretical prebehavioral activity. The higher mental processes are the best examples of theories of this sort; neurological parallels have not been well worked out. The appeal to theory is encouraged by the fact that choosing (like discriminating, matching, and so on) is not a particular piece of behavior. It is not a response or an act with specified topography. The term characterizes a larger segment of behavior in relation to other variables or events. Can we formulate and study the behavior to which these terms would usually be applied without recourse to the theories which generally accompany them?

Discrimination is a relatively simple case. Suppose we find that the probability of emission of a given response is not significantly affected by changing from one of two stimuli to the other. We then make reinforcement of the response contingent upon the presence of one of them. The well-established result is that the probability of response remains high under this stimulus and reaches a very low point under the other. We say that the organism now discriminates between the stimuli. But discrimination is not itself an action, or necessarily even a unique process. Problems in the field of discrimination may be stated in other terms. How much induction obtains between stimuli of different magnitudes or classes? What are the smallest differences in stimuli that yield a difference in control? And so on. Questions of this sort do not presuppose theoretical activities in other dimensional systems.

A somewhat larger segment must be specified in dealing with the behavior of choosing one of two concurrent stimuli. This has been studied in the pigeon by examining responses to two keys differing in position (right or left) or in some property like color randomized with respect to position. By occasionally reinforcing a response on one key or the other without favoring either key, we obtain equal rates of responding on the two keys.

The behavior approaches a simple alternation from one key to the other. This follows the rule that tendencies to respond eventually correspond to the probabilities of reinforcement. Given a system in which one key or the other is occasionally connected with the magazine by an external clock, then if the right key has just been struck, the probability of reinforcement *via* the left key is higher than that *via* the right since a greater interval of time has elapsed during which the clock may have closed the circuit to the left key. But the bird's behavior does not correspond to this proba-

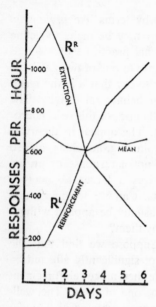

Figure 11.

bility merely out of respect for mathematics. The specific result of such a contingency of reinforcement is that changing-to-the-other-key-and-striking is more often reinforced than striking-the-same-key-a-second-time. We are no longer dealing with just two responses. In order to analyze "choice" we must consider a single final response, striking, without respect to the position or color of the key, and in addition the responses of changing from one key or color to the other.

Quantitative results are compatible with this analysis. If we periodically reinforce responses to the right key only, the rate of responding on the right will rise while that on the left will fall. The response of changing-from-right-to-left is never reinforced while the response of changing-from-left-to-right is occasionally so. When the bird is striking on the right, there is no great tendency to change keys; when it is striking on the left, there is a strong tendency to change. Many more responses come to be made to the right key. The need for considering the behavior of changing over is clearly shown if we now reverse these conditions and reinforce responses to the left key only. The ultimate result is a high rate of responding on the left key and a low rate on the right. By reversing the conditions again the high rate can be shifted back to the right key. In Figure 11 a group of eight curves have been averaged to follow this change during six experimental periods of 45 minutes each. Beginning on the second day in the graph responses to the right key (R^R) decline in extinction while responses to the left key (R^L) increase through periodic reinforcement. The mean rate shows no significant variation, since periodic reinforcement is continued on the same schedule. The mean rate shows the condition of strength of the response of striking a key regardless of position. The distribution of responses between right and left depends upon the relative strength of the responses of changing over. If this were simply a case of the extinction of one response and the concurrent reconditioning of another, the mean curve would not remain approximately horizontal since reconditioning occurs much more rapidly than extinction.[5]

The rate with which the bird changes from one key to the other depends upon the distance between the keys. This distance is a rough measure of the stimulus-difference between the two keys. It also determines the scope of the response of changing-over, with an implied difference in sensory feedback. It also modifies the spread of reinforcement to responses supposedly not reinforced, since if the keys are close together, a response reinforced on one side may occur sooner after a preceding response on the other side. In Figure 11 the two keys were about one inch apart. They were therefore fairly similar with respect to position in the experimental box. Changing from one to the other involved a minimum of sensory feedback, and reinforcement of a response to one key could follow very shortly upon a response to the other. When the keys are separated by as much as four inches, the change in strength is much more rapid. Figure 12 shows two curves recorded simultaneously from a single pigeon during one experimental period of about 40 minutes. A high rate to the right key, and a low rate to the left had previously been established. In the figure no responses to the right were reinforced, but those to the left were reinforced every minute as indicated by the vertical dashes above curve L. The slope of R declines in a fairly smooth fashion while that of L increases, also fairly smoothly, to a value comparable to the initial value of R. The bird has conformed to the changed contingency within a single experimental period. The mean rate of responding is shown by a dotted line, which again shows no significant curvature.

What is called "preference" enters into this formulation. At any stage of the process shown in Figure 12 preference might be expressed in terms of the relative rates of responding to the two keys. This preference, however, is not in striking a key but in changing from one key to the other. The probability that the bird will strike a key regardless of its identifying properties behaves independently of the preferential response of changing from one key to the other. Several experiments have revealed an additional fact. A preference remains fixed if reinforcement is withheld. Figure 13 is an example. It shows simultaneous extinction curves from two keys during seven daily experimental periods of one hour each. Prior to extinction the relative strength of the responses of changing-to-R and changing-to-L

---

[5] Two topographically independent responses, capable of emission at the same time and hence not requiring change-over, show separate processes of reconditioning and extinction, and the combined rate of responding varies.

yielded a "preference" of about 3 to 1 for R. The constancy of the rate throughout the process of extinction has been shown in the figure by multiplying L through by a suitable constant and entering the points as small circles on R. If extinction altered the preference, the two curves could not be superimposed in this way.

These formulations of discrimination and choosing enable us to deal with what is generally regarded as a much more complex process—matching to sample. Suppose we arrange three translucent keys, each of which may be

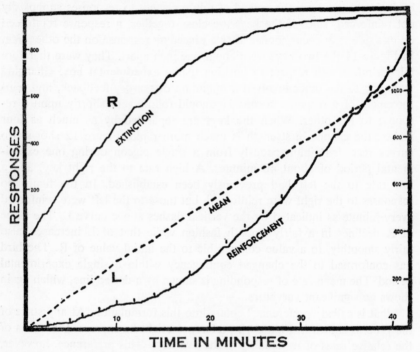

TIME IN MINUTES

Figure 12.

illuminated with red or green light. The middle key functions as the sample and we color it either red or green in random order. We color the two side keys one red and one green, also in random order. The "problem" is to strike the side key which corresponds in color to the middle key. There are only four three-key patterns in such a case, and it is possible that a pigeon could learn to make an appropriate response to each pattern. This does not happen, at least within the temporal span of the experiments to date. If we simply present a series of settings of the three colors and reinforce successful responses, the pigeon will strike the side keys without respect to color or pattern and be reinforced 50 per cent of the time. This is, in effect, a schedule of "fixed ratio" reinforcement which is adequate to maintain a high rate of responding.

Nevertheless it is possible to get a pigeon to match to sample by reinforcing the discriminative responses of striking-red-after-being-stimulated-by-red and striking-green-after-being-stimulated-by-green while extinguishing the other two possibilities. The difficulty is in arranging the proper stimulation at the time of the response. The sample might be made conspicuous—for example, by having the sample color in the general illumination of the experimental box. In such a case the pigeon would learn to strike red keys in a red light and green keys in a green light (assuming a neutral illumination of the background of the keys). But a procedure which holds more

closely to the notion of matching is to induce the pigeon to "look at the sample" by means of a separate reinforcement. We may do this by presenting the color on the middle key first, leaving the side keys uncolored. A response to the middle key is then reinforced (secondarily) by illuminating the side keys. The pigeon learns to make two responses in quick succession—to the middle key and then to one side

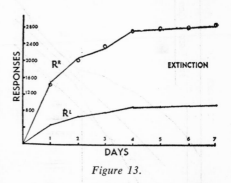

Figure 13.

key. The response to the side key follows quickly upon the visual stimulation from the middle key, which is the requisite condition for a discrimination. Successful matching was readily established in all ten pigeons tested with this technique. Choosing the opposite is also easily set up. The discriminative response of striking-red-after-being-stimulated-by-red is apparently no easier to establish than striking-red-after-being-stimulated-by-green. When the response is to a key of the same color, however, generalization may make it possible for the bird to match a new color. This is an extension of the notion of matching that has not yet been studied with this method.

Even when matching behavior has been well established, the bird will not respond correctly if all three keys are now presented at the same time. The bird does not possess strong behavior of looking at the sample. The experimenter must maintain a separate reinforcement to keep this behavior in strength. In monkeys, apes, and human subjects the ultimate success in choosing is apparently sufficient to reinforce and maintain the behavior of looking at the sample. It is possible that this species difference is simply a difference in the temporal relations required for reinforcement.

The behavior of matching survives unchanged when all reinforcement is withheld. An intermediate case has been established in which the correct matching response is only periodically reinforced. In one experiment one color appeared on the middle key for one minute; it was then changed or not changed, at random, to the other color. A response to this key illuminated the side keys, one red and one green, in random order. A response to a side key cut off the illumination to both side keys, until the middle key had again been struck. The apparatus recorded all matching responses on one graph and all nonmatching on another. Pigeons which have acquired matching behavior under continuous reinforcement have maintained this

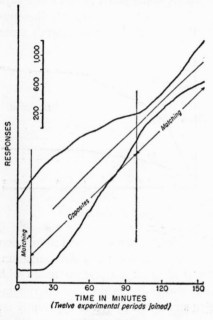

TIME IN MINUTES
(Twelve experimental periods joined)

Figure 14.

behavior when reinforced no oftener than once per minute on the average. They may make thousands of matching responses per hour while being reinforced for no more than sixty of them. This schedule will not necessarily develop matching behavior in a naïve bird, for the problem can be solved in three ways. The bird will receive practically as many reinforcements if it responds to (1) only one key or (2) only one color, since the programming of the experiment makes any persistent response eventually the correct one.

A sample of the data obtained in a complex experiment of this sort is given in Figure 14. Although this pigeon had learned to match color under continuous reinforcement, it changed to the spurious solution of a color preference under periodic reinforcement. Whenever the sample was red, it struck both the sample and the red side key and received all reinforcements. When the sample was green, it did not respond and the side keys were not illuminated. The result shown at the beginning of the graph in Figure 14 is a high rate of responding on the upper graph, which records matching responses. (The record is actually stepwise, following the presence or absence of the red sample, but this is lost in the reduction in the figure.) A color preference, however, is not a solution to the problem of opposites. By changing to this problem, it was possible to change the bird's behavior as shown between the two vertical lines in the figure. The upper curve between these lines shows the decline in matching responses which had resulted from the color preference. The lower curve between the same lines shows the development of responding to and matching the opposite color. At the second vertical line the reinforcement was again made contingent upon matching. The upper curve shows the reestablishment of matching behavior while the lower curve shows a decline in striking the opposite color. The result was a true solution: the pigeon struck the sample, no matter what its color, and then the corresponding side key. The lighter line connects the means of a series of points on the two curves. It seems to follow the same rule as in the case of choosing: changes in the distribution of responses between two keys do not involve the over-all rate of responding to a key. This mean rate will not remain constant under the spurious solution achieved with a color preference, as at the beginning of this figure.

These experiments on a few higher processes have necessarily been very briefly described. They are not offered as proving that theories of learning are not necessary, but they may suggest an alternative program in this difficult area. The data in the field of the higher mental processes transcend single responses or single stimulus-response relationships. But they appear to be susceptible to formulation in terms of the differentiation of concurrent responses, the discrimination of stimuli, the establishment of various sequences of responses, and so on. There seems to be no *a priori* reason why a complete account is not possible without appeal to theoretical processes in other dimensional systems.

Conclusion

Perhaps to do without theories altogether is a *tour de force* that is too much to expect as a general practice. Theories are fun. But it is possible that the most rapid progress toward an understanding of learning may be made by research that is not designed to test theories. An adequate impetus is supplied by the inclination to obtain data showing orderly changes characteristic of the learning process. An acceptable scientific program is to collect data of this sort and to relate them to manipulable variables, selected for study through a common sense exploration of the field.

This does not exclude the possibility of theory in another sense. Beyond the collection of uniform relationships lies the need for a formal representation of the data reduced to a minimal number of terms. A theoretical construction may yield greater generality than any assemblage of facts. But such a construction will not refer to another dimensional system and will not, therefore, fall within our present definition. It will not stand in the way of our search for functional relations because it will arise only after relevant variables have been found and studied. Though it may be difficult to understand, it will not be easily misunderstood, and it will have none of the objectionable effects of the theories here considered.

We do not seem to be ready for theory in this sense. At the moment we make little effective use of empirical, let alone rational, equations. A few of the present curves could have been fairly closely fitted. But the most elementary preliminary research shows that there are many relevant variables, and until their importance has been experimentally determined, an equation that allows for them will have so many arbitrary constants that a good fit will be a matter of course and a cause for very little satisfaction.

References

1. MOWRER, O. H., and JONES, H. M. Extinction and behavior variability as functions of effortfulness of task. *J. exp. Psychol.*, 1943, **33,** 369–386.
2. SKINNER, B. F. *The behavior of organisms.* New York: D. Appleton-Century Co., 1938.
3. ———. The nature of the operant reserve. *Psychol. Bull.*, 1940, **37,** 423 (abstract).
4. ———. Differential reinforcement with respect to time. *Amer. Psychol.*, 1946, **1,** 274–275 (abstract).
5. ———. The effect of the difficulty of a response upon its rate of emission. *Amer. Psychol.*, 1946, **1,** 462 (absract).

16. *The Contiguity Principle in Learning Theory* [*][1]

FRED D. SHEFFIELD, *Yale University*

THE LAST twenty years of basic learning theory has reflected a period of the supremacy of the law of effect and the discounting of contiguity. This trend started when conditioned-response people began noticing that conditioning was often complicated by selective learning which did not seem

* From Fred D. Sheffield, "The Contiguity Principle in Learning Theory," *The Psychological Review,* 58 (September, 1951), 362–67. Reprinted by permission of the author and the publisher.
[1] Presented at a symposium on single-process versus multiple process theories of learning at the 1950 meetings of the American Psychological Association and along with other papers at the symposium was published in *The Psychological Review.*

to follow the Pavlovian rubric. We can perhaps identify the starting point of this era with the 1928 article by Miller and Konorski (12) on a special type of conditional reflex—later to be named the conditioned or discriminated "operant" (19), the "instrumental" conditioned response (7), and so forth. The development subsequent to Miller and Konorski has been one of rediscovering the law of effect—and relegating contiguity to a minor role either as a primitive learning principle among dualists or as a necessary but insufficient factor among the single-process effect theorists.

Now, I suspect, we are on the threshhold of a rediscovery of contiguity. I think Mowrer's paper announcing his switch to dualism in the 1947 *Harvard Educational Review* (13) is one of the signs of the times. Also the 1949 Birch and Bitterman (1) critique of the effect position—and support of Maier and Schneirla (10) on dualism—I interpret as an undercurrent of dissatisfaction with the recent pre-eminence of effect as the major learning principle. Mowrer has elevated contiguity to an equal status with effect as a sometimes-sufficient condition for learning. Birch and Bitterman have hinted that their sensory integration version of contiguity will handle phenomena which even previous dualists have considered the exclusive property of effect. In each case these authors suggest a trend toward reinstating the significance of contiguity as a sufficient condition for some learning.

At the same time there seems to be another sort of trend underway in favor of contiguity. This second trend I would say is more relevant to contiguity as a *factor* than contiguity as sufficient. It consists of the discovery that contiguity is a powerful source from which to derive learning phenomena without regard to one's position as to whether contiguity is sufficient—or only necessary. A good illustration is seen in Estes' (3) recent article in which he disowns the reinforcement problem and proceeds to deduce a mathematical model of selective acquisition based on a very Guthrian (6) set of assumptions flowing from contiguity alone. Other illustrations are seen in modern interpretations of partial reinforcement, as presented in the Jenkins and Stanley (9) review article, and in the interpretations of extinction and spontaneous recovery in Skinner's (20) very recent paper challenging theories in general and S-R reinforcement theories in particular.

Perhaps my perception of the current situation is biased, but I feel that we are getting further and further in handling the major phenomena of learning with less and less worry about reward as a factor. Perhaps we can carry it all the way and eliminate the law of effect from a general treatment of learning. I do not feel entirely optimistic about this parsimonious outcome but I think it is worth a concerted effort. And at the moment I would place the dualist position as a halfway point in such an effort. It strikes me as an easy out—with defeatist consequences—for a current situation in which neither contiguity nor effect can make a convincing universal case.

On a less intuitive basis my objections to dualism are easily classified: (1) there appears to be strong evidence that learning—when properly defined—is a single process, and (2) the arguments of the dualists are unconvincing whether one takes a single-principle contiguity approach or whether one plays devil's advocate and takes a single-principle effect approach.

Starting with the first of these—the evidence for a single process—my point is simply that the phenomena exhibited in selective learning are so similar to those of Pavlovian conditioning that it is hard to believe in any differences in physiological process. One should of course be prepared to expect that two different physiological mechanisms will have the same overall outcome—as when temperature regulation is achieved both by perspiration and by vasodilation. But one should not be prepared to expect that two different mechanisms will exhibit point-by-point similarity in their detailed properties. Yet this is the case in a conditioned modification and a selectively acquired one. The ease with which the S-R reinforcement people have been able to appropriate Pavlov's findings attests to the similarity of the details of the two forms of learning. In such matters as acquisition, extinction, spontaneous recovery, generalization, differentiation, effects of partial reinforcement, and so forth, it makes no difference whether we are talking about a Thorndikian or a Pavlovian learning situation. The impressive fact is that we can translate from one discipline to the other by the simple expedient of interchanging appropriately the terms "reward" and "unconditioned stimulus." To me this makes it very improbable on *a priori* grounds that there is not a common process. The notable differences are not in properties but rather in inferred experimental operations in reinforcing with an unconditioned stimulus on the one hand and with a reward on the other. This suggests looking extensively for a hidden similarity in operations or process—it does not readily suggest that there is a different process to go with each experimental operation.

In my second objection to dualists—that their arguments are not convincing—I shall not attempt to cover all dualists. Instead I will mention only present company. I am not impressed by the Birch and Bitterman argument because it hinges primarily on what I consider to be an incorrect analysis of avoidance training. Here I have to play devil's advocate and defend the law of effect. Their main objection to a single-principle effect theory is that they believe the findings of avoidance learning disprove the Hullian hypothesis that cessation of pain is a reward. Their disproof is too easy to be true. The argument runs as follows: in avoidance training *pain* and its termination is invariably correlated with failure to respond; *no pain* is invariably correlated with the correct response. Therefore, they argue, according to Hull, failure to respond is rewarded by pain termination whereas performance of the correct response is subjected to extinction through nonreward. Since the facts of avoidance learning are just the opposite, Hull's notion of the reward value of pain termination is said to be disproven.

However, Birch and Bitterman have ignored entirely the factor of conditioned fear as a drive—and reduction of fear as a reward. These factors play a critical role in modern effect interpretations of avoidance learning as formulated by Mowrer (13) and others (14, 16). In this interpretation the critical fact is that failure to make the correct response becomes very frightening because it invariably produces pain. At the same time performance of the correct response cannot become frightening because it is invariably not correlated with pain. Thus in avoidance training we create an instrumental learning situation—with fear as drive—and in which the only way to convert a frightening situation into a nonfrightening one is by lifting the paw, leaping into the air, or whatever else the experimenter might require. This can be handled by Hull (8) in drive-reduction terms or by Guthrie (4) in stimulus-change terms.

I am more impressed with the Birch and Bitterman argument that sensory preconditioning is an exception to the law of effect, although I am also familiar enough with effect dialectics to know that there are several ways out. For one we can postulate an investigatory drive which is satisfied by attending to any and all environmental changes. For another we can note that with strong stimuli the mere cessation of the stimluation is reinforcing to whatever response the animal makes to the stimuli. Thus we may predict that the response to S_1 becomes connected to S_2 and vice versa —and will mediate just about the amount of transfer actually obtained —namely, a *small* amount in most cases. Moreover, the usual smallness of transfer in sensory preconditioning appears to be inconsistent with their sensory-integration interpretation of Pavlovian conditioning. Thus the Birch and Bitterman argument can be said to backfire considerably if the question is asked as to why the phenomenon is always such a weak counterpart of direct conditioning. If all conditioning by contiguity is afferent modification, why did Brogden (2), in the original experiment on this topic, find that some subjects failed to show any transfer, the average transfer was only 21 per cent of direct conditioning, and what little transfer was obtained initially extinguished very rapidly?

The Mowrer and Suter (15) experiment will also be attacked by single-process effect theorists. For example, does a signal that precedes shock, accompanies shock, and terminates with shock become a cue for fear or a mixed cue for fear and the relaxation of fear that accompanies the termination of shock? Or, since the animal is free to move about on a grill, what evidence is there that all animals do not momentarily stop shock immediately by partial hops from the grill? Or, to be technical, what control is offered for an Adrian-type "on effect"—with an immediate and sharp pain reduction through sensory adaptation—as suggested by Miller and Dollard (11) when a cue is correlated with onset of pain?

Personally I think the Mowrer and Suter experiment *is* embarrassing for the effect position but not a crucial exception. On the other hand, it goes almost without saying that the experiment would not convince a contiguity theorist that one is forced into dualism; rather it is merely further support that contiguity is sufficient. Similarly Mowrer's (13) "collateral support" for dualism, while it helps make the dualistic position reasonable, does not at all show one is forced into dualism. The hypothesis that contiguity applies only to visceral-autonomic-involuntary effectors whereas effect applies only to skeletal-central-voluntary effectors is intriguing but unconvincing. Skeletal responses can be conditioned and primarily visceral responses can be selectively learned. At least this is the way I interpret eyelid conditioning and the use of rewards and punishments in teaching control of bowel and bladder sphincters.

Moreover, the voluntary-involuntary breakdown does not seem to be particularly neuroanatomical. It is well known that many visceral responses can become voluntary, and skeletal responses which are not ordinarily useful never come under voluntary control. Few people can wiggle their ears, cross their eyes at will, or move each toe independently, although all of these can become voluntary with practice. A reasonable alternative to the Mowrer hypothesis is that, while skeletal responses are continually determining whether rewards are forthcoming, visceral systems rarely get exposed to selective learning. Instead, visceral systems are reared in the constant and predictable type of environment which promotes the evolution of innate reflexes and prevents selective learning from getting a chance to occur. However, selective learning apparently can take over in the autonomic when, for example, a conflict makes acquisition of a psychosomatic symptom rewarding.

These foregoing single-process arguments can of course be as well utilized by an effect theorist, and do not particularly support contiguity except in a roundabout way. I would now like to drop the role of devil's advocate and argue that there is so much room for theoretical expansion within the framework of *any* theory of selective learning that a contiguity approach is at least as promising as the effect one.

The room for expansion comes chiefly from the fact that nobody knows what "effect" is. It is an odd law that contains a term so interdeterminate in advance. It is analogous to the law of sleep which states that "sleep is produced by soporific agents." As currently used, effect is defined as any-thing which strengthens instrumental responses. We can collect an empirical list of such events and get a workable statement of the law of effect as fol-lows: "If a response occurs contiguously with a neutral stimulus pattern, it will become connected to that pattern if it is followed by one of the things in the list." However, this workable law gives only a circular description of the operations producing "effect." We are essentially defining effect as any event which makes the law of effect true. Descriptively this procedure may be practical but it leaves us up in the air about the outcome with an untried event. It also makes the law of effect exceptionless and untestable from a reductionist standpoint.

The reductive alternative to this handbook type of "law" is to seek a common factor in the empirical list of rewards. If we hit upon the right factor, we can predict the outcome when a new untried event is put in the reward position in a trial and error situation. The search for such a factor has been hampeerd because of one fairly common factor in the items of the empirical list collected so far. It is the property of being events which we feel are desirable from the standpoint of the organism. This leads to one of the most common and reprehensible versions of the law of effect— a version which merely says that responses with "adaptive" outcomes get fixated, and does not state the procedure for determining the adaptivity of a response. Such formulations probably constitute the most common way of conceptualizing the law of effect.

All such purposive conceptions of the law of effect are probably merely statements of the biological significance of learning. Selective learning is bound to be dominated by adaptive outcomes if the animal is left to his own devices in a maladaptive situation. He got the learning process through natural selection and it would be a surprise if it did not turn out to be a bodily process which helped him adapt to his environment. But survival-need reduction is no more a cause of an individual instance of learning than is cooling of the body a cause of a person's perspiring when hot.

A more mechanistic, and therefore more acceptable, interpretation of effect is the drive reduction hypothesis of Mowrer (13), Miller and Dollard (11), Hull (8), and others in the S-R reinforcement group. There are numerous difficulties in Hull's use of "need reduction," but when he and his followers speak of "drive reduction"—or still more tangibly, of "stimulus-intensity reduction"—we have a principle which can predict that most learn-ing will be adaptive but also can account for such examples as the maladaptive drug addict who acquires a habit which is adjustive but not adaptive.

But a good mechanist is also not going to ignore the Smith and Guthrie (21) hypothesis that effect is removal from the situation. If one is endowed with a variety of adaptive reflexes, what could be more adaptive, when next thrown into a previously experienced maladptive situation, than to do whatever got you out of it the last time you were in it? The response that changes a maladaptive situation into an adaptive one is inevitably going to be a wise choice from an adaptive standpoint—and a last-response factor may well have been incorporated into the learning process by natural selection.

The Smith and Guthrie hypothesis—which they deduce from contiguity —is a hard one to test experimentally and it has survived without real disproof for about thirty years. It has the advantage over the drive reduction position in that it accepts contiguity as sufficient and therefore does not have the awkwardness of the drive reduction position in coping with the conditioning of such responses as the knee jerk, vasodilation, salivation based on acid, and so forth. Moreover, the drive reduction position is faced with problems even in its home territory of accounting for instances of *selective learning* where the "reward" is not drive reducing in any obvious way.

Thus in a collaborative study with Dr. Thornton Roby (17) we found that hungry rats would learn responses for which reward was only a very sweet solution of saccharine and water. Hungry rats gorge themselves on such a nonnourishing solution and even after weeks of acquiring sophistication in this form of sham feeding they readily learn to dash to the correct side of a T-maze to get a few minutes at the saccharine bottle.

In some other experiments in collaboration with Jepson Wulff and Robert Backer (18) we found that male rats reared from infancy in segregation from females readily learned an instrumental response that led to a chance to copulate with a female in heat even though copulation was always stopped short of ejaculation. That is, the "reward" for selective learning was an opportunity to initiate copulation but the female was always removed considerably before ejaculation. By some standards the "reward" would be called sexual frustration. The animals had never ejaculated before the experiment so acquired drive reduction was ruled out; and they did not ejaculate during the experiment so primary drive reduction was ruled out. Yet the response instrumental in producing the female in heat showed steady acquisition compared with controls receiving only a male companion in the goal box.

These findings seem contrary to the drive-reduction hypothesis of the nature of "effect," although they might be thought to follow the beneception mechanism of Troland (22). Perhaps the proper generalization is that the common factor is the execution of an innate and prepotent consummatory response, regardless of whether it reduces the drive state. Whatever the correct inductive generalization, the results are more in line with a Guthrian contiguity analysis of selective learning than they are in line with a Hullian drive-reduction analysis. According to Guthrie the common factor in the empirical list of rewards is that they radically change the environment from just before to just after reward. The kinds of changes Guthrie (5) considers important indicate that it should be unimportant whether or not the animal's drive is reduced so long as the consummatory behavior remains prepotent and therefore able to take the animal "out of the situation."

I cite these experimental findings more to prove the fluid stage of our knowledge about reinforcement than to bolster the Guthrian contiguity analysis. My opinion is that Guthrie is still a long way from exhausting the implications of contiguity for instrumental learning. In the meantime my hunch is that we will eventually be forced to conclude that rewards are critical only as the means of motivating practice and performance and that the contiguity factor will turn out to be sufficient in describing the effects of practice *per se*. In terms of the main topic of our symposium my chief argument is that disproof of the universality of the law of effect does not force us into dualism as the only alternative—at least not until an all-out modern attempt has been made to see if association by contiguity is the common process both in selective learning and conditioning.

Bibliography

1. BIRCH, H. G., and BITTERMAN, M. E. Reinforcement and learning: the process of sensory integration. *Psychol. Rev.*, 1949, **56**, 292–308.
2. BROGDEN, W. J. Sensory pre-conditioning. *J. exp. Psychol.*, 1939, **25**, 323–332.
3. ESTES, W. K. Toward a statistical theory of learning. *Psychol. Rev.*, 1950, **57**, 94–107.
4. GUTHRIE, E. R. *The psychology of learning*. New York: Harper, 1935.
5. ———. The effect of outcome on learning. *Psychol. Rev.*, 1939, **46**, 480–484.
6. ———. Association and the law of effect. *Psychol. Rev.*, 1940, **47**, 127–148.
7. HILGARD, E. R., and MARQUIS, D. G. *Conditioning and learning*. New York: Appleton-Century, 1940.
8. HULL, C. L. *Principles of behavior*. New York: Appleton-Century, 1943.
9. JENKINS, W. O., and STANLEY, J. C. Partial reinforcement: a review and critique. *Psychol. Bull.*, 1950, **47**, 193–234.
10. MAIER, N. R. F., and SCHNEIRLA, T. C. Mechanisms in conditioning. *Psychol. Rev.*, 1942, **49**, 117–134.
11. MILLER, N. E., and DOLLARD, J. *Social learning and imitation*. New Haven: Yale Press, 1941.

12. MILLER, S., and KONORSKI, J. Sur une forme particulière des réflexes con- ditionelles. *C. R. Soc. Biol. Paris,* 1928, **99,** 1155–1157.

13. MOWRER, O. H. On the dual nature of learning—a re-interpretation of "conditioning" and "problem-solving." *Harvard educ. Rev.,* 1947, **17,** 102–148.

14. ———, and LAMOREAUX, R. R. Fear as an intervening variable in avoid- ance conditioning. *J. comp. Psychol.,* 1946, **39,** 29–50.

15. ———. *Learning theory and personality dynamics.* New York: Ronald Press, 1950.

16. SHEFFIELD, F. D. Avoidance training and the contiguity principle. *J. comp. physiol. Psychol.,* 1948, **41,** 165–177.

17. ———, and ROBY, T. B. Reward value of a non-nutritive sweet taste. *J. comp. physiol. Psychol.,* 1950, **43,** 471–481.

18. ———, WULFF, J. J. and BACKER, R. Reward value of copulation without sex-drive reduction. *J. compy. physiol. Psychol.,* 1951, **44,** 3–8.

19. SKINNER, B. F. *The behavior of organisms.* New York: Appleton-Century, 1938.

20. ———. Are theories of learning necessary? *Psychol. Rev.,* 1950, **57,** 193–216.

21. SMITH, S., and GUTHRIE, E. R. *General psychology in terms of behavior.* New York: Appleton, 1921.

22. TROLAND, L. T. *The fundamentals of human motivation.* New York: Van Nostrand, 1928.

17. *Gestalt Psychology Today* [*][1]

WOLFGANG KÖHLER, *Dartmouth College*

IN 1949, the late Herbert Langfeld gave a lecture in Europe in which he described what appeared to him to be the major trends in American psychology. He also mentioned Gestalt psychology; but he added that the main observations, questions, and principles characteristic of this school had become part of every American psychologist's mental equipment. I was not so optimistic. And, in fact, the very next year attempts were made to explain the molar units in perception by processes which gradually connect neural elements. Soon afterwards, a theory of conditioning was developed,

[*] From Wolfgang Köhler, "Gestalt Psychology Today," *The American Psychologist,* 14 (December, 1959), 727–34. Reprinted by permission.

[1] Address of the President at the Sixty-Seventh Annual Convention of the American Psychological Association, Cincinnati, Ohio, September 6, 1959.

according to which more and more components of a stimulus object are gradually conditioned, and the course of the whole process can be explained in this fashion. Such theories may prove to be very useful, but one can hardly say that, at the time, their authors were greatly influenced by Gestalt psychology. It is for this and similar reasons that a new discussion of old questions seems to me indicated.

I should like to begin with a few remarks about the history of Gestalt psychology—because not all chapters of this history are generally known. In the eighties of the past century, psychologists in Europe were greatly disturbed by von Ehrenfels' claim that thousands of percepts have characteristics which cannot be derived from the characteristics of their ultimate components, the so-called sensations. Chords and melodies in hearing, the shape characteristics of visual objects, the roughness or the smoothness of tactual impressions, and so forth were used as examples. All these "Gestalt qualities" have one thing in common. When the physical stimuli in question are considerably changed, while their relations are kept constant, the Gestalt qualities remain about the same. But, at the time, it was generally assumed that the sensations involved are individually determined by their individual stimuli and must therefore change when these are greatly changed. How, then, could any characteristics of the perceptual situation remain constant under these conditions? Where did the Gestalt qualities come from? Ehrenfels' qualities are not fancy ingredients of this or that particular situation which we might safely ignore. Both positive and negative esthetic characteristics of the world around us, not only of ornaments, paintings, sculptures, tunes, and so forth, but also of trees, landscapes, houses, cars—and other persons—belong to this class. That relations between the sexes largely depend on specimens of the same class need hardly be emphasized. It is, therefore, not safe to deal with problems of psychology as though there were no such qualities. And yet, beginning with Ehrenfels himself, psychologists have not been able to explain their nature.

This holds also for the men who were later called Gestalt psychologists, including the present speaker. Wertheimer's ideas and investigations developed in a different direction. His thinking was also more radical than that of Ehrenfels. He did not ask: How are Gestalt qualities possible when, basically, the perceptual scene consists of separate elements? Rather, he objected to this premise, the thesis that the psychologist's thinking must begin with a consideration of such elements. From a subjective point of view, he felt, it may be tempting to assume that all perceptual situations consist of independent, very small components. For, on this assumption, we obtain a maximally clear picture of what lies behind the observed facts. But, how do we know that a subjective clarity of this kind agrees with the nature of what we have before us? Perhaps we pay for the subjective clearness of the customary picture by ignoring all processes, all functional interrelations, which may have operated before there is a perceptual scene and which thus influence the characteristics of this scene. Are we allowed to impose on perception an extreme simplicity which, objectively, it may not possess?

Wertheimer, we remember, began to reason in this fashion when experimenting not with perceptual situations which were stationary, and therefore comparatively silent, but with visual objects in motion when corresponding stimuli did not move. Such "apparent movements," we would now say, occur when several visual objects appear or disappear in certain temporal relations. Again in our present language, under these circumstances an interaction takes place which, for instance, makes a second object appear too near, or coincident with, a first object which is just disappearing, so that only when the first object, and therefore the interaction, really fades, the second object can move toward its normal position. If this is interaction, it does not, as such, occur on the perceptual scene. On this scene, we merely observe a movement. That movements of this kind do not correspond to real movements of the stimulus objects and must therefore be brought about by the sequence of the two objects, we can discover only by examining the physical situation. It follows that, if the seen movement is the perceptual result of an interaction, this interaction itself takes place outside the perceptual field. Thus, the apparent movement confirmed Wertheimer's more general suspicion: we cannot assume that the perceptual scene is an aggregate of unrelated elements because underlying processes are already functionally interrelated when that scene emerges, and now exhibits corresponding effects.

Wertheimer did not offer a more specific physiological explanation. At the time, this would have been impossible. He next turned to the problem of whether the characteristics of stationary perceptual fields are also influenced by interactions. I need not repeat how he investigated the formation of molar perceptual units, and more particularly of groups of such objects. Patterns which he used for this purpose are now reproduced in many textbooks. They clearly demonstrate that it is *relations* among visual objects which decide what objects become group members, and what others do not, and where, therefore, one group separates itself from another. This fact strongly suggests that perceptual groups are established by interactions; and, since a naive observer is merely aware of the result, the perceived groups, but not of their dependence upon particular relations, such interactions would again occur among the underlying processes rather than within the perceptual field.

Let me add a further remark about this early stage of the development.

Surely, in those years, Gestalt psychologists were not satisfied with a quiet consideration of available facts. It seems that no major new trend in a science ever is. We were excited by what we found, and even more by the prospect of finding further revealing facts. Moreover, it was not only the stimulating newness of our enterprise which inspired us. There was also a great wave of relief—as though we were escaping from a prison. The prison was psychology as taught at the universities when we still were students. At the time, we had been shocked by the thesis that all psychological facts (not only those in perception) consist of unrelated inert atoms and that almost the only factors which combine these atoms and thus introduce action are associations formed under the influence of mere contiguity. What had disturbed us was the utter senselessness of this picture, and the implication that human life, apparently so colorful and so intensely dynamic, is actually a frightful bore. This was not true of our new picture, and we felt that further discoveries were bound to destroy what was left of the old picture.

Soon further investigations, not all of them done by Gestalt psychologists, reinforced the new trend. Rubin called attention to the difference between figure and ground. David Katz found ample evidence for the role of Gestalt factors in the field of touch as well as in color vision, and so forth. Why so much interest just in perception? Simply because in no other part of psychology are facts so readily accessible to observation. It was the hope of everybody that, once some major functional principles had been revealed in this part of psychology, similar principles would prove to be relevant to other parts, such as memory, learning, thinking, and motivation. In fact, Wertheimer and I undertook our early studies of intellectual processes precisely from this point of view; somewhat later, Kurt Lewin began his investigations of motivation which, in part, followed the same line; and we also applied the concept of *Gestaltung* or organization to memory, to learning, and to recall. With developments in America, Wertheimer's further analysis of thinking, Asch's and Heider's investigations in social psychology, our work on figural aftereffects, and eventually on currents of the brain, we are probably all familiar.

In the meantime, unexpected support had come from natural science. To mention only one point: Parts of molar perceptual units often have characteristics which they do not exhibit when separated from those units. Within a larger visual entity, a part may, for instance, be a corner of this entity, another part its contour or boundary, and so on. It now seems obvious; but nobody in psychology had seen it before: the same happens in any physical system that is pervaded by interactions. These interactions affect the parts of the system until, eventually, in a steady state, the characteristics of all parts are such that remaining interactions balance one another. Hence, if processes in the central nervous system follow the same rule, the dependence of local perceptual facts on conditions in larger entities could no longer be regarded as puzzling. Comparisons of this kind greatly encouraged the Gestalt psychologists.

In America, it may seem surprising that enthusiastic people such as the Gestalt psychologists were intensely interested in physics. Physics is generally assumed to be a particularly sober discipline. And yet, this happened to us most naturally. To be sure, our reasoning in physics involved no changes in the laws of physics, and no new assumptions in this field. Nevertheless, when we compared our psychological findings with the behavior of certain physical systems, some parts of natural science began to look different. When reading the formulae of the physicist, one may emphasize this or that aspect of their content. The particular aspect of the formulae in which the Gestalt psychologists became interested had, for decades, been given little attention. No mistake had ever been made in applications of the formulae, because what now fascinated us had all the time been present in their mathematical form. Hence, all calculations in physics had come out right. But it does make a difference whether you make explicit what a formula implies or merely use it as a reliable tool. We had, therefore, good reasons for being surprised by what we found; and we naturally felt elated when the new reading of the formulae told us that organization is as obvious in some parts of physics as it is in psychology.

Incidentally, others were no less interested in this "new reading" than we were. These other people were eminent physicists. Max Planck once told me that he expected our approach to clarify a difficult issue which had just arisen in quantum physics—if not the concept of the quantum itself. Several years later, Max Born, the great physicist who gave quantum mechanics its present form, made almost the same statement in one of his papers. And, only a few weeks ago, I read a paper in which Bridgman of Harvard interprets Heisenberg's famous principle in such terms that I am tempted to call him, Bridgman, a Gestalt physicist.

We will now return to psychology. More particularly, we will inspect the situation in which American psychology finds itself today. The spirit which we find here differs considerably from the one which characterized young Gestalt psychology. Let me try to formulate what members of this audience may have been thinking while I described that European enterprise. "Enthusiasm?" they probably thought. "Feelings of relief when certain assumptions were found less dreary than those of earlier psychologists in Europe? But this is an admission that emotional factors and extrascientific values played a part in Gestalt psychology. We know about the often pernicious effects of the emotions in ordinary life. How, then, could emotions be permitted to influence scientific judgments and thus to disturb the objectivity of research? As we see it, the true spirit of science is a critical spirit. Our main obligation as scientists is that of avoiding mistakes. Hence our emphasis on strict method in experimentation and on equally strict procedures in the evaluation of results. The Gestalt psychologists seem to have been guilty of wishful thinking. Under the circumstances, were not some of their findings unreliable and some of their concepts vague?"

I will at once admit two facts. Almost from its beginning, American psychology has given more attention to questions of method and strict proof than Gestalt psychology did in those years. In this respect, American psychology was clearly superior. Secondly, sometimes the Gestalt psychologists did make mistakes. Not in all cases was the reliability of their findings up to American standards, and some concepts which they used were not immediately quite clear. I myself once used a certain concept in a somewhat misleading fashion. I had better explain this.

What is insight? In its strict sense, the term refers to the fact that, when we are aware of a relation, of any relation, this relation is not experienced as a fact by itself, but rather as something that follows from the characteristics of the objects under consideration. Now, when primates try to solve a problem, their behavior often shows that they are aware of a certain important relation. But when they now make use of this "insight," and thus solve their problem, should this achievement be called *a solution by insight?* No—it is by no means clear that it was also insight which made that particular relation *emerge.* In a given situation, we or a monkey may become aware of a great many relations. If, at a certain moment, we or a monkey attend to the right one, this may happen for several reasons, some entirely unrelated to insight. Consequently, it is misleading to call the whole process a "solution by insight."

This will be particularly obvious when the solution of the problem is arbitrarily chosen by the experimenter. Take Harlow's excellent experiments in which primates are expected to choose the odd item in a group of objects. "Oddity" is a particular relational fact. Once a monkey attends to it, he will perceive it with insight. But why should he do so during his first trials? His first choices will be determined by one factor or another, until he happens to attend, once or repeatedly, to the oddity relation just when he chooses (or does not choose) the right object. Gradually, he will now attend to this particular relation in all trials; and he may do so even when entirely new objects are shown. Surely, such a process should not simply be called "learning by insight." If Harlow were to say that, under the circumstances, it is learning of one kind or another which gives the right relation and corresponding insight their chance to operate, I should at once agree. What, I believe, the monkeys do not learn is insight into which object in a given group is the odd one; but they must learn to pay attention to the oddity factor in the first place. I hope that this will clarify matters. They have not always been so clear to me.

When the solution of a problem is not arbitrarily chosen by the experimenter, but more directly related to the nature of the given situation, insight may play a more important role. But, even under these circumstances, it is not insight alone which brings about the solution. The mere fact that solutions often emerge to the subjects' own surprise is clear proof that it cannot be insight alone which is responsible for their origin.

But I intended to discuss some trends in American psychology. May I confess that I do not fully approve of all these trends?

First, I doubt whether it is advisable to regard caution and a critical spirit as *the* virtues of a scientist, as though little else counted. They are necessary in research, just as the brakes in our cars must be kept in order and their windshields clean. But it is not because of the brakes or of the windshields that we drive. Similarly, caution and a critical spirit are like tools. They ought to be kept ready during a scientific enterprise; however, the main business of a science is gaining more and more new knowledge. I wonder why great men in physics do not call caution and a critical spirit the most important characteristics of their behavior. They seem to regard the testing of brakes and the cleaning of windshields as mere precautions, but to look forward to the next trip as the business for which they have cars. Why is it only in psychology that we hear the slightly discouraging story of mere caution over and over again? Why are just psychologists so inclined to greet the announcement of a new fact (or a new working hypothesis) almost with scorn? This is caution that has gone sour and has almost become negativism—which, of course, is no less an emotional attitude than is enthusiasm. The enthusiasm of the early Gestalt psychologists was a virtue, because it led to new observations. But virtues, it has been said, tend to breed little accompanying vices. In their enthusiasm, the Gestalt psychologists were not always sufficiently careful.

In American psychology, it is rightly regarded as a virtue if a man feels great respect for method and for caution. But, if this virtue becomes too strong, it may bring forth a spirit of skepticism and thus prevent new work. Too many young psychologists, it seems to me, either work only against something done by others or merely vary slightly what others have done before; in other words, preoccupation with method may tend to limit the range of our research. We are, of course, after clear evidence. But not in all parts of psychology can evidence immediately be clear. In some, we cannot yet use our most exact methods. Where this happens, we hesitate to proceed. Experimentalists in particular tend to avoid work on new materials resistant to approved methods and to the immediate application of perfectly clear concepts. But concepts in a new field can only be clarified by work in this field. Should we limit our studies to areas already familiar from previous research? Obviously, this would mean a kind of conservatism in psychology. When I was his student, Max Planck repeated this warning over and over again in his lectures.

Our wish to use only perfect methods and clear concepts has led to Methodological Behaviorism. Human experience in the phenomenological sense cannot yet be treated with our most reliable methods; and, when dealing with it, we may be forced to form new concepts which, at first, will often be a bit vague. Most experimentalists, therefore, refrain from observing, or even from referring to, the phenomenal scene. And yet, this is the scene on which, so far as the actors are concerned, the drama of ordinary human living is being played all the time. If we never study this scene, but insist on methods and concepts developed in research "from the outside," our results are likely to look strange to those who intensely live "inside."

To be sure, in many respects, the graphs and tables obtained "from the outside" constitute a most satisfactory material; and, in animal psychology, we have no other material. But this material as such contains no direct evidence as to the processes by which it is brought about. In this respect it is a slightly defective, I am tempted to say, a meager, material. For it owes its particular clearness to the fact that the data from which the graphs and tables are derived are severely selected data. When subjects are told to say no more than "louder," "softer," and perhaps "equal" in certain experiments, or when we merely count how many items they recall in others, then we can surely apply precise statistical techniques to what they do. But, as a less attractive consequence, we never hear under these circumstances how they do the comparing in the first case and what happens when they try to recall in the second case.

Are such questions now to be ignored? After all, not all phenomenal experiences are entirely vague; this Scheerer has rightly emphasized. And, if many are not yet accessible to quantitative procedures, what of it? One of the most fascinating disciplines, developmental physiology, the science investigating the growth of an organism from one cell, seldom uses quantitative techniques. And yet, nobody can deny that its merely qualitative description of morphogenesis has extraordinary scientific value. In new fields, not only quantitative data are relevant. As to the initial vagueness of concepts in a new field, I should like to add an historical remark. When the concept of energy was first introduced in physics, it was far from being a clear concept. For decades, its meaning could not be sharply distinguished from that of the term "force." And what did the physicists do? They worked and worked on it, until at last it did become perfectly clear. There is no other way of dealing with new, and therefore not yet perfect, concepts.

Hence, if we refuse to study the phenomenal scene, because, here, few concepts are so far entirely clear, we thereby decide that this scene will never be investigated—at least not by us, the psychologists.

Now, I had better return to Gestalt psychology. Let me try to show you how Gestalt psychology tends to work today by discussing a more specific issue, an issue on which scores of American psychologists have worked for years. We shall thus be enabled to compare the way in which they approach this issue with the Gestalt psychologists' approach.

The issue in question refers to the concepts of conditioning and motivation. One school seems to regard conditioning as almost *the* process with which the psychologist has to deal. In a famous book with the general title *Principles of Behavior,* the late Clark Hull, then the most influential member of the school, actually dealt with little else—although he often used other terms. He felt that even such facts as thinking, insight, intentions, striving, and value would eventually be explained by a consistent investigation of the various forms of conditioning. We are all familiar with the basic concepts of his theory. Hence I will say only a few words about it. When conditions in an animal's tissue deviate from an optimal level, a state of need is said to exist in this tissue. Such needs produce, or simply are, drives —which means that they tend to cause actions in the nervous system, some more or less prescribed by inherited neural connections, others of a more random nature. Drives are also called motivations. None of these terms is to be understood in a phenomenological sense. They always refer to assumed states of the tissue. The main point is that, for biological reasons, states of need must, if possible, be reduced and that this may be achieved by certain responses of the organism to the given situation. In case first responses are of a random character, learning or conditioning will often select such responses as do reduce the needs in question. In a simple formulation, the well-known rule which governs such developments is as follows: when a response has repeatedly occurred in temporal contiguity with the neural effects of a certain stimulus, then this stimulus will tend to evoke the same response in the future—provided the response has caused a reduction of the need. I will not define such further concepts as habit strength, reaction potential, afferent stimulus interaction, reactive inhibition, and so forth, because they will play no role in my discussion.

But one term seems to me particularly important. Many recent, and important, investigations are concerned with so-called "learned drives," an expression which has, of course, this meaning: if a neutral stimulus is repeatedly followed by conditions which cause a primary state of drive such as pain, and the corresponding fear, then the fear with its usual effects on behavior will gradually become connected with that neutral stimulus, so that the stimulus alone now evokes the fear and its overt consequences.

Certain drives are therefore said to be "learnable" in the sense that they can be attached to facts which, as such, are not related to the drive and hence would originally not evoke corresponding responses.

Some experiments in the field of conditioning in general are most interesting. I will only discuss the concepts used in the interpretation of this work and the conclusions which it is said to justify.

To begin with these conclusions: They refer to certain human experiences which, if the conclusions were justified, would have to be regarded as strange delusions. I mean our cognitive experiences. Suppose somebody discovers by accident that every time he subtracts the square of a given integer from the square of the next integer in the series, the result is an odd number. A more learned friend now explains to him why this is a necessary rule, undoubtedly valid beyond any tests ever done by a person. The explanation refers to simple relations and to relations among relations —all readily understandable—and the final outcome is convincing. Now, is the understanding of the relations involved to be explained in terms of conditioning? Nothing in conditioning seems to give us access to the psychological fact which I just called understanding; and, since an understanding of relations is essential to all cognitive achievements, the same applies to the whole field.

Explanation of our intellectual life in terms of conditioning would simply mean its reduction to the operations of an often most practical, but intrinsically blind, connection of mere facts. Promises that such an explanation will nevertheless be achieved cause in the present speaker a mild, incredulous horror. It is not the business of science to destroy evidence. Behaviorists would perhaps answer that arguments which refer to human thinking as an experience are irrelevant, because science is only concerned with facts observable from the outside, and therefore objective. This answer would hardly be acceptable. The Behaviorist's own objective observations are invariably observations of facts in his perceptual field. No other form of objective observation has ever been discovered. Consequently, the Behaviorist cannot, without giving more particular reasons, reject reference to other individual experiences merely because they are such experiences.

Thus we are justified in considering a further example of human experience. A need or drive, we are sometimes told, is a motivation. I do not entirely agree with this statement for the following reasons. A need or drive, we remember, is supposed to be a particular state in the tissue. There is no indication in Hull's writings that such a state "points beyond itself" toward any objects—although it may, of course, cause movements, or actions of glands. Now it is true that the same holds for certain needs as human experiences; because, when a need is felt, it does not always point toward an object, attainment of which would satisfy the need. At the time, no such object may be in sight; in fact, no such object may yet be known. But when the proper object appears, or becomes known, then the situation changes. For now the subject feels attracted or (in certain instances) repelled by this object. In other words, an object may have characteristics which establish a dynamic relation between the subject and that object. According to common experience, it is this dynamic relation which makes the subject move toward, or away from, the object. We ought to use different terms for a mere need *per se* and the situation in which a subject is attracted or repelled by an object. Otherwise, the dynamic aspect of the latter situation might easily be ignored. I suggest that we reserve the term "motivation" for this dynamic situation. Here we are, of course, on familiar ground. Motivation as just described was Kurt Lewin's main concern in psychology. He clearly recognized the part which certain characteristics of an object play in establishing the dynamic relation between this object and the subject. He called such characteristics of objects *Aufforderungscharaktere,* a term which then became "valences" in English.

So far as I know, there are no valences in objects, no attractions and no repulsions between objects and subjects in the Behaviorist's vocabulary. I am afraid that, in this fashion, he misses a point not only important in human experience but also relevant to what he regards as true science.

How would a Gestalt psychologist handle motivation in the present sense? He would begin with the following psychological facts. I do not know up to what point Lewin would have accepted what I am now going to say. My facts are these: (*a*) In human experience, motivation is a dynamic vector, that is, a fact which has a direction and tends to cause a displacement in this direction. (*b*) Unless there are obstacles in the way, this direction coincides with an imaginary straight line drawn from the object to the subject. (*c*) The direction of the experienced vector is either that toward the object or away from it. In the first case, the vector tends to reduce the distance in question; in the second, to increase it. (*d*) The strength of both the need present in the subject and of the valence exhibited by the object can vary. Both in man and in animals it has been observed that, when the strength of the valence is low, this reduction can be compensated for by an increase of the need in the subject; and, conversely, that, when the need is lowered, an increase of the strength of the valence may compensate for this change.

When considering these simple statements, anybody familiar with the elements of physics will be reminded of the behavior of forces. (*a*) In physics, forces are dynamic vectors which tend to change the distance between one thing (or event) and another. (*b*) Unless there are obstacles in the way, a force operates along a straight line drawn from the first object (or event) to the other. (*c*) The direction in which a force operates is either that of an attraction or of a repulsion, of a reduction or of an increase of the given distance. (*d*) The formula by which the intensity of a force between two objects is given contains two terms which refer to the sizes of a decisive property (for instance, an electric charge) in one object and in the other. It is always the product of these two terms on which, according to the formula, the intensity of the force depends. Consequently, a reduction of the crucial term on one side can be compensated for by an increase of the term on the other side.

We have just seen that the behavior of vectors in motivational situations is the same as the behavior of forces in nature. Gestalt psychologists are, therefore, inclined to interpret motivation in terms of such forces or, rather, of forces which operate between certain perceptual processes and processes in another part of the brain, where a need may be physiologically represented. We have no time to discuss the question how cortical fields or forces would cause overt movements of the organism in the direction of these forces.

Now, not everybody likes the term "force." Its meaning, it has been said, has anthropomorphic connotations. But, in human psychology, we simply must use terms which—if I may use this expression—"sound human." If we refused to do so, we would not do justice to our subject matter which (to a high degree) is human experience. To be sure, in physics, Heinrich Hertz once tried to do without the concept "force." He actually wrote a treatise on mechanics in which he avoided this term. And what happened? He had to populate the physical world with unobservable masses, introduced only in order to make their hidden presence substitute for the much simpler action of forces. Ever since that time, physicists have happily returned to the old concept "force," and nobody has ever been harmed by the fact.

The present reasoning leads to a conclusion which distinguishes this reasoning from the treatment of motivation in the Behaviorist's system. Clark Hull was a great admirer of science; but, to my knowledge, he hardly ever used the concepts characteristic of field physics. The fundamental distinction between physical facts which are scalars (that is, facts which have a magnitude but no direction) and vectors (which have both an intensity and a direction) played no decisive part in his theorizing. His main concepts were obviously meant to be scalars. There is no particular spatial direction in a habit strength, none in a reaction potential, and none even in what he called a drive state. Hence, the core of modern physics as developed by Faraday and Maxwell had no influence on his system. For this reason, and also because he refused to consider motivation as an experienced vector, he could not discover that the operations of motivation appear to be isomorphic with those of fields or forces in the brain.

But, if motivation is to be interpreted in this fashion, certain assumptions often made by Behaviorists may no longer be acceptable. Take the concept of learned drives. As I understand this term, it means that learning can attach a drive state to a great variety of stimuli which, as such, are neutral facts. Now, so long as a drive is not regarded as a vector, this seems indeed quite possible. But, if the drive in Hull's sense is replaced by a motivational force which operates between a subject and some perceptual fact, no arbitrary connections of this kind can be established. For now motivation becomes the experienced counterpart of a force in the brain, and this force depends entirely upon the relation between conditions in the subject and the characteristics of the perceived object. There can be no such force if the object is, and remains, a neutral object. Forces only operate between objects which have the right properties. Any example of a force in nature illustrates this fact.

How, then, are the observations to be explained which are now interpreted as a learning of drives? After all, some learning must be involved when an originally neutral object gradually begins to attract or repel a subject. From the present point of view, only one explanation is possible. Supposing that the subject's need does not vary, learning must change the characteristics of the object, and thus transform it into an adequate motivation object. One instance would be what Tolman calls a sign Gestalt; in other words, the neutral object would become the signal for the appearance of something else which is a proper motivational object. This expected object would now be the object of the motivation. Or also, when a neutral object is often accompanied by facts which are natural motivational objects, the characteristics of such facts may gradually "creep into" the very appearance of the formerly neutral object and thus make it a proper motivational object. Years ago, comparative psychologists in England stressed the importance of such processes, to which they gave the name "assimilation." They regarded assimilation as a particularly effective form of an association. And is it not true that, as a consequence of learning, a coffin *looks* forbidding or sinister? I also know somebody to whom a bottle covered with dust and just brought up from the cellar *looks* most attractive.

As a further and particularly simple possibility, the subject might just learn more about the characteristics of the given object itself than he knew in the beginning; and the characteristics revealed by this learning might be such that now the same object fits a need. It seems to me that all these possibilities ought to be considered before we accept the thesis that motivations in the present sense can be attached to actually neutral objects. Incidentally, similar changes of objects may also be responsible for the developments which Gordon Allport once regarded as evidence of "functional autonomy."

You will ask me whether my suggestions lead to any consequences in actual research. Most surely, they do. But, since I have lived so long in America, and have therefore gradually become a most cautious scientist, I am now preparing myself for the study of motivation by investigating, first of all, the action of dynamic vectors in simpler fields, such as cognition and perception. It is a most interesting occupation to compare motivational action with dynamic events in those other parts of psychology. When you do so, everything looks different, not only in perception but also in certain forms of learning. Specific work? There is, and will be, more of it than I alone can possibly manage. Consequently, I need help. And where do I expect to find this help? I will tell you where.

The Behaviorist's premises, we remember, lead to certain expectations and experiments. What I have just said invites us to proceed in another direction. I suggest that, in this situation, we forget about schools. The Behaviorist is convinced that his functional concepts are those which we all ought to use. The Gestalt psychologist, who deals with a greater variety of both phenomenal and physical concepts, expects more from work based on such premises. Both parties feel that their procedures are scientifically sound. Why should we fight? Many experiments done by Behaviorists seem to me to be very good experiments. May I now ask the Behaviorists to regard the use of some phenomenal facts, and also of field physics, as perfectly permissible? If we were to agree on these points, we could, I am sure, do excellent work together. It would be an extraordinary experience— and good for psychology.

18. An Eclectic View of Some Theories of Learning *

W. N. KELLOGG, *Indiana University*

Introduction

TO ANYONE who is interested in the explanation of learning, the various theories and interpretations which are current today present a bewildering picture. Many of the students of learning are aligned into separate groups or camps, each of which is intent upon furthering its own concep-

* From W. N. Kellogg, "An Eclectic View of Some Theories of Learning," *The Psychological Review*, 45 (July, 1938), 165–84. Reprinted by permission.

tions. So it is with some of the conditioned response adherents, who have pushed their doctrine to the point where it accounts for all learning, from habit-breaking to the development of elaborate skills. Among the Gestaltists, on the other hand, are those who would reduce conditioning to the development of insights. And between these views lies the trial-and-error hypothesis which seems to take little notice of the other schools. To the "plain psychologist" who does not wish to take sides in the issue, the situation is certainly perplexing. If a single all-inclusive view of learning is correct, then competing views must certainly be wrong. Which of the theories shall he pick?

In the attempt to introduce clarity into this confusion, some authors have subdivided the field of learning into a few major categories of increasing difficulty. Different theories or interpretations of learning, so far as they fit the different categories proposed, are taken to apply to different kinds of learning. Thus Harlow has distinguished four major levels of learning, viz., (1) nonvoluntary or forced conditioning, (2) skills, (3) perceptual learning and (4) conceptual or symbolic learning.[1] Tolman in an earlier analysis has also listed four classes of learning, although they are not the same as those which Harlow lists.[2] More recently Tolman has expanded his list to seven.[3]

A second method which makes for unity in the field of learning is that employed by Dashiell.[4] This author, who starts with the three primary divisions of trial-and-error learning, conditioning and Gestalt learning, has pointed to the common ground in each and has tried to show that real and basic distinctions do not exist. Such fundamental conditions as motivation, multiplicity of response, increase in general activity and selection or least action are common to each supposed kind of learning. It is Dashiell's point, therefore, that the discrepancies which appear between different interpretations have arisen from the bias and emphasis of particular theorists.

To the present writer, it would seem only reasonable to admit that any interpretation which has achieved the status of a well-known theory cannot be wholly wrong or will ever be completely outmoded. The enormous amount of observation and experimentation, which backs up such views, assures a basis of scientific accuracy. Are we then to believe that each interpretation applies only to a special kind of learning, and that there are,

[1] H. F. Harlow, The neuro-physiological correlates of learning and intelligence, *Psychol. Bull.,* 1936, 33, 479–524.

[2] E. C. Tolman, Theories of learning, in *Comparative Psychology,* edited by F. A. Moss, New York: Prentice-Hall, 1934, pp. 367–408.

[3] E. C. Tolman, The acquisition of string-pulling by rats—conditioned response or sign-gestalt?, *Psychol. Rev.,* 1957, 44, 195–211.

[4] J. F. Dashiell, A survey and synthesis of learning theories, *Psychol. Bull.,* 1935, 33, 261–275.

as a consequence, as many discrete sorts of learning as there are theories to account for them? Or are the principal theories of learning, as Dashiell has suggested, simply viewpoints of the same set of facts—viewpoints which are determined by the training and experience of the viewer? It is our purpose in this paper to examine four of the better-known theories of learning and to point out, if possible, some unrecognized relationships between them, so as to assist in a further clarification of the field. These theories are trial-and-error learning, Gestalt insight, conditioning and sign learning.

Low and High Learning

No one can deny that there are complex problems and simple problems in learning. For any given organism, some tasks are learned quickly and others are unsolvable. It is likewise true that certain of the theories of learning apply more readily to simple learning of a low or mechanical sort; and that other theories assume higher capacities on the part of the organism. A distinction of this kind has long been recognized, and is typified on the low or mechanical side by the terms "motor," "muscular," and "physiological" learning; on the side of higher learning, by the terms "ideational learning," "inferential learning" and "symbolic learning."

If learning is divisible into simple and complex varieties, then it would appear that Gestalt learning must belong in the latter group. There is certainly an affinity between symbolic learning and learning of the Gestalt type. For one thing, the organism is responding to more than one stimulus in each case. It makes a kind of relational reaction, the success of which depends upon several factors. Some of the stimuli may be kinesthetic or symbolic. But this does not alter the fact that what may be called the "field of stimulation," is, in each case, broad. Again, each view seems willing to attribute to the organism an ability beyond that which is directly observable through its behavior. Obviously, they are liberal interpretations. They give the animal the benefit of the doubt. It is a question whether symbolic or Gestalt learning should be described at all in purely mechanistic terms.

Conditioned response learning and trial-and-error learning, on the other hand, are simple types of learning, not necessarily because, as Tolman has put it, each is based upon neural or upon other sorts of "connections," but rather because they are fundamentally objective and automatic. They are mechanistic interpretations freed for the most part from symbolism or "ideas." The learning in a sense takes place itself, providing the requisite conditions for learning are satisfied. The learning organism assumes a kind of passive part in the learning situation. What he does seems to a greater extent to be forced upon him, and less a contribution of his own, than is the case in higher learning.

Trial-and-Error Learning

Having raised a distinction of this sort on traditional and logical grounds, let us now ask whether the distinction can be bridged, and whether there is really any fundamental qualitative difference between "low" learning and "high." The answers to these questions can be discovered most easily by means of a series of diagrams, in terms of which the four theories of learning to be discussed can be more clearly presented. Let us take first the trial-and-error view as proposed by Thorndike and as described by numerous writers today. *Trial-and-error learning is essentially a process of selecting*

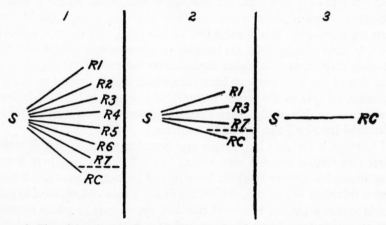

Figure 1. The trial-and-error theory in diagram form. 1, 2, and 3 represent successive time periods in the learning. Step 1 depicts the process at the beginning of a series of trials. Step 2 represents a "sample" trial in the middle of the learning process. And Step 3 shows the final stage when the learning is complete.

one response from among many, the selection taking place as a result of the operation of the Law of Exercise, the Law of Effect, and more recently the Law of Belonging.[5] In order to show the progress of learning over a period of time, let us break up the process into three phases or steps. The most elementary or initial stage would represent the situation as it exists at the start or beginning of the learning process. The second or intermediate stage then represents the situation as the learning is taking place, and the final or completed stage would depict the situation after the learning has been accomplished.

In Figure 1, these three stages are diagramed as they exist according to

[5] A detailed consideration of these principles is omitted entirely from the present discussion, which seeks only to examine the theory as it exists.

the trial-and-error hypothesis. S is the stimulus situation (maze, problem box, puzzle, etc.) and $R1 \ldots R7$ are incorrect responses or errors. RC is the correct response leading to a solution of the problem at the termination of any given presentation of the stimulus. In Stage 1 (Figure 1) the conditions are those which exist at the start of the learning process. A great many errors are made (and often the same error is repeated) before the correct response, RC, occurs. Progress in learning is shown in Stage 2 where the number of errors is considerably reduced, but not entirely eliminated. In Stage 3, the learning is complete. Any presentation of S now calls forth RC immediately, without the occurrence of any other R's at all. The gradual decrease in the number of errors, if recorded at each presentation of the stimulus situation, gives the "error" learning curve typical of situations of this sort.

If learning is now regarded as the gradual development of an insight into the nature of the problem, as Wheeler [6] has suggested, then there is no point in distinguishing between trial and error learning and learning by insight. Trial-and-error observations become simply an objective record of the development of "an insight." Conversely, learning by insight becomes the subjective or introspective aspect of trial-and-error learning. They are one and the same activity conceived (1) from the point of view of the experimenter and (2) from the point of view of the subject.

Sudden Insights and Trial and Error

But if the insight comes suddenly, according to the traditional method described by Köhler in his *Umweg* experiments,[7] then it may at first appear that there can be no similarity between trial-and-error learning and Gestalt learning. Yet it is our contention that such a similarity exists, and that the two are only variants of one and the same process except that trial-and-error learning is the more elementary version ("low" learning) and learning by sudden insight is the more complex version ("high" learning). The diagrams in Figure 2 may serve to make this clear.

Unless the solution of the problem is *immediately apparent* to the subject so that no false attempts (errors) are made at all, the condition which exists at the beginning of the learning is as indicated in Stage 1, Figure 2. *The subject does make errors,* despite popular misconceptions to the contrary, providing the problem is difficult enough to require any new adjustments at all and cannot be "seen into" as soon as it is presented.[8] The

[6] R. H. Wheeler, *The Science of Psychology,* New York: Crowell, 1929, p. 252.

[7] W. Köhler, *The Mentality of Apes,* 2nd ed., New York: Harcourt-Brace, 1927, p. 336.

[8] In such cases, it may be argued there is no real problem of *learning* at all, and hence the situation is not a typical learning situation.

classical description by Köhler of the solution of the jointed stick problem by the chimpanzee, Sultan, may be taken as an illustration of this point. The statements which are capitalized in the quotation below describe successive trials and errors.[9]

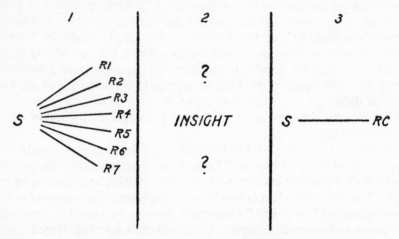

Figure 2. A diagrammatic arrangement of the process of learning by sudden insight. 1, 2 and 3 refer to separate time sequences as they do in Figure 1.

Are the two sticks ever combined so as to become technically useful? This time Sultan is the subject of experiment. His sticks are two hollow, but firm, bamboo rods, such as the animals often use for pulling along fruit. The one is so much smaller than the other, that it can be pushed in at either end quite easily. Beyond the bars lies the objective, just so far away that the animal cannot reach it with either rod. They are about the same length. NEVERTHELESS, HE TAKES GREAT PAINS TO TRY TO REACH IT WITH ONE STICK OR THE OTHER, EVEN PUSHING HIS   ERROR RIGHT SHOULDER THROUGH THE BARS. When everything proves futile, Sultan commits a "bad error," or, more clearly, a great stupidity, such as he made sometimes on other occasions. HE PULLS A BOX FROM THE BACK OF THE ROOM   ERROR TOWARDS THE BARS; true, he pushes it away again at once as it is useless, or rather, actually in the way. Immediately afterwards, he tries something which, although practically useless, must be counted among the "good errors"; HE PUSHES ONE OF THE STICKS OUT AS FAR AS IT WILL GO, THEN TAKES THE   ERROR SECOND, AND WITH IT POKES THE FIRST ONE CAUTIOUSLY TOWARDS THE OBJECTIVE, pushing it carefully from the nearer end and thus slowly urging it towards the fruit.

[9] Capitalizing is mine.

This does not always succeed, but if he has got pretty close in this way, he takes even greater precaution; HE PUSHES VERY GENTLY, WATCHES THE MOVEMENTS OF THE STICK THAT IS LYING ON THE GROUND, AND ACTUALLY   ERROR TOUCHES THE OBJECTIVE WITH ITS TIP. Thus, all of a sudden, for the first time, the contact "animal-objective" has been established. . . . THE PROCEEDNG IS REPEATED; WHEN THE ANIMAL HAS PUSHED THE STICK ON THE GROUND SO FAR OUT THAT HE CANNOT POSSIBLY GET IT BACK   ERRORS BY HIMSELF, IT IS GIVEN BACK TO HIM. . . . SULTAN, AS BEFORE, PUSHES ONE STICK WITH THE OTHER TOWARDS THE OBJECTIVE, and as this pseudo-solution does not satisfy him any longer, he abandons his efforts altogether, and does not even pick up the sticks when they are both thrown through the bars to him. The experiment has lasted over an hour, and is stopped for the present. . . . As we intend to take it up again after a while, Sultan is left in possession of his sticks; the keeper is left there to watch him.

Keeper's report: Sultan first of all squats indifferently on the box, which has been left standing a little back from the railings; then he gets up, picks up the two sticks, sits down again on the box and PLAYS CARELESSLY WITH THEM. While doing this,   ERRORS? it happens that he finds himself holding one rod in either hand in such a way that they lie in a straight line; he pushes the thinner one a little way into the opening of the thicker, jumps up and is already on the run towards the railings, to which he has up to now half turned his back, and begins to draw a banana towards him with the double stick. I call the master: meanwhile, one of the animal's rods has fallen out of the other, as he has pushed one of them only a little way into the other; whereupon he connects them again.[10]

What Sultan did (and what any organism does in learning of this sort), *up to but not including the final successful response,* is schematically represented in the first stage of Figure 2. The final response is indicated in Stage 3. It would also be possible to diagram the correct solution, *RC,* at the bottom of the series of responses in Stage 1, and still obtain a true and accurate picture of the situation. The arrangement shown in Figure 2 was chosen because it can be more easily compared with the diagrams in Figure 1. The essential fact here is that, as usually recorded, there is *not* a gradual reduction in the number of errors, from Stage 1 (before the learning has taken place) to the final stage of complete learning. Step 2 of the trial-and-error process (2, Figure 1) is missing in the present instance and a "sudden insight" is substituted for it. The insight, however, has the same effect as a

[10] Köhler, *op. cit.,* 125–127.

long and gradual elimination of errors, in that it places the learner at the same point of efficiency he would have reached at the culmination of a regular trial-and-error process. In each instance, after the learning has been completed, succeeding presentations of the stimulus lead to the immediate calling out of *RC*. Trial-and-error learning and learning by sudden insight are similar then as to the initial and final steps, but differ chiefly in the intermediate one. The principal distinctions may be summarized as follows:

T and E	*Sudden Insight*
Gradual elimination of errors	Abrupt elimination of errors
The learning is not complete upon the first occurrence of *RC*	After *RC* has once been *insightfully* made, it is always thereafter called out upon subsequent presentations of *S*
Time of learning usually long	Time of learning shorter
(Gradual building up of insight?)	Sudden insight

To what are these differences ascribable? It is certainly not to a difference in organisms, since a gradual elimination of errors has been shown to exist over almost the whole phyletic scale, and since learning by insight has been demonstrated even in chickens and rats.[11] The same organism may at different times learn by trial-and-error and learn by insight. Are we then to suppose that the organism itself possesses a kind of reservoir of learning techniques, from which it selects this, that or the other as the occasion demands?

There is one obvious source to which the differences listed above are traceable, and when this source is taken fully into account, the differences become simply differences in degree rather than in kind. They become quantitative rather than qualitative differences. That source, as has been previously pointed out, is the fundamental difference in the degree of difficulty of the problems which are solvable by the two methods. A very difficult learning problem which cannot be solved at once, leads to a gradual elimination of errors and so to trial-and-error learning. A problem well within the grasp of the organism may be solved immediately. There need therefore be no sharp rift between these two interpretations since each is reducible to the other if the difficulty of the problems involved is considered. Learning of the sudden insight variety is equivalent to trial-and-error learning that occurs upon a single presentation of the stimulus situation. The final stage of learning is reached after a single correct insightful response, as

---

[11] Köhler, *op. cit.*, p. 14; H. Helson, Insight in the white rat, *J. Exper. Psychol.*, 1927, 10, 378–397; G. D. Higginson, Visual perception in the white rat, *J. Exper. Psychol.*, 1926, 9, 337–347.

demonstrated by the fact that subsequent presentations of the problem situation lead at once to correct solutions. This means that the problem must have been simple enough for the organism to retain completely the methods used in its solution, after having solved it but a single time. When such a retention is not possible because the difficulty of the problem prevents the immediate formation of a Gestalt, then—motivation being maintained for successive presentations of S—some of the errors originally made in Stage 1 are bound to be repeated before the learning is complete. If a difficult task, which would ordinarily require a trial-and-error solution, can be decreased in difficulty, learning by sudden insight may result. The apparent difference between the two varieties of learning arises, therefore, simply from the great difference in the difficulty of the learning situations habitually employed in each case. To obtain evidence of trial-and-error learning, use difficult learning problems. To get sudden insights in the same organism, use relatively simple problems. Where insight is clearly a special case of positive transfer, which is undoubtedly true in some instances, then a second difficult problem, presented after a former similar one has been mastered by trial-and-error, may demonstrate insight. The second problem in such instances has lost its difficulty because of the previous learning the subject is able to bring to bear upon its solution.

Cases of learning, like those diagrammed in Figures 1 and 2, are best conceived as extreme examples. Between them we would suppose there may exist almost any combination or degree of the two. Instances in which sudden drops occur in otherwise orthodox learning curves are a case in point, as are, perhaps, some situations in which the appearance of the insight is not immediate but develops by more easy stages. We would suppose, therefore, a sort of scale or continuum, of which "pure" trial-and-error learning and Gestalt sudden insights are the poles. The intermediate degrees would be determined in the main by the relative difficulty of the problems employed.

Conditioning

Let us now turn to conditioning and its possible relationship to the other types.[12] It will be remembered that the writer has already suggested that conditioning and trial-and-error learning can, with some justification, be called "low" interpretations of learning in the sense that they are generally supposed not to involve as many of the higher mental or psychic processes as are assumed in symbolic and insightful learning. Learning of the condi-

[12] For a detailed analysis of this questions in its experimental aspects, see E. R. Hilgard, The relationship between the conditioned response and conventional learning experiments, *Psychol. Bull.,* 1937, **34,** 61–102.

tioned response variety, although customarily diagramed without reference to its temporal aspects, is shown in Figure 3, divided into three progressive steps. Step 1 (Figure 3) may serve, as in Figures 1 and 2, to represent the situation before learning has taken place. Step 3 shows the situation after the learning is complete, and Step 2 gives a picture of the intermediate state.

It should be noted that the *S*'s in this diagram do not carry quite the same significance as the *S*'s in Figure 1 or Figure 2. In Figure 3, *S*1 and *S*2 stand for specific features of the general situation commonly analyzed or conceived as elementary or unitary stimuli. In Figures 1 and 2, on the other

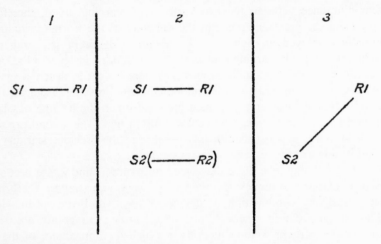

Figure 3. Showing conditioned-response learning, after Guthrie, diagramed in three stages so as to show the progress of the learning (see text).

hand, *S* was used to represent the whole stimulus situation, or field, which included many elementary stimuli.

Stage 1 (Figure 3) shows that a given functional unity must exist between a stimulus and a response before conditioning can begin. In traditional Pavlovian terms, *S*1 is the unconditioned stimulus and *R* is its response. The learning process itself is characterized by the introduction of *S*2 which may or may not possess a readily observable *R* itself. Step 2 in the diagram then represents the many repetitions of *S*1, *S*2, and *R*1 which are necessary for the completion of the conditioning process. *S*2 has been drawn immediately below *S*1 to suggest a simultaneous temporal order of *S*'s and *R*'s. The arrangement pictured in Step 2 may, therefore, be taken to follow the position of Guthrie who has held that all conditioning is simultaneous conditioning, if the true stimuli and responses can be adequately discovered.[13] In Step 3, which represents the situation after the learning has been completed, $S2$ calls out $R1$ with $S1$ no longer present.

Figure 3 as a whole covers the elementary types of conditioned reflexes studied by Pavlov and his followers. It needs no insightful or symbolic assumptions but serves as a simple description of this mechanical type of low or physiological learning.

Sign Learning

Probably the most direct connection that can be traced between elementary conditioned-response processes of this sort and more psychic or higher varieties of learning lies in the direction of Tolman's sign-Gestalt theory. According to Tolman, learning is essentially a matter of discovering and retaining "what leads to what." [14] It is a matter of reacting to certain stimuli, which always come before other stimuli, as signs or signals that the other or secondary stimuli are about to arrive. Learning reduces itself to anticipation of a sort and the conditioned response itself is explained by Tolman as definitely anticipatory. The learner forms new Gestalts or perceptual patterns by bringing the new stimulus into relationship with the old when it was not originally a part of the same Gestalt. Tolman's view has the advantage of explaining those cases of conditioning in which it has been definitely established that the conditioned response is not the same as the unconditioned one.[15] It also applies nicely to instances in which the conditioned stimulus invariably precedes the unconditioned stimulus ("forward" conditioning).

A diagram of sign-Gestalt learning, modified from Tolman so as to follow

---

[13] E. R. Guthrie, *The Psychology of Learning*, New York: Harpers, 1935. It is Guthrie's view that the response conditioned must occur simultaneously with the stimulus which later calls it out. The diagram in Step 2, Figure 3 does not fully picture this arrangement unless (1) the R's are imagined to extend back to the S's or (2) unless the lines between the S's and the R's are taken to represent the passing of no more time than the reaction time of the organism.

[14] E. C. Tolman, *Purposive Behavior in Animals and Men*, New York: Century, 1932; Theories of learning, in *Comparative Psychology*, edited by F. A. Moss, New York: Prentice Hall, 1934, pp. 367–408.

[15] *Cf., e.g.*, C. R. Garvey, A study of conditioned respiratory changes, *J. Exper. Psychol.*, 1933, **16**, 471–503; E. R. Hilgard, and D. G. Marquis, Acquisition, extinction, and retention of conditioned lid responses to light in dogs, *J. Comp. Psychol.*, 1935, **19**, 29–58; E. R. Hilgard, and A. A. Campbell, The course of acquisition and retention of conditioned eyelid responses in man, *J. Exper. Psychol.*, 1936, **19**, 227–247; H. D. Scott, Hypnosis and the conditioned reflex, *J. Genet. Psychol.*, 1930, **4**, 113–130; L. H. Warner, An experimental search for the 'conditioned response,' *J. Genet. Psychol.*, 1932, **41**, 91–115; G. R. Wendt, An analytic study of the conditioned knee-jerk, *Arch. Psychol.*, 1930, No. 123, p. 97; E. G. Wever, The upper limit of hearing in the cat, *J. Comp. Psychol.*, 1930, **10**, 221–234.

the three-step arrangement employed in this paper, is given in Figure 4.[16]
Here, as in Figure 3, $S1$—$R1$ represents the situation which exists before
any learning takes place. $S2$ is the new (conditioned) stimulus which may
or may not have a clear-cut response of its own. It is introduced during the
learning, *so that it invariably occurs prior to* $S1$.[17] When the learning is
complete (Step 3, Figure 4), $S2$ calls out *a new response, RN,* which was
formerly not associated either with $S2$ or with $S1$. $S2$ has then become a
sign or signal to $S1$. In responding to $S2$ with RN the organism may be said
to demonstrate that "it knows" $S1$ is coming. It makes, in other words, an

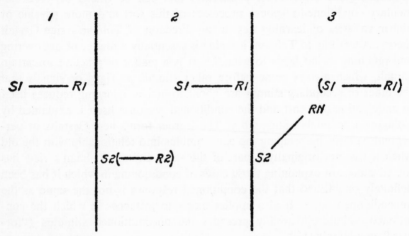

Figure 4. Sign learning, diagramed in three steps comparable to those in Figure 3.

anticipatory or preparatory reaction by means of which it gets ready for $S1$.
RN will thus appear after $S2$, even though $S1$—$R1$ is not included in the
situation. This follows from the fact that $S2$—RN always precedes $S1$—$R1$.
The nonexperimental example given below, chosen from among those suggested by Tolman, will show the operation of this sequence in terms of Figure 4.

. . . My dog has come to react to the noise of my returning automobile [$S2$]
before she can see the machine [$S1$] and I find her waiting for me on the side-
walk [RN] when I and the car finally loom into sight. She has learned to respond to the sound [$S2$] as a "sign" for the car and me in it [$S1$]. Further the
response she has thus attached to the sign is not the same as the response she

[16] E. C. Tolman, Theories of learning, in *Comparative Psychology*, edited by F. A.
Moss, New York: Prentice-Hall, 1934, pp. 367–408.
[17] S2 and RN have been drawn to the left of S1 to indicate that they occur before
S1.

makes to the car when I finally arrive [R1]. The response [RN] to the sign [S2] is a preparatory coming forward, that to the actual car with me in it, one of scrabbling up and wet kisses [R1].[18]

The close similarity between the formation of a new Gestalt of this character (*i.e.,* between the dog's getting insight into the meaning of the sound of the automobile) and the lower or more elementary conditioned reflex type of learning should now appear from a comparison of Figures 3 and 4. If Figure 3 represents conditioning on a physiological level, then Figure 4 may be said to represent conditioning on a psychological level. The principal objective differences between the two processes appear to be (1) the setting of S2 (—R2) invariably in advance of S1—R1, and (2) the introduction of a new response, RN, in place of the formation of a connection between S2 and R1.

It would be our view that "low" conditioning, as diagramed in Figure 3, is one extreme of this pattern of learning and that sign-learning, as diagramed in Figure 4, is a higher aspect of the same general process. In the language of Guthrie,[19] who has pointed to the common ground between conditioning and association by contiguity, we may say that there are here two varieties of association—one elementary and the other more complex. Or, to use Gestalt terminology, we have in each case a new configuration of elements (stimuli and responses) not originally Gestalted. The present analysis assumes a sort of continuum from simple to complex instances of conditioned learning. Between the two examples discussed we would suppose there lies a range of intermediate possibilities. The relationship between conditioning and sign learning is similar then, as we conceive it, to that already outlined between trial-and-error and insightful learning.

A Single Principle of Learning

The step which would logically follow in a simplification of this sort would now be to bring together the two groups of theories which have been pointed out. There are several ways in which they could be united under the heading of a single general principle. Any of the ways would be consistent with the present argument.

1. We could, for example, follow the methods of Frank,[20] Hull,[21] Smith

[18] E. C. Tolman, Theories of learning, in *Comparative Psychology,* edited by F. A. Moss, New York: Prentice-Hall, 1934, pp. 368–369.

[19] E. R. Guthrie, *The Psychology of Learning,* New York: Harpers, 1935, p. 23.

[20] J. K. Frank, Suggestion for a theory of learning, *Psychol. Rev.* 1923, **30,** 145–148.

[21] C. L. Hull, A functional interpretation of the conditioned reflex, *Psychol. Rev.,* 1929, **36,** 498–511; Simple trial and error learning—a study in psychological theory, *Psychol. Rev.,* 1930, **37,** 241–256.

and Guthrie,[22] Wilson [23] and others, and reduce trial-and-error learning, as demonstrated in the maze and problem box, to conditioning. Since conditioning, according to our reasoning, includes sign learning, and since trial and error is but an extreme variety of Gestalt, all would become particular cases of the conditioned response.

2. Or, to start from the Gestalt point of view, we might use the system of Tolman [24] and explain trial-and-error learning as the building up of discriminatory sign-Gestalts.

3. It would also be possible to follow more exactly the deductions of the present paper, and combine these with the fundamental geometrical theorum, "Things equal to the same or equal things are equal to each other." Since it has already been shown that trial-and-error learning is a variety of Gestalt (and vice versa), and that conditioning is but an aspect of sign-Gestalt learning, we could then say that conditioning and trial and error are equivalent, since they are both reducible to a common or equivalent base.

It is doubtful whether much would be gained from such procedures, or whether they would serve to give complete, yet unstrained, interpretations of the facts. There are certain special characteristics of conditioning which appear to us at the present writing to make a separate classification of it, of some convenience. Learning of the conditioning, or association type, is always more simple and more easily broken up into units than trial-and-error learning. There is often no "problem" to "solve" in the customary sense of the word as there is in trial-and-error and other kinds of learning. Again, conditioning and sign-learning, like association, are in a sense *positive processes,* comparable to the process of addition. Something is added, or hooked on, or connected, to something else. Although the additive process can also be seen in trial-and-error learning, it is not so clear or prominent as the subtractive process or the elimination of errors. Conditioning, therefore, might almost be called, "learning by addition," and trial and error, which is a kind of *negative process,* "learning by subtraction."

That such a distinction cannot be carried too far, however, is apparent when it is considered that both of these processes go on in any complicated learning situation. There is not only an elimination of wrong activities, but there is also an introduction of new responses which were not originally called out by the stimuli or objects of the situation. The individual has to

[22] S. Smith, and E. R. Guthrie, *General Psychology in Terms of Behavior,* New York: Appleton, 1921, p. 124f.

[23] W. R. Wilson, Principles of selection in 'trial and error' learning, *Psychol. Rev.,* 1929, **36**, 481–487.

[24] E. C. Tolman, *Purposive Behavior in Animals and Men,* New York: Century, 1932, pp. 339–370.

learn *what not to do* as well as *what to do*. He is frequently learning both at the same time.

It can be said, in fact, of the different theories, that each has taken some part or feature of the learning situation and has emphasized it to the exclusion of other parts. Trial-and-error learning emphasizes the wrong responses which are made at the beginning of a gradual learning process.

SCHEMA SHOWING RELATIONSHIPS BETWEEN FOUR THEORIES OF LEARNING

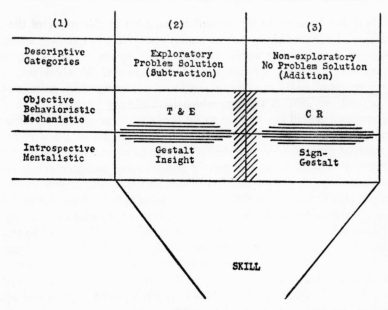

Figure 5. Some similarities and differences between the trial-and-error hypothesis, conditioning, sign learning and gestalt insight are represented in this diagram. See text for meaning of shaded and angular lines.

Conditioning emphasizes stimulus-response units and the principle of association. The Gestaltists make much of the introspective or psychic side of learning, or sometimes of the suddenness of the transition from wrong to right responses. And Tolman has pointed to the temporal sequence of stimuli and responses. He has emphasized the time element in learning.

The relationships between the four theories discussed, together with special characteristics applying to each of them, have been diagramed in Figure 5. The top row in columns 2 and 3 lists a few of the objective features of the learning which stand out, while column 1 gives some psychological and descriptive terms applying to the views indicated. Continua must be imagined to exist in columns 2 and 3 between the upper and lower entries. The vertical line separating these two columns is a hazy one to indicate that the boundary is not hard and fast. It is a boundary which can easily be bridged. Difficult or elaborate problems, in actual practice, may be said to include learning which is describable in terms of any, or of all, of the theories.

Skills

There has been up to the present no mention in this paper of the acquisition of complex skills such as mastery in typing, in speaking a foreign language, or in playing tennis. Is it necessary to invent an entirely new hypothesis to account for this sort of development? We think not. The development of a skill can be explained as the learning which goes on after or beyond the sorts of learning which have already been discussed. The perfection of a skill has nothing to do either with "addition" or "subtraction" in learning. It is not concerned with the beginning of a new response or series of responses, or with the elimination of old responses. Rather is it concerned with the giving of a certain fluency, speed and precision to complete reactions after their nature has already been determined. Improvement in skill is not a matter of finding out what is to be done, but of doing it better and better. Skills may, therefore, be placed under the heading of overlearning. Their single most important principle is the Law of Exercise, upon which their efficiency must ultimately depend. They start from a point where the theories already considered end and they move forward from that point. An attempt has been made to indicate this relationship, in the schema of Figure 5, where skills have been placed beyond and apart from descriptions of the original learning.

Summary

Some of the proponents of different theories of learning have so zealously defended their positions that psychologists who are not committed to one view or another may find the field a complex and confusing jumble. It has been the aim of this paper to assist in clarifying the situation. To this end the trial-and-error hypothesis, insightful learning, conditioning, and sign learning have been separately discussed and analyzed. Each theory has been reduced, for purposes of simplification, to a series of three-stage diagrams. Examination of these diagrams has shown:

1. A close correspondence between trial-and-error learning and learning by insight. A continuum has been proposed between these two extremes.

2. A further correspondence between conditioning, as described by

Guthrie, and sign learning, after Tolman. These also have been viewed as varieties of a common process.

3. It has been pointed out that each particular theory has served to emphasize some special feature of the learning situation to the exclusion of other features.

4. The writer sees no point in trying to reduce all learning to a single general principle, but holds that it may be of some convenience to classify learning in which the elimination or reduction of responses is emphasized (as in trial-and-error learning) separately from learning in which new stimulus—response relationships are emphasized (like conditioning). Both go on, however, in any complex learning situation.

5. In difficult or involved learning, therefore, activities which can be adequately accounted for in terms of any, or of all, of the learning theories take place.

6. It is proposed that the term "skill" be reserved for the development of fluency and precision of response, *after the right reactions have been integrated*. Skill is then a matter of overlearning, which is apart from, and beyond, the learning theories discussed.

19. The Concept of the Stimulus in Psychology [*][1]

JAMES J. GIBSON, *Cornell University*

IT SEEMS to me that there is a weak link in the chain of reasoning by which we explain experience and behavior, namely, our concept of the stimulus. The aim of this paper is to find out what psychologists mean by the term stimulus, with the hope of deciding what they *ought* to mean by it. After a short look at the history of the term, I will try to uncover the sources of confusion in modern usage. In the end, perhaps, the concept will be clarified. If not, certain contradictions will have been brought to light.

The experimental study of the stimulus began in the eighteenth century, so far as I can tell, with an investigation of the curious things that could be done to make a frog's leg twitch. The experimenters discovered what is now called the nerve-muscle preparation. Galvani and later Volta gave their names to electricity as well as to physiology by their experiments. In the early nineteenth century Johannes Müller applied these discoveries to the philosophers' problem of the human senses, the gates of knowledge. The nerves of sense, he pointed out, can be excited by a variety of unnatural agencies such as electrical current. Since the mind is acquainted only with the qualities specific to the sensory nerves, not with the stimuli, how it gets knowledge of the material world became more puzzling than ever. Later in

[*] From James J. Gibson, "The Concept of the Stimulus in Psychology," *The American Psychologist,* 15 (November, 1960), 694–703. Reprinted by permission.

[1] Presidential Address to the Eastern Psychological Association, New York, New York, April 1960.

the century, Sherrington was to emphasize the extent to which receptors are naturally protected against such irrelevant stimuli by the structural specialization of sense organs. But meanwhile it had been discovered that the skin would yield sensations only at certain discrete points. Here was a fresh puzzle. The separate receptor cells of all the sense organs came to be seen under the microscope, and the punctate character of the sensory process seemed to be established.

During all this time, the physical scientists were discovering the laws of energy and triumphantly measuring it in its various forms, electricity, momentum, light, heat, sound, and the results of chemical reaction. It became possible to measure certain variables of energy at sense organs, at least the simple ones like frequency and amount. Thresholds of reportable sensation were established. Fechner, following Weber, conceived the grand scheme of a measurement formula for consciousness, relating its judged intensity to a simple variable of the stimulus. Psychophysics was born.

Whatever could be controlled by an experimenter and applied to an observer could be thought of as a stimulus. In the growing science of human psychology, it became evident that this was the independent variable of an experiment, to be isolated and systematically varied. Much more complex things than physical energies could be presented to the sense organs— words for instance. These were also called stimuli, although the stimulus conditions manipulated, recency, frequency, meaningfulness, were vastly different from the variables of the psychophysical experiment.

In the latter part of the nineteenth century the concept of the reflex arc was applied to the adaptive behavior of animals. It had been thought to explain the strictly mechanical actions of the body ever since Descartes. Reflexes had stimuli. The situations of animals could be systematically altered and the reactions observed. Organisms obviously responded to such stimuli, and the experimenter could apply them more freely than he could venture to do with human beings. To shorten a long story, such experiments came to be merged with human experiments and the outcome was a general stimulus-response psychology. This was a great success, especially in America. But stimuli for animal psychologists were not the same as stimuli for sensory physiologists and stimuli were still different for the students of perception and learning.

Enough has been said to show that in the twentieth century we have inherited a mixed batch of ideas about the stimulus. We constantly use the word but seldom define it. We take it for granted. We have behavior theory in full bloom, and perception theory in ripened complexity, but who ever heard of stimulus theory? As a preliminary effort in this direction, I have made a survey of what modern writers seem to mean by the term. Some writers define it, but not many. My method was to collect quotations from books. I then put them in opposition to one another. The ways of conceiving the stimulus are often in flat contradiction. Occasionally one book can be quoted against itself. The issues interlock, of course, but I have separated them into eight areas of disagreement and will treat them separately. In what follows, I will quote without comment, for the most part, keeping my own opinions to the end.

I. For Freud, the only use of the term stimulus that is discoverable in the *Collected Papers* (1949) is to refer to a motivating force. This, after all, is the dictionary meaning of the word—something that arouses or impels to action. In ordinary speech we refer to the stimulus of hunger or fear, which may compel extreme forms of behavior. Freud does not often use the term, but when he does, a stimulus is something to be satisfied or warded off.

Psychologists and physiologists, however, have generally used the term for the arousing of a sense organ instead of a whole individual. But they do not wholly agree about this. Some accept both meanings. Neal Miller asserts that "any stimulus has some drive value" (Miller and Dollard, 1941, page 59). However, Skinner believes that "a drive is not a stimulus," and that although "the term has the unfortunate connotation of a goal or spur to action," we must not be misled by this popular meaning of the word (1938, p. 375). Here, then, is a first area of disagreement in our way of conceiving the stimulus: *does a stimulus motivate the individual or does it merely trigger a response?*

II. Pavlov said that "a stimulus appears to be connected with a given response as cause with effect" (1927, page 10). This is a forthright assertion. Similarly Watson took as the whole aim of psychology the predicting of the response, given the stimulus, and the specifying of the stimulus, given the response (1924, page 10). But contrast this with the caution of Hilgard and Marquis. "We refer to a stimulus as an instigator [and] no more is intended than that the stimulus is in some sense the occasion for the response" (1940, page 73). Evidently what Pavlov and Watson meant by a stimulus is not what Hilgard and Marquis meant. Nearly all psychologists now follow the second line. It is allowed that a stimulus may cause a reflex, but not an act. Woodworth was one of the first to emphasize that the stimulus does not in itself determine the response; factors in the organism intervene to help determine it. The discussion of intervening variables or mediating processes has by now filled volumes.

The same rule is taken to hold for experience. It is allowed that a stimulus may cause a sensation, but not a perception. M. D. Vernon, for example, states that "the nature of the percept is not . . . determined by the physical qualities of the stimulus, but is largely a function of constructive tendencies in the individual" (1952, page 47). But I have been arguing the opposite for some time, that the percept is in very good correspondence with the physical variables of the stimulus. *Can a stimulus be taken as the sufficient cause of a response, or can it not?* This is a second area of confusion in our concept of the stimulus.

. III. Skinner has recently noted that "we frequently define the stimulus by the very doubtful property of its ability to elicit the response in question, rather than by any independent property of the stimulus itself" (1959, page 355). He suggests no remedy, however, for this doubtful scientific behavior, and he seems to be confessing a sin without pointing the way to salvation. In truth many psychologists do give a circular definition of the stimulus. Skinner himself believed in his first book that "neither term [stimulus or response] can be defined as to its essential properties without the other" (1938, page 9). Neal Miller has said "a response is any activity by or within the individual which can become functionally connected with an antecedent event through learning; a stimulus is any event to which a response can become so connected" (Miller and Dollard, 1941, page 59). Miller, in fact, has argued that this circular definition of the stimulus is not only necessary but is theoretically desirable (Koch, 1959, page 239). He seems to have abandoned completely the specifying of a stimulus by variables of physical energy. But listen to Estes. "By *stimulus,* I refer to environmental conditions, describable in physical terms without reference to the behavior of an organism" (Koch, 1959, page 455), and Hayek says, "the distinction between different stimuli must be independent of the different effects they have on the organism" (1952, page 9).

Here is a disagreement. The student of psychophysics will argue that we must define our stimulus by certain operations of physical science, not by the judgments of our subject. Otherwise how are we ever to discover what stimuli can be discriminated and what cannot? When the stimulus is difficult to specify in objective physical terms, however, investigators tend to avoid the difficulty and describe it as that which is responded to, or that which is perceived. A few go further and, by arguing that an experimenter cannot define the stimulus anyway except in terms of *his* perception, reach a philosophical position of subjectivism. There is an ancient puzzle to which students of philosophy are treated—whether there exists any sound when a tree crashes in the forest with no living being there to hear it. It is a question of how to conceive the auditory stimulus. It seems to remain a puzzle for a good many psychologists.

I think the central question is the following. Is a stimulus that which *does* activate a sense organ or that which *can* activate a sense organ? Some writers imply that a stimulus not currently exciting receptors is not a stimulus at all. Others imply that a stimulus need not excite receptors to be called such. They allow of *potential* stimuli. Witness Guthrie's assertion that stimuli are "potential occasions" for the initiation of sensory activity, and that "the physical stimuli, though present, may not be effective" (Koch, 1959, page 178). The former conception allows physical energy to be called a stimulus only when some response can be observed; the latter allows of the possibility that stimulus energy may be present without necessarily being responded to. The latter seems the better concept. With the former meaning, one could never speak of a subthreshold stimulus, and this is a useful term. An effective stimulus on one occasion may be ineffective on another. And there are various response criteria by which a threshold can be measured.

The distinction between effective and potential stimuli is made by a few theorists, but its implications have not been traced, and the idea remains undeveloped. The concept of a permanent environment of *objects* is widely accepted, but not the concept of a permanent environment of *potential stimuli.*

The third area of disagreement is this: *must a stimulus be defined independently of the response it produces—in physical terms rather than terms of behavior or sensory process?*

IV. For Pavlov a stimulus could be anything in the terrestrial world. Any event he could think of to use in an experiment he would call a stimulus, and he employed tones, bells, the sound of bubbling water, lights, rotating objects, pictures on a screen, acid in the mouth, food, a scratch on the back, or electric shock. This common sense usage of the term persists among a good many behaviorists. Spence has said that the term stimulus means to him, "the physical or world situation, with its different aspects or features" (1956, page 39). For Neal Miller anything that is discriminable is a stimulus or, as he calls it, a cue, these terms having the same meaning. For Skinner, a stimulus is simply "a part, or modification of a part, of the environment" (1938, page 235). To be sure, he says, it must "refer to a class of events the members of which possess some property in common" (page 34). Because stimuli have this "generic nature," the practice of calling a bell an auditory stimulus and a book a visual stimulus is, as he puts it, "frequently successful" (page 235). All these writers persist in believing that somehow the things of the environment can *stimulate* us, and they refuse to be worried by the paradox that only receptors at the skin of an individual can actually be stimulated.

This definition of the stimulus is considered naive by perception psychologists. Stimuli are energies, not objects. In Troland's words, "the stimulus may be defined as the specific physical force, energy, or agency which brings about the stimulation of the given receptor system" (1930, page 9). This conception has the authority of a century's research on the senses. In 1834, Johannes Müller argued that a stimulus was whatever excited one of the "nerves of sense." To the modern neurophysiologist, a stimulus is energy that depolarizes a living cell—especially, but not exclusively, a nerve cell. For Jennings in 1906, studying the ameba, a stimulus was a type of change in the immediate environment that produced a change in behavior (1906, page 19) and there existed precisely five types: chemical, mechanical, thermal, photic, or electrical. Woodworth says that "a stimulus is any form of energy acting upon a sense organ and arousing some activity of the organism" (1929, page 223). Koffka wishes to call stimuli "the causes of the excitations of our sense organs" (1935, page 79), but he, more than any other theorist, faced up to the contradictory meanings of the term and proposed a formal distinction between the "proximal" stimulus and the "distal" or "distant" stimulus. He made us consider the paradox that although perception and behavior seem to be determined by the distal object, they can in fact only be aroused by the proximal stimulus.

Not all psychologists are willing to grapple with this paradox and, in truth, it is baffling. If the proximal stimulus for a given object is altered with every change of the observer's position in space, if it is different on different occasions, we are faced with an absurdity. We must suppose that a countless family of different stimuli can all arouse the same percept. Most behaviorists speak of the stimulus-object as if, by hyphenating two words with different meanings, the absurdity were removed. As men of common sense they see the need of reducing to one the countless number of stimuli that can arouse a single percept, and in this surely they have a point. But perceptionists, being unable to take this easy way out, struggle to construct theories of how different stimuli might arouse the same percept, the theories of perceptual constancy. So far, no theory has been agreed on. Is it possible that common sense is right without knowing it, and that every family of proximal stimuli arising from one object *is,* in a sense, one stimulus?

Here is a fourth disagreement: *do stimuli exist in the environment or only at receptors?* There is a suggestion that both usages of the term are somehow correct, but it has not been explained.

V. Osgood says that "a stimulus may be defined as that form of physical energy that activates a receptor" (1953, page 12). But he does not tell us whether he means by a receptor a single cell or a mosaic of receptor cells, that is, a sense organ. Others besides Osgood are undecided about this question, or have not thought about it. Hull knew what he thought. For him, the retinal image was a pattern of stimuli (1943, page 37) and a single light ray was a stimulus (page 33). "A stimulus element is a stimulus energy which activates a single receptor-organ" (page 349). This is straightforward. Woodworth says that "of course the light entering the eye and striking many rods and cones is a collection of stimuli rather than a single stimulus," but in the next paragraph he suggests that "the sudden cessation of a light" is a stimulus (1929, page 28). Köhler was fairly explicit on the question, saying that an organism responds to "an objective constellation of millions of stimuli" (1929, page 179) and Koffka also assumed that stimuli on the retina or the skin were local events (1935). But Nissen, on the other hand, asserts that "a stimulus involves a pattern of stimulation, spatial or temporal" (Stevens, 1951, page 374). Many other writers define stimuli as the occasions for activation of a sense organ, not of a receptor cell, and speak as if a pattern were a stimulus. There is a vast difference between a pattern of stimuli and a stimulus pattern, but we have not sufficiently thought about it. Is a "pattern" a single stimulus or is it a number of separate stimuli?

The notion that a stimulus is what excites a cell, and is therefore *punctate,* seems to many theorists the only rigorous definition. On this account Hull had to introduce the postulate of afferent neural interaction to explain molar behavior as distinguished from molecular responses. The gestalt psychologists had to develop the theory of sensory organization in order to explain perception. But Lashley once said that—

the stimulus to any reaction above the level of a spinal reflex involves not the excitation of certain definite sensory cells but the excitation of *any* cells of a system in certain ratios, and the response may be given to the ratio even though the particular cells involved have not previously been excited in the same way (Murchison, 1934, page 476).

This passage suggests the idea that higher levels of reaction require us to define higher orders of stimulation. Lashley seems to be saying that a ratio may be itself a stimulus, not just a relation between two stimuli. But note that the gestalt theorists, by conceiving all stimuli as local events, did not come to think in this way.

A controversy has long been going on over the question of how an individual could respond to a relation. It began with Köhler's evidence that a chick will select the brighter of two gray papers instead of the absolute brightness of a particular paper. Köhler thought it demonstrated a relational process in the brain; Spence has gone to great lengths to show that it could be explained in terms of absolute responses to each piece of paper, subject to the so-called principle of stimulus generalization. But the simplest explanation would be that the effective stimulus in the experiment was the direction of the difference in brightness in the field of view. In line with this solution to the problem, students of vision conceive that a margin is a visual stimulus, perhaps *the* visual stimulus, and a margin in the array of light to an eye is strictly a ratio, that is, a relation between measured intensities.

Here is a fifth source of confusion: *when is a pattern or relation to be considered a single stimulus and when a number of separate stimuli?*

VI. The notion that a stimulus can only be something punctate is related to the notion that a stimulus can only be something *momentary*. The gestalt psychologists pointed out that a melody is perceived, but they never suggested that a melody was a stimulus. The notes of the melody were taken to be the stimuli. But what about the transitions between notes, or the "transients" of acoustical engineering? Are they stimuli? The investigators of speech sounds seem to think so, but the auditory literature of sensation is vague on this question. And if a short transition is a stimulus, why not a long transition or temporal pattern?

In vision, experimenters have not been able to make up their minds as to whether an optical motion was a stimulus or a series of stimuli. The retina and also the skin are very sensitive to motion. It ought to be simple, but the facts of the stroboscope and the phi-phenomenon have been interpreted to imply that it is complex. Motion is taken to be change of location, as it is in classical physics, and it is then reasoned that the impression of location must be fundamental to any perception of a change of location.

On the other hand the generalization is frequently met with that a stimulus is *always* a change. This is very confusing, in fact it is one confusion piled on another. I think that writers who make this assertion have in mind the experiments showing that an unchanging stimulus soon ceases to be effective for perception. They are thinking of sensory adaptation. What changes in that case is not the stimulus but the process of excitation. For the retina, the skin, and the olfactory organ, sensory adaptation does occur. For example, the steady application of an image to a human retina, by the method of artificially stabilizing the image, eventuates in a wholly ineffective stimulus. But note that the steady application of focusable light to a human eye does not. This stimulus never becomes wholly ineffective, even with the best voluntary fixation, because of slight movements of the eye itself. This means that retinal stimulation is by no means the same thing as optical stimulation. They are different stages in the chain of events that leads to vision. A "change in stimulation" means something quite different when it is produced by some adjustment of the sense organ itself than when it is produced by an external event.

Is optical motion, then, meaning a change in the pattern of focusable light to the eye, to be considered a stimulus? Experiments based on this assumption are beginning to appear. In the recent Cornell research with optical transformation (Gibson and Gibson, 1957) we not only think of this as a stimulus, we have come to think of nonchange of pattern as simply a special case. Stability, after all, is only definable as absence of motion. Similarly, a form is definable as a nontransformation. In this conception, sequence is a dimension of stimulation whether or not change occurs.

The great virtue of this conception of sequence is that it suggests a simple solution to the puzzle of perceptual constancy. Two types of nonchange are distinguishable, first, nonmotion of a pattern and, second, invariance of a pattern during motion. The invariant contained in a family of the perspectives arising from a single object is a single stimulus. Hence there is only one stimulus for a single object, and the common sense opinion is right after all.

The sixth conceptual issue is this: *when does a sequence constitute a single and when a number of separate stimuli; also, can a single enduring stimulus exist throughout a changing sequence?*

VII. Users of the Rorschach test assume that a stimulus field can be either structured or, as they put it, *unstructured.* I could find no explicit definition of unstructured stimulation in the literature but only examples of the material to which the term is applied—inkblots and other items used in the so-called projective tests. The idea of structured stimulation comes from gestalt theory but only from a vague, tentative, and undeveloped hypothesis of gestalt theory—the external forces of organization as distinguished from the internal forces of organization. Koffka, for example, was so preoccupied with the ways in which the individual *structured* his stimulus field that he scarcely considered the ways in which it might already *have* structure (1935). In fact, he wrote sometimes as if it had none, as if all structure had to be imposed on it, because the stimuli themselves were meaningless points.

This uncertainty about the existence of structure in the stimulus for perceived form still persists. But since Koffka's time, and partly inspired by him, some experimenters are beginning simply to assume it, and to apply mathematics to the structure of a stimulus. They would not agree that an inkblot is in any sense an unstructured stimulus. A picture has one structure, an inkblot has another, but it does not lack structure. That can be said only of a film-color or the cloudless blue sky. The structure of an array may have ambiguous or equivocal components, as Koffka showed, but that is not the same thing. The capacity of light to carry structure to an eye may be impoverished or reduced experimentally but it remains. The structure of light may not specify anything familiar to the subject, or to any observer, but it is a geometrical fact. The subject may be unable to register the structure because it is nonsense to him, or he overlooks it, or he was not told to look for it, or his eyes are defective, or he is too young, or for a dozen other reasons, but it is still in the light. So, at least, some experimenters would argue.

What can be meant by an unstructured stimulus field is thus a matter of disagreement. The seventh question is: *how do we specify the structure of a stimulus?*

VIII. The conception of stimuli as physical energies seems to imply that, in themselves, they have no significance or meaning. Especially if they are considered to be only spots of energy at brief moments of time it is clear that they specify little or nothing about the environment. Light, heat, mechanical, acoustical, chemical, and electrical energy are far from being objects, places, events, people, words, and symbols, but nevertheless they are the only stimuli that can affect receptors. This theory of the meaningless stimulus has been an accepted doctrine for a long, long time in the study of the senses. It leads to the notion of the sense datum—the bare sensation, or raw sensory impression, and thence to the persistent problem of how animals and men can be supposed to perceive objects, places, events, and one another.

Students of behavior, however, without questioning the doctrine of the empty stimulus, often act as if they did not believe it. Beach speaks for comparative psychologists when he says, in describing how birds feed their offspring, "young birds exhibit a gaping response which *stimulates* the parent to place food in the nestling's mouth" (Stevens, 1951, page 415). He takes it for granted that light rays can specify the event called gaping and refuses to worry about it further. Students of perception do worry about this question, but they are not consistent. On the one hand, they firmly assert that nothing gets into the eye but light of variable wave length and intensity, not objects, or events, or facts of the environment. On the other hand, they often say that light "carries" information about the environment, or that stimuli "provide" information to the perceiver. If this is so, the stimuli must specify something beyond themselves, and they cannot be empty of meaning.

A sort of compromise between the informative stimulus and the empty stimulus is provided by the use of the term *cue*. According to Woodworth, "a cue, as used in psychology, is a stimulus which serves as a sign or signal of something else, the connection having previously been learned" (1958, page 60). Stimuli are conceived by analogy with messages, or communication in code. Brunswik thought of stimuli as *indicators* of environmental facts, by analogy with pointer readings, emphasizing, however, that they had only a probable connection with the fact in question (1956). Boring has suggested that stimuli may be taken as *clues,* and this term points to Helmholtz's theory of unconscious rational inference from the sense data (Harper and Boring, 1948).

Merely to call the stimulus a cue, sign, signal, message, indicator, or clue does not tell us what we need to know. The question is to what extent does the stimulus specify its source, and how does it do so? Is it possible that the use of these verbal metaphors only prevents us from facing the problem? Or consider the use by modern information theorists of a neutral term like *input.* When they compare the organism to a communication system or to a black box, the internal working of which has to be discovered, are they avoiding the obligation to consider the environment of an organism and the relation of stimuli to the environment?

The problem of the connection between stimuli and their natural sources has not been taken seriously by psychologists. Stimuli have not even been classified from this point of view, but only with respect to the sense organs and the types of energy which carry stimuli. It is a problem of ecology, as Brunswik realized when he wrote about the "ecological validity" of cues (1956). I think the problem has been obscured, and our recognition of it delayed, by our failure to separate it into parts. The connection between natural stimuli and their sources is not the same as the connection between *social* stimuli and their sources, for example, the connection between words and their referents. This latter problem, surely, is distinct. Semantics is one thing, ecology is another; and a science of environmental stimuli may not prove to be as difficult as a science of symbols, once we put our minds to it.

I have maintained that optical stimuli, for example, gradients of texture in the light to an eye, specify environmental objects by the relation of *projection.* To me this is not at all the same as the relation by which words specify objects, which I would call one of *coding.* But however this may be, we face another unanswered question, the eighth: *do stimuli carry information about their sources in the world, and how do they specify them?*

Some Positive Hypotheses

Can anything useful be salvaged from these various contradictory usages and definitions? No one could be blamed for being pessimistic about it. S. S. Stevens, who has thought hard and long about stimuli, concluded that it is futile even to attempt a general definition of the stimulus in psychology. Psychology as a whole, he says, can be equated with the problem of defining the stimulus, that is, giving a complete definition of the stimulus for a given response. To be able to do so would require that we specify "all the transformations of the environment, both external and internal, that leave the response invariant." And "for no response have we yet given a complete definition of the stimulus" in this sense (Stevens, 1951, pages 31f.). If I understand him, what Stevens chiefly had in mind is the puzzle of constancy. He was saying that we do not know how to specify, in the chaos of literal proximal-energy stimulation, the actual cause of a given response. This is a discouraging truth.

But, unlike Stevens, I have hopes, and even some positive hypotheses to suggest. Once the contradictory assumptions about stimulation are made explicit, we can try to resolve them. For one thing we might search for an invariant component in the bewildering variety of functionally equivalent stimuli. Perhaps there is an invariant stimulus for the invariant response, after all. Many sorts of higher order variables of energy may exist, only awaiting mathematical description. They will have to be described in appropriate terms, of course, not as simple functions of frequency and amount. We must not confuse a stimulus with the elements used for its analysis. We must learn to conceive an array not as a mosaic of stimuli but as a hierarchy of forms within forms, and a flux not as a chain of stimuli but as a hierarchy of sequences within longer sequences.

Molar stimuli. Ever since Tolman, behavior theorists have been agreeing that psychology is concerned with molar responses, not molecular ones. Accordingly we try to observe and measure what an organism is doing, not how all its muscles are contracting. With this kind of observation on the response side there should be a corresponding kind of observation on the stimulus side. We should try to discover what an organism is responding *to,* not what excites all the little receptors. Of course all the muscles may be contracting and all the receptors may be excited, but observation at that level is the job of the physiologists.

The same recommendation can be made for the study of perception. The gestalt theorists have demonstrated the fact of molar experience, but they did not look for molar stimuli. These may very well exist outside the laboratory and, with ingenuity, can perhaps be isolated in the laboratory. If so, we shall have a new and powerful kind of psychophysics.

This conception of molar stimuli is not wholly new. Forty-five years ago, E. B. Holt was convinced that cognition, along with behavior, was a constant function of stimulation. In this he agreed with Pavlov and Watson. But Holt emphasized that the stimulus *of which* cognitive behavior was a function was more abstract and more comprehensive than the stimulus of classical psychophysics. As one passes from reflexes to behavior, the effective stimulus "recedes," as Holt put it (1915, *passim*). By the *recession* of the stimulus he meant that it seems to be located far out in the environment rather than close by in the receptors. And he also meant that as cognition develops, the stimulus of which it is a function recedes more and more. Following this suggestion, one might conclude that a change in response implies a change in the stimulus to which the response is made. Learning would then involve not only an alteration of behavior but also an alteration in the effective stimulus. Presumably its molar character has gone up a stage in the hierarchy.

   Potential stimuli. Evidently the hypothesis of potential stimulation, accepted casually by some theorists, has quite radical but unrecognized implications. We have long acknowledged the almost unlimited possibilities for new responses in learning theory; why not equally vast possibilities of new stimuli? The environment, so considered, would consist of a sort of reservoir of possible stimuli for both perception and action. Light, heat, sound, odor, gravity, and potential contacts with objects surround the individual. But this sea of energy has variables of pattern and sequence which can be registered by sense organs. They can be explored, either at one station-point or by moving around in the environment. The fields of radiating sound and odor, together with the flux of light rays reflected from surfaces, make it possible to respond to things at a distance. The changes of pattern in time serve as controlling stimuli for locomotion and manipulation. The variables and covariables and invariables of this stimulus environment are inexhaustible.

   Surprisingly little has been written about potential stimuli. The sensory physiologists, of course, have read their physics and chemistry. But physical science portrays a sterile world. The variables of physics make uninteresting stimuli. Why is this true? I think it is because psychologists take for stimuli only the variables of physics as they stand in the textbooks. We have simply picked the wrong variables. It is our own fault. After all, physicists are not primarily concerned with stimuli. They have enough to do to study physical energies without worrying about stimulus energies. I think that we will have to develop the needed discipline on a do-it-yourself principle. It might be called ecological physics, with branches in optics, acoustics, dynamics, and biochemistry. We cannot wait for the physical scientists to describe and classify potential stimuli. The variables would seem to them inelegant, the mathematics would have to be improvised, and the job is not to their taste. But it is necessary. And if successful, it will provide a basis for a stimulus-response psychology, which otherwise seems to be sinking in a swamp of intervening variables.

   Consider, for example, the physics (that is to say the acoustics) of speech sounds. As recently as 1951, in the *Handbook of Experimental Psychology* (Stevens, page 869), the fact that a word is perceptually the same when whispered as it is when shouted was taken to prove that the physical characteristics of sound waves, frequency, intensity, and so on, cannot tell us about speech. Speech perception would require a psychological theory, not physical, measurement. But the invention of the sound spectrograph seems to have shown that certain higher order variables of acoustic energy are the critical constituents of speech and the stimuli for hearing it. These newly discovered invariant patterns of sound are completely physical, even if they had not previously been studied in physics. What was needed to understand the psychophysics of hearing words was not more psychology but more physics.

For another example consider the optics of an array of light. The physical variables applying to the point source and the image point do not explain the seeing of a surface. But my own work shows that the variables of an optical *texture* do account for the seeing of a surface, and that by manipulating textures an experimenter can produce synthetic perceptions of objects (Gibson, Purdy, and Lawrence, 1955). Gradients, patterns, and other invariants are not part of existing geometrical optics, but they are physical facts. What was needed for a psychophysics of visual perception was not more theorizing about cues but more attention to geometrical optics.

Effective stimuli. An effective stimulus can now be defined. It is one which arouses receptor activity, or recorded neural impulses, or sense organ adjustments, or overt responses, or verbal judgments—whichever criterion one chooses. Note that the idea of fixed innate thresholds of sensation is rejected. It always was a myth, for every psychophysical experimenter knows that the threshold obtained depends on the method used and the response criterion chosen.

In short, whether or not a potential stimulus becomes effective depends on the individual. It depends on the species to which he belongs, on the anatomy of the sense organs, the stage of maturation, the capacities for sense organ adjustment, the habits of attention, the activity in progress, and the possibilities of educating the attention of the individual. Such facts make up the field of perceptual development and perceptual learning. At the lower levels they are called facts of sensory physiology; at the higher levels, facts of attention or exploration, but they are all one problem. Animals seem to be driven to make potential stimuli effective. They use their receptor equipment, probably, in as great a variety of ways as they use their motor equipment. From this point of view, it seems to me, the senses begin to make sense.

Stages of specificity. Johannes Müller began the study of the way in which the modes of experience are specific to the excitations of nerve fibers. Sherrington and others showed how the excitations of fibers were generally specific to the patterns of the stimulus. Ecological physics will tell us the extent to which the proximal stimuli are specific to their sources in the world. If experience is specific to excitation, and excitation to stimulation, and stimulation to the external environment, then experience will be specific to the environment, within the limits of this chain of specificities. The first two stages have long been under investigation. The last is ripe for study. There has been a controversy over whether or not visual stimuli can specify their objects (for example, Cantril, 1950), but it can be settled, for the facts are discoverable, and arguments should await evidence.

The informative capacity of molar stimuli. If the structure and sequence of stimulus energy can be analyzed, potential stimuli can be described and arranged in a hierarchy. There will be subordinate stimuli and superordinate stimuli, of lower order and higher order. So conceived it is reasonable to assume that stimuli *carry information* about the terrestrial environment. That is, they specify things about objects, places, events, animals, people, and the actions of people. The rules by which they do so are to be determined, but there is at least enough evidence to warrant discarding the opposite assumption under which we have been operating for centuries—that stimuli are necessarily and intrinsically meaningless.

Natural stimuli, pictorial stimuli, and coded stimuli. I have suggested that, instead of continuing to employ the careless analogies of our present loose terminology for stimuli—cues, clues, signals, signs, indicators, messages, inputs, and the like—we make a systematic study of the laws by which stimuli specify their sources. We need to know the laws of stimulus information. Almost certainly these will not be the laws which govern the transmission of information in human systems of communication. The natural world does not literally *communicate* with the sense organs. The potential physical stimuli arising from an event are not to be compared to the physical stimulus arising from the *word* for that event. We cannot hope to understand natural stimuli by analogy with socially coded stimuli, for that would be like putting the cart before the horse. Just this, however, is what we tend to do when we speak of the "signs" for depth perception and the "messages" of the senses. We cannot afford to speak of coded information for the sense organs when we mean stimuli, for some of these are coded and some are not.

A systematic study of the specifying power of stimuli will put the problem of meaning in perception on a new footing. It will take several forms, depending on the kinds of relations discovered. My guess is that there will be at lease three, corresponding to the stimuli from things, from pictures, and from words. It is true that men, besides learning to perceive objects, also learn to apprehend things by way of perceiving pictures and words. These mediated perceptions get mixed with direct perceptions in the adult. But we shall have to disentangle them before we can have a complete theory of human perception.

Conclusion

The foregoing distinctions and assumptions seem promising to me. But I would agree that a stimulus theory cannot be established by merely asserting it. The scientific question is whether all these new kinds of stimuli exist. I suggest that we look for them in the environment and then try to bring them into the laboratory.

It is still true that the stimulus is the prime independent variable of a psychological experiment. I quote from Underwood (1957):

One may vary more than one stimulus condition in a given experiment . . . but to draw a conclusion about the influence of any given variable, that variable must have been systematically manipulated alone somewhere in the design. Nothing in analysis of variance, covariance, Latin squares, Greco-Latin squares, or Greco-Arabic-Latin squares has abrogated this basic principle (page 35).

If Underwood is right, the secret of a good experiment is to discover the relevant stimulus before doing the experiment. The moral of my argument is that a systematic search for relevant stimuli, molar stimuli, potential stimuli, invariant stimuli, specifying stimuli, and informative stimuli will yield experiments with positive results. Perhaps the reservoir of stimuli that I have pictured is full of elegant independent variables, their simplicity obscured by physical complexity, only waiting to be discovered.

References

BRUNSWIK, E. *Perception and the representative design of experiments.* Berkeley: Univer. California Press, 1956.

CANTRIL, H. *The "why" of man's experience.* New York: Macmillan, 1950.

FREUD, S. *Collected papers.* London: Hogarth Press, 1949.

GIBSON, J. J., and GIBSON, E. J. Continuous perspective transformations and the perception of rigid motion. *J. exp. Psychol.,* 1957, **54,** 129–138.

———, PURDY, J., and LAWRENCE, L. A method of controlling stimulation for the study of space perception: The optical tunnel. *J. exp. Psychol.,* 1955, **50,** 1–14.

HARPER, R. S., and BORING, E. G. Cues. *Amer. J. Psychol.,* 1948, **61,** 343–351.

HAYEK, F. A. *The sensory order.* Chicago: Univer. Chicago Press, 1952.

HILGARD, E. R., and MARQUIS, D. G. *Conditioning and learning.* New York: Appleton-Century-Crofts, 1940.

HOLT, E. B. *The Freudian wish.* New York: Holt, 1915.

HULL, C. L. *Principles of behavior.* New York: Appleton-Century-Crofts, 1943.

JENNINGS, H. S. *Behavior of the lower organisms.* New York: Columbia Univer. Press, 1906.

KOCH, S. (Ed.) *Psychology: A study of a science.* Vol. 2. New York: McGraw-Hill, 1959.

KOFFKA, K. *Principles of gestalt psychology.* New York: Harcourt, Brace, 1935.

KÖHLER, W. *Gestalt psychology.* New York: Liveright, 1929.

MILLER, N. E., and DOLLARD, J. *Social learning and imitation.* New Haven: Yale Univer. Press, 1941.

MURCHISON, C. *Handbook of general experimental psychology.* Worcester: Clark Univer. Press, 1934.

OSGOOD, C. E. *Method and theory in experimental psychology.* New York: Oxford Univer. Press, 1953.

PAVLOV, I. P. *Conditioned reflexes.* (Trans. by G. V. Anrep) London: Oxford Univer. Press, 1927.

SKINNER, B. F. *The behavior of organisms.* New York: Appleton-Century-Crofts, 1938.

————. *Cumulative record.* New York: Appleton-Century-Crofts, 1959.

SPENCE, K. W. *Behavior theory and conditioning.* New Haven: Yale Univer. Press, 1956.

STEVENS, S. S. (Ed.) *Handbook of experimental psychology.* New York: Wiley, 1951.

TROLAND, L. T. *Psychophysiology.* Vol. 2. New York: Van Nostrand, 1930.

UNDERWOOD, B. *Psychological research.* New York: Appleton-Century-Crofts, 1957.

VERNON, M. D. *A further study of visual perception.* Cambridge: Cambridge Univer. Press, 1952.

WATSON, J. B. *Psychology from the standpoint of a behaviorist.* Philadelphia: Lippincott, 1924.

WOODWORTH, R. S. *Psychology.* New York: Holt, 1929.

————. *Dynamics of behavior.* New York: Holt, 1958.

20. Perceptual Development: Some Tentative Hypotheses [*][1]

GARDNER MURPHY, *City College, New York*
AND
JULIAN HOCHBERG, *Cornell University*

SUCH AN abundance of new material is coming to hand from experimental psychology and clinical psychology regarding the dynamics of perception that we have—as have others (6, 61)—been interested in attempting an integration utilizing both sources. The primary conception which we have exploited (at its root not so very different from John Dewey's 1896 formulation) is that perception is a form of continuous adjustment to environmental requirements, involving not simply a "sensorium" or seat of cognitive functions, but the whole organism. But from this basic idea, empirical facts and personal idiosyncrasies may lead speculation in any one of many directions; and the one which has especially interested us is the conception of perceptual learning, the conception that the whole organism, in coping with its environment, progressively alters its modes of perception and develops more and more complex ones that serve it better. What we are trying to say will be presented under a series of eighteen hypotheses. It would be good if these hypotheses could be prepared in the form of postulates, but they are neither as clearly thought through nor as coherent as are the usual postulates of science, and on the other hand some of them take the form of propositions regarding which a good deal of empirical material has been assembled. They are presented here, however, neither as substantiated principles nor as original and unfounded theses, but rather as a very tentative system of ideas to be worn "like a loose garment," a makeshift which may be replaced by more appropriate garments when the facts are clearer and their interrelations more evident.

The Hypotheses

(1) *Perception is typically, if not always, both unitary and structured—a* unitas multiplex. The tree-frog's piping or the roll of drums gives tonal

* From Gardner Murphy and Julian Hochberg, "Perceptual Development: Some Tentative Hypotheses," *The Psychological Review*, 58 (September, 1951), 332–49. Reprinted by permission.
[1] The main outlines of this paper were presented by the senior author on June 7, 1949, to the British Psychological Society in London. The present form of the paper represents both authors' views equally, not by compromise but by coalescence.

elements, but elements in temporal order and with a quality which reflects the whole context of the hearing. This first hypothesis involves the recognition of the difference between an assemblage of parts and an organized structure, and also the conception that, in this whole, differentiable aspects can still be observed. There are phenomenal aspects which can be noted separately although they are held in a sort of central coherence: such "parts" (objects, extended forms, etc.) display considerable stability and separable identity insofar as they are of defined extent, and can with relative independence be shuffled and manipulated; thus, a leaf or a robin in the visual field may change its spatial location, size, orientation, and may even be partially occluded by other objects and still maintain its individual identity and form (23). However (as is attested by their constancy in the face of changing stimulation), the existence and the characteristics of such spatially delimited "parts" cannot be ascribed to the action of any comparably separable or spatially delimited aspects of the pattern of stimulus excitation (i.e., perceived size is not a univocal function of visual angle, or retinal shape, or retinal stimulus intensity, etc.). Instead, the characteristics of any phenomenal "part" depend upon relationships within the total *extended* field of impinging stimulation, and upon many diverse and, frequently, mutually reinforcing (8) aspects of the stimulus distribution.[2]

(2) *A primordial aspect of the structure of the percept is differentiation between figure and ground.* Here are emphasized facts such as the following: that the phenomenal content of visual perception consists of shaped regions and relatively unshaped ground, and not of immutable fixed elements such as mosaic points; and that accent, or anchorage, is always well marked. There may be a moment of instability, when wood-thrush song is melted into "forest murmurings," but figure-ground relations are quickly established, and any changes in organization must either occur within the relationships first laid down or pass through only transitory and limited periods of ambiguous dominance. This figure-ground differentiation exhibits greater or lesser degrees of sharpness (62). It is not a single bipolar process, with one figure stably superposed upon one ground. Rather, it is capable of extreme complication (23)—as the listener at *Parsifal* finds it hard to "take it all in"—especially as we leave the static fixation of the laboratory for the free glance and the moving observer of more natural perceptual conditions (56).

---

[2] Thus, the perceived brightness of a particular region depends upon the distribution of stimulation in other regions (58); upon preceding conditions (18) and "memory" (12); upon stimulation in other modalities (52); upon the extremely complex relationships of contours, proprioception, *brightness itself,* etc. which determine perceived space (20), etc.

(3) *Structure depends genetically upon two processes:* (a) *differentiation within a more-or-less homogeneous matrix, and* (b) *integrations of the differentiated phases.* Here reference is made to Herbert Spencer's conception of progress from homogeneous to heterogeneous; likewise, to the evidence of Werner, Piaget, and others that diffuseness (and even a "syncretic" lack of differentiation between self and environment) is characteristic of the child's earliest percepts, and that the development of parts can actually be observed as the child takes hold of, points to, and names specific aspects, while other aspects of the environment remain "blurred" or completely undifferentiated. The elephant may stand out in the child's apprehension of the circus—just as the elephant in the circus poster stands out against the painted jungle behind.

Integration of the differentiated phases comes only as a result of differentiation and only as interaction occurs between the differentiated phases. Thus, in perceiving words as compounds of letters, it is at first necessary to differentiate the letters (which are not, in general, sufficiently "good" forms to insure such discrimination on autochthonous grounds alone), and then to integrate those letters into larger, characteristic word units (the modern teacher may teach words before letters; this means simply postponing, until the child is ready, the analytical learning of letters).

The same processes of perceptual development can be observed in the adult by presenting new "micro-scales" (60), *within* the musical intervals now in use, in which the initial indiscriminability of the "notes" gives way to ready perception of tones which still later integrate to form "micro-melodies" (it is probably in such culturally unstressed areas, as tactile and olfactory perception, that the most fruitful investigations of perceptual development will be made); children presumably acquire our normal musical scales in like fashion.

The assumption of integration as a process which may at least tentatively be considered as separable from differentiation is supported by the inadequate integration of already differentiated parts (evidenced by relatively independent spatial lability) found in children (60); by those cases of visual agnosia (44) in which the parts of complex presentations are perceived but not the interrelations between them; by the drawings of primitives in which ". . . particulars often appear as self-subsistent things which do not necessarily become synthesized into larger entities" (60, page 139).

Progression from (a) homogeneous through (b) differentiated to (c) integrated characterizes, in principle, not only the stages through which the perceptual development of the maturing child passes, but also (with important qualifications later discussed) the course of every perceptual process, regardless of age. (a) We hear Japanese spoken—a melodious blur; (b) we learn a few words and pick them out as we listen; (c) we follow a conversation. The initial response even in the adult is diffuse and undifferentiated. It may be incompletely separated from the "ego," unlocalized in space and time, undifferentiated as to form and modality; and it may contain strong affective and conative as well as cognitive components (**5, 9**). Although the course of such development is, with familiar stimulus configurations, altered by prior differentiations and integrations, and although the durations of these stages are in most cases much shorter in the adult than in the child (perhaps simply because of his greater experience, and quite aside from the matter of neural maturation), the basic nature of the process is assumed to be the same.[3]

It is not implied here that the stimulus situation automatically determines the development of any percept, since there are usually many ways in which boundaries can be cut across any inhomogeneous field, and a large number of ways in which such boundaries can serve as figural contours. Admittedly, in some limiting cases the autochthonous forces of organization restrict perceptual development to configurations of highest stability (23, pages 106–210); with increased stimulus complexity, however, the number of almost equally "good" organizations may increase, i.e., in terms of stimulus considerations alone the situation may become ambiguous and any number of organizations equally possible.

(4) *The phenomenal aspects of the resulting integration are interdependent and exhibit membership character in the whole*. The fear in a child's voice is fully apprehended only in a context of perceiving the child and his situation. Whatever *ultimate* independence may characterize receptor processes or afferent conduction, the percept as we actually know it exhibits interdependence of phenomenal phases, and no phase can be brought into relation with a punctiform stimulation whether of the periphery or of the cortex.[4]

Assuming interrelatedness of the physiological processes underlying the interrelated psychological ones, and recalling that even the most spatially delimited perceptual "part" depends for its existence and characteristics

[3] It is not here implied that tachistoscopic exposure achieves a corresponding fractionation of percept development. Reduced exposure time probably does little more than reduce the efficacy of the stimulus.

[4] It *may* be possible to recognize a relative independence of sensory-neurone processes preceding their convergence at central levels; however, evidence such as that of retinal field effects paralleling the phenomenal field relations (39), etc., makes doubtful isolation even at peripheral levels. Be that as it may, we can here admit of no trace of punctiform sensation in perception. Although the belief probably still exists that it is possible under special attitudes to inspect one's sensations, such attempts generally reveal only some reduction of phenomenal constancy, explicable as a perceptual reorganization which rotates the region considered into a plane frontal-parallel to the observer, thus yielding percepts similar *in some ways* to the physical image on the retina.

upon the total extended field of stimulation, we should expect that the *integration* of delimited "parts" involves likewise the *integration or mutual adjustment* of the extended processes upon which they depend. Thus, the whole field of physiological processes is altered in perceptual integration, and each integrated part is conditioned by—is "keyed" to—the whole field (cf. 23, page 554).

(5) *Exteroceptive, interoceptive, and proprioceptive components enter fully and on an equal footing, but not always with equal weight, into the dynamics of perception.* Those sense organs which make contact with the outer world, those which make contact with the vital organs, and those which make contact with our own muscular adjustments to our environment pool their sensory contributions. Rejecting the view that perception is necessarily heavily loaded with exteroceptive components and that it therefore "mediates reality," it is here urged that it is simply the prejudice of psychologists to emphasize the distance receptors to an extraordinary degree and, therefore, to build our whole theory of perception upon a somewhat warped notion of how the organism works. The spatial world in which we live is *not* constituted by exteroception alone. In the very grossest sense, the proprioceptive pattern provides an important base to perception (anatomically, the sensory and motor functions of the nervous systems are extremely intimate, if not inextricably interrelated [13]). We observe actively, muscularly, with head, eyes, neck, and much else besides. Visual information must be pooled with proprioceptive information as to the position and motion of the receptor surfaces if effective contact with the outside world is to be maintained, and it is the excellent agreement of the percepts based upon these *two* factors with the world as we know it from other grounds which leads to the frequent neglect of the obvious inadequacy of either, and to the acceptance of a largely mythical version of visual exteroception as the basis of perception. The term "mythical" is used because the information yielded by any momentary fixation (devoid of scanning, of motion parallax, and clearly articulated only in the foveal region) bears little resemblance to the "visual" percepts upon which we tend to base not only our normal activities but (in considering the "stimuli" to which an organism responds) our scientific analyses as well. It may be possible, of course, to restrict the term "perception" to that process which occurs during such momentary fixations (although this raises the question as to where such fractionation should cease), but this course makes most of what we normally call perception the province of "judgment," "inference," "memory," etc.

Although perception is based, in part, upon both proprioceptive and exteroceptive "information," *both* components are in large part "silent" in the formation of the visual percept. We are no more directly aware of the continually fleeting and changing transformations and patterns of retinal stimulation than we are of the proprioceptive stimulation occasioned by physiological nystagmus, by the acceleration of gravity, and by the relative positions of eye, head, and trunk. It is only in special cases that the influence of one or the other becomes evident, as in situations where either component is manipulated in an "artificial" manner (i.e., without reciprocal or corresponding change of the other) or in situations in which careful analysis of the psychophysical relationships reveals systematic discrepancies from what would be expected by exteroceptive components alone. Numerous studies dealing with the effects of the distribution of muscular tension on the perception of visual stimuli, and of exteroceptive stimulation on the perception of muscular tension, are summarized by Werner and Wapner (61), who conclude that perception is the product of a fusion of dynamically equivalent sensory and tonic factors—a viewpoint close to the one here accepted.

It is here urged that the same approach can be applied to the interoceptive excitation patterns which yield "information" as to the state of our internal organs and our tissue needs. Unless we postulate an isolation between the exteroceptive and proprioceptiv portions of the nervous system, on the one hand, and the interoceptive tracts, on the other, we must expect some interrelationship. Such isolation appears improbable (22); and even if anatomical isolation were complete, relationship would be expected through proprioceptive changes due to autonomic activity. It is therefore assumed that our "visual" percepts are based upon information delivered by all afferent tracts, whether they be exteroceptive, proprioceptive, or interoceptive in origin. Moreover, any effector excitation pattern aroused by those cortical excitations correlated with a percept will, through consequent muscular and visceral effects, feed back through exteroceptive, proprioceptive, and interoceptive tracts to modify the perceptual organization of the preceding moment. Thus, our conceptions of the external world are in part a product of what goes on inside us, and our conceptions of what goes on inside us are to some degree loaded by our responses to the external world.

Consonant with the view of perceptual development, it is assumed that in the most primitive forms of perception all three sources of sensory information are present in an undifferentiated or partially differentiated state and that subsequent differentiation gradually achieves more and more separation of these factors. We would expect that in primitive stages, perception of environmental objects would prove inextricably fused with the motion, position, and feeling state of the observer. Considerable evidence that the behavior of very young children, of the drug-intoxicated, and of brain-damaged patients can best be understood as the effects of such undifferentiated fusion of sensorial, affective, and motor phenomena has been collected and compellingly presented by Werner (60). The hammer is not perceived as a visual object only; it is directly perceived as heavy, and as hard, and as "a thing you strike with." In children before such areas are well differentiated, in cases of brain injury involving considerable dedifferentiation, and in schizophrenics in whom ego-object polarity is lost, it is difficult or impossible to get reactions in terms of such highly static, differentiated abstractions as objects-in-isolation or shapes-as-such. The adult separation between subject and object may be viewed as being as much a product of differentiation as is the distinction between modalities, which is likewise decreased in children, in patients suffering from drug intoxication, etc., and is not always perfect even in normal adults (52). Even in the sophisticated adult, such fusion of contributions from all sources provides the basis of perception: the initial stages of perception are, like the earliest responses of childhood, a fusion of external and internal information. Undifferentiated affective, conative "presensations" not specifically localized in space or time are not completely differentiated as to modality (5).

After differentiation is completed, the evidence of interaction is more difficult to come by. The very structure of our language is designed to make almost impossible a report on process or context rather than static and abstract identity (24), and in the laboratory an added effort has been made to rule out the "subjective" variable presumably so removed from science. Even in the laboratory, however, one no more normally perceives objects completely outside of any affective and conative setting than one perceives them without spatial characteristics. Such affective characteristics may be attributed to the perceived object, but they probably tend to shift, with development, toward a subjective tension or need attributed to the observer's perceived self, in line with the general developmental tendency toward stabilization of environmental objects and abstraction from their context.[5]

It is suggested, then, that as the proprioceptive components may contribute "silently" to our perception of spatially localized objects, the information from the vital organs may in most cases also be silent, yet contribute heavily, together with proprioception and exteroception, to those relationships (between the perceived self and perceptual objects) which may be subsumed under Tolman's concept of "sign-gestalten" (55), those action-

[5] Similar relationships appear in the cooperation of exteroception and proprioception, *e.g.*, in the way in which motion, if perceived in the object, may not at the same time be ascribed to the self and vice versa (57); in the same fashion, the affective components perceived as characteristics of the object may not at the same time be perceived simply as information concerning subject's needs—a stage of incomplete differentiation very similar to phenomena subsumed under the concept of "projection."

impelling attributes of the perceived world which, in order to achieve "objectivity," we so rigorously train ourselves to ignore. After dinner, not before, is the time to present our case. Much of what we term "affection" would then consist (at least originally) in the contribution of interoception to the exteroceptive-proprioceptive pool; similarly, much of what we term "conation" depends upon the proprioceptive information contributed. There is, however, no warrant for identifying cognition solely with exteroceptive processes, e.g., with visual, tactual, auditory sensations, and excluding organic sensations; and there is no warrant for relating affection solely to interoception, nor for relating conation solely to proprioception.

(6) *It is meaningless to separate sharply the cognitive, affective, and conative aspects of perception.* A process must be cognitive if it is to be called perception, but it may be affective and conative as well. In the normal intact organism retaining interoceptive and proprioceptive neural components, it would not only be difficult to get the exteroceptors to work at the same time that one prevented the interoceptors and proprioceptors from working; it would also be improbable that the resulting process would be anything like perception as we know it. Indeed, the terms "cognition," "affection," and "conation" become matters for phenomenological investigation rather than psychological categories. The fact that a particular phenomenal region within the field carries the "flavor" of objectivity and cognition, and another region carries those of affection or conation, does not necessitate ascribing to them separable sensory origins. We cannot identify cognition with exteroception, affection with interoception, etc., since we have seen that cognition itself *includes* necessary interoceptive and proprioceptive elements, and we cannot talk of perception as *modified* by conative or affective factors, any more than we can talk of perception as modified by kinesthesis. Cognition, affection, and conation are therefore independent only in the sense of a necessary and sometimes rather laborious scientific task of abstraction. Perception as such can (and, moreover, must) be loaded or weighted with any one of these three processes and still remain perception.

This interdependence may perhaps also throw light on the problem of motive or "drive." Interoceptive processes, whether we are aware of them of not, are of course important aspects of many drives, e.g., hunger. Hunger, while physiologically a response to tissue needs, may at the same time be just as sensory as is a patch of color. Proprioceptive processes, such as restlessness, or the impulse to change from one posture to another, likewise have a drive quality. Frequently the drive toward a goal-satisfying object, like apple pie, involves both interoceptive and proprioceptive (goal-seeking) components. Impulses from such interoceptive and proprioceptive sources may fuse freely with exteroceptive sources, and as the apple pie in the kitchen is smelled or seen, we do not merely perceive it; we perceive it hungrily. Hunger does not necessarily becloud the cognitive situation, for the flaky crust, the spicy aroma, are more vividly apprehended than when we are neutral toward such things. From such a homely example of the fusion of exteroceptive, interoceptive, proprioceptive components we may proceed by gradations to Robert Burns's "for to see her was to love her" and to Spinoza's "intellectual love of God."

To become aware of our drives, in contradistinction to becoming aware of the things we want, is usually a form of perception in which the interoceptive processes receive emphasis; but all drives, insofar as we are aware of them at all, become, from this viewpoint, *perceptual phenomena*. There is no need for two independent categories in our basic psychology of immediate experience, one for perception, one for drive. Both perception and drive are cognitive; both are affective; both are conative. It is just a question of convenient scientific abstraction and emphasis.

It may be asked whether, as we listlessly loll on the riverbank and eye the clouds, we perceive in the same affective and conative fashion. In reply, we suppose that if we became so perfectly neutral to the summer's day as to be free of any desire to drink it lusciously in, the interoceptive and proprioceptive components which we call drowsiness would dominate the situation. We should conclude by perceiving it neither conatively nor, indeed, in any other way than by going to sleep.

(7) *Perception develops through experience as well as through neural maturation.* It was suggested earlier that there is systematic perceptual "growth" dependent upon a general developmental principle of differentiation and integration. It seems likely, however, that experience also results in this kind of development, and that growth may be to some extent subsumable under differentiation and integration; i.e., the high degree of perceptual structure characteristic of the adult may be a direct consequence of the child's successful passage through the developmental sequence of differentiation and integration in a large variety of stimulus conditions. The members of different cultural groups have learned to perceive as culture requires. Certainly the present evidence (48) as to the roles of use and experience would make it unwise to set limits to the relative importance of these factors in determining the perceptual repertory of the organism. On this assumption, individual differences in experience, in interaction with the environment, will alter the rate and form of perceptual development. Environments differ in the direction and extent to which they force us to make distinctions and then to integrate what has been distinguished (it was for this reason that it was previously implied that experiments with adult human beings on percept development would not yield simple developmental laws uncontaminated by the effects of past experience [15]).

Cognition in a given situation is a function not only of the pattern of stimulation, but of the "schema," framework, or matrix within which the cognitive contact is made, as has been demonstrated by the work of Sherif (54) and Bartlett (4), and by the many experiments in perceptual "set" (10, 29, 45). If we assume that the matrix within which each percept develops may itself be so altered through experience that it guides in an altered fashion the direction and extent of the growth of the percept, then, although the initial developmental phase of each percept in the adult may be as undifferentiated as that of the child, subsequent differentiation will occur in directions previously found successful or satisfying if such growth is possible within the limits set by the stimulus distribution. If the stimulus distribution "blocks" the growth of the percept at any stage, either the development will have to take a new course within the framework or, if no successful resolution is possible, an altered or new matrix ("cued," perhaps, by the preceding perceptual development) will be brought to bear. The successive mutual adjustment of matrix, stimulus distribution, and percept in the attempt to mesh into a coherent, stable organization may *appear,* at least superficially, like trial-and-error behavior. However, where the matrix and the limits imposed by the stimulus coincide; where stimulus distribution is strong and simple, allowing of only one organization of overwhelmingly superior stability; or where the matrix is relatively strong and the stimulus distribution weak or complex and permissive of many alternative organizations, there should be no "trial-and-error" but, rather, a smooth perceptual development.

Moreover, the point at which further articulation ceases should depend not only upon what, in the abstract, constitutes a configuration of maximum autochthonous stability but also upon the demands of the situation and upon the extent to which differentiation has progressed in the past. The level at which the tourist admires masses of foliage involves far less articulation than that which the native, searching for camouflaged game, must employ; on the other hand, identifying simple geometrical forms may prove a more difficult task for the jungle native than for the tourist, to whom such "signals" are a matter of daily importance (41).

(8) *It is possible to control experimentally the phenomenal aspects of the genetic process, i.e., to teach the subject how to perceive.* Although it is granted that the sensory neurones feed specific stimulus-determined impulses to the brain, and that the basic "autochthonous" laws of organization described by Gestalt psychology impose further conditions upon what can be perceived, repeated experience with particular attributes of the environment builds up, first, different types of differentiation and then different types of coherence between the differentiated "parts."

Consider the vast difference in the perception of a complicated electronic gadget by one who has built it and by someone else who, with knowledge neither of the gadget nor of electronics, reports a mass of colored spaghetti with anchorage points perhaps determined by brightness of color, the purely "autochthonous" simplicity of form, etc. Learning to read must certainly impose new grouping upon the perception of material printed in the appropriate alphabet; indeed, the individual letters are apparently now perceived more readily under reduced stimulus conditions than are their mirror images (19), which are presumably equivalent configurationally. Insofar as individuals have learned to make distinctions and to interrelate those distinctions in ways which serve their needs, they must pereceive in a manner unlike those with different experiences and with different needs.

Of special interest are examples of "interference" with the factors which determine the figure-ground differentiation: Schafer and Murphy (53) rewarded their subjects along with the perception of certain patterns, punished them with others; later, with both stimuli presented simultaneously, figure and ground consistently followed the direction of reward and punishment. Subjects failed to see in these combined presentations the materials which had been seen just before they were punished, and saw in the presentation what they had seen earlier, just before they were rewarded. Apparently, they literally learned to perceive one way rather than another.[6] Proshansky and Murphy, (47) by giving arbitrary rewards after the presentation of long lines and punishment after short ones, caused increased estimates of line length; by similar procedure, they also produced a tendency to underestimate lifted weights. Another interesting example can be found in an experiment by Krechevsky (26) in which the autochthonous perceptual "law of proximity" was found operative in the rat only when reward-achievement was helped by such operation. The process of learning by reward and punishment appears, then, to apply to perceptual development —perhaps to the same extent and subject to the same limitations that appear in any generalization about learning.

(9) *Repeated stimulation alone, without either known satisfaction or known frustration, also leads directly to analysis and to synthesis, i.e., differentiation and integration.* The same passage from homogeneity to a differentiated, and from a differentiated to an integrated, level is likely to be obtained by sheer repetition without involving neural growth in the

---

[6] Recent repetition by I. Rock and F. S. Fleck (49) has failed to duplicate the results of this experiment. It is difficult to accept their conditions as comparable inasmuch as the design of the experiment was somewhat altered. Further work is certainly needed. (It seems likely, also, that the motivation afforded by rewards of four cents has probably changed both qualitatively and quantitatively since 1943.)

usual maturational sense and without involving satisfaction or frustration of any known nature.[7] Here we can appeal to everyday experience on the stabilization of perception; to Rubin's demonstration (51) that familiarity can determine which of two alternate figures will be seen; to a follow-up study by Schafer (53, page 341), in which this kind of stabilization of perception occurred without external rewards and punishment; to Leeper's study on the organization of incomplete figures (32); to Hanawalt's findings (16) that increased recognition of concealed figures, as a result of practice, was at least in part dependent upon the "unessential" parts of the concealing design becoming ground; and to a striking example of the effects of sheer experience in the recently reported work of Wallach and O'Connell (59) showing that perceiving the projection of a wire figure on a flat surface as the projection of a three-dimensional structure depended upon specific past experience with the projection of that form while in rotation.

It would seem reasonable, here, to assume the operation of something very much like Woodworth's "drive to perceive" (66), i.e., that even in the absence of *external* pressures, the integration of the main "anchorage points" into a coherent, stable unit is an end in itself, an assumption in close accord with the Gestalt concepts. "Sheer repetition" might then serve the function of providing opportunity for the operation of this process.[8]

(10) *Integration tends to achieve homeostasis or stability and offers maximal resistance to change.* Integration involves a decrease in the freedom of each differentiated part, with mutual support and reinforcement of such parts by each other and by the whole (23). This reduction of freedom may tentatively be assumed as due, at least in part, to bringing the configuration of cohesive field forces (43) to the stable state of lowest energy (3); that is, once integrated, the percept would resist change. (It would be interesting to explore the problem of whether the achievement of stability is related to rigidity as it is known to psychiatrists and clinical psychologists. Perhaps the contemporary study of feedback systems will ultimately show that the maintenance of stability in a perceptual system is formally analogous both to the physiological maintenance of homeostatic balance [27] and to psychopathic rigidity.)

(11) *"Association by contiguity" results directly from such synthesis.* Something phenotypically like "association by contiguity" must occur if integration is a direct result of repeated or extended presentations of a stimulus distribution. The *integration* into a stable percept of the various simul-

---

[7] Hebb (17) has recently proposed a neurological model involving something very much like differentiation and integration through sheer repetition.

[8] Perhaps perception passes through substages of *relatively* stable organization, depending either upon temporal processes (as are ambiguous figures [25]) or upon repetition under slightly altered circumstances, to be "jogged" out of the substages and to achieve maximal integration.

taneously present differentiated "parts" must change the components so that they now bear membership character in the same organization (38), and each one, no longer independent, "leads to" the others through their mutual relationships with the whole. This, of course, is not association by contiguity in the usual sense inasmuch as the "elements" do not maintain their identity and inasmuch as "association" is not by addition of elements but by the modification of each part by its role in the original percept. In a sense, the "part" now bears the "keyed" imprint of the distribution of stresses in the original percept, and separate presentation of that part therefore tends to re-establish something which may be close to the percept aroused under the original conditions of stimulation. Thus, with the perception of such a "keyed" part the development of the rest of the field is guided along those paths (where permitted by the stimulus material) of differentiation and integration traversed by the original percept. This "leading-to" based upon previous structure (21) would constitute at least a large part of the matrix within which perception develops, although we should expect not the ideal operation of such tendencies under stationary stimulus distributions but, rather, continually changing, temporally extended interrelations of partially aroused and incomplete frameworks, shifting stimulus distributions, and the feedback from the developing percept to both.

Matrices may affect not only perceptual selection but reintegration, or closure, as well: an evoked matrix directs the development of the percept toward recreation of the original integration; and where the stimulus situation is close to that which evoked the original percept, this must result in what appears to be a "lowered threshold." Even poorly defined or incomplete fragments of previously well-integrated wholes should lead to the reintegration of something close to that whole. Thus, with impoverished and even fragmentary stimulation, we would expect lower thresholds for reporting familiar forms than for configurationally equivalent unfamiliar forms. The data reported by Henle (19), who found lower threshholds for letters than for their mirror images; by Duncker (12), who found evidence of a "memory color" evoked by shape, etc.; by Postman and Bruner (45), who found closure of incomplete circles attributable to an experimentally induced "set" to see circles; and, possibly, by Postman, Bruner, and McGinnies (46), who found lower tachistoscopic thresholds for words most consonant with "personal values," may be called upon to support this hypothesis. Such effects presumably require that the stimulus distributions permit such organization. Thus, Duncker found that memory color may increase a given hue, not create one completely absent from the stimulus; and Djang (11) found that past experience with forms affects their perception when embedded in other forms only if the autochthonous organization of the latter is not determinate, permitting alternate organization, etc.

We would expect that such reconstituted aspects of the original percept might have effects as though actually sensorially present (28). Perhaps the "conditioned response" may come under this principle, in the sense that from appropriate excitations there arise behaviors appropriate to a stimulus (or to expectation [55, 66] of a stimulus) which is not sensorially present (14) but which is part of the integrated, temporally extended world-of-action with which the organism is faced.[9]

Guidance by such matrices in no way guarantees the *validity* of the percepts, or of the behavior thereby aroused: the completion of autochthonously strong figures, or of familiar ones (7), may very well involve erroneous perception of the environment, and behavior directed toward a strongly expected event may prove unrealistic. Far away, we recognize a friend by his walk; but on closer view the walk attaches itself to an alien form—and turns out to be not quite the walk we knew.

(12) *The processes of autistic perception are only relatively distinct from realistic or objective perception insofar as the phenomenal content of a percept is concerned.* The extent to which such perceptual development deviates from what would be expected from the environment, *as we know it on other grounds,* constitutes "perceptual distortion." Where the percept is "distorted" toward an environment more consonant with the observer's "needs," such distortion is called *autism.*[10] However, *all* perception involves adjustment between matrix and stimulus distribution; whether or not such adjustment "reconstitutes" the environment, the process remains fundamentally the same. It is, of course, perfectly possible to separate autistic and realistic processes if one refers to the degree of success in "adapting" to the external environment, or to performing certain tasks according to certain criteria of the experimenter. It is evident, however, that if we do this, we are emphasizing external criteria of success or failure, not actually describing a perceptual process. Indeed, if the environment changes somewhat while retaining certain identifiable features, the same perceptual response may be "realistic" today and "autistic" tomorrow. The man who sees at a lower tachistoscopic threshold those words which fit his "value system" (46) is only displaying autism if the stimulus distributions around

[9] It is probable that, as Koffka arguered (23), any hypothesis of this nature must assume the existence of memory traces; however, it does not seem essential at this stage to make explicit assumptions as to their characteristics.

[10] "Needs," especially in human adults, may often be less directly related to metabolic deprivations than to the highly complex "egotensions" concerning which we can learn much more from the personologist than from the physiologist; e.g., the ego mechanism may include ways of coping with threat which, phenotypically, may be revealed by distortions apparently aimed at perceiving that which the organism fears.

which his percepts developed actually constitute other words, but the perceptual process remains the same in either case. Realism and autism are functional terms, not terms which relate to the content of experience.

(13) *By varying experimentally the exteroceptive, interoceptive, and proprioceptive components which affect perception, one may define a full continuum from realism to autism.* The experimenter may reduce one and increase another component, and he may alter their balance so as to increase realism or autism or to get determination to a varying extent by the three components considered. Sometimes the percept is almost completely exteroceptively predetermined: with well-articulated visual stimulus situations, a proprioceptive excitation pattern can be one which would, alone, result in the perception of the vertical, for example, considerably different from that indicated by vision, yet the perceived vertical will, for most observers, remain that of the exteroceptive pattern (65). Vary, however, the strength of the proprioceptive stimulation relative to that of the exteroceptive stimulation (or the extent to which the individual habitually relies upon one or the other [64]), and the perceived vertical apparently may assume compromise positions anywhere between those dictated by the proprioceptive and by the exteroceptive excitation (cf. 2, 34, 42). Altering the balance of interoceptive and exteroceptive components will probably likewise alter the closeness with which the response is anchored to the external stimulus situation.

As a first approximation, we may assume that increased domination of perception by nonexteroceptive components can be achieved by increasing the intensity of the nonexteroceptive components and decreasing the effectiveness of the exteroceptive determinants. The latter may be achieved by any method which increases the ease with which alternative figural organizations can be fitted to the exteroceptive stimulation. Such situations often occur before differentiation is complete (when alternative boundaries may be set up), and after bounded regions have separated but before they have been integrated into a stable structure. The probability of meeting these conditions can be increased by (*a*) the use of any method which impairs structuring of the exteroceptive pattern, whether it be by the use of short exposure (46), low illuminations (50), or decreased clarity of the stimulus-inhomogeneities upon which contours may form (as by the use of ground-glass diffusing screens [33]); or (*b*) the presentation of complex unfamiliar patterns (32) or material yielding unstable (i.e., of more than one equally "good" alternative structure) or potentially reversible figure-ground differentiation (53). These are the situations most explored in studies of autism, perceptual defense, and in projective techniques.

(14) *Satisfying aspects of percepts tend to become figure in a progressively more focused manner.* The organism is often sensitive to several goals

at once, its neuromuscular system being incompletely focused, but it becomes more and more focused or set toward those specific goals which have in the past proved satisfying (figure-ground segregation is not necessarily all-or-none but may be a matter of degree).

In terms of the hypotheses presented, with perception a temporally extended developmental process, integration must involve the bringing together of temporally separated parts (if only through the interaction between those parts which overlap temporally). The extent to which such integration occurs determines the extent to which each part is modified so as to "lead" to the future pattern (as a few notes from a melody lead to its completion) as well as contemporary "keyed" parts.

Where such integration—or structural resolution—depends *chiefly* upon the limitations set by the exteroceptive stimulus conditions we may, if we wish, refer the resultant integration to the reinforcement of a drive-to-perceive, as does Woodworth (66), or to the achievement of a configuration of maximum stability, as would the Gestaltists. Where integration awaits the resolution of interoceptive components aroused by tissue needs, the perceptual integration of greater stability will usually be the one that generates actual behaviors which reduce the tissue need (33). Upon rearousal of perceptual parts to which such interoceptive information has contributed, those parts will "lead to" the completed perceptual integration and, therefore, indirectly to that kind of action which relieves the needs. Here, as before, we can refer either to the concept of reinforcement or to the achievement of stable perceptual configurations and still be referring to the same process; *from this viewpoint the controversy regarding the Law of Effect is purely terminological.*

Thus, the strength of different needs with which the individual is faced and the history of their satisfaction or their frustration become fundamental in the determination of any characteristic differences in personal outlook.

(15) *The trend toward integration tends to be irreversible.* This hypothesis is certainly both controversial and far from capable of full verification. It has been assumed (page 333) that progressive differentiation tends to occur *within* the major boundaries already laid down, and we know (23) that those regions of the field having the greatest internal articulation tend toward figural status; since integration occurs at each successive level, reversal, in the sense of eliminating boundaries or contours already in existence and creating new ones, would be difficult. Once "insight" was gained, for example, in Boring's ambiguous figure of the old-and-young woman, Leeper found it almost impossible to see the other aspect (32). Leeper also found that in material of the type of Street's Gestalt Completion, figures once perceived in a given way were difficult to get rid of, and

apparently prevented reorganization. Such percepts represent convergences of high order, so that their destruction is improbable. In order to see any other figure, the integration would have to be rent asunder and dedifferentiation occur, often through many concentric levels. Thus, the earliest anchorages and "associational" integrations precondition later perceptual development and tend to be permanent or to have permanent effects on further perception and behavior.

It should be pleaded here that there is a good deal of evidence from Freud's studies of cathexis that early trends in this direction are never outgrown. Childhood loves, whether of mothers or of doughnuts, are never wholly lost. In fact, psychoanalysis and other therapies are here presumed to be necessary in part because of early accentuation of certain satisfying aspects of the perceptual field which the organism cannot later leave or submerge effectively under new cathexes. The attempt is made elsewhere (40) to show that this principle, called canalization, is supported by considerable evidence, and to suggest that while such canalizations may be overlaid or disguised, the moment that the overlay is removed, they rebound and reappear in full force.

(16) *Those aspects of a percept which are only prominently "associated" with "satisfaction" tend toward the role of figure but are displaced when this connection ceases.* This hypothesis refers to the evident daily fact that much which tends to attract our notice, and which plays a rather large dynamic part in our feeling and acting, is nevertheless pushed aside when it is no longer related to the satisfaction of our wants. The dinner bell rung repeatedly as a practical joke becomes sheer clanging nuisance. Signals of various sorts which key us up and give us joy hold this role as long as the anticipated satisfaction is actually forthcoming, or as long as we maintain an expectancy (having no reason to believe otherwise); but when the relationship is broken, the role is quickly lost. This may be what is denoted by the extinction of the conditioned response: what was once perceived as "to-be-followed-by" satisfaction, now has lost those *sign-gestalt* characteristics; what once held the center of the stage retreats into relative obscurity.

The difference between these last two points (hypotheses 15 and 16) dealing with "canalization" and "conditioning," respectively, lies in the fact that those anchorages which are themselves directly "satisfying," within which further stable organization has been achieved, cannot be readily discarded; but those which owe their connection with satisfaction only to the temporary advantageous position of "signal" or subgoal status lose it when the connection is broken. In Schafer's experiment, the contours which achieved dominance through reward lost this dominance when reward was discontinued, since such contours were of differential importance in achieving a stable integration only insofar as they were seen as leading to reward.

Lambert, Solomon, and Watson (30) found that the size of a poker chip was consistently overestimated (a phenomenon for which no clear-cut explanation exists at present) while that chip served as a subgoal in the path to obtaining a reward. When the reinforcement ceased, the relative overestimation of the poker chip also ceased.

It would accord with these assumptions (13–16) if all learning should prove reducible to a matter of perceptual restructuring. There is a widespread tendency at present to emphasize the flexibility or malleability of perception and to point out that changes in behavior follow directly from changes in the way in which a situation is viewed, so that it is an easy step from this point to the proposition that learning follows from perceptual reorganization. Education and therapy, as many alert observers have suggested, consist of fresh perception.

(17) *Perceptual restructuring can occur at any level of awareness, so that learning while asleep, or learning by invertebrates, etc., need offer no exceptions.* It is suggested that awareness may be regarded as a question of degree, and, therefore, that while the most explicit, sharply differentiated and richly structured percepts occur at a level upon which introspection can report, there may well be—and probably are—in adults, in children, and in animals, less well-defined perceptual structures which, as a consequence of poor differentiation, defy the precise analysis necessary for introspective report and conscious manipulation. Indeed, one might follow the older suggestions of Leibnitz in carrying awareness down one step at a time until we conceive very vaguely a most primitive and blurred type of experience. Functionally we might go down *below* that and say that even at a level which we cannot regard as conscious at all, processes of structuring and organization occur *as if* they had that quality we know as awareness. Moreover, there is considerable evidence of the existence of *sets* (perhaps directly analogous to what have here been dealt with as perceptual matrices), or "unconscious determining tendencies," of considerable complexity of differentiation (10, 29), whose effects (while obtained without conscious participation) are so similar to those of conscious discrimination and inspection as to suggest the existence of a "preperceptual observer" in much the same fashion as that evidenced by many of the "perceptual defense" studies (35, 36). We see what is coming, so we manage not to see it. The organizational structure of such percepts, and of others suggesting "unconscious perception" (37), is not as yet separable from that of processes in which awareness is evidently present but the processes involved are unmistakably perceptual in nature.

(18) *The more complex phenomena of conflict, ego defense, and psychoanalytic dynamics generally may be viewed as anchorage and differentiation phenomena in which two or more aspects of a perceptual field can*

make a sharp bid for the role of figure. Here it is suggested that instead of being completely unconscious of our own struggling and conflicting tendencies, there are phenomena essentially like those of perceptual conflict within us at all levels of awareness. Awareness of ourselves, of our own inadequacies, of the different directions in which we might like to move; awareness of the modes of escape and of reconciliation of wishes—are all there according to the present thesis, in varying degrees of clarity or obscurity, dissociation or integration.

There is more than one way in which, from this viewpoint, our behavior may be determined by material of which we are unaware, and it would prove instructive to examine the behavioral material presently considered homogeneously as "repression," to determine whether or not it can be fitted into such diverse categories. To select a few possibilities: those aspects of the field which are relegated to ground status still affect the organization but are not noticeable as forms (23). An individual might react to several different objects or situations in the same fashion, not because of an unconscious perception of their similarities—as expressed in the concept of substitution—but because of an inadequate differentiation between them, a lack of perception of their differences (31). Repression might in some cases be analogous to the process by which Schafer's subjects rejected perceptual possibilities which led to frustration, or to that by which Chapman's subjects were unable to report the attributes not included in the *Aufgabe* (10). In other cases perceptual repression might be analogous to an inability to allocate phenomenal causal responsibility to any portion of a relatively amorphous, insufficiently differentiated field; etc.

All that psychoanalysis and the other depth psychologies have taught us may easily be conceived in terms of the learning process, governed by needs and their cognitive expression, exactly as in the simpler experimental examples, except that continuous conflict and inadequate differentiation contribute to the low degree of awareness which some components enjoy, and except that perception of the self in all its rich and complex manifestations must receive cardinal emphasis. But perception of the self could still exhibit the characteristics of perceptual development, figure-ground dynamics, canalization, and the rest of the principles suggested.

Summary

Our hypotheses have dealt with the interaction of exteroceptive, interoceptive, and proprioceptive components in the determination of perception, and with the likelihood that both growth and learning modify the form of this interaction.

It has long been emphasized and, under the stimulus of feedback theory, it is currently being re-emphasized (63), that as we react to our percepts, our bodies feed in impressions proprioceptively just as our distance receptors feed in, at the same time, reports on the changing situation. What has here been suggested is that it is unjustified to consider one of these components alone as the basis for perception by the normal, functioning organism in its intercourse with its environment, and that the visceral-affective components may also be vitally concerned in perception; that the study of perception includes the affective and conative phenomena and their interrelations with the cognitive in such a way that the whole, living individual participates in every perceptual act; and lastly, a possible relationship has been suggested with the learning process and with those personality dynamics which the psychoanalysts and other clinicians have stressed.

These hypotheses are, of course, only programmatic and worth but little till the hard work of thinking them out, testing them, and modifying them has been done. It is hoped that personality research methods may in time justify the conception that the perceptual dynamics to which these methods point are ultimately the same perceptual dynamics which in the laboratory can be investigated in terms of figure-ground differentiation and other parameters. There is only one psychology of perception, and it should be equally good in the laboratory and in social reality if it is solidly constructed.

References

1. ABEL, T. M. Unsynthetic modes of thinking among adults: A discussion of Piaget's concepts. *Amer. J. Psychol.*, 1932, **44**, 123–132.
2. ASCH, S. E., and WITKIN, H. A. Studies in space orientation: I. Perception of the upright with displaced visual fields. *J. exp. Psychol.*, 1948, **3**, 325–337.
3. ASHBY, W. R. Dynamics of the cerebral cortex: The behavioural properties of systems in equilibrium. *Amer. J. Psychol.*, 1946, **59**, 682–686.
4. BARTLETT, F. C. *Remembering*. New York: Macmillan, 1932.
5. BICHOWSKY, F. R. The mechanism of consciousness: Pre-sensation. *Amer. J. Psychol.*, 1925, **36**, 558–596.
6. BRUNER, J. S., and POSTMAN, L. Perception, cognition, and behavior. *J. Personality*, 1949, **18**, 14–31.
7. ———. On the perception of incongruity: A paradigm. *J. Personality*, 1949, **18**, 206–223.
8. BRUNSWIK, E. Psychology as a science of objective relations. *Phil. Sci.*, 1937, **4**, 227–260.
9. CATTELL, R. B. The subjective character of cognition and the pre-sensational development of perception. *Brit. J. Psychol. Monogr. Suppl.*, 1930, No. XIV.
10. CHAPMAN, D. W. Relative effects of determinate and indeterminate *Aufgaben*. *Amer. J. Psychol.*, 1932, **44**, 163–174.

11. DJANG, S. The role of past experience in the visual apprehension of masked forms. *J. exp. Psychol.,* 1937, **20,** 29–59.

12. DUNCKER, K. The influence of past experience upon perceptual properties. *Amer. J. Psychol.,* 1939, **52,** 255–265.

13. DUSSER DE BARENNE, J. G., GAROL, H. W., and McCULLOCH, W. S. The "motor" cortex of the chimpanzee. *J. Neurophysiol.,* 1941, **4,** 287–323.

14. ELLSON, D. G. Hallucinations produced by sensory conditioning. *J. exp. Psychol.,* 1941, **28,** 1–20.

15. FEHRER, E. V. An investigation of the learning of visually perceived forms. *Amer. J. Psychol.,* 1935, **47,** 187–221.

16. HANAWALT, N. G. The effect of practice upon the perception of simple designs masked by more complex designs. *J. exp. Psychol.,* 1942, **31,** 134–148.

17. HEBB, D. O. *The organization of behavior.* New York: Wiley, 1949.

18. HELSON, H. Adaptation-level as a basis for a quantitative theory of frames of reference. *Psychol. Rev.,* 1948, **55,** 297–313.

19. HENLE, MARY. An experimental investigation of past experience as a determinant of visual form perception. *J. exp. Psychol.,* 1942, **30,** 1–22.

20. HOCHBERG, J. E. Brightness as a function of perceived spatial form. Paper given at EPA meetings, March, 1951.

21. HUMPHREY, G. *The nature of learning in its relation to the living system.* New York: Harcourt Brace, 1933.

22. KENNARD, MARGARET A. Autonomic interrelations with the somatic nervous system. *Psychosom. Med.,* 1947, **9,** 29–36.

23. KOFFKA, K. *Principles of gestalt psychology.* New York: Harcourt Brace, 1935.

24. KÖHLER, W. Psychological remarks on some questions of anthropology. *Amer. J. Psychol.,* 1937, **50,** 271–288.

25. ———. *Dynamics in psychology.* New York: Liveright, 1940.

26. KRECHEVSKY, I. An experimental investigation of the principle of proximity in the visual perception of the rat. *J. exp. Psychol.,* 1938, **22,** 497–523.

27. KREEZER, G. L. The derivation of the transfer functions of homeostatic systems from experimental response curves. *J. Psychol.,* 1949, **28,** 487–493.

28. KROLIK, W. Über Erfahrungwirkungen beim Bewegungssehen. *Psychol. Forsch.,* 1934, **20,** 47–101.

29. KÜLPE, O. Versuche über Abstraktion. *Ber. ü. d. I. Kongr. f. exper. Psychol.,* 1904, 56–68.

30. LAMBERT, W. W., SOLOMON, R. L., and WATSON, P. D. Reinforcement and extinction as factors in size estimation. *J. exp. Psychol.,* 1949, **39,** 637–641.

31. LASHLEY, K. S., and WADE, MARJORIE. The Pavlovian theory of generalization. *Psychol. Rev.,* 1946, **53,** 72–87.

32. LEEPER, R. W. A study of a neglected portion of the field of learning—the development of sensory organization. *J. genet. Psychol.,* 1935, **46,** 41–75.

33. LEVINE, R., CHEIN, I., and MURPHY, G. The relation of the intensity of a need to the amount of perceptual distortion: A preliminary report. *J. Psychol.,* 1942, **13,** 283–293.

34. MANN, C. W., BERTHELOT-BERRY, N. H., and DAUTERIVE, H. J., JR. The perception of the vertical: I. Visual and nonlabyrinthine cues. *J. exp. Psychol.*, 1949, **39**, 538–547.

35. McCLEARY, R. A., and LAZARUS, R. S. Autonomic discrimination without awareness: An interim report. *J. Personality*, 1949, **18**, 171–179.

36. McGINNIES, E. Emotionality and perceptual defense. *Psychol. Rev.*, 1949, **56**, 244–251.

37. MILLER, J. G. Discrimination without awareness. *Amer. J. Psychol.*, 1939, **52**, 562–578.

38. MOORE, J. H. The role of determining tendencies in learning. *Amer. J. Psychol.*, 1936, **48**, 559–571.

39. MOTOKOWA, K. Field of retinal induction and optical illusion. *J. Neurophysiol.*, 1950, **13**, 413–426.

40. MURPHY, G. *Persoruality.* New York: Harper, 1947.

41. NISSEN, H. W., MACHOVER, S., and KINDER, ELAINE F. A study of performance tests given to a group of native African Negro children. *Brit. J. Psychol.*, 1935, **25**, 308–355.

42. NOBLE, C. E. The perception of the vertical: III. The visual vertical as a function of centrifugal and gravitational forces. *J. exp. Psychol.*, 1949, **39**, 839–850.

43. ORBISON, W. D. Shape as a function of the vector field. *Amer. J. Psychol.*, 1939, **52**, 31–45.

44. PATERSON, A., and ZANGWILL, O. L. Disorders of visual space perception associated with lesions of the right cerebral hemisphere. *Brain*, 1944, **67**, 331–358.

45. POSTMAN, L., and BRUNER, J. S. Unpublished manuscript.

46. ———, and McGINNIES, E. Personal values as selective factors in perception. *J. abnorm. soc. Psychol.*, 1948, **43**, 142–154.

47. PROSHANSKY, H., and MURPHY G. The effects of reward and punishment on perception. *J. Psychol.*, 1942, **13**, 295–305.

48. RIESEN, A. H. The development of visual perception in man and chimpanzee. *Science*, 1947, **106**, 107–108.

49. ROCK, I., and FLECK, F. S. A re-examination of the effect of monetary reward and punishment on figure-ground perception. *J. exp. Psychol.*, 1950, **40**, 766–776.

50. ROSENSTOCK, I. M. Perceptual aspects of repression. *Amer. Psychologist*, 1950, **5**, 306–307. (Abstract.)

51. RUBIN, E. *Visuell Wahrgenommene Figuren: Studien in Psychologischer Analyse.* Copenhagen: Glydendal, 1921.

52. RYAN, T. A. Interrelations of the sensory systems in perception. *Psychol. Bull.*, 1940, **37**, 659–698.

53. SCHAFER, R., and MURPHY, G. The role of autism in a visual figure-ground relationship. *J. exp. Psychol.*, 1943, **32**, 335–343.

54. SHERIF, M. *The psychology of social norms.* New York: Harper, 1936.

55. TOLMAN, E. C. Gestalt and sign-gestalt. *Psychol. Rev.*, 1933, **40**, 391–411.

56. VERNON, M. D. *Visual perception.* New York: Macmillan, 1937.

57. VOGEL, P. Über optokinetische Reaktionsbewegungen und Scheinbewegungen. *Arch. ges. Physiol.*, 1931, **228**, 632–644.

58. WALLACH, H. Brightness constancy and the nature of achromatic colors. *J. exp. Psychol.*, 1948, **38**, 310–324.

59. WALLACH, H., and O'CONNELL, D. N. Perception of tri-dimensional form. *Amer. Psychologist*, 1950, **5**, 487. (Abstract.)

60. WERNER, H. *Comparative psychology of mental development.* Chicago: Follett, 1948.

61. ———, and WAPNER, S. Sensory-tonic field theory of perception. *J. Personality*, 1949, **18**, 88–107.

62. WEVER, E. G. Figure and ground in the visual perception of form. *Amer. J. Psychol.*, 1927, **38**, 194–226.

63. WIENER, N. *Cybernetics.* New York: Wiley, 1948.

64. WITKIN, H. A. The nature and importance of individual differences in perception. *J. Personality*, 1949, **18**, 145–170.

65. WOOD, H. C. The "haunted swing" illusion. *Psychol. Rev.*, 1895, **2**, 277–278.

66. WOODWORTH, R. S. Reënforcement of perception. *Amer. J. Psychol.*, 1947, **60**, 119–124.

21. *Perceiving as Innately Determined* [*][†]

NICHOLAS PASTORE,[1] *Queens College, New York*

THE NOTION that significant aspects of perceiving are learned is quite old and its controversial status is far from resolution. We may wonder why the growth of psychology as a science has made such meager inroads in establishing a reliable body of interrelated facts and in inducing a uniform approach to theoretical and experimental issues. Perhaps philosophical issues and questions of value, as was the case in the nature-nurture controversy, exert a strong influence in this regard. Berkeley's *New Theory of Vision* (1709), for example, was doubtlessly shaped by a special attitude toward

[*] From Nicholas Pastore, "Perceiving as Innately Determined," *The Journal of Genetic Psychology,* 96 (March, 1960), 93–98. Reprinted by permission.

[†] Accepted for publication by Leonard Carmichael of the Editorial Board, and received in the Editorial Office on August 12, 1958.

[1] Slightly revised version of paper read at the Symposium on "Problems, Experiments, and Issues in the Transfer Effect of Early Exposure on Perceptual Discrimination," Eastern Psychological Association, New York, April, 1957.

idealism and materialism. Nowadays, it is possible that the wish to stress the significance of the individual strengthens an empirical approach. The individual is not a passive or helpless recipient of external forces; rather, the world itself may image his needs and training. Given the subjectivism that prevails in some quarters, the actual status of the real world is thrown into doubt. Everyone seems to construct a world in line with his wishes and needs to a degree that a common measure of the collection of private worlds cannot be defined. A common measure, even if it were defined, simply would represent an excursion into a particular individual's private view of things. These attitudes, in so far as they exist, suggest that the *nativism* vs. *empiricism* controversy ultimately may be resolved along the lines of clarifying philosophical and other extrascientific issues (1, page 89). Rather than pursue this approach further, let us turn to a few of the vexing scientific issues which plague the question under discussion. But, first, to state our thesis: *All of the significant aspects of perceiving are unlearned.*[2] These aspects include pattern and depth perceptions, the so-called laws of organization, figure-ground relationship, solidity, the illusions, the constancies, the phi phenomenon, figural aftereffects, and the perception of the world as upright. The scope of this thesis will be delimited by drawing a distinction between the origin and the modification of a perceptual achievement.

By origin we refer to the rôle of factors—whether innate, maturational, or experiential—which shape a perceptual process in a characteristic direction from the moment an organism comes in contact with the visual environment. By modification we refer to those changes which may occur in an already achieved perception through some learning factor. The bulk of experiments purporting to demonstrate the role of empirical factors actually deal with the question of modification, and not of origin. In this regard, for example, we think of experiments on memory color. The underlying assumption of such experimental work is that if a given perception is modified by some contemporary experiential factor then it must have been due to experience in the first place. Thus, Helmholtz wrote: "Whatever, therefore, can be overcome by factors of experience, we must consider as being itself the product of experience and training" (8, page 13). This view is fallacious since from the fact of modification no direct inference about origin can be drawn. A parallel example exists in the field of genetics; the environmental modification of a trait does not preclude its genetic determination. For example, let us suppose that knowledge of an object influences the degree of size constancy; it would not follow thereby that size constancy is initially the outcome of learning. In view of the foregoing distinction, we shall restrict the thesis to questions of origin.

[2] In stating and developing this thesis the writer's debt to Koffka (10) and Köhler (11) is obvious; see also Pratt (21).

Partial evidential and inferential support for the thesis lies in the following. (*a*) Evidence suggests that there is a similarity, if not identity, in perceptual functioning in man and in lower animals (14) despite obvious differences in anatomical structures and in modes of responding to the environment. Such perceptual functioning common to man and lower animals includes form perception, depth perception, apparent movement, illusions, size constancy, and brightness constancy.[3] Apparently there must be some communality in the nervous tissue underlying perceiving or, alternatively, there must be common laws which govern the functioning of nervous tissue in relation to retinal stimulation. (*b*) In some species important aspects of perceptual functioning are apparent shortly after birth or hatching. Brightness constancy and size constancy have been demonstrated in the duckling at the respective ages of two days and seven days and discrimination among closely related geometrical figures before the fourth week (19, 20). Frantz has shown that chicks have marked form preferences before the age of four days (6). Within a few days after hatching chicks and ducklings can discriminate different heights (22). On a nonexperimental level it is reported that the mound bird can fly immediately upon hatching and, on the same day, perch on a branch (2, page 99). The swift, after hatching and growing to a fledgling stage, leaves the nest to spend practically its entire life on the wing. It gathers all food and nesting material, and may even mate, while in flight (13). It seems clear that the perceptual abilities of this bird must be complete at the time of leaving the nest. Such early perceptual achievements are not restricted to birds. Following a lead supplied by Carmichael (4, page 69 f.), the writer was able to show depth discrimination (by using platforms of varying heights) in the guinea pig within six hours after birth. Carmichael observed an infant giraffe that could respond visually to its environment 20 minutes after birth (5, page 324). Tinklepaugh and Hartman reported that a rhesus monkey reached for and grasped objects during delivery itself (27). The activities of the monkey reported on by Lashley and Watson (16) suggest that its perceptual apparatus is complete by the age of 21 days. These results, partly experimental and partly observational,[4] show that for these species perceptual functioning is due to innate factors. The two foregoing points strongly suggest that similar features of perception in higher phylogenetic levels (chimpanzee and man) are also outcomes of autochthonous factors.

A principal difference among the species discussed above concerns the degree to which animals are able to function at birth or hatching. In some species, the nervous tissue is practically complete—at least in so far as the optical sector is concerned—at birth or hatching, whereas in higher species

[3] For discussions of such evidence see references 14, 17, 25, 26, 28.
[4] Observations are invaluable in providing direction for research.

the optic system attains completion after birth. Consequently, in animals higher up in the phylogenetic series postnatal maturational processes can be confounded with concomitant experiential factors. Such experiential factors may merely supply the occasion for the unfolding of developmental processes and need not be of causal significance in the shaping of perceptions. Efforts that control postnatal experience by rearing animals under some restrictive condition (for example, light deprivation) may impede the rate of maturation and may actually lead to structural or functional impairment of the optic system (3, 6). By virtue of such impairment, the results of deprivation experiments could not be decisive against the thesis that perceiving is determined by innate mechanisms. In this regard it is interesting to note the word of caution stated by Spalding in 1872, perhaps the first investigator to use animals for the purpose of testing an empirical approach to perception. With reference to his own experiments on chicks reared under some restrictive condition, he wrote: ". . . it would seem that any early interference with the established course of their lives may completely derange their mental constitution, and give rise to an order of manifestations, perhaps totally and unaccountably different from what would have appeared under normal conditions" (23, page 7).

Let us consider briefly the critical term *learning*. Unfortunately, this term does not have a precise definition in general psychology and, in so far as it is related to perception, its meaning is quite vague. What are the criteria for distinguishing among learning, satiation, maturation, and adaptation? Is reinforcement an essential factor in "learning to perceive" and does such learning exhibit generalization and extinction effects? Although discussion of these questions is a topic in its own right several issues can be defined. If we are to speak of "learning to perceive" there must be some demonstration that different training sequences lead to different perceptual outcomes. This means that there should be specifications of the percept prior to learning and after learning. Furthermore, it would be desirable to advance some theory that would deal with the processes intervening between the initial and final perceptual states. In current discussions we usually do not find a clear specification of the percept prior to learning, the postlearning situation being quite clear. However, sometimes we do find statements, explicitly or implicitly, concerning the initial state. Some of these statements include the following: a percept is "amorphous" or "blurred"; a triangle cannot be distinguished from a circle; the percept is correlated with retinal size; the animal is "form-blind"; there is no differentiation of figure from ground; there is no seen depth; the conditions under which the phi phenomenon is obtained yield punctate percepts; a human infant sees the world upside down. With regard to mediating processes, the main task of a theory of learning is to show how the initial perceptions are transformed into the perceptions we know them to be. *S-S* theory and *S-R* reinforcement theory are the two main candidates advanced for dealing with this task. Both, I believe, are inadequate as presently formulated. Both theories assume initial perceptual variability in relation to a proximal stimulus. For instance, it has been suggested that a percept, prior to the learning which is presumed to lead to size constancy, is determined by the visual angle (10, page 87 f.). From the organism's standpoint, changing distance from the distal stimulus means perceptual variability. It has been shown elsewhere that the effect of such an assumption makes adaptive responses to stimuli impossible (18). With regard to *S-R* theory there is the additional difficulty of defining the way in which reinforcement serves to stabilize perceptions. With regard to *S-S* theory there is the problem, by no means unique to it, as to why certain aspects of the stimulus field become organized in one way rather than in some other way. For example, contour is phenomenally part of the figure and not of the ground. Yet, in a physical sense, the contour is as much a part of the ground as it is of the figure. Or, the contour (physically) is as often associated with the points interior to a figure as it is with the points exterior to the figure. On contiguity grounds alone, therefore, there is no rationale for the unique association of the contour with the enclosed points. The fact that depth perception offers a difficult obstacle for both theories since on the retina there is no identifiable stimulus correlate for depth. Appeal to eye movements or other peripheral factors also entails difficulties.

Generally, the learning approach to perception thrives on two types of discrepancies. One type pertains to the discrepancy between the proximal stimulus and the percept, as is exemplified by depth perception or by the constancies. This discrepancy necessarily forces the theorist to postulate various experiential factors—knowledge, unconscious reasoning, probabilistic weighting of cues, palpation of the stimulus object, muscular movements—providing he makes that special assumption which the gestalt psychologists have labeled as the "constancy hypothesis." Such postulated factors introduce the further question as to how they are able to effect changes in perception. The difficulties entailed by the "constancy hypothesis" can be circumvented if we accept an alternative assumption advanced by gestalt psychologists; namely, the neural medium which is the locus of a percept imposes characteristic transformations on the impulses propagated from the retinae. The outcomes of such transformations need not be isomorphic with the retinal pattern. Thus, stimulation of the retina—a two dimensional surface—can, under certain conditions, lead to a three dimensional central process. The alternative assumption, attractive as it seems to be, has not won general acceptance. One objection to it, anticipated by Helmholtz (9, page 274), is that the investigation of perceptual processes is thereby removed from scientific scrutiny. However, Köhler's theory of satiation and the related experiments (cf. 12), some of the experiments of Sperry and his colleagues (24), and of Lashley and his colleagues (15) would seem to weaken the force of this objection since information is obtained on the neural correlates of perceptual processes.

The second type of discrepancy is the one which supposedly obtains between the proximal stimulus and the distal stimulus. It is said, for example, that a rectangular proximal stimulus can be projected by an infinity of external configurations. Yet a specific perception can be matched to the given proximal stimulus, not an infinitude of perceptions. The theoretical import of this discrepancy for an empirical approach to perception is uncertain since it implies the "constancy hypothesis" as a hidden assumption and initial perceptual variability. Moreover, if we adopt Gibson's approach (7), one which assumes a one to one correspondence between the retinal distribution and the external visual situation, it may turn out that this discrepancy actually represents a pseudo problem.

Certainly there are many other issues not touched upon but lack of time forbids their discussion. I should like to conclude by asserting that the most parsimonious position to take with regard to perceiving is that its major features are determined by intrinsic properties of the nervous system and that learning factors have no determinative influence. At most, learning factors must be assigned a secondary rôle; they may exert an influence but only when the perception-to-be-modified is already an existent one.

References

1. ALLPORT, F. H. Theories of Perception and the Concept of Structure. New York: Wiley, 1955.
2. BARRUEL, P. Birds of the World. New York: Oxford Univ. Press, 1954.
3. BEACH, F. A., and JAYNES, J. Effects of early experience upon the behavior of animals. *Psychol. Bull.*, 1954, **51,** 239–263.
4. CARMICHAEL, L. (*Ed.*) Manual of Child Psychology. New York: Wiley, 1946.
5. ———. Letter to the editor. *Contemp. Psychol.*, 1957, **2,** 323–324.
6. FANTZ, R. I. Form preferences in newly hatched chicks. *J. Comp. & Physiol. Psychol.*, 1957, **50,** 422–430.
7. GIBSON, J. J. The Perception of the Visual World. New York: Houghton Mifflin, 1950.
8. HELMHOLTZ, H. VON. Physiological Optics. (Ed. by J. P. S. Southall.) Vol. III. Optical Society of America, 1925.
9. ———. Popular Lectures on Scientific Subjects. (2nd Series.) London: Longman's Green, 1881.
10. KOFFKA, K. Principles of Gestalt Psychology. New York: Harcourt, Brace, 1935.

11. KÖHLER, W. Gestalt Psychology. New York: Liveright, 1947.
12. ———, HELD, R., and O'CONNELL, D. An investigation of cortical currents. *Proc. Amer. Philos. Soc.*, 1952, **96**, 290–330.
13. LACK, D., and LACK, E. The home life of the swift. *Sci. Amer.*, 1954, **191**, 60–65.
14. LASHLEY, K. S. The mechanism of vision: XV. Preliminary studies of the rat's capacity for detail vision. *J. Gen. Psychol.*, 1938, **18**, 123–193.
15. ———, CHOW, K. L., and SEMMES, J. An examination of the electrical field theory of cerebral organization. *Psychol. Rev.*, 1951, **58**, 123–136.
16. ———, and WATSON, J. B. Notes on development of a young monkey. *J. Anim. Beh.*, 1913, **3**, 114–139.
17. MUNN, N. L. Handbook of Psychological Research on the Rat. Boston: Houghton Mifflin, 1950.
18. PASTORE, N. An examination of one aspect of the thesis that perceiving is learned. *Psychol. Rev.*, 1956, **63**, 309–316.

22. *Visual Perception and Personality* [*] [1]

WARREN J. WITTREICH

WHEN WE watch a person walk away from us, his image shrinks in size. But since we know for a fact that he is not shrinking, we make an unconscious correction and "see" him as retaining his full stature. Past experience tells us what his true stature is with respect to our own. Any sane and dependable expectation of the future requires that he have the same true stature when we next encounter him. Our perception is thus a prediction; it embraces the past and the future as well as the present.

From such considerations psychology has taught us all by now that perception is not a simple act. We do not merely see what is "out there" in the here and now. Perception is an ongoing process that involves our image of our own self, our needs, values and purposes, as fully as it involves the image of the object perceived. In this "transaction" between the viewer and

---

[*] From Warren J. Wittreich, "Visual Perception and Personality," *Scientific American* (April, 1959), pp. 56–60. Reprinted with permission. Copyright © 1959 by Scientific American, Inc. All rights reserved.
[1] NOTE: Most of the pictures that illustrate the points made in the article are omitted here. They can be seen by reference to the April, 1959, issue of *Scientific American*.

the viewed it seems evident that emotional relationships between people must also condition how they see each other. Would anyone deny that beauty is in the eye of the beholder?

Six years ago we began a series of experiments designed to measure the degree to which the emotional feeling of one person toward another may modify that person's image of the other. At Princeton University and subsequently at the Naval Medical Research Institute at Bethesda, Maryland, we studied how one person's perception of another is influenced by emotions arising out of the marriage relationship, out of one person's subordination to another and out of perceiving that the other person is disfigured or mutilated. We have found that the emotions do not only involve such intangible qualities as beauty; they may also significantly affect a person's perception of such "objective" attributes as the stature of the person perceived.

For the experimental devices and procedures employed in our study we are indebted to the late Adelbert Ames, Jr., of Hanover, New Hampshire, whose work has inspired so many other lines of investigtion in psychology during the past 25 years. This gifted investigator (who before he turned to psychology had been a lawyer, then a painter, then a physiologist) developed a number of powerful demonstrations of the transactions involving the perceiver and the perceived [see "Experiments in Perception," by W. H. Ittelson and F. P. Kilpatrick; *Scientific American,* August, 1951]. For one series of experiments we employed one of Ames's famous distorted rooms. The floor of this room slopes upward to the right of the viewer, the rear wall recedes from right to left, the windows in the rear wall are different sizes and trapezoidal in shape. When the room is viewed from one vantage point, however, it looks like an ordinary room: the floor appears level, the rear wall is at right angles to the line of sight and the windows are rectangular and of the same size. Out of his past experience with the cues provided by perspective, the viewer has assembled a set of assumptions that he brings to the occasion and applies to the immediate experience.

Ames built one of these rooms large enough for people to walk about in it. A surprising thing now happens. When the viewer sees another person walk across the room, he typically observes an extraordinary alteration in that person's size. Depending on which way the person walks, he appears to grow or shrink. A smaller model of this room permits hands or faces to be seen at the rear windows. As with the larger room, the hands or faces appear to be abnormally large or small, depending upon whether they are framed in the window to the viewer's right or to his left. Thus in the typical experience the viewer sticks to his assumptions about the shape of the room, even to the extreme of accepting distortion in the appearance of another person.

On one occasion a decade ago, however, Hadley Cantril and his associates at Princeton University observed a striking departure from the usual pattern of response to the Ames room. A viewer, observing the faces of her husband and another man at the windows of the small room, reported that her husband's face remained unchanged though she observed the expected distortion in the face of the other man. Similarly, the other man appeared to grow or shrink as he walked to and fro in the larger room, while her husband underwent no change in size whatever. Cantril called this reaction the "Honi" phenomenon, after the woman's nickname.

Suspecting that the emotional relationship of this woman to her husband might in some way underlie the Honi reaction, a group of us at Princeton set out to repeat the experiment with other married couples. Of the 10 couples we enlisted, it happened, most had been married for a brief time, several for less than a year. The majority of these individuals saw their partner grow and shrink in the usual manner and to the same apparent degree as a stranger who acted as the "control" in each experiment. Six viewers, however, reported that their partners altered less than the stranger or did not change at all.

All six turned out to be recently married. Indeed, at least one member of every couple married less than a year reported the Honi reaction. Only one subject married more than a year displayed it, and he had been married only two years. We also noted with interest that the "Honi" subjects tended to see the room as distorted when their partners entered it. Faced with the choice of seeing their partner or the room distorted, they chose the latter.

Our tape recordings of the subjects' spontaneous comments support the authenticity of the response recorded in each case; several expressed surprise when they observed that their partners did not change size. In search for a more objective standard of determining the subject's response, however, we enlisted six new couples, all married less than 15 months. This time we asked each subject to tell us at what point the partner and the stranger appeared to assume normal size as they walked from wall to wall in the larger room. The location of this point varied considerably in each trial, but in every case the marital partner was required to walk a shorter distance than the stranger to be judged of normal size. We also asked each subject for detailed "before and after" descriptions of the room's appearance. When we totaled the number of distorted items in each description, we found that the "distortion score" increased sharply after the partner's entrance. As one would expect, the subjects with the strongest tendency to perceive their partners unchanged showed the highest scores with the partner in the room.

The completion of this experiment left us in something of a quandary. We had demonstrated differences in perception that seemed somehow related to marriage, but were hard put to explain the differences. It could not be ascribed to mere familiarity with the person perceived, since the effect was most marked among newlyweds. On the other hand, the "Honi" couple had been married for more than 25 years. This troublesome fact pointed up an almost self-evident truth: Marriage, though it has a very clear legal meaning, has diffuse meaning in psychological terms. The relationship between marriage partners obviously differs from that between unmarried people. But specifically and precisely in what way does it differ that is relevant to our finding? Indeed, the marriage relationship itself changes with the years. To explain our results we obviously needed to experiment with a simpler and more clear-cut relationship, subject to more precise definition.

An opportunity to conduct such experiments presented itself in 1953 at the Naval Medical Research Unit in connection with the psychiatric adjustment of patients who had been seriously mutilated or disfigured. In this investigation we employed another Ames technique that involves the use of "aniseikonic" lenses. These lenses had originally been devised to correct a defect in the mechanism of stereoscopic vision (aniseikonia), which has been found to affect about 2 per cent of the population. When a person with normal vision looks through the corrective lenses, his vision is distorted as if he were troubled with aniseikonia. Another person viewed through aniseikonic lenses of one type appears to lean forward; the lower portion of his body seems to broaden to give him almost a pyramidal shape. Individual parts of his body may also suffer corresponding distortion. The kind and degree of distortion depend partly on the distortion power of the lenses, but lenses of a given power still produce different degrees of distortion for different people.

When we fitted amputees with these lenses and asked them to view other persons, including other amputees, we at once made a significant finding. Each amputee reported that he saw considerably less distortion in the appearance of other amputees than he did in normal, whole persons. By way of experimental control, we fitted normal persons with the lenses and got the same report from them. They too saw amputees and even simulated amputees as less distorted than other people.

Since each type of aniseikonic lens is available in graded degrees of distortion power, we were able to reduce these differences in the perception of each subject to a quantitative expression. We had each of 12 enlisted men, selected at random from the staff, view a normal person and a simulated amputee through a succession of lenses of increasing power. For 11 of our 12 subjects it took a lens of higher power to cause him to see the "mutilated" figure as distorted. The average difference was about 25 per cent; in one case it was 150 per cent.

As compared to our first series of experiments with married couples, the finding of this study was susceptible to somewhat more precise and reliable interpretation. It is not too difficult to specify the one overriding emotion involved when one person views another who is, or appears to be, mutilated and disfigured. Almost invariably it is a feeling of uncertainty and anxiety. Few of us have had enough experience with mutilated people to be sure of ourselves in dealing with them. Thus, it may reasonably be supposed, the subjects of our experiment were moved to reject the distor-

THREE STUDENTS of about the same height seem to be of radically different sizes in a larger Ames room. The student on the left is actually nearly twice as far from the camera as the one on the right, but the distorted perspective of the room conceals this fact.

tion of the mutilated figures conveyed to them by the distorting lenses. One might think that the amputees who had taken part in our preliminary studies would not have reacted in this way, because they had presumably become used to seeing other mutilated men. All these men, however, were receiving psychiatric help in adjusting to their own mutilation, and the sight of another amputee still set off their more intense anxieties.

To test our hypothesis that an anxiety-inducing figure would be less easily distorted than a "neutral" one, we devised a third experiment. We had noted quite by accident that when one of our assistants, an enlisted man, looked through aniseikonic lenses, his immediate superior, an officer, appeared less distorted than other enlisted men. Intrigued by this observation, we conducted a series of interviews to assess the feelings of enlisted men toward their officers. We were not surprised to find that most of them reported some feeling of anxiety and that the feeling was most marked among recruits. We therefore selected at random 24 Navy recruits, or "boots," and had each of them view two different men through the lenses. One man wore the insignia of the recruits' immediate petty-officer superiors; the other, the insignia and canvas leggings ("boots") of a recruit. All but two of our subjects required lenses of higher distortion power to perceive the "officer" as distorted. The increase in lens power averaged about 50 per cent.

Apparently anxiety and an intensified need for reliable guides to action explained both the "mutilation" and the "authority" results. Did they also explain the findings of our experiments with married couples? At first glance there certainly seemed little connection between the emotions associated with the sight of a marital partner, an amputee and a person in authority. Newlyweds, however, may be regarded in one sense as "recruits," uncertain and anxious about their relationship to their spouse. In the case of Honi, a veteran of 25 years of marriage, one may surmise that her husband had the role of an "authority figure." On the other hand, marriage remains a complex relationship, and some entirely different process may have been at work. Further studies will doubtless reveal many emotional factors other than anxiety that may influence perception just as powerfully.

A number of experiments at the Naval Medical Research Institute and elsewhere suggest the unexplored possibilities. Some of the most interesting studies concern the way in which we perceive ourselves. Children who view themselves in a mirror through aniseikonic lenses report different kinds of distortion at different ages. Girls, who are typically more anxious about their appearance than boys, consistently report less distortion than boys of the same age. Both children and adults report that their own mirror image is distorted in different ways from that of another person. One's own image changes mainly in detail; the other person's, in over-all size and shape.

Most intriguing of all, some "mirror" experiments with psychotics indicate that they see the over-all distortion in their own image that a normal person sees in a stranger. Although the exact meaning of these experiments is not clear, one is tempted to say that the psychotic is a stranger to himself. Such measurement of perception may eventually prove useful in diagnosing mental disease. In any case, a knowledge of how the psychotic "sees" himself and other people should help us to understand his peculiar behavior.

Though I have spoken here of reacting to people and perceiving them as two distinct processes, these processes should not be regarded as being so separable as this wording suggests. In using such terms we are simply abstracting two aspects of a single process. The evidence points to the fusion of feeling and perceiving in a deeper understanding of the process of living.

23. Toward a Workable Psychology of Individuality * [1]

LEONA E. TYLER, *University of Oregon*

A S LONG as I can remember, I have been fascinated by human individuality. To me it has always seemed a strange and wonderful thing that every person is indeed unique. The attempt to comprehend this uniqueness —to grasp what is the distinctive quality in another person's life—is a common thread that has run through my experience with literature and music, counseling and therapy, and the psychology of individual differences. It is tied in also with my research on the meaning of likes and dislikes in children and adults. Out of the interaction between these major concerns in my own life has come a set of ideas with a certain amount of coherence and pattern, a product somewhat different from any of the raw materials that went into it. It is this product, rough and unfinished as it is, that I should like to place before you.

It was hard to decide what to call it. It is not complete or rigorous enough to be considered a theory. It is not close enough to the evidence that generated it to be considered a research report. It is essentially a different set, a different approach to familiar facts. Because it is this change in direction that I wished to chart, I decided just to do what various other recent authors have done and begin my title with the noncommittal word "Toward."

Individuality has many champions these days. "Conformity" has become almost a nasty word. "Adjustment," for years a central concept in psychology and mental hygiene, is coming to be regarded with suspicion. Riesman's portrayal of other-directedness seems to have stimulated in most of his readers a firm resolve not to be that way. Lindner's prescription for rebel-

* From Leona E. Tyler, "Toward a Workable Psychology of Individuality," *The American Psychologist,* 14 (February, 1959), 75–81. Reprinted by permission.
[1] Condensed and adapted from the Presidential Address to the Western Psychological Association, delivered in Monterey, California, on April 25, 1958.

lion woke echoes in thousands of psyches. Colin Wilson's collection of "outsiders" was lauded by reviewers and critics. Right now practically everyone is recoiling in horror from Whyte's picture of the organization man. An increasing number of existentialist novelists and playwrights are highlighting the individual's search for his own identity. In intellectual circles, at least, it is getting so that a person must be something of a non-conformist in order to conform to the prevailing standards. But I am afraid something like the much-quoted weather remark applies here: Everybody talks about individuality, but nobody does anything about it.

This is where the psychologists come in. What we have often been able to do is to take an idea that teachers, politicians, playwrights, philosophers, or theologians were concerned with, and make it *workable*. I do not mean this in any narrow sense. When I say a workable psychology of individuality, I mean one that would generate good research ideas, which, in turn, would lead to steady increases in dependable knowledge. I mean one that would produce a technology of assessment useful to clinical workers, teachers, and personnel men. I mean one that could be applied in the day-to-day activities of people who are not psychologists, such as diplomats, business men, and construction foremen. The problem as I see it is: How can we modify the system of psychological principles and skills that are now being applied in all these situations so that the uniqueness of the individual is really taken into account?

In differential psychology we have been concerned with this for something like 60 years. We have worked out techniques for measuring hundreds of traits. We have attempted to match particular individuals with particular situations, in schools, in industry, and in military settings. We have developed skills that enable us to help individuals make their decisions, solve their problems. Out of this activity has come a sort of model that we use in thinking about the general phenomena of individuality. The basic concept is that of dimension. Each of the traits that have been identified can be thought of as an axis along which any one person's position can be located. In this system the *uniqueness* of the individual is defined by his *combination* of measurements along all possible dimensions. A person is represented by a point in n-dimensional space. No one else occupies exactly the same position.

Useful as this approach has been, I have found myself questioning more and more whether it is really adequate at this stage in the development of our science. For one thing, it does not *feel* quite right. Most people find it hard to think of themselves as points in n-dimensional space. Occasionally I encounter an unusually articulate student who reacts violently against the whole conception, and I think that at a lower level of awareness many of the others show a kind of passive resistance to it. For another thing, the system shows signs of becoming completely unworkable, in the sense I have defined workability, because of the proliferation of dimensions. It looked for a time as though factor analysis would enable us to simplify it, but there are now so many factors and their relationships with each other are so complex that factor theory does not really constitute a simplification. But the most important reason I see for questioning the adequacy of this way of looking at things is that we are no longer making the progress with it that we have a right to expect. Correlations with criteria significant for theory or for practice are not going up very much. Seldom do we find a cross-validated multiple correlation with any criterion that exceeds .6. The addition of new dimensions and the increasing refinement in the ways we measure the old ones are not really "paying off" very well. The possibility is at least worth considering that we are approaching the limit of what can be done with this particular system.

In the more general psychology of personality, not all research workers and theorists have been particularly concerned with the question of individual uniqueness and how it can best be conceptualized. But a number of them have considered this problem, and developed some potentially useful ways of looking at it. Holistic Gestalt theories have never accepted the additive assumptions made in trait and factor work and have stressed individuality of pattern or organization. The Freudian conception of developmental stages has furnished one framework for analyzing differences between individuals. The Freudian concept of defense mechanisms, differentially developed in different persons, constitutes another such framework. The whole concept of cathexis and object choice would seem to furnish an even richer system within which the uniqueness of individuals could be described. Adler's concept of style of life is a way of thinking about individuality. So are Jung's psychological types. Gordon Allport has maintained a continuous emphasis on the ideographic as contrasted with the nomothetic. Henry Murray's system for detailed intensive study of individuals has been a dominant influence in personality research for more than 20 years.

When one examines these concepts drawn from personality theory to see which ones are really workable, however, it becomes plain that hardly any of them have as yet led to what one might call an adequate *technology*. By and large, the vast majority of so-called personality *tests* are measures either of general maladjustment, the extent to which an individual deviates from some hypothetical average of general "normality," or they are measures of the particular *variety* of neurotic or psychotic trends he shows. The utilization of the other theoretical treatments of individuality has been spotty and haphazard. A number of workers, for example, have tried to measure introversion-extraversion, but they have not taken into account the rest of the Jungian system for describing individuals. There have been attempts to make dimensions of Freudian oral and anal systems, but no one has really utilized the cathexis concept as a basis for standardized techniques of individual assessment. Of the personality theorists, Murray has come closest to developing a usable technology. A number of other workers, such as Allen Edwards, have devised ways of measuring the different needs or motives which are the most basic variables in the Murray system.

Even in cases like this, however, where concepts from personality theory have led to methods for the appraisal of the individual, the assumption is still being made that differences between persons can be measured in terms of traits or dimensions. A score on a personality test purports to tell how far the testee is above or below the mean of some reference group. This kind of comparison in terms of trait measurements is involved even in projective tests, although when they are used, the final clinical report may add some extra nonquantitative descriptions.

What I have been coming to believe is that individuality will continue to elude us as long as we restrict our thinking to models based on dimensions or trait continua. Little by little, evidence has been accumulating that some of the crucial defining features of psychological individuality are to be found in two aspects of experience and behavior that are not easily expressed as dimensions and that can best be thought of as *dis*continuous. I call these two aspects of individuality *choice* and *organization,* though I am by no means certain that these are the best labels. But whether the terms are adequate or not, I hope at least to be able to tell you what I mean by them.

Partly what led me to a reorganization of my ideas about individuality around these concepts was a sort of inherent reasonableness about them. With the swift passage of the years one becomes acutely aware that human life is finite. It lasts only a limited time, and each person has only a limited number of hours each day at his disposal. Only a small fraction of the potentialities with which his life begins can ever become realities. By the time his infancy is over, a considerable number of them have already been ruled out by the fact that he has spent his most formative years in one particular kind of home rather than another. But the person is still confronted at each step of his life with an incredibly complex assortment of stimulating conditions and behavior possibilities. In order to function at all, each of us must choose from this plethora of possibilities and organize what he has chosen.

Consider, for example, Barker's report on the Midwest study (Barker and Wright, 1955). If even in one little town there are 585 distinguishable behavior settings, 60 to 79 per cent of them open to children, and if during the course of a single day one child engages in almost 2,500 behavior transactions with 749 different behavior objects, the *possibilities* for influence that might help to determine individuality are absolutely staggering. It seems plausible to me to assume that one of the main things that happens as the boy or girl interacts with this complex milieu is that he develops patterns of choices that serve to let some things in and to keep others out. If to this screening function we add some sort of organizational process acting upon the experience choice has admitted, we begin to come close to the meaning of individuality. In counseling and therapy we are actually using this sort of conceptualization in our attempts to understand clients, although it is not always expressed very clearly, and, as we shall see, some research workers have been developing methods of assessment that can be considered pilot projects on the way to a new technology.

Let us then take a look at choice and organization separately, realizing as we do so that they are not independent and do not actually occur separately. I have mentioned that I do not think choice is a very good word for the phenomenon, but I have not been able to think of a better one. Perhaps some other figurative statements can serve to make its meaning clearer, however. I have compared it a moment ago to a screen. This is really too fixed and static a picture. We might see life instead as a restaurant with a large number of items on the menu from which two or three are to be selected. Or we might take our cue from the poets who have seen life as a road, which forks every now and then requiring that the traveler go in one direction or the other.

All these analogies have the merit of reminding us that a person's life is always bounded by limits of one kind or another. He is not free to do anything he wants to or to go in any direction. I do not think it is necessary to get into the old controversy over determinism versus free will at all. Certainly at any one time a large number of behavior possibilities are ruled out by external circumstances, by personal inadequacies, and by previous commitments. But within these analyzable limits there is a larger or smaller space in which movement of different sorts is possible. It is this movement in one direction rather than another, within defining limits, that I am calling choice.

It seems clear to me also that a large part of the choice process is unconscious. The individual's choice of the aspects of a complex stimulating situation to which he will respond is a universal process, constantly going on. It is only the small part of it of which we are aware that we call freedom. In a very real sense it *is* freedom, because in human choices, awareness makes a difference. It changes the nature of the total situation and thus leads to choices that may be different from those that would have been made unconsciously. And in this small margin of difference that awareness makes lies our best hope for progress in living our own lives wisely and helping those it is our responsibility to help.

A workable psychology of individuality would provide us with ways of recognizing significant patterns of choices that have been made at previous stages of life, consciously or unconsciously, and of widening the margin of awareness in any individual's present experience. To accomplish this we need a different approach, a different kind of assessment from the customary measurements of traits or dimensions. Let us go back for a moment to our restaurant analogy. Two men are having dinner together. One orders jambalaya, artichokes, and crepe suzette. The other orders fried chicken, corn on the cob, and apple pie. Conceivably we could scale the degree of liking for each of these foods and compare the two men on these several scales. But if we did just this, we would miss the main distinction here. It is the choice of the particular *combination* of foods, jambalaya *and* artichokes *and* crepe suzette, or chicken *and* corn *and* apple pie that reveals something about each person. Measuring the strength of these preferences is unnecessary and irrelevant.

It is here, in connection with the assessment of the meaning of combinations of choices, that the research activity on which I have been principally engaged enters the picture. In one way or another I have been dealing for some 20 years with the responses men and women, boys and girls make to Like and Dislike items on the blanks we have been calling interest tests. But it was not until a couple of months ago that it suddenly dawned on me that the major significance of all of this work is that it points the way to a kind of assessment quite different from trait measurement, namely, the direct assessment of choice patterns. True, we have been expressing what we found in terms of traits or dimensions that we labeled "interest in science," "masculinity-femininity," or "occupational level." But when we did this, the findings never fit the labels very well. On the Strong test, for example, the correlations of the numerical scores people make on the various scales with criteria purporting to represent degrees of success and satisfaction have almost always turned out to be rather low. The really impressive relationships Strong (1955) has obtained in his 20-year followup of Stanford students have been based on *letter grades* as predictors of a special kind of criterion—that of remaining in the original occupation vs. shifting to another.

The letter grades on the Strong are derived from the scores but carry a different meaning from customary trait measurements. An "A" means "Yes" with regard to the question of whether a certain person belongs in a certain occupation, a "C" means "No," and a "B" means "We cannot be sure." We can relate these grades to the concept of choice we have been considering by putting it this way: An A signifies that the person's characteristic pattern of acceptance and rejection of life's varied possibilities is like the choice pattern characteristic of persons in a certain occupation.

What we should expect then to be able to predict from such a score is not how well the person will do the work of his chosen occupation, or how much satisfaction he will express with his job, but simply the way he will make his choices at later junctures of his life. This makes sense of the high degree of validity Strong's recent studies have shown for the test. What they are telling us is that an indicator of the nature of an individual's complex pattern of choices in the occupational area predicts well later complex choices in the same area.

My own special research activities have focused on an attempt to trace such choice patterns backward into childhood rather than forward into maturity. In 1946 I entered upon a longitudinal study of about 200 children, beginning at the time they entered school. The first half of this group is graduating from high school this year. They have taken the Strong test each year during the high school period, so that I have a clear picture of what their interests are like now at the end of adolescence. I am attempting to relate these interest patterns (or choice patterns, as I should now prefer to call them) to various personality characteristics, background factors, and special abilities, measured now and at earlier periods of the subjects' lives.

At the outset I was thinking of each of the variables as a trait and planning to correlate them with one another. The shift to this concept of choice patterns has changed my plans for analyzing the data. The appropriate type of measurement for these problems is *nominal,* not ordinal or interval—that is, simple categorization rather than continuous distribution. And to relate one of these choice categories to another, the appropriate statistic is not correlation, but some nonparametric significance test leading to a statement of probabilities. What this means concretely so far as my particular body of data is concerned is that I will classify my subjects in various ways, based on their final Strong scores, and then ask specific questions of the data from earlier stages. For example, I shall place all boys whose scores point to the choice of some science career in one group, those who definitely are not in the science group in another. I will then tabulate other test results and biographical data for these groups, using total scores, subscores, and in some cases separate items, and look for patterns or combinations of characteristics related to this particular choice pattern. (Such findings will of course need to be cross-validated. For some of the relationships, supplementary data on other groups not in the main study will serve this purpose; in other cases extra studies will need to be run.)

The main point I am trying to make here is that to work out a technology of choice measurement we must use classifications with regard to choices rather than continua, validate our assessments using choice criteria rather than measures of degrees of happiness or success, and state the relationships as probabilities that one thing will lead to another rather than as correlation coefficients. The work with the Strong Vocational Interest Blank is important to all of us who are concerned about personality assessment not just because it has a great deal of demonstrated practical value, but because it demonstrates that this kind of assessment, of choice patterns rather than traits, does work. Eventually we may have many such assessment devices, covering a much wider variety of patterned choices. Measures of preferences, values, and attitudes would seem to be clearly in this area, but as yet we are still trying to score and interpret them as traits or dimensions.

The work with the Strong test demonstrates that we need not abandon the concept of predictive validity when we shift from traits to discontinuous patterns of choices. The only difference is that we need to find criteria that represent choices rather than distances along some scale. There are many of these. My impression is that criteria are far less of a problem here than in customary validation studies. In the academic area they would include things like staying in school vs. dropping out, selecting one major rather than another, choosing "easy" or "hard" electives, going in for social success or for academic success. In a broader social framework, choice criteria would include such things as suing for divorce vs. attempting to work out marital problems, or parole keeping vs. violation. Choice criteria in the clinical area would include such things as the development of one kind of symptom rather than another, or the decision to seek psychotherapy vs. reliance on tranquilizers. These have all been used in research but not for the purpose for which they would seem to be particularly appropriate—research on the relationship of choice patterns to one another.

It is quite feasible, then, for us to carry on research that will enable us eventually to make much sounder inferences about individuals by observing what they choose. But this is only part of the story. I have been convinced, primarily as a result of my counseling activities, that the *how* is as important as the *what*. There are several aspects of choice we must consider. I have already touched briefly on the matter of differences in *awareness*. To understand an individual we must know how conscious he is of the choices he is making. Another aspect probably related to this is the age or developmental stage at which the first step in this direction was taken. It seems probable that some of the most important choices of all are made in the earliest years, long before the child is clearly aware of the direction he is taking. Whether to be active or passive in one's encounters with life, whether to seek security through dependence or independence, whether to relate oneself to persons or nonpersons (to use Anne Roe's terms), these are the kinds of fundamental early choices I have in mind. Research on concepts of sex role seem to show that a basic decision to accept one's own sex and to live by the code that goes with it is often made by the age of three. The Freudian concept of cathexis is clearly relevant here. Existentialist writers like Sartre have also emphasized unconscious choices and their significance in personality.

Another aspect of choice, perhaps somewhat easier to study, is the question of whether it has been made positively or negatively. It may make a considerable difference in the quality of an individual's life whether the choices that constitute its basic structure have been made by grasping what one wants or by rejecting what one does not want. I ran into this problem years ago when I first began to work with blanks calling for Like and Dislike responses. I became convinced that this negative choice process is far more significant in human life than we are assuming it to be. If we examine the scoring weights for most scales of the Strong test we find that so-called interest scores are based more on what we reject or rule out than on what we wish to do. Dislikes influence scores more than Likes do. My work with children in grade school suggests that interest development is primarily a matter of learning to rule out clusters of things and activities one once liked.

There are probably clear-cut individual differences in this area of positive vs. negative choices, and they would be well worth some special study. In our own profession, for example, it is conceivable that some of us are here because no other direction for our efforts was open to us. We needed to avoid, say, low prestige, low pay, mathematics, routine activties, and religious dogma. When we got through ruling out the occupations that would not do for one or another of these reasons, we found ourselves in a graduate psychology program. Others of us may be here because of an intense curiosity about human behavior and motivation, a strong urge to try out different experimental procedures and see what happens. Probably most of us have some of both kinds of motivation. Probably most of us score A on the Strong key for Psychologist, but that in itself does not show whether positive or negative choices predominate, since there are different combinations of items that will produce such a score.

Another of these "How" questions in which I am interested has to do with the *basis* upon which choices have been made. Do they grow out of identification with a parent or some other significant person? Do they reflect the point of view of some group to which the person belongs? Have they been influenced by particular experiences or by specific kinds of information? How much thoughtful consideration of possible alternatives has gone into them?

There is one more aspect of choice as a clue to individuality which is in some ways the most important of all, though it is the hardest to investigate. I mean the question as to how *central* or deeply rooted any given pattern of

choice is for an individual. It is these basic *unalterable* choices that give
a person a firm sense of self. Just making choices with regard to separate
objects and actions is not enough. It is necessary that a person in some
way *choose to be himself.* The idea is beautifully expressed in the words
Yourcenar attributes to Hadrian in the novel *Hadrian's Memoirs.*

Whatever I had I chose to have, obliging myself only to possess it totally, and
to taste the experience to the full. . . . And it is in such a way, with a mixture
of reserve and of daring, of submission and revolt carefully concerted, of extreme demand and prudent concession, that I have finally learned to accept
myself.

There is no derth of discussion of self concepts, self-acceptance, and
identity in psychology today. What I have been thinking about a great deal
is how to make these ideas more "workable." Here too I think we can use
interest tests as tools for work on the larger problem.

To sum up, the thing that distinguishes the kinds of research studies
I have been using as examples from much of the previous work on individual differences in personality is a design based on classification rather
than measurement (or on nominal rather than interval measures, if we wish
to use Stevens' terminology). We select a group that appears to be homogeneous with regard to one particular aspect of their choices. By contrasting
them with another group, we can obtain evidence about what this aspect
of choice means—the kind of previous experience that is associated with it,
the kind of subsequent choice behavior to which it leads. But because we
are interested in the choices made by *individuals,* we will not stop with the
statement that a relationship is significant at a given probability level but
will attempt also to explore the differences between the persons who do
and those who do not follow the prevailing trend.

I hope that nothing I have said will be taken to mean that I think we
should discard the measuring techniques we now have for appraising the
individual, or the knowledge that has accumulated from their use. Certainly
the differences in physical and biochemical characteristics, that can be
measured with considerable accuracy and expressed as continuous variables,
are very significant. The research that has been going on for many years
at the California Institute for Child Welfare has shown us how meaningful
such a variable as age of reaching sexual maturity can be when we try to
understand individual growth patterns. Certainly the differences in mental
abilities and achievements that we pick up by means of our standardized
tests represents important components of individuality. What I am trying
to suggest is that, when we have recognized that there are choice patterns
that are *not* continuous variables, we will be able to *utilize* more effectively
all the resources we now have. We can still use our measures of physical
characteristics, intelligence, special abilities, and personality traits to give us

an approximate picture of an individual. The information about his distinctive patterns of choices will enable us to sketch in the finer lines of his portrait—to make it definitive.

As I stated in the beginning, individual uniqueness for me is described primarily in terms of *choice* and *organization,* and I consider it the task of psychologists to make those concepts workable—to bring them into the general stream of thinking in research, assessment, and practical activities. I have used up about nine-tenths of my time talking about choice. This is not because I consider it the more important of the two, but simply because my own research activity has been in that area and I have done more thinking about it. Fortunately, an increasing number of psychologists have been presenting interesting new methods of assessing the ways individuals organize their experience. Perhaps the best known of these methods is Stevenson's *Q* sort. Other sorting techniques, originally developed as research tools in the study of concepts now are being applied to the study of individuals. George Kelly's Role Construct Repertory Test is an ingenious way of finding out something about the organiaztion of the person's relationships to other people who are significant in his life. Osgood's semantic differential represents still another approach to the assessment of individual patterns of organization. While a number of other things could be mentioned, perhaps these examples are sufficient to indicate directions I should like to have us move in our attempts to understand individuality.

There are many related areas we might consider if time permitted. We might turn to the experimental work on choice and decision in general psychology. We might look at the flourishing new mathematics of decision processes. We might attempt to relate some philosophical systems to these ideas. We might take up the implications of these ideas for psychotherapy and education.

What interests me most right now, however, is the significance of concepts of choice and organization in an inclusive psychology of the *development* of the human individual. We are coming to see development as a lifelong process in which choice and organization play a crucial part. In a certain sense each person *is* a "self-made man." At each stage of our lives, we impose limits on the next stage, by the choices we make and the ways in which we organize what we have experienced. There is an important something that each individual must do for himself.

References

BARKER, R. G., and WRIGHT, H. F. *Midwest and its children.* Evanston, Ill.: Row, Peterson, 1955.

STRONG, E. K., JR. *Vocational interests 18 years after college.* Minneapolis: Univer. Minnesota Press, 1955.

24. Intelligence: Its Nature and Measurement *

RICHARD HARSH, *Assistant Director, Division of Research and Guidance, Los Angeles County Public Schools, California.*

THE HUMAN mind is our fundamental resource. Such a statement has been a frequent pronouncement in recent literature. Descriptions of man have always included characterizations of individual differences as well as similarities. However, the products and refinements of the various sciences have led to more explicit definitions of the various aspects of man. The term intelligence is one reflection of this endeavor to describe a dimension of man.

Intelligence has been the term or label used to refer to a quality or condition of individual difference. As individuals showed differing speed and accuracy in solving a problem, assembling a device, or devising a plan of action, the comment was made that one person had a lot and another person had less of this quality called intelligence. Intelligence has been a construct devised to explain the potentialities of the human being for learning, for producing, and for adjusting to the environment.

From the inception of modern mental measurement, a variety of issues have been of concern in defining the nature of intelligence. The emergence of contemporary thought regarding the nature of mental abilities or intelligence probably relates in part to the research which has been concerned with:

* From Richard Harsh, "Intelligence: Its Nature and Measurement," *The National Elementary Principal* (September, 1961), pp. 23–28. Reprinted by permission.

The distribution and extent of individual differences found in the total population.

The contribution of heredity and environment to human abilities.

The relationship between physiological status and the behavioral characteristics attributed to intelligence.

The relationship of education or training to measured mental abilities.

The qualitative and quantitative characteristics of extremes in human abilities as represented by mental deficiency and genius.

The effect of social, class, and cultural environments on the development of mental abilities.

The development and validation of a theory of mental organization.

The results of these research findings have pointed out the complexity of the concept referred to by the term intelligence. One part of the complexity deals with the multiple factors which may facilitate or retard the development of human abilities. A second aspect of the complexity was revealed by attempts to validate the practical significance of the existing measures of intelligence in predicting excellence of human behavior in product and adjustment.

Recognizing the danger of oversimplification, it is nevertheless felt that some brief summarization of these research findings would be helpful in relation to this discussion of the nature of intelligence and the aspects of intelligence measured by some of the more commonly used tests.

Degree of Individual Differences

The research suggests that individual differences are qualitative as well as quantitative. The normal curve appears to be a reflection of quantitative differences found by a variety of measures of mental abilities. In some cases, sampling irregularities, special environmental conditions, or characteristics of the measuring instrument produced other than bell-shaped curves. These exceptions, however, have not disproven the concept that human abilities tend to be distributed in a normal curve.

There is substantial agreement that the quest for absolute measurements of extent and variability of different traits is unfruitful. The degree of individual differences is a relative quantity in any measured dimension. This is due both to the lack of comparable units for measuring various traits and to the absence of a means of establishing absolute zero points on psychological scales.

Effects of Heredity and Environment

Research dealing with heredity and environment suggests that their effects are inextricably intertwined. Heredity sets certain limits within which the organism may develop. In the case of psychological traits, these limitations for most persons may be so wide as to allow almost unlimited variation. At the same time, there seems to be little evidence that a given intellectual trait can be directly dependent upon heredity. The variations in the extent of development of the inherited potentials are a reflection of the stimulation of the environmental conditions.

Specific research concerned with heredity has directed attention toward such aspects as family resemblance, similarities of the biological organism, organic conditions limiting human development, physical deficiencies, and selective breeding. Specific researches concerned with heredity have attempted to determine the contribution of the structural properties of the organism. There is agreement that a healthy, optimally reacting organism is essential for maximum development. It is also recognized that certain congenital conditions may limit or enhance mental development. More recent research with the basic neuromechanism suggests the contribution of this fundamental element for learning potential and reactivity of the individual. So far, the attempts to determine precise differences or measurements of the contributions of heredity and environment have been inconclusive. Agreement is found regarding the constant interaction and mediation of these two contributors to the development of human potential. Although some might suggest that heredity and environment should be viewed only as separate contributors, they appear to be like two courses of water mixing together in a stream that is subsequently reflected in levels of human development.

The studies of identical twins have illustrated that impoverished environments tend to depress the possible development and, conversely, rich and stimulating environments tend to accelerate and expand the person's development.

The studies of the Kentucky Hollows illustrate that the demands of the society or culture may offer specific requirements and stimulations to the development of mental abilities. Other studies which noted the change of mental abilities as individuals were moved from impoverished to rich environments give additional evidence of cultural impact upon human development.

Research dealing with the relationship of education to developmental abilities has consistently shown a direct positive relationship. Generally, the higher measured mental abilities of children have been found in families engaged in the occupations requiring greater amounts of educational training. Research has produced similar findings when relating the children of parents of different occupational groups to mental ability. These relationships, however, which suggest a substantial positive correlation between education and mental ability, also are apparently related to the type of measurement or method of assessing intellectual differences.

Other research has suggested a positive relationships between emotional and personality factors and the development of human abilities. Still other research studies have pointed up the impact of social class and cultural environments in stimulating mental abilities. These studies are similar to those dealing with education and occupational differences. It should be mentioned, however, that studies with canal-boat children, migrant gypsies, or mountain children typically reveal less satisfactory stimulation of such cultures on measured abilities. These findings might lead to the hypothesis that the deficiencies noted may be the result of both the nature of the functions tested as well as the influence of the environmental deprivation. A similar kind of hypothesis might also be drawn in relation to the wide differences found when measuring urban and rural population with the same instrument.

Some studies suggest that differences between social classes or regions may be related to the specific functions tested. It is hypothesized that each cultural group tends to foster the development of a characteristic pattern of aptitudes as well as values and personality traits. If a test which is used to assess mental ability measures a pattern of aptitudes, values, or traits dissimilar to those of a particular culture, conclusions might be drawn that the measured group was inferior to that on which the test was standardized. Thus, many studies have concluded that tests constructed within a particular subculture (eastern urban, for example) tend to measure aspects of that culture and, thus, obviously favor individuals reared in that culture. We must conclude that assessment of intelligences or mental abilities must be interpreted in terms of the criteria from which the test was constructed and validated.

Viewpoints on Intelligence

Within this century, definitions of intelligence have featured many different views. Some definitions have featured learning, others memory, others adjustment, and others abstraction. Some scientists reacting to this question of what intelligence is have replied, "Intelligence is what my test measures." Such circular thinking, although somewhat humorous, has unfortunately led to limited concepts and behavioral definitions of the nature of intelligence. Furthermore, it has tended to promote the concept that intelligence is a single substance or quality.

Everyday observation of the layman, or statistical validations of measurement results by the psychometrician, or attempts to predict success in various educational or occupational areas have led to a common conclusion. This conclusion is that none of the widely used measures of mental ability which suggest a single quotient to characterize the abilities of man are comprehensive measurements. Convergence of thought and concept in relation to intelligence has pointed toward the variety of mental abilities which have qualitative as well as quantitative differences among members of the population. The description of mechanical, social, verbal, abstract, or spatial-perceptual abilities is a reflection of convergence of concepts that a man is characterized by a variety of mental abilities. Each person represents a profile of abilities. Each person's abilities reflect the stimulation and opportunity provided by the heredity, culture, family, education, and other contributors to human development.

Some of the limited concepts of intelligence are specifically related to the somewhat limited means of measurement which have been in wide usage. Concepts have tended to be in advance of the development of the technical measures. Hence, many of our school paper-and-pencil measures of intelligence or mental ability were really only measures of word meaning, manipulation, or fluency. They were further mainly reflections of convergent thinking dealing with common educational contents of an urban culture. The perceptual, the mechanical, or the spatial were frequently unmeasured dimensions when an intelligence quotient was cited for an individual.

At the present, broader concepts are presenting theoretical models which more adequately describe the variety of mental abilities of man. J. P. Guilford suggests that:

Intellectual abilities may be classified according to operation (cognition, memory, production, and evaluation).

Intellect may be classified in terms of content such as figural, symbolic, or semantic.

Intelligence may be classified according to product such as elements, classes, relations, systems, or implications.

In this area of product, Guilford's model has suggested the importance of convergent as well as divergent thinking. An emerging dimension may be the social or behavioral abilities which have previously been related to personality patterns, but are apparently inextricably related to the manner in which the individual receives, focuses, and produces in the various intelligences he possesses.

This model by Dr. Guilford obviously highlights the fallacious concept of the intelligence quotient. Intelligence is not a unitary substance. Research clearly points to the intelligences of man.

Intelligence has been used by many to mean the innate ability with which a person is born. Hence, intelligence was seen as that which a person inherited, as unchanging or unmodifiable and constantly predictive of the amount a person could learn. The research dealing with heredity and environment, physiological conditions, education, and cultural influences has shattered the myth that intelligence is solely a reflection of the inherited capacities of the person.

Meaning of IQ

Reference made to the intelligence quotient is frequently done in a manner which suggests an immutable inherited characteristic. We know, however, that the intelligence quotient is merely a numerical representation of how well a given child performs on a particular series of test items in relation to the performance of other children of similar age. This is certainly quite different from an exact measurement of the inherited capacties of the person. When the individual is subsequently tested with a different series of items or tests, it is not uncommon to find an intelligence quotient that varies considerably from the first measurement. This is not only under-standable, but expected when one considers the tasks required by the test items.

Some educators have been troubled as they viewed cumulative records and saw the Goodenough IQ of 140, the CTMM IQ of 120, and the Otis IQ of 110. Such results have prompted a variety of reactions. Some would debate, "Which score is correct?" Others would suggest, "Take the last test score. It is probably the most accurate." Still others would suggest, "Average all the scores together and you probably have the best indi-cation." Still others would suggest, "Well, I guess none of the tests are very accurate when they vary this much."

None of these suggestions or explanations sound very appropriate if we consider merely the item content of these several tests. The Goodenough Draw-A-Man IQ is based upon the graphic motor representation of the human figure which the subject is able to draw on a blank sheet of paper. The California Test of Mental Maturity at the primary level presents pictorial material to be classified according to similiarities and differences; forms to be interpreted or imaginably manipulated; pictures of objects for which verbal classifications and meanings must be identified; quantitative concepts and manipulations; and appraisal of the vocabularly development. The test items present verbal as well as nonverbal materials. Material is presented to and suggested for the subject to react to. Still an IQ is derived based upon items which are testing very different qualities from the Good-enough. The Otis Test presents items which are mainly verbal descriptions of word meaning, reasoning or classification, and numerical reasoning. Skill in reading comprehension and the level of vocabulary development become crucial items to success on this particular test. Here, too, an IQ is computed.

These general characteristics of these three measures should reflect the difference in performance and task for the student. The IQ's have only one thing in common. They compare the subject's performance with others of the same age or classification. Their differences lie in the task assigned the subject to complete and the degree of excellence suggested or expected by the norms established in the standardization of the instrument.

Scholastic Aptitude Tests

To suggest that any one or all of these measures gives a comprehensive picture of the intelligences of man seems totally fallacious. Paper-and-pencil tests in wide usage in the schools tend to be most commonly subjecting students to verbal and numerical tasks presented in printed abstraction. Many of these items have been specifically selected because they tend to have good predictive value in relation to subsequent scholastic progress of the students. The common use of the term intelligence test for these paper-and-pencil instruments widely administered in the schools should probably be discontinued. A more appropriate term would be a measure of scholastic aptitude or a test of academic aptitude. These are not tests of pure inherited qualities. What is measured by these tests are the developed abilities which reflect a combination of what the person inherited in organic characteristics and the variety of environmental influences and training he has received. Scholastic aptitude should be defined as those inherited and acquired capacities which indicate the relative speed, accuracy, and breadth of scholastic learning.

Some tests included in measures of "intelligence" are assessments of abilities which are poor predictors of scholastic success. For example, test problems asking the individual to visualize the movement of forms or objects in space or organize parts of the device have been found to be relatively unpredictive of scholastic success. These test items probably do an effective job in describing a perceptual or spatial ability which may be important for other types of learning and productivity.

Achievement versus Scholastic Aptitude Tests

Some persons question whether the paper-and-pencil measures of scholastic aptitude are any different from the conventional achievement tests which are administered. Yes, they are different. Measures of scholastic aptitude present test items which assess the generalized accumulation of learning and development which is obviously a reflection of both the inherited capacities as well as the environmental stimulation. Since the measurement of capacity may only be made through devising problems of situations the individual must react to, it is necessary to use some of the same content which is found in achievement tests. The crucial element of difference, however, is in the specificity of content assessed. For example, a scholastic aptitude test frequently presents a complex reading comprehension problem for the individual to pick out the most logical solution or cause. The content tends to be sufficiently general so that it might be applicable in any school regardless of the particular curriculum content.

In contrast, an achievement test in history or geography would probably deal with those specific informations required in a history or geography course. The scholastic aptitude test is a measure of the generalized achievements which may be focused and utilized in the solutions of new and unique problems. The score is a reflection of the speed, accuracy, and breadth of this problem solution. The achievement test is the reflection of the extent and depth of comprehension and retention of the specified content of a given subject field, such as arithmetic, French, or economics.

Differences in Performance

The dimensions of intellect defined by Dr. Guilford make specific reference to the variety of intelligences possessed by man. This description of the nature of intellect is an attempt to make further realistic refinements of the broad and ambiguous concept which for so many years was referred to as intelligence. The distinction between aptitude and achievement is applicable for these new dimensions of intellect as well as the distinction drawn between the more commonly used tests of scholastic aptitude, such as the Kuhlman, California, or Otis tests.

The commonly used paper-and-pencil test of scholastic aptitude tends to measure such things as mastery of previous learnings, attention span, memory, comprehension, analogies of dissimilar association, organization of ideas or facts, vocabulary, associational implications, recognition of rules, principles, or operation. All paper-and-pencil tests do not measure the same functions. The Otis, CTMM, Chicago Non-verbal, Kuhlman-Anderson, PMA, and SCAT make rather different assessments of intellect. Rather wide differences might be anticipated in IQ performance on the Chicago Non-verbal and Otis, or the Terman-McNemar and the PMA.

The measurement of intelligence is mental measurement. Mental measurement is indirect measurement. Indirect measurement is dependent upon items designed to sample behavior of the subjects. The behavior sampled is directed by the particular directions or content of the items. Various tests present different content and situations for the subjects to respond to.

Variations in item content suggests probable variations in IQ's which will result. Our conclusion would most naturally be severalfold.

Variation in IQ may be expected when measured by different tests.

The variable performance on a variety of tests is helpful rather than discouraging in that these variations may point up a profile of abilities as reflected by the differences in the various measures.

Predictive use of measures of various kinds of intellect may be tremendously increased when diligent attention is given to the psychological functions employed and the products or outcomes demanded by the items in the particular tests.

Conclusions about Human Intelligence

Finally, the result of this research leads me to certain conclusions regarding a verifiable concept of intelligence as well as practical uses of the measurement of human intelligence. Obviously, our conclusions have rather direct relationship to educational interpretations as well as to the provisions made in the educational program.

First, I conclude that the IQ or intelligence quotient is a misleading and fallacious concept if it is used to describe the comprehensive intelligence of an individual. The IQ suggests that a single measurement characterizes the diversity and quantity of human abilities which we make reference to as a person's intelligence. I believe it is fallacious to refer to a person's intelligence in the singular. Research clearly shows us that we must speak of the intelligences of man.

In education, we have used measures of intelligence as estimates of expected achievement. There are certainly many types of mental abilities which show no high relationship to academic success. Thus, we make reference to measures of mental abilities that have high relationship (or predictive value) for academic success. Such measures might realistically be referred to as indications of scholastic aptitude. In a similar vein, there are measures of spatial, mechanical, and social abilities which are apparently quite separate from these scholastic or academic abilities.

The research with various types of thinking suggests that there may be several types of scholastic aptitudes rather than the dominant one we have used in the past. I refer to the verbal meanings and abstractions measured by convergent thought items. There is high probability that other scholastic aptitudes related to divergent thinking with various symbols or content may be meaningful dimensions for educational prediction and planning.

Some are of the opinion that if an individual has high ability in academic aptitude he consequently has high ability in all other aptitudes. Such an assumption appears unsubstantiated; however, there is still doubt regarding the degree of relationship between the variety of intelligences or aptitudes within any person. The evidence of the variation of abilities demonstrated by any individual suggests that high aptitude in one type of intelligence is not necessarily a predictor of high aptitude in all others.

A third conclusion would suggest that the description or characterization of any person should be made in terms of a profile of his various mental abilities. Recent research suggests that the profile would probably need to be tridimensional so that the motivation, products, and expressions illustrating the variety of interpretations might be adequately represented. We have heard the statement, *"He looks at the person and he is reading him."* This is not a conventional description of the reading process, but it is perhaps analogous to a type of human ability which is quite different from the comprehension of verbal abstraction measured on either a reading or abstract verbal intelligence test.

Of course, the final implication of all this is obvious but worthy of mention. Educational experiences must be realistically planned for the diversity of human abilities which are known to be existent and capable of development. It would further imply that rather separate and discrete measurements are necessary to describe adequately the variety of human abilities which exist in a student population encompassing the variety of geographical and cultural settings in the many schools of our country.

25. *Aptitude, Intelligence, and Achievement* *

ALEXANDER G. WESMAN, *The Psychological Corporation*

WHICH is more helpful—an aptitude test or an achievement test?—a general mental ability test or a differential aptitude test battery? There are purposes for which each kind of test is superior; there are circumstances in which all are useful; there are conditions when any one of these types may be pressed into service to yield information ordinarily obtained from

* From *Test Service Bulletin* of The Psychological Corporation (December, 1956), No. 51, pp. 4–6. Reprinted by permission.

another type of test. What are these purposes, circumstances and conditions? When should an achievement test be used rather than an intelligence
test, or an aptitude test? What advantages do multiple-score aptitude batteries have over single-score intelligence tests?

As a preliminary, let us look at the basic characteristics of achievement
tests, intelligence tests and aptitude tests. By definition, an achievement
test measures what the examinee has learned. But an intelligence test
measures what the examinee has learned. And an aptitude test measures
what the examinee has learned. So far, no difference is revealed. Yet three
of the traditional categories into which tests are classified are intelligence,
aptitude and achievement. Now these categories are very handy; they permit publishers to divide their catalogs into logical segments, and provide
textbook authors with convenient chapter headings. Unfortunately, the
categories represent so much oversimplification as to cause confusion as to
what is being measured. What all three kinds of tests measure is what the
subject has learned. The ability to answer a proverbs item is no more a
part of the examinee's heredity than is the ability to respond to an item
in a mechanical comprehension test or in a social studies test. All are
learned behavior.

Moreover, all are intelligent behavior. It takes intelligence to supply the
missing number in a number series problem. It also requires intelligence to
figure out which pulley will be most efficient, or to remember which president proposed an inter-American doctrine. We can say, then, that an intelligence test measures intelligent behavior, an aptitude test measures intelligent behavior and an achievement test measures intelligent behavior.

Finally, all three types of tests measure probability of future learning or
performance, which is what we generally mean when we speak of "aptitude." In business and industry, the chances that an employee will profit
from training or will perform new duties capably may be predicted by
scores on an intelligence test, by scores on one or more specific aptitude
tests, or by some measure of the degree of skill the employee already
possesses. Similarly, test users in the schools know that an intelligence test
is usually a good instrument for predicting English grades, a social studies
test is often helpful for prediction of future grades in social studies, and a
mechanical comprehension test is likely to be useful in predicting for scientific or technical courses. So, intelligence tests are aptitude tests, achievement tests are aptitude tests and aptitude tests are aptiude tests.

Content—What the Test Covers

On what basis are the types to be differentiated? One possible basis is
that of content. Quite often, we can look at the subject matter of a test and

classify the test as achievement or intelligence or aptitude. But content is not a sure guide by any means.

Let us take a specific item. A student is taught to multiply $(x - y)$ by (x). If he demonstrates that he can perform this operation correctly, we accept this item as an achievement measure. Next, without specific formal instruction, he is asked to multiply $(p + q)$ by $(p - q)$, and again answers correctly. Is this achievement? The mathematics teacher would say it is. Is it aptitude? Certainly the ability to perceive the analogy between the taught and untaught algebraic problems is indicative of future learning ability in algebra. Is it intelligence? The demonstrated ability to generalize is clearly symptomatic of intelligence.

The same point can be made with regard to entire subtests. In the *Metropolitan Achievement* series there is a spelling test; one of the *Differential Aptitude Tests* is also a test called spelling. Tests of arithmetic comprehension may be found in most achievement batteries; one of the subtests in each of the *Wechsler Intelligence Scales* measures arithmetic comprehension. What does all this mean? Have we demonstrated that the authors of these tests are confused, or is our classification system less neat and simple than it appears to be on the surface?

We believe the classification system is at fault. The teacher who has taught pupils how to solve arithmetic problems is perfectly justified in claiming that the pupils' performance on tests in these abilities represents achievement—both hers and theirs. At the same time, the learning of the skills and appreciations by the pupils is evidence of intelligence. Furthermore, the possession of the skills and of the ability to learn demonstrates the possession of aptitude for further learning in those same school subjects, and probably in other subjects as well. For example, scores on the *DAT* Spelling Test provide excellent prediction of success in learning stenography.

Process—What the Examinee Has To Do

It would appear, then, that test content is not entirely adequate to discriminate among intelligence, achievement and aptitude testing. Can we use process to discriminate among them? Shall we say that achievement is measured when the subject is tested for recall of what he has been taught, and that intelligence is shown in the ability to generalize from the facts?

Every modern educator and every modern test constructor would reject such classification outright. Rare is the teacher who will admit her students are merely memorizing facts; rare is the curriculum which is not aimed at developing the ability to generalize, to apply learned principles in new situations. Furthermore, inspection of the items in some of our most highly regarded intelligence tests will reveal many items which are as direct questions of fact as any to be found in the least imaginative achievement tests. Processes of recognition, recall and rote repetition may be distinguishable from processes of generalization, appreciation, and problem solving—but apparently they are not satisfactory for distinguishing between intelligence and achievement.

Function—How the Test Results Are Used

If test content will not serve, nor test process, what will successfully discriminate intelligence or aptitude from achievement measures? A logical candidate would seem to be function. What are we trying to accomplish with the test scores? How are the results to be used? What inferences are to be drawn concerning the examinee? If a test's function is to record present or past accomplishment, what is measured may be called achievement. If we wish to make inferences concerning future learning, what is measured is thought of as aptitude. One kind of aptitude test, usually some combination of verbal and numerical and/or abstract reasoning measures, is sometimes called an intelligence test; more properly, in educational settings, it is called a scholastic aptitude test.

In Educational Testing . . .

If the purpose is to evaluate the effectiveness of teaching or training, and the test is designed to measure what has been specifically taught, we have an achievement situation. The more closely the test reflects what has been taught, the better it suits the purpose. The statement holds equally well if the intent is to grade students on the basis of what they have learned in a course. If, in addition, we wish to infer how well a student will learn in the future, we have an aptitude situation. The greater the similarity between what has been learned and what is to be learned, the better the achievement test suits the aptitude purpose. A test of achievement in first term algebra is likely to be an excellent test of aptitude for second term algebra. On the other hand, such a test is likely to predict less well future course grades in physics, French and shop. Nor can an achievement test in algebra be used effectively to predict course grades before the students have been exposed to algebra. Some other measure of aptitude is required.

If we are interested only in predicting algebra grades, a numerical aptitude test is likely to prove best. The chances are, however, that we are also interested in predicting success in other subjects at the same time. In that case, we have several choices. We can select achievement tests in as many relevant or nearly relevant subjects as are available, and use these tests as predictors. This approach will obviously be most effective where past and future courses are most alike; it will be least effective where past and future courses are least alike. Concretely, achievement tests can function as aptitude measures best in the early school years, less well as the junior and senior high school levels where courses become increasingly differentiated.

Another possible choice for predicting success in various courses is the scholastic aptitude or so-called group intelligence test. To the extent that various courses demand verbal and/or numerical facility for successful learning, a test which measures those aptitudes will probably prove useful. Again, this verbal-numerical ability is likely to play a more pervasive role in the elementary grade subjects than in the high school. Even at the high school level, grades are so often affected by the student's verbal expression that scholastic aptitude tests often correlate well with those grades even in subjects such as mechanical drawing and music. In such courses when grades are assigned on the basis of what the student can *do,* rather than how well he can speak or write about it, the predictive value of verbal or verbal-numerical aptitude tests is likely to be less.

A third alternative is the use of differential aptitude test batteries. These batteries ordinarily include measures of verbal and numerical aptitude, just as the scholastic aptitude intelligence tests do; they also provide measures of other aptitudes as well—spatial, mechanical, clerical, and the like. The instruments yield a set of scores which recognize intraindividual differences, accepting the fact that a student may be fairly high in verbal ability, average in numerical, very high in mechanical aptitude, and very poor in clerical speed and accuracy. These multi-score batteries provide broader coverage of mental functioning than is obtainable from the more limited scholastic aptitude test.

Is this broader coverage worth the effort? It depends on what the user wants to accomplish. If only the probability of success in an English class is of interest, a scholastic aptitude test might well suffice—information concerning other abilities may not improve prediction enough to be worth obtaining. If several varied criteria are of interest, as in guidance into an academic, trade or commercial curriculum, the additional information provided by differential aptitude batteries should be well worth the effort. Interest in broad and varied criteria is greatest at the secondary school level, where the pupil reaches points of decision. At this time, the pupil and the school should be considering what kind of curriculum is best for him, what are appropriate directions and levels of aspiration for the immediate and the more distant future. Educational and vocational guidance are of tremendous importance; therefore, the broadest scope of ability testing is both desirable and eminently worth-while. True, differential aptitude testing takes more time and costs more money. A two-, three-, or four-hour difference in time, or a dollar per pupil difference in cost, should be seen in the perspective of all the years of each student's educational and occupational future. The choices to be made may well set the pattern of the student's life; information to help guide those choices warrants the additional expenditure of minutes and pennies.

And in the Business World

The use of the educational frame of reference should not be taken to mean that the points do not apply to industry. They do. Readers engaged in personnel work in business and industry will have seen parallels between the last few paragraphs and their own problems, but will be conscious of some differences, too. For example, multi-score employment tests are often more useful than single-score tests in employee selection simply because they give a clearer picture of several aspects of ability that are mixed in unknown proportions in the single score. On the other hand, it is more often necessary for the industrial man than for the educator to make do with a less appropriate test. Many of the specific aptitude or achievement tests industry needs simply do not exist as yet, or do not work very well. In such cases, a general mental ability test or a semirelevant aptitude test may be better than nothing even though we realize that a proficiency test would give us still more useful information about the applicant.

In Summary

Which kinds of tests are most helpful? Any test is helpful or harmful only as it is used properly or misused. The information which can be obtained from group tests of general intelligence, so-called, is often valuable. The information can be misinterpreted, and perhaps the use of the word "intelligence" predisposes somewhat to misinterpretation; but *any* test score can be misinterpreted. The issue is really whether scholastic aptitude or general mental ability tests provide *enough* information, and here one can only say "enough for what?" For some important decisions, and at some educational levels, the information is probably adequate. For other decisions, and at other levels, the additional information provided by differential ability tests is needed.

Whether achievement, intelligence or differential aptitude tests should be used depends on the functions to be served. The test user should ask, "What inferences do I want to make; what information do I need to make those inferences?" The user who answers those questions will show intelligence, achievement of proficiency in test usage, and special aptitude for further advances in psychometrics.

26. The Four IQ's *

EDGAR A. DOLL, *Consulting Psychologist, Bell-ingham Public Schools, Belling-ham, Washington.*

THE IQ IS now used as if it were a household word which the users under-stand as well as m.p.h. and degrees Fahrenheit; as if it were an absolute; that given a high IQ there should, if the schools were adequate to their job, be high achievement. And, conversely, that given a low IQ, there is little hope for success. These are fallacies. There are in reality four IQ's which must be recognized as factors in achievement. These are:

1. *The Intelligence Quotient:* which is a measure of intellectual poten-tial, a measure of brightness—not of capacity or maturity level.
2. *The Inner Quest:* which is the individual's answer to "What am I?" and "What am I living for?" It is made up of aspirations and values, not always in the conscious mind. It is a strong lever for education.
3. *The Ideal Qualities:* which are the traits of personality which evaluate and maintain a balance between the Inner Quest and the Intelligence Quotient.
4. *The Innate Quirks:* which are the obstacles which lie between us and the fulfillment desired by our Inner Quest, made possible by our Intelligence Quotient, to the extent determined by our Innate Qual-ities. Some of these quirks are in the person; some are environmental.

The Intelligence Quotient is a relative measure, indicating where the candidate stands among his age peers in the performances called for by the test which has been chosen. These tests, generally, call for (1) rational comprehension of a situation, and (2) an effective response. Many of the tests used are heavily weighted toward the academic, requiring the verbal comprehension and response prized in education. For making the most of one's self, other measures of rational comprehension and response are needed as in the following:

1. of and to *social situations*—the intelligence which enables us to get along with other people. This is most certainly a factor in success or failure in school as well as in the world outside.
2. of and to *things*—like machinery, for example.

* From Edgar A. Doll, "The Four IQ's," *International Journal for Exceptional Children* (October, 1957), pp. 56–57, 66. Reprinted by permission. (Reprints of this article are available from CEC.)

These two factors of intelligence should not be relegated to separate fields and degraded, as many educationalists do. Nor should verbal intelligence be made a prerequisite for opportunity.

Intelligence test results depend upon many variables—what test, who administers, when, where, and why. Implicit assumptions are that the child hears (or reads) and understands, that there is no emotional interference with either comprehension or response, that there is no malingering, that there is no handicap. In testing situations, severe impairments are obvious, and usually compensated for, but that mild impairments which are not observed can handicap a candidate considerably.

It is a fallacy that the tests actually measure true intelligence. The candidate's performance is measured, but it is always the minima. We can get no better than his best, but often get far less. What we do get might often better be termed Expressive Intellectual Performance—not Intelligence. Something more is needed to determine potential.

Hence, the assumption that there is a 1-1 relationship between intelligence and learning is based upon a fallacy. Relatively large numbers of the intellectually gifted are underachievers in school and out. The reasons for this underachievement *may* be found by making a study of the other three IQ's.

The Inner Quest produces "drive." Whence it derives, no one knows. Some suspect the adrenals; some blame thyroid deficiency. We do know that it is highly variable, both from person to person, and within the same personality. We do know that it is sometimes more than we can stand, as parents or teachers; that it can be smothered by an overenthusiastic parent or teacher as effectively as by one who is indifferent. It is as elusive as an instinct when we attempt to locate its origin, and quite as powerful. To one who is born "goose," water is for swimming, but not to one who is born "chicken." To require swimming for both is as great a folly as to prohibit it for both. With this example, we are asked to consider the effects upon achievement produced by a blocking of the Inner Quest through the demands of conformity in curricula. Neither the duck nor the chicken *knows* its attitude towards water, it only *feels* the rightness or wrongness. . . .

Children need assistance in developing their self-concepts—their Inner Quests—discovering whether they are duck or chicken, or rabbit or squirrel, in their nature, and all who deal with children must appreciate the power, differences and the variabilities of Inner Quests.

The Ideal Qualities: Observe Miss B. leaving her apartment at eight in the morning, tastefully but rather plainly dressed, her expression interested, but rather prim and quite virtuous, on her way to be a teacher. The ideal qualities are evident; there will be interest, work, and no nonsense in her classes.

Observe Miss B. leaving her apartment at eight in the evening, on her way to be a "date." Are the same qualities now ideal? If she goes out prim, plain, and in no mood for nonsense, she might better stay home and put her feet up, for she will be on them in the classroom for another 40 years. . . .

The Ideal Qualities which maintain a productive balance between Intellectual Capacity and Inner Quest are those which enable the individual to achieve peace of mind. They protect the ego and the sense of dignity and worth. They enable one to achieve enough acceptance to satisfy the gregarious drive. They provide a sense of status, neither overestimating nor undervaluing either the capacity or the quest.

In school we recognize this need for status and acceptance when the reactions of a child are dramatically evident. We cannot teach the sick child, the unruly child, the unhappy child, or the disturbed child. They have no peace of mind, no inner quietude which will permit learning. When there are no dramatic evidences, we tend to think that all is well when we may well be faced by a lack of balance, soon to erupt in a dramatic scene. It is urged that teachers, being more mature, go more than halfway to bring about that sense of tranquility which comes from status. Without this inner quietude there can be no concentrated effort at learning.

In some areas of our curriculum, we tend to be hide-bound ritualists, especially in subjects like arithmetic. There we often let the "training" aspect of the work inhibit "the spontaneous learning which should characterize the school performance."

The Innate Quirks: These are the handicaps and the obstacles which stand between us and the goal set by our Inner Quest, within our Intellectual Capacity, kept in balance by our Ideal Qualities. Some of these obstacles are in the person; some in the environment. The teacher is part of the environment.

In general, we tend to pressure pupils toward the typical; we are so concerned with scholastic achievement that we are, in effect, punishing the handicapped child for his handicap; we are so concerned with our planned program of progress for the class as a whole we punish the gifted child for his giftedness.

Quirks may be points of view, attitudes, values, or prejudices. They may be common to our family, our social group, or our community, or we may be mavericks in these respects.

Quirks may be in our physical environment. Barren or lush, it is a factor which must be considered and compensated for. We must not as teachers, think of environment as only that of the home. The street, the playground, the community, and the general social climate are all important factors making for success or failure. Above all, let us consider the environment of the school and the classroom. Is it lush or barren—in space? in numbers? in staff? in equipment? in services?

These then are the four IQ's—Intelligent Quotient, which is not an absolute; Inner Quest, which is the most potent factor in achievement; Ideal Qualities, which maintain balance; Innate Quirks, of which we all have our share. Educators, then, should not glibly compare achievement and intelligence quotient. Each individual's progress is the product of a great array of factors, often hard to identify, and often still more difficult to influence.

This does not mean that we must adopt a laissez-faire attitude to achievement. Rather, it emphasizes the need for continuous and greatly expanded research which will, in time, enable us to act with more assurance than we now can do.

27. *Three Faces of Intellect* * 1

J. P. GUILFORD

M Y SUBJECT is in the area of human intelligence, in connection with which the names of Terman and Stanford have become known the world over. The Stanford Revision of the Binet intelligence scale has been the standard against which all other instruments for the measurement of intelligence have been compared. The term IQ or intelligence quotient has become a household word in this country. This is illustrated by two brief stories.

A few years ago, one of my neighbors came home from a PTA meeting, remarking: "That Mrs. So-And-So, thinks she knows so much. She kept talking about the 'intelligence *quota*' of the children; 'intelligence *quota*'; imagine. Why, everybody knows that IQ stands for 'intelligence *quiz*.'"

The other story comes from a little comic strip in a Los Angeles morning newspaper, called "Junior Grade." In the first picture a little boy meets a little girl, both apparently about the first grade level. The little girl remarks, "I have

* From J. P. Guilford, "Three Faces of Intellect," *The American Psychologist,* 14 (August, 1959), 469–79. Reprinted by permission.
1 The Walter V. Bingham Memorial Lecture given at Stanford University on April 13, 1959.

a high IQ." The little boy, puzzled, said, "You have a what?" The little girl repeated, "I have a high IQ," then went on her way. The little boy, looking thoughtful, said, "And she looks like such a nice little girl, too."

It is my purpose to speak about the analysis of this thing called human intelligence into its components. I do not believe that either Binet or Terman, if they were still with us, would object to the idea of a searching and detailed study of intelligence, aimed toward a better understanding of its nature. Preceding the development of his intelligence scale, Binet had done much research on different kinds of thinking activities and apparently recognized that intelligence has a number of aspects. It is to the lasting credit of both Binet and Terman that they introduced such a great variety of tasks into their intelligence scales.

Two related events of very recent history make it imperative that we learn all we can regarding the nature of intelligence. I am referring to the advent of the artificial satellites and planets and to the crisis in education that has arisen in part as a consequence. The preservation of our way of life and our future security depend upon our most important national resources: our intellectual abilities and, more particularly, our creative abilities. It is time, then, that we learn all we can about those resources.

Our knowledge of the components of human intelligence has come about mostly within the last twenty-five years. The major sources of this information in this country have been L. L. Thurstone and his associates, the war-time research of psychologists in the United States Air Forces, and more recently the Aptitudes Project [2] at the University of Southern California, now in its tenth year of research on cognitive and thinking abilities. The results from the Aptitudes Project that have gained perhaps the most attention have pertained to creative-thinking abilities. These are mostly novel findings. But to me, the most significant outcome has been the development of a unified theory of human intellect, which organizes the known, unique or primary intellectual abilities into a single system called the "structure of intellect." It is to this system that I shall devote the major part of my remarks, with very brief mentions of some of the implications for the psychology of thinking and problem-solving, for vocational testing, and for education.

The discovery of the components of intelligence has been by means of the experimental application of the method of factor analysis. It is not necessary for you to know anything about the theory or method of factor analysis in order to follow the discussion of the components. I should like to say, however, that factor analysis has no connection with or resemblance to psychoanalysis. A positive statement would be more helpful, so I will

[2] Under Contract N6onr-23810 with the Office of Naval Research (Personnel and Training Branch).

say that each intellectual component or factor is a unique ability that is needed to do well in a certain class of tasks or tests. As a general principle we find that certain individuals do well in the tests of a certain class, but they may do poorly in the tests of another class. We conclude that a factor has certain properties from the features that the tests of a class have in common. I shall give you very soon a number of examples of tests, each representing a factor.

The Structure of Intellect

Although each factor is sufficiently distinct to be detected by factor analysis, in very recent years it has become apparent that the factors themselves can be classified because they resemble one another in certain ways. One basis of classification is according to the basic kind of process or operation performed. This kind of classification gives us five major groups of intellectual abilities: factors of cognition, memory, convergent thinking, divergent thinking, and evaluation.

Cognition means discovery or rediscovery or recognition. Memory means retention of what is cognized. Two kinds of productive-thinking operations generate new information from known information and remembered information. In divergent-thinking operations we think in different directions, sometimes searching, sometimes seeking variety. In convergent thinking the information leads to one right answer or to a recognized best or conventional answer. In evaluation we reach decisions as to goodness, correctness, suitability, or adequacy of what we know, what we remember, and what we produce in productive thinking.

A second way of classifying the intellectual factors is according to the kind of material or content involved. The factors known thus far involve three kinds of material or content: the content may be figural, symbolic, or semantic. Figural content is concrete material such as is perceived through the senses. It does not represent anything except itself. Visual material has properties such as size, form, color, location, or texture. Things we hear or feel provide other examples of figural material. Symbolic content is composed of letters, digits, and other conventional signs, usually organized in general systems, such as the alphabet or the number system. Semantic content is in the form of verbal meanings or ideas, for which no examples are necessary.

When a certain operation is applied to a certain kind of content, as many as six general kinds of products may be involved. There is enough evidence available to suggest that, regardless of the combinations of operations and content, the same six kinds of products may be found associated. The six kinds of products are: units, classes, relations, systems, transformations, and implications. So far as we have determined from factor analysis, these are the only fundamental kinds of products that we can know. As such, they may serve as basic classes into which one might fit all kinds of information psychologically.

The three kinds of classifications of the factors of intellect can be represented by means of a single solid model, shown in Figure 1. In this model, which we call the "structure of intellect," each dimension represents one

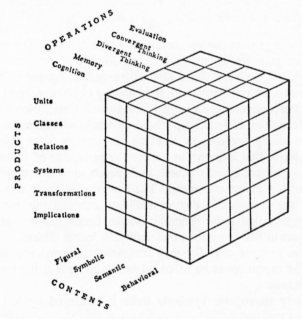

Figure 1. A cubical model representing the structure of intellect.

of the modes of variation of the factors.[3] Along one dimension are found the various kinds of operations, along a second one are the various kinds of products, and along the third are various kinds of content. Along the dimension of content a fourth category has been added, its kind of content being designated as "behavioral." This category has been added on a purely theoretical basis to represent the general area sometimes called "social intelligence." More will be said about this section of the model later.

In order to provide a better basis for understanding the model and a better basis for accepting it as a picture of human intellect, I shall do some exploring of it with you systematically, giving some examples of tests. Each

[3] For an earlier presentation of the concept, see J. P. Guilford, "The Structure of Intellect," *Psychological Bulletin*, 53 (1956), 267–93.

cell in the model calls for a certain kind of ability that can be described in terms of operation, content, and product, for each cell is at the intersection of a unique combination of kinds of operation, content, and product. A test for that ability would have the same three properties. In our exploration of the model, we shall take one vertical layer at a time, beginning with the front face. The first layer provides us with a matrix of eighteen cells (if we ignore the behavioral column for which there are as yet no known factors) each of which should contain a cognitive ability.

THE COGNITIVE ABILITIES

We know at present the unique abilities that fit logically into fifteen of the eighteen cells for cognitive abilities. Each row presents a triad of similar abilities, having a single kind of product in common. The factors of the first row are concerned with the knowing of units. A good test of the ability to cognize figural units is the Street Gestalt Completion Test. In this test, the recognition of familiar pictured objects in silhouette form is made difficult for testing purposes by blocking out parts of those objects. There is another factor that is known to involve the perception of auditory figures —in the form of melodies, rhythms, and speech sounds—and still another factor involving kinesthetic forms. The presence of three factors in one cell (they are conceivably distinct abilities, although this has not been tested) suggests that more generally, in the figural column, at least, we should expect to find more than one ability. A fourth dimension pertaining to variations in sense modality may thus apply in connection with figural content. The model could be extended in this manner if the facts call for such an extension.

The ability to cognize symbolic units is measured by tests like the following:

Put vowels in the following blanks to make real words:

P___W___R
M___RV___L
C___RT___N

Rearrange the letters to make real words:

R A C I H
T V O E S
K L C C O

The first of these two tests is called Disemvoweled Words, and the second Scrambled Words.

The ability to cognize semantic units is the well-known factor of verbal comprehension, which is best measured by means of a vocabulary test, with items such as:

GRAVITY means _____
CIRCUS means _____
VIRTUE means _____

From the comparison of these two factors it is obvious that recognizing familiar words as letter structures and knowing what words mean depend upon quite different abilities.

For testing the abilities to know classes of units, we may present the following kinds of items, one with symbolic content and one with semantic content:

Which letter group does not belong?
XECM   PVAA   QXIN   VTRO
Which object does not belong?
clam   tree   oven   rose

A figural test is constructed in a completely parallel form, presenting in each item four figures, three of which have a property in common and the fourth lacking that property.

The three abilities to see relationships are also readily measured by a common kind of test, differing only in terms of content. The well-known analogies test is applicable, two items in symbolic and semantic form being:

JIRE : KIRE : : FORA : KORE KORA LIRE GORA GIRE
poetry : prose : : dance : music walk sing talk jump

Such tests usually involve more than the ability to cognize relations, but we are not concerned with this problem at this point.

The three factors for cognizing systems do not at present appear in tests so closely resembling one another as in the case of the examples just given. There is nevertheless an underlying common core of logical similarity. Ordinary space tests, such as Thurstone's Flags, Figures, and Cards or Part V (Spatial Orientation) of the Guilford-Zimmerman Aptitude Survey (GZAS), serve in the figural column. The system involved is an order or arrangement of objects in space. A system that uses symbolic elements is illustrated by the Letter Triangle Test, a sample item of which is:

What letter belongs at the place of the question mark?

The ability to understand a semantic system has been known for some time as the factor called general reasoning. One of its most faithful indicators is a test composed of arithmetic-reasoning items. That the phase of understanding only is important for measuring this ability is shown by the fact that such a test works even if the examinee is not asked to give a complete solution; he need only show that he structures the problem properly. For example, an item from the test Necessary Arithmetical Operations simply asks what operations are needed to solve the problem:

A city lot 48 feet wide and 149 feet deep costs $9,432. What is the cost per square foot?

A. add and multiply
B. multiply and divide
C. subtract and divide
D. add and subtract
E. divide and add

Placing the factor of general reasoning in this cell of the structure of intellect gives us some new conceptions of its nature. It should be a broad ability to grasp all kinds of systems that are conceived in terms of verbal concepts, not restricted to the understanding of problems of an arithmetical type.

Transformations are changes of various kinds, including modifications in arrangement, organization, or meaning. In the figural column for the transformations row, we find the factor known as visualization. Common measuring instruments for this factor are the surface-development tests, and an example of a different kind is Part VI (Spatial Visualization) of the GZAS. A test of the ability to make transformations of meaning, for the factor in the semantic column, is called Similarities. The examinee is asked to state several ways in which two objects, such as an apple and an orange, are alike. Only by shifting the meanings of both is the examinee able to give many responses to such an item.

In the set of abilities having to do with the cognition of implications, we find that the individual goes beyond the information given, but not to the extent of what might be called drawing conclusions. We may say that he extrapolates. From the given information he expects or foresees certain consequences, for example. The two factors found in this row of the cognition matrix were first called "foresight" factors. Foresight in connection with figural material can be tested by means of paper-and-pencil mazes. Foresight in connection with ideas, those pertaining to events, for example, is indicated by a test such as Pertinent Questions:

In planning to open a new hamburger stand in a certain community, what four questions should be considered in deciding upon its location?

The more questions the examinee asks in response to a list of such problems, the more he evidently foresees contingencies.

THE MEMORY ABILITIES

The area of memory abilities has been explored less than some of the other areas of operation, and only seven of the potential cells of the memory matrix have known factors in them. These cells are restricted to three rows: for units, relations, and systems. The first cell in the memory matrix is now occupied by two factors, parallel to two in the corresponding cognition matrix: visual memory and auditory memory. Memory for series of letters or numbers, as in memory span tests, conforms to the conception of memory for symbolic units. Memory for the ideas in a paragraph conforms to the conception of memory for semantic units.

The formation of associations between units, such as visual forms, syllables, and meaningful words, as in the method of paired associates, would seem to represent three abilities to remember relationships involving three kinds of content. We know of two such abilities, for the symbolic and semantic columns. The memory for known systems is represented by two abilities very recently discovered.[4] Remembering the arrangement of objects in space is the nature of an ability in the figural column, and remembering a sequence of events is the nature of a corresponding ability in the semantic column. The differentiation between these two abilities implies that a person may be able to say where he saw an object on a page, but he might not be able to say on which of several pages he saw it after leafing through several pages that included the right one. Considering the blank rows in the memory matrix, we should expect to find abilities also to remember classes, transformations, and implications, as well as units, relations, and systems.

THE DIVERGENT-THINKING ABILITIES

The unique feature of divergent production is that a *variety* of responses is produced. The product is not completely determined by the given information. This is not to say that divergent thinking does not come into play in the total process of reaching a unique conclusion, for it comes into play wherever there is trial-and-error thinking.

The well-known ability of word fluency is tested by asking the examinee to list words satisfying a specified letter requirement, such as words beginning with the letter "s" or words ending in "-tion." This ability is now regarded as a facility in divergent production of symbolic units. The parallel semantic ability has been known as ideational fluency. A typical test item calls for listing objects that are round and edible. Winston Churchill must have possessed this ability to a high degree. Clement Attlee is reported to

[4] R. E. Christal, "Factor Analytic Study of Visual Memory," *Psychological Monographs*, Vol. 72, No. 13 (Whole No. 466) (1958).

have said about him recently that, no matter what problem came up, Churchill always seemed to have about ten ideas. The trouble was, Attlee continued, he did not know which was the good one. The last comment implies some weakness in one or more of the evaluative abilities.

The divergent production of class ideas is believed to be the unique feature of a factor called "spontaneous flexibility." A typical test instructs the examinee to list all the uses he can think of for a common brick, and he is given eight minutes. If his responses are: build a house, build a barn, build a garage, build a school, build a church, build a chimney, build a walk, and build a barbecue, he would earn a fairly high score for ideational fluency but a very low score for spontaneous flexibility, because all these uses fall into the same class. If another person said: make a door stop, make a paper weight, throw it at a dog, make a bookcase, drown a cat, drive a nail, make a red powder, and use for baseball bases, he would also receive a high score for flexibility. He has gone frequently from one class to another.

A current study of unknown but predicted divergent-production abilities includes testing whether there are also figural and symbolic abilities to produce multiple classes. An experimental figural test presents a number of figures that can be classified in groups of three in various ways, each figure being usable in more than one class. An experimental symbolic test presents a few numbers that are also to be classified in multiple ways.

A unique ability involving relations is called "associational fluency." It calls for the production of a variety of things related in a specified way to a given thing. For example, the examinee is asked to list words meaning about the same as "good" or to list words meaning about the opposite of "hard." In these instances the response produced is to complete a relationship, and semantic content is involved. Some of our present experimental tests call for the production of varieties of relations, as such, and involve figural and symbolic content also. For example, given four small digits, in how many ways can they be related in order to produce a sum of eight?

One factor pertaining to the production of systems is known as expressional fluency. The rapid formation of phrases or sentences is the essence of certain tests of this factor. For example, given the initial letters:

W_____c_____e_____n_____

with different sentences to be produced, the examinee might write "We can eat nuts" or "Whence came Eve Newton?" In interpreting the factor, we regard the sentence as a symbolic system. By analogy, a figural system would be some kind of organization of lines and other elements, and a semantic system would be in the form of a verbally stated problem or perhaps something as complex as a theory.

In the row of the divergent-production matrix devoted to transformations, we find some very interesting factors. The one called "adaptive flexibility" is now recognized as belonging in the figural column. A faithful test of it has been Match Problems. This is based upon the common game that uses squares, the sides of which are formed by match sticks. The examinee is told to take away a given number of matches to leave a stated number of squares with nothing left over. Nothing is said about the sizes of the squares to be left. If the examinee imposes upon himself the restriction that the squares that he leaves must be of the same size, he will fail in his attempts to do items like that in Figure 2. Other odd kinds of solutions are

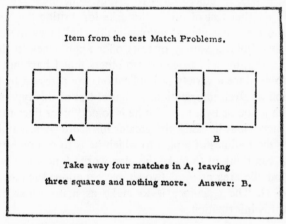

Item from the test Match Problems.

A   B

Take away four matches in A, leaving
three squares and nothing more.   Answer: B.

Figure 2. A sample item from the test Match Problems. The problem in this item is to take away four matches and leave three squares. The solution is given.

introduced in other items, such as overlapping squares and squares within squares, and so on. In another variation of Match Problems the examinee is told to produce two or more solutions for each problem.

A factor that has been called "originality" is now recognized as adaptive flexibility with semantic material, where there must be a shifting of meanings. The examinee must produce the shifts or changes in meaning and so come up with novel, unusual, clever, or farfetched ideas. The Plot Titles Test presents a short story, the examinee being told to list as many appropriate titles as he can to head the story. One story is about a missionary who has been captured by cannibals in Africa. He is in the pot and about to be boiled when a princess of the tribe obtains a promise for his release if he will become her mate. He refuses and is boiled to death.

In scoring the test, we separate the responses into two categories, clever and nonclever. Examples of nonclever responses are: African Death, Defeat of a Princess, Eaten by Savages, The Princess, The African Missionary, In Darkest Africa, and Boiled by Savages. These titles are appropriate but commonplace. The number of such responses serves as a score for ideational fluency. Examples of clever responses are: "Pot's Plot, Potluck Dinner, Stewed Parson, Goil or Boil, A Mate Worse Than Death, He Left a Dish for a Pot, Chaste in Haste, and A Hot Price for Freedom. The number of clever responses given by an examinee is his score for originality, or the divergent production of semantic transformations.

Another test of originality presents a very novel task so that any acceptable response is unusual for the individual. In the Symbol Production Test the examinee is to produce a simple symbol to stand for a noun or a verb in each short sentence, in other words to invent something like pictographic symbols. Still another test of originality asks for writing the "punch lines" for cartoons, a task that almost automatically challenges the examinee to be clever. Thus, quite a variety of tests offer approaches to the measurement of originality, including one or two others that I have not mentioned.

Abilities to produce a variety of implications are assessed by tests calling for elaboration of given information. A figural test of this type provides the examinee with a line or two, to which he is to add other lines to produce an object. The more lines he adds, the greater his score. A semantic test gives the examinee the outlines of a plan to which he is to respond by stating all the details he can think of to make the plan work. A new test we are trying out in the symbolic area presents two simple equations such as $B - C = D$ and $z = A + D$. The examinee is to make as many other equations as he can from this information.

THE CONVERGENT-PRODUCTION ABILITIES

Of the eighteen convergent-production abilities expected in the three content columns, twelve are now recognized. In the first row, pertaining to units, we have an ability to name figural properties (forms or colors) and an ability to name abstractions (classes, relations, and so on). It may be that the ability in common to the speed of naming forms and the speed of naming colors is not appropriately placed in the convergent-thinking matrix. One might expect that the thing to be produced in a test of the convergent production of figural units would be in the form of figures rather than words. A better test of such an ability might somehow specify the need for one particular object, the examinee to furnish the object.

A test for the convergent production of classes (Word Grouping) presents a list of twelve words that are to be classified in four, and only four, meaningful groups, no word to appear in more than one group. A parallel test (Figure Concepts Test) presents twenty pictured real objects that are to be grouped in meaningful classes of two or more each.

Convergent production having to do with relationships is represented by three known factors, all involving the "education of correlates," as Spearman called it. The given information includes one unit and a stated relation, the examinee to supply the other unit. Analogies tests that call for completion rather than a choice between alternative answers emphasize this kind of ability. With symbolic content such an item might read:

pots stop bard dram rats ?

A semantic item that measures education of correlates is:

The absence of sound is _____.

Incidentally, the latter item is from a vocabulary-completion test, and its relation to the factor of ability to produce correlates indicates how, by change of form, a vocabulary test may indicate an ability other than that for which vocabulary tests are usually intended, namely, the factor of verbal comprehension.

Only one factor for convergent production of systems is known, and it is in the semantic column. It is measured by a class of tests that may be called ordering tests. The examinee may be presented with a number of events that ordinarily have a best or most logical order, the events being presented in scrambled order. The presentation may be pictorial, as in the Picture Arrangement Test, or verbal. The pictures may be taken from a cartoon strip. The verbally presented events may be in the form of the various steps needed to plant a new lawn. There are undoubtedly other kinds of systems than temporal order that could be utilized for testing abilities in this row of the convergent-production matrix.

In the way of producing transformations of a unique variety, we have three recognized factors, known as redefinition abilities. In each case, redefinition involves the changing of functions or uses of parts of one unit and giving them new functions or uses in some new unit. For testing the ability of figural redefinition, a task based upon the Gottschaldt figures is suitable. Figure 3 shows the kind of item for such a test. In recognizing the simpler figure within the structure of a more complex figure, certain lines must take on new roles.

In terms of symbolic material, the following sample items will illustrate how groups of letters in given words must be readapted to use in other words. In the test Camouflaged Words, each sentence contains the name of a sport or game:

I did not know that he was ailing.
To beat the Hun, tin goes a long way.

For the factor of semantic redefinition, the Gestalt Transformation Test may be used. A sample item reads:

From which object would you most likely make a needle?

A. a cabbage
B. a splice
C. a steak
D. a paper box
E. a fish

The convergent production of implications means the drawing of fully determined conclusions from given information. The well-known factor of numerical facility belongs in the symbolic column. For the parallel ability

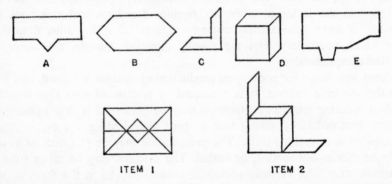

Figure 3. Sample items from a test, Hidden Figures, based upon the Gottschaldt figures. Which of the simpler figures is concealed within each of the two more complex figures?

in the figural column, we have a test known as Form Reasoning, in which rigorously defined operations with figures are used. For the parallel ability in the semantic column, the factor sometimes called "deduction" probably qualifies. Items of the following type are sometimes used.

Charles is younger than Robert
Charles is older than Frank
Who is older: Robert or Frank?

EVALUATIVE ABILITIES

The evaluative area has had the least investigation of all the operational categories. In fact, only one systematic analytical study has been devoted to this area. Only eight evaluative abilities are recognized as fitting into the evaluation matrix. But at least five rows have one or more factors each, and also three of the usual columns or content categories. In each case, evaluation involves reaching decisions as to the accuracy, goodness, suitability, or workability of information. In each row, for the particular kind of product of that row, some kind of criterion or standard of judgment is involved.

In the first row, for the evaluation of units, the important decision to be made pertains to the identity of a unit. Is this unit identical with that one? In the figural column we find the factor long known as "perceptual speed." Tests of this factor invariably call for decisions of identity, for example, Part IV (Perceptual Speed) of the GZAS or Thurstone's Identical Forms. I think it has been generally wrongly thought that the ability involved is that of cognition of visual forms. But we have seen that another factor is a more suitable candidate for this definition and for being in the very first cell of the cognitive matrix. It is parallel to this evaluative ability but does not require the judgment of identity as one of its properties.

In the symbolic column is an ability to judge identity of symbolic units, in the form of series of letters or numbers or of names of individuals.

Are members of the following pairs identical or not:

825170493_____825176493
dkeltvmpa_____dkeltvmpa
C. S. Myerson_____C. E. Meyerson

Such items are common in tests of clerical aptitude.

There should be a parallel ability to decide whether two ideas are identical or different. Is the idea expressed in this sentence the same as the idea expressed in that one? Do these two proverbs express essentially the same idea? Such tests exist and will be used to test the hypothesis that such an ability can be demonstrated.

No evaluative abilities pertaining to classes have as yet been recognized. The abilities having to do with evaluation where relations are concerned must meet the criterion of logical consistency. Syllogistic tests involving letter symbols indicate a different ability than the same type of test involving verbal statements. In the figural column we might expect that tests incorporating geometric reasoning or proof would indicate a parallel ability to sense the soundness of conclusions regarding figural relationships.

The evaluation of systems seems to be concerned with the internal consistency of those systems, so far as we can tell from the knowledge of one such factor. The factor has been called "experiential evaluation," and its representative test presents items like that in Figure 4 asking "What is wrong with this picture?" The things wrong are often internal inconsistencies.

A semantic ability for evaluating transformations is thought to be that known for some time as "judgment." In typical judgment tests, the examinee is asked to tell which of five solutions to a practical problem is most adequate or wise. The solutions frequently involve improvisations, in other words, adaptations of familiar objects to unusual uses. In this way the items present redefinitions to be evaluated.

A factor known first as "sensitivity to problems" has become recognized as an evaluative ability having to do with implications. One test of the factor, the Apparatus Test, asks for two needed improvements with respect to each of several common devices, such as the telephone or the toaster. The Social Institutions Test, a measure of the same factor, asks what things are wrong with each of several institutions, such as tipping or national

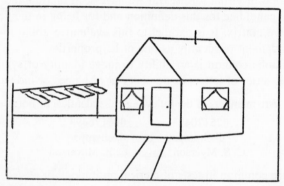

Figure 4. A sample item from the test of unusual details. What two things are wrong with this picture?

elections. We may say that defects or deficiencies are implications of an evaluative kind. Another interpretation would be that seeing defects and deficiencies are evaluations of implications to the effect that the various aspects of something are all right.[5]

Some Implications of the Structure of Intellect

FOR PSYCHOLOGICAL THEORY

Although factor analysis as generally employed is best designed to investigate ways in which individuals differ from one another, in other words, to discover traits, the results also tell us much about how individuals are alike. Consequently, information regarding the factors and their interrelationships gives us understanding of functioning individuals. The five kinds of intellectual abilities in terms of operations may be said to represent five ways of functioning. The kinds of intellectual abilities distinguished according to varieties of test content and the kinds of abilities distinguished

[5] For further details concerning the intellectual factors, illustrative tests, and the place of the factors in the structure of intellect, see J. P. Guilford, *Personality* (New York: McGraw-Hill Book Co., 1959).

according to varieties of products suggest a classification of basic forms of information or knowledge. The kind of organism suggested by this way of looking at intellect is that of an agency for dealing with information of various kinds in various ways. The concepts provided by the distinctions among the intellectual abilities and by their classifications may be very useful in our future investigations of learning, memory, problem-solving, invention, and decision making, by whatever method we choose to approach those problems.

FOR VOCATIONAL TESTING

With about fifty intellectual factors already known, we may say that there are at least fifty ways of being intelligent. It has been facetiously suggested that there seem to be a great many more ways of being stupid, unfortunately. The structure of intellect is a theoretical model that predicts as many as 120 distinct abilities, if every cell of the model contains a factor. Already we know that two cells contain two or more factors each, and there probably are actually other cells of this type. Since the model was first conceived, twelve factors predicted by it has found places in it. There is consequently hope of filling many of the other vacancies, and we may eventually end up with more than 120 abilities.

The major implication for the assessment of intelligence is that to know an individual's intellectual resources thoroughly we shall need a surprisingly large number of scores. It is expected that many of the factors are intercorrelated, so there is some possibility that by appropriate sampling we shall be able to cover the important abilities with a more limited number of tests. At any rate, a multiple-score approach to the assessment of intelligence is definitely indicated in connection with future vocational operations.

Considering the kinds of abilities classified as to content, we may speak roughly of four kinds of intelligence. The abilities involving the use of figural information may be regarded as "concrete" intelligence. The people who depend most upon these abilities deal with concrete things and their properties. Among these people are mechanics, operators of machines, engineers (in some aspects of their work), artists, and musicians.

In the abilities pertaining to symbolic and semantic content, we have two kinds of "abstract" intelligence. Symbolic abilities should be important in learning to recognize words, to spell, and to operate with numbers. Language and mathematics should depend very much upon them, except that in mathematics some aspects, such as geometry, have strong figural involvement. Semantic intelligence is important for understanding things in terms of verbal concepts and hence is important in all courses where the learning of facts and ideas is essential.

In the hypothesized behavioral column of the structure of intellect, which may be roughly described as "social" intelligence, we have some of the most interesting possibilities. Understanding the behavior of others and of ourselves is largely nonverbal in character. The theory suggests as many as thirty abilities in this area, some having to do with understanding, some with productive thinking about behavior, and some with the evaluation of behavior. The theory also suggests that information regarding behavior is also in the form of the six kinds of products that apply elsewhere in the structure of intellect, including units, relations, systems, and so on. The abilities in the area of social intelligence, whatever they prove to be, will possess considerable importance in connection with all those individuals who deal most with other people: teachers, law officials, social workers, therapists, politicians, statesmen, and leaders of other kinds.

FOR EDUCATION

The implications for education are numerous, and I have time just to mention a very few. The most fundamental implication is that we might well undergo transformations with respect to our conception of the learner and of the process of learning. Under the prevailing conception, the learner is a kind of stimulus-response device, much on the order of a vending machine. You put in a coin, and something comes out. The machine learns what reaction to put out when a certain coin is put in. If, instead, we think of the learner as an agent for dealing with information, where information is defined very broadly, we have something more analogous to an electronic computor. We feed a computor information; it stores that information; it uses that information for generating new information, either by way of divergent or convergent thinking; and it evaluates its own results. Advantages that a human learner has over a computor include the step of seeking and discovering new information from sources outside itself and the step of programing itself. Perhaps even these steps will be added to computors, if this has not already been done in some cases.

At any rate, this conception of the learner leads us to the idea that learning is discovery of information, not merely the formation of associations, particularly associations in the form of stimulus-response connections. I am aware of the fact that my proposal is rank heresy. But if we are to make significant progress in our understanding of human learning and particularly our understanding of the so-called higher mental processes of thinking, problem-solving, and creative thinking, some drastic modifications are due in our theory.

The idea that education is a matter of training the mind or of training the intellect has been rather unpopular, wherever the prevailing psychological doctrines have been followed. In theory, at least, the emphasis has been upon the learning of rather specific habits or skills. If we take our cue from factor theory, however, we recognize that most learning probably has both specific and general aspects or components. The general aspects may be along the lines of the factors of intellect. This is not to say that the individual's status in each factor is entirely determined by learning. We do not know to what extent each factor is determined by heredity and to what extent by learning. The best position for educators to take is that possibly every intellectual factor can be developed in individuals at least to some extent by learning.

If education has the general objective of developing the intellects of students, it can be suggested that each intellectual factor provides a particular goal at which to aim. Defined by a certain combination of content, operation, and product, each goal ability then calls for certain kinds of practice in order to achieve improvement in it. This implies choice of curriculum and the choice or invention of teaching methods that will most likely accomplish the desired results.

Considering the very great variety of abilities revealed by the factorial exploration of intellect, we are in a better position to ask whether any general intellectual skills are now being neglected in education and whether appropriate balances are being observed. It is often observed these days that we have fallen down in the way of producing resourceful, creative graduates. How true this is, in comparison with other times, I do not know. Perhaps the deficit is noticed because the demands for inventiveness are so much greater at this time. At any rate, realization that the more conspicuously creative abilities appear to be concentrated in the divergent-thinking category, and also to some extent in the transformation category, we now ask whether we have been giving these skills appropriate exercise. It is probable that we need a better balance of training in the divergent-thinking area as compared with training in convergent thinking and in critical thinking or evaluation.

The structure of intellect as I have presented it to you may or may not stand the test of time. Even if the general form persists, there are likely to be some modifications. Possibly some different kind of model will be invented. Be that as it may, the fact of a multiplicity of intellectual abilities seems well established.

There are many individuals who long for the good old days of simplicity, when we got along with one unanalyzed intelligence. Simplicity certainly has its appeal. But human nature is exceedingly complex, and we may as well face that fact. The rapidly moving events of the world in which we live have forced upon us the need for knowing human intelligence thoroughly. Humanity's peaceful pursuit of happiness depends upon our control of nature and of our own behavior; and this, in turn, depends upon understanding ourselves, including our intellectual resources.

28. Measurement of Learning and Mental Abilities *[1]

HAROLD GULLIKSEN, *Princeton University and Educational Testing Service*

ABOUT TWENTY-SEVEN YEARS ago, a small group of students met with Professor Thurstone in Chicago to discuss methods of encouraging quantitative work in psychology. The initial group that was concerned about the slow rate of development of quantitative work in psychology included Jack Dunlap, Al Kurtz, Marion Richardson, John Stalnaker, G. Frederic Kuder, and Paul Horst. They had discussed the problem, had been helped a bit by Donald Paterson, and had decided that possibly if a magazine were set up to publish quantitative psychological material this would facilitate the development of the field. Persons who did good quantitative work, either theoretical or experimental, would thus have a forum where it would be accepted because it was high quality quantitative work, rather than being rejected because it was quantitative and hence "not of too great interest" to the readers.

It developed after discussion that possibly the best method of supporting such a journal would be to have a society which would have this journal as its major organ. This was the nucleus of the Psychometric Society and of the magazine *Psychometrika,* a quarterly journal devoted to the development of psychology as a quantitative rational science.

Thus, in March of 1936, Volume 1, Number 1 of *Psychometrika* was issued with Marion Richardson as Managing Editor, and Horst and Thurstone as members of the editorial board. From this small beginning with five or ten people interested in furthering the development of the field, it is interesting to look back now and consider what has happened during the intervening 25 years.

Let us look at the state of quantitative rational psychology at that time. Thurstone's work over the preceding ten years, from 1925 to 1935, might well be thought of as typifying the field then. He had done some work

* From Harold Gulliksen, "Measurement of Learning and Mental Abilities," *Psychometrika,* 26 (March, 1961), 93–107. Reprinted by permission.

[1] Prepared as a technical report in connection with research partially supported by Office of Naval Research contract Nonr 1858–(15) and National Science Foundation Grant G-3407 to Princeton University, and by the Educational Testing Service. Reproduction of any part of this material is permitted for any purpose of the United States Government.

in the area of learning (Thurstone [44, 46]), developing certain learning curves and checking on the fit of these curves to learning data. He had also considered some of the typical material in psychophysics, had become somewhat dissatisfied with the emphasis in psychophysics on measuring brightness of lights or heaviness of weights, had thought that it would be tremendously more fruitful and interesting to measure the strength of an attitude, the beauty of a picture, the degree of preference for a belief, for a nationality, or for a political candidate. This was the genesis of Thurstone's psychophysics—the Law of Comparative Judgment set up to analyze data collected by the experimental method of paired comparisons. Later Thurstone initiated what Torgerson has termed the Law of Categorical Judgment to deal with the data collected by the experimental method of successive intervals. Successive intervals was developed for the situation in which one could not reasonably require that the subject make all intervals equal (method of "equal-appearing intervals") or where there was doubt that he could or would do so, even if requested. At this time also, Thurstone (45) had completed his beginning text on test theory, a photo-offset version, and had started his developments of factor analysis for the further study of mental abilities. Thus he had worked in the various areas which today represent the major areas in which the quantitative rational approach in psychology has achieved the most success.

It is of interest that Professor Boring (5) in a recent discussion of quantitative developments in psychology specified four areas that had been particularly fruitful for such developments. These were psychophysics, learning, mental measurements, and reaction time. Thurstone's work between 1925 and 1935, as indicated above, dealt with three of these four areas.

During the subsequent 25 years there has been relatively little quantitative development in the study of reaction time. There has, however, been a tremendous growth in psychophysics or psychological scaling, in learning, and in mental measurements represented by developments in test theory and in factor analysis. As to the work in psychophysics or psychological scaling, I shall simply refer to the symposium held this morning as an illustration of the development in this field over the last 25 years, and will consider here in some detail Learning, Test Theory, and Factor Analysis.

In order to set the stage for the discussion here I should like to illustrate one view of the relationship between scientific theory, mathematics and statistics (Gulliksen [18]). One always, of course, initially has the psychologically meaningful verbal statements of the postulates, the basic assumptions of any system. The characteristic thing about the mathematical rational approach is that at a very early stage these postulates, that is, the functioning postulates that would have some impact on deducing the nature of experimental results, are translated into the language of mathematics. We then have the stage of mathematical development of the concepts eventuating in various equations some of which contain two or more terms that can be subject to experimental observation. These then may be termed the observation equations for which one can gather data. One then designs an experiment and collects data from the experiment and then (with statistics) checks on the degree of agreement between the observation equation and the data. Frequently when one speaks of quantitative methods in psychology, he is thinking only of the use of statistics to check on the agreement between a hypothesis and data.

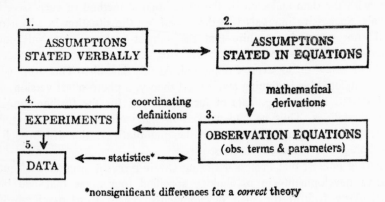

Figure 1. Mathematical formulation of psychological theories.

In this discussion I will not deal with statistics which is essentially the last step in the development. I will discuss the complex indicated by the verbal psychological statements of the postulates, the mathematical statements of these same postulates, and the derivations from which one gets various implications of the initial postulates eventuating then in mathematical equations that could be in agreement with data from experiments or that could be in disagreement with data.

Statistics (the estimation procedures, testing of hypotheses, and the determination of confidence intervals) is a field that has undergone such tremendous developments in the last 25 years that again it could not possibly be covered even in a symposium devoted entirely to statistics.

Omitting both Psychophysics and Statistics is reminiscent of Sherlock Holmes in "The Adventure of Silver Blaze." When asked for the most significant item in the case to date, he said, "The strange behavior of the dog in the nighttime." Watson, after thinking a moment, replied, "But the dog did nothing in the nighttime." "That," said Holmes, "is the strange behavior."

In the consideration of developments in the last 25 years, in a single symposium, it is necessarily true that the most significant items in development are those that are being omitted because they are too extensive to deal with short of several symposia. Areas essentially nonexistent 25 years ago are now too extensive to be considered in a single session.

Learning

One area in which there has been considerable development of mathematical translation of verbal postulates and derivation of their consequences is the area of learning (Hilgard [21]). Thurstone (44, 46) in the early thirties developed a theory based on an analogy of sampling from an urn, and showed that the equations derived from such assumptions were in reasonable agreement with data. Since then there have been a number of learning theories stated in mathematical form. Gulliksen (16, 17) has generalized Thurstone's initial equations and developed others based directly on Thorndike's law of effect showing that these equations are identical with those that Thurstone developed in terms of an urn model. Rashevsky (35) has taken an approach from basic ideas of the functioning of the nervous system, utilizing inhibition and facilitation, and has developed some equations of learning on this basis.

Hull (24) has utilized as his starting point the conditioning model where each repetition has an effect of increasing the strength of the response. He also used the concept of confusability of various responses to account for the lack of, shall we say, immediate learning to explain different degrees of difficulty of learning in serial lists. The probabilistic model that expresses its postulates in terms of operators increasing and decreasing the probabilities of response has also been developed during this time (Bush and Mosteller [7]).

I should also mention the work of Audley (3) in London. He has developed probabilistic equations of learning and devised methods of fitting these to individual learning curves so that one can obtain parameters for each individual from data on learning curves and also from data on changes in reaction time with learning. This is a rather interesting development, first, because it develops the probabilistic model so that parameters can be computed for each individual, and, second, because it relates the right-wrong response data to the reaction time data. One of the characteristics of learning is that the reaction time usually decreases. This theory tries to show that these two curves are two different manifestations of the same basic set of parameters. Roger Shepard (39) has related work in learning to psychophysics showing that generalization in learning is related to psychological similarity.

There have also been some recent interesting attempts to develop these models of learning and to express them in terms of electronic computing machine programs where the machine is instructed to compute probabilities in accordance with the numbers in certain cells. Under reward conditions it adds something to the numbers in those cells, under punishment conditions it subtracts something. The information-processing language (described by Green [14]) developed by Newell, Shaw, and Simon is an illustration of this particular approach (see also Newell and Simon [34]). Also Block, Rosenblatt, and others at Cornell have been working on the perceptron (see Rosenblatt [37]). This is a mechanical gadget in which the initial connections are purely random. However, there is a programming of an increase and decrease in resistance of certain circuits corresponding to reward and punishment and it turns out that this machine with purely random connections is capable of learning. Other discussions of complex behavior of computers are found in the Western Joint Computer Conference proceedings (53), the Teddington National Physical Laboratory symposium (33), Hagensick (20), Shannon and McCarthy (38), and Uhr (51).

A very interesting thing to note as one surveys these various theories by Audley, Estes, Bush, Mosteller, Hull, Rashevsky, Thorndike, Gulliksen, and Thurstone is the essential similarity in the basic framework of each theory. This can be indicated as follows.

1. There is some procedure to effect the "stamping in," the "facilitation," or the "increase in probability" of a response that in some sense is a correct response, a rewarded response, or a response that is at least dominantly rewarded.

2. There is a corresponding postulate regarding the "stamping out," "inhibition," or "decrease in probability" of a response that may be thought of as a wrong response, an incorrect response, an unrewarded response, or at least a dominantly nonrewarded response.

3. Many of the theories also have some provision regarding resemblance or similarity of stimuli either in their sensory characteristics or in their position, such as position near to each other in a rote learning series. This sort of similarity or contiguity leads in certain contexts to confusion and slows up learning; in other contexts it is termed "generalization of response to similar stimuli," or "transfer of training," or "equivalence of stimuli." Some mechanism, in other words, whereby a response which has initially been learned to one stimulus tends to be given to other stimuli. Depending on the particular learning setup designed by the experimenter this tendency

may either delay learning in one situation, or facilitate generalization in another situation.

4. There is also some sort of decrease in probability or fading out of a response, "forgetting" due either to passage of time or due to confusion with other stimuli. In some guises it has been termed retroactive inhibition. Rashevsky has shown how a differential decline rate for inhibition and facilitation could produce a "reminiscence" effect. This decline with time again enters into a number of the different learning theories.

5. There is also a change in reaction time that is often made a part of the theory. Hull utilized this as one of his postulates. One of the manifestations of learning is a decrease in response latency. Audley (3) has also used this to give a very interesting possibility for a sort of reliability check on a single learning situation.

During the last 25 years we have had a reasonable proliferation of slight variants on the increase or decrease of strengths and probabilities. These various sets of postulates result in somewhat different observation equations. However, the basic observation equations would all be in a superficial sense fairly similar so that it would probably take rather a precise test of a fit in various experiments to determine that one of these theories was a better fit to the data than others. Bush and his coworkers at Pennsylvania are embarking on such a program now. It is to be hoped that others will follow and that in the next 25 years we will be able to specify more accurately the kind of learning situation for which a given model or equation is most appropriate.

RELIABILITY OF LEARNING PARAMETERS

I want to mention here a development that is not, strictly speaking, quantitative, but one that may have a tremendous influence in the quantitative development and testing of learning theory. This stems from the work of Sperry (40). He has found it possible to divide a brain into two halves by sectioning the corpus callosum and the optic chiasma; he reports that not only is it found that habits learned by one half do not transfer to the other half, but for a given animal the peculiarities manifested by him in "right brain learning" are again exhibited in "left brain learning." Should this turn out to be verified, or generally true, we now have a possibility never before envisaged by workers in the field of learning, the "split brain reliability."

In my opinion one of the great handicaps under which work in learning has labored over the last hundred years has been the fact that, unlike the mental test area, it has been essentially impossible to do a repeat experiment and to determine a reliability. Every respectable achievement or aptitude test has some device of odd-even, first and second half, or repeat test, whereby one attempts to do the same thing twice and measures the accuracy of the technique by the correlation between these two halves—the reliability coefficient. In the case of learning the experimenter could always obtain a learning curve to determine parameters. However, when he attempted to get another learning curve, there was always a dilemma. He could experiment on animals which had not been used for the first set of learning curves, in which case there was simply a sort of species reliability. It would be considered extremely poor procedure, in the case of an intelligence test, to correlate one person's score with another person's score in order to determine the test reliability. Or he could have the same subjects learn another problem, in which case there was always the question, "Was the subject learning the second problem better because of the influence of the first one, or was he hindered in his learning of the second problem because of the influence of the first one?" The experimenter could never be particularly certain which was the case and, as a result, measures of learning have not had reliability coefficients attached. One just does not know the extent to which the lack of agreement is a result of a difference in the psychological function being tested, the psychological ability being tested, or simply the result of poor experimental techniques. Certainly this contribution of Sperry and others is worth an extremely careful look to see if the initial possibility that it holds for "split brain reliability" coefficients in the case of learning tasks is really borne out.

RELATION OF INTELLIGENCE TO LEARNING

I should also like to emphasize that while one purpose of learning theories is, of course, to describe the course of learning, this in itself should not stand as a final goal. Important questions can be raised regarding the relationship of these learning parameters to other parameters characterizing behavior of the individual. I can illustrate this point with the studies by Stake (41) and Allison (1). They both have raised a question regarding the relationship between mental abilities and learning. As we know, for decades intelligence has been defined as the ability to learn, yet intelligence tests have measured the ability to learn not directly but only by inference. They have concentrated on what has already been learned. Both Stake and Allison have set up a variety of learning problems, have fitted equations of the learning curve to the data obtained from 200 or 300 persons who took these learning tests, have also given these people some 30 or 40 aptitude and achievement tests and then have entered the entire material into a factor study. The purpose of these studies is to determine how many different learning abilities there are, and to see how these learning abilities are related to the abilities measured by aptitude and achievement tests.

First we can say that, as a result of these two studies, the learning area is definitely a complex area that cannot be represented in terms of one learning ability. There are many different kinds of learning ability—how many we will not know until a good many more studies have been made. Second, it is clear that some of the abilities required for the learning tasks are *not* represented in any of the intelligence measures. The nature and the importance of these abilities that have been missed by the one-shot aptitude and achievement measures constitutes a very important problem for further investigation.

I should also indicate that studies such as Stake's and Allison's could not have been conducted without electronic computers. Stake estimated that by Monroe-Marchant methods in use a few years ago his analysis would have taken one hundred and twelve man-years. With electronic computers the job was done in about six months.

MASTER- OR REFERENCE-LEARNING CURVES

In the first volume of *Psychometrika,* Eckart and Young (11) published a very important paper. It dealt with the approximation of one matrix by another of lower rank. It applied in general to any matrix, square or rectangular, and furnished the essential basis for the use of matrix theory for expressing and testing a large number of quite different psychological hypotheses. (See also Hohn [22] for an elementary treatment of matrices.)

One interesting application of the Eckart-Young theorem is to learning matrices. For many years, people have analyzed group learning data, plotted group learning curves, and criticized others on the ground that there are individual differences in learning which averages ignore. The Eckart-Young procedure has been used by Tucker (48, 50) for analyzing learning data. The matrix of trials by individuals is factored to give a minimum number of "reference" or "master" learning curves. Each individual receives a set of weights indicating the extent to which he has utilized each curve. If the matrix is rank one, then there is only one master learning curve, and the average curve is a good representation for each individual. In general, for ranks greater than one the individuals will not be correctly represented by the average curve.

Tucker (48, 50) has applied this method of handling learning matrices to some probability learning data collected by R. Allen Gardner. He finds that in a simple probability learning situation where the subject is distinguishing between probabilities of .70 and .30, the matrix is of rank one. Only one learning curve is necessary to explain the data. In another situation, where four objects were presented with relative frequencies 70, 10, 10, and 10 per cent, three different learning curves were needed to explain the data. There were apparently (shall we say) early learners, medium learners, and people who caught on to some of the ideas very late in the

series of trials, so that one of the learning curves was a rapidly rising negatively accelerated curve, and the other two were inflected *S*-shaped curves.
The different subjects had different weighted combinations of these curves.

Weitzman (52) has utilized the Eckart-Young procedure for analyzing
matrices of learning data (animals by trial matrices) for a combined group
of rats and a group of fish, putting them together as successive rows of the
same matrix and applying a uniform analysis. The question is, "Will the
learning curves that are necessary for the rats be the same as those that are
exhibited by the fish, and will the weights of the learning curves needed for
the rats be the same as or different from the weights needed for the fish?"
In his particular case he found a rather clear-cut rank-two structure which
means that the same two, shall we say, master learning curves were necessary to explain the learning data for the rats and for the fish.

Test Theory

The area of mental measurement, which in the thirties was represented
by Thurstone's (45) small photo-offset manual, now covers a huge literature (Anastasi [2], Cronbach [9], Guilford [15], Thorndike and Hagen
[43], Lindquist [27], Remmers and Gage [36], and Meehl [31]).

Reliability and error of measurement are no longer the simple concepts
they were 25 years ago (Cureton [10], Jackson and Ferguson [25]). Guttman (19) has developed formulas for lower bounds of reliability coefficients. Cronbach (8) has suggested many different kinds of reliability
coefficients taking account of various types and combinations of factors
which can affect test performance. Perhaps one generalization would be to
point out that there are k different factors which may influence test performance such as fatigue, practice, additional learning, time of day, state of
health, emotions, distractions, maturation, and growth. There are then 2^k
different reliability coefficients, depending on which particular set of factors
is of interest for the particular use to be made of the test. The more important ones have been explicitly dealt with by Cronbach, Guttman, and
others.

Error of measurement is no longer a single number to attach to a test
to represent variance of observed test scores for persons with the same true
score. The error of measurement is a function of true score, so that the
discriminating power of the test will be different at different ability levels.
Mollenkopf (32) initiated some work in this area. The problem is being
studied in greater detail by Birnbaum (4) and Lord (30). The goal of this
work would be to develop procedures so that it would be possible to specify
the discriminating power desired in various ability ranges, and then to
construct a test having the desired characteristics.

The personnel classification problem is the problem of assigning or recommending the most efficient utilization of each person in a group to perform the set of jobs to be done by that group. Votaw, Brogden (6), and others have suggested solutions for the problem.

The central problem of test theory is the relation between the *ability* of the individual and his *observed score* on the test. A third concept, that of the true score of an individual on a test, has also been introduced in an effort to clarify the problem. Psychologists are essentially in the position of Plato's dwellers in the cave. They can know ability levels only through the shadows (the observed test scores) cast on the wall at the back of the cave. The problem is how to make most effective use of these shadows (the observed test scores) in order to determine the nature of reality (ability) which we can know only through these shadows. Birnbaum (4), with his studies of test theory, and Lazarsfeld (26), with his use of various trace lines in latent structure analysis, have proposed various types of solutions to this problem.

An attempt to develop a consistent theory tying test scores to the abilities measured is typified by Lord's recent work (28), including his Psychometric Society presidential address (30), in which he formulated at least five different theories of the relationship between test scores and abilities, and showed how it was possible to test certain ones of these. It is to be hoped that during the next 10 or 20 years a number of these tests will be carried out so that we will have not five different theories of the relationship between ability and test score and various possible trace lines, but we will be able to say that, for certain specified tests constructed in this way, here is the relationship between the score and the ability measured, and this is the appropriate trace line to use.

Factor Analysis

Another one of the major developments over the last 25 years has stemmed from the work in factor analysis of mental tests. It is interesting to note that when Thurstone worked for the military during the first world war, the contribution of psychologists under Dr. Yerkes was to set up a single measure of ability, the Army Alpha, or a measure of lower level ability, the Army Beta, and to range all men along the single scale of the Army Alpha test and on the strength of this information to assign jobs.

I remember in teaching beginning psychology classes in the late twenties that I repeatedly explained to doubting freshmen that it was merely a popular superstition that some people had high verbal ability and others had high mathematical ability. These various abilities were perhaps matters of differential interest, but basically there was only one intelligence as indicated by the Spearman so-called two-factor theory, which of course was one general factor with various sorts of specific factors, and that any belief in various factors had the status purely of an unverified popular superstition.

In the early thirties Thurstone took the view that very possibly we had failed to find different types of intelligence simply because we had not looked carefully enough with sufficiently powerful methods. He developed the factor methods, found that there was a mathematics—the mathematics of matrix theory—that was possibly relevant, and devoted his time to studying this and applying it in the analysis of mental abilities. I remember Thurstone telling that he had presented his factor problem to some of the mathematicians at a Quadrangle Club lunch one noon, pointing out that he had a square array of numbers here (the set of correlation coefficients), that he wanted to get one rectangular array such that when multiplied together in a certain way the sum products of the numbers in these two rectangular arrays would equal the correlations in the one larger square array. He said they smiled at each other and said, "Oh, the square root of a matrix is all that is." He insisted on pursuing the inquiry further, found that there was a field that possibly dealt with this topic that he should be interested in, tutored in it for some years, and developed as a result the vectors of mind and multiple-factor analysis. Tremendous numbers of studies stemmed from this work. Other theoretical developments in the area were made by Truman Kelly and Harold Hotelling, who also generalized Spearman's one general-factor view to include the possibility of a large number of factors. This was the beginning of literally hundreds of factor studies which led to the development of a variety of tests of various mental abilities. One illustration of the impact of this work is the difference in the testing program in the second world war. None of the services utilized only a single measure of general intelligence. There were tests of a variety of abilities—verbal, quantitative, spatial, mechanical. Placement for different types of assignments was dependent on different weighted combinations of these abilities.

THEORY OF FACTOR ANALYSIS

With respect to the theoretical developments in factor analysis, we have had a considerable growth in the area of statistical tests for significance of factors or of ranks of matrices, although considerable still remains to be done in this area. The development of methods of comparing factor analyses results of one battery with those of another—the interbattery method —constitutes an extremely significant contribution (Tucker [49]). The other lack, until recently, was the lack of methods for comparing one study on a given set of tests with another study using the *same* set of tests on a *different* sample of people (Tucker [47]). So we now have precise methods for comparing different groups given the same battery, and different batteries given to the same group. These are powerful extensions of the factor method.

The recent development of high-speed computing methods is also critical for this field. Twenty years ago there was a considerable argument between persons with a mathematical bent, such as Hotelling, who insisted that one must use the principal axis solution, and experimenters, such as Thurstone, who maintained that, while the principal axis solution was very nice, he had never seen anyone utilize it with 50 tests on 200 or 300 people. We now of course have computing routines that give the principal axis solution at a feasible time and cost so that this controversy is now technologically obsolete. Thurstone would clearly have adopted the principal axis solution as soon as it was feasible from the point of view of cost involved and time consumed.

Many of the problems in test theory and factor analysis are essentially problems of multivariate analysis in mathematical statistics. It is very encouraging to note that many psychologists are developing proficiency in mathematical statistics, and also that mathematical statisticians, such as T. W. Anderson, Frederick Mosteller, David Votaw, Allan Birnbaum, D. N. Lawley, M. G. Kendall, S. S. Wilks, John Tukey, and others, are becoming interested in some of the statistical problems associated with test theory and other branches of psychology, and are providing the psychologists with solutions to these problems.

APPLICATIONS OF FACTOR ANALYSIS

There have been various conferences on factor analysis and its results lately. Two monographs by French (12, 13) on the various achievement and aptitude factors and the various personality factors indicate the degree to which this field has proliferated. The need now seems to be for more systematization, boiling down, determining which of the factors are important and which are not, rather than added proliferation of the factors.

Typically, the work in factor analysis has dealt with a battery of *predictors*. However, increasing attention is being directed toward the problem of using a battery for efficient prediction, differential prediction, of multiple criteria. The Psychological Corporation has a differential prediction battery. Horst (23) at the University of Washington has been developing the theory for differential prediction, and developing such a battery.

Achievement Tests

I probably should also mention that the field of achievement testing has developed considerably since the early 1900's, when three-hour essay examination graded by crews of readers was the standard procedure for the College Entrance Examination Board. There is some appreciation of the fact that evaluation of the essay is not very precise, and that teachers need to be taught the appropriate methods for preparing and evaluating class-room tests. This is an extremely large job on which only a relatively small start has been made as of now. In the next 25 years I would hope for considerably greater sophistication of the classroom teacher in the development and evaluation of tests than we find now.

Summary

We have considered developments over the last 25 years in the area of measurement of mental abilities. Marked advances have been made in determining the relationship between the ability measured and the test score, in methods of item analysis, in the differentiation and classification of various methods of dealing with reliability. The big development in this area though has been the change from the emphasis on a single general intelligence to the differentiation of a large number of different aptitudes. This has been made possible by the development of the factor analysis methods.

Note that factor methods were just at their beginning when *Psychometrika* was started, that the initial paper by Young and Householder on multidimensional scaling techniques had not yet been written, the Eckart-Young paper dealing with the expression of one matrix as a product of two other matrices of minimum rank, a fundamental factor analysis theorem, had not yet been written, and that the factor computations were done entirely with Monroe-Marchant methods. We can see that during the last 25 years there has been, first, a terrific growth in the basic theory related to mathematical formulation of psychological problems—basic theory in the area of testing, in the area of aptitude measurement and factor analysis, in the area of learning, and in the area of psychophysics. Second, there has been a tremendous development of computational methods, enabling us to do studies now that were essentially impossible because of time and cost factors even five or ten years ago.

The findings resulting from these methods have an impact in various areas. The development of multiple factor tests has changed the entire picture of the testing field from what it was during the first world war. The development of a variety of learning theories gives some promise that in the next 25 years we will be able to specify the types of conditions, if any, under which these various theoretical approaches are appropriate.

The development of the unidimensional and multidimensional scaling methods and their use in a variety of areas, in measuring sensations, in measuring preferences or values for objects, should have considerable impact. Various fields such as linguistics, sociology, and economics should benefit tremendously from some of these methods that have been developed during the last 25 years since this small group of students met with Thurstone and decided to form the Psychometric Society to publish *Psychometrika,* and to further the development of psychology as a quantitative rational science.

References

1. ALLISON, R. B., JR. Learning parameters and human abilities. Princeton Univ., Psychol. Dept., 1960. (multilith)

2. ANASTASI, A. *Psychological testing.* New York: Macmillan, 1954.

3. AUDLEY, R. The inclusion of response times within a stochastic description of the learning behavior of individual subjects. *Psychometrika,* 1958, **23,** 25–31.

4. BIRNBAUM, A. Probability and statistics in item analysis and classification problems: on the estimation of mental ability. Ser. Rep. 15. Pensacola, Florida: Sch. of Aviation Medicine USAF, 1957.

5. BORING, E. G. The beginning and growth of measurement in psychology. Paper presented at the N. R. C. and S. S. R. C. conference on "The history of quantification in the sciences," Nov., 1959.

6. BROGDEN, H. E. Least squares estimates and optimal classification. *Psychometrika,* 1955, **20,** 249–252.

7. BUSH, R. and MOSTELLER, F. *Stochastic models for learning.* New York: Wiley, 1955.

8. CRONBACH, L. J. Test "reliability": its meaning and determination. *Psychometrika,* 1947, **12,** 1–16.

9. ———. *Essentials of psychological testing.* New York: Harper, 1949.

10. CURETON, E. E. The definition and estimation of test reliability. *Educ. psychol. Measmt,* 1958, **18,** 715–738.

11. ECKART, C. and YOUNG, G. The approximation of one matrix by another of lower rank. *Psychometrika,* 1936, **1,** 211–218.

12. FRENCH, J. W. The description of aptitude and achievement tests in terms of rotated factors. *Psychometric Monogr. No. 5.* Chicago: Univ. Chicago Press, 1951.

13. ———. The description of personality measurements in terms of rotated factors. Princeton: Educ. Testing Serv., 1953.

14. GREEN, B. F., JR. IPL-V: The Newell-Shaw-Simon programming language. *Behav. Sci.,* 1960, **5,** 94–98.

15. GUILFORD, J. P. *Psychometric methods.* (2nd ed.) New York: McGraw-Hill, 1954.

16. GULLIKSEN, H. Rational equation of the learning curve based on Thorndike's law of effect. *J. gen. Psychol.,* 1934, **11,** 395–434.

17. ———. A generalization of Thurstone's learning function. *Psychometrika,* 1953, **18,** 297–307.

18. ———. Mathematical solutions for psychological problems. *Amer. Scientist,* 1959, **47,** 178–201.

19. GUTTMAN, L. A basis for analyzing test-retest reliability. *Psychometrika,* 1945, **10,** 255–282.

20. HAGENSICK, P. W. Logic by machine: programming the LGP-30 to solve problems in symbolic logic. *Behav. Sci.,* 1960, **5,** 87–94.

21. HILGARD, E. R. *Theories of learning.* (2nd ed.) New York: Appleton-Century-Crofts, 1956.

22. HOHN, F. E. *Elementary matrix algebra.* New York: Macmillan, 1958.

23. HORST, P. and MACEWAN, C. Optimal test length for multiple prediction: the general case. *Psychometrika,* 1957, **22,** 311–324.

24. HULL, C. L. *Principles of behavior.* New York: Appleton Century, 1943.

25. JACKSON, R. and FERGUSON, G. Studies on the reliability of tests. Toronto: Dept. Educ. Res. Bull. No. 12, 1941.

26. LAZARSFELD, P. F. Latent structure analysis. In S. Koch (Ed.), *Psychology: A study of a science.* Vol. III. New York: McGraw-Hill, 1959.

27. LINDQUIST, E. F. (Ed.) *Educational measurement.* Menasha, Wis.: Banta, 1951.

28. LORD, F. M. A theory of test scores. *Psychometric Monogr. No. 7.* Chicago: Univ. Chicago Press, 1952.

29. ———. Tests of the same length do have the same standard error of measurement. *Educ. psychol. measmt,* 1959, **19,** 233–239.

30. ———. An approach to mental test theory. *Psychometrika,* 1959, **24,** 283–302.

31. MEEHL, P. E. *Clinical and statistical prediction.* Minneapolis: Univ. Minnesota Press, 1955.

32. MOLLENKOPF, W. G. Variation of the standard error of measurement. *Psychometrika,* 1949, **14,** 189–230.

33. NATIONAL PHYSICAL LABORATORY, Teddington, England. *Mechanisation of thought processes.* London: Her Majesty's Stationery Office, 1959.

34. NEWELL, A. and SIMON, H. A. The simulation of human thought. Santa Monica, Calif.: The RAND Corp., 1959. (mimeo)

35. RASHEVSKY, N. *Mathematical biophysics.* (Rev. ed.) Chicago: Univ. Chicago Press, 1948.

36. REMMERS, H. H. and GAGE, N. L. *Educational measurement and evaluation.* New York: Harper, 1955.

37. ROSENBLATT, F. The perceptron: a probabilistic model for information storage and organization in the brain. *Psychol. Rev.,* 1958, **65,** 386–408.

38. SHANNON, C. E. and MCCARTHY, J. (Eds.) *Automata studies.* Princeton: Princeton Univ. Press, 1956.

39. SHEPARD, R. Stimulus and response generalization: tests of a model relating generalization to distance in psychological space. *J. exp. Psychol.,* 1958, **55,** 509–523.

40. SPERRY, R. W. Physiological plasticity and brain circuit theory. In H. F. Harlow and C. N. Woolsey (Eds.), *Biological and biochemical bases of behavior.* Madison, Wis.: Univ. Wisconsin Press, 1958. Pp. 401–424.

41. STAKE, R. Learning parameters, aptitudes and achievements. Princeton Univ., Psychol. Dept., 1958. (multilith)

42. THORNDIKE, E. L. *The fundamentals of learning.* New York: Columbia Univ. Bur. Publ., 1932.

43. THORNDIKE, R. L. and HAGEN, E. *Measurement and evaluation in psychology and education.* New York: Wiley, 1955.

44. THURSTONE, L. L. The learning function. *J. gen. Psychol.*, 1930, **3**, 469–493.

45. ———. *The reliability and validity of tests.* Ann Arbor, Mich.: Edwards Brothers, 1931.

46. ———. The error function in maze learning. *J. gen. Psychol.*, 1933, **9**, 288–301.

47. TUCKER, L. R. A method for synthesis of factor analysis studies. Dept. of the Army, Personnel Res. Br., AGO, Rep. 984, 1951.

48. ———. Determination of parameters of a functional relation by factor analysis. *Psychometrika*, 1958, **23**, 19–23.

49. ———. An interbattery method of factor analysis. *Psychometrika*, 1958, **23**, 111–136.

50. ———. Determination of generalized learning curves by factor analysis. Princeton Univ., Psychol. Dept., 1960. (multilith)

51. UHR, L. Intelligence in computers: the psychology of perception in people and in machines. *Behav. Sci.*, 1960, **5**, 177–182.

52. WEITZMAN, R. A. A comparison of the performance of rats and fish on a probabilistic, discriminative learning problem. Princeton: Educ. Testing Serv. Rep., 1959.

53. WESTERN JOINT COMPUTER CONFERENCE. *Proceedings of the 1955 Western Joint Computer Conference.* New York: Amer. Inst. of Elect. Engineers, 1955.

29. Influence of Intelligence on Anxiety and Perception of Self and Others[*][1]

BEEMAN N. PHILLIPS,[†]
EDWIN HINDSMAN, AND
EARL JENNINGS, *The University of Texas*

THE VIEW that anxiety is associated with dissatisfaction with self and others is widely held, and it has found support in a number of studies (2, 3, 5, 7, 13, 17). However, in previous research only slight attention has been given to the characteristics of the *Ss* which were studied. Consequently, little is known about the effects which such characteristics have on anxiety relationships. Yet, it seems reasonable to believe that the development of anxiety and the occasions in which anxiety occurs are conditioned by and depend to some extent on the individual's personal characteristics and experiences.

As an underlying assumption of this research, it was reasoned that differences in relationships between anxiety and attitudes toward self and others would be explicable in terms of the theoretical formulations of Rogers, Sarason, and others (4, 9, 10, 12, 15). This rationale may be briefly summarized as follows: When an individual is unable to make responses which lead to success, frustration is produced and anxiety is aroused. In the beginning, this anxiety leads to self-dissatisfaction and increased goal-oriented reactions. The self tends to be perceived as responsible for the frustration, and there is increased awareness of needs, of the obstacles to the satisfaction of needs, and of instrumental ways of overcoming obstacles. But as frustrations continue and anxiety grows more intense, behavior becomes more and more centered on the reduction of anxiety through defense mechanisms. As a result, defense-oriented reactions increase and others are perceived as responsible for the frustrations.

The specific purpose of the study reported here was to investigate the effects of intelligence on relationships between anxiety and attitudes toward self and others. If bright *Ss* tend to be less frustrated and more successful, then they should also show less anxiety than mentally dull *Ss*, as the results

[*] From Beeman N. Phillips, Edwin Hindsman, and Earl Jennings, "Influence of Intelligence on Anxiety and Perception of Self and Others," *Child Development*, 31 (March, 1960), 41–46. Reprinted by permission.

[1] The research reported herein is being performed pursuant to a contract with the United States Office of Education, Department of Health, Education and Welfare.

[†] Department of Educational Psychology, University of Texas, Austin 12.

of previous research have indicated (8, 11, 14, 16, 18). As a consequence, on the basis of the rationale, we should also expect relationships between anxiety and dissatisfaction with others to be higher for mentally dull *S*s than for *S*s with high intelligence.

Procedures

The 709 *S*s used in the study were seventh graders selected from the population of the Human Talent Project which is being conducted in four Texas communities. A more detailed description of this project is found in a report by Duke and Hindsman (6).

As part of the talent project, a variety of ability, achievement, and personality instruments were administrated to these *S*s by the project's testing team. In this study use was made of the California Test of Mental Maturity, scales developed in the Texas Cooperative Youth Studies (CYS), the Castaneda-McCandless Anxiety Scale, and the Brown-Holtzman Survey of Study Habits and Attitudes (SSHA).

From the CYS and SSHA inventories eight scales were selected. Four of these were used as measures of the way individuals perceive themselves (social inadequacy, lack of personal adjustment, family tension, and school inadequacy). The other four were selected as measures of the way individuals perceive others (criticism of youth, low teacher valuation, criticism of education, and negative orientation to society).

To facilitate machine computations, all raw scores were converted to stanines before correlation coefficients were computed for subsamples based on intelligence and sex. Stanine values used to assign *S*s to the three levels of intelligence were: HI = 7–9, MI = 4–6, and LI = 1–3.

Results

From Table 1 it can be seen that anxious *S*s expressed more dissatisfaction with themselves and others than less anxious *S*s, although the relationships are higher for indices of self-dissatisfaction. In general, then, there is good agreement between these results and those of previous studies and some support for the sufficiency of the rationale.

However, the major proposition of the study, that relationships between anxiety and other dissatisfaction would be higher for *S*s with below average intelligence, is only partially supported by the data in Table 1. Results for criticism of youth and negative orientation to society are as predicted. But the relationship for criticism of education is not significantly different for high and low intelligence adolescents. In addition, the relationship for teacher valuation is opposite to predictions, being higher for high intelli-

Table 1

CORRELATIONS BETWEEN ANXIETY AND SELF-DISSATISFACTION AND OTHER-
DISSATISFACTION SCORES OF ADOLESCENTS CLASSIFIED BY LEVEL OF
INTELLIGENCE AND SEX

	HIGH INTELLIGENCE			MEDIUM INTELLIGENCE			LOW INTELLIGENCE			
Scales (N):	*Boys* (74)	*Girls* (86)	*Total* (160)	*Boys* (269)	*Girls* (205)	*Total* (474)	*Boys* (43)	*Girls* (32)	*Total* (75)	*Total* (709)
Self-dissatis- faction										
Social inade- quacy (CYS)	58	65	62	55	62§	58	77	62	70	60
Lack of per- sonal adjust- ment (CYS)	56	41	47	46	44	45	48	53	50	46
School inade- quacy (SSHA)	42	52‡	47*	25	29	27	31	19	23	32
Family tension (CYS)	34	22	27	35	34	35	28	55	39	35
Other dissatis- faction										
Criticism of Youth (CYS)	67†	17‡	12*	25	26	25	45	57	48	26
Low teacher valuation (SSHA)	35	46‡	40*	11	21	13	12	02	06	20
Criticism of education (CYS)	26	44	36	23	25	24	38	34	36	29
Negative orienta- tion to society (CYS)	40§	14‡	26*	38	34	37	54	51	53	37

NOTE—All decimal points have been omitted.

* Differences between rHI and rLI (Totals) significant at .05 level.

† Differences between rHI and rLI (Boys) significant at .05 level.

‡ Differences between rHI and rLI (Girls) significant at .05 level.

§ Differences between rBOYS and rGIRLS and (Within intelligence levels) significant at .05 level.

gence Ss. With respect to sex differences, it should be noted that relationships for girls followed predictions better than those for boys.

In interpreting these findings, an issue of some importance concerns
the degree of intercorrelation among the various indices of self- and other-
dissatisfaction, and the relationship of these scales to intelligence. For the
set-up as a whole, the intercorrelations among the indices of self and other
dissatisfaction ranged from .13 to .74, with most highly correlated measures
being school inadequacy, low teacher valuation, and criticism of education.

These latter relationships are particularly significant in view of the large differences in Table 1 on two of these measures. In addition, the correlation between intelligence and anxiety was —.15, while the correlations between intelligence and the various measures of self- and other-dissatisfaction ranged from statistical insignificance to .28.

Noteworthy, also, is the general lack of mean differences between the 3 samples on the various scales. In an analysis of variance of anxiety, self, and other scores of a random sample of 144 of these Ss, the following results, pertinent to the present study, were obtained: (a) There were no significant interactions between intelligence and sex. (b) There were significant differences between levels of intelligence on anxiety and school inadequacy (SSHA), with HI Ss reporting less anxiety and fewer feelings of school inadequacy. (c) Boys differed significantly from girls on low teacher valuation (SSHA), with girls reporting more favorable opinions of teachers than boys.

In addition, factor analytic studies have been in progress using varimax procedures. In one such analysis the Ss of the present study were classified by levels of intellectual functioning. Findings pertinent to the present investigation may be briefly summarized as follows: For HI Ss, anxiety had significant loadings on two factors. The factor with the higher anxiety loading also had high loadings on social inadequacy, lack of personal adjustment, and family tensions. Loadings of the other tests used in this study were either low or insignificant. Low teacher valuation and school inadequacy had the highest loadings on the other anxiety-loaded factor. However, these loadings were opposite in sign to the anxiety loading. Other tests with significant loadings on this factor included criticism of education, negative social orientation, and social inadequacy. For LI Ss, anxiety loaded significantly on only one factor. Other tests loading on this factor included social inadequacy, lack of personal adjustment, family tensions, negative social orientations, criticism of youth, and criticism of education.

Discussion and Conclusions

The results of this study substantiate the generally accepted hypothesis that anxiety produces dissatisfaction with self and others, for it was found that anxious Ss expressed more self- and other-dissatisfaction than less anxious Ss. However, as predicted by the rationale of the study, these relationships were modified to some extent when the intelligence of the Ss was considered. Within the limits of this study, then, it can be concluded that relationships between anxiety and attitudes toward self and others have only limited generality, the nature of such relationships depending to some extent on the characteristics of the sample studied.

As results indicate, the rationale was less successful in predicting relationships for boys than it was for predictions for girls. A possible explanation of this, which is suggested by Sarason's findings, is that a high anxiety score does not have the same significance for boys as it does for girls (1, 17). Due to cultural pressures and training, boys may find it more difficult to admit anxiety during adolescence. In addition, boys may express anxiety differently than girls. This raises the issue of whether scores on the same self- and other-dissatisfaction measures have comparable meaning for boys and girls.

Particularly noteworthy, also, was the failure of the rationale to predict results for school-related attitudes. Clear-cut differences on these attitudes were obtained between high and low intelligence *S*s, but differences were not in accord with predictions. In two of the three measures relationships were significantly higher for *S*s with high intelligence. From the rationale there is the presumption that this means that bright *S*s become more ego-involved in school activities, develop higher expectations and goals, and consequently suffer more frustration and anxiety in school situations than *S*s with low intelligence. However, such an explanation is at variance with previous findings (12, 13, 16). A more definitive explanation must await further research.

References

1. BENDIG, A. W. Age, sex, and the manifest anxiety test. *J. consult. Psychol.*, 1954, 18, 16.
2. BLOCK, J., and THOMAS, H. Is satisfaction with self a measure of adjustment? *J. abnorm. soc. Psychol.*, 1955, 51, 254–259.
3. CALVIN, A. D., and HOLTZMAN, W. H. Adjustment and the discrepancy between self concept and inferred self. *J. consult. Psychol.*, 1953, 17, 39–44.
4. CASTANEDA, A., PALERMO, D. S., and McCANDLESS, B. R. Complex learning and performance as a function of anxiety in children and task difficulty. *Child Develpm.*, 1956, 27, 327–332.
5. DORIS, J., and SARASON, S. B. Test anxiety and blame assignment in a test situation. *J. abnorm. soc. Psychol.*, 1955, 50, 335–338.
6. DUKE, R. L., and HINDSMAN, E. Educational utilization of human talent: note on research project. *Psychol. Rep.*, 1959, 5, 252.
7. FEY, W. F. Correlates of certain subjective attitudes toward the self and others. *J. clin. Psychol.*, 1957, 13, 44–49.
8. GRICE, G. R. Discrimination reaction time as a function of anxiety and intelligence. *J. abnorm. soc. Psychol.*, 1955, 50, 71–74.
9. HILLSON, J. S., and WORCHEL, P. Self concept and defensive behavior in the maladjusted. *J. consult. Psychol.*, 1957, 21, 83–88.
10. JESSOR, R., and HAMMOND, K. Construct validity and the Taylor Anxiety Scale. *Psychol. Bull.*, 1957, 54, 161–170.

11. McCandless, B. R., and Castaneda, A. Anxiety in children, school achievement, and intelligence. *Child Develpm.*, 1956, 27, 379–382.

12. Mandler, G., and Sarason, S. B. A study of anxiety and learning. *J. abnorm. soc. Psychol.*, 1952, 47, 166–173.

13. ——, and ——. The effect of prior experience and subjective failure on the evocation of test anxiety. *J. Pers.*, 1953, 21, 336–341.

14. Phillips, B. N., McGuire, C., and King, F. J. Studies on anxiety: I. Anxiety and performance on psychometric tests varying in complexity. *Child Develpm.*, 1959, 30, 253–259.

15. Rogers, C. R. *Client-centered therapy.* Boston: Houghton-Mifflin, 1951.

16. Sarason, S. B. A test anxiety scale for children. *Child Develpm.*, 1958, 29, 105–113.

17. ——, *et al.* Rorschach behavior and performance of high anxious and low anxious children. *Child Develpm.*, 1958, 29, 277–285.

18. Zweibelson, I. Test anxiety and intelligence test performance. *J. consult. Psychol.*, 1956, 20, 479–481.

30. Satisfactions and Interests *[1]

EDWARD K. STRONG, JR., *Stanford University*

THE TOPIC is "Satisfactions and Interests." During the last 37 years I have learned some things about interests, but I confess I have taken satisfaction for granted—which I think is pretty much what most psychologists have done. The term is employed in everyday language and defined in the dictionary. It plays an important role in all theories of motivation. For over three decades surveys of job satisfaction of employees have been conducted costing thousands of dollars. Nevertheless I am very doubtful if any ten experts would agree on a specific definition of the term.

Years ago I contended that there was "no better criterion of a vocational interest test than that of satisfaction enduring over a period of years" (10, page 385). I have actually never used satisfaction as a criterion on the ground that there seemed to be no good way to measure it. Such correlations as have been reported between interest scores and satisfaction have been for the most part too low to be of practical significance.

Job Satisfaction and Job Success

Most people have assumed that job satisfaction or morale contributes to production. It came as a shock to me, as it must have had to many others, to read Brayfield and Crockett's (1) review of the literature and to learn that there is little or no evidence to support the assumption. In a

* From Edward K. Strong, Jr., "Satisfactions and Interests," *The American Psychologist,* 13 (August, 1958), 449–56. Reprinted by permission.
[1] This paper is based on the fifth Walter Van Dyke Bingham Memorial Lecture given at the University of Minnesota on April 10, 1958.

still more recent review, Herzberg, Mausner, Peterson, and Capwell (2) report some relationship between morale and production, but in most of the investigations where there were positive relations they were low correlations. Reading these two reviews and that of Viteles (11) and many of the articles on which these reviews are based leaves one bewildered. Definitions of the key terms are conspicuous by their absence and must differ greatly, judging by the context. Many statements by one writer are contradicted by another.

What is satisfaction? Some say it is a kind of feeling as simple as pleasantness; others contend it is a complex of feeling, emotion, and sensation. If the latter, do the proportions of these three ingredients vary each time? Contrast the satisfaction of eating dinner and resting afterwards with a full stomach with the satisfaction of finding a house to rent after hunting many weary days. The mother tells her daughter as she leaves the home to have a good time and asks when the girl returns: "Did you have a good time?" Is having a good time what is meant by satisfaction?

Employee surveys are called attitude or job satisfaction or morale surveys. The terms are sometimes used synonymously and sometimes not. In the absence of generally accepted definitions it is suggested that job satisfaction be employed when the worker is thought of as an individual and that morale be used when the worker is thought of as a member of a group. Perry defines morale as "a state of mind which characterizes groups of men when they are engaged in some action. . . . The essence of it is that the group holds together and holds to its objective, despite events that are calculated to divide and dishearten" (7). An employee is an individual and a member of one or more groups. It is appropriate to consider both his job satisfaction and his morale. But seemingly there should be some difference in the inventories designed to measure these two attitudes towards one's job. Inventories regarding morale should contain items relative to the man's involvement with his company, his union, and the members of his department. Are the low correlations between production and job satisfaction caused in part at least by inadequate measurement of job satisfaction? Consider briefly how job satisfaction has been measured.

Employee surveys since the pioneer days of Houser have typically consisted of two parts: the first part asking a few questions as to the man's overall satisfaction with his job; the second asking whether he liked or was satisfied with all manner of factors, such as income, supervision, cafeteria, pension system, and so on. A summary of the responses in the first part was supposed to measure the employee's overall satisfaction. Responses to the items in the second part that pertained to each job factor were summarized in order to show how satisfied or dissatisfied employees were regarding the various factors. The purpose of such surveys has been to aid management to improve production by determining the causes of dissatisfaction and by identfying the departments with low morale. Much of the literature is devoted to the causes or job factors presumably associated with dissatisfaction, their relative importance, and what can be done to improve conditions. Surveys have been worth-while to the extent that management has made intelligent use of the results—which has not always been done.

One reason why job satisfaction inventories do not correlate with production is that the items do not furnish good measures of the specific job factors. In one investigation, for example, four questions were used to measure each of four factors; the intercorrelations among the four items ranged from .39 to .52. A summary of the responses of four such questions can only roughly approximate what they purport to measure.

Even if we had good measures of job factors, which we do not have, some of the factors would not correlate particularly with production. Seemingly, health should be directly related to production. But some employees who suffer from poor health plug along regardless, and other employees absent themselves whenever they have the sniffles. Consider one very simple example of physical condition, that of toothache. If we rate production on a scale of −3 to +3 (where −3 represents absence from work and zero production, and +3 represents maximum production) and similarly rate satisfaction-dissatisfaction from toothache (where −3 represents such severe pain the man is absent at his dentist, the rating of −2 represents a decrease of 2 from normal rating in production, and the rating of − 1 represents a decrease of 1 from normal production), then we will have a correlation of .42 when 35 per cent of employees have ratings of −3, −2, and −1 in dissatisfaction from toothache. If the percentage of employees so affected drops to 15 per cent, the correlation is .26; if the percentage is further decreased to 10 per cent, the correlation is .20. It is unlikely that the percentage of employees seriously affected by toothache is ever as high as 10 per cent, so that the correlation would be appreciably below .20 although the data were arranged so that there was high correlation between suffering from toothache and decrease in production.

In order to obtain a significant correlation between satisfaction-dissatisfaction and production, we must have a situation where dissatisfaction produces decrease, and satisfaction produces increase, in production; and, furthermore, where a fair percentage of employees rate the factor high or low. It is doubtful if most job factors are so related to production.

Consider a second condition, that of being in love. Here we might obtain very high or very low overall satisfaction-dissatisfaction responses depending upon the current behavior of the loved one. It seems probable that those suffering from this malady, whether satisfied or not, would exhibit decrease in production since the employee's attention would be distracted by day-dreaming about last night and what will happen on the next date.

The factor of age has a curvilinear relationship with production. The youngest and oldest employees are more satisfied than those about 30 years of age. The factor of age will reduce the correlation when it is mixed in with other factors.

Those of you who are interested should consider how satisfaction-dissatisfaction relative to each aspect of a job could be related to success on the job and also estimate what percentage of employees would be particularly satisfied or dissatisfied on any one day.

A still more serious difficulty arises when responses to all the items on an inventory are summarized on the assumption that, if job satisfaction is to be measured, all aspects of the job should be taken into account. Here, inadequate measures of each factor are combined without much consideration as to the relationships between the factors—a procedure which makes our statisticians fairly froth at the mouth. A way must be found to consider only those who are really satisfied or dissatisfied with each job factor and to disregard those who don't really care about the factor. In the case of toothache there may be perfect correlation with production among the very few suffering with toothache and zero correlation among the great majority. Data based on all of them will not correlate as high as .10. How can you expect to learn how production is related to satisfaction with the job and with expectation of advancement when people with such attitudes are combined with girls who expect to marry and quit work? We need to develop adequate measures of each factor and determine the relationship to an adequate criterion before attempting a summary of all factors.

One way to discover what a test should measure is to note the nature of its items. Four types of questions are found in survey questionnaires: questions asking for facts, opinions, likings, and satisfactions. The proportions of these types vary greatly among survey inventories.

The evidence is clear that facts and opinions about working conditions are colored by feeling—as is every aspect of behavior. It is therefore appropriate to use fact and opinion questions to indicate feeling. Responses should, however, differ according as one is asked: Does your supervisor treat all alike? Do you like your supervisor? Are you satisfied to work under your supervisor? Most inventories ask many interesting questions: "Do you like or dislike this and that?" Considering that the inventory is to measure job satisfaction or morale, it is surprising that there are not more items which ask: "Are you satisfied or not with this and that?" Relatively few items inquire as to the man's involvement with his fellows and the company.

The correlations between job satisfaction and production are low not only because measures of job satisfaction are inadequate but because measures of success on the job are also inadequate. It is well recognized that production is not a complete measure of success on the job. There is possibly no more difficult problem in industrial psychology than the determination of adequate criteria of success. Furthermore, in a surprisingly high proportion of jobs there is no way to measure amount of production, and in many cases where it can be measured, as on an assembly line, the measure is far more a measure of flow of work, determined by management, than it is a reflection of the man's ability and willingness to do the work. It is not surprising that psychologists resort so often to ratings of supervisors as their criterion of success. Psychologists have so far contributed relatively little to this task. I have great faith in the ability of psychologists to develop an adequate test of any specifically defined activity; but, if the activity is not definitely defined, the first step should be to define the activity, not to attempt to devise tests that correlate .20, maybe .30, with something that it is hoped represents the activity. It would seem at the present time that both psychologists and management should concentrate on what is meant by success on a given job. When that is accomplished, management ought to be able to measure success on the job, and psychologists should aid in the analyses and devise tests which will predict in advance who will be successful and, I hope, also who will be interested and reasonably satisfied.

What shall be done with job surveys? Three alternatives are evident. First, continue the surveys for their practical value to business management but discontinue trying to prove that morale increases production appreciably. Second, accept the necessity of morale for its own sake. Modern personnel practice stresses that men must be selected so as to be both useful and happy. Maybe we should assume that good morale means general contentment, happiness, satisfaction on the part of all, top management as well as employees. No instructor, supervisor, or army officer wants the people under him to be complaining and criticizing everything that has to be done. Third, develop adequate measures of morale and success on the job. If there were adequate measures, might there not be much higher correlations between them?

Unquestionably much has been learned from job satisfaction surveys of practical use to business and of theoretical value to psychology. It is doubtful, however, if additional surveys will add much more of theoretical value. It now seems highly desirable to isolate and define the basic components and find some way to measure each of them. These are problems for psychologists to tackle. They are not easy or we would know more about them than we do today.

Opinion, Attitude, Interest, and Satisfaction

Consider now four basic concepts: opinion, attitude, interest, and satisfaction. First, what is *opinion,* often referred to as attitude? An opinion is a mental reaction to the relationship between this and that. Many items in an employee survey are opinion items, such as: "Do you work better on a clear or rainy day?" Responses to the questions are either "Yes" or "No" based on facts, more or less, but primarily indicating belief or disbelief. Belief is a feeling comparable to pleasantness, liking, and satisfaction. Opinions concerning religion and membership in the Republican or Democratic party are about as stable as anything we have in life. But many judgments are based on conversation, hearsay, not personal experience, and change about as readily as styles. The hullabaloo following the appearance of Sputnik is a striking example of a whole country losing faith in what they had previously believed. Because opinion items are not as stable as interest items, it is doubtful that they can be as useful as interest items in predicting future behavior. Research is needed to answer this and many other related problems well set forth by Sherif and Cantril (8) and by McNemar (3).

A second term is *attitude.* This term has a great vogue today. But what does it signify? Nelson (5) lists 23 rather distinct characterizations of the term. Sherif and Cantril tell us the term is in a very confused state, and McNemar reminds us that "no one has ever seen an attitude." Seemingly its best usefulness is its ambiguity. When a psychologist does not want to disclose his real purpose, as is typically the case with employee surveys, he may call his inventory a job attitude survey.

Several have given definitions of attitude. Peak's definition of attitude is useful here. She defines attitude (6) as "a hypothetical construct which involves organization around a conceptual or perceptual nucleus *and* which has affective properties." Concepts and percepts are acquired reactions to a combination of sensations. They are mental activities, and most of them initiate overt activities. It is not merely that sensations are organized into a concept so that no two persons have exactly the same concept but that such concepts are *used* in some manner that is important. What happens when I say the word "baseball"? Do you see the word, or think of keeping score, as you used to do in high school, or do you think of watching a game, or of playing the game, of playing short stop, or knocking out a home run? If the concept is emphasized, then according to Peak we have an attitude; if the activity is emphasized, we have a habit, a skill, or an interest. Psychologists are prone to call activities by many names depending upon the aspect that is emphasized. Thus the activity of skating is called a habit or a skill when its motor coordination acquired by repetition is emphasized; it is called an interest when its feeling quality is emphasized.

Five characteristics of *interests* may be mentioned. First, they are acquired in the sense that feeling becomes associated with the activity. We are not referring to the learning of an activity itself, such as writing one's name, which usually requires many repetitions. We are referring to the associating of feeling with an activity. Such association results from one or only a few experiences—once stung by a bee, one dislikes bees the rest of his life. About all that can be said about the associating process is that, when an activity is useful, aids in reaching some goal, pleasant feeling is attached to it; when the activity is not useful, brings some disagreeable consequence, unpleasant feeling is attached.

Second, interests are persistent. Sometimes disliking is replaced by liking and vice versa; many start out disliking olives and acquire a taste, a pleasant feeling, for them. But, all in all, interests are surprisingly permanent.

A third characteristic of interests is intensity. One can not only immediately indicate whether he likes or dislikes an activity, but one can also immediately indicate his relative preferences for different activities.

The fourth and fifth characteristics are acceptance-rejection and readiness to act. For example, the waitress says: "Will you have some garlic bread?" My wife's response is, "Yes, please"; my own response is, "No, thanks." She likes garlic and goes toward it, I dislike garlic and reject it. Such acceptance-rejection implies action, direction, choice. Such preferences typify readiness to act in the sense that a habit or memory is a readiness to act. The query of the waitress is a stimulus, and the already acquired interest, habit, memory, whatever one wants to call it, functions. The associated value, or feeling quality, determines whether the activity will be accepted or rejected, whether the organism will go toward or away from, whether it will continue the status quo or discontinue it. It must also be noted that many activities develop in time so as to bring sufficient pleasure to be employed for their own sake. So we smoke, chew gum, play bridge, or golf for the fun of it.

It is not surprising that interest tests predict the direction in which a person will go, for each item is indicative of preference, choice, direction to go. Interest tests are diagnostic because no two persons have acquired the same list of activities nor are the activities classified in the same manner as liked or disliked. Moreover, people engaged in an occupation have to a marked degree similar interests, and so people in one occupation can be differentiated from the members of other occupations.

How shall *satisfaction* be defined? Here again there are many definitions of satisfaction, but most of them emphasize three aspects: first, arrival at a goal, Webster says "fulfillment of a need or desire"; second, pleasant feeling or contentment; and third, a relatively quiescent condition. A sleepy cat purring on a rug, or contented cows, come to mind. But satisfaction occurs not merely when the goal is reached but also long before. These two satisfactions may be referred to as actual and anticipated satisfaction. Anticipation of one's date next Friday night is often much more exciting than the actuality.

Dissatisfaction is the opposite of satisfaction as far as feeling goes, but the overt activities accompanying satisfaction and dissatisfaction are quite different. In the case of actual satisfaction, the series of activities has been completed or nearly so, tension is released, and quiescence follows. In the case of anticipated satisfaction, activities may continue for years, as in the case of the boy planning to be a physician. Here is long range planning, continuing effort. Dissatisfaction arises because the individual is prevented from reaching his goal. He must find some way to circumvent the obstacle, or he must forego his desire. Any interference with one's purpose is frustrating with release of energy and anger. Such explosive behavior is very different from the quiescence of reaching a goal or the long term planning associated with anticipated satisfaction. Expressed in another way, anticipated satisfaction accompanies progress toward a goal, while dissatisfaction arises when progress is prevented.

I have had a lot of fun asking my colleagues what is the difference between interests and satisfactions. They start out quite sure they know and often end up quite confused. One distinction is that interests are associated with activities, and satisfactions are not. It is true that there are certain activities regularly employed to satisfy bodily needs, but the striking characteristic in securing satisfaction is that one uses whatever activities are available and may use a different combination of activities each time a goal is sought. Aside from the final, consummatory activity, satisfaction cannot be identified in terms of activities, as can interests.

Can interests and satisfactions be differentiated in terms of feeling? Interests are liked or disliked; there seems to be no qualitative difference in the liking of different activities. Satisfactions of bodily needs differ in quality. But possibly this is so because of the presence of different sensations. If the sensations were eliminated, would the remaining satisfactions be similar in such cases? What about goals other than bodily needs? Are there qualitative differences in the satisfactions of earning an *A* grade, in winning the high jump, in finding a house to rent, and so on? On the negative side, disliked activities tend to be ignored. But if one is forced to employ a disliked activity, as fixing a flat tire, the reaction is more typically dissatisfaction than disliking; then one grumbles, complains, swears, and even exhibits all the symptoms of anger.

Finally how can satisfaction-dissatisfaction be measured? We have already mentioned how job satisfaction is measured and that improvements are greatly needed before adequate measurements can be obtained as to how much satisfaction-dissatisfaction is associated with each job factor. Before considering a different procedure, let us eliminate measurement of satisfaction-dissatisfaction of past events on the grounds that they cannot be measured with any accuracy; and even if they could, they would be of little value.

A man who liked to fish and to golf but no longer does so because of old age continues to say he likes such activities. It is possible that, if he were asked to arrange a long list of activities in order of preference, he would not rank fishing and golf as high as he would have done 20 years earlier. Nevertheless he still likes them. The question is: Can one feel satisfaction for past events in similar fashion? I once hiked through heavy brush in hot weather for over 24 hours without food or water. It must have been very rugged, but I cannot now conjure up the thirst and fatigue I must have experienced. I can only recall the incident and enjoy talking about it as I am doing now. My old friend Hollingworth would have exclaimed: "That exemplifies the oblivescence of the disagreeable." My present feeling of pleasure at having done it is very different from how I must have felt at the time. Consider another incident. A violent argument arises in the machine shop as to how a job is to be done. The man who wins feels satisfied, the other dissatisfied. Now, if as so often happens the incident is forgotten the next day and there is no bad feeling on either side, then there is no existing satisfaction or dissatisfaction. And if so, is there any value today in trying to measure the feelings of yesterday? But if the loser in the argument continues to be sore, then such existing dissatisfaction may have a bearing on his over-all satisfaction-dissatisfaction.

What about satisfaction-dissatisfaction concerning a goal not yet attained. Here three components are evident: the goal, the dissatisfaction of today, and the anticipated satisfaction of tomorrow. The difference between the last two is, however, more significant than either, or both, considered separately.

In attempting to explain persistence of motivation Peak suggests that it is the "discrepancy rather than the affect which is the important source of continuing action." It is the difference between "Harry's feeling about his present job . . . and his feeling for the ideal job that he imagines" that is the source of persistent efforts to achieve the ideal. This agrees with what I have long taught: that motivation, or "intensifying the want of a prospect in selling, involves, first, making him realize how unpleasant his present situation is, and second, making him anticipate as much as possible the enjoyment he will have when he reaches his desired goal" (9). Morse

(4) has this same conception in mind when she says that "satisfaction depends basically upon what an individual wants from the world and what he gets." We would suggest substituting what "he expects to get" for "what he gets."

Measurement of Motivation

What we are proposing is the measurement of motivation rather than satisfaction of a given moment. Motivation is a more dynamic aspect of behavior than satisfaction and should prove more useful in predicting future behavior. It is worth-while to know how an employee feels toward this or that right now, today. But it is more important to know whether he is going to continue in his present type of work, to continue with the company, or to do something else. Job surveys have asked: "How satisfied are you with this and that?" In contrast we ask: "What do you want?" "What do you expect to get?" and "What do you think are the chances you will get what you want?" The difference between aspiration and expectation affords a basis of estimating degree of dissatisfaction; but likelihood that the expectation will be achieved must also be taken into account. The greater the expectation, the greater is the anticipated satisfaction.

It should be noted in passing that measurement of motivation is similar to measurement of interests in that neither predict how far or how fast one will go, for success is primarily a matter of ability, but both indicate direction, which of many activities will be engaged in.

Specific goals must be considered as well as present dissatisfaction and anticipated satisfaction. It is futile to compare the feelings of a girl who is working hard to make good and become office manager with those of a girl who is planning to quit work, marry, and have a home of her own, even though at the moment they are both dissatisfied with their progress toward their different goals.

Goals are phantasies, wishes, daydreams, aspirations, plans. Goals are often called needs. Some of them are needs but most have evolved as the result of social pressures, often expressed as "Keeping up with the Joneses." Many of these seem imperative, but does one have to keep up with the Joneses in every respect?

Have we any idea of how many different goals the men and women in this country possess, if all were expressed in standard terminology? Does a given man possess during his lifetime all possible goals or only a few? If the latter, why has he these particular goals? Again, how many goals does a man have at a given time? It is also important to know whether each goal is accompanied by its own satisfaction-dissatisfaction quality or do all these qualities more or less fuse together? In other words, does unhappiness because of one's wife affect one's attitude toward one's job, and vice versa? Does the dissatisfaction at being fired from one's job and the satisfaction from one's girl's promise to marry him alternate so that he fluctuates from dissatisfaction to satisfaction; or do the two fuse, and if so is the fusion a mere average or a weighted average in terms of their relative significance?

Goals differ also in complexity. There are simple goals as getting to class on time and complex goals such as planning to graduate from college while still in high school. Such long distant goals necessitate careful planning in terms of many subgoals, as selecting the courses necessary to enter college, getting good enough grades, selection of a college, etc.

It is necessary to determine not only a man's goals but the chance, the likelihood, of his attaining his goal. Likelihood is dependent here not upon the actual facts but upon the man's opinion or belief. A former student resigned because he saw no future in being moved from one job to another, not knowing that he was being groomed for an important position. The greater the chance, the greater is the anticipating satisfaction; the less the chance, the greater is the dissatisfaction. When there is no chance, the man may quit (a friend of mine committed suicide), or nurse a grudge, or abandon his goal (often not easy to do), or find a substitute goal. Likelihood may be expressed in terms of money as in buying an auto or home; or it may be expressed in terms of effort, that is, practice or study; or in terms of willingness to forego other goals, often called pleasures.

With many goals there is a cycle from dissatisfaction to satisfaction, repeated over and over. A simple example is eating. Three times a day we want to eat, are satisfied, and quit thinking about eating for a short while. Another example pertains to salary. Start with dissatisfaction, then anticipated satisfaction when the grapevine reports there will be raises, then satisfaction when the increase is received, then little thought of the subject gradually changing to dissatisfaction. Answers to the static question, "Are you satisfied with your salary?" depends upon where the man is in such a cycle. The more dynamic questions of: "What salary do you want a year hence, five years hence?" and "What do you think the chances are of obtaining such salaries?" should provide a more forward looking picture of the man's reaction to his salary. Whether men can look five years ahead or not is something to be determined. A few years ago I tried out such questions with college seniors; the great majority could not or would not give anything like definite answers.

Satisfaction in the long run necessitates improvement, progress. A golfer who had never had a better score than 85 would be elated with 84. But if he had 84 everytime for several weeks, he would become steadily more dissatisfied; only an 83 or better would give him satisfaction. Many investigators have pointed out that men about 30 years old are more dissatisfied than younger and older men. Is this not due to the fact that such 30-year-old men have come to realize that future progress is limited, that they are not going to realize their aspirations? Some remain disgruntled, but many seek satisfaction in other activities.

The term "level of aspiration" has considerable vogue today. Presumably it represents fairly well formulated to clear-cut formulation of one's goals. Why does one young man aspire to be a lawyer and his brother follow in the footsteps of his father, a coal miner? We always come back to the old, old problem: did the two go in different directions because of environmental educational pressures or because their genes were different? I have a hunch that many adult goals have evolved out of phantasies and daydreams. A 10-year-old girl dreamed of accompanying Allan Quartermain on wild adventures in Africa; later on she has always said "Yes" to her husband's harum-scarum expeditions. Is there any connection? Why did she indulge in exploration and physical danger instead of being a movie actress, a princess, or a Cinderella? How can one ascertain what daydreams a person has, considering that daydreams are usually viewed as too personal, too self-revealing, to be divulged to anyone? No psychologist will achieve fame by predicting future behavior on the basis of well-formulated plans; the really tough task is to predict behavior in terms of the antecedents of such plans.

I hope it has occurred to you that there are two great problems: What can this person do, what are his abilities, what can he accomplish if his abilities are properly trained; and, second, what does he want to do, which way does he want to go in life? His satisfaction, happiness, contentment is dependent upon the direction he is permitted to go. Happiness and success are interrelated, but all counseling services both educational and industrial must seek reasonable success for their counselees and also happiness now and in the future. Such counseling is dependent upon a determination of capacities on the one hand and goals on the other hand. We have made far more progress in measuring capacities than in ascertaining men's goals.

I have asked many questions for which I don't know the answers. There are hundreds of difficulties in all this—I am tempted to say a million difficulties. A good research man ought not to be dismayed; rather he should glory in the complexities—a tough job is far more fun than an easy one.

References

1. BRAYFIELD, A. H., and CROCKETT, W. H. Employee attitudes and employee performance. *Psychol. Bull.*, 1955, **52**, 396–424.

2. HERZBERG, F., MAUSNER, B., PETERSON, R. O., and CAPWELL, D. F. *Job attitudes: Review of research and opinion.* Pittsburgh: Psychological Services of Pittsburgh, 1957.

3. MCNEMAR, Q. Opinion-attitude methodology. *Psychol. Bull.,* 1946, **43,** 289–374.

4. MORSE, N. C. *Satisfaction in the white-collar jobs.* Ann Arbor: Institute for Social Research, 1953.

5. NELSON, E. Attitudes: I. Their nature and development. *J. gen. Psychol.,* 1939, **21,** 367–399.

6. PEAK, H. Attitude and motivation. In *Nebraska symposium on motivation,* 1955.

7. PERRY, R. B. National morale. *Educ. Rec.,* 1942, **23,** Supple. No. 15.

8. SHERIF, M., and CANTRIL, H. The psychology of attitudes. Part I. *Psychol. Rev.,* 1945, **52,** 295–319.

9. STRONG, E. K., JR. *Psychological aspects of business.* New York: McGraw-Hill, 1938.

10. ———. *Vocational interests of men and women.* Stanford: Stanford Univer. Press, 1943.

11. VITELES, M. S. *Motivation and morale in industry.* New York: Norton, 1953.

31. The Perception of Social Attitudes *[1]

SAMUEL J. MESSICK,[2] *University of Illinois*

THE ATTITUDES of others may be perceived as organized in different ways by different groups of people. Consider an attitude area composed of attitude toward war, attitude toward capital punishment, and attitude toward the treatment of criminals (correction versus punishment).

* From Samuel J. Messick, "The Perception of Social Attitudes," *The Journal of Abnormal and Social Psychology,* 52 (January, 1956), 57–66. Reprinted by permission.

[1] This study was supported in part by the Office of Naval Research contract N60nr-270–20 with Princeton University and also in part by funds from the National Science Foundation. The opinions and conclusions expressed are, of course, those of the author and do not represent the views of the Office of Naval Research or of the National Science Foundation. The initial portion of this study was carried out when the author was an Educational Testing Service Psychometric Fellow at Princeton University.

[2] Postdoctoral Fellow for Research in Personality, Ford Foundation Grant to the University of Illinois.

Certain people may perceive others as varying from an extreme humanitarian to a correspondingly extreme nonhumanitarian viewpoint. In such a situation some particular person might be seen as being antiwar, anticapital punishment, and procriminal correction in the sense that one attitude directly implies the other and that no alternatives are possible (see Figure 1). Such a person might be called a "humanitarian." In the same

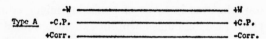

Figure 1. Conceptualization of the attitudes toward war, toward capital punishment, and toward treatment of criminals as a unidimensional system.

type of schema, some other person, who would be called inhumane, might be seen as being prowar, procapital punishment, and anticriminal correction. This would be a one-dimensional system, since the attitudes are not perceived separately but as one composite "humane-inhumane" attitude. People with such a point of view could not conceive of a person who was both antiwar and procapital punishment.

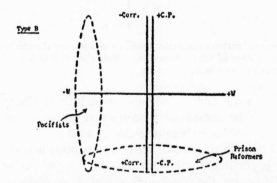

Figure 2. Conceptualization of the attitude toward capital punishment combined with the attitudes toward correction of criminals while the attitude toward war is seen as an independent dimension.

Another group of people may perceive the attitudes of others as being structured in a different way (see Figure 2). In this type of structure capital punishment of extreme criminals is equated with punishment of criminals in general as a deterrent to crime, but war is seen as something independent. This dimensional configuration provides a "frame of reference" in which Type B finds it possible to conceive of people in each of the four quadrants. In this perceived structuring, two pacifists could be conceived of as having widely different views toward capital punishment.

Although they are both viewed as being against war, one could be seen as in favor of capital punishment as a protection to society and a deterrent to crime and the other as against it because "it is just as uncivilized as war." Type B would also feel it possible for two people to be violently anticapital punishment and yet have different views toward war, because war is considered to be essentially independent of attitudes toward criminals. It would be difficult under these circumstances, however, for Type B to conceive of a person who was in favor of punishing minor criminals and at the same time against capital punishment for extreme criminals.

In Type C war and capital punishment are equated as two means of taking human life, but criminal correction is seen as something independent. Thus, Type C might conceive of two religious conscientious objectors as

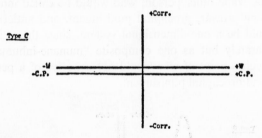

Figure 3. Conceptualization of attitudes toward war and capital punishment combined as two means of taking human life while the attitude toward correction of criminals is seen as independent.

being against both war and capital punishment because killing is involved, and yet one may be considered procorrection for humanitarian reasons and the other propunishment because evildoers must pay.

For Type D these three attitudes are viewed as being independent of each other, and it is possible for this group to conceive of people in each of the octants. Of course, the dimensions in any of the above types may be related in various ways—the lines drawn at angles instead of perpendicularly.

It must not be construed from the above discussion that a given group of people perceive the attitudes of others in only one way. The above types may be considered to be "points of view," and it is certainly possible for an individual to hold several different points of view with respect to the attitudes of others, depending upon the characteristics of the "other" people considered. Some individuals may be able to conceive of a different attitude structure for every group of people specified, because they perceive different types of people in different ways. However, it is also possible that these individuals perceive one particular attitude structure more often than an-

other, and that in the absence of specific knowledge or a detailed characterization of the other person, they may ascribe to his attitudes this modal
structure. It is this modal, or dominant, way in which individuals generally
structure the attitudes of others with which the present study is concerned.

In psychophysics multidimensional scaling methods (12, 13) have been
developed which yield dimensional configurations for psychophysical judgments. These methods may be promising for the analysis of attitudes. The
fundamental concept involved in these techniques is psychological distance,
a construct that has been widely used by many psychological theorists.
Psychological distance in the attitude realm can be thought of in terms of
the degree of agreement or disagreement shown between two statements.

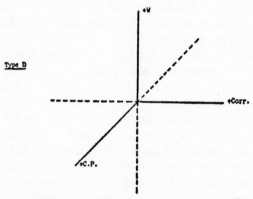

Figure 4. Conceptualization of the attitudes toward war, toward capital punishment,
and toward the correction of criminals as three completely independent
dimensions.

If a person who strongly agrees with one statement would also be likely to
agree strongly with another, then these two statements can be considered
to be psychologically close together. If a person who strongly agrees with
one statement would not be very likely to agree with the other, then
those two statements can be considered to be psychologically far apart. If
the psychological distances among attitude statements can be analyzed in
a Cartesian space, it will be possible to obtain a configuration of the way
in which an individual perceives attitudes as being structured in a given
domain.

The Problem and an Approach to Its Solution

As was seen in the introduction, it is possible on a priori grounds to
structure the attitudes of others in terms of several different, yet reasonable,

dimensional arrangements. The actual attitude arrangements perceived by individuals, however, has seldom been investigated, mainly because of a lack of appropriate methods. Knowledge of the ways in which individuals perceive attitudes as being structured in others is important psychologically, since such perceptions affect an individual's understanding of others, his relationships and adjustments with others, and his actions toward others. It might be possible to obtain some information about these perceived attitude structures by utilizing multidimensional scaling techniques.

The purpose of this study, then, is first of all to see whether a set of perceived attitude relationships can be adequately represented in dimensional terms and, secondly, to see if two groups, which probably differ with respect to these attitudes, perceive them as being structured in different ways. The adequacy of the dimensional representation can be evaluated in terms of the requirements of the multidimensional psychophysics model (see 7, 13, 18). This model provides for a Euclidean dimensionalization of the data, and if the data do not have Euclidean properties, one of the requirements of the model will not be met, i.e., the matrix of distance scalar products (see 7, 18), which must be positive semidefinite for Euclidean distances, will be found to have large negative roots. Therefore, if large negative roots are found, the suitability of the model is in question, and dimensions should not even be extracted. Unfortunately, however, statistical tests for the size of latent roots are not available, so arbitrary acceptance regions must be set (7, 13). Under such conditions, it might sometimes be possible for a matrix to be dimensionalized when it is actually nonEuclidean. Even in this case, however, there are indications of the unsuitability of the model, for a forced Euclidean description of non-Euclidean distances would lead to an increase in dimensionality. Thus, whenever the number of dimensions extracted approaches the number of stimuli, not only is the fruitfulness of the approach in that area in doubt, but the suitability of the model is also in question.

Multidimensional scaling methods have been utilized by Richardson (method of triadic combinations [10] and Torgerson (method of complete triads [13]) which could be applied for this purpose. These methods are essentially extensions of the method of paired comparisons to the multidimensional case. The method of complete triads could be applied to attitude statements as it stands, but it has the undesirable property that for n statements $n(n - 1)(n - 2)/2$ judgments would be required from each S. The task becomes prohibitive with more than 10 statements. It would be more reasonable to apply a multidimensional extension of the method of successive intervals (3, 11), which would require only $n(n - 1)/2$ judgments. The procedure for such a method would require S to arrange $n(n - 1)/2$ pairs of stimuli on a distance continuum according to the degree of similarity of the members of each pair. This question of similarity or relatedness can be approached in the attitude realm by asking for a judgment of the agreement or disagreement shown between two statements. The judgment involved can be set up in terms of the attitudes of some *other* person in the following way: S is asked to imagine the type of person who would strongly agree with Statement A and then to decide how this same person would also feel about Statement B. In this way, S is asked to estimate the attitude relationships of others, and the multidimensional analysis of these data will provide a dimensional configuration of these perceived attitude relationships. Minimal information about the "other" person is provided in this procedure, i.e., he is characterized only as being in complete agreement, with a single statement. Perhaps, in this highly unstructured situation, this agreement will act as a cue to the complex characterization which S most often ascribes to other people in general, and S will respond in terms of this modal, or dominant, characterization.

Since there is a persistent correlation between a person's own attitudes and his estimates of the attitudes of others (5, 14, 16), the procedure suggested here for investigating the structure of perceived attitudes bears certain similarities to projective instruments. However, such correlations characteristically range from .4 to .6. Such a relationship seems to indicate the possibility of assessing a person's own attitudes by giving him the seemingly objective task of estimating the opinions of others, but this is not the intent of the present experiment. The suggested procedure as it stands does not necessarily yield the structure of S's own attitudes or the actual structure of attitudes in others, but it does yield information about the ways in which people *perceive* attitudes "out there" in others. Two groups were used in the present experiment, which were thought to be diverse with respect to the attitudes involved. Any differences in the attitude configurations obtained from these groups might possibly be traced not only to differences in perception but also to differences in the Ss' actual attitudes which had been projected into the situation. Since the primary concern of the present study was with the perception of attitudes, the directions and the task were so formulated as to minimize the effects of projection. The success of this intention and the projective aspects of the task as formulated will be considered in a later section.

Method

In the present study a multidimensional method of successive intervals (1, 6) was applied to a set of attitude statements in an attempt to discover the number and the nature of the relevant dimensions perceived. The attitude statements were chosen from three of Thurstone's scales—attitude toward war, attitude toward capital punishment, and attitude toward the treatment of criminals. The procedure was applied using two diverse groups in an attempt to discover any differences which may exist in the structuring of these perceived relationships. The groups chosen for this purpose were a theological seminary class and an Air Force officer candidate class.

The Stimulus Statements and Their Experimental Presentation

Seven statements were selected from each of the three Thurstone scales on attitude toward war (9), attitude toward the treatment of criminals (17), and attitude toward capital punishment (8). These statements, which were selected in such a way as to be fairly evenly distributed over the favorable-unfavorable continuum for each of the three atttiudes, are listed below.

1. On the whole, wars do the world some good.
2. Peace and war are both essential to progress.
3. War is sometimes necessary because right is more important than peace.
4. War has some benefits, but it's a big price to pay for them.
5. Although war is terrible, it has some value.
6. War is hardly necessary in the modern world.
7. There is no conceivable justification for war.
8. All criminals are victims of circumstances and deserve to be helped.
9. One way to deter men from crime is to make them suffer.
10. Correction is more effective than punishment in preventing crime.
11. Harsh imprisonment merely embitters a criminal.
12. Criminals must be punished.
13. Petty offenders can be reformed without punishment.
14. Failure to punish the criminal encourages crime.
15. The death penalty should be given for major crimes.
16. Capital punishment is good because it deters others from crime.
17. I think capital punishment is necessary but I wish it were not.
18. Until we find a more civilized way to prevent crime we must have capital punishment.
19. No thinking individual can believe in capital punishment as a method of preventing crime.
20. Criminals are pathological people who should be corrected, not executed.
21. The death of a comrade in prison embitters all the inmates against the state.

In this procedure, it is not at all necessary to use previously scaled attitude statements. Any other set of statements, scaled or otherwise, which was thought to be of possible relevance to the domain in question could have been used. The selection of previously used items for the present investigation was for the purpose of gaining some incidental information about the claimed unidimensionality of the Thurstone scales.

The statements were arranged in booklet form in order to make the task more amenable to group presentation. One statement was printed at the top of each page, followed by a list of statements at the left. To the right of each of these statements appeared a series of 11 boxes, with the first box labeled "Strongly

Disagree," the sixth box labeled "Neutral," and the eleventh box labeled "Strongly Agree." The *S* was asked to imagine the type of person who would strongly agree with the statement at the top of the page and then to decide how this same person would also feel about each of the statements on the left. The *S* was then to indicate the extent of this person's agreement or disagreement with each statement by placing a cross in one of the boxes to the right. In constructing the booklet the order of appearance of the statements on each page and the order of the pages in the booklet was determined by random number techniques.

The Judgments Required

The multidimensional method of successive intervals requires that the subject arrange all possible pairs $[n(n-1)/2 = 210]$ of the 21 statements on a distance continuum according to the degree of relatedness or agreement shown between the members of each pair. In order to obtain judgments about perceived attitudes, the question of relatedness was set up in terms of the attitudes of some other person as described above. In terms of the multidimensional model this task can be considered as asking *S* to estimate the distance between Statements A and B, while located at A and looking at B. The reverse judgment for each pair of statements was also obtained in the present experiment, i.e., *S* was also asked to imagine the type of person who would strongly agree with Statement B and then to decide how this same person would also feel about Statement A. This task may be considered as judging the distance from Statement B to Statement A, while located at B and looking at A. Thus, the procedure requires two judgments for each of the 210 pairs of statements, making a total of 420 judgments required from each subject.

The two judgments of the same distance taken from opposite directions were obtained in the present experiment in order to see whether the data met one of the basic requirements of the multidimensional scaling model. The multidimensional attitude scaling model is an interpoint-distance model, i.e., attitude statements and people are represented in the same space by points. The extent of the individual's agreement or disagreement with the statements in the space is represented by the distance between the person and the statement. The person agrees with items close to him in any direction and disagrees with items far away. One property of this model, then, is that the probability of an affirmative response to any statement decreases as the distance between the statement and the person increases, without regard to direction. Statements selected by Thurstone scaling methods such as equal-appearing intervals, paired comparisons, or successive intervals usually have this property. Such statements are commonly referred to as "point" statements, and the multidimensional scaling model can be properly applied only to such items. The requirement that the probability of an affirmative response should vary inversely with distance independent of direction is another way of saying that the distance between two points in Euclidean space should be the same in both directions.

In the present experiment, then, an attempt was made to see whether judgments of the same distance taken from opposite directions would come out similar. The two judgments elicited for each pair of statements were considered as independent estimates, and scale values were obtained for both the distances AB and BA for each pair. If the multidimensional scaling requirement that the distance between two points be the same in both directions is met by the data, the differences between corresponding AB and BA distances should be small. Systematic groupings of large differences would probably indicate the type of asymmetric relationships that might reasonably be expected to occur with cumulative items (4) as opposed to the symmetric relationships expected from point items. If a few large differences occur, then, the statements involved in these differences should be deleted from the study on the grounds of a failure to meet certain requirements of the model. However, great care should be exercised in evaluating these differences, since a few large discrepancies might occur by chance alone. Also, large differences would be expected for statement pairs at either extreme of the similarity scale, since such scale values are based on only a few cases and, hence, are very unstable.

The Subjects

The two diverse groups selected for this experiment were a seminary class and an Air Force officer candidate class. The seminary group consisted of 40 third-year male students at the Princeton Theological Seminary in Princeton, New Jersey. A regularly scheduled class hour had been made available for the purposes of this experiment, and the enlisting of Ss was put on a purely voluntary basis. Forty volunteers were obtained from the class, and the rest of the students were permitted to leave the room.

The Air Force group consisted of 82 male officer candidates who had just finished the first half of their O.C.S. training at Lackland Air Force Base, San Antonio, Texas.

No direct measure of the actual attitudes of these two groups was obtained in the present investigation for several reasons. Instead, attitude differences were inferred from the widely different backgrounds of the Ss. It seemed reasonable that factors which had led to such divergent career choices might also be reflected in divergent attitudes, especially in an attitude area dealing with war and punishment. However, the main reason why these actual attitudes were not "measured" in the present study was that it would have made it difficult, if not impossible, to obtain the cooperation of suitable populations of Ss, but other reasons did exist.

An investigation of the actual attitudes of these groups would have to be set up in multidimensional terms, not only to be comparable to the analysis of perceived attitudes, but also because some important differences between groups are probably reflected in relationships among dimensions rather than in responses to single scales. On the surface, then, the proper approach would appear to be to obtain responses to the three Thurstone scales, intercorrelate items, and factor-analyze. However, the vector model of factor analysis and the interpoint distance model of multidimensional scaling are not directly comparable (6), so the actual and perceived attitude structures could not be compared anyway.

Results [3]

Each attitude booklet contained responses to 210 AB statement combinations and to 210 BA combinations. Each response, which was signified by a cross in one of a series of 11 boxes, indicated the judged extent of the imaginary other person's agreement with Statement B. This set of responses, 420 per booklet, constituted the raw data, which were analyzed separately for the seminary and Air Force groups.

THE SEMINARY GROUP DATA

The 420 combinations of statements were scaled by a graphical successive-intervals technique developed by Gertrude W. Diederich and described in (6). The 210 scale values for the AB statement-pairs represented the 210 possible distances among the 21 statements, all distances being estimated in one specified direction. The scale values for the 210 BA statement pairs represented the same distances, estimated in the opposite direction. There was adequate agreement between corresponding AB and BA values, so the two estimates were averaged for each distance. The general multidimensional scaling procedure described by Messick and Abelson (7) was then used to obtain a multidimensional configuration for these interstatement distances.

The end product of the multidimensional scaling procedure is a matrix of projections, which is analogous to the factor matrix of multiple-factor analysis. The rank of this matrix is equal to the dimensionality, r, of the Euclidean space defined by the experimentally obtained distances, and the elements of the matrix represent the projections of the statements on a set of r orthogonal axes placed at the centroid of the statements (13, 18). In the present experiment, this matrix of projections was of Rank 2, and when the two-dimensional configuration was plotted, two distinct streaks of points were evident. The structure was translated slightly in order to place the origin at the intersection of the streaks and then was rotated orthogonally until the largest streak of points was in a horizontal position. This particular orientation has the advantage of producing the maximum number of zero projections for this two-dimensional space, thus permitting simple psychological interpretation. The rotated, translated configuration obtained from the seminary group appears in Figure 5.

The horizontal dimension in this figure contains all 14 statements from the scales of attitude toward the treatment of criminals and attitude toward capital punishment, and thus it represents a "propunishment versus antipunishment" dimension. Statements 9, 12, 14, 15, 16, and to a slightly

[3] The data, along with a complete description of analytical procedures, appear in the writer's dissertation (6).

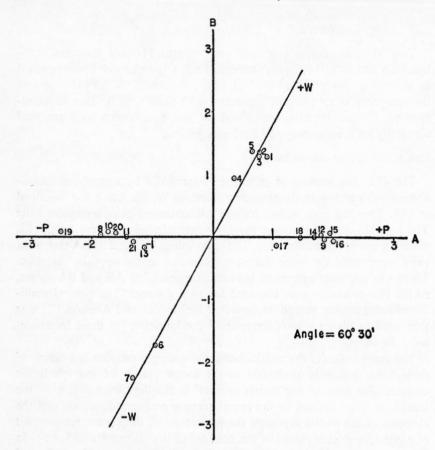

Figure 5. Dimensional configuration of 21 attitude statements for the theological
            seminary group.

lesser extent 17 and 18 define the propunishment end of the continuum, and Statements 8, 10, 11, 13, 19, 20, and 21 define the antipunishment end. A "war" dimension is located oblique to the "punishment" dimension at an angle of approximately 60°, with Statements 1, 2, 3, 4, and 5 lying in the prowar direction and Statements 6 and 7 in the antiwar direction. The 60° angle between the dimensions indicates a positive correlation between the prowar and propunishment attitudes perceived by the seminary group.

THE AIR FORCE GROUP DATA

The graphical scaling technique used to analyze the seminary data is a simple, quick iterative routine which yields a very good approximation to a computationally laborious least-squares solution for successive intervals, which was also developed by Diederich (see 6). After the seminary data had already been analyzed graphically, an IBM routine for the computational procedure was developed, so the Air Force data were treated according to the punched-card technique (15). When the 420 scale values obtained in this way were examined, it was again found that there was adequate agreement between corresponding AB and BA values, so the two estimates were averaged for each distance. The resulting 210 averages represented all possible distances among the 21 statements. The general multidimensional scaling technique (7) was used to obtain the configuration of the statements, and the matrix of projections was again found to be of Rank 2.

Two distinct streaks of points were again evident in the two-dimensional configuration, and the structure was translated slightly and rotated orthogonally to the same orientation as for the seminary data. This rotated, translated configuration for the Air Force group appears in Figure 6. The horizontal factor in this figure represents a punishment dimension, having Statements 9, 12, 14, 15, 16, 17, and 18 in the propunishment direction and Statements 8, 10, 11, 13, 19, 20, and 21 in the antipunishment direction. A war dimension is located oblique to the punishment dimension at an angle of approximately 68°, with Statements 1, 2, 3, 4, and 5 lying in the prowar direction and Statements 6 and 7 in the antiwar direction. The 68° angle between these dimensions indicates a positive correlation between perceived prowar and propunishment attitudes for the Air Force group.

The two configurations described above can be considered to be adequate dimensional representations of the experimentally obtained distances, since, apart from small residuals, only two dimensions were necessary to account for relationships among 21 stimuli, and no indications of non-Euclidean properties were found, i.e., there were no markedly negative latent roots.

A COMPARISON OF THE STRUCTURES OBTAINED FROM
THE SEMINARY AND AIR FORCE GROUPS

A comparison between the final rotated structures obtained from the seminary and Air Force groups (Figure 5 versus Figure 6) indicates an extremely high amount of agreement. It is quite evident from these figures that the two structures are essentially identical. The angle between the two dimensions in the seminary structure is 60°, while in the Air Force structure the angle is 68°. This shift in axis position is in an expected direction in terms of the probable differences between the "actual" attitudes of the Air Force and seminary groups. One might expect a theological seminary population to be more "humanitarian" than a military population. If this is the case, the "actual" attitudes of the seminary group would be

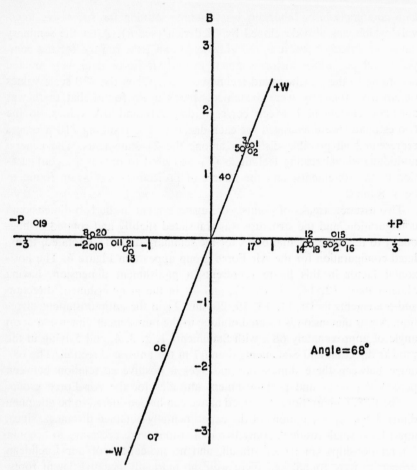

Figure 6. Dimensional configuration of 21 attitude statements for the Air Force officer candidate group.

expected to exhibit a higher correlation between antiwar and antipunishment attitudes than the "actual" attitudes of the Air Force group. If the "actual" attitudes of the *S*s in this particular experimental situation affect attitudes as perceived in others, then the shift in axes toward a higher correlation for the seminary than for the Air Force group is in an expected direction. However, the angular difference of 8° is probably not significant.

Discussion

The dimensional configurations obtained from both the seminary and Air Force groups certainly demonstrate that perceived relationships among attitudes toward war, capital punishment, and the treatment of criminals can be adequately represented in dimensional terms. Apparently, then, individuals do think of these attitudes as having a definite structure, and when asked to make judgments concerning attitude statements, they respond in terms of such dimensional frames of reference. The configuration obtained from both the Air Force and seminary groups is essentially the same as Type B given in Figure 2, with the war dimension drawn obliquely to the punishment dimension. Within this frame of reference, the two groups find it possible to conceive of people in each of the four quadrants, but it should be noted that certain kinds of people would be almost inconceivable to them. For instance, both groups would have difficulty in conceiving of a person who was in favor of capital punishment of extreme criminals and at the same time against punishing minor criminals.

The finding of an underlying structure in an attitude domain, when considered along with some of the specific properties of the structure, has important implications for attitude measurement and theory. Since one of the more reasonable ways to measure multidimensional attributes is to apply appropriate unidimensional scales along each of the dimensions involved, dimensional configurations such as those found in the present experiment would aid considerably, first of all, in determining the number and the nature of the relevant dimensions and, second, in selecting and evaluating the appropriate unidimensional scales. It is striking that the attitude statements in both the Air Force and seminary structures form straight lines, indicating a unidimensionality in the original Thurstone scales, at least for the items considered in the present experiment. Similar studies investigating the linearity of other scales would be interesting and very important in justifying the use of these scales in attitude measurement. Another important aspect of these configurations is the fact that the scales on attitude toward capital punishment and attitude toward the treatment of criminals, which are admittedly similar in content but nevertheless had been independently established by equal-appearing interval techniques, should be perceived as precisely the same unidimensional continuum. This finding has important theoretical implications, since it suggests that different attitude variables, which had been separately abstracted on a priori grounds, can be reasonably thought of in terms of a single dimension. These results, however, pertain only to "perceived" attitudes and, no matter how suggestive they are, the structure of "actual" attitudes should be investigated before such a finding is incorporated into attitude theory. It well may be, for instance, that the "actual" attitudes of Ss in the present experiment were three-dimensional, even though the groups *perceived* the attitudes in others in terms of a two-dimensional configuration. In other words, the results of the present study are immediately applicable to considerations of the ways in which individuals conceive of attitudes as being structured "out there," but further research is necessary before they may be applied to considerations of individuals' own attitudes. In any event, multidimensional analysis applied in attempts at a systematic understanding of the psychology of attitudes offers the hope that the host of trait names and labels in the attitude area can be represented in terms of a limited number of variables.

The high correlation between the configurations obtained from the Air Force and seminary groups indicates a definite similarity in the ways in which these groups perceive attitudes in this particular domain as being structured. It is not unreasonable that perceived attitude structures should be similar for two diverse groups, since similar frames of reference are important for efficient communication, but the essential identity of the two structures requires comment.

Previous studies (5, 14, 16) have shown a persistent correlation between a person's own attitudes and his estimates of the attitudes of others. If the seminary and Air Force groups differ, as they probably do, with respect to attitudes toward war and punishment, the seemingly projective nature of the task of estimating the opinions of others would lead one to expect a difference between the structures obtained in the multidimensional analysis. However, the above studies are not really comparable to the present experiment, since they involved estimates of group opinion obtained from subjects who were themselves members of the group. Also, as Campbell (2, page 23) has pointed out, ". . . in a group of any size, the respondent has an uneven acquaintanceship, and probably associates more with those of tastes like his own. Basing his estimates of group opinion upon his own experience in the group, his error may be in part a 'sampling bias' as well as biased perception."

The information supplied the subject in the present experiment was such as to be favorable to objective perception and unfavorable to projection. In one sense the information supplied was minimal; the other person, whose attitude relationships were to be estimated, was characterized only by complete agreement with a single statement. In the absence of a detailed characterization of the other person, the S evidently ascribed to his attitudes some kind of modal or average structure. It might be argued that minimal information is a favorable condition for eliciting projective responses, but the information supplied in the present case, although minimal in characterizing the other person, was quite specific concerning isolated aspects of his attitudes. A great deal of specific information is given to the subject when he is told that another person strongly agrees with the statement, "There is no conceivable justification for war," and it is not difficult to evaluate objectively the extent of this person's agreement with the statement, "On the whole, wars do the world some good." Projection is favored by conditions of insufficient or conflicting information, but when specific and relevant information is available concerning a particular judgment, an objective response is probably favored.

Summary

The primary purpose of this study was to see whether a set of perceived attitude relationships could be adequately represented in dimensional terms and, if so, to discover the number and the nature of the relevant dimensions involved. A secondary purpose was to investigate judgments made by two diverse groups in order to discover whether they perceive attitudes as being structured in different ways. Accordingly, a multidimensional method of successive intervals, which is a Euclidean distance model, was applied to judgments of attitude relationships. The procedure required S to arrange all possible pairs of a set of attitude statements on a distance continuum according to the degree of similarity of the members of each pair.

Seven statements were selected from each of the three Thurstone scales on attitude toward war, capital punishment, and the treatment of criminals, and these 21 statements were set up in booklet form for group presentation. The attitude booklets were administered to 40 third-year, male students at a theological seminary, and to 82 male Air Force officer candidates.

The multidimensional attitude structures perceived by the two diverse groups were essentially identical, the relationships among statements of the three attitudes being adequately represented in terms of two oblique dimensions, a war dimension and a punishment dimension. Apparently individuals do perceive attitudes, at least in this particular attitude area, in terms of a definite structure, and when called upon to make judgments concerning attitude relationships, they respond in terms of this dimensional frame of reference.

References

1. ABELSON, R. P. A technique and a model for multidimensional attitude scaling. *Publ. Opin. Quart.*, in press.
2. CAMPBELL, D. T. The indirect assessment of social attitudes. *Psychol. Bull.*, 1950, **47**, 15–38.
3. GULLIKSEN, H. A least squares solution for successive intervals assuming unequal standard deviations. *Psychometrika*, 1954, **19**, 117–139.
4. GUTTMAN, L. A basis for scaling qualitative data. *Amer. sociol. Rev.*, 1944, **9**, 139–150.

5. KATZ, M. R. A hypothesis on anti-Negro prejudice. *Amer. J. Sociol.,* 1947, **53,** 100–104.

6. MESSICK, S. J. The perception of attitude relationships: a multidimensional scaling approach to the structuring of social attitudes. Unpublished doctoral dissertation, Princeton Univ., 1954. Also, Princeton: Educational Testing Service, 1954.

7. ————, and ABELSON, R. P. The additive constant problem in multidimensional scaling. *Psychometrika,* in press.

8. PETERSON, R. C. *Scale for the measurement of attitude toward capital punishment.* Chicago: Univer. of Chicago Press, 1931.

9. ————. *Scale for the measurement of attitude toward war.* Chicago: Univer. of Chicago Press, 1931.

10. RICHARDSON, M. W. Multidimensional psychophysics. *Psychol. Bull.,* 1938, **35,** 659–660.

11. SAFFIR, M. A comparative study of scales constructed by three psychophysical methods. *Psychometrika,* 1937, **2,** 179–198.

12. TORGERSON, W. S. A theoretical and empirical investigation of multidimensional scaling. Unpublished doctoral dissertation, Princeton Univer., 1951.

13. ————. Multidimensional scaling: I. Theory and method. *Psychometrika,* 1952, **17,** 401–419.

14. TRAVERS, R. M. W. A study in judging the opinions of groups. *Arch. Psychol.,* N. Y. No. 266, 1941.

15. TUCKER, L. R., MESSICK, S., and GARRISON, H. A punched card procedure for the method of successive intervals. Princeton: Educational Testing Service, 1954.

16. WALLEN, R. Individual's estimates of group opinion. *J. soc. Psychol.,* 1943, **17,** 269–274.

17. WANG, C. K. A., and THURSTONE, L. L. *Scale for the measurement of attitude toward the treatment of criminals.* Chicago: Univer. of Chicago Press, 1931.

18. YOUNG, G., and HOUSEHOLDER, A. S. Discussion of a set of points in terms of their mutual distances. *Psychometrika,* 1938, **3,** 19–22.

32. *Motivating Students of All Levels of Ability* *

RACHEL DUNAWAY COX

EXPERIENCE suggests that not only deans and teachers but parents, as well, more often get stirred up about the motivation of young people than about almost any other aspect of their behavior. No matter what the child's intelligence or the nature of the young person's problem we are always, and perhaps primarily, aroused about the intention, and the implementation of the intention, which the child brings to his life situation. Intelligence alone will not produce good citizenship or good scholarship. In the long run the intention, the motive, must support and thrust forward whatever abilities exist.

Students of motivation make the distinction between the primary or primitive drives which serve survival, and the secondary or symbolic drives which include both the need to be respected, accepted, and loved, and the drive to find satisfaction in the so-called conflict-free areas of curiosity, imagination, and thinking. Whether or not these are two levels of the same underlying matrix is a matter of some controversy. But, as Melton (7) puts it, "there is accumulating evidence of the efficacy of symbolic rewards in the learning of sub-human animals so that it now appears that the efficacy . . . of stimuli other than those which actually remove the physiological need is so great that secondary or symbolic reinforcement is becoming a basic postulate of learning theory." It is these secondary or derived motives with which the family, the school, the dean, and the community deal, and certainly our efforts at motivation in normal peacetime society are invariably confined to that area.

All we know about motivation from the animal laboratory, and surely all we know about personality, points to the conclusion that motivation is not a special booster or overdrive that can be attached to the learning apparatus to make the machine function. The drive the individual exerts in response to the motivating stimulus is rather a dynamic summation of the total personality, including intellectual and physical attributes, emotional states and hopes for the future, interacting with the present environment.

It is therefore inappropriate to lay total responsibility for the students'

* From Rachel Dunaway Cox, "Motivating Students of All Levels of Ability," *Journal of National Association of Women Deans and Counselors,* (October, 1960), pp. 16–22. Reprinted by permission.

motivation upon the educating institution, although this is often done, either directly or by implication. It would be a misguided institution or teacher who accepts this total responsibility, for the mainspring of the will to achieve lies at the very core of personality, with its basis in the earliest years of life. This infant direction and force is confirmed by the recurring themes in parent-child relationships, and these are in turn picked up and reenacted in the teacher-child relationship.

Vigor in pursuing goals, any goals, depends in the first place upon an innate drive of the organism to approach and pursue objectives. Recent and sensitive research in infant development indicates that there are quantifiable individual differences in this trait. Sybille Escalona and Grace Heider in their recent book, *Prediction and Outcome in Child Development* (4), observe that "mothers who have reared more than one child usually find the term 'decisiveness and goal striving' a meaningful description of one characteristic of infant behavior. They will readily say that one of the children always knows his mind, where with another it is difficult to tell, because he is changeable."

Significantly, this goal-directedness is one of the modes which these investigators found appearing most clearly as a continuing pattern from early to later stages in the development of the individual child. All this gives scientific validation to what mothers have long known—babies are individuals with strengths and persuasions of their own, and some are more easily than others diverted from a desired end.

However, there is also accumulating evidence that parent attitudes and expectations are likewise powerful determiners of the child's engagement with achievement. An ingenious study by Winterbottom (6) has demonstrated that the striving of young boys is related to the efforts of their mothers to establish independence in them and that the early lifting of restrictions allowing the child to act responsibly is accompanied by the son's thinking positively about trying to achieve. The converse was also found to be true.

Another approach to the study of motivation deals with the parallel between the striving of an individual and the achievement drive of his family or tribal group. This is an especially rich vein and has been mined by Ericksen, and more recently by David McClelland. In brief, the achievement motive as revealed in folk lore, including that of us modern Americans, seems to be faithfully echoed in the attitudes and behavior of individuals living within the culture.

Psychoanalytic theory avers that one of the earliest and most powerful modes of personality formation is that of identification (5). It is perhaps not too much to say that if we want well-motivated children, we should provide them with well-motivated grandparents. This point received support in the Student Council Study, a piece of research carried on at Bryn Mawr, Haverford and Swarthmore (3). A significant number of the students said they felt they must make good in the college experience because their families had a tradition of doing one's best.

Children identify with the parents' demands upon *themselves* too and in some ways this is the most subtle and pervasive influence the parent exercises. Not what they say but what they *are* charges the air the children breathe and enters into their judgments of people and events, including the child's judgment of himself and what he does. For as the analysts point out, the child patterns his own superego upon the superego of the parents.

Remember the earnest Scottish mother who said to her son, "Jaimie, I may not have raised ye so ye won't sin, but I have fixed ye so ye'll nae enjoy it." Just so. Not only the parents' striving is likely to be catching, but the general direction of the striving is contagious too. Years ago, when I made a study of school counselors, I found this an impressive datum (2). A high proportion of the hundred counselors selected for the study were the children of parents in a humanitarian calling. Quite a number of them were children of ministers. One said, "I am a son of a dentist with a small income. Small because of his social service ideals and low fees." Another said, "My social service ideals were developed early by stories of my grandfather, a country doctor, with a wide practice. His emphasis was upon service regardless of fees." A third reported, "My father and mother were much interested in helping people who were in trouble— financial and emotional trouble." Said one, "My home life gave me a set of values that I try to pass on to young people." I remember one fine counselor from upstate Pennsylvania, who said quietly, "I come from the plain people. It is just natural that I should be in work of this sort." Only eight out of the hundred counselors in the study failed to give material on the point of how their lives as children had been instrumental in bringing them into the occupation of school counselor.

In our dealing with adolescents and young adults, counselors face a crucial question: Are we altogether too late to have any genuine influence upon the way in which the student responds to present experience? Is there any hope for motivating the student at the stage in which he reaches us? If we took the determinist position that the individual's life has been irrevocably shaped by the time he is of school age, we would be free to waive all responsibility for motivating him. While unquestionably some of the most crucial time is past by the time that the six-year-old is faced with reading, we cannot believe we are powerless. This would be to deny the very dynamism of personality which is at the basis of our belief in the importance of the parent-child relationship. As John Anderson (1) puts it, each new stage in growth not only rests on what has gone before, but interacts with what current experience offers. "In order to modify the stream of organism-environment relations, there must be reiteration; that is, a mechanism similar to that which produces over-learning in the case of a skill or memory must be present. It then becomes important to examine the environment for recurring stimulation, and the individual for manifestations of an internal process that can exercise 'carrier function'—a carrier function, which operating again and again, will keep alive the sub-system of responses which are crucial in personality organization."

Thus in the case of the child from good background we must accept some responsibility for motivating the student because it is this reiteration which must be done by school, college, and community in the altered context of later childhood and adolescence. It is the reiterated concern of the parent, as expressed now in the teacher and the personnel officer, that will confirm the young person in the direction he has earlier taken. It is true that the school or the college can never supply the deficit that is left by a poor home and an unfortunate parent-child relationship. But a poor and unstimulating school, college, or community experience can go a long way toward scarring and spoiling something that a good home experience has started.

The dynamic past experience summed up in the individual child interacts with the present experience, and therefore the teacher initiating the child into reading may be dealing either with one who has already learned to reach out vigorously and to find satisfaction at the breast or bottle, or with one who having met ungivingness, restriction, and irritation, has learned not to expect very much and so, in defensiveness, will less eagerly reach out to a new task. At whatever level, the learner can probably be motivated only within the limits already roughly bounded by his past success or failure and by the level of confidence he brings to a new experience.

On the whole this is true, and yet any counselor may recall some individual who apparently gives the lie to this whole theory. There are indeed always some extraordinary persons, the exceptions who try the rule, and prove that we deal not with an unbendable law but only with a probability. I rather expect we could find a significance beyond the 1 per cent of confidence that the constellation I have described above will occur in any sample we might draw. Yet there remains that unexplained 1 per cent, and we are deeply grateful for that improbable boy or girl who, coming from the most unpromising situation, upsets our neat calculations and shines like a gem. Our certainty that the improbable individual *may* turn up at any time keeps deans and counselors alert and makes our work exciting. Because he or she *does* turn up now and again, we know that the mystery of personality is not yet fully revealed.

We take heart too from the certainty that the child as a living organism does not rigidly pursue a trajectory determined by his past, but is dynamically related to the present. Further, there are some things upon which we are able to count as we undertake the job of motivating students. Chief of these is the fact that the human mind seems to be naturally inquiring. Once survival needs are satisfied, the need to reach out and explore is immediately evident. Watch an infant explore the platform of his high chair with hands, eyes and tongue; watch the growing boy make his collections and get himself into all sorts of jams as he tries to learn about and master his world; recall the college student genuinely grateful for the opening up of a new field of knowledge. All teachers need minds well stocked with the things children and students want to know, or can be interested in discovering.

Yet the teacher who merely issues the "come-and-get-it call to learning" is not likely to motivate the learner, for new learning is best mediated by direct infection from one person to another, television and other audio-visual aids notwithstanding.

The unquestionable merits of learning by doing, by finding immediate practical employment for the thing learned, raises the question of how we shall motivate students for content which has no clear application to practical devices. For capable students great ideas and great personalities *can* speak directly, and with an extraordinary impact. How many students have wept for Socrates accepting the cup? With what an answering joy have young readers heard, "Bliss was it in that dawn to be alive, and to be young was very heaven." These ideas and emotions take lodging in the mind and become resources for all the future.

Good teaching is teaching infused with emotion, whether the actual material be in the sciences or the humanities. At the college level we often tend to play emotion down, feeling that we may make ourselves a little ridiculous. Whether the teacher gains his own excitement by opening up new and undiscovered territory in his discipline, or through rediscovery and reexperiencing of content already well traveled by his predecessors, he can most effectively create an emotional impact upon the student if he is himself emotionally stirred. It is in the nature of our enthusiasms that they are strongest and most contagious when they are recently experienced. The teacher will in all probability be a better teacher if he is himself a discoverer of new facts, ideas, or insights. The discoveries may be made in the diggings at Urr, or in the laboratory, or through investigations of blighted neighborhoods. But for the student to be motivated by his learning experience, the teacher himself must be well-motivated for the task which his discipline sets him, for as in the relation of the child with the parent, the student's excitement for learning comes through the excitement of his teacher.

Of course, there are times with every one of us when we come upon arid stretches when we do not seem able to "give out," and then certain devices may be used to help support the intention of the student. First, when the general goals are clearly defined the meaning of any given block of material can be related specifically to them and this helps some students. Second, since distant goals have less pulling power than nearerby goals, it is well for the morale both of the teacher and of the learner that partial goals be set up and be clearly defined. Third, it is helpful to report frequently and in detail to the learner where he stands in relation to the partial goal. Students are blocked in their growth when they receive low grades for which the instructor gives little accounting. Even the eager learner is brought to a standstill when unfavorable comments on his paper are made in such a general way that he does not know how to deal with them, and it is a devoted teacher who will take the time to point out just how and why he has fallen short.

A fourth technique is that of a reformulating, redifining, and restating the long-range goals as the development of the student makes it possible for him to direct his course more concisely toward educational and vocational goals. We must be aware of what he is capable of doing and what he probably ought not to attempt, so that the difficulty level of the task is always appropriate to the student. It is unjust to expect a two-year-old to manage a fork at the table and likewise to demand work far above a student's capacity. As the mother who permits her three-year-old to use a nursing bottle wrongs her child, so the school which permits a top-flight intelligence to slide by with merely a good performance wrongs the student. Both stultify motivation. Fifth, nurture of the student's growth is supported by confronting him with himself. We need to let the learner know what is possible for him and to convey to him gently, but with some definiteness, what reasonable expectations for him are. Sixth, we must inform him of the available outlets for his particular talents. Here again teachers and guidance specialists have a joint responsibility, though the latter will of course carry a major load.

A further important aspect of motivating the student is to free him to use himself. This responsibility belongs first and fundamentally to parents, but it is as well a responsibility of teachers, guidance specialists, and institutions. Ego psychology stresses the so-called conflict-free aspects of experience, dwelling on learning as a normal goal of the organism. Nevertheless, in school and in college too many students are not able to give rein to healthy curiosity, imagination, and reason. The conflict-free aspects of the learner's growth have been invaded by conflicts indigenous to affective aspects of experience.

When this occurs, dislocations in motivation occur. These invasions often take place when early problems of relationship have remained unsolved and are carried forward into a time of life which should be relatively untroubled by such problems. The complex tasks of adolescence cannot be properly discharged when the parents of disturbed learners are still engaged on the unfinished business of early childhood relationships. Learning which should be satisfying in and for itself becomes a weapon against the parents, the society, and the self.

Conflicts of early days which are often refought in the learning sphere include, *first:* the struggle around the need to accept the fact that the learner is only one among many persons who are loved and valued by their parents or their surrogates; *second,* the struggle to forego some ego satisfactions in the interest of group membership; *third,* the conflict concerning the hard fact of big and little, a principle re-encountered at every stage of life and in successive contexts. A *fourth* difficulty is the pain and threat of accepting one's essential separateness from every other person and the attendant necessity to assert courageously one's own values and even one's own equity. The dependence of early childhood must gradually be given up if one is to be a self-sustaining personality. Yet how unwelcome it is to relinquish this mode of assuring one's self of love and protection.

The struggles in these four areas are never wholly won. But for learning to go forward they must be under reasonable control, a control appropriate to the time of life and to the external setting. Perhaps in his being unable to go on to the mastery of skills and knowledge the learner is guided by a kind of primitive wisdom. In this the organism refuses to accept the task of cognitive learning until it has come to grips with profounder issues.

Some educators complain that to give attention to this unfinished business is to coddle the student and to weaken him. Others say that these are problems for the psychiatrist, and beyond the parish of the educating institution. But we cannot escape the consequences of the conflicts, since their presence blocks our own undertakings as educators. Guidance people, because of their professional training, are in a better position to recognize the problems without emotional involvement. They know the educative experience is in itself a therapy if it is properly used. They know sources of more specialized help and have the responsibility to get confused learners to them. To be sure the role of the educating agency differs with the time of life of the learner and the degree of responsibility which the mandate of the institution makes possible.

Finally we must recognize the fact that the educative experience is not wholly intellectual nor yet wholly emotional. It is in a far greater degree than we often recognize a social experience and as our guidance services become more adequate and sophisticated, we shall move toward the team approach within the college setting, with various levels of training and directions of specialization banded together in the service of the student.

References

1. ANDERSON, JOHN. "Personality Organization in Children," in *Readings in Child Development*, Wayne Dennis, editor. New York: Prentice Hall, 1951. P. 486.
2. COX, RACHEL DUNAWAY. "The Normal Personality," *Journal of Projective Techniques*, Vol. 20, No. 1, 1956.
3. ————. *Counselors and Their Work;* Harrisburg, Pa.: Archives Press, 1945.
4. ESCALONA, SYBELLE, and HEIDER, GRACE. *Prediction and Outcome in Child Development*. New York: Basic Books, 1960. Pp. 81 and 82.
5. FREUD, ANNA. *The Ego and the Mechanisms of Defense*. New York: International Universities Press, 1946.
6. McCLELLAND, DAVID. *Studies in Motivation*. New York: Appleton-Century-Crofts, Inc., 1953. Pp. 297–304.
7. MELTON, ARTHUS W. "Motivation and Learning," *Encyclopedia of Educational Research,* W. S. Monroe, editor. New York: Macmillan, 1952. Pp. 672–673.

33. Attitude Change through Modification of Attitude Structure [*]

EARL R. CARLSON, [3] *University of Michigan*

THERE is wide agreement that "attitudes" are complex, in that they are composed of a number of components, characteristics, or dimensions. Psychologists generally agree, also, that changes in attitudes may come through the operation of different processes (4). There have been few

[*] From Earl R. Carlson, "Attitude Change through Modification of Attitude Structure," *The Journal of Abnormal and Social Psychology,* 52 (March, 1956), 256–61. Reprinted by permission.

[1] This study is one of a series undertaken by the Attitude Change Project at the University of Michigan. It was supported in part by the U. S. Air Force under Contract AF 33(038)–26646, monitored by the Human Resources Research Institute.

[2] The present paper is based upon a thesis submitted to the Department of Psychology of the University of Michigan in partial fulfillment of the requirements for the degree of Doctor of Philosophy. The writer wishes to express his appreciation to Dr. Helen Peak for her generous advice and assistance given throughout the study.

[3] Now at Michigan State College.

studies, however, which have attempted to differentiate either components of attitudes or the processes of change experimentally. The present study is of this nature—an investigation of the importance of two independent sources of *affect* (the liking or favorableness-unfavorableness aspect) of an attitude.

The importance of the individual's system of general goals in life, or values, has been suggested by many theorists as of crucial significance in determining the affect associated with specific aspects of the person's experience. A recent study by Rosenberg (3), building upon and improving the methodology and conceptualization of earlier experimental studies (5, 6), demonstrated the relationship between attitudinal affect, i.e., the attitude position, or what is generally termed simply "attitude," and two components of "attitude structure." Rosenberg differentiated as structural components (*a*) the intensity of affect of a person's values, i.e., the expected satisfaction from these values, and (*b*) the perceived importance of the attitude object (situation, event) in leading to or blocking the attainment of the values. He measured "value satisfaction" and "perceived instrumentality" independently, and found each to correlate significantly with the attitude of the person. The best predictor of attitude, however, was found to be an index of "affective loading" which combined the two measures. The results clearly indicated that value satisfaction and perceived instrumental relations were separate and important components of the attitude structure.

Attitude change, it follows from this theory, should result from changes in either the expected satisfaction from goals, or in the instrumental relationship perceived between the attitude object and the goal. The present study was designed to test this latter hypothesis—that changes in attitude (affect) result from altering perceptions of the attitude object (situation or event) as leading to the attainment of valued goals. This hypothesis is consistent with experimental findings on animal and human learning, but has not been clearly tested in the area of social attitudes.

A second important source of affect is hypothesized to be mediated through generalization from affect associated with related attitude objects or situations. Following principles of generalization developed in learning studies, tests were made of two further hypotheses: (*a*) attitude change generalizes to related issues, and (*b*) the degree of generalization is a function of the similarity of the attitude objects or situations.

Method

The experimental procedure of the study was designed to increase the subjects' perception that "allowing Negroes to move into White neighborhoods" would be a means for attaining four specified goals, or values. The attitude issue of Negro housing segregation was selected as the vehicle for studying attitude and attitude structure change, since the subjects varied widely in attitude on the issue, the attitude was relatively stable, yet some change could be produced using a limited experimental procedure. Attitudes on five related issues were also measured in order to test for generalization of attitude change.

The four values discussed in the experimental communication were (*a*) American prestige in other countries, (*b*) protection of property values, (*c*) equal opportunity for personal development, and (*d*) being experienced, broadminded, and worldly-wise. These values were selected on the basis of their probable importance for this issue.

The data were collected in three major stages. Early in the semester experimental and control *S*s were given attitude and value measures during regular class periods. Code numbers were used to maintain anonymity for the *S*s. The experimental change procedure was administered to the experimental *S*s in two parts: the first consisted of an assignment given by the instructor to be completed outside of class, one to two weeks after the initial measures were obtained; the second, five to ten days later, consisted of a prepared discussion given orally by the experimenter. After a further interval of three weeks the attitude and value measures were readministered to both experimental and control *S*s. Finally, a follow-up questionnaire was given a few days later to obtain judgments of the perceived similarities between Negroes, Jews, and Mexicans.

In order to minimize the *S*s' awareness of the nature of the study, the change procedure was presented as a separate experiment by a person not involved in the measurement of attitudes and value. The follow-up questionnaire indicated that *S*s did not attempt to distort their responses deliberately.

Attitude measures. The measures of attitude toward the primary issue of study, Negro housing segregation, and the five related attitude issues required the *S* to rank six alternatives (ranging from "I am completely opposed to allowing Negroes into White neighborhoods" to "I am completely in favor of allowing Negroes into White neighborhoods") in terms of the degree to which they represented the person's own opinion. The measure of the person's attitude position used in the analysis was coded directly from the *S*'s first choice of the six alternatives. The measure of attitude change was obtained through coding the first three ranks given of the six alternative positions; using only transitive rankings, the three ranks gave a 16-point scale, ranging from position 1 (subject choosing alternatives in the order ABC), to position 2 (BAC), position 3 (BCA), and on to position 16 (FED). The Negro housing segregation measure had an uncorrected reliability of .67 for the control group.

To test the hypotheses concerning generalization of attitude change, five attitude issues similar to the Negro housing segregation issue on two dimensions were also measured in the same manner before and after the change procedure, these being (*a*) Mexican housing segregation, (*b*) Jewish housing segregation, (*c*) command of White enlisted men by Negro officers, (*d*) command of non-Mexican enlisted men by Mexican officers, and (*e*) command of non-Jewish enlisted men by Jewish officers.

Value measures. The measures of "value satisfaction" and "perceived instrumentality" required the Ss to rate each of the 25 value items given in Table 1. Two items, using different words but identical in meaning, were used within the set to measure each of the four areas selected for experimental change. The four sets of experimental items were items 5 and 19, items 8 and 11, items 10 and 22, and items 6 and 17. The remaining 17 values were selected to cover the broad range of further general goals in life that individuals regard as important in some degree. The items were presented on cards in random order, with a randomly assigned number on the card being used to record judgments of the value.

Table 1

VALUE ITEMS USED IN THE SATISFACTION AND INSTRUMENTALITY RATINGS

Value Item

1. Everyone being assured of a good standard of living
2. People sticking to their own groups
3. People looking out for the welfare of others
4. Being looked up to by others
5. America having high prestige in other countries
6. Being well-rounded, enlightened and sophisticated about life
7. Serving the interests of the group to which one belongs
8. Security of the value of one's real estate
9. Having power and authority over people
10. All persons having the chance to realize their potentialities
11. Having the value of property well-protected
12. Self-discipline————overcoming my irrational emotions and desires
13. All human beings having equal rights
14. Complying with the wishes of persons in authority
15. Being like others in general; having the same interests, opinions and ways of behaving as other people have
16. People having strict moral standards
17. Being a person who is experienced, broadminded, and worldly-wise
18. The open expression of disagreement between people
19. People in other nations respecting our principles and standards
20. Being allowed to maintain the privacy of one's opinions and beliefs
21. Being with other people; socializing
22. Everyone having opportunity to develop himself and his capacities
23. Letting others make their own decisions
24. People being strongly patriotic
25. Not being ashamed of one's own feelings and behavior

The value satisfaction index was obtained from Ss' ratings of the extent to which each value represented goals from which the S gets, or would get, satisfaction. Each value was judged independently in terms of 11 categories on a graphic rating scale. The scale of positively-valued goals was defined by three descriptive phrases: "No satisfaction from the goal" (Category 0), "Medium satisfaction from the goal" (Category 5), and "Maximum satisfaction from the goal" (Category 10). One further category was for judgments of "Dissatisfaction from the goal." The index of value satisfaction for the four experimental values was then obtained through arithmetic summation of the ratings of the eight items, coding "dissatisfaction" ratings minus 5. This index yielded an uncorrected test-retest reliability of .79.

The measure of "perceived instrumentality" required the *S*s to judge each value in terms of the "probability that the goals will be attained by allowing Negroes to move into White neighborhoods." The judgments were made on an 11-point graphic rating scale defined by three descriptive phrases: "Maximum probability that the goal will be blocked by allowing Negroes to move into White neighborhoods" (Category −5), "Allowing Negroes to move into White neighborhoods is irrelevant to achieving the goal" (Category 0), and "Maximum probability that the goal will be achieved by allowing Negroes to move into White neighborhoods" (Category +5). The index of perceived instrumentality was a summation of the ratings of the eight experimental value items, and had an uncorrected test-retest reliability of .66.

An index of "affective loading," used by Rosenberg to predict attitude, was computed separately for the total set of 25 value items, the eight experimental items, and the 17 nonexperimental value items. Since, according to the theory, attitude is a function of both value satisfaction and perceived instrumentality, attitude change should covary with change in an index combining measures of these separate components. The index of affective loading was computed by algebraically summing, over the set of values, the products of the satisfaction and instrumentality ratings of each value.

Change procedure. The change procedure was designed to increase the *S*s' awareness that "allowing Negroes to move into White neighborhoods" would tend to bring about the attainment of the four values. This procedure consisted of two parts: (*a*) a task which was presented as a "Test of Objectivity," and (*b*) a verbal discussion which ostensibly reported the results of the test. The "Test of Objectivity," completed as an assignment by the students outside of class, was introduced as a test of one's "ability to take a certain viewpoint and support it logically and objectively regardless of your own viewpoint." It was presented as a small experiment illustrating the scientific method, studying whether men or women were better able to take an objective viewpoint in reasoning. The test required the *S*s to support four propositions, each stating that "allowing Negroes to move into White neighborhoods" would lead to one of four values listed above.

In the second part of the change procedure the experimenter, in reporting the results of the study on objectivity in reasoning, presented a prepared discussion of the four propositions. The discussion, covering each of the values in 350 to 400 words, attempted to make clear several important and reasonable points which would be accepted by the *S*s, and which demonstrated the instrumentality of "allowing Negroes to move into White neighborhoods" for attaining each of the four values.

Subjects. One hundred eighty-three students in eight introductory psychology sections at the University of Michigan participated as experimental *S*s; 126 of these received both parts of the experimental procedure (the "Test of Objectivity" and the verbal discussion of the test results), and 58 received only one or the other of the two parts. The analyses reported in this paper are based upon the combined group of 183 experimental Ss.[4] Thirty-eight students in two classes participated as control subjects. The experimental and control groups were equated for initial attitude toward Negro housing segregation, and for both groups initial attitudes approximated a rectangular distribution.

Results and Discussion

EFFECTS OF THE EXPERIMENTAL PROCEDURE

Before testing the basic hypotheses of the study, it must first be shown that the experimental procedure in fact altered both attitude and attitude structure as anticipated. The proportion of Ss changing attitude in a positive direction (toward less prejudice) on the Negro housing segregation issue was significantly greater for the experimental group than for the control group. Similarly, a significant proportion of experimental Ss changed in the predicted direction on instrumentality ratings of the eight experimental value items ($x^2 = 9.91, p < .01$).

Change in the value satisfaction ratings was not predicted, since the experimental procedure was directed only toward change in perceived instrumentalities, and no change was found. A significant proportion of experimental Ss, however, changed on the indices of affective loading based upon the eight experimental items ($x^2 = 17.79, p < .001$) and on the total set of 25 items ($x^2 = 4.19, p < .05$). Although not predicted, this change is consistent with the theory and with the rationale of the index, which is a direct function of instrumentality ratings as well as value satisfaction ratings. No systematic change was observed for the control group on the Negro segregation attitude scale or on any of the attitude structure measures.

It was anticipated prior to analyzing the data that Ss with different initial attitudes toward Negro housing segregation would react differently to the experimental procedure, but specific predictions were not made concerning the form of the relationships. No systematic differences were found for attitude structure changes, but the data clearly indicated a curvilinear relationship between initial attitude and attitude change for the experimental Ss, as shown in Figure 1. Tests comparing positive changes against the combination of no-change and negative-change Ss indicated that a significantly smaller proportion of Ss at position 1 (extreme prejudice) changed posi-

---

[4] Separate analyses for the experimental subjects receiving both parts of the experimental procedure and for those receiving only one part demonstrated the same relationships throughout (1). The subjects receiving only one part generally showed less total change, as would be expected, but since the relationships between types of change were identical for both groups, the analyses reported here are based upon the combined group.

tively than Ss at positions 2 ($p < .05$) and 3 ($p < .05$); at position 4 the
difference was at the .10 level. Similarly a significantly smaller proportion
of Ss at position 5 changed positively than at positions 2 ($p < .01$), 3
($p < .01$) and 4 ($p < .02$). The Ss at the moderate positions (positions
2, 3, and 4) were found to be significantly influenced by the experimental
procedure, while extremely prejudiced (position 1) and extremely nonprejudiced (positions 5 and 6) persons were not found to change systematically. An analysis of change in the control group is not meaningful as a
result of the small number of Ss at each initial attitude position.

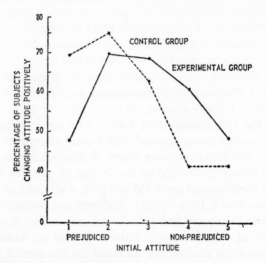

Figure 1. Relationship between initial attitude and attitude change.

A study of change on the five related attitude issues also supports this
curvilinear relationship. Combining the data from all six scales showed
that experimental Ss at position 1 were significantly less likely to change
positively than Ss at position 2 ($p < .01$), position 3 ($p < .01$) and position 4 ($p < .01$), and that Ss at position 5 were also significantly less likely
to change than those at position 2 ($p < .001$), position 3 ($p < .001$) and
position 4 ($p < .05$). A further analysis of change for the generalization
scales studied separately indicated basically the same curvilinear relationship for all six scales.

For the control group, however, the more prejudiced Ss changed more in
attitude than those at less prejudiced positions. A significantly larger proportion of Ss at positions 1 and 2 combined changed positively than Ss at
positions 4 and 5 combined, suggesting the operation of other change influences during the period of the study.

What accounts for this curvilinear relationship between initial attitude and change? The smaller proportion of positive changes at the nonprejudiced positions can be explained by the fact that the Ss already largely agreed with the change communication, and by the ceiling placed on change by the measuring instrument itself. The finding for experimental Ss of fewer positive changes in attitude for prejudiced Ss than for those at intermediate positions can be accounted for in terms of the possible wide range on the attitude continuum over which Ss at this extreme position may be spread. Some prejudiced Ss may have actual attitudinal positions far below the cutting-point between positions 1 and 2, and the same amount of actual positive change would result in fewer position changes than for Ss initially at other positions.

These findings indicate the importance of considering the possible interaction of initial attitude on effects of attitude change techniques. In the present study the absence of attitude change for Ss at the extreme positions prevented tests of the major hypotheses for these Ss. Consequently the analysis of relationships between attitude structure change and attitude change, and the generalizations from the findings, must be restricted to persons with moderate initial attitudes toward the issue.

RELATIONSHIPS OF ATTITUDE CHANGE TO ATTITUDE STRUCTURE CHANGE

The hypothesis that Ss who changed in perceived instrumental relationships would also change in attitude was clearly supported by the data. Experimental Ss with moderate initial attitudes (positions 2, 3, and 4) who altered their perception of the relation of segregation to the values discussed also tended to change their attitude toward Negro housing segregation, this difference being significant at the .01 level ($x^2 = 24.01$, $n = 69$, $df = 9$).

Changes in the value satisfaction measures, if occurring, should covary with changes in attitude, but the amount of value satisfaction change was too slight to enable an adequate test of this relationship. Changes in attitude, however, were significantly related to the indices of affective loading, which reflected both instrumentality and value satisfaction changes. The relationship for the total set of 25 value items was significant at the .02 level ($x^2 = 5.27$, $n = 69$, $df = 1$), and the relationship for the eight experimental items was significant at the .05 level, measured in terms of a correlation coefficient ($r = .27$, $df = 68$), but not significant tested by chi-square analysis ($x^2 = 1.43$, $n = 70$, $p < .15$). A relationship found between attitude change and change in the index of affective loading for the 17 nonexperimental values ($x^2 = 5.47$, $n = 70$, $p < .01$) is also consistent with the theory, since the basic relationship between perceived instrumentality and attitude should hold for all values, whether experimentally manipulated or not.

What are the implications of these findings? This test does not account for all of the variance of attitude-affect change, certainly, but it has tested experimentally the significance of *one* important source of affect of an attitude. The role of perceived instrumental relations was demonstrated for *S*s with nonextreme attitudes, but was not tested for persons extremely prejudiced or extremely nonprejudiced. The underlying theory would predict that changes in value satisfaction would covary similarly with changes in attitude, but this hypothesis was not tested in the present study.[5]

GENERALIZATION OF ATTITUDE CHANGE

The data demonstrated generalization of attitude change to certain related issues, but the hypothesis of a gradient of generalization varying as a function of the similarity of the attitude objects or situations was not confirmed. Comparison of the proportions of *S*s in the experimental group changing attitude positively, not changing, and changing negatively with changes in the control group indicated generalization of change to the Jewish housing segregation issue ($x^2 = 5.15$, $p < .03$), the Jewish officer issue ($x^2 = 8.43$, $p < .01$), and the Negro officer issue ($x^2 = 3.38$, $p < .07$). Because of the limited change in attitude for *S*s with extreme initial attitudes, the analysis here was also restricted to *S*s with initial positions 2, 3, and 4.

A sign-test analysis of positive changes compared to negative changes, i.e., discarding the no-change cases, rejected the null hypothesis (of no change in the positive direction) at the .05 level for all six attitude scales. A significant proportion of control *S*s summed over all six scales changed positively ($p < .05$), and a significant proportion changed positively on the two Mexican issues taken together; the other control group comparisons, however, were not statistically significant.

Judgments on a follow-up questionnaire item of "Which group do you believe is most like Negroes? ———— Jews ———— Mexicans" indicated that Mexicans were judged as "most like" Negroes by almost all *S*s, but, as reported, generalization of attitude change was not demonstrated for the two Mexican issues, though it was for the two Jewish issues. Actually significant proportions of experimental *S*s did change attitude positively on the Mexican scales, but the proportion changing in the control group, though less, was also significant. With the relatively small number of control *S*s the differences between groups were not statistically significant.

The failure to confirm the hypothesis of a gradient of generalization can be accounted for in terms of recognized limitations in the measure of "similarity" used in the study. Conceptual similarity between these issues is

[5] This problem is currently under study in a program of research on attitude change processes by Dr. Helen Peak and her colleagues at the University of Michigan.

undoubtedly multidimensional, and the dimensions used by the Ss in judging similarity may differ considerably from those over which generalization took place. Also several sources of evidence indicated that the Mexican issues were not well-structured or stable for these Ss, and that changes occurring on them were due more to this lack of structure, and consequent instability, than to influence of the experimental procedure.

Further study of the process of generalization of change of social attitudes will depend upon systematic analyses of the gradients of conceptual similarity involved. Methodology for handling this problem has not been thoroughly developed, though an approach formulated by Osgood (2), using a combination of associational and scaling procedures, may provide a systematic basis for such measurement and dimensionalizing of conceptual meaning.

Summary

This experiment was designed to test the hypothesis that attitudes toward an object, or situation, may be changed through altering the person's perception of the significance of the object as a means for attaining valued goals. It sought further to test whether attitude change generalizes to related objects, and whether the degree of generalization is a function of the similarity of the objects.

One hundred eighty-three experimental Ss responded to three sets of measures before and after a change procedure: (*a*) measures of attitude toward "allowing Negroes to move into White neighborhoods" and five related issues, (*b*) a measure requiring ratings of 25 general values in terms of the expected satisfaction from each, and (*c*) a rating measure of the 25 values in terms of the probability that "allowing Negroes to move into White neighborhoods" would lead to, or block, the attainment of each of the values. Thirty-nine control Ss took the same measures but did not receive the change procedure. The change procedure was designed to increase the Ss' awareness that nonsegregation would lead to the attainment of each of four important values.

The experimental procedure changed perceptions of the role of Negro housing segregation in attaining the four values, and changed attitude toward Negro housing segregation for Ss with moderate initial attitude on the issue. Insufficient attitude change was produced in extremely prejudiced and extremely nonprejudiced subjects to permit tests of the hypotheses for these Ss. Satisfaction ratings were not affected by the change procedure.

Changes in attitude were related significantly to changes in perceived instrumental relationships, and to changes in an index based upon both satisfaction and instrumentality ratings. Attitude change generalized to three

related attitude issues, but not to two further issues. The extent of generalization of attitude change was not shown to vary with the similarity of the
attitude issues.

References

1. CARLSON, E. R. Attitude change through modification of attitude structure. Unpublished doctor's dissertation, Univer. of Michigan, 1953.
2. OSGOOD, C. E. The nature and measurement of meaning. *Psychol. Bull.,* 1952, **49,** 197–237.
3. ROSENBERG, M. J. The experimental investigation of a value theory of attitude structure. Unpublished doctor's dissertation, Univer. of Michigan, 1953.
4. SARNOFF, I., and KATZ, D. The motivational bases of attitude change. *J. abnorm. soc. Psychol.,* 1954, **49,** 115–124.
5. SMITH, M. B. Personal values as determinants of a political attitude. *J. Psychol.,* 1949, **28,** 477–486.
6. WOODRUFF, A. D., and DIVESTA, F. J. The relationship between values, concepts, and attitudes. *Educ. psychol. Measmt,* 1948, **8,** 645–659.

34. Some Cognitive Aspects
of Motivation * [1]

W. C. H. PRENTICE, *Swarthmore College*

IDEALLY, a presidential address should be a contribution to knowledge.
Unfortunately, we are not always wise enough to choose presidents who
can provide such a contribution. In my case, I can plead circumstance and
thereby assure you without what might seem like false modesty that I am
a president who cannot supply you with new and exciting facts. For reasons
that are unimportant to you, I have been unable to get back into the laboratory for a number of years. Instead I dream about what I would like to
do were I free to enter a new field of research and explore a new set of

* From W. C. H. Prentice, "Some Cognitive Aspects of Motivation," *The American Psychologist,* 16 (August, 1961), 503–11. Reprinted by permission.

[1] Delivered September, 1960, in Chicago, Illinois, as the Address of the retiring President of the Division of General Psychology of the American Psychological Association.

techniques. Perhaps I shall regain that freedom. In the meantime, I should like to share with you some of my dreams and hope that you may be inspired to do some of the exploring yourselves.

Off and on for a number of years, I have been identified with a controversial point of view, namely, the view that perception is not governed by motivation. Today I shall introduce a new element of controversy by turning the topic upside down and asking you to consider the possibility that what we call motives are really a particular kind of perceptual or cognitive event. To some of you that may sound like nonsense or worse, but let me see if I cannot make some kind of sense out of it for you. Certainly motivational theory is in the doldrums, and if I can suggest a new slant on old problems, some good may result even from views that you ultimately reject, just so long as you reject them on empirical grounds— which will mean doing new research and adding to our pathetically small store of facts in the field of human motivation.

Partly because scientists are intelligent and versatile and diligent in their search for chinks in the armor of nature through which to peer for understanding, partly because of the extraordinary complexity of human psychological problems, and partly through accidents of the history of our discipline, we have come to mean several different things when we refer to understanding or explanation in psychology. To some of us, it is clear that a satisfactory explanation of a human activity must be made in neurological terms; to others, the explanatory framework can only be that of depth psychology; to still others, introspection or self-description may provide satisfactory accounts; and finally, a large group of us feels that some kind of formal theoretical model ultimately provides the only satisfactory clarification of the question "Why?" as it relates to human behavior. The approaches I have listed are not mutually exclusive, some combinations and overlap are possible; or some of us may hold to one for certain kinds of problem and another for certain others, depending on the stage of development of information in the particular case.

What I wish to suggest, however, is that our stage of development in the field of motivation is so primitive that none of these implicit definitions of "understanding" in psychology is appropriate, and that instead we should be searching for laws of behavior in what I can only call, with gratitude to (but also with apology to) Kurt Lewin, cognitive structure.

Consider with me a single case. Smith has struck Jones a violent blow. The psychologist is called on to tell why he did it.

In our present state of ignorance, no neurological answer is possible, and if it were, it would merely push the question back one step: why did that set of neurological patterns occur?

An account in terms of unconscious wishes and fears or of struggles between ego and superego may provide some intellectual satisfaction, but it leaves us in doubt about how we may ever predict such outbreaks in the future or how we may prevent them. In short, it gives us an idiosyncratic account that cannot be generalized very usefully. Moreover, there are systematic difficulties resulting from our ignorance and the consequent necessity of our relying on a large number of highly questionable assumptions.

If we turn instead to the culprit's own account of his motivation, we may get some interesting information, but we are very likely to get one of the following answers or some variant of it. "I don't know." "I don't like him." "I was angry." "It seemed like a good idea at the time." None of these helps much. Even the three last, which seem to hint at something useful, inspire primarily the further question, "But why?" When we ask it in such cases, we increase our chances of finally getting the inevitable, "I don't know."

Formal models are appealing. Modern behavior theory in its several forms does give at its best the possibility of deducing from antecedent conditions the behavior that must occur. A highly satisfactory kind of "understanding" to be sure, and probably for most of us an ultimate one. The trouble is that behavior theory is based on very primitive postulates, ones drawn from research on sharply limited kinds of behavior, and in 1960 it simply is not capable of encompassing our problems. It will not be able to help us until the complexities of human adult behavior have been reduced to manageable dimensions by careful descriptive investigation. Only then will we be able to discover whether or not the dimensions of maze and Skinner box can be adapted to fit the psychological problems of everyday life. And it is in the hope of stimulating your interest in that task that I stand before you today.

We desperately need to discover the dimensions of motivated behavior, and I think we are ready to make a start on that voyage of discovery if we will only take a careful and systematic but unbiased look at the phenomena of motivation. I think we can find there clues for a structural approach to our common problems that can lead in time to the construction of genuinely helpful formal models and deductive systems.

Let me return to Smith. There is one kind of comment the psychologist might make that strikes me as helpful. He may say, "He was jealous." There is a surprising amount of psychological content and tentative understanding of Smith's behavior embedded in that simple statement. We at least think we understand what it means to be jealous and what sort of behavior can be expected to ensue. By saying he was jealous, we are describing in a crude way a moderately complex psychological pattern. Jealousy can only be understood as involvement in a particular kind of interpersonal relationship and the holding of certain kinds of cognitive attitude and belief about it.

Now, to be sure, the kind of understanding is partial and incomplete, but I am suggesting that it carries with it the seeds of a progressively more complete and more satisfying understanding, if we are willing to do the requisite research. We are in somewhat the same intellectual position as the man who explains the origin of a fire as spontaneous combustion in a pile of oily rags on the cellar floor. The fire is explained very satisfactorily for certain purposes, but, since not all piles of oily rags burst into flames, we are given insufficient information to let us predict where the next fire will occur or to tell householders exactly when such conditions are or are not dangerous. But merely knowing that the heat was generated in that place under those roughly describable conditions gives us a start and suggests numerous experiments with the variables of temperature, moisture, pressure, materials, etc. which should in principle give us detailed and generalizable answers to our questions.

Clearly my example of Smith hitting Jones because of jealousy is a randomly chosen example. Innumerable other situations would illustrate the same methodological point. In everyday discourse we treat each other as having chosen or avoided particular activities because they appear to be attractive or threatening, respectively; because they look easy or hard; because they appear to belong to (or be antithetical to) a particular social role. But we do not probe further to try to discover what, in detail, it means for something to seem "difficult" or "threatening" or "appropriate to my role." Systematic analysis of the phenomena of motivation has been almost entirely omitted from psychology. We recognize dimly that our understanding of Smith is furthered somehow by knowing that he was jealous, but we do not really know why or how, because we have not tried to dissect the thing called jealousy and classify it. And the same is true of almost every other motivational situation.

It is interesting though ironic that we know much more about motivation as a set of techniques than we do about motivational principles. In various ways, we do successfully create for others psychological situations that lead them to do what we hoped and predicted they would do. Almost never are we able to give a systematic account of why our efforts were effective. Salesmen and advertisers, teachers and political leaders, parents and orchestra directors, friends and neighbors, and husbands and wives dimly understand and certainly use a principle that has never been part of scientific theory, namely, that you can influence another person, create motives in him, if you like, by manipulating his conception of the situation in which he finds himself.

The admirable parsimony of behavior theories like Hull's, or the learning theory of Thorndike to which it owes so much, has led several generations of academic theorists to persist in the attempt to deal with motivation without reference to cognition as such. We have, in fact, continued to hope that we could do away with motivational problems by explaining all behavior in terms of instigation by stimuli, merely noting that the conditions of instigation include the prior influence of what we call positive and negative reinforcement on the formation of habits. But the system has not worked. The motivational problems will not go away. Let me remind you of two roughly symmetrical ones dealing respectively with the long-term effects of positive and negative reinforcement.

One way of asking the question I have in mind, would be in terms of behavior theory itself. "Can the conditions of reinforcement (either positive or negative) be themselves changed by training?" Or, a bit less obscurely, "May learned responses take on permanently the character of what Thorndike called states that the animal will seek or avoid?"

In everyday language, the problem is this. When we repeatedly reward a kind of behavior, do we ever reach a state where that behavior is now permanently attractive in its own right and as predictable and characteristic an aspect of the organism as was the tendency to repeat responses followed by (e.g.) food in the first place? Of course, this is the problem of what Gordon Allport calls functional autonomy. Is it really true that states of affairs to be sought or prolonged by the organism can be *created* by training, or does training only strengthen the probability of responses leading to states innately sought by that animal?

As long ago as 1937, Allport provided us with convincing examples of just such acquired motives, and all the attempts of alternative theories to explain them away have failed. We must take as a fact of nature the finding that, in man at least, genuine and permanent "reinforcers" may be acquired during the individual's lifetime. Some adult motives do seem to have all the characteristics of bodily needs despite having obviously been acquired through some kind of training or experience. The grave difficulty is that we know nothing about the conditions of such training, if indeed the training is to be held responsible. Some acts long performed in the service of a basic satisfaction ultimately seem to become self-sustaining; others do not. Which are the differences among them? Does the difference really lie, as is so often proposed, in the nature of the reinforcement or in its frequency? Or should we not ask whether it lies in the nature of the acts themselves?

Functional autonomy has, of course, a parallel case on the negative side. When certain behavior is followed repeatedly by unsatisfactory states and finally ceases to occur, have we created new motives or merely created a habit that is inconsistent with the old response? When we reduce the frequency of a particular response by punishing it, have we weakened the instigation to that response or merely blocked its expression? There is a brand of radical behaviorism that would claim my question is trivial or meaningless or both, but that is a mistaken view. We cannot shrug off as merely verbal the question of whether the psychological nature of the organism may be so changed that a state of affairs natively satisfying becomes permanently discomforting. Our question is roughly equivalent to asking of a physical system whether we prevented an explosion by building thicker walls and thus containing the pressure or whether we got rid of the pressure. The two answers have genuinely different consequences for many uses to which we might wish to put the system. And so they do for the psychological parallel. Psychoanalytic theory emphasizes this problem, and clinical evidence of continued strong tendencies toward acts long suppressed by punishment is pretty impressive. Rats which are taught to press a bar for food, then shocked for the same response, and finally allowed to return to the bar pressing situation without shock sometimes show comparatively little loss of the originally learned instigation toward bar pressing, though the shock may have temporarily reduced the response level to zero.

But what about the cases where the opposite appears to occur? A child becomes ill after eating a favorite food and later finds that food permanently distasteful. A game or a place of residence or a companion once loved is made hateful by continual disappointment or injustice and thereafter serves as a negative reinforcement for activities connected with it, though it used to play a positive role. If indeed such things really occur, they raise the same kinds of questions as those raised by claims for functional autonomy. Under what conditions does such fundamental psychological change occur? And under what conditions does mere suppression of a response occur? Is it only the strength and frequency of the punishment that are important, as traditional theories would hold? Or are not other more complex matters worth investigating?

Surely it is naive, for example, to persist in using Thorndike's "state of affairs which the animal avoids and abandons" as the definition of negative reinforcement and to treat it without differentiation. It is one thing to abandon a bad-tasting food; it is quite another to abandon an unhappy marriage; and it is still another to abandon a burning building. Even a simple slap from a parental hand can be a very different matter taken in play from what it is when set in the context of deterrence.

I have probably digressed far enough in trying to make clear some illustrations of my conviction that we have persisted too long in the use of artificial unidimensional concepts instead of investigating the variety and richness that we know exists within what we call reward or punishment. We will not answer the fundamental questions about how motives are acquired until we give up the fiction that the psychological consequences of an act may vary only in one dimension, ranging from strongly negative to strongly positive. We must start with a more naturalistic approach and try to discover what are the true dimensions of effect and then proceed to manipulate experimental situations in terms of those dimensions. Perhaps we will thus finally begin to throw some light on the differences between habitual responses that become autonomous and those that extinguish, between punished responses that bounce back with all their original vigor when threat of punishment is removed and those that become instead the basis of phobic reactions, motivating in turn new complexes of behavior.

I may have seemed to imply that it is only the behavior theorists whose treatment of motivation is inadequate. But of course physiological psychology, comparative psychology, and clinical psychology all have their own inadequacies in this respect. All have failed to make clear what kind of answers we are seeking in the study of motivation.

Everyone's explanations have tended to attempt to reduce motives to something else. Almost no attempt has been made to study the unique properties of acts that are carried on for their own sake. Esthetics and play offer an almost infinitely fertile field for such investigation. What is satisfying about looking at something we call "beautiful"? What properties must the object have? What properties must the observer have? What other properties must be present in the situation? How could any part of the total be changed so as to make it discomforting instead of satisfying? Or take games and unorganized play. What are the properties that make a game or a hobby enjoyable? Clearly those properties are not entirely objective, since the game may be exciting to me and boring to you, or deeply satisfying to you and irritating to me. What kinds of interaction are involved? What dimensions of the person are important, and how do they relate to the structure of the objective situation?

Let me suggest a few examples of what I have in mind, taking my first examples from games. Most games involve built-in *difficulty*. It is no fun to move pieces across a chessboard without constraint or to fill up blanks in a crossword puzzle with any old letters that come into our heads. One of the things we seek from games is somehow related to the overcoming of obstacles or barriers or competition from an opponent. But "difficulty" is not a property of objects or situations; it is a property of interactions between objects or sets of objects and a person. The degree of difficulty depends on the person as well as the task. We must develop a technique for quantifying the degree of difficulty of a task that makes it attractive or gives it reinforcing properties, and the measure will clearly have to be one that involves personal parameters of some sort.

Novelty is another positive factor in games. Satiation, boredom, ennui result from sameness. A game that does not offer new situations does not hold one's attention or provide continuing satisfaction. But novelty is also "in the eye of the beholder" in some sense. What is new to me may be old to you. Or the newness may result only from a subtle change that you are bright enough to detect while I miss what charms you. Or the reverse may occur. Your superior intelligence may lead you to notice that despite superficial variations, the game in question really offers only one or two basic problems endlessly repeated with perfectly predictable variations, and you may then find the game no longer appealing, while I remain enchanted with what I consider infinite novelty. We shall never be in a position to discover to what extent novelty is an important factor in human choosing until we discover how to define novelty as an interaction between a particular observer and a situation.

Suppose that a research program were to be undertaken along these lines. What other properties of motivational situations would we wish to investigate? If I suggest a few, I think you will find others springing to mnd in large numbers.

For instance, in the same general category as novelty will be *change, unpredictability,* and *surprise.* The McGill studies on sensory deprivation and some early explorations of satiation in Lewin's laboratory suggest that the most discomforting of all conditions other than severe sensory pain may turn out to be lack of change. Prolonged periods with only a little change may be more than enough to counteract the initial attractiveness of any activity. I am here distinguishing change from novelty in the sense that church on Sunday is a change from the rest of the week though by no means a novelty; mere alternation between two perfectly familiar patterns may be a great deal more satisfying (or less discomforting) than complete lack of change. Experiments should be designed to explore this relationship.

Unpredictability seems to have charms of its own. It would be interesting to inquire whether church, for example, would be even more inviting if we never knew which day was going to be appointed church-going day or whether a job would be more attractive if our day off sometimes came on Thursday, sometimes on Monday, etc. without predictable pattern.

Surprise is still different. Surprise appears when the predictable does not occur. We make a prediction in confidence, and something goes awry. Some interesting quantitative problems arise here. How do we establish the kind of expectation that can be surprised? Must the expected event have invariably occurred in the past, or in what proportion of cases, and how often? Once the expectation is established, under what conditions of timing is surprise attractive? For, though some surprises can surely be unattractive, there is considerable evidence of a homely kind that surprise as such, stripped of everything but the formal relation of an expected event that does not appear, is a "state that the organism will tend to prolong or repeat." Small children are delighted by any form of repeated behavior that is suddenly replaced by something else. Much of our humor is based on such a switch in the direction of thought: the humorist or clown leads you to expect one kind of idea or action and then hands you something else. It is funny, and it is fun. The fun lies partly in proper timing, and another interesting quantitative problem here presents itself. Both the "suddenness," or rate of exposure of the switch, and the properly dramatic moment for producing it are relationally determined. When we come to study them systematically, we must, of course, deal not with a simple measure like a number of seconds from part of the sequence to another but instead with a second—or higher—order relationship among time intervals. I am not proposing that the content of the surprise is without importance, but it is striking that proper timing can often change what seems to be inherently frightening or distasteful into something pleasurable.

Within the more general category of *difficulty,* already alluded to, we need to investigate the seemingly desirable qualities of barriers having certain properties. What follows is speculation, but careful observation should lead to specific hypotheses that are subject to empirical study. It appears to be true that barriers, in order to be enticing, must seem not to be insuperable but must nevertheless seem to offer a test and a challenge to one's self-esteem. No adult would spend much time jumping over a stick raised 2 feet off the ground, nor would he spend time trying to jump over one 10 feet up. But quite a few young men spend many afternoons trying to jump over ones between 4.5 and 7.5 feet high.

If you watch a small child involved in spontaneous play, you will recognize that so simple a matter as opening a door or turning a faucet on and off can be a source of interest and enjoyment so long as it is both new and a bit difficult. When it becomes too easy, it is abandoned; but we can also lead the child to abandon it by making it too hard. Lock the door, and the struggle with it soon ceases. Think how helpful it would be if we could uncover the laws that operate on such ranges of difficulty. Sporting activities, college courses, professional problems, and social roles can all be made more or less attractive within limits by adjusting their difficulty. We know in a general way that they may be unattractive because they are too easy, offering no sense of achievement, or because they are too difficult, permitting either no achievement at all or too little to compete successfully with other activities. We must learn to identify optimum ranges of difficulty for different tasks. The problem will, of course, be a tough one, because the measures we need will have to take account of the abilities of the person himself and deal with information available to him about the task. Still, since the research problem is difficult but not insuperable, it should fall in an optimum range for someone and seem attractive to a psychologist or two.

Perhaps the same psychologists will also take up a closely related set of problems. The setting of personal goals seems to be enhanced by the opportunity to see a graded series of achievements. It would take a bolder theorist than I to assert that as a general law of human motivation, but I think we have the tools to find out whether or not it is one. The first step must be to learn how to measure the kind of graded goals that lead to choice behavior and how to distinguish them from ones that lead to avoidance. Let me illustrate. If I asked a 15-year-old boy to attempt to high jump 7 feet, he would almost certainly give up very soon. But if I let him start with a height that can be achieved and show him how practice and training can help him to inch his way upward over a period of years, I may be able to make a high jumper out of him. Or suppose I invite you to run for President. A realistic view of what that would mean were you to set out on your own would probably make the program unappealing. It would fall in the "too difficult" category. But the apparent degree of difficulty might change if I presented you with a series of stratagems leading to successive subgoals of precinct leader, city chairman, governor, etc.

Our knowledge in this area is slight, indeed, but we do have a few facts. Studies of levels of aspiration show that success typically leads to the setting of higher sights but that success also leads to more realistic goals than failure does. Apparently it is important to permit the aspirant to very distant goals an opportunity to avoid the cognitive confusion that can be produced by failure. It is necessary not only for a properly graded series of steps to exist, but also for them to be apprehended. And that fact emphasizes the importance of recognizing the motivational differences that may exist between clearly presented situations and a less clearly presented one, but also between people capable of understanding what lies ahead and those unable to do so. The attractive progression from subgoal to subgoal can occur only when it is cognitively available to the actor.

It may be valuable in this connection to note that in games we typically arrange things so that the direction of the paths to the goal is much clearer than it is likely to be in life's ordinary tasks. Even in a game like chess or bridge, where uncountable combinations of steps are available, the game provides strict constraints, and the shrewd player may know within reasonably narrow limits the probabilities of success on any one play. The dull player will probably find the same game confusing and, therefore, unattractive. It seems likely that the clarity of paths toward the goal is a part of the attractiveness of the entire enterprise. At least we may note that people who are skillful in handling human beings make regular use of this motivational principle (if it can be dignified with that title). The salesman or politician will typically attempt to diminish uncertainties for you with respect to the next step and where it will lead, while at the same time showing you the magnificent possibilities of the steps to come. Any theory of motivation will have to find room for an assessment of the clarity with which the path to the goal is delineated.

Earlier I spoke of the charms of uncertainty and surprise; now I am asking you to consider the attractiveness of a diminution of alternatives and a maximizing of clarity. There is really no contradiction. It is simply a fact of life that the attractiveness of most situations increases with uncertainty up to some recognizable point and then decreases. If we can learn to measure such things, we can discover empirically the optimum ranges of uncertainty just as I have proposed that we seek the optimum ranges of difficulty.

The observation of games and recreations, activities that are seemingly without extrinsic goals but are instead indulged in for their own attractive properties, suggests still another kind of pattern that seems to create attractiveness. That is the pattern of tension followed by release. The playground roller coaster is a classic example. So is a horror movie. So is the game of hide-and-seek between parent and small child. So to some extent are skiing, mountain climbing, automobile racing, and others. I should certainly not maintain that any of these occupations has as its only charm the building up of fear or tendencies like fear only to find out that one comes out safely in the end. But the fact is that the tension release pattern appears over and over again throughout observations of human motivation, taking forms as various as the taking of snuff, the seeking of sexual arousal that it may then be dispelled, and the half-serious tales of women who buy shoes that are too tight because it feels so good to take them off. What we do not know, and what so desperately needs careful study, is the objective meaning of what we call tension. The word has been used by psychologists to refer to physical changes (as in muscle), to experiences (like anxiety), to conditions of the nervous system, and to purely formal constructs (as in the writings of Lewin). In general we tend to feel that these uses are not unrelated, that there is a kind of basic common sense to justify the same word's being assigned in the different contexts. But the common core, if any, has not been identified. And we should not continue trying to use the word for scientific purposes until it is. All the uses seem to have in common a reference to some kind of constriction of behavioral possibilities combined with a probability, increasing with time, that the constriction will be replaced by relatively diffuse and undirected expenditure of energy. Can we find a mathematical statement of those relationships that is adequate to enable us to try it for size on the various things called tension?

Another formal problem has to do with the rates at which tension is built up and released. It seems likely that the explosive relief of the sneeze is a very important part of the snuff-taker's pleasure and that if the nasal tickle merely faded slowly away, the point would be lost. Conversely, the fear and uncertainty of the roller-coaster- or horror-movie-type of thrill can sometimes be built up for so long that the fun is destroyed. Genuine problems of temporal patterning exist here, and I see no reason why they should not be amenable to experimental investigation.

We have made here only a small beginning. We have hardly scratched the surface of the things that people do "for their own sake." The afternoon of a small child is a gold mine of suggestions for research on the structural properties of situations that motivate behavior. What are the structural properties of the task of taking apart and putting together a simple object that make it attractive? How could we make it more attractive, or less so? What are the *temporal* characteristics of that same task? How long can play continue before interest flags? After what might be likened to experimental extinction does take place, does spontaneous recovery occur? How soon? Under what conditions does permanent extinction occur?

We have tended to think of extinction only in terms of inhibition by a competing response or in terms of the weakening of a stimulus-response bond by punishment or by reactive inhibition. But the problem is bigger than that. Human beings do, after all, find that block piling and percolator dismantling permanently pall before adulthood. When I became a man, I put away childish things. What, psychologically speaking, are childish things?

Visitors from other cultures often strike us as childish because of their delight with what is new to them but old to us. Adults who "discover" a new art form go rapidly through stages of excitement followed by boredom with particular styles in the art until, as we say, their taste matures. Perhaps maturing taste means only that increasing opportunity to experience the various sensory relationships inherent in an art form leads to a gradual recognition of the difference between experiences that are, for some inherent structural reason, readily satiated and those that are not. As in games, *difficulty* may play a part in maintaining interest. Or sheer complexity may provide a sense of unending novelty and variety within a familiar framework. We do not know what is important here, but someone ought to be finding out. Experimental esthetics seems to hold little interest for the artist or art historian, but it may hold the key to many important motivational issues and should thus be of great interest to psychologists.

In fact, nowhere is the cognitive approach to motivation so clearly promising as in esthetics. Successive re-exposures to a work of art produce genuine cognitive changes that are in turn clearly related to changes in esthetic satisfaction and value. A work seen or heard for the sixth or sixtieth time comes to be more familiar, perhaps more orderly, sometimes more complex as we begin to appreciate details that escaped us at first, and finally in at least some cases to be apprehended so differently from the first time that we genuinely have difficulty believing that we are dealing with the same work of art. These cognitive changes affect the degree of satisfaction or dissatisfaction that we have with the experience and determine whether or not we seek to experience that work again.

But to return to the matter of maturing taste and putting away childish things, it should be apparent that some kinds of experience do lose their charm after numerous exposures. If the process is a cognitive one, it would not be surprising that adults develop more rapidly than children and, if started at the same stage, run faster through the various delights that (for whatever reason) seem not to hold experienced human beings despite their early charm.

The problem gains added interest when we look at it from the point of view of the now classic problem of functional autonomy. Allport supplied us many years ago with numerous examples of human activities first engaged in as a way of reaching some more distant goal and later accepted as attractive in their own right. A typical example is that of the fisherman who first went to sea to earn a living but who now finds that the ocean exerts an irresistible pull when he no longer makes his living that way. Or consider the man who first learned to play the violin in order to win the favor of his parents and now, though parental favor is no longer an issue, seeks out the violin as his favorite relaxation. Why is it true that in both cases only part of the activity acquires motivational force? The fisherman has given up all the things he used to do on the boat as a commercial fisherman; he does not feel the need to cast nets and clean fish. The violinist has given up doing his homework before dinner, riding his bicycle to music lessons, and all the other things he used to do as part of the same activity. Our problem is to discover what factors select out the particular parts that become and remain intrinsically attractive. It is important that we investigate the properties of activities which drop out as well as the properties of the activities that remain.

The idea that one may "discover" in a genuinely cognitive sense the undesirability of a course of action that appeared superficially to be desirable is, so far as I know, an unexplored one. But the cognitive approach might conceivably clear up the present mystery and confusion about the role of punishment. Let us, in a purely speculative way, consider the possibility that punishment produces three distinguishable results.

In one case, punishment may deter the attractive response. A child, knowing that he will have his hands slapped if he steals the cake, eyes it greedily from afar but does not touch it. Continued contemplation does not diminish the desirability of the forbidden object. Indeed, in some cases, deterence may result in just such opportunity for contemplation as will bring out hitherto unforeseen attractions in the forbidden response.

In the second case, punishment having deterred the response itself, study and contemplation of the total situation may follow and have the opposite result. That is, a child punished for playing in the street may live to understand the situation as his parents understood it and thus find it no longer inviting. The punishment may serve primarily to focus attention on the problem and to provide a respite from the activity that was indulged in so automatically that suitable contemplation never occurred.

The third case, that in which a relatively strong response tendency seems to be permanently destroyed, may come about not through the discovery of unsuspected properties in the original situation, but more directly by the addition of punishment to that situation. Perhaps there, too, hypothetical answers can be proposed in terms of cognitive structure. At least two aspects deserve investigation. To what extent is punishment made to appear intrinsic to the situation? Touching a hot stove or walking into areas posted for dangerous radiation provides a deterrent very different psychologically from the intrinsic fear of detection and punishment by a policeman. If an activity can be made to appear *inherently* painful or destructive or sinful, that may in itself be sufficient to produce permanent withdrawal and distaste. Secondly, the structural characteristics of the punishment itself, already hinted at above, deserve the most careful investigation. To be scolded by Mother and to be scolded by Teacher are two different matters. Mother's scolding when angry is itself different from her scolding when she is apparently otherwise in a good mood. A punishment accepted as personal rejection is different from mere retributive payment of a symmetrical kind such as blows or angry words exchanged by boys on a playground.

Oviously we do not have the theoretical tools for dealing with such differences in cognitive pattern, and we must begin to forge them. I have seemed to describe all motivation in terms free of self-reference, and many of you will be uneasy about the seeming disappearance of the self from the motivational stage. There is not time to develop the thesis fully, but I want to suggest that the self too is a cognition and that it appears as a single factor in relation to others in experience. The kinds of relationship between self and others or between self and objects that lead to particular kinds of action simply need the same kind of careful descriptive account that we need in dealing with other cognitive facts. "Self-realization," "self-esteem," and similar words describe cognitions. When we recognize certain kinds of failure or opportunity or threat involving ourselves we behave in particular ways. We must seek the regularities in such self-involved behavior as we would seek those in more objective situations.

To summarize: The sizes and shapes and colors of objects determine in part their attractiveness. Temporal patterns of stimulation may be pleasant or unpleasant. Invitations from persons in one social role produce a different response from those in another. The clarity with which we grasp the details of a situation may affect our interest or lack of interest in dealing with it in a particular way. Complex matters of cognitive organization that can only be described crudely by words like novelty and difficulty and threat seem to play a critical part in the selection of playful activities. Choice of particular foods, particular mates, and particular vocations seems to depend on characteristics of patterns of sensory stimulation or relations between such patterns and memories or ideas. In short, the cognitive contribution to why we do what we do is an important one. It is also one that we know very little about. I have tried to present some suggestions for ways of looking at these problems, ways that might lead to empirical research of the kind we need so badly.

It is my hope that the establishment of lawful relationships among cognitive variables and patterns of choice may some day give us a genuine theory of motivation at a prephysiological level. I have no objection to physiology. In fact, I look forward to the day when we will have a psysiological account of every behavioral fact or relationship, but the behavioral facts and relationships must come first. And we must not delay longer in finding out what kinds of psychological situation produce what kinds of behavior, writing first approximations to laws about the structure of such situations, and then beginning to seek the biological substrate.

35. *The Acquisition and Retention of Skills* *

LESTER D. CROW AND ALICE CROW,
Brooklyn College

E SSENTIALLY, skill is the performance of a task. During his lifetime, an individual engages in many tasks, such as various forms of locomotor activity, riding a bicycle, driving an automobile or flying an airplane, speaking, playing a musical instrument, pitching a baseball, typing, reciting, a poem, playing chess, or any other form of activity that requires muscular coordination and motor control.

Some psychologists classify skills as *motor* and *verbal*. In general, motor skills involve activities that represent overt bodily movement. In a verbal skill, such as reciting aloud a list of words, language activities are utilized, although movement of the vocal musculature is needed. Also, as an individual is learning a motor skill he may engage in implicit verbal activities, as he reviews the steps needed to acquire the skill.

Motor control and coordination. The acquisition of competence in any skill is based upon the development of motor control. The primary pattern of motor development is gross bodily movements, in which most or all of the large muscles are involved, as in walking, jumping, running, skating, or swimming. In the secondary pattern, coordination and control of the smaller muscles are needed, e.g., writing, drawing, and working

---

* From Lester D. Crow and Alice Crow, *An Outline of General Psychology*, (Paterson, N.J. Littlefield, Adams and Company, 1959), pp. 200–204. Reprinted by permission.

with tools or other implements. The learning of most skills requires the coordinated movements of both gross and fine muscles.

Readiness for skill acquisition. Progress in acquiring a motor skill is dependent upon maturation of the muscular system. Learning a skill also is closely associated with sensory acuity and power of perception. Usually there is a felt need for a drive toward or an interest in the mastery of the skill. No matter how great the inner urge or the outer pressure may be, the learning process involved in skill mastery cannot begin effectively until a state of readiness for such learning has been reached.

The many experiments conducted with both animals and human beings in the field of motor development have yielded data that would seem to indicate that the patterns and rate of learning are determined by maturation or internal growth rather than by experience or training. This principle is becoming more or less generally accepted as applying to gross body activities. Yet, many children still are being "forced" to begin learning tasks, such as speaking intelligently, writing, and reading before they have matured sufficiently to profit from their learning efforts.

Significant factors of skill mastery. Competence in a skill is achieved only through learner activity. The learner is conscious of his own muscular movements. Hence motor learning is associated with kinesthetic sensations.

Awareness of Goal. It is important that a learner be aware of the goal toward which he is striving and know the amount and kind of activity needed to reach that goal. These understandings help the learner recognize errors and improve his performance. Hence the power to discriminate among responses has a significant effect upon the attainment of skill competence.

Observation of Model. Much can be discovered about skill competence by observing, analyzing, and understanding the performance of a highly skilled person who serves as a model. The imitation of an excellent model has value throughout the learning process but is especially helpful when the learner has reached the stage of adequate performance, provided he is interested in attaining greater than average competence in it.

First Attempts. Initial attempts at mastering a skill usually are *awkward* and imperfect. The learner may become so discouraged by his first failures that he may appear to have developed a mental "block" that will cause further learning in the skill area to be mediocre in quality, if not impossible.

Positive Attitude. The adverse attitude toward continuance of learning can be avoided or ameliorated only if (1) there is a strong urge to master the skill, (2) the learner understands that skill perfection cannot be achieved without the ability to persevere in spite of annoying results, (3) too high standards are not set for the beginner, (4) the first feeble attempts are accepted by the teacher, accompanied by encouragement to continue the learning.

Learning a skill. Degree of proficiency in a skill depends upon the extent to which correct motor responses result finally in automatic performance. For effective skill mastery, the learner must develop *steadiness* or *control, precision* or *accuracy, speed,* and *strength in his voluntary movements.* After these essential qualities are achieved, the learner then is free to perfect the *form* or style of his performance.

Basic Principles. The learner needs to be motivated. His first attempts often are of the trial and error variety. Correct responses are substituted for incorrect ones, sometimes by means of the use of reward and punishment.

A learner may seem to be making poor progress; then, almost unconsciously, he gains new insights that initiate much improved performance. Important as other learning approaches may be, a skill cannot be perfected unless the learner engages in correct and consistent practice or drill.

Aspects of Practice. For a motor skill to become automatic and relatively independent of the functioning of the higher mental processes, accurate and sufficient practice is needed. Mere repetition does not constitute practice, however. The results of psychological studies indicate that for practice to be effective it must be well planned, suited to the learner's abilities, and conducted according to certain psychologically derived principles.

Overlearning. More than one repetition is needed in the development of a skill. In this connection, learning can be regarded as a single correct response to a stimulus situation. In order to fix a response or a series of responses so that they become automatic, many repetitions are needed.

It is possible for some simple activities, such as the spelling of the word *cat* or the saying of *Yes* or *No,* to have been repeated so often in day-by-day experiences that the adult scarcely can believe that there ever was a time in his life when such responses were not a part of him. Continued practice has resulted in automatization.

Practice or constant repetitions of learning material is referred to as *overlearning.* It is possible that incorrect as well as correct responses can be overlearned. Hence drill or practice must be correct or accurate. The learner needs help in recognizing and discarding incorrect responses as soon as they occur, and substituting the correct for the incorrect. Moreover, if unimportant details of the learning situation are stressed and consequently overlearned, they may interfere with the fixing through practice of more needed responses.

Length of Practice Periods. The rate at which an individual practices a task is an important factor in skill development. The length of time needed to gain proficiency in a skill varies with individual ability and interest, as well as with previous learning.

Practice or drill is most effective when it is well motivated and appropriately spaced. Because of the relative shortness of their attention span, young children can learn a skill better if the practice periods are short. Practice periods for older learners can be somewhat longer.

In the beginning of the learning stage, the practice periods should be shorter than they may need to be during the advanced stages. The practice periods may be lengthened when the learner has mastered the fundamentals of the skill, and wishes to refine his performance or develop a particular form or style. These periods should not be so short that nothing is accomplished, neither should they be so long that physical fatigue or boredom causes the learner to make errors.

Distribution of Practice Periods. The distribution of practice periods depends partly upon the kind of skill to be learned and partly upon the age and ability of the learner. Distributed practice yields more effective mastery than does mass practice. This principle holds for the learning of most skills, from the simple to the relatively complex.

The spacing of practice periods has been found to be important. Too short rest periods may fail to relieve fatigue; too long rest periods may interfere with the learner's desire to improve his performance. Also important is the location of the rest periods. For each area of skill learning there probably is an optimal distribution of practice and rest periods to obtain rapid and effective progress.

36. The Learning of Motor Skills as Influenced by Knowledge of Mechanical Principles *

FRANCES M. COLVILLE

MANY GENERAL PRINCIPLES of mechanics are relevant to the teaching, learning, and performance of activities included in the physical education curriculum. These principles may describe the motion of objects such as balls and racquets, movement of the body itself, or a combination of both.

The question has been raised as to whether knowledge of these general principles and an understanding of their application to these activities will facilitate the learning and improve the performance of pupils in physical education classes. Also of interest are questions concerning the influence of knowledge of these principles as applied to one activity upon subsequent learning of other activities to which the same principles apply. Results of a few experiments suggest that a pupil who understands a principle related to one skill may master a related skill more readily than the pupil whose experience has been restricted to specific instruction in technique without explanation of pertinent principles.

With reference to the teaching of a motor skill in which a specific principle of mechanics is involved, then, two questions have been raised:

1. What is the effect of knowledge of a principle upon immediate learning of a skill to which the principle applies?

2. What is the effect of knowledge of a principle learned in relation to one skill upon subsequent learning of a different or more complicated skill to which the same principle is applicable?

Reported investigations bearing on the acquisition and transfer of principles are limited, and although most authorities agree that general principles are probably transferable, little strong experimental evidence is available to support such a claim. Apparently, little or no experimentation has been done in the field of physical education on the effect of knowledge of principles of mechanics in learning situations involving body movement and large muscle activities.

* From Frances M. Colville, "The Learning of Motor Skills as Influenced by Knowledge of Mechanical Principles," *The Journal of Educational Psychology*, 48 (October, 1957), 321–26. Reprinted by permission.

Judd, and Hendrickson and Schroeder reported that knowledge of the principle of refraction was beneficial in dart throwing and rifle shooting at a target under water. Cox found that knowledge of principles involved in manipulating electrical equipment facilitated the assembling and stripping of such equipment. Other experimenters have reported similar results from investigations involving mathematics, mental games, spelling, card tricks, and mechanical puzzles. In contrast to these findings are a number of investigations in which the method of including instruction in the principles involved did not appear to be more effective. In studying the effect of drill versus the learning of generalizations related to addition and subtraction, Olander found that the two methods appeared to be equally effective. Babitz and Keys found similar results with college chemistry classes, and Hendrix reported only one difference, significant at the 12 per cent level, in her experiment with teaching algebraic generalizations.

With the exception of the experiments by Judd, Hendrickson and Schroeder, and Cox, all of the reported investigations have dealt with various types of learning other than motor learning, and only Judd's experiment involved skills requiring the coordinated use of large muscles of the body as well as fine coordinations of the fingers. Judd, and Hendrickson and Schroeder, while reporting a difference in favor of instruction in principles, included this instruction in such a way that additional time was allotted to the group receiving the instruction. Thus, the experimental groups had the advantage of additional time as well as additional information. Furthermore, Judd supplied no statistical analysis of his early experiment, and the other differences reported were significant at a statistical level below that which is usually considered acceptable.

In the present investigation, an attempt was made to control these ambiguities by using an experimental design which insured that both the experimental and the control groups spent equal amounts of time in learning and performing and by considering only those differences which were significant at the 5 per cent level of confidence or above.

Method

PURPOSE OF THE STUDY

It was the purpose of this study to investigate certain questions related to the teaching of physical education activities in which specific principles of mechanics are involved. This problem was approached by: (a) selecting three principles of mechanics which are pertinent to motor skill; (b) selecting three motor skills, each of which utilizes one of the principles (c) establishing for each skill two comparable groups of Ss, one of which was taught without reference to the principle involved, and the other of which was taught to understand and apply the principle; (d) comparing for each skill the performance of the two groups, one of which spent the entire time practicing the skill without reference to the principle involved, and the other of which spent part of the time practing the skill and part of the time in learning the principle; (e) comparing for each skill the performance of the two groups in a similar or more complicated form of the skill to which the same general principle applies.

SELECTED PRINCIPLES AND SKILLS

The selected principles and the skills in which they are utilized were as follows:

Principle I: The angle of incidence is approximately equal to the angle of reflection. Skill: Rolling a ball against a surface, or surfaces, from which it would rebound.

Principle II: In stopping a moving object, the force opposing the momentum must be equal to the force of the momentum, and if the object is to be caught, this momentum must be dissipated by reducing the resistance of the catching surface. Skill: Catching a tennis ball in a lacrosse stick and catching a badminton bird on a tennis racquet.

Principle III: An object set in forward motion through the air by an external force is acted upon by the force of the momentum and by gravital acceleration. Skill: Archery.

PROCEDURE

Three parallel experiments were devised, each of which was designed to investigate performance of one of the three skills. The Ss for all three experiments were undergraduate women students at the University of Southern California. There were thirty-six Ss in the Ball Rolling experiment, forty in the Catching experiment, and forty-two in the Archery experiment. (The Ss in the Archery experiment included some men whose scores were treated separately from those of the women.) For each of the experiments the Ss were divided into two groups, one of which spent the entire time learning and practicing the skill, and the other of which spent part of the time learning about the principle and the rest of the time learning and practicing the skill. Each experiment consisted of two tests. During the first test the Ss of the nonprinciple group learned the skill and practiced. The Ss of the principle group learned the principle, and the skill, and practiced. The total amount of time spent by both groups was the same. During the second test both groups practiced a similar or more complicated skill. Each group spent the same amount of time and no mention was made of the principle involved.

The Ball Rolling Experiment. The Ball Rolling experiment was designed to illustrate the principle describing the rebound of a ball. The apparatus consisted of a modified pinball machine plunger, a squash ball, a felt-covered table surface four feet wide and six feet long, and a target made of colored construction paper. The overall size of the target and each of its scoring divisions was determined by recording the hits made by a group of comparable *S*s who were not used in the experiment. These *S*s rolled the ball so that it would rebound from one side of the table as close as possible to the center of the adjacent side which was marked with a square of white paper. The rest of the side was covered with brown wrapping paper, and spots on this paper to which the balls rolled were marked in red pencil. This scoring sheet provided the basis for establishing a six-standard deviation scale, and from this scale the scoring areas of the target were derived.

The *S*s were asked during the first test to roll the ball against one side of the table in such a manner that it would rebound to the target placed against the adjacent side. For the second test they were asked to roll the ball so that it would rebound from two adjacent sides to the target set at right angles on the third side.

The Catching Experiment. The Catching experiment consisted of two tests each involving the skill of catching a moving object. The first test involved catching a tennis ball in a lacrosse stick. For the second test, they caught a badminton bird on a tennis racquet. The apparatus for this experiment, in addition to balls, birds, crosse, and racquet, included a homemade device for projecting the tennis ball and the badminton bird. This device proved to have high reliabilty.

The Archery Experiment. The Archery experiment was planned to illustrate the principle of gravital acceleration and its action on arrow flight and the relation of line of flight to line of sight. The first test involved shooting from twenty yards. The second test included ends shot from thirty yards, from forty yards, and a Junior Columbia Round.

Analysis of Data. In each experiment, the reliability of the scores was established by use of the split-half technique, the odd scores being correlated with the even scores. Use of the Spearman-Brown Prophecy Formula for predicting reliability of the whole test resulted in coefficients which ranged from .81 to .94 and thus it was felt that these scores were sufficiently reliable to permit further analysis and comparison.

All of the data were analyzed by means of analysis of variance using Edwards' technique for repeated measurements of the same subjects. This technique tests differences between methods, between trials, and between the interaction of trials and methods. In each experiment the initial ability of the two groups, as evidenced by preliminary trials, was tested and found not to differ significantly.

Findings

In the Ball Rolling experiment, no significant difference in the performance levels of the two groups was found on either test. A difference between trials significant at the 1 per cent level of confidence was found on both tests.

In the Catching experiment, no significant differences were found in performance levels, and a difference between trials significant at the 5 per cent level of confidence was found only on the first test.

In the Archery experiment no significant difference in performance levels was found. A difference significant at the 1 per cent level for men and at the 5 per cent level for girls was found on the second test at all distances except forty yards.

The following general findings were noted:

1. A significant amount of learning took place under both methods of instruction.

2. This learning was not only similar in amount but also in pattern. Exceptions occurred in the second test of the Catching experiment where no significant increase in scores occurred in either group, and in the Junior Columbia Round for men in the Archery experiment, where both groups increased in scoring ability, but the group which had been taught the principle was significantly better at twenty yards.

These findings are in general agreement with those of some published investigations and are opposed to those of some others. However, most of the reported experiments have dealt with various types of learning other than motor learning. The ability to use understood principles in performing a motor skill presents a complex problem since more than one type of learning is involved. As Ragsdale has pointed out, a learner may understand a principle when applied to inanimate objects, but he may not understand and be able to apply it to his own movements. In general, it seems that the findings of this study support Ragsdale's observation, at least in the initial stages of acquiring an unfamiliar motor skill.

Conclusions

Within the limitations of the three parallel experiments which constitute the present investigation, there is no evidence:

1. That instruction concerning mechanical principles utilized in the performance of a motor skill faciltates the initial learning of the skill to any greater extent than an equivalent amount of time spent in practicing the skill.

2. That such knowledge facilitates subsequent learning as evidenced in the performance of a similar or more complicated skill to which the same principle is applicable.

However, since it appears that some part of the learning period may be devoted to instruction concerning general principles without detriment to the motor learning of the students, it would seem desirable to include such instruction in order to provide this additional opportunity for acquiring some related knowledge about principles of mechanics and the application of forces.

37. Learning Curves and Sequence of Skills *

JAMES DEESE, *The Johns Hopkins University*

Types of Learning Curves

There are many ways in which components of skills can be measured. For skills in which the components can be classified into errors and correct responses, curves can be plotted which show the way in which errors decrease with practice (trials) or the way in which correct responses increase. In addition we can plot curves which show the length of time it takes to complete a unit of practice at the task. This is the kind of curve one would obtain if the length of time it took an individual to assemble a jigsaw puzzle were measured. Obviously, time per trial decreases with practice, or we do not have evidence for learning. If, for example, the same individual assembled the same jigsaw puzzle several times in succession and there was no decrease in time of assembly, we should conclude that the individual had not shown evidence of learning to assemble the puzzle.

* By permission from James Deese, *The Psychology of Learning,* Second Edition, pp. 183–87. Copyright 1958 by McGraw-Hill Book Co., Inc., New York.

In many tasks we can obtain measures based upon both errors and time. In maze learning, for example, we can plot both the number of blind alleys a subject enters on a given trial and the time that it takes him to go through the maze.

In addition, in some tasks, we may be interested in plotting the way in which accuracy changes with an increase in the number of trials. If we were studying the ability of an individual to learn to fire at a stationary target, for example, we might plot a learning curve in terms of his deviation from the center of the target for each trial. Or, if an individual were tracking a constantly moving target, we might plot the amount of time he stayed on the target for each trial.

It should be noted that the measures of improvement are not all necessarily independent of one another. In maze learning, for example, number of errors and time per trial will be highly correlated. This is simply because the fewer the entrances into blind alleys, the less time it takes to go through the maze. There are fewer mechanical correlations as well. In general, for example, an increase in accuracy will go along with a decrease in the amount of time necessary to accomplish a unit of work. In other words, improvement in one aspect of a task is usually accompanied by improvement in other aspects as well. This is not necessarily so, but it is generally true of learning outside of the laboratory.

In addition there are many other changes in behavior during learning which often do not get charted. Usually there is a change in attitude of the individual toward the task. A task may be regarded as difficult at the outset of learning and as easy after much practice. There may be a change in the degree of tension which an individual shows during learning. In the beginning there may be much tension and anxiety which may be reduced by the learning of a task. Finally the mode of attack of the learner will most surely vary throughout the course of learning. Thus it is clear that there are many aspects of the change in performance with practice, and some of these are often ignored.

Many times learning curves are obtained by averaging together the performance of a number of individuals at each trial. The learning curve then is a kind of average learning curve. "Kind of average" is sometimes apt, for there are frequently serious distortions introduced by this procedure. This has been pointed out many times, most recently by Estes (1956). Most generally this is true because the form of the curve for averaged measurements is not necessarily the same as that for the individual subjects. For example, suppose we plotted learning curves for a group of individuals who always learned instantaneously (as would be the case if the learners had "insight"). Thus on some one trial an individual's score would go from zero to the maximum possible score. If some of these individuals learned at *different* trials, the result could be a smooth, gradual learning curve for the average of all these individuals. If we looked only at the average curve we should infer that the learning of this task proceeded in a gradual way, with, perhaps, more learning in the early trials than in the later trials.[1] Thus, because learning curves for individuals are not always the same as those for groups, we must be careful about the inferences we draw.

Plateaus

If we look at learning curves for individuals an interesting phenomenon occasionally turns up. This is illustrated by the curve in Figure 37. The task this individual was practicing was receiving telegraphic code. Notice that there was a period of about six weeks during which the subject did not appreciably increase his ability to receive code signals. After this period, there was a sudden spurt in letters received per minute which gradually leveled off to a final asymptote. Such a period of little or no improvement is known as a plateau.

The particular curve in Figure 37 comes from a well-known older study by Bryan and Harter (1897, 1899), who were trying to determine the reason for this plateau, which they thought fairly typical of learning tasks like receiving code. They put forward the notion that a plateau occurs when an individual has learned all of the primary skills in a complicated

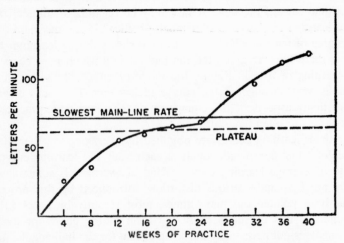

Figure 37. Learning curve for receiving telegraphic code. A plateau occurs in the middle of the curve just before the minimum rate is reached. (*After Bryan and Harter,* 1897.)

[1] This would be true if the distribution of occurrences of "insight" were logarithmic.

task but has not yet organized them into broader units so that he can learn the higher-order skills. They argued that learning any skill like telegraphy involves a hierarchy of habits; that is to say, the learning of the higher-order skills depends upon mastery of the lower-order skills. In learning to receive telegraphic code, for example, individuals first learn to receive individual letters. Then as they master the skill involved in this, they can take advantage of the redundancy, or predictability, in English and learn to receive by words instead of by letters. Finally, they can receive phrases or words as units.

Bryan and Harter argued that the plateau ought to occur at the transition between learning to receive individual letters and learning to receive words. They were able to justify this interpretation by a study of the way in which people learned to receive jumbled letters rather than real words. They found that the plateau for meaningful material occurred at just about the point at which there was no further improvement in the ability to receive disconnected letters and words. Thus, the plateau occurs where the limit on the lower-order habits has been reached and where the higher-order habits have not yet begun to appear. The results of this comparison of disconnected and connected material can be seen in Figure 38.

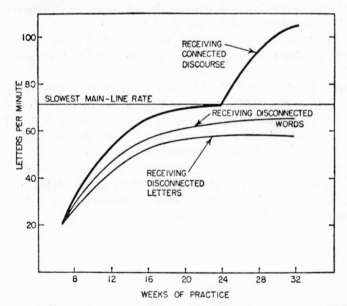

Figure 38. Learning curves for receiving connected discourse, disconnected words, and disconnected letters. Notice that the plateau in the curve for connected discourse occurs at the point where there is no further improvement in the curves for disconnected material. (*After Bryan and Harter, 1899.*)

It is obvious that the notion of hierarchy of habits is useful whether we are interested in plateaus or not. Something like this hieararchical structure must occur in all tasks in which there is opportunity to recode the material into larger and larger units. Thus, learning to typewrite, read music, and the basic skill of learning to read itself must involve something like hierarchies of habits.

Plateaus do not always occur. Indeed, in telegraphy they seem to be the exception rather than the rule (Taylor, 1943). The transition between orders of skills is more often a smooth one. Also, there seem to be other causes of plateaus in the learning curve. Swift (1918) argued that plateaus are caused by a decline in the learner's motivation. He pointed out that plateaus for all learners occur in about the same place; furthermore they occur in many tasks which do not involve a hierarchy of habits. Book (1925), in his handbook on learning to typewrite, located the lapses in attention and drop in motivation at the point where letter habits were making a transition into word habits. Thus the failure to improve generated discouragement, which furthered the failure to improve. Individuals may become so discouraged at failure to improve that they lose motivation for further practice. Indeed, plateaus may well be a fact which keeps adult learners from acquiring such skills as playing tennis or playing the piano. A well-motivated adult can learn the fundamentals of these skills quite easily, but there then follows a long period when devoted practice brings no fruits. At this point interest drops and the individual will cease taking lessons.

Frequently, the limit of performance which learners finally reach is a plateau. The author doubts that his typing has improved much in the past fifteen years, but there is certainly room for improvement. A little practice would eliminate some bad habits and bring in some new levels of organization which would no doubt quickly raise his level of typing. Thus, while he is currently at a limit of performance in typing, practice would raise that limit. There are surely real physiological limits to our ability to perform specific skills; we cannot type faster than our fingers will move. Most of us, however, seldom push ourselves to this limit.

38. Motor Paired-Associate Learning and Stimulus Pretraining [*][1]

HAYNE W. REESE,[†] State University of Iowa

SEVERAL studies (e.g., 1, 2, 6, 7) have indicated that performance on motor paired-associate task is facilitated if S first learns to associate distinctive verbal responses with the stimuli. Miller and Dollard's hypothesis that the acquired distinctiveness of cues (5) provides an explanation of this phenomenon and leads to the prediction that greater facilitation will result from (a) higher levels of learning in task I and (b) greater degrees of distinctiveness of the verbal responses learned in task I. The prediction is concerned with the effects of the transfer of specific associations; therefore, it is necessary to control the effects of performance set or nonspecific transfer in testing the prediction. It is assumed that the verbal responses provide cues and that these cues affect the similarity of the stimulus complexes. The probability that the cue-producing responses will be elicited in task II is presumably a function of the level of conditioning of these responses in task I. Further, if the cues are more distinctive than the stimulus complexes, the similarity of the complexes will be reduced by the addition of the cues that will be increased if the cues are less distinctive than the complexes.

Experimental evidence relevant to the first part of the prediction is inconclusive (1, 4). With respect to the second part of the prediction, one study (2) failed to obtain support, but two experiments by Norcross (7) provided support.

The specific predictions tested in the present experiment were: (a) With performance set controlled, a high level of pretraining will lead to better performance on task II than a low level, and the low level will lead to better performance than no pretraining. (b) There will be greater facilitation in a group that has learned distinctive names for the stimuli than in a group that has learned similar names for them.

[*] From Hayne W. Reese, "Motor Paired-Associate Learning and Stimulus Pretraining," *Child Development*, 31 (September, 1960), 505–13. Reprinted by permission.

[†] Department of Psychology, University of Buffalo, Buffalo 14, New York.

[1] This paper is based on a dissertation submitted to the Graduate College of the State University of Iowa in partial fulfillment of the requirements for the Ph.D. degree. The writer is indebted to Dr. Charles C. Spiker for his aid and advice throughout the course of the investigation.

Six stimuli were used in task II, four of which were also used in task I. In task I, one group learned to associate distinctive nonsense syllables with the stimuli, and a second group learned to associate similar nonsense syllables with the stimuli. Each S learned the associations with two stimuli to a high criterion in task I. The other stimuli were presented only one-third as many times as these two. In task II, Ss learned to associate button-pushing responses with the six stimuli.

Method

APPARATUS

The apparatus is essentially the same in operation and design as that described in detail by Spiker and Holton (9). It was designed to present motor paired-associate learning tasks in which S learns to associate push buttons with stimulus lights differing in hue. It consists of four parts: a stimulus-exposure unit, a response unit, a control box, and a timing unit. It permits the presentation of one stimulus at a time for a selected anticipation time interval, followed by a timed joint-presentation interval during which the stimulus is presented jointly with an informational light beside the correct button, followed in turn by a timed interstimulus interval. The S is instructed to respond prior to the onset of the informational light. A bell sounds immediately if the response is correct, and whether or not it is correct, the informational light is automatically turned on at the end of the anticipation interval.

The response unit consists of a black panel on which six push-buttons are arranged in a semicircle. A small 115-volt pilot (informational) lamp is located beside each button. The buttons are numbered, starting at the left, from one to six with one-inch high white numerals.

The stimulus-exposure unit contains on its front face a single aperture covered with flashed opal glass, through which stimulus lights differing in hue are filtered. Glass color filters obtained from the Corning Glass Company were used. The stimuli were two reds, a light red (No. 2434) and a dark red (No. 2030); two greens, a light green (No. 3718 and No. 4784) together and a dark green (No. 3384, No. 3389, and No. 5031); and two blue, a light blue (No. 5572) and a dark blue (No. 5543).

The task I response words were three-letter nonsense syllables. There were two pairs of similar syllables, *zim* and *zam* (pair A) and *wug* and *wog* (pair B), and two pairs of distinctive syllables, *lev* and *mib* (pair C) and *wug* and *zam* (pair D). In terms of common elements the within-pair similarity of the similar syllables is greater than their between-pair similarity, and both the between- and within-pair similarity of the distinctive syllables is low.

PROCEDURE

Pretraining task. The Ss were divided into two experimental groups. Group S learned to associate the similar syllables with the four stimulus lights used in task I, and group D learned to associate the distinctive syllables with these stimuli. The syllables of a given pair were associated with stimulus lights of similar hue.

The response unit was concealed throughout the pretraining task. The Ss were first taught the appropriate set of nonsense syllables and were then told which syllable was to be associated with each of the four stimuli. The stimuli were then presented one at a time in blocks of eight stimulus presentations. When S gave an incorrect response, he was told the correct syllable in the "joint-presentation" interval and was required to repeat it aloud. The joint-presentation and interstimulus intervals were each 2 seconds. The anticipation time was 4 seconds for the first 16 presentations, and was 2 seconds thereafter. During task I the bell signaled the end of the anticipation time, and correct responses were reinforced verbally by E.

In each block of stimulus presentations each of the two high-pretraining stimuli (the N_2 stimuli) was presented three times, and each of the two low-pretraining stimuli (the N_1 stimuli) was presented once. The learning criterion was two consecutive blocks with no errors to the N_2 stimuli, excluding the two blocks in which the anticipation time was 4 seconds. Therefore, each S was given at least four blocks of stimulus presentations, and, whatever the number of blocks required to reach criterion, the N_2 stimuli were presented three times more often than the N_1 stimuli. All Ss who failed to reach criterion within 20 blocks, excluding the first two blocks, were eliminated from the experiment.

Transfer task. Immediately after S reached the task I learning criterion, the response unit was placed in position in front of the stimulus-exposure unit and below the stimulus aperture. The procedure outlined along with the description of the apparatus was followed in task II. Only one response to each stimulus presentation was permitted. Training was continued until S reached a criterion of four consecutive errorless trials, or until he had been given 20 trials, whichever was sooner. A trial consisted of the presentation of all six stimuli in some order. A different order was used in each of the first six trials, after which the six orders were repeated. The anticipation time was 3 seconds throughout task II, and the joint-presentation and interstimulus intervals were each 2 seconds.

COUNTERBALANCING

To counterbalance syllable pairs with levels of pretraining, each of the two experimental groups was divided into two subgroups. A given pair of syllables was associated with the N_1 stimuli in one subgroup and with the N_2 stimuli in the other subgroup. These subgroups are designated S-I, S-II, D-I, and D-II, and each contained 18 Ss.

Each of the four subgroups was divided into nine further subgroups to counterbalance pairs of stimuli and pairs of buttons with the pretraining levels by the application of a Graeco-Latin square design. Each pair of stimuli and each pair of buttons was used once under each of the three pretraining levels in each of the four major subgroups. (The three pretraining levels in were High, Low, and None or N_0.) The button pairs were buttons 1 and 4, 2 and 5, and 3 and 6.

SUBJECTS

The Ss were 72 fourth-, fifth-, and sixth-grade school children obtained in a single public school in Ottumwa, Iowa.[2] They were assigned to the experimental groups in a random manner. Twelve additional Ss were eliminated, two because of procedural errors, and 10 because of failure to reach the task I criterion within the allotted number of presentations. Six of them were eliminated from group S-I, two from group D-I, and two from Group D-II.

Results

PRETRAINING TASK

Two questions relevant to the experimental hypotheses may be answered by examining the task I data. First, since groups S-I, S-II, D-I, and D-II learned to associate different pairs of syllables with the N_2 stimuli, it is possible that they differed in the number of stimulus presentations required to reach the task I criterion. If there were such differences, it is likely that task II performance would be differentially affected by differences in performance set. Secondly, the criteria used to construct the syllables differing in similarity, while probably adequate for visually presented materials, may be inadequate for materials presented orally as in the present

[2] The writer is indebted to Mr. R. O. Wright, Director of Curriculum, Ottumwa Public School System, Ottumwa, Iowa, for his generous permission to use the Ss of this experiment. Thanks are also due Mr. Cecil M. Van de Venter, Principal, Horace Mann Elementary School, and his teaching staff, for their fine cooperation in providing facilities and for their assistance in many other ways.

experiment. One measure which may be used to check the effective similarity of the syllables is the number of within-pair errors. A within-pair error is a response which is inappropriate to the stimulus presented, but appropriate to the stimuli similar in hue to the one presented.

The mean numbers of presentations of the N_2 stimuli required to reach the task I learning criterion are presented in the first line of Table 1. Group S-I required an average of about 36 per cent more presentations than the other groups, and the latter groups differed very little. Hence, the possibility of differential performance set must be considered in the analysis of the task II data.

Table 1

TASK I RESPONSE MEASURES

| | SYLLABLE PAIRS | | | |
| | Pair A | Pair B | Pair C | Pair D |
Response Measures	zim, zam	wug, wog	lev, mib	wug, zam
Mean Presentations of N_2 Stimuli	50.67	68.00	50.33	49.00
Mean Within-Pair Errors to N_2 Stimuli	4.94	10.11	1.89	2.56

NOTE—Pair A was associated with the N_1 stimuli in group S-I and the N_2 stimuli in group S-II. Pair B was associated with the N_1 stimuli in group S-II and the N_2 stimuli in group S-I. Pair C was associated with the N_1 stimuli in group D-I and the N_2 stimuli in group D-II. Pair D was associated with the N_1 stimuli in group D-II and the N_2 stimuli in group D-I.

The mean numbers of within-pair errors to the N_2 stimuli are given in the second line of Table 1. There were more within-pair errors on associations with pairs A and B, the similar pairs, than on those with pairs C and D, the distinctive pairs, and more on pair B than on pair A. Analysis of variance showed that the effect of syllable pairs was significant ($F = 9.90$; $df = 3, 60$; $p < .001$), and t tests, with the standard errors based on ms_w and with df of ms_w (3, p. 214), indicated that the mean for pair B was significantly greater than the other means ($t = 3.08$, 4.89, and 4.49 for the comparisons with pairs A, C, and D, respectively). Pair A did not differ significantly from pair C or D ($t = 1.82$, 1.42, respectively), and pairs C and D were not significantly different ($t < 1.00$). Hence, the effective within-pair similarity of pair B was greater than that of the other pairs, suggesting that the effect of similarity of syllables on transfer must be determined by comparison of individual pairs of syllables rather than combinations of pairs.

TRANSFER TASK

A within-pair error measure of task II performance is appropriate to the tests of the experimental hypotheses, and the measure selected was the percentage within-pair errors, defined as $100 \times$ number of within-pair errors on a given pair of stimuli divided by the total number of errors on that pair of stimuli.

The mean percentages are presented in Table 2, where a lower score reflects better performance. The best test of the effects of levels of pretraining is with groups D-I and D-II since the differences between these two groups on the task I measures were small and nonsignificant. Performance on the N_2 stimuli was about the same as that on the N_1 stimuli, but superior to that on the N_0 stimuli. This effect was statistically significant ($F = 5.26$; $df = 2, 36$). The mean for the N_0 level was significantly larger than the N_1 mean ($t = 2.79$; $df = 36$) and the N_2 mean ($t = 2.83$; $df = 36$), and the latter two means did not differ significantly ($t < 1.00$). Hence, both levels of pretraining with the distinctive syllables led to facilitation, but not to different amounts of facilitation.

Table 2

MEAN PERCENTAGE WITHIN-PAIR ERRORS ON TASK II

	LEVEL OF PRETRAINING		
Group	N_0	N_1	N_2
S-I	29.44	34.61	38.56
S-II	39.78	38.22	26.94
Both	34.61	36.42	32.75
D-I	43.61	39.39	31.28
D-II	49.11	28.28	36.06
Both	46.36	33.83	33.67

For the analysis of the effect of similarity of syllables, the possible differences in performance set among the groups were controlled by subtracting each S's N_1 and N_2 scores from his N_0 score. This adjustment yields direct measures of the effects of specific transfer, since the effects of nonspecific, transfer are subtracted out. The adjusted means are presented in Table 3, where a positive score represents facilitation. Pairs C and D have been combined, since the differences between these pairs on the task I measures were small and nonsignificant.

At the N_1 level there was greater facilitation with the combined distinctive syllables than with pair A or B, and slight interference with pair A.

At the N_2 level there was as much facilitation with pair A as with the combined distinctive syllables and interference with pair B. Differences between pairs of means were tested at each level of pretraining separately by analyses of variance. At the N_1 level the mean for the combined distinctive syllables was significantly greater than the pair A mean ($F = 4.25$ $df = 1, 36$), but not significantly different from the pair B mean ($F = 2.02$; $df = 1, 36$). The latter two means did not differ significantly ($F < 1.00$). At the N_2 level the mean for pair B was significantly smaller than the mean for pair A ($F = 6.79$; $df = 1, 36$) and the mean for the combined distinctive syllables ($F = 6.50$; $df = 1, 36$). The latter two means did not differ significantly ($F < 1.00$).

Table 3

ADJUSTED MEANS SHOWING SPECIFIC TRANSFER EFFECTS

Syllable Pairs	LEVEL OF PRETRAINING	
	N_1	N_2
Pair A	− 5.17	12.83
Pair B	1.56	− 9.11
Combined Distinctive Syllables	12.53	12.69

It was previously noted that both levels of pretraining with the distinctive syllables led to significantly greater facilitation than the no-pretraining condition. That is, pretraining with these syllables produced significant specific transfer. To test the significance of the specific transfer produced by pretraining with pairs A and B, the significance of the adjusted means for these pairs was determined with t tests, in which the standard errors of the means were based on the appropriate ms_w and with df of ms_w from the preceding analyses. At the N_1 level the adjusted means for pairs A and B were not significantly greater than zero ($ts < 1.00$). At the N_2 level the mean for pair A was significantly greater than zero ($t = 2.16$; $df = 36$), but the pair B mean was nonsignificant ($t = 1.53$; $df = 36$).

Discussion

Learning distinctive names for the stimuli led to facilitation of motor paired-associate learning in task II, but different levels of learning did not lead to different amounts of facilitation. With one of the pairs of similar syllables (pair A), facilitation was produced only by the high level of pretraining, and with the other pair (pair B) neither level of pretraining led to facilitation. The task I data indicated that pair A syllables were more distinctive than pair B syllables and suggested that the former were less distinctive than the pair C and pair D syllables; that is, pairs C and D were distinctive, pair B highly similar, and pair A syllables were of intermediate similarity. These findings suggest that the effect of level of pretraining depends on the similarity of the stimulus names learned in pretraining, more pretraining being required to produce facilitation the more similar the syllables are. There was no statistically reliable evidence that learning similar stimulus names led to interference with task II performance, but rather that it either had no effect or led to facilitation. These implications may be explained on the assumptions that, if the syllables are learned well enough to transfer to task II, facilitation will be produced, and overlearning the syllables will not increase the probability that they will transfer and therefore will not increase the facilitation; and that a higher level of learning is required to bring about transfer of similar syllables than distinctive ones. The facilitation produced, when the syllables transfer can be accounted for by the mechanism postulated by Miller and Dollard (5), increased distinctiveness of stimulus complexes by the addition of response-produced cues to the complexes. An alternative mechanism has been suggested by Spiker (8). If the names transfer to task II, *S* uses them to rehearse the stimulus-response connections during the interval between stimulus presentations. If the names are highly similar, they will not be used for rehearsal otherwise, they will be used, and facilitation will result.

Summary

It was predicted that better performance on a motor paired-associate task will result from (a) higher levels of verbal pretraining and (b) greater degrees of distinctiveness of the verbal responses learned during pretraining.

The *S*s were fourth-, fifth-, and sixth-grade school children. One group learned similar nonsense-syllable names for four stimuli in task I, and the second group learned distinctive nonsense-syllable names for the stimuli. Two of the association were learned to a high level, and the other two to a low level. In task II, *S*s learned to associate button-pushing responses with six stimuli, including the four pretraining stimuli and two nonpretraining stimuli. The latter served as a performance-set control.

It was found that the effect of level of pretraining depended on the similarity of the task I responses. For distinctive syllables each level of pretraining produced better performance on task II than the control condition, but increasing levels did not produce increasing amounts of facilitation. For syllables of intermediate similarity (as determined by task I analysis) only the high level of pretraining produced better performance than under control condition. For syllables of extreme similarity neither level of pre-training produced facilitation.

References

1. CANTOR, J. H. Amount of pretraining as a factor in stimulus preferentiation and performance set. *J. exp. Psychol.*, 1955, 180–184.
2. GERJUOY, I. R. Discrimination learning as a function of the similarity of the stimulus names. Unpublished doctoral dissertation, State Univer. of Iowa, 1953.
3. Lindquist, E. F. *Design and analysis of experiments in psychology and education.* Boston: Houghton Mifflin, 1953.

39. Straight and Crooked Thinking *

R. RODERICK PALMER, *Ohio State University*

ALTHOUGH the teaching of straight thinking is greatly emphasized by both traditionalists and progressives in education, the method by which this objective is to be achieved differs very sharply in the two groups. For many of the traditionalists, reliance is to be placed mainly upon the teaching of rhetoric and formal logic. For the progressives it is to be placed mainly upon the furnishing of daily experiences in solving problems by the scientific method. To a neutral it would seem that both kinds of training have their advantages. Even if it is true, as many conservatives maintain, that the use of the experimental method of science has very limited possibilities in the curriculum as a whole, it is still possible to make clear to the pupils its great advantages where it can be used. And if it is true, as the progressives maintain, that the study of formal deductive reasoning does little to improve the reasoning powers of the student, it is still possible that it can make him more keenly aware of the kinds of fallacious reasoning against which he is to guard himself in studying the conclusions of others. It may serve him well in his dealings with the paid propagandist.

Ambiguity is probably the commonest of all sources of difficulty. We are led to erroneous conclusions because the meaning of certain words shifts during the discussion without our noticing that it has done so. Ambiguities may sometimes be discovered by condensing an argument and reducing it to the form of a syllogism. A syllogism may be defined as three propositions

* From R. Roderick Palmer, "Straight and Crooked Thinking," *The Clearing House* (May, 1958), pp. 542–46. Reprinted by permission.

so related that one of them is involved or implied in the other two. In sound syllogistic reasoning the terms used must be employed in the same sense throughout. Other sources of difficulty are hypostatization, circular argument, special pleading, false analogy, false assumptions, feelings that dictate thinking, and cause-effect relationships.

False disjunction is one of the commonest of the misleading sorts of reasoning in education. We argue that we must either stress classical education or vocational education, and that since vocational education is inadequate, we must revert to classical or liberal education. The many other kinds of education possible to use we ignore. We argue that since the function of the university is not to develop athletes or to build character or to produce the fine gentleman or to train for a particular vocation, it must be to produce the thinker. The error again lies in assuming that we have stated all the alternatives.

Sometimes our error lies rather in ignoring intermediate stages. As Dewey has said, "Mankind likes to think in terms of extreme opposites. It is given to formulating its beliefs in terms of *Either-Ors,* between which it recognizes no intermediate possibilities. When forced to recognize that the extremes cannot be acted upon, it is still inclined to hold that they are all right in theory but that when it comes to practical matters circumstances compel us to compromise. Educational philosophy is no exception. The history of educational theory is marked by opposition between the idea that education is development from within and that it is formation from without; that it is based upon natural endowments and that education is a process of overcoming natural inclination and substituting in its place habits acquired under external pressure." [1]

Just as in politics we force a choice between democracy and communism, without inquiring how much these doctrines have in common and how much each might assist in removing the deficiencies of the other, and a choice between private enterprise and public ownership, without considering the possibility that for some industries one might be better and for other industries the other. So in education we insist on a choice between doctrines as wholes. The remedy is not compromise. It is not a resort to eclecticism. It lies in a more careful study of the facts as they are, and inquiry as to whether all alternatives have been considered and all intermediate stages examined.

We need to stop debating whether a given man is normal or subnormal in intelligence, as if these stages were sharply divided, and to recognize that intelligence shades off very gradually from genius to imbecile in degrees

[1] John Dewey, *Experience and Education* (New York: The Macmillan Co., 1938), p. 1.

that can be represented by an unbroken curve. We need similarly to recognize that there is the same unbroken transition from those called sane to those called insane.

Educationists with their love for clear distinctions have too long attempted to settle vexing questions by choosing among specious alternatives. Even in their researches they frequently go no farther than to demonstrate that one familiar method of teaching is better than another, ignoring the possibility that a third or fourth is immensely superior to either. Conclusions drawn from the method of disjunction should always be stated with their limitations. They indicate only that one alternative is better than another, that one alternative must be accepted if we can be sure that all the others have been duly considered, and so on. Ordinarily we cannot from such evidence draw any conclusions that are forthright and unqualified.

So far we have been concerned with developing ability to evaluate the thinking done by others. Let us now consider the possibility of developing the pupil's ability to think for himself. Perhaps in the long run one of his best defenses against propaganda and crooked thinking is an offense, an independent investigation of his own problems.

That an improvement in thinking power can be effected seems to be indicated by the results obtained in experimental schools. The investigations by J. W. Wrightstone and by the Evaluation Staff of the Eight-Year-Study of the Progressive Education Association appear to indicate that when the development of power in constructive thought is taken as a definite objective and intelligently striven for, such development can be secured. As the belief in the "constancy of the IQ" fades out before other experimental evidence, hope for a contrived enhancement of the average man's capacity for constructive thinking seems more and more thoroughly justified.

Teaching children to do constructive thinking has meant in experimental schools giving them practice and help in carrying on the kind of investigations that we have just seen to be engaged in by persons whose thinking has proved successful. As they make such investigations, the pupils are studied by their teachers, their individual deficiencies with reference to any of the various stages of thinking are located, sometimes with the aid of objective tests, and remedial measures are undertaken. Thus the teaching of thinking appears to proceed very much like that teaching which has been found valuable in reaching other educational objectives. Although such work is comparatively new and is still in the experimental stage in many schools, we may delineate a few of the measures which have so far proved most effective.

(1) To develop the pupil's ability to recognize and formulate problems,

he must be given a considerable amount of experience with unorganized materials and encouraged to state clearly the problems arising therefrom. Such experiences can be furnished by the shop or laboratory, the excursion, the film, the interview, or by written statements giving incomplete descriptions and inconsistent explanations. Practice in stating problems clearly can be given the pupil by such devices as asking him to look for topic sentences in his reading; placing him in contact with confused accounts of an issue in which he has become interested; allowing him to study the irrelevancies of court testimony and the many restatements of the issue by the attorneys in the case, and similarly to study the records of hearings of legislative committees and the attempts of the committee members to keep the issues in sharp focus; permitting the pupil to act as chairman of discussion groups and to practice the same art himself; encouraging him to state clearly the problems torturing a confused and futile character in fiction; assisting him to state clearly the issues in propaganda which deliberately attempts to divert attention to irrelevancies more likely to win approval; and using similar devices commonly employed in progressive schools but ignored in those traditional schools which believe it the duty of the teacher or the textbook to supply a clear initial statement of the problem that is to be attacked.

(2) To develop the pupil's ability to collect data bearing on the problem before him, it is necessary to develop his power to observe accurately and his skill in using printed sources of information. But since "the essential condition of better seeing is definiteness of purpose," [2] the requisite sharpening of observation will usually be attained through that clarification and amplification of his problem which we have just described. Skill in the use of printed materials may be developed by systematic instruction and practice.

To develop the ability to use the library intelligently, the teacher may construct practice exercises involving questions on the classification of books and the order in which they are arranged in an open-shelf library, on the intelligent use of the card catalogue, on the principal reference books and source books, and on general type of content characteristic of the leading periodicals.

(3) To develop the pupil's ability to originate promising hypotheses, it is necessary to supply at the very minimum the time in which reflection may take place. Though this fact seems too obvious to be stated, many teachers rush so rapidly from one topic to another, in an effort to "cover the ground," that no real opportunity for thought is provided. Since fer-

[2] M. T. McClure, *How to Think in Business* (New York: McGraw-Hill Book Co., Inc., 1923), p. 51.

tility in ideas depends partly on native ability and partly on familiarity with the field in question, it is obvious that if we cannot increase our inherent brightness we can at least increase our knowledge of relevant facts.

A valuable habit to develop is that of occasional complete relaxation. After the problem is put aside, say many men of originality, and you are engaged in something else, excellent ideas often come to you as from a clear sky. Many times has this tale been told. A relaxed state of the organism may be important in mental as in athletic achievement. A class enterprise that is engrossing enough to absorb the pupil's efforts for several weeks may thus be expected in the course of time to produce some first-class ideas. If it is impossible to force the appearance of ideas—as indeed it is—at least certain of the conditions can be provided which, experience has shown, are likely to be favorable to the appearance of ideas.

(4) To develop the pupil's ability to trace out the implications of hypotheses or tentative solutions the teacher, after calling attention to the way clever investigators have followed out "leads," may well permit class discussion of proposed solutions for a problem within the group's interests, in order that the richness of relationship of the simplest proposal may become evident. Here again the teacher will need to restrain his impatient urge to teach more facts. For if the pupils learn how to solve problems systematically, they learn something much more important than other people's solutions of given problems. They learn a method which may enable them to solve their most important problems after all factual instruction has been forgotten.

Class discussion allows the various implications of a given proposal to be discovered and pointed out by the various types of persons within the group. What is not seen by one may be seen by another. But precautions must be taken against making the pupils dependent upon discussion for ideas. In some schools this sort of work is carried so far that individuals are unable to think alone. To counteract such a tendency, it is desirable that for some of the problems the individual pupils be required to work toward a solution without the aid of others. Practice in following out the implications of proposed solutions is as necessary as practice in any other phase of intellectual work.

The qualities most important to develop here are thoroughness and persistence in exploring all possibilities. These are an aspect of intellectual honesty. They insure a careful and systematic examination of the implications of an hypothesis to reach an understanding of all that is involved in it. They prevent hasty conclusions and thoughtless action that may be harmful either to oneself or to others.

Through the study of sound and unsound syllogisms, the pupil may be helped to distinguish, in certain types of cases, those implications which are genuinely involved in a hypothetical solution and those which are only apparently involved. Attention may be called both to characteristic errors in deductive reasoning and to intentional distortions of the issue to lead attention away from sound inferences.

(5) To develop the pupil's ability to verify his conclusions, the school must keep closely in touch with real problems. Preschool and kindergarten children rarely fail to test out their theories. Ideas there arise in concrete situations and are immediately put into effect, and their soundness or unsoundness is at once evident. As problems become more bookish and further removed from reality, the tendency to verify one's decisions is lost. Conclusions are reached but not acted upon or otherwise checked up.

To restore the normal tendency to verify one's conclusions by some sort of overt action, it is primarily desirable to change the curricular emphasis from a series of subjects to a series of activities, projects, enterprises, investigations, and the like. This shift means the frank acknowledgment that to "master the race experience" as a set of facts is no longer possible and that such an undertaking should be replaced by the attempt to learn the most successful method by which these facts have been acquired. This method involves the validation of conclusions.

The teacher must also abandon outright that Herbartian variety of teaching in which, after the examination of a considerable number of concrete instances, the solution is assumed to roll out into clear sight, to be obviously true, and to wait not for validation but only for "application." It is necessary to recognize that the most obvious Herbartian "generalization" is in need of verification before it can be given more than tentative acceptance.

How this verification can be done is clear enough in those activities in which we make or do something—informal constructions, more technical shop practice, still more technical laboratory experimentation. It is clear in mathematics. The difficulties lie in the social sciences and the humanities. But here, too, improvement on current practice is possible.

In the social sciences the teacher can make evident the desirability of verification by encouraging the pupils to carry over their own conclusions from the schoolroom and try them out whenever possible in the community. The teacher can do much toward this result by lending particular encouragement to those proposed activities which promise to eventuate in conclusions that will be thus testable. He can also be of help by enabling the pupils to leave the school building and make a test of their ideas by lending aid to local improvements. So the conception of money saving through co-operative buying may lead to the formation of buyers' cooperatives in the community, as the study of health may lead to better nutrition in the homes or to the establishment of a medical clinic.

In the humanities the pupils can be shown that masterpieces are not masterpieces because they meet certain rules of writing or painting or the like, but because they achieve certain effects, attain certain objectives. Their effectiveness in reaching these objectives can be tested only by producing them and trying them out on those for whom they were made.

When young people have been habituated by daily practice to the use of systematic reflective thought and have found by experience how sound ideas originate and how they are verified, they are probably better prepared as citizens than by any other kind of training we might give them. They are independent of the propagandist in certain areas because they can think their own problems through. They are constructive.

They can not only fend against the crooked thinking of others but forge out a piece of straight thinking of their own. They will probably be able to stand on their own feet and they will probably be willing to co-operate with others in adult life as they have done through their school life.

40. The Learning of Concepts *

JAMES DEESE, *The Johns Hopkins University*

THE WORLD presented through our senses is a vast jumbled confusion of different sensations. We are able to deal with it only by cutting it down to the size of our own mental processes. The primary way we do this is by setting up equivalences and identities among separate parts of our experience. In short, we categorize and assign names to the categories. Thus, the deep maroon color of the book on my desk and the tomato-colored stripes in my tie both are characterized as "red." This process of categorizing so that all the infinite variety of the external world may be dealt with by our mental processes and language, is one of the most essential elements in human thinking. We call this process *concept attainment,* or *concept formation.* In the next few pages we shall examine some of the experimental

* By permission from James Deese, *The Psychology of Learning,* Second Edition, pp. 291–93. Copyright 1958 by McGraw-Hill Book Co., Inc., New York.

literature on concept attainment and see how special problems in the organization of concepts are related to the basic principles of learning.

FORMING CONCEPTS

Categorization. Most of us are so familiar with the conceptual categorization of our world that we do not stop to think about the process of arriving at categories. We may even naïvely believe that our conceptual categories have independent existence. The habit of accepting the reality of conceptual categories may be so firmly established that it will interfere with scientific progress and thinking. Only in the past few years have systematic biologists generally come to the view that "species" of animals are not fixed classes into which animals do or do not belong, but rather that "species" are simply convenient classes into which we can group animals with similar characteristics. Nature is often continuous and will not fit the boundaries of our categories. Thus, frequently there is a continuous gradation in essential characteristics from one species of animals to another.

Every college student at one time or another has run into a homely example of the conflict between categories and the continuity of things. Registrars and deans demand that instructors categorize students in classes usually labeled A, B, C, D, and F. There may be only the faintest difference between the student with the highest B and the lowest A, but because human society and thinking cannot function with continuously graded events, and must resort to categorization, we are required to place these students in different classes.

We form classes by isolating attributes of things which are to be classed as identical or equivalent. There are two ways of doing this. We may take a heterogeneous collection of things and examine them for common attributes so that we can sort them into classes, or we may come to examine a number of things with some preconceived notion about the classes into which they ought to be placed. In either case, we assign names to the classes (thus recoding our experience).

Our categorization is usually done in accordance with social reinforcement. Thus, children learn at an early age to discriminate between dogs, cats, and rabbits, though they may make mistakes during the early stage of learning to assign the proper names to the individual animals.

Learning conceptual categories. Osgood (1953) reminds us that the formation of concepts involves verbal mediating responses which permit us to recode the continuity of our experience. The classical experimental literature on the formation of concepts has dealt with the ways in which such verbal mediating responses are established.

For example, Hull (1920) studied the way in which students learned to find identity relationships between stimuli possessing common elements. He presented subjects with Chinese characters paired in a certain way with English words. Chinese characters are compounded of certain elements, called radicals. These may vary in position or size within the character, but whenever they are present it means that the character has something in common with other characters which also contain the same radical. They are roughly analogous to certain syllables (mainly suffixes) in English. Thus, the words "repeat" and "return" have in common a syllable (actually, a bounded morpheme) which carries the connotation of coming back over the same event. In Hull's experiment, whenever a certain radical occurred it was always combined with a certain English word. The problem for the subjects was to recognize and associate the radical with the appropriate English word.

As might be supposed, such learning is much the same as any other kind of paired-associate learning. There were, however, some cases in which subjects obviously had learned to associate the proper English word with the proper radical, but these subjects could not recognize the radical. Thus they were reacting to something they could not verbalize. They had learned the correct pairing of the Chinese characters with English words, but they had not acquired a mediated recognition of this.

Other experimenters (Heidbreder, 1924; Smoke, 1932) have studied the role of hypothesis formation in the discovery of concepts. Smoke (1932) reports that his subjects systematically tested and rejected a number of hypotheses—thus making use of transfer—until they finally came upon one which gave them enough correct responses to be satisfying. Heidbreder (1924) emphasized the fact that the learner does not always have to be actively engaged in hypothesis formation in order to arrive at a solution of the problem. In especially difficult problems some subjects engaged in what Heidbreder called "spectator" behavior; these subjects would resign themselves to responses which were more or less random and would spend their time in passive observation of the material presented to them. Under these conditions, subjects eventually solved the problems. Thus a period of quiescent observation may be just as valuable as a period of active hypothesis formation.

41. Confusion and Problem Solving *

WILLIAM J. PAULI, *Woodrow Wilson Junior High School, San Jose, California*

A STUDENT solves a problem when his initial state of confusion ends in understanding. If his initial state is understanding, he is not confronted with a problem. If the terminal state is confusion, the student has not solved the problem.

Relating confusion to problem solving is not a new thought. Professor Brownell, in defining problems, included this sentence in his definition: "The subject experiences perplexity in the problem situation, but he does not experience utter confusion." [1] In the same thoughtful article Professor Brownell stressed the subjective character of problems. One student's difficult problem may be another student's simple exercise. The subjective nature of problems adds another element of confusion to teaching.

John Dewey in his classic work on the thinking process wrote: ". . . The origin of thinking is some perplexity, confusion, or doubt." [2] According to Dewey, confusion, the feeling of difficulty in a situation, is the stimulus as well as the origin of thinking. Without this felt difficulty, appeals to an individual to think would be futile.

My purpose is to discuss problems and problem solving explicitly in terms of the confusion surrounding both. As a classroom teacher I see confusion and the subjective character of problems revealed both visibly and audibly on the brows and lips of my students. As a teacher searching for better ways of teaching the solution of problems, I find myself threading through a maze of confusion on the meaning of problems, their uses, their uselessness, their psychology, the opinions of experts, and the contradictory opinion of other experts.

Everybody would agree that learning to think and learning to solve problems are the highest and most important objectives of education. While all would agree on the objectives, few would reach these objectives by the same route. Indeed, there are some who even doubt whether thinking and problem solving can actually be taught. Such doubts—most teachers at

* From William J. Pauli, "Confusion and Problem Solving," *The Clearing House* (October, 1960), pp. 79–82. Reprinted by permission.
[1] William A. Brownell, "Problem Solving," *The Psychology of Learning*, 41st Yearbook, Part II, National Society for the Study of Education (Chicago, 1942), p. 416.
[2] John Dewey, *How We Think* (Boston: D. C. Heath and Co., 1910), p. 12.

some period of their life must experience such doubts—present the teacher with a most frustrating contradiction. If thinking and problem solving are the noblest objectives of education, and if these objectives cannot be taught, how then can they be reached? The solution of this contradiction begins with confusion and ends with the creation of necessary weapons to overcome the confusion. Before we trace the connection of confusion to problem solving, let us define our terms more clearly.

Problem Solving and Problems Defined

Problem solving as used here denotes all learning of a conceptual nature. Problems may be solved alone by the student or they may be solved with the help of the teacher. When the student is taught how a particular problem is solved, he learns how others have solved the problem. The skill of the teacher in that case determines how much problem solving takes place in the mind of the student and how much takes place in the mind of the teacher. The latter may take a flying trip with the student to reach the destination; or he may lead the student by the hand, pointing out the interesting and important landmarks along the way, the bridges that link vital centers, and the foundations on which the connecting links rest. In this case the teacher is more concerned with the student's acquiring expert knowledge of the terrain and the route traveled than he is with the final destination. When to fly and when to explore are themselves problems for the teacher. The student and teacher do not always agree on the best way of traveling.

I like Professor Fehr's short definition of a problem as a "situation in which there is need for attaining a goal, but the route to the goal is unknown." [3]

Professor Fehr believes that problem consciousness needs to be developed in the student. What a good problem attitude should be he states in these words: "A problem is something with which I am supposed to have difficulty. It is a situation which I must explore to bring to bear all my past learning in order to get the answer. It will take a little time and a lot of thinking to solve it." [4]

The literature on problem solving often arises out of the attempts to make the solution of problems in mathematics easier and more palatable. Regardless of how the issue is approached, whether from the standpoint of interest, need, or meaning, the objective is to improve the problem-solving

[3] Howard F. Fehr, "Teaching the Solution of Verbal Problems in Algebra," California Mathematics Council *Bulletin*, XII (May, 1954), p. 2.
[4] *Ibid.*, p. 4.

ability of the student. This is as it should be. We want to be able to transform problems, which are initially confusing and difficult, into tasks that are clear, simple, and easy. Problem solving may be defined as the process of transforming the difficult into the easy, the complex into the simple, and the confusing into the clear and understandable. Teachers who are searching for ways of teaching the solution of problems free of the element of confusion are seeking in vain for a modern philosopher's stone. It is the characteristic of problems to be confusing, as it is the characteristic of the whole to contain parts.

Conclusions on the nature of problem solving are by no means limited to mathematics, but are applicable to all fields where problems exist. Indeed, it is precisely the conviction that problem solving is a general process which keeps alive the hope that a mastery of the process will improve the amount of transfer of learning. No one, of course, any longer believes that exercising some particular faculty of the mind is the path through which maximum transfer can be accomplished. Nevertheless, faculty psychology, like the old soldier, never completely dies, but merely fades away to reappear in modern dress. Instead of exercising the mind on "tough" subjects the modern version is to learn all about a process called "problem solving," master this process, and then use this knowledge as a master key to unlock all doors labeled "Problems."

Serious writers on problem solving—most writers on this topic are quite serious—would emphatically disclaim any intent to fabricate a magic wand with which to solve any and all problems. Yet these same writers would readily agree that their hope is to improve or to facilitate the solution of problems. How can this be done without creating the illusion that problem solving is an "it" whose mastery will open even the strangest doors? Can problem solving really be taught? Or to phrase the question in a more answerable light, what is there in the study of the problem-solving process which is most likely to be useful in all problem situations? This last question is much more modest in its hope and expectations, and, for that very reason, more conducive of a fruitful answer. In answering this question, we shall find that confusion is the one common ingredient in all problem situations. Wherever there are problems begging to be solved, there will be found people in various states of confusion. In the broadest sense, thinking, problem solving, and transfer of learning are synonymous terms in which individuals are confronted by confusion. The process of thinking, of solving problems, of discovering identical and related elements in seemingly unrelated and different situations is the process of overcoming confusion.

Confusion Defined

Confusion is used here in the sense of a discomfiture of mind, a state of being disconcerted, of experiencing perplexity, doubt, and uncertainty. Confusion is not used here in the psychiatric sense of a mental state characterized by unstable attention, poor perception of reality, disorientation, and inability to act coherently. The former state implies that the individual has the intelligence and experience to penetrate the confusion blocking his goal. The latter state applies to the confusion of patients who need clinical help. The confusion in their case is so overwhelming, or their perception of reality so poor, that they see no problem and experience no confusion. The confusion in their situation is noted by the observer.

The confusion we are concerned with is the subjective confusion of the learner as he faces a problem. We are, of course, also concerned with objective forms of confusion which prevent active and concerted concentration. The confusion which we couple with bedlam is the objective kind of confusion we try to avoid, because that kind of confusion obstructs problem solving. There is one kind of objective confusion which does grow out of the subjective confusion of the learner. Not all students can contain their excitement within bounds. Excessive confusion within the immature creates visible agitation. This outward manifestation of inward confusion appears whenever problems are not solved within reasonable time limits. Some students can stand inward confusion only a short time before they demonstrate their capacity to stand external confusion a much longer period of time. Daily the teacher faces the problem of providing exactly the right kind of confusion. In one case the students may not have the necessary background to overcome the confusion; in other cases the confusion is not great enough to be challenging. Dewey expressed the mental juggling the teacher must practice in these words: "The best thinking occurs when the easy and difficult are duly proportioned to each other. The easy and familiar are equivalents, as are the strange and the difficult. Too much that is easy gives no ground for inquiry; too much of the hard renders inquiry hopeless." [5]

Learning to mix the easy and difficult, the clear and the confusing, so that they are "duly proportioned to each other," means learning to become an effective teacher. This kind of mixing problem always exists in teaching. It is the most important aspect of the problem of individual differences. The question here is that of producing the most effective kind of thinking by providing the most carefully organized material fitted to the learner's

[5] Dewey, op. cit., p. 222.

past experience out of which can grow the most fruitful inquiry. The difference between a good teacher and a poorer one is that the former solves this mixing problem more often than does the latter. The effective teacher anticipates the kind of confusion the learner is capable of overcoming and plans his lesson accordingly. The teacher who wants his students to pause and reflect must set the stage and frame the goal in such a way that the answer the student is made to seek corresponds to the solution the understanding teacher wishes him to discover. This is no simple trick but one which calls forth the highest creative talents of the teacher. The role of science and methodology is in organizing the material to be learned and in mapping the terrain with necessary landmarks to help the faltering explorer maintain his quest. The teacher can help the student most by exciting him enough to make the solution of the problem both fascinating and possible.

Confusion Resolved

For any individual the key to successful problem solving lies in his attitude toward confusion. For all of us, no matter what the problem might be, in whatever field we might be engaged, if we desire the solution of the problem seriously enough, we must also decide at the same time how much confusion we can stand. We can learn to overcome confusion or we can be overcome by it. The first step in overcoming confusion is to acquire a realistic attitude toward it. Part of this attitude is a skepticism of all approaches to problem solving which purport to be clear and simple. Techniques which remove the confusion from problems are at best methods of reaching the goal without knowledge of the path. Shortcuts through dense forests are sometimes necessary, but if the necessary is understanding of the forest, shortcuts will enable us to see the least. In learning, our objective is not merely to reach a specific goal, an answer which can be found in a book or which someone can tell us, but to attain understanding of the relationships which connect the answer to the question. In personal problems, such as a painful illness, relief from pain is our only quest. How the physician solves the problem for us is purely academic and of little interest except to those who like to dwell upon their operations.

In solving problems we move from the complex to the simple. Simplicity is always an ultimate goal, but to reach this goal many problems have to be solved and much confusion overcome. Simplicity follows understanding and does not precede it. The teacher, of course, has the obligation and the problem of breaking the complex into simple steps which the learner can follow. Only after the learner has followed in the footsteps of those whose knowledge of the terrain is superior to his can he arrive at the simplicity which is the result of understanding. The more the learner is led to discover each step along his path of learning, the greater will be his confusion and the greater will be his conquest.

The desire to make our teaching problems simple and free of confusion will always prove to be chimerical. The more difficult the learning, the more confusion both teacher and learner must learn to overcome. Teaching of problem solving, or, perhaps more accurately, providing fruitful problem-solving experiences for pupils, will never become a simple effortless task. To be sure, specific problems can be solved very often in extremely simple ways. For the teacher, the key question must always be: Simple for whom? For the teacher or for the learner? An equally important question must also be: Is the simplest method the one in which the most learning takes place? New knowledge, new research, and more discovery can bring us more effective ways of overcoming confusion. We should not expect to learn new ways of avoiding confusion unless we are also resigned to avoiding learning. Confusion is not to be regarded as an intrusion to make problem solving needlessly difficult, but as the essential barrier to hurdle. Confusion is the catalytic agent that generates the problem-solving process, and thinking is the solvent.

42. *Judgment of Size in Relation to Geometric Shape* *

BETSY WORTH ESTES, †[1] *University of Kentucky*

THIS IS an investigation of perceived size comparisons for figures of the same shape and figures of different shape.

Previous investigators have studied the development of simple perceptual tasks, such as the ability of very young children to select the middle size

* From Betsy Worth Estes, "Judgment of Size in Relation to Geometric Shape," *Child Development*, 32 (June, 1961), 277–86. Reprinted by permission.

† Department of Psychology, University of Kentucky, Lexington.

[1] The author is appreciative of the statistical assistance given by the Computing Center, University of Kentucky.

of three shapes (3, 8, 9), and concepts of roundness (4) and of largest size (5). In these studies the authors were concerned essentially with the development of meanings, of concepts.

Many studies have been concerned with judgment of size as related to constancy and thus to learning and concept formation. Some have questioned whether the tasks which have been used are of a simple perceptual nature or whether more complex judgment is involved. Relevant variables which have been investigated are the experimental situation, attitudes of subjects, age, and intelligence. Osgood agrees with Boring (1) that Martius' almost perfect constancy "looks more nearly like judgment than immediate perception" (6, page 275). The kind of situation set for Ss apparently influences the degree of constancy. Brunswik (2) used a quite natural situation in which Ss were instructed to select from a number of cubical blocks the one which appeared equal in size to the standard. In this natural situation, Ss showed considerable constancy. Thouless (7) has been interested in the distinction between object-orientation and critical-stimulus orientation and found that the former is associated with an increase in constancy, whereas the critical-stimulus attitude is used more by professional artists and results in less constancy. Thouless hypothesized that the engineer, because of his practical training, will come closer to the "real" aspects of objects and will thus show more "phenomenal regression" toward these "real" characteristics. The increase of constancy with increase in age has been studied, but the results are conflicting. Osgood (6) reports that Burzloff, in a natural situation, using both adults and children, found (a) a high level of constancy and (b) no significant differences according to age. Osgood states: "Considerable interest has attached to the age variable . . . this whole question is very much up in the air at this time" (6, page 279). The influence of intelligence may be concomitant with increase in age.

The present study approximates the natural situation and object-oriented attitude in the task presented and in the instructions given to Ss and includes both children and adults. However, it is not concerned with the usual variables found in constancy experiments, namely, distance and retinal shape and angle.

This study investigated (a) accuracy of judgments of same-shaped figures and (b) the bases or cues used to estimate equality of different-shaped figures, e.g., comparing the size of a square with a circle or comparing the size of a circle with a triangle. Comparing here means comparing in direct perception, not by measurement or computation. There are several possibilities. A person may base his judgment on estimated areas or the diameter of a circle may be equated with the side of an equilateral triangle. Still another possibility is that a figure may be compared with another by inscribing or circumscribing. Such specific possibilities are termed the pre-designated figures and are included in the variable series.

Subjects

Table 1 presents the grade levels, ages, and number of *S*s in each group. None of the *S*s in the Arts and Sciences group had had geometry; all the engineering students had had geometry and were in their second semester of mechanical drawing. Each group except the engineers included males

Table 1

SUBJECTS

Grade	MEAN AGE			N
	Years	Months	Range	
Kindergarten	6	1	± 3 months	15
Second	7	3	± 3 months	15
Fourth	9	5	± 4 months	15
Sixth	11	5	± 3 months	15
Eighth	14	3	± 2 months	15
Arts and Sciences students				15
Engineering students				15
All subjects				105

and females. The children attend the University School of the University of Kentucky; from the experience of the author in intelligence testing at this school, a conservative estimate of the mean Stanford-Binet IQ is 120. The adults, of course, are college students.

Method

*S*s were presented a standard figure (a triangle, a square, or a circle) and were asked to select, from a series varying in size, called the variable series, the figure most nearly equal to the size of the standard figure. Each *S* made a total of 135 judgments. Forty-five of these judgments were similar-figure trials; i.e., the standard figure and the variables were the same shape. The remaining 90 trials were different-figure trials (e.g., the standard figure might be a triangle to be compared with a variable series of circles).

Both the standard series and the variable series were constructed of lemon yellow, antique finish, 80 weight, Buckeye cover paper obtained from the Beckett Paper Company, Hamilton, Ohio.

The standard series consisted of five of each of the following forms: equilateral triangles 15 inches on a side, 10 inches on a side, 5 inches on a side; squares, 15 inches on a side, 10 inches on a side, 5 inches on a side; and circles, 15 inches in diameter, 10 inches in diameter, and 5 inches in diameter. Thus, there were three shapes and three sizes of each shape making nine different combinations. Five random orders of this 45-member

Table 2

SIZES OF THE VARIABLE SERIES

Triangles		Squares		Circles	
22.80*	12.00	20.00	9.87*	20.00	9.00
21.21*	11.55*	19.00	9.19*	19.00	8.66*
20.20*	11.00	18.00	9.00	18.00	8.00
20.00	10.00*	17.00	8.66*	17.31*	7.42*
19.00	9.00	16.00	8.00	16.92*	7.00
18.00	8.66*	15.00*	7.00*	16.00	6.00
17.32	8.00*	14.00	6.58*	15.00*	5.64*
17.00	7.60*	13.26*	6.00*	14.00	5.00*
16.33*	7.00*	13.00*	5.00*	13.00*	4.33*
16.00	6.73*	12.00	4.43*	12.00	4.00*
15.00*	6.00	11.31*	4.00	11.55*	3.00*
14.00*	5.77*	11.00	3.54*	11.28*	
13.47*	5.00*	10.61*	3.00*	11.00*	
13.00*	4.33*	10.00*		10.00*	

NOTE—Values indicate length in inches of sides of equilateral triangles, sides of squares, and diameters of circles.
   * Predesignated values.

standard series were prepared; each S was examined with three of these orders.

There were three variable series: squares, circles, and triangles. The size gradations in linear measurements are shown in Table 2. The size intervals are not equal.

In each series, certain predesignated sizes are indicated by asterisks in Table 2. The other values in Table 2 were inserted to provide series of sufficient length and of a higher level of difficulty than was possible with only the predesignated sizes. Table 3 shows the precise values for figures of different shapes when different cues are used as the standard of equality; these are the predesignated values in Table 2. The predesignated figures were constructed to the nearest 0.1 inch; there was no figure constructed whose linear dimension was larger than 22.80 inches because material that large could not be obtained.

Table 3

EXPLANATION OF PREDESIGNATED VALUES

Standard	Variable	Possible Cues	15-Inch Size	10-Inch Size	5-Inch Size
Triangle ..	Squares ...	Side of T = side of S	15.00	10.00	5.00
		Altitude of T = side of S	12.99	8.66	4.33
		Side of T = diagonal of S	10.61	7.07	3.54
		Altitude of T = diagonal of S ..	9.19	6.12	3.06
		Area of T = area of S	9.87	6.58	3.29
Triangle ..	Circles	Side of T = diameter of C	15.00	10.00	5.00
		Altitude of T = diameter of C ..	12.99	8.66	4.33
		Area of T = area of C	11.14	7.42	3.72
		C inscribed in T	8.66	5.77	2.89
		C circumscribed around T	17.31	11.55	5.77
Square ...	Triangles ..	Side of S = side of T	15.00	10.00	5.00
		Diagonal of S = side of T	21.21	14.14	7.07
		Side of S = altitude of T	17.32	11.55	5.77
		Diagonal of S = altitude of T ..	24.49	16.33	8.16
		Area of S = area of T	22.80	15.19	7.60
Square ...	Circles	Side of S = diameter of C	15.00	10.00	5.00
		Diagonal of S = diameter of C ..	21.21	14.14	7.07
		Area of S = area of C	16.92	11.28	5.64
Circle	Triangles ..	Diameter of C = side of T	15.00	10.00	5.00
		Diameter of C = altitude of T ..	17.32	11.55	5.77
		Area of C = area of T	20.20	13.47	6.73
		T inscribed in C	12.99	8.66	4.33
		T circumscribed around C	25.98	17.32	8.66
Circle	Squares ...	Diameter of C = side of S	15.00	10.00	5.00
		Diameter of C = diagonal of S ..	10.61	7.07	3.54
		Area of C = area of S	13.26	8.86	4.43

NOTE—T = triangle, S = square, C = circle.

Procedure

Each *S* was used for three sessions, spaced at least 24 hours apart. The sessions differed in the figures used as variables; in one session, triangles were used, in another, squares, and in the remaining session, circles were the variable figures. To control practice effects, each set of variable figures was used for the first, second, and third sessions by an equal number of *S*s.

In each session, 45 standard figures, in one of the random orders, were compared, one at a time, against a variable series. The variable series was

Table 4

RESULTS FOR SIMILAR-FORM JUDGMENTS IN LINEAR INCHES

Standard	Variable		Kinderg.	2nd Grade	4th Grade	6th Grade	8th Grade	Coll. Stud.	Engineers	All Groups
15-Inch T	T	Mean	14.9	15.5	15.4	15.6	15.5	15.8	16.0	15.5
		SD	1.1	.9	.6	.6	.5	.5	.5	.8
10-Inch T	T	Mean	10.3	10.4	10.2	10.2	10.3	10.4	10.6	10.3
		SD	.7	.6	.5	.8	.3	.4	.5	.6
5-Inch T	T	Mean	4.9	5.1	5.1	5.1	5.0	5.1	5.1	5.1
		SD	.5	.6	.1	.1	.1	.2	.0	.1
15-Inch S	S	Mean	15.4	16.8	14.8	15.2	15.1	15.1	14.2	15.2
		SD	1.3	2.4	.9	.6	.5	.5	2.0	1.6
10-Inch S	S	Mean	9.8	11.3	10.2	10.3	10.2	10.2	10.4	10.3
		SD	.7	1.5	.4	.3	.2	.4	.4	.8
5-Inch S	S	Mean	4.8	5.6	5.1	5.1	5.0	5.0	5.2	5.1
		SD	.4	1.0	.2	.0	.0	.1	.3	.5
15-Inch C	C	Mean	15.2	14.9	14.5	14.8	14.8	15.0	15.5	15.0
		SD	.8	.6	.4	.4	.5	.3	.6	.6
10-Inch C	C	Mean	10.1	10.3	9.9	10.2	10.2	10.3	10.5	10.2
		SD	.8	.6	.3	.3	.3	.4	.5	.5
5-Inch C	C	Mean	4.9	5.2	5.0	5.0	5.0	5.1	5.1	5.0
		SD	.4	.6	.1	.0	.0	.0	.5	.3

NOTE—T = triangle, S = square, C = circle.

arranged in order of size on a large table in front of *S*. On each trial the standard figure was placed on the table and *S,* who walked around the table at will, was told: "Look over all these figures and find the one which is the same size as this one." At the higher age levels, an occasional *S* asked what was meant by size. *E*'s reply was: "I want to find out what *you* mean. Please choose from the table the one which is the same size as this one."

The total number of judgments made was 14,175: *N* equals 105; there were five judgments per combination and three sizes, three shapes, and three standard-variable combinations.

Results

Each *S*'s score is a mean of five trials; for each group, the mean is for 15 *S*s.

EQUALITY JUDGMENTS FOR SIMILAR-FORM FIGURES

The accuracy of equality judgments for similar-form figures was high at all age levels. The kindergartners were as accurate as the college students. Variability decreased (a) with increase in age and (b) with decrease in size of figure. Table 4 shows the results for similar-form judgments.

EQUALITY JUDGMENTS FOR DIFFERENT-FORM FIGURES

In a comparison of figures of different shapes it is not meaningful to establish an arbitrary measure of accuracy as a criterion. Some other basis or cue must be used. Table 3 shows the possible ways by which figures of different shapes could be compared. That is, *S* might use area or equal sides or altitude equal to diameter. The *t* test was used to compare the mean of each group for every size-shape comparison with each of the predesignated values or possible cues. Table 5 shows the apparent cue used for each standard-variable comparison. The last column shows the number of groups, out of a total of seven age groups, who apparently used the cue; i.e., no statistical difference between the mean of each group and the actual dimension for the specific cue was shown by the *t* test.

Size of figures and grade level of *S*s are omitted in Table 6.[2] Size did not influence the cue used; when a 15-, 10-, or 5-inch triangle was compared

---

[2] Results are presented by groups and sizes in Table A which has been deposited as Document number 6605 with the ADI Auxiliary Publications Project, Photoduplication Service, Library of Congress, Washington 25, D.C. Copies may be secured by citing the Document number and by remitting $1.25 for photoprints, or $1.25 for 35 mm. microfilm. Advance payment is required. Make checks payable to: Chief, Photoduplication Service, Library of Congress.

Table 5

RESULTS FOR DIFFERENT-FIGURE COMPARISONS IN LINEAR INCHES
FOR THE SEVEN GROUPS

Standard	Variable	Mean	SD	Apparent Cue Used	No. of Groups Using Cue
15 T	S	12.57	1.71	altitude = side	7
10 T	S	8.62	1.13	altitude = side	5
5 T	S	4.24	.53	altitude = side	6
15 T	C	12.92	1.84	altitude = diameter	7
10 T	C	9.13	1.34	altitude = diameter	5
5 T	C	4.52	.69	altitude = diameter	4
15 S	T	19.84	1.86	diagonal = side	2
10 S	T	13.90	2.11	diagonal = side	5
5 S	T	7.12	1.14	diagonal = side	6
15 C	T	18.94	2.13	equal areas	5
10 C	T	12.99	1.88	equal areas	5
5 C	T	6.60	1.16	equal areas	7
15 C	S	14.84	1.73	diameter = side	6
10 C	S	9.96	1.11	diameter = side	6
5 C	S	4.86	.58	diameter = side	4
15 S	C	16.46	1.52	equal areas	6
10 S	C	11.45	1.01	equal areas	6
5 S	C	5.78	.61	equal areas	6

NOTE—T = triangle, S = square, C = circle. The seven groups are the seven grade levels, as kindergarten, 2nd grade, 4th grade, etc.

with squares, Ss consistently, over all three sizes, equated altitude of triangle with side of square. Age or grade of Ss did not influence the cue used; kindergarten through college students used the same apparent cues. All conclusions based upon *t* tests were confirmed by analyses of variance. No sex differences were found. Ss were very consistent within themselves in

Table 6

COMBINED RESULTS FOR DIFFERENT-FIGURE COMPARISONS

Standard	Variable	Apparent Cue Used	No. of Groups Using Cue *
Square	Circle	equal areas	18
Square	Triangle	diagonal = side	13
Circle	Square	diameter = side	16
Circle	Triangle	equal areas	17
Triangle	Square	altitude = side	18
Triangle	Circle	altitude = diameter	16

* Total $N = 21$ groups (seven grade levels and three sizes).

overestimation or in underestimation as measured by the coefficient of concordance.

Discussion

The results suggest that fairly accurate judgment of similar-shaped figures develops before six years of age.

The results also suggest that the cues used as the basis for judgments did not differ according to age of Ss or size of figures, but rather according to the figures themselves. Area was used when the standard was a square and circles were the variable and when the standard was a circle and triangles were the variable figures. Altitude was used when the triangle was the standard; i.e., altitude was made equal to the side of a square or the diameter of circles. In the other two comparisons, the longest dimension was most commonly used; i.e., the diagonal of the square was made equal to the side of the triangle and the diameter of circles was equated with the side of squares. Thus, multiple cues were used, and these cues seem to have depended on which shape was the standard and which was the variable.

In general, variability decreased with increase in age. Except for the engineering students, there was a fairly sharp break between the second and fourth graders, the older children showing less variability in their judgments. The engineering students walked around the table, looked at the variable stimuli, and muttered formulas to themselves. Of course, they did not know the sizes of the figures, and, therefore, these formulas were of no help. Their attempts to go beyond the task presented (comparing the figures spread on the table) by doing formulas in their heads when they did not know the true sizes of the figures, may not have remembered the formulas correctly, and may have made miscalculations probably accounted for the greater error in their judgments.

An interesting finding was the greater variability in judgments of squares and least variability in judgments of circles. This may be related to a decrease in the number of angles, from squares to triangles to circles.

Graphs were drawn showing each S's score on each of the 27 combinations of standards, sizes, and variables to investigate whether the means were obscuring real differences in behavior. There was a possibility that some Ss, for example, might equate the side of a triangle with the side of a square and that other Ss might make the side of a triangle equal to the diagonal of a square. If this occurred, the mean for the group might indicate that the basis for judgment was altitude of triangle equal to side of square. The graphs show that this did not occur. Most Ss' scores fell close to the point indicated by the mean of the group which, in turn, did not differ significantly from the value to be expected if altitude of triangles were equated with side of squares. These graphs are not presented since they merely confirm previous statistical analysis.

The possibility that area is the commonly used basis for comparing the size of all figures was not borne out by the results of this study. Area was used in only two of the six comparisons of different-shaped figures. Further validation appears in the responses of Ss. At the end of the three sessions, each S was asked: "Can you tell me how you decided which square was equal to a triangle, etc.?" They frequently mentioned height, sides, and diameter as determinants of equality. They mentioned area in the judgment of circles, and the apparent cues in Table 4 indicate that area was used in two of the major comparisons of circles. Some Ss declared they "never thought of area" as a basis for their judgments.

Summary

Ss ranging in grade from kindergarten through college were presented with a standard series of figures and were asked to select from a variable series the figure which was most nearly equal in size to the standard. Forty-five of these judgments were similar-figure trials; 90 were different-figure trials.

On the similar-figure trials (a) Ss were accurate in estimation of equality of size; (b) young children were as accurate as adults; (c) variability of group judgments decreased with increase in age; (d) variability of group judgments decreased with decrease in size of the standard presented.

On the different-figure trials (a) the basis for judgments differed according to whether figures were in the standard or variable series; (b) cues differed according to the shapes of the figures; (c) the same cues were used by all groups regardless of size of figures; (d) there were no age or sex differences; (e) in one-third of the comparisons, area was used in estimating equality of size.

43. *Freedom through Creativity* *

GENE D. PHILLIPS, *Boston University*

THERE IS a need today as never before for a reaffirmation of faith in human experience and potential. This can be called creativity. It has content. It has meaning. It can be understood. To believe that it can be developed provides much of the motivation needed to seek out its meanings. The late Viktor Lowenfeld said it in this manner. ". . . creativity is an instinct which all people possess, an instinct with which we were born. It belongs to one of the basic drives, a drive without which man cannot exist." If, as teachers, we believe this, then we act on it. The mandate is to seek out the conditions of freedom which permit it to flourish.

The exploratory attempt to be made here will not debate the subjective-objective character of creativity, whether it comes from somewhere or nowhere, whether we can know it totally or experience it partially, or the importance of including the most recent experimental evidence. At best, we can examine some of the conditions and relevancies of and for its encouragement and existence.

Stages of Creativity

The following discussion has its genesis in the thinking of Gardner Murphy, although many students of the topic include these stages in this or a similar manner. (1) *Immersion* involves the development of a sensitivity to some particular medium. Then the task is to steep oneself in it.

"From Gene D. Phillips, "Freedom through Creativity," *Educational Horizons* (Summer, 1961), pp. 121–24. Reprinted by permission.

Picasso immersed himself in a knowledge of color: his Blue and Pink period, his famous black, white, and gray "Guernica." Through his knowledge, some of the most lasting effects have been imprinted upon our visual memories. Others might work at the problem of tone as did Beethoven. Or there is the knowledge of movement in the dance of Isadora Duncan, Martha Graham, and George Balanchine. There is power in the imagery of a Dickinson poem. One reads Shakespeare and recognizes with wonderment his knowledge of words. Some people choose to immerse themselves in the science of social relationships. This knowing and feeling deeply about a particular interest lead the way to the next step, and that is (2) *incubation*—which is the stage of consolidation and where this developmental readiness leads one to have the creative insights necessary for seeing and feeling an object, which is in part preparatory to (3) *illumination*—which is the sudden inspiration resulting from one and two but makes the next stage possible, (4) *verification*—which is the process of evaluating, perfecting, revising, and trying. There is a strong similarity here between the act of thought-involving problem-solving and creativity in an artistic sense.

The conditions which stimulate *immersion* need further study by the psychologists and philosophers. Every teacher is included here, for he has beliefs about the nature of growth in the learner and about the values which make this growth possible. Thus, a deep concern for the causes of motivation, the stimulation of curiosity, the development of will, and the permissiveness needed for the expression of moods require further study from all who prize the earlier contention that creativity can be developed. Just to have tensions, confused excitements of a higher pitch are not enough. There must be an attending interest in building knowledge in a special field and providing the child with the necessary skills for satisfying the tension or problem.

Since the stage of *incubation* is that point when an idea might flourish, there is a need here for patience, discipline of suspended judgment, and (above all) a critical exploration of possible alternatives for proceeding to the solution of the problem.

The exercising of the will to create is involved in the stage of *verification*. Here courage is demanded, for the individual faces uncertainties. Questing amidst uncertainties demands a certain amount of eccentricity, for the lines are not clearly drawn, the outline not set. Thence, industry, control, and direction are essential for realization of the goal.

If today's teacher is looking for a new conception of discipline, it seems to be inherently a part of the way in which the child creates. This process, if it's genuine, provides for integrity of expression. Here we are reminded that, in order to build a theory of creativity, we must also build a basic theory of human behavior. Murphy's suggested ingredients of creativity seem to have a forceful and dynamic behavior orientation.

The New Physics and Creativity

Recent explorations of the relationships existing between principles of quantum physics and the human brain lead us to question the oldest and one of the most persistent notions of creativity. Plato proposed that the creative imagination has a divine origin outside of man. Medieval theology supported this view, only to be questioned by Shaftesbury and Young in the eighteenth century. They thought the origin of creativity was located in that aspect of human nature called "genius." A further manifestation of this notion of human involvement was Freud's and Jung's placing the problem in the unconscious. This gave a breath of excitement and vitality to the time-worn explanation of the imaginative self.

Another effect of this exploration has led man to realize that the brain is amazingly fluid and, at the same time, amazingly precise. Erwin Schrödinger likens this precision to the *quantum jump*. Werner Heisenberg's *uncertainty principle* maintains that there is an inherent uncertainty in subatomic activity. The real is not to be found in this realm, but things exist as a kind of *potentia,* he insists. Thus, this can be one problem of mental activity for creativity in teaching.

If the scientists are successful in their relating mental activity to hypotheses involving energy and evolution, it might be said that man can utilize the creative powers of his mind for entering into communion with, or becoming a part of, the great creative process that runs through all nature. In him, this process is concentrated. He can refine it, accelerate it, because it is to be likened with a force running through all nature. This kind of a scientific variation places man as the creative source. This does not make man and nature one; rather, it makes the particular duty of intelligent men today more dutiful toward themselves rather than to nature itself. Nature can be modified. Such problems of struggles among nations and classes, too, can be modified, controlled, and ultimately eliminated if we understand them as scientific phenomena. Man, according to Julian Huxley, has the assignment to further the evolutionary process, for he is the only organism capable of this. This has been ordained by nature. This challenging destiny is his because he possesses the tools of experience, mind, and spirit. The content of this knowing is not merely for formalized science as fact rather than as a way or ways to behave but from the equally important humanities and social sciences. This could be a second problem of mental activity for the teacher.

Because man has been able to come by certain new knowledges, he has been (or will be) able to build new and more adequate beliefs about himself, his place in nature, his place in the universe, his role in the universal cosmic process. The peculiar range and scope of this new knowledge excite further inquiry and creative imagination. When man discovered that the atom was not the ultimate unit of matter, he made radiation studies, inquired into quantum theory and atomic physics; thus it was the bringing of matter and energy together; the new discoveries in medical and physiological sciences are the result of hormone and vitamin, chemotherapy and antibiotic, nervous action and muscular contraction studies, along with many others; thus an emerging coherence of the working of the body in disease and health. This list of discoveries in much less than the sixty years could include the rediscovery of Mendelism which led to studies in heredity and organic evolution; the discoveries of psychology—human and comparative—involving repression and the unconscious, the measurement of intelligence and temperament, conditioned reflexes and Gestalt perception, the language of bees, the homing of birds, and the behavior of apes, which led us towards a fuller picture of the evolution, the individual development, and the working of mind. A final concern for mental activity encouraged by the teacher is this seeking out the method by which and through which knowledge of the past has been produced and the knowledge of the future is promised.

The outpouring of knowledge coming from the study of prehistory, archaeology, and palaeontology has given us a fuller view of human development as a whole, as well as having given us new kinds of history: social and economic, art, science, education, religion, and the rest—leading toward a fuller view of civilized man's cultural and social evolution.

Already mention has been made of man's control of nature, but this must not be mistaken for its point of emphasis. This is largely his external world. For his inner or own nature remains to be achieved.

Man's own proliferation is coming to be a sobering realization. Julian Huxley reminds us ". . . that population must be limited if man is not to turn into a cancer of the planet." The creative management of this explosive human affair needs the attention and help of every teacher in the world.

These encapsulated reminders bring us to our next concern. They remind us further of man's past creative efforts. What about those in the future? This leads to the question: in what kind of a social climate, a cultural milieu can human creativity be developed optimally?

Conditions of Freedom to Encourage Creativity

If one were to ask the question, what kind of nature? one might answer that it is and can be found in *a free universe*. To continue this questioning: what kind of human nature? *The free man*. What kind of society? *The free society*. What kind of consciousness? *The free mind*. What kind of education? *The freedom to grow*. What kind of philosophy? *The freedom to create*.

Teaching as Expressive

A teacher who shares in the development of creativity in others must also be a participator in the expressive arts or an appreciator of them. There is a needed recognition for the fact that, in all ages, art is the expression of mood, feeling, and spirit. Art is expressive rather than merely descriptive. Are we recognizing that the will to create is first a social response, and we use science for materials and descriptions, and we use art for expression? From this it might be said that the three ingredients in the life of every child might be experiences of a social, scientific, and aesthetic nature. The order of their importance might be questioned. The degree of emphasis of each phase of the experience might be puzzled over. The value of each discrete experience would need to be assessed carefully. And whether they are all parts of a continuum would require extended consideration.

If creativity is developed in individuals, then from this can come an art which can provide man with social values not yet known. We recall how the troubadours and the poets developed the ideal of romantic love; how Sophocles with his "Oedipus Rex," how Giotto with his "Entombment," Michelangelo with his "Pieta," and Brahms with his *Requiem Mass* gave to death a majestic beauty; how Gothic cathedrals, Gregorian chants, and Buddhist statues have exalted man's religious attitudes; how Brueghel, Van Gogh, and Walt Whitman have enriched our democratic sympathies; how the Renaissance painters developed the interest in perspective and depth space; and how the impressionist painters taught us to delight in sunshine and brilliant color. If this is what our past has given us aesthetically and an earlier assessment was made of our recent scientific heritage, what then can our future be if we come to know the ingredients of creativity?

The mysteries of productive personalities, sources of energy, change and variation, peace, and other problems of man in only a partially-explored universe can be the ventures of the mind tomorrow. No limits to human inquiry need to be set. Why then must the teacher create artificial and limiting standards of achievement, conduct, performance, expression? When so much uncertainty surrounds us, why all the prescriptions?

When and if the teacher sets his charges to question after the answers to the unexplored, making intelligent uses of the explored, the standard will be set which can make education an energetic force for human survival. Otherwise, our course shall be one of imitation, not creation. Our assisting in the adding to culture through releasing creative energy in children seems to be a moral assignment for our day. To discover the method for doing this is our most pressing task.

44. The Act of Discovery *

JEROME S. BRUNER, *Harvard University*

MAIMONIDES, in his *Guide for the Perplexed*,[1] speaks of four forms of perfection that men might seek. The first and lowest form is perfection in the acquisition of worldly goods. The great philosopher dismisses such perfection on the ground that the possessions one acquires bear no meaningful relation to the possessor: "A great king may one morning find that there is no difference between him and the lowest person." A second perfection is of the body, its conformation and skills. Its failing is that it does not reflect on what is uniquely human about man: "he could [in any case] not be as strong as a mule." Moral perfection is the third, "the highest degree of excellency in man's character." Of this perfection Maimonides says: "Imagine a person being alone, and having no connection whatever with any other person; all his good moral principles are at rest, they are not required and give man no perfection whatever. These principles are only necessary and useful when man comes in contact with others." "The fourth kind of perfection is the true perfection of man; the possession of the highest intellectual faculties. . . ." In justification of his assertion, this

---

* From Jerome S. Bruner, "The Act of Discovery," *Harvard Educational Review*, 31 (Winter, 1961), pp. 21–32. Reprinted by permission.
[1] Maimonides, *Guide for the Perplexed* (New York: Dover Publications, 1956).

extraordinary Spanish-Judaic philosopher urges: "Examine the first three kinds of perfection; you will find that if you possess them, they are not your property, but the property of others. . . . But the last kind of perfection is exclusively yours; no one else owns any part of it."

It is a conjecture much like that of Maimonides that leads me to examine the act of discovery in man's intellectual life. For if man's intellectual excellence is the most his own among his perfections, it is also the case that the most uniquely personal of all that he knows is that which he has discovered for himself. What difference does it make, then, that we encourage discovery in the learning of the young? Does it, as Maimonides would say, create a special and unique relation between knowledge possessed and the possessor? And what may such a unique relation do for a man—or for a child, if you will, for our concern is with the education of the young?

The immediate occasion for my concern with discovery—and I do not restrict discovery to the act of finding out something that before was unknown to mankind, but rather include all forms of obtaining knowledge for oneself by the use of one's own mind—the immediate occasion is the work of the various new curriculum projects that have grown up in America during the last six or seven years. For whether one speaks to mathematicians or physicists or historians, one encounters repeatedly an expression of faith in the powerful effects that come from permitting the student to put things together for himself, to be his own discoverer.

First, let it be clear what the act of discovery entails. It is rarely, on the frontier of knowledge or elsewhere, that new facts are "discovered" in the sense of being encountered as Newton suggested in the form of islands of truth in an unchartered sea of ignorance. Or if they appear to be discovered in this way, it is almost always thanks to some happy hypotheses about where to navigate. Discovery, like surprise, favors the well-prepared mind. In playing bridge, one is surprised by a hand with no honors in at all and also by hands that are all in one suit. Yet all hands in bridge are equiprobable: one must know to be surprised. So too in discovery. The history of science is studded with examples of men "finding out" something and not knowing it. I shall operate on the assumption that discovery, whether by a schoolboy going it on his own or by a scientist cultivating the growing edge of his field, is in its essence a matter of rearranging or transforming evidence in such a way that one is enabled to go beyond the evidence so reassembled to additional new insights. It may well be that an additional fact or shred of evidence makes this larger transformation of evidence possible. But it is often not even dependent on new information.

It goes without saying that, left to himself, the child will go about discovering things for himself within limits. It also goes without saying that there are certain forms of child rearing, certain home atmospheres that lead some children to be their own discoverers more than other children. These are both topics of great interest, but I shall not be discussing them. Rather, I should like to confine myself to the consideration of discovery and "finding-out-for-oneself" within an educational setting—specifically the school. Our aim as teachers is to give our student as firm a grasp of a subject as we can, and to make him as autonomous and self-propelled a thinker as we can—one who will go along on his own after formal schooling has ended. I shall return in the end to the question of the kind of classroom and the style of teaching that encourages an attitude of wanting to discover. For purposes of orienting the discussion, however, I would like to make an overly simplified distinction between teaching that takes place in the *expository mode* and teaching that utilizes the *hypothetical mode*. In the former, the decisions concerning the mode and pace and style of exposition are principally determined by the teacher as expositor; the student is the listener. If I can put the matter in terms of structural linguistics, the speaker has a quite different set of decisions to make than the listener: the former has a wide choice of alternatives for structuring, he is anticipating paragraph content while the listener is still intent on the words, he is manipulating the content of the material by various transformations, while the listener is quite unaware of these internal manipulations. In the hypothetical mode, the teacher and the student are in a more cooperative position with respect to what in linguistics would be called "speaker's decisions." The student is not a bench-bound listener, but is taking a part in the formulation and at times may play the principal role in it. He will be aware of alternatives and may even have an "as if" attitude toward these and, as he receives information he may evaluate it as it comes. One cannot describe the process in either mode with great precision as to detail, but I think the foregoing may serve to illustrate what is meant.

Consider now what benefit might be derived from the experience of learning through discoveries that one makes for oneself. I should like to discuss these under four headings: (1) The increase in intellectual potency, (2) the shift from extrinsic to intrinsic rewards, (3) learning the heuristics of discovering, and (4) the aid to memory processing.

1. Intellectual potency. If you will permit me, I would like to consider the difference between subjects in a highly constrained psychological experiment involving a two-choice apparatus. In order to win chips, they must depress a key either on the right or the left side of the machine. A pattern of payoff is designed such that, say, they will be paid off on the right side 70 per cent of the time, on the left 30 per cent, although this detail is not important. What is important is that the payoff sequence is arranged at random, and there is no pattern. I should like to contrast the behavior of subjects who think that there *is* some pattern to be found in the sequence—who think that regularities are discoverable—in contrast to subjects who think that things are happening quite by *chance*. The former group adopts what is called an "event-matching" strategy in which the number of responses given to each side is roughly equal to the proportion of times it pays off: in the present case R70:L30. The group that believes there is no pattern very soon reverts to a much more primitive strategy wherein *all* responses are allocated to the side that has the greater payoff. A little arithmetic will show you that the lazy all-and-none strategy pays off more if indeed the environment is random: namely, they win 70 per cent of the time. The event-matching subjects win about 70 per cent on the 70 per cent payoff side (or 49 per cent of the time there) and 30 per cent of the time on the side that pays off 30 per cent of the time (another 9 per cent for a total take-home wage of 58 per cent in return for their labors of decision). But the world is not always or not even frequently random, and if one analyzes carefully what the event-matchers are doing, it turns out that they are trying out hypotheses one after the other, all of them containing a term such that they distribute bets on the two sides with a frequency to match the actual occurrence of events. If it should turn out that there is a pattern to be discovered, their payoff would become 100 per cent. The other group would go on at the middling rate of 70 per cent.

What has this to do with the subject at hand? For the person to search out and find regularities and relationships in his environment, he must be armed with an expectancy that there will be something to find and, once aroused by expectancy, he must devise ways of searching and finding. One of the chief enemies of such expectancy is the assumption that there is nothing one can find in the environment by way of regularity or relationship. In the experiment just cited, subjects often fall into a habitual attitude that there is either nothing to be found or that they can find a pattern by looking. There is an important sequel in behavior to the two attitudes, and to this I should like to turn now.

We have been conducting a series of experimental studies on a group of some seventy school children over the last four years. The studies have led us to distinguish an interesting dimension of cognitive activity that can be described as ranging from *episodic empiricism* at one end to *cumulative constructionism* at the other. The two attitudes in the choice experiments just cited are illustrative of the extremes of the dimension. I might mention some other illustrations. One of the experiments employs the game of Twenty Questions. A child—in this case he is between 10 and 12—is told that a car has gone off the road and hit a tree. He is to ask questions that can be answered by "yes" or "no" to discover the cause of the accident. After completing the problem, the same task is given him again, though he is told that the accident had a different cause this time. In all, the procedure is repeated four times. Children enjoy playing the game. They also differ quite markedly in the approach or strategy they bring to the task. There are various elements in the strategies employed. In the first place, one may distinguish clearly between two types of questions asked: the one is designed for locating constraints in the problem, constraints that will eventually give shape to an hypothesis; the other is the hypothesis as question. It is the difference between, "Was there anything wrong with the driver?" and "Was the driver rushing to the doctor's office for an appointment and the car got out of control?" There are children who precede hypotheses with efforts to locate constraint and there are those who, to use our local slang, are "pot-shotters," who string out hypotheses noncumulatively one after the other. A second element of strategy is its connectivity of information gathering: the extent to which questions asked utilize or ignore or violate information previously obtained. The questions asked by children tend to be organized in cycles, each cycle of questions usually being given over to the pursuit of some particular notion. Both within cycles and between cycles one can discern a marked difference on the connectivity of the child's performance. Needless to say, children who employ constraint location as a technique preliminary to the formulation of hypotheses tend to be far more connected in their harvesting of information. Persistence is another feature of strategy, a characteristic compounded of what appear to be two components: a sheer doggedness component, and a persistence that stems from the sequential organization that a child brings to the task. Doggedness is probably just animal spirits or the need for achievement—what has come to be called *n-ach*. Organized persistence is a maneuver for protecting our fragile cognitive apparatus from overload. The child who has flooded himself with disorganized information from unconnected hypotheses will become discouraged and confused sooner than the child who has shown a certain cunning in his strategy of getting information—a cunning whose principal component is the recognition that the value of information is not simply in getting it but in being able to carry it. The persistence of the organized child stems from his knowledge of how to organize questions in cycles, how to summarize things to himself, and the like.

Episodic empiricism is illustrated by information gathering that is unbound by prior constraints, that lacks connectivity, and that is deficient in organizational persistence. The opposite extreme is illustrated by an approach that is characterized by constraint sensitivity, by connective maneuvers, and by organized persistence. Brute persistence seems to be one of those gifts from the gods that make people more exaggeratedly what they are.[2]

Before returning to the issue of discovery and its role in the development of thinking, let me say a word more about the ways in which information may get transformed when the problem solver has actively processed it. There is first of all a pragmatic question: what does it take to get information processed into a form best designed to fit some future use? Take an experiment by Zajonc [3] as a case in point. He gives groups of subjects information of a controlled kind, some groups being told that their task is to transmit the information to others, others that is merely to be kept in mind. In general, he finds more differentiation and organization of the information received with the intention of being transmitted than there is for information received passively. An active set leads to a transformation related to a task to be performed. The risk, to be sure, is in possible overspecialization of information processing that may lead to such a high degree of specific organization that information is lost for general use.

I would urge now in the spirit of an hypothesis that emphasis upon discovery in learning has precisely the effect upon the learner of leading him to be a constructionist, to organize what he is encountering in a manner not only designed to discover regularity and relatednes, but also to avoid the kind of information drift that fails to keep account of the uses to which information might have to be put. It is, if you will, a necessary condition for learning the variety of techniques of problem solving, of transforming information for better use, indeed for learning how to go about the very task of learning. Practice in discovering for oneself teaches one to acquire information in a way that makes that information more readily viable in problem solving. So goes the hypothesis. It in still in need of testing. But is is an hypothesis of such important human implications that we cannot afford not to test it—and testing will have to be in the schools.

2. Intrinsic and extrinsic motives. Much of the problem in leading a child to effective cognitive activity is to free him from the immediate control of environmental rewards and punishments. That is to say, learning that starts in response to the rewards of parental or teacher approval or the avoidance of failure can too readily develop a pattern in which the child is seeking cues as to how to conform to what is expected of him. We know

---

[2] I should also remark in passing that the two extremes also characterize concept attainment strategies as reported in *A Study of Thinking* by J. S. Bruner *et al.* (New York: J. Wiley, 1956). Successive scanning illustrates well what is meant here by episodic empiricism; conservative focussing is an example of cumulative constructionists.

[3] R. B. Zajonc, [Personal Communication, 1957].

from studies of children who tend to be early overachievers in school that they are likely to be seekers after the "right way to do it" and that their capacity for transforming their learning into viable thought structures tends to be lower than children merely achieving at levels predicted by intelligence tests. Our tests on such children show them to be lower in analytic ability than those who are not conspicuous in overachievement.[4] As we shall see later, they develop rote abilities and depend upon being able to "give back" what is expected rather than to make it into something that relates to the rest of their cognitive life. As Maimonides would say, their learning is not their own.

The hypothesis that I would propose here is that to the degree that one is able to approach learning as a task of discovering something rather than "learning about" it, to that degree will there be a tendency for the child to carry out his learning activities with the autonomy of self-reward or, more properly, by reward that is discovery itself.

To those of you familiar with the battles of the last half-century in the field of motivation, the above hypothesis will be recognized as controversial. For the classic view of motivation in learning has been, until very recently, couched in terms of a theory of drives and reinforcement: that learning occurred by virtue of the fact that a response produced by a stimulus was followed by the reduction in a primary drive state. The doctrine is greatly extended by the idea of secondary reinforcement: any state associated even remotely with the reduction of a primary drive could also have the effect of producing learning. There has recently appeared a most searching and important criticism of this position, written by Professor Robert White,[5] reviewing the evidence of recently published animal studies, of work in the field of psychoanalysis, and of research on the development of cognitive processes in children. Professor White comes to the conclusion, quite rightly I think, that the drive-reduction model of learning runs counter to too many important phenomena of learning and development to be either regarded as general in its applicability or even correct in its general approach. Let me summarize some of his principal conclusions and explore their applicability to the hypothesis stated above.

I now propose that we gather the various kinds of behavior just mentioned all of which have to do with effective interaction with the environment, under the general heading of competence. According to Webster, competence means fitness or ability, and the suggested synonyms include capability, capacity, effi-

[4] J. S. Bruner and A. J. Caron, "Cognition, Anxiety, and Achievement in the Preadolescent," *Journal of Educational Psychology* (in press).

[5] R. W. White, "Motivation Reconsidered: The Concept of Competence," *Psychological Review*, LXVI (1959), 297–333.

ciency, proficiency, and skill. It is therefore a suitable word to describe such things as grasping and exploring, crawling and walking, attention and perception, language and thinking, manipulating and changing the surroundings, all of which promote an effective—a competent—interaction with the environment. It is true of course, that maturation plays a part in all these developments, but this part is heavily overshadowed by learning in all the more complex accomplishments like speech or skilled manipulation. I shall argue that it is necessary to make competence a motivational concept; there is *competence motivation* as well as competence in its more familiar sense of achieved capacity. The behavior that leads to the building up of effective grasping, handling, and letting go of objects, to take one example, is not random behavior that is produced by an overflow of energy. It is directed, selective, and persistent, and it continues not because it serves primary drives, which indeed it cannot serve until it is almost perfected, but because it satisfies an intrinsic need to deal with the environment.[6]

I am suggesting that there are forms of activity that serve to enlist and develop the competence motive, that serve to make it the driving force behind behavior. I should like to add to White's general premise that the *exercise* of competence motives has the effect of strengthening the degree to which they gain control over behavior and thereby reduce the effects of extrinsic rewards or drive gratification.

The brilliant Russian psychologist Vigotsky [7] characterizes the growth of thought processes as starting with a dialogue of speech and gesture between child and parent; autonomous thinking begins at the stage when the child is first able to internalize these conversations and "run them off" himself. This is a typical sequence in the development of competence. So too in instruction. The narrative of teaching is of the order of the conversation. The next move in the development of competence is the internalization of the narrative and its "rules of generation" so that the child is now capable of running off the narrative on his own. The hypothetical mode in teaching by encouraging the child to participate in "speaker's decisions" speeds this process along. Once internalization has occurred, the child is in a vastly improved position from several obvious points of view—notably that he is able to go beyond the information he has been given to generate additional ideas that can either be checked immediately from experience or can, at least, be used as a basis for formulating reasonable hypotheses. But over and beyond that, the child is now in a position to experience success and failure not as reward and punishment, but as information. For when the task is his own rather than a matter of matching environmental demands, he becomes his own paymaster in a certain measure. Seeking to gain control over his environment, he can now

[6] *Ibid.*, pp. 317–18.

treat success as indicating that he is on the right track, failure as indicating he is on the wrong one.

In the end, this development has the effect of freeing learning from immediate stimulus control. When learning in the short run leads only to pellets of this or that rather than to mastery in the long run, then behavior can be readily "shaped" by extrinsic rewards. When behavior becomes more long-range and competence-oriented, it comes under the control of more complex cognitive structures, plans and the like, and operates more from the inside out. It is interesting that even Pavlov, whose early account of the learning process was based entirely on a notion of stimulus control of behavior through the conditioning mechanism in which, through contiguity, a new conditioned stimulus was substituted for an old unconditioned stimulus by the mechanism of stimulus substitution, that even Pavlov recognized his account as insufficient to deal with higher forms of learning. To supplement the account, he introduced the idea of the "second signalling system," with central importance placed on symbolic systems such as language in mediating and giving shape to mental life. Or as Luria [8] has put it, "the first signal system [is] concerned with directly perceived stimuli, the second with systems of verbal elaboration." Luria, commenting on the importance of the transition from first to second signal system, says: "It would be mistaken to suppose that verbal intercourse with adults merely changes the contents of the child's conscious activity without changing its form. . . . The word has a basic function not only because it indicates a corresponding object in the external world, but also because it abstracts, isolates the necessary signal, generalizes perceived signals and relates them to certain categories; it is this systematization of direct experience that makes the role of the word in the formation of mental processes so exceptionally important." [9, 10]

It is interesting that the final rejection of the universality of the doctrine of reinforcement in direct conditioning came from some of Pavlov's own students. Ivanov-Smolensky [11] and Krasnogorsky [12] published papers showing the manner in which symbolized linguistic messages could take over the

[7] L. S. Vigotsky, *Thinking and Speech* (Moscow, 1934).

[8] A. L. Luria, "The Directive Function of Speech in Development and Dissolution," *Word*, XV (1959), 341–464.

[9] *Ibid.*, p. 12.

[10] For an elaboration of the view expressed by Luria, the reader is referred to the forthcoming translation of L. S. Vigotsky's 1934 book being published by John Wiley and Sons and the Technology Press.

[11] A. G. Ivanov-Smolensky, "Concerning the Study of the Joint Activity of the First and Second Signal Systems," *Journal of Higher Nervous Activity,* I (1951), 1.

[12] N. D. Krasnogorsky, *Studies of Higher Nervous Activity in Animals and in Men,* Vol. I (Moscow, 1954).

place of the unconditioned stimulus and of the unconditioned response (gratification of hunger) in children. In all instances, they speak of these as *replacements* of lower, first-system mental or neural processes by higher order or second-system controls. A strange irony, then, that Russian psychology that gave us the notion of the conditioned response and the assumption that higher order activities are built up out of colligations or structurings of such primitive units, rejected this notion while much of American learning psychology has stayed until quite recently within the early Pavlovian fold (see, for example, a recent article by Spence [13] in the *Harvard Educational Review* or Skinner's treatment of language [14] and the attacks that have been made upon it by linguists such as Chomsky [15] who have become concerned with the relation of language and cognitive activity). What is the more interesting is that Russian pedagogical theory has become deeply influenced by this new trend and is now placing much stress upon the importance of building up a more active symbolical approach to problem solving among children.

To sum up the matter of the control of learning, then, I am proposing that the degree to which competence or mastery motives come to control behavior, to that degree the role of reinforcement or "extrinsic pleasure" wanes in shaping behavior. The child comes to manipulate his environment more actively and achieves his gratification from coping with problems. Symbolic modes of representing and transforming the environment arise and the importance of stimulus-response-reward sequences declines. To use the metaphor that David Riesman developed in a quite different context, mental life moves from a state of outer-directedness in which the fortuity of stimuli and reinforcement are crucial to a state of inner-directedness in which the growth and maintenance of mastery become central and dominant.

3. Learning the heuristics of discovery. Lincoln Steffens,[16] reflecting in his *Autobiography* on his under graduate education at Berkeley, comments that his schooling was overly specialized on learning about the known and that too little attention was given to the task of finding out about what was not known. But how does one train a student in the techniques of discovery? Again I would like to offer some hypotheses. There are many ways of coming to the arts of inquiry. One of them is by careful

[13] K. W. Spence, "The Relation of Learning Theory to the Technique of Education," *Harvard Educational Review,* XXIX (1959), 84–95.

[14] B. F. Skinner, *Verbal Behavior* (New York: Appleton-Century-Crofts, 1957).

[15] N. Chomsky, *Syntactic Structure* (The Hague, The Netherlands: Mouten & Co., 1957).

[16] L. Steffens, *Autobiography of Lincoln Steffens* (New York: Harcourt, Brace, 1931).

study of its formalization in logic, statistics, mathematics, and the like. If a person is going to pursue inquiry as a way of life, particularly in the sciences, certainly such study is essential. Yet, whoever has taught kindergarten and the early primary grades or has had graduate students working with him on their theses—I choose the two extremes for they are both periods of intense inquiry—knows that an understanding of the formal aspect of inquiry is not sufficient. There appear to be, rather, a series of activities and attitudes, some directly related to a particular subject and some of them fairly generalized, that go with inquiry and research. These have to do with the *process* of trying to find out something and while they provide no guarantee that the *product* will be any *great* discovery, their absence is likely to lead to awkwardness or aridity or confusion. How difficult it is to describe these matters—the heuristics of inquiry. There is one set of attitudes or ways of doing that has to do with sensing the relevance of variables—how to avoid getting stuck with edge effects and getting instead to the big sources of variance. Partly this gift comes from intuitive familiarity with a range of phenomena, sheer "knowing the stuff." But it also comes out of a sense of what things among an ensemble of things "smell right" in the sense of being of the right order of magnitude or scope or severity.

The English philosopher Weldon describes problem solving in an interesting and picturesque way. He distinguishes between difficulties, puzzles, and problems. We solve a problem or make a discovery when we impose a puzzle form on to a difficulty that converts it into a problem that can be solved in such a way that it gets us where we want to be. That is to say, we recast the difficulty into a form that we know how to work with, then work it. Much of what we speak of as discovery consists of knowing how to impose what kind of form on various kinds of difficulties. A small part but a crucial part of discovery of the highest order is to invent and develop models or "puzzle forms" that can be imposed on difficulties with good effect. It is in this area that the truly powerful mind shines. But it is interesting to what degree perfectly ordinary people can, given the benefit of instruction, construct quite interesting and what, a century ago, would have been considered greatly original models.

Now to the hypothesis. It is my hunch that it is only through the exercise of problem solving and the effort of discovery that one learns the working heuristic of discovery, and the more one has practice, the more likely is one to generalize what one has learned into a style of problem solving or inquiry that serves for any kind of task one may encounter—or almost any kind of task. I think the matter is self-evident, but what is unclear is what kinds of training and teaching produce the best effects. How do we teach a child to, say, cut his losses but at the same time be persistent in trying out an idea; to risk forming an early hunch without at the same time formulating one *so* early and with so little evidence as to be stuck with it waiting for appropriate evidence to materialize; to pose good testable guesses that are neither too brittle nor too sinuously incorrigible; etc. Practice in inquiry, in trying to figure out things for oneself is indeed what is needed, but in what form? Of only one thing I am convinced. I have never seen anybody improve in the art and technique of inquiry by any means other than engaging in inquiry.

4. Conservation of memory. I should like to take what some psychologists might consider a rather drastic view of the memory process. It is a view that in large measure derives from the work of my colleague, Professor George Miller.[17] Its first premise is that the principal problem of human memory is not storage, but retrieval. In spite of the biological unlikeliness of it, we seem to be able to store a huge quantity of information —perhaps not a full tape recording, though at times it seems we even do that, but a great sufficiency of impressions. We may infer this from the fact that recognition (i.e., recall with the aid of maximum prompts) is so extraordinarily good in human beings—particularly in comparison with spontaneous recall where, so to speak, we must get out stored information without external aids or prompts. The key to retrieval is organization or, in even simpler terms, knowing where to find information and how to get there.

Let me illustrate the point with a simple experiment. We present pairs of words to twelve-year-old children. One group is simply told to remember the pairs, that they will be asked to repeat them later. Another is told to remember them by producing a word or idea that will tie the pair together in a way that will make sense to them. A third group is given the mediators used by the second group when presented with the pairs to aid them in tying the pairs into working units. The word pairs include such juxtapositions as "chair-forest," "sidewalk-square," and the like. One can distinguish three styles of mediators and children can be scaled in terms of their relative preference for each: *generic mediation* in which a pair is tied together by a superordinate idea: "chair and forest are both made of wood"; *thematic mediation* in which the two terms are imbedded in a theme or little story: "the lost child sat on a chair in the middle of the forest"; and *part-whole mediation* where "chairs are made from trees in the forest" is typical. Now, the chief result, as you would all predict, is that children who provide their own mediators do best—indeed, one time

[17] G. A. Miller, "The Magical Number Seven, Plus or Minus Two," *Psychological Review*, LXIII (1956), 81–97.

through a set of thirty pairs, they recover up to 95 per cent of the second words when presented with the first ones of the pairs, whereas the uninstructed children reach a maximum of less than 50 per cent recovered. Interestingly enough, children do best in recovering materials tied together by the form of mediator they most often use.

One can cite a myriad of findings to indicate that any organization of information that reduces the aggregate complexity of material by imbedding it into a cognitive structure a person has constructed will make that material more accessible for retrieval. In short, we may say that the process of memory, looked at from the retrieval side, is also a process of problem solving: how can material be "placed" in memory so that it can be got on demand?

We can take as a point of departure the example of the children who developed their own technique for relating the members of each word pair. You will recall that they did better than the children who were given by exposition the mediators they had developed. Let me suggest that in general, material that is organized in terms of a person's own interests and cognitive structures is material that has the best chance of being accessible in memory. That is to say, it is more likely to be placed along routes that are connected to one's own ways of intellectual travel.

In sum, the very attitudes and activities that characterize "figuring out" or "discovering" things for oneself also seems to have the effect of making material more readily accessible in memory.

45. Creative Thinking through the Language Arts *

E. PAUL TORRANCE,[1] *University of Minnesota*

"**Y**OUR ideas are important! But their value is lost unless you record them—write them down. People have their best ideas at the funniest times and places. In fact, many of the world's greatest inventors and scientific discoverers say that their great ideas occurred to them when they were in the bathtub, in church, or just walking along. It pays to have an 'idea-trap'—a small note pad or something similar to record your ideas when they occur before they are forgotten and lost."

Value of Own Ideas

The above introduction to the third, fourth, fifth, and sixth graders of one elementary school marked the beginning of an exciting six-week experiment in creative writing. We hoped that through this experiment these children would be stimulated to do a great deal of writing on their own and form the habit of recording their ideas, something that children do not do naturally. Above all, we hoped that they would learn that their ideas are important and that others will enjoy them and find them useful, if they are recorded.

Each child was given a large brown envelope. This was to serve as the "bag" for the "trapped ideas." They were urged to write down their ideas for poems, stories, jokes, songs, opinions, inventions, and cartoons. Pupils were instructed: "If you think of an idea in the middle of an arithmetic lesson, you will not be able to write it out just that minute. You can jot down a few words to remind you of your idea later. Then you can pay better attention to your arithmetic work because your idea is safely trapped. Then, the first chance you have, you can write it out in detail."

On Fridays, I visited all classrooms and asked each pupil to select from his envelope the idea he thought others would enjoy most. Selections were then made for a weekly magazine named by the children *Ideas of the Week*. Every issue had an attractively illustrated colored cover, using drawings

* From E. Paul Torrance, "Creative Thinking through the Language Arts," *Educational Leadership* (October, 1960), pp. 13–18. Reprinted by permission.

[1] The research described herein was supported in part by the U.S. Office of Education.

submitted by participants in the study. On Thursdays, when the magazine was delivered, the person making the delivery was almost mobbed, the children were so eager for copies. There was intense interest among the children, their parents and teachers, and the research staff.

To help evaluate the effects of this experiment, subjects were given a test story to write at the beginning and end of the experiment. Topics such as the following were suggested:

    The dog that doesn't bark
    The man who cries
    The woman who can but won't talk
    The doctor who became a carpenter.

A different set of topics was used for the pre- and the post-tests. At the end of the experiment, each subject was interviewed by the editor of the magazine and asked to fill out a brief questionnaire evaluating his experience in writing down his ideas.

The data collected have not yet been analyzed but several important conclusions are obvious. Children in the third through sixth grades can be stimulated to record their ideas on their own. All of this writing was done outside the regular curriculum of the school. No special time was allowed by the teachers, although they could write and illustrate their ideas when they had completed their regular work. Third graders were highest in productivity. Almost all contributed regularly, most of them writing down their ideas when they had finished with other work. The only noncontributors were a few slow learners who "didn't ever get through with their regular work." The least productive grade was the fourth. Many of the fourth graders confided to the interviewer that they didn't have enough time to write down their ideas, because it took all of their spare time to write 500 times, "I will not make noise in German class' or "I will not run in the hall." Productivity among fifth and sixth graders fluctuated. Some weeks they were just too busy to record their thoughts.

There were many evidences that the subjects learned to value more highly their own ideas and even the nonparticipants showed great enthusiasm for the ideas of their classmates. In fact, they accepted so well the notion that their ideas are important, that they objected rather violently to the small amount of editing done. During the fourth week, there were several irate complaints. The following by a fifth grader is a sample: "I don't think you should change our poems, stories, etc., around. I know you are trying to make them better, but sometimes the way people write things—no matter whether it makes sense or not—is the way people want them. . . . I thought you said our ideas are important but we are beginning to wonder if we are mistaken. Please try and understand the way we feel about it."

Many of the stories and poems gave us fresh insight into the emotional problems and conflicts of highly creative children. The symbolism contained in the following story of "The Green Pig," by a creative fifth-grade girl describes what appears to be the essential problem of many children in the intermediate grades and causes them to sacrifice their creativity:

> Once upon a time in a far-off land, there was a magic farm that no one has ever visited. Many different animals lived there. The odd thing about these animals was that they were different colors from regular animals.
>
> The cows were pink, the horses were purple and hens and chicks were blue! All the pigs were green. That is, all except for one little fellow who was just plain pink. Nobody wanted to be near him because he wasn't green. And this little pig was very, very sad.
>
> One day when he was walking along he saw a great big puddle of mud. He splashed and rolled in it because he loved the mud. When the little pig came out of the puddle, he was all *green!* And he stayed green for all of his life. And all the other pigs began to play with him.

Developing through Creative Activities

The experiment described here represents an attempt to develop creative thinking through more or less self-initiated activities. The subjects were stimulated to write on their own during their "spare time."

Another experiment conducted in 21 fourth-, fifth-, and sixth-grade classes relied upon creative activities in the language arts as a part of the curriculum. Teachers participating in this study were given a 34-page manual, a collection of ideas for developing the creative thinking abilities through language arts activities. The manual was presented and discussed in a two-hour workshop and the participating teachers agreed to try out in their classes as many of the suggestions as seemed reasonable.

At the beginning and end of the experiment, pupils of the participating teachers and four control teachers were administered the same creative writing tests used in the first experiment. Language arts activities were suggested for developing each of eight abilities thought to be involved in creative thinking. A 60-item check-list was developed to determine the extent to which the suggested activities were applied. The following are sample items from the check-list:

Ideational Fluency

"Brainstorming" as a technique for stimulating ideas, developing fluency of ideas, etc.

Practice in playing word games

Pupil dictation of stories, ideas, etc., on a tape recorder or other electrical recording device

Competition to stimulate fluency of ideas

Associational Fluency

Introduction to Roget's *Thesaurus,* some book of synonyms, or other word reference in addition to dictionary

Exercises in recognizing word relationships, words of similar meaning, words of opposite meaning, etc.

Spontaneous Flexibility

Having pupils think of new uses for some device or product

Having pupils think of many alternative solutions to a problem.

Adaptive Flexibility

Writing the same message or story in several forms, for different audiences, for different effects, etc.

Rewriting story or other composition in a different setting, with different characters, etc.

Originality

Practice in writing unusual titles or captions for cartoons, pictures, news items, etc.

Book reports in an original manner

Writing humorous stories, anecdotes, etc.

Sensitivity

Critical reading of comic books and suggestion of changes to make them more realistic, accurate, etc.

Practice in creative listening, thinking how the speaker really feels about what he says

Expression of ideas and feelings stimulated by music.

Elaboration

Writing original plays

Writing a book or carrying out some other sustained writing project

Pupils tell entire stories through pictures, cartoons, photographs, drawings, etc.

Curiosity

Exercises to improve ability to ask good questions

Exercises to improve ability to make guesses from limited clues.

General

    Encouragement of "idea-trap" habit for creative writings

    Keeping folders of creative writings

    Practice exercises or periods which "don't count" on grades, etc.

    "Writer's Corner," a quiet retreat where pupils can go to think and to work out ideas.

Data analysis has not been completed. Results thus far, however, indicate that teachers using the manual applied a larger number of the activities included in the check-list than the control teachers and that their pupils made greater gains in the quality of their creative writing as measured by the pre- and post-tests.

Rewarding Creative Thinking

Children and adults learn and develop along whatever lines they find rewarding. We reward children for spelling words correctly, dotting *i's* and crossing *t's,* and for being neat, polite, clean, cooperative, honest, and punctual. In other words, we reward those who meet "behavioral norms." In a recent study I found that about 60 per cent of the language arts objectives for the activities of a particular day were concerned with conformity to behavioral norms. Less than 9 per cent of the objectives were related to creative thinking.

To help teachers in rewarding creative thinking a manual entitled *Rewarding Creative Thinking* was developed by the author and his colleagues. A set of six principles were also developed and used in an in-service training program in a field experiment. Briefly stated, these principles are:

1. Treat questions with respect.
2. Treat imaginative, unusual ideas with respect.
3. Show pupils that their ideas have value.
4. Give opportunities for practice or experimentation without evaluation.
5. Encourage and evaluate self-initiated learning.
6. Tie in evaluations with causes and consequences.

Manual users were asked to describe and evaluate specific attempts of their own in applying these principles.

These data have helped us to understand the difficulties most teachers experience in rewarding creative thinking and what happens in successful attempts. It is already clear that many teachers find it quite difficult to apply these principles. Many teachers, however, respond favorably to workshop experiences and suggestions provided by manuals. Skillful application of these principles appears to lead to creative growth.

The following incident described by a first-grade teacher illustrates a successful application of the principle of having respect for imaginative ideas:

Occasion: I was introducing a poem, "February Twilight," and asked the class what "twilight" meant. One boy said that it meant "Twilight Zone." When asked what that meant he said that it had something to do with the brain.

Immediate teacher reaction: I asked him how "Twilight Zone" made him feel, and he answered, "Kinda funny—like it's different," and then he seemed confused as to how to express himself. I then said that I liked his idea and maybe we could think better if we knew what "twilight" was. When everyone seemed puzzled, I suggested it was a time of day. Several then suggested "not really light," "almost night," "when the sun is going down," etc.

Immediate class Reaction: Intense interest and desire to contribute their ideas.

Way respect shown: I was very interested in his ideas and encouraged others to add to them.

Effects: Lee told us that he knew it was like imagination. The discussion led to that time between night and day—wakefulness and sleep—daydreaming —real and unreal. It sparked their imagination.

Three experimental approaches have been outlined for developing creative thinking abilities through language arts:

1. Helping youngsters recognize the value of their ideas
2. Providing activities which give practice or exercise in creative thinking
3. Rewarding creative thinking in the classroom.

Although evaluation of these three approaches is incomplete, all appear promising.

46. Motivating the Pupil's Creativity in the Classroom *

HARTLEY KERN, *Sequoia High School, Redwood City, California*

A MID THE furor that the Sputniks have aroused in our educational system today, there is the ever-present concern with pupil motivation. Teachers are worried about student apathy in their classes and many a finger has been pointed and an abundance of solutions offered. This article will be concerned with the methods the writer has found rewarding in stimulating student motivation.

The problem of getting students interested in their work has always been with us. It is a well-recognized fact that if the students are interested in their class work, many of the other problems a teacher has to face are minimized. Before any methods can be presented for stimulating motivation, it is necessary that the nature of the student himself be understood.

Secondary school teachers often make the mistake of assuming that their pupils are endowed with less intelligence than they actually possess. They are in agreement with the legal code and assume that persons below the age of eighteen are not responsible for their conduct and must be treated in a different manner than are members of the adult community. Such teachers spoon-feed the subject matter to their students and coddle them in all academic pursuits. This writer maintains that students will always measure up to their teachers' expectations. If the teacher looks upon them as immature and irresponsible infants, they will be so; if treated as young adults with important responsibilities, they will react accordingly. The fact is that secondary school students have the mental capabilities of adults and must be expected to use these abilities.

The purpose of academic work is to help the student learn about the past and to think critically and objectively about the present. One way this goal can be reached is by looking once again to the foundations of our democratic society. Our country is founded upon the ideals of freedom of the intellect and freedom of the individual. It is considered good that a man be allowed to think for himself, especially when this thinking involves

* From Hartley Kern, "Motivating the Pupil's Creativity in the Classroom," *California Journal of Secondary Education* (May, 1959), pp. 263–68. Reprinted by permission.

value judgments, ethical norms, and rational explanations. One must not be subjected only to one ideology or one point of view. For those who are seeking a method of pupil motivation, the writer suggests a classroom situation where every student is encouraged to express his own ideas freely and where these ideas are acknowledged as being worth-while by his classmates and teacher. If a student realizes he will not be ridiculed or put under pressure for any original ideas or questioning of traditional ideas, he will begin using his mind more critically. If he realizes that he has some thing to offer to his classmates and to the teacher, then this is the necessary motivating force.

Basic to this concept of free expression within the classroom is the acknowledgment that not all ideas are good ideas. Students will be taught to discriminate between logical analysis and emotional attachments. Experts will be recognized as people who possess greater ability to interpret a situation through their better training. The opinions of the doctor, the lawyer, and the historian concerning their special fields are considered more valid than those of the layman. However in a democracy where it is believed that all men intrinsically possess the ability to think for themselves, it must be realized that no one point of view concerning any particular area is ever totally correct. Within this point lies the crux of this article. Each individual possesses the right and the ability to discover for himself and for others a new approach or answer to a heretofore noncontroversial and accepted point of view.

It might be asked how this is related to the actual classroom situation. If a teacher allows his students to think in a creative fashion without feeling threatened, if he actively promotes original work, if time is allowed for controversial discussion, if students are encouraged to disagree critically with each other, the text, and the teacher, if a teacher shows by his actions that he favors these activities, then he is on the road to motivating his students. Pupils will work hard and become interested in applying themselves if they feel that they really have something to offer to the class.

Many teachers feel it is necessary to start out the beginning of each new semester with work in the subject matter. It should be realized that it takes time to create the type of situation wanted, and that if the teacher takes a few days or a week to get to know the students first, and to explain to them what he is trying to accomplish, then the rest of the semester will flow more smoothly.

The first thing that a teacher must do in a class if he hopes to motivate all students is to explain to them his philosophy of education. He must tell them that he considers the role of education in our schools to be the development of the mind and the ability to think for oneself on one's own feet, not just for the presentation of facts accepted without question and committed to memory.

During the first few days of the term it must be stressed that the classroom will be run in a democratic manner. We have all heard about democratic atmosphere in the classroom; but here the writer means a democracy based on law, not anarchy. The teacher is to be considered the leader because of his training, not because he is a better or more intelligent person. Once the framework of rules has been established, the teacher can create a situation whereby the students and teacher become better acquainted. At this point there will be further talks on the teacher's philosophy and orientation to what will be taking place in the classroom during the term.

For some teachers, creating this type of classroom environment presents problems. When you encourage free discussion it is difficult to cover all the material and impossible to follow any preconceived plans, since the work will be based upon the interest and inclination of the group in problem areas. Therefore, daily lesson plans are frustrating and you will soon find yourself using well-developed unit plans covering the broad areas you want developed. In this way your time sequences will be less restricted. It is helpful to pass out unit assignment sheets to the students. These sheets should list the basic ideas behind the entire unit, followed by a list of discussion questions on the most pertinent problems in the area of study. At the bottom of each sheet should be a category of extra credit work that students can do should they finish their work before the rest of the class. All extra work should be of an original nature with the exception of a research paper done in collegiate form. Students appreciate these assignment sheets because they are enabled to work ahead of the class, or, when absent, to know just what they have missed. They also are able to see the over-all general plan of the unit through these sheets.

The mind cannot function creatively and enthusiasm will vanish if pupils are forced to conform to many specific rules. Once students become stimulated, the teacher must provide the necessary equipment to direct their enthusiasm in a thought-provoking channel. This means the students must make use of the library frequently, book lists must be developed, and interesting work projects and displays created. Pupil interest usually evolves into group and committee work, panels, and debates. This often requires double assignments, multiple texts, and, most of all, very efficient planning.

Once a class starts moving, the situation is generally as follows: The class as a whole is studying the present assignment, each student is working on one or more projects, and the class is divided up into research, audio-visual, and debate teams. This is a far cry from the "read book, answer questions, test" variety of activity. It should be realized that there is no halfway point. If your object is to teach *everyone* in the class and not just the few gifted and the problem children, then you will either have a highly motivated steamed-up group of fireballs or a lethargic watch-the-clock group of bored individuals.

Each teacher should realize that in every class there is a large group of divergent interests represented and that not all of the students will possess a fervent interest in the subject matter at hand. Therefore the teacher should attempt to cross subject lines and tie in different areas of study in order to bring as many students into the fold as possible. For example, if you are studying any historic period, attempt to tie in literature, the arts, music, science, religion, the military, clothing, foods, transportation, etc. Some students become interested in the Roman Wars simply by bringing into the classroom information concerning the type of weapons or money used. Others may be interested in the dress of the period, etc.

Creative expression and activities that tend to promote it, must be stressed, such as: individual and group projects, debates, committee work, plays, and role-playing. Silent reading, frequent tests of factual information, or discussion of specific answers to lists of questions cannot promote a process of critical thinking nor motivate the students to do any original work.

Many teachers feel it is important to start the classroom period with work on written assignments, their object being to occupy the students for the first few minutes while certain routine matters are taken care of. Such activities as writing down lists of words, or answering specific questions are methods that are often employed. However, the writer feels it is also quite important to start the class *thinking,* so that their minds will be receptive to what will follow during the period. Defining proverbs or quotations pertaining to the present unit of study, restating the point behind the last days' lesson in a paragraph, or answering some broad general question by stating an opinion rather than a fact, are examples of the types of activities that might be employed.

One thing that must be stated over and over in the classroom is that the teacher is looking for original work. This means that no type of homework, project work, or written reports should ever be copied. However, this will not be fruitful unless the student is paid for his originality by getting good grades. He must be made to realize that the primary criteria for grading are not neatness, size, nor amount of time put in, but thorough involvement. If you ask a student to turn in a term paper concerning the arguments for and against the Monroe Doctrine, and Student A turns in a definitive ten-page critical analysis with no bibliography, and Student B turns in an unoriginal, less comprehensive fifty-page report with a long bibliography consisting mostly of standard sources, then Student A must receive a higher grade than Student B. The writer is opposed to giving an A grade for any written work unless there are some well thought out, original (not copied) views contained within it.

Much has been written about the type of tests that should be given in the classroom. Actually, the most important thing is not the type of test that is given, but what the student is being tested for. It is much more important to test for understanding than for retention. If the students know that they are going to be tested on their ability to retain a series of facts, they will not be motivated toward a broad understanding of the course nor become involved in their own specific areas of interest. Therefore the questions, whether they be objective or subjective, should test for a broad comprehension of the subject matter and should include only the pertinent facts studied within the unit.

If the students are confronted with the idea that all problems have been solved for them and all they have to do is learn the answers, this is not going to motivate them to try to create anything new and original. However, if the teacher presents a problem to the class and informs the students that the solution to the problem, held true for centuries, was later disproved, then it will become apparent to the students that present-day problems and their solutions might some day in the future be also disproved. This may motivate them to use their own reasoning in relation to the facts.

Never answer a student's specific question! Never let the student come to the conclusion that the teacher is there to supply factual information as if he were a walking dictionary. If the question requires an answer of factual nature, then it is the role of the teacher to point out to the student where this information can be obtained. On the other hand, if the answer requires a logical analysis, then it is the teacher's job to aid the student in analyzing the situation, always allowing the student to arrive at his own conclusion. If a student asks whether or not the solution he reached is absolutely correct, it should again be pointed out that no answers are *absolutely* correct, but that his answer is perhaps a good one or one accepted by a recognized authority. It could be pointed out to some students that there are other interpretations that might warrant a research project on their part. If the student comes up with a weak answer, you should let him know that his is one of many answers, but that the experts in the field today are in disagreement with it.

A teacher who is interested in helping students to think for themselves will always let them disagree with him and with each other. In any area of study you will find among learned people different evaluations and contradictory ideas. One is forced to conclude that in almost any discussion there is no one final interpretation. In the classroom the textbooks and the teacher will usually accept one system of thought. If the teacher wants to motivate student thinking, however, he must never reject a *logical* deviation from the "accepted" point of view. He must let the students know that even mathematics and history are explained in terms of certain assumptions which may be wrong. The student must be aware of the fact that there are other less popular interpretations. This does not mean that there are not correct answers, but simply that all answers should be accepted on their own merits because of the logical proof contained within them. Proof should never rest on the laurels of authority. This also does not mean the teacher should allow the students to express all ideas indiscriminately or that all student ideas should be given equal weight with those that come from the teacher and the book. Ideas should be considered only on the basis of thought and logical defense.

It must be remembered that the whole key to the problem of motivation lies in provoking the students to think on their own. Thinking promotes motivation and motivation promotes thinking, since the two are permanently interwoven.

47. Teaching Machines and Programmed Learning: What Support from the Psychology of Learning? *

ERNEST R. HILGARD, *Stanford University*
California

PROGRAMMED learning has come upon the scene very rapidly and brought with it both the possibility of a radically different (and, hopefully, successful) method of instruction and the possibility of providing a new look at the process of learning itself. It derives support from established principles in the psychology of learning, six of which I shall mention here.

1. Programmed learning recognizes *individual differences* by beginning where the learner is and by permitting him to proceed at his own pace. It is possible that programmed learning may succeed in reducing individual differences because of these features.

2. Programmed learning requires that the learner be *active.* Learning by doing is an old educational slogan, and it is still a good one. The teaching machine (or program in other form) fights the tendency for the pupil to be passive and inattentive by requiring his participation if the lesson is to move.

3. Programmed learning provides immediate *knowledge of results.* Whether because it provides reinforcement, reward, or cognitive feedback, there is abundant testimony that knowledge of results is important in learning. It favors learning the right thing; it prevents repeating and fixating the wrong answers.

4. Programmed learning emphasizes the *organized nature of knowledge* because it requires continuity between the easier (earlier) concepts and the harder (later) ones. Again, all learning theories have some place for meaningfulness, for understandable relationships, for assimilating the new to the familiar. The program builder cannot be as arbitrary about content as the ordinary laboratory student of learning (with his multiple-unit mazes or nonsense lists of varying lengths); the programmer has to make one step fit the next and provide the hint or cue for the next. He has to examine the subject matter very carefully in order to find out what

* From Ernest R. Hilgard, "Teaching Machines and Programmed Learning: What Support from the Psychology of Learning?" *NEA Journal,* November, 1961, pp. 20–21. Reprinted by permission.

has to be known before something else can be learned, and he eliminates side issues that do not lead to cumulative learning.

5. Programmed learning provides **spaced review** in order to guarantee the high order of success that has become a standard requirement of good programs. Review with application, if properly arranged, permits a high order of learning on the first run through a program. While there is no rule against going through a program a second time if there have been many errors, the aim is to produce essentially errorless learning the first time around.

6. Programmed learning reduces anxiety because the learner is not threatened by the task: He **knows** that he can learn and is learning, and gains the satisfaction that this knowledge brings. Lest this seem to be a trivial observation, we need only to be reminded that many children have been so frustrated by school learning tasks that they have never had the satisfaction of coming up to expectations; we have no way of knowing the costs we have had to pay for this accumulated frustration.

Having said this much in favor of the teaching machine and programmed learning in relation to what we know about learning, let me say that a general principle of learning can never be tagged to a practical procedure as a validation of that procedure; the validation comes in other ways. Thus any successful instructional device must accord with learning principles, or there is something wrong with those principles. Psychological principles do not tell us just what to do in practice; that is why we need educational as well as psychological research.

Let me turn now to the teacher's role in the midst of the new technology. If through teaching machines and programmed instruction we free the teacher of the drudgery of straightforward instruction in the imparting of information and questioning about facts, computations, and the like, the teacher will then have time to do the things that he can do better than any machine.

The hope, as I see it, is not that the machine will relieve the teacher shortage, but that it will relieve teacher fatigue, permitting the teacher to devote himself to the essential task of inspiring, stimulating, and encouraging students to feel a sense of their own significance in the scheme of things, to see themselves as creative individuals who can set tasks for themselves and can achieve at a level that will increase their self-respect and give them a favorable self-image. The teaching machine will help, so far as the student's competency in routine achievement is concerned, but the teacher will still have many opportunities for recognizing and rewarding individuality, initiative, and creativity.

Let us spell this out a little more clearly:

Let us agree first that you cannot think at a high level unless you have some facts to think about and unless you have some tools by which to manipulate concepts. At the same time, no person can store in his head the kinds of facts he needs to think about all sorts of complex problems, so even at the factual level he needs to learn how to find facts.

Thus the dictionary habit, the encyclopedia habit, and the library-catalog habit are fully as important as memorized facts. While a teaching machine can give some of these facts, the search for facts is not a sedentary habit; no matter how well-organized a library, you have to walk around a little to use the reference works. This is then a task that the teacher is needed for: to teach the student how to search out the facts he needs to know for a given purpose.

Let us also agree that in a changing world we cannot teach formulas by which to solve problems; we have to prepare the pupil for new situations by teaching more general aspects of problem solving. The puzzle-form of problem (where there is one right answer to discover) can easily be taught by the teaching machine, but the full-scale problem is harder to teach. The feature that impresses me most about really good problem solvers (and I include research scientists among these) is their capacity to see a problem where others do not see one or to define a manageable problem in the midst of a situation so complex that others feel merely baffled.

A good teacher can help pupils to discover problems for themselves and to have the satisfaction of working out answers to problems they discover or set for themselves. The real yield in transfer of learning necessarily comes in the kinds of problem-solving skills that are content indifferent; that is, that will permit the attack on a problem regardless of what the content of the problem is.

In addition to teaching the search for facts, and problem solving in general, we also wish to teach creativity. Guilford makes a useful distinction between convergent thinking and divergent thinking. Convergent thinking is that which focuses down to a precise answer, as in puzzle solving. You surround the problem, so to speak, and then marshal your forces for an attack at its heart. In divergent thinking, you work in the opposite way: Starting with a familiar topic or idea, you let it flower and grow in novel and interesting ways, and thus create something new. Several creative people given the same starting point will end up at very different places. Hence the process is divergent rather than convergent.

How can we teach the kind of flexibility that yields creative divergent thinking? The answer is that it must be encouraged, rewarded, just as anything else is that we try to teach. Taking a cue from the teaching machine, if you will, I favor the encouragement of small evidences of creativity.

Here is where a skilled teacher comes in. He can encourage a pupil to take pride in his own creative efforts even though they are very limited by external standards. A small tune invented on the piano, a limerick (instead of a sonnet), a string tied to the key of an alarm clock that turns on the radio instead of sounding the alarm—it does not matter how trivial the invention may be. If it gives the individual the sense that he can create something, he learns to see himself as potentially creating something more.

The last aspect of teaching that I wish to point to is the group process of living with diversity, of discovering compromises that permit community life to go on, of seeing individual behavior in terms of its consequences for others, of developing a sense of responsibility. There is no way to learn this but to participate responsibly in group processes. Here is clearly an area where the teacher cannot be replaced. Any group activity—especially one that involves planning, division of labor, moderating conflicting value systems, taking of responsibility, cooperating and competing—is significant for the teaching of social process.

By relieving the teacher of much that is routine, the teaching machine and program permit these other opportunities greater play. If much of the *science* of teaching is taken over by the machine, the *art* of teaching will again come into its own, residing where it should, in the teacher as a person.

48. Educational Measurement: A Broad Perspective *

RALPH W. TYLER, *Director, Center for Advanced Study in the Behavioral Sciences, Stanford, California.*

EDUCATIONAL measurement is important for the elementary school principal not as an end in itself but as one of the means by which he exercises his responsibility for instructional leadership. In the selection and use of educational measures, the goals of elementary school instruction are clarified and information is obtained which is helpful in teaching and counseling, and in curriculum development, supervision, and administration. Measurement is not a method of rating teachers but it is a process of great value for teachers.

Educational measurement is an effort to refine and make more objective and precise our observations of pupils' behavior as they are engaged in learning and in using what they have learned. Measurement is not a substitute for informal observations by the school staff but it is an aid in interpreting these observations. It does not take the place of thinking, planning, and working creatively but it serves to appraise the results of curriculum planning and instructional activities. It is not the only means of evaluation but it is an essential part of it.

* From Ralph W. Tyler, "Educational Measurement: A Broad Perspective," *The National Elementary Principal* (September, 1961), pp. 8–13. Reprinted by permission.

USES OF EDUCATIONAL MEASUREMENT

The many uses of educational measurement in the elementary school can be easily illustrated.

Assessing subject achievement by grade: Perhaps the most common use, but certainly not the most significant, is in assessing the level of pupil achievement in the school subjects, grade by grade. One or more standardized tests in such fields as reading and arithmetic are given at several grade levels. Using the results, it is possible to: 1) estimate the amount of learning in these fields during the time since the same pupils were tested previously; 2) compare the indicated amount of learning (that is, the change in achievement since the previous measurement) with that indicated in previous years—this is one index of improvement in the school's educational accomplishments; and 3) compare the mean and the variability of the pupils' achievement in these fields with the mean and variability of similar schools in the city, state, region, or nation.

Providing data for individual guidance: A second common use of educational measurement is to provide data for individual guidance and conseling. A pupil's scores on achievement tests, intelligence tests, tests of special aptitudes, and tests of interests, social behavior, and personality supplement teacher and parent observations in identifying talents and abilities, problems and difficulties. This data is also helpful in parent interviews and reports.

Diagnosing learning difficulties: Educational measurement aids teachers in identifying the strong and weak points in a class' work. For example, through the use of a test on reading and interpreting narrative materials, the teacher may recognize more clearly the fact that a class is making good progress in getting the main plots of stories but is not growing in ability to interpret their implications. A test in arithmetic may show that a class is making good progress in problem solving but not in speed and accuracy of computation. Finding these areas of difficulty enables the teacher to focus his instructional efforts more efficiently.

Similarly, measurement can be helpful in identifying the strengths and weaknesses in achievement of individual pupils. As the teacher and pupil find the respects in which his achievement is less than adequate, individual learning efforts can be directed more efficiently.

In diagnosing learning difficulties of a class or an individual pupil, more than educational achievement should be measured. The outcome of instruction is influenced by the learner's personal characteristics as well as by his achievement level. Among the significant characteristics, in addition to age, sex, and mental test scores, are social class, educational and occupational goals, cultural level of the home, parents' attitudes toward education, interests, types of motivation, social acceptance by peers, physical growth, and work experience. A number of these characteristics can be measured. The results are useful in understanding the extent and limitations of achievement by a class or individual pupil and in working out an instructional plan to improve learning.

Evaluating new methods and materials: Most elementary schools, concerned with improving their effectiveness, devise and try out new teaching methods and materials. Some of these new things may turn out in practice to be a distinct improvement; others may not. In determining the value of new devices, educational measurement is important. One's subjective judgment about how well something is working is greatly affected by his habits, expectations, and moods. It is necessary to supplement personal judgments with objective comparisons of educational results. There are several useful comparisons. One may compare the results obtained in using the new device with previous educational outcomes with the same class, with outcomes obtained in control groups, or with outcomes commonly obtained by classes similar to the ones in which the new device is used. Hence, educational measurement is a necessary tool in improving methods and materials.

Contributing to in-service education: One of the most important values of educational measurement for the elementary school principal is in its contribution to the continued in-service education of the school staff. It assists in developing the school staff in two ways: 1) by calling for clarity and concreteness in discussing, planning, and appraising educational programs; and 2) by focusing attention on pupil learning rather than on teaching procedures per se.

Many discussions of educational objectives are expressed so vaguely that they do not serve to guide the selection of learning experiences. Saying that the school is to teach thinking, develop character, and enable pupils to master the tools of learning will not get to the level of concreteness needed to focus effort and guide instruction. In planning a program of educational measurement, the staff must go beyond these general phrases and define the goals clearly in terms of the behavior the school seeks to help its pupils acquire. The staff must be able to state the kinds of thinking, feeling, and acting the school expects to help children develop. For an elementary school, this involves an actual listing, for both the primary and intermediate grades, of the things the staff expects pupils to understand, the skills it expects them to acquire, the interests it hopes they will develop, the values it hopes they will appreciate, and the habits it wants them to develop. This listing is basic to planning a measurement program. One cannot select appropriate measures until he knows what it is he wants to measure. Hence, planning a measurement program requires the staff to clarify its goals. The concrete results of this thinking are useful not only in selecting measures but also in planning the curriculum.

Planning a measurement program focuses attention upon what pupils are expected to learn; study of the results of measurement directs attention to what pupils have learned or have not learned and to pupil characteristics and learning conditions which may facilitate or interfere with learning. Thus, the pupils and their learning occupy the center of attention. This concern leads naturally to further observations, to additional study of pupil needs, motivations, habits, attitudes, and the like, and to a consideration of conditions which facilitate learning and of the ways in which the instructional program may increase learning. These are important subjects in the in-service education of the staff.

PUBLIC PRESSURE FOR CRITICAL APPRAISAL

Although it can serve such important purposes, many elementary schools are not using educational measurement and many others are utilizing it inadequately or inappropriately.

During the past few years, there has been more than a fivefold increase in the use of standard tests in American schools. But this increase has not been accompanied by a corresponding growth in the use of tests for the purposes mentioned above. The major influences in the current emphasis on testing have been those provisions of the National Defense Education Act which support the use of tests in educational guidance and, secondly, the public demand for evaluation of our educational efforts. The NDEA has been primarily an influence on the high schools in the use of tests, but the public demand for evaluation has affected the elementary schools fully as much as the secondary schools.

One of the reasons for the current limitations in utilizing educational measurement is the concern of many of us in the schools to defend our work against public criticism. Not since the great debates of a century ago on the development of the American system of public schools has there been so much general public interest in education. Local school boards, state legislatures, the Congress, and the public generally are deeply concerned with the quality of education. Seeking appraisals of the public schools, they find conflicting reports.

These increasing demands for critical evaluation must be met. But appraisal of the work of an elementary school is not a simple procedure. It requires consideration of the school's several objectives, of the educational backgrounds from which children come since there is a wide range in the extent to which the home contributes constructively to children's educational development, and of the quality and quantity of resources the community devotes to the school. While educational measurement is an important part of the appraisal process, its value depends upon proper use.

The present emphasis upon critical appraisal of American schools can be a good and powerful influence toward strengthening educational programs if the evaluation is adequate, constructive, and intelligently used. But it can also do great damage both within and without the school if the appraisal is inadequately conceived, poorly planned, and unwisely used. To serve most effectively, educational measurement needs to be planned and used as an integral part of the school's instructional program.

SHORTCOMINGS OF EARLY TESTING MOVEMENT

Another factor which contributes to the inadequate use of measurement in the elementary school is our earlier experience with group testing which reached its peak in the 1920's. This was called the "scientific movement" in education.

During this period, the products of learning were measured on tests which carefully reflected the content of teaching materials, but were not built on a systematic analysis of the educational values to which good schools and teachers were dedicated. In subjects like geography and history, pupils were tested on their recall of specific items appearing in commonly used textbooks. Yet thoughtful teachers of geography and history strongly believed that the most important values to be sought in teaching these subjects lay not in mere memorization but in perceiving relationships among things and events and in being able to interpret human activities through geographical and historical concepts and generalizations. As a result, they were unhappy about the "measurement movement" of the period because it did not base its appraisal upon a careful consideration of the educational values involved.

Reading tests were constructed on detailed analyses of vocabulary and of the percentages of pupils answering questions correctly, but without systematic examination of the major educational values sought in the teaching of reading. Most test items required only simple comprehension of reading passages or an unanalyzed mixture of pupil responses. Experienced teachers were certain that a number of values in addition to "plain sense comprehension" could be and often were achieved in teaching reading. Interpretation of varied types of reading materials involves much more than straightforward comprehension. Life-long reading interests and sensitive responses to poetry are two illustrations of values which loom large in a reading program. These were minimally reflected in educational appraisals of the time.

The arithmetic tests were also inadequate in terms of the values sought by able teachers. They usually included only exercises in computation and verbal problems to be solved by computation. They, too, were based on a compilation of the exercises found in widely used textbooks, and on an analysis of the percentages of pupils answering questions correctly. There was no direct effort to appraise such values as understanding arithmetic concepts and the ability to think in quantitative terms. Yet these values were considered of great importance by many competent teachers.

Because of these serious limitations, many educators became disillusioned with the tests of the period.

DEFINING EDUCATIONAL OBJECTIVES

The Eight-Year Study, which began in 1933, worked out a new and broader concept of educational measurement in connection with the program of evaluation. The study used the term "evaluation" to accent the fact that it was seeking to appraise the educational values actually developing in a school program. The first step in the study was to identify the educational objectives teachers were seeking in order to plan appraisals that would measure how well they were being attained.

To say that evaluation should begin with the educational objectives since its purpose is to appraise pupil progress toward each of these objectives is simple enough. But obtaining a list of clearly defined objectives is not easy.

Many teachers have not stated their objectives—in fact, some which they consider most important may not have been written down or even explicitly formulated in their own minds. Hence, the listing of objectives requires a great deal of thought and discussion. It should be guided by such questions as: "What are we trying to help students acquire in and through our reading program? Our social studies program? Our arithmetic program? Our arts program? What abilities, skills, knowledge, attitudes, interests, habits, and the like do students need in order to get the most out of reading? Out of social studies? Out of arithmetic? Out of music? Why are we using these materials or these procedures? Do they suggest certain results or objectives that we are or ought to be seeking?" These are simply different ways of reminding ourselves of possible objectives. Often several different questions are needed to stimulate teachers to reflect on their own experiences and purposes.

Once identified, objectives must be clearly defined. The objectives of education are to facilitate various kinds of desirable learning on the part of pupils. But learning is the acquisition by the pupil of ways of behaving—that is, ways of thinking, feeling, and acting which he has not previously followed. Thus, a child in the primary grades may develop a mode of attacking unfamiliar words which he has not previously used, or a sixth-grade child may acquire an interest in learning more about the peoples of Africa. To evaluate, we need to know what kinds of pupil behavior we are looking for. When we talk about comprehension as a reading objective, we should ask what kind of behavior is involved and with what kind of reading materials. Our objectives must be defined in terms of pupil behavior.

Skill and ability objectives are easier to define than objectives concerning interests and appreciations. Working over the years with teachers, we have found some fairly common agreements in defining many of these less tangible objectives. Interest in reading, for example, is often defined in terms of the following behavior: "The pupil likes to read. He gets satisfaction in reading. When he has free time, he often chooses voluntarily to spend time in reading." Usually, teachers are concerned that pupils become interested not only in reading but also in reading varied types of stories, articles, and books, and that the content of the reading they choose voluntarily show increased complexity and maturity as time goes on.

Such definitions of objectives in terms of behavior make it possible to plan appraisals based on the important educational objectives. This was a first significant phase in the development of the older measurement into a process more appropriate for educational evaluation.

BROADER DEFINITION OF EDUCATIONAL TESTS

Since the purpose of educational appraisal is to find out to what extent each of the important educational objectives is actually being realized, means for measuring actual pupil behavior are essential. This is a necessary check on hopes and fears, on expectations and doubts. Without real evidence of what pupils are learning, we tend to rely heavily on our own preconceptions, and our temperaments—optimistic, skeptical, or pessimistic as they may be—will largely color our conclusions. Empirical tests are necessary.

Some 25 years ago, the prevailing concept of an educational measurement was the administration of a paper-and-pencil test, usually consisting of true-false or multiple-choice items. These devices could provide evidence of the amount of information the student could recall and indicate his ability to spell words, define terms, and make computations. They could also furnish some indication of his ability to comprehend reading passages. But they were not relevant to some other important objectives. They did not provide evidence of habits, attitudes, interests, appreciations, and a variety of problem-solving abilities.

As we sought to develop means for evaluation, it became clear that we must broaden the concept of an educational test. We now think of an educational test as a series of situations which call forth from the pupil the kind of behavior defined in the objective and permit a record to be made of the pupil's actual behavior. For example, a test of reading interpretations should consist of a series of situations in which the pupil is stimulated to read and to interpret what he is reading, and in which a record can be made of the pupil's interpretations.

This conception of an educational test makes possible the use of a variety of devices for measurement. In addition to paper-and-pencil exercises, such procedures as observations, interviews, questionnaires, samples of products made, and records obtained in other connections can serve as evaluation devices. To appraise habits, for example, observation may be employed or, under certain circumstances, questionnaires may be useful. To appraise appreciation of literature, interviews focused on the pupil's responses to his reading and his feelings and judgments are sometimes helpful. Although the realization that comprehensive educational measurement requires evidence about each of several important objectives made the task seem more difficult, the further recognition that a variety of appraisal methods could be used helped to encourage us.

NEED TO MEASURE PUPIL CHARACTERISTICS

The early notions of educational measurement drew heavily upon the natural sciences for their rationale. To determine the melting point of aluminum, any sample of pure aluminum would do. The results did not vary appreciably with the particular sample tested. Biological science, however, recognized the differences in genetic composition. The effect of limited rainfall on wheat is partly dependent on the genetic composition of the wheat. Similarly, the early experimenters in education quickly went beyond J. M. Rice's pioneer effort to find out whether different amounts of time devoted to spelling made any difference in the ability of children to spell. In his study, no attention was given to differences among the children taking spelling. But the influence of Terman, Thorndike, and others resulted in general recognition of differing "mental abilities" which had to be taken into account in studying the effects of differing teaching methods. By the beginning of the Eight-Year Study, educational appraisal often involved testing for mental ability and frequently the use of control groups similar in age and sex as well as in mental test scores.

The Eight-Year Study included a great diversity of boys and girls. As we began to appraise pupil learning and observe the effects of different procedures, materials, and teaching personalities, it became clear that the educational effects often were related to a number of pupil characteristics. A free reading program in the eighth grade which showed great influence on the quality of reading interests in one school seemed to have much less effect on the quality of interests in another school. Yet the appraisal of mental ability revealed no appreciable differences in the distribution of these scores. These findings led us to recognize the need to evaluate a variety of student characteristics if we were to understand and report the values of different kinds of educational experience. Instructional procedures and materials and principles of curriculum organization were often effective for students with certain characteristics and not for others.

Hence, the conception of educational measurement developed to include the measurement of characteristics of the learners. Some of these characteristics were mentioned earlier in this article. The appraisal of characteristics is similar to the appraisal of what students are learning. Except for categories like sex and age, each characteristic needs to be defined in terms of pupil behavior and a variety of test devices selected which call forth the desired behavior and provide opportunity for recording the pupil reactions.

NEED TO ASSESS LEARNING CONDITIONS

When the Eight-Year Study began, it was commonly assumed that curricular plans, teaching methods, and instructional materials were in themselves clearly defined factors which could be assessed in terms of their effectiveness in producing desired learning. Educational experiments had compared the "look-say" method of teaching beginning reading with the "syllabic analysis" method, the "systematic method" of teaching spelling with the "incidental method," the "incidental method" of teaching arithmetic with the "drill method," and so on. Often, several investigations of the same "methods" yielded quite different results.

In the Eight-Year Study, several schools explored such innovations as "pupil-teacher planning" and the "core curriculum." As we observed the development in different schools of what was thought to be the same innovation and talked with teachers about them, we realized that a phrase like "pupil-teacher planning" assumes concrete meaning in terms of the way in which it is conceived, developed, and actually carried on by the teacher. The phrase is a stimulus for thought and planning. But this and similar terms are not precisely defined entities like a specific injection of penicillin. We sometimes found as much variability in results among classes which were purportedly using the same "method" as we found among classes which were using several different methods.

From such experiences, it was apparent that a comprehensive program of educational measurement should include an assessment of the *conditions* of learning if the results of the appraisal of *what* pupils were learning were to be adequately understood. The conditions of learning which should be assessed depend to some extent on those that appear to be critical for the educational program under study. Generally, an estimate of the following conditions of learning will give a very useful picture of the teaching methods, materials, and organization.

Pupil motivation: What proportion of the pupils are interested in the work of the class? What proportion are deeply involved in the work?

Recognition of need to learn new behavior: What proportion of the pupils recognize that they are facing new problems and are acquiring new understanding, new techniques, and new attitudes to deal with these problems effectively?

Guidance of new behavior: What proportion of the pupils are obtaining needed guidance rather than being left to trial-and-error when they attempt new behavior?

Availability of appropriate materials: To what extent are pupils provided with materials that give them the opportunity to practice the kind of behavior to be learned?

Time for effective learning: What proportion of the pupils have time to carry on the behavior and practice it?

Satisfaction from the desired behavior: What proportion of the pupils are deriving satisfaction from learning the desired behavior?

Provision for sequential practice: To what extent do the learning experiences from day to day—and over longer periods—provide for sequential rather than repetitious practice of desired behavior?

Pupil standards of performance: What sort of standards of performance do the pupils have? To what extent does each pupil have a standard which is high for him, but attainable?

Means for the pupil to judge his performance: What proportion of the pupils have ways which they use to judge the quality of their own learning? Are the methods they use valid and practical?

Conditions for learning such as the foregoing provide a more useful way of describing teaching procedures than to describe them in terms of "direct" or "incidental" methods or in terms of "teacher-dominated" or "pupil-directed" methods. Creative teachers can facilitate learning by a variety of procedures. But whatever methods they use or however they stimulate reactions, teachers can more clearly understand their effectiveness in terms of the extent to which the conditions of learning are provided.

In the light of the history of the past quarter century, educational measurement is seen as a growing concept. It has developed into a process involving educational objectives, educational tests, the appraisal of the characteristics of the learner, and the assessment of learning conditions. Beginning as a procedure used only by educational and psychological research workers, it has become a process of great value to the elementary school principal in discharging his responsibilities for educational leadership.

49. The Place of Testing
and Evaluation in Learning *

HOWARD A. BOWMAN, *Los Angeles City
School District,
California*

OCCASIONALLY, when this writer has spoken to a group of teachers on the subject of measurement and evaluation, someone rises to ask, "Why do we have evaluation?" What such an individual probably means is, "Why do we, in our school system, have the particular kind of an evaluation program that we have?" The question as originally asked always elicits the same reply, which is that evaluation is one of the most basic of human activities.

Almost every human choice, unless deliberately made on the basis of chance, results from evaluation of some sort. Often, such evaluation is of the most casual sort, and one is scarcely conscious of having made it. Moreover, the basis upon which an evaluation is made often is somewhat irrelevant to the totality of the problem which has elicited the evaluation. Thus the question should not be, "Why do we have evaluation?" Rather, more appropriately it should be "What kinds of evaluation shall we have?"

It is, perhaps, unfortunate but understandable that tests have too frequently become synonomous with evaluation. In certain instances, as, for example with various physical tests on inanimate objects, there is no good reason why the two may not be considered synonymous. However, the problem of evaluation in learning is substantially different, mainly because people are primarily involved. It is also different because of its background,

* From Howard A. Bowman, "The Place of Testing and Evaluation in Learning," *California Journal of Secondary Education* (January, 1960), pp. 61–65. Reprinted by permission.

reaching back to the dawn of history in which human beings are satisfied with the kind of evaluation based on feelings rather than facts. Human opinion might be placed in the same category. . . .

The traditional kind of formal evaluation in schools is the report card. In recent years the report card has been, in some schools, supplanted by the "interview" or "conference," in which the teacher gives the good (or bad) news to each pupil's parents. This, of course, is also evaluation. Lying behind the report card or conferences are numerous minor evaluations of pupil status or progress, likes or dislikes, sins or salvations, errors or accuracies, and so on, until the teacher's mind becomes so crammed with them that the chief problem is deciding which shall hold sway at this "moment of truth."

Unfortunately, there is evidence to show that teachers rely at times more on their memories of small incidents, performances, assignments, recitations, than they do on records of them. This is even more apt to be true if the school employs a marking system which requires the teacher to make a quantitative evaluation of "character traits." Here opinion, unsupported by fact, may run rampant.

The foregoing analysis is no protest against opinion. Opinion is a powerful and worthy instrument. However, to be worth-while, opinion must be informed. In the present context, opinion should be solidly backed by evidence, gathered in a manner appropriate to the situation. Memory can not be trusted. Evidence should be recorded, and to the best of the teacher's capacity such evidence should be as objective as possible.

What then is the relationship of evaluation to learning? Learning is an accretive process, and for each new "layer" of skills, facts, attitudes, and knowledges, the learner must be properly prepared. It is precisely in judging the degree of preparation which exists that the teacher should accomplish one of his more important functions. This diagnosis should be accomplished with skill and insight. It should not be carelessly made of unsecured opinion.

The teacher has many opportunities to evaluate each pupil's performance. For example, the class is taught how to perform a particular operation in mathematics and each pupil in his assigned work demonstrates that he can perform the operation *at that time*. However, unless the operation has some relationship to the totality of instruction in that subject, it was not worth teaching. Assuming then, that this relationship to the totality of instruction exists, the question arises, "How well will the pupil be able to perform this operation tomorrow, next month, or next year, and in context, not in isolation?" This is where the function of the test arises. A test is a sampling of presumptive learnings. The word "sampling" implies a greater range of learnings than may conveniently be tested *in toto*. In turn, this implies a time relationship between the extent of the learnings to be sampled and the length and complexity of the test. Test length and complexity are largely governed by the amount of time the teacher is willing to devote to the process of making, administering, scoring, and interpreting the test. If the test is a commercial one, there are some obvious short cuts. But almost always the commercially prepared test will suffice only for relatively long periods of instruction—a semester, or a year, or even more. It is not economically feasible for a publisher to produce a test for shorter units. It is feasible and desirable for the teacher to do this, and most teachers do.

What is the relationship of the teacher-made test to learning? There are few teachers who do not, at intervals throughout the school year, devise tests or quizzes. From the scores which pupils attain on these, they hope to be able to draw conclusions as to how well these pupils have learned that which was presumed to have been taught. These teacher-made tests will not have, on the whole, the degree of excellence of professionally made instruments. Teachers do not have the time, the knowledge, or the facility for the detailed analysis which professional test makers count on to reduce errors of measurement in the instruments they produce. On the other hand, the teachers have factors working to their advantage. They are closer to what has actually been done, and they are certainly better acquainted with the objectives of instruction and the philosophy behind the work in their own classrooms.

The teacher can profit by the techniques which have been devised by others, building these techniques upon his already excellent foundation of teaching skill, his intimacy with the philosophy of education which prevails in his school, and his pervasive feeling of what he is trying to do in his classroom. This writer has known a number of teachers who have concluded that the only way they could do a decent job of evaluating the progress made within the classrooms for which they were responsible was to learn how to make tests. Undoubtedly thousands of others have reached the same conclusion. We still have to worry about those who make the kind of test in which, automatically, "ten right answers is an A, nine a B, eight a C, seven a D, and if you have fewer than seven correct you fail."

There are certain steps which the teacher may profitably take when constructing tests for classroom use. Some of them have more philosophical overtones than do others, but all are practical and tangible.

1. Come to a decision as to the real purposes of a given unit of work and write out these purposes. What skills, attitudes, knowledges, or other factors are to be developed in this unit?

2. In connection with each purpose, answer the question: What evidences of attainment of this objective are acceptable and subject to measurement within the scope of your skill at writing test items?

3. Borrow or buy one of the several available books which give examples of various kinds of test items, and which tell how to put together a test. Such a book is to be used not for mastery, necessarily, but as a reference source. More than one such source would be helpful if available, and faculty or departmental study groups will provide more good outcomes than the same number of people working independently.

4. Try writing various kinds of test items and use them with the class. Some may be subjective, some objective, and some in between. Try to observe the rules laid down in the reference book in use, especially with respect to scoring the items. One of the easiest ways to get into trouble is to use both positive scores (for correct responses) and negative scores (for incorrect items) on, say, a matching item. It is much better to play safe and use only positive scores.

5. Keep a record of how pupils respond to each item. This is easily done if each item is written on a card. The data can be recorded on the back of the card. The principal matter is to realize that the pupils who do best on the test as a whole should also tend to do better on each item than do those whose total scores are lowest. A crude but satisfactory form of "item analysis" is to divide the scored papers into thirds. On each item, more of the pupils in the top third should respond correctly than do those in the lowest third. If the opposite is true, that item is detracting from the measuring capacity of the test and should be eliminated.

6. Save the good items in a card file. Steps one through five are laborious at the time, but, over the long haul of several years, the accumulation of usable test items will save many hours. Moreover the teacher's function in the evaluative process will have improved and he will be a better teacher.

7. As a final step, learn that when a test is first put together, there is no way of knowing how difficult it is. There are many variables to take into account, and these are not always apparent. Don't fall into the earlier mentioned trap of assuming that it is possible to tell in advance how many correct responses constitute a level of "C" or "A." Let the test scores provide this information. Better still, let the scores of several successive tests provide it. The more times one measures, the better his chances of measuring correctly.

Learning and following the foregoing steps will not make the teacher a test expert. It will, however, help him to be a better teacher because it will make him more aware of the strong and weak spots in the learning of his pupils. If the weak spots are known they can be "beefed up," a process which may require no more than reallocation of time spent on various aspects of the subject. Moreover, an additional advantage lies in the fact that pupils are more satisfied that a fair system has been used to rate them.

In summary, the following points have been made to support the thesis that testing and evaluation have an important place in learning.

1. Evaluation is a basic human activity; teachers are constantly evaluating whether or not they realize it.
2. Much evaluation carried on by teachers is informal and subjective. However, informed opinion is a powerful and proper instrument.
3. The teacher has the final job of evaluating a semester's work or a year's work by placing a mark on a report card. His opinion of the pupil's achievement should be solidly backed by evidence in recorded form.
4. All kinds of pupil performances, properly evaluated, provide the necessary evidence.
5. Tests are the source of one important kind of evidence. Unfortunately, too many teacher-made tests are constructed without a realization of what constitutes a good test, and are improperly interpreted. This need not be so.
6. Making good tests is not easy, but neither is it extremely difficult. The teacher can learn to do it, and both he and his pupils will profit as a result of the exercise of this skill.

50. On the Assessment of Academic Achievement *

HENRY S. DYER, *Educational Testing Service Princeton, New Jersey*

IN THESE DAYS of ferment in the curriculum, any large producer of educational tests is likely to get strange and wonderful requests from teachers suddenly smitten by the need to evaluate the new things they are doing. The following letter, though purely imaginary, is not untypical. It reflects

* From Henry S. Dyer, "On the Assessment of Academic Achievement," *Teachers College Record* (November, 1960), pp. 164–72. Reprinted by permission.

a few of the mistaken ideas about testing and the assessment of achievement which are prevalent:

Dear Sir:

During this past academic year I have been giving a new course, Marine Wild Life 106. I need some incontrovertible evidence to prove to my suspicious colleagues that Marine Wild Life 106 is more comprehensive and effective than the course it has replaced, namely, Marine Wild Life 102.

Will you therefore please send me 92 copies of your standardized objective test in ichthyology? I am particularly interested in showing that my students have developed a true and deep appreciation of the love-life of our underwater friends.

Please rush the shipment, since I want to give the test as part of my final examination next Thursday.

Sincerely yours,
Professor Finn

Although Professor Finn does not exist, he has many educational cousins who do, and who think, with him, that the purpose of educational evaluation is to demonstrate the truth of a foregone conclusion. It has never occurred to him that an investigation of Marine Wild Life 106 should be so planned as to permit negative findings to appear if, in fact, the course is not all he firmly believes it to be.

But what most bothers the professional tester about the many Professor Finns who are experimenting with new courses is the series of bland assumptions that lie behind the letters they write. The first such assumption is that one can prove something by giving a single test after the show is all over. The second is that a standardized objective test is standard and objective in some absolute sense, as though it had been made in heaven. The third is that testing agencies are like vending machines: All you have to do is put your nickel in the right slot, and out will come precisely the test you are looking for. All of which would be just dandy if true, but unfortunately none of these assumptions bears any noticeable relation to the facts of testing as the assessment of achievement.

The Human Side of Tests

What Professor Finn does not appear to realize is that an educational test of any kind is primarily a human process, not a physical thing. It is a process that begins and ends in human judgment. It is a process that requires time, effort, and hard creative thinking, not only of the professional tester, but of the test user as well. It is a process than can take an infinite number of forms, depending on the purposes to be served and the conditions under which the testing is to be done. It is a process that can hardly be confined to the use of multiple choice questions and paper-and-pencil techniques if it is to provide the sort of rewarding illumination of the educational scene that some people hope for.

In what follows I shall discuss some of the essentials of the testing process as applied to the assessment of academic achievement and pay my respect to several of the knotty problems that bedevil the whole enterprise. The discussion will turn up more questions than answers, but if the questions are sufficiently disturbing, the outcome should be such as to nudge Professor Finn toward deeper wisdom in approaching his evaluation problem.

What do we mean by "academic achievement?" If it is something we are trying to assess, then it seems reasonable to ask first of all what it is. In current usage, it is a fuzzy term that may mean any one of a dozen unspecified things: the sum total of information a student has at his command when he finishes a course of instruction, the getting of a passing grade in a course regardless of what may lie behind the grade, the score on a test that has "achievement" in the title, and so on.

There are two ideas that can be used to pin down the notion of academic achievement a bit more precisely. The first idea is that academic achievement refers to the *identifiable operations* a student is expected to perform on the materials of a course, that is, on the facts, theories, problems, principles, and points of view which he encounters while taking the course. The second idea is that academic achievement refers to the *differences* between the number and kinds of operations a student can and does perform at the beginning of a course and the number and kinds of operations he can and does perform at the end of a course.

The key terms in this definition of achievement are *identifiable operations* and *differences*. The emphasis on operations is supposed to suggest that it is what the student actually *does* that counts. We should think of achievement as something composed of transitive verbs with direct objects —verbs like *infer, generalize, recall, compare, analyze, evaluate, organize, criticize.* And we need to be sure that we can identify these operations by reference to specific tasks or questions that require them. ("What inferences can you draw from the following set of data?" "What general principle can you find that explains the behavior of the following political figures?" etc.)

The emphasis on the *differences* between what a student does at the beginning of a course and what he does at the end of a course calls attention to the fact that academic achievement is a dynamic, not a static, concept; it is what has happened between then and now, not just what is happening now. Can the student now solve differential equations that he found impossible last October? Can he detect differences between Beethoven and Brahms that were not apparent to him earlier? Can he organize his thoughts in written form better than he did at the outset?

Clearly, under this definition, the assessment of academic achievement is a complicated business; it is not something that can be done merely by going out and buying a standardized test two weeks before the final examination. It requires that the teacher responsible for a course must himself be a major participant in the assessment job from start to finish. He may be able to get supplementary aid from published tests; he may find that the professionals in testing can give him useful ideas and point the way to sound strategy; but the substance of the job of sizing up what he has done to his students rests with him.

How shall he proceed?

Clarity of Goals

Obviously, the first step is for him to get a clear idea of what he is trying to have his students achieve. What operations does he want them to perform in June that they could not perform last September? This may be an "obvious" first step, but a look around the classrooms of the country suggests that it is a step rarely taken. Almost invariably teachers are more concerned with what *they* are going to do in their courses than with what their *students* are going to do. Lessons and lectures are outlined, reading lists are laid out, visual aids are planned, but few teachers give much concentrated attention to what the fuss is really all about from the standpoint of the student. If a syllabus is prepared, it almost never gives any detailed description of what students are supposed to be able to do as a result of having been exposed to the instructor and the subject matter. There is usually a hope that students will be impressed, that they will remember something, and in a vague sort of way it is felt that the course experiences will do them good, that is, make better thinkers or better citizens of them. But there is very little disposition to get down to brass tacks and specify what kinds of student performance are deemed to reflect better thinking or better citizenship.

All of which is hardly surprising. Setting the goals of a course in a highly concrete manner takes more energy and imagination than most teachers have time for. One of the very practical problems in developing a sound assessment program is to find the time needed to carry out this essential first step.

Generally speaking the goals of achievement fall into three broad classes:

informational goals, proficiency goals, and attitudinal goals. The informational goals refer to those items of information that students are expected to know and give forth on demand by the time they have completed a course. It would appear that these can be readily described simply by listing the topics, subtopics, and subsubtopics the course is expected to cover. But this is only half the story. A fact in human knowledge is not just the name of something standing all by itself; it is a subject and a predicate. It is not just the name "sodium"; it is the sentence, "Sodium is a metal." Progress toward the informational goals of a course, therefore, is measured by the number and complexity of these subject-predicate relationships which the student can reproduce. In making the informational goals useful as a basis for assessing achievement, some explicit attention must be given to these relationships and to their degree of complexity. It is not sufficient to list topics and subtopics and subsubtopics.

The large majority of teachers would disown the idea that the *only* kinds of goals they have in mind for their courses are informational goals. They would argue, and quite properly, that information is one of the goals, and a necessary one, but certainly not one of ultimate importance. This they argue, but their arguments are too often confounded by their own examinations, which demand facts and facts only. One of the hoariest criticisms brought against objective tests is that they test only for factual information, while essay tests get at the higher aspects of learning. This would be a cogent criticism except for two things: First, a well-made objective test need not be limited to the measurement of factual information; and second, essay tests are too frequently graded solely by counting the number of relevant facts that each student churns up.

Most of what we think of as "the higher aspects of learning" is contained in the proficiency goals of academic achievement, that is, proficiency in various kinds of skills, both manual and mental—manipulative skills, problem-solving skills, evaluative skills, and organizational skills. Taken together, they add up to effective thinking and sound execution. But to be useful as guides in the assessment of achievement, they must *not* be taken together; they must be elaborated in detail and expressed in terms of the multitude of different kinds of specific tasks a student is expected to perform and in terms of the specific kinds of operations he must follow in performing them.

Unless the proficiency goals are elaborated in this fashion, they may be too easily overlooked or forgotten. Back in the 1930's a number of experiments in the teaching of science led to the conclusion that science courses without laboratory instruction were just as effective as science courses with laboratory instruction. The typical setup was to divide science classes into two groups, one of which received laboratory work in addition to the regular course work and the other of which received no laboratory exercise. At the end of the course, the two groups would be compared by means of an achievement test in science. The differences in test scores between the two groups were generally negligible. Why? Because in setting up the tests, the proficiency goals peculiar to laboratory instruction had been overlooked. The only measures used had been measures related mainly to informational goals that have little or nothing to do with what goes on in a laboratory. Under these conditions, the finding of no difference in achievement between the two groups is essentially meaningless, since the relevant proficiency variables had not been taken into account. More recently Kruglak and his associates at Minnesota have taken a second look at this problem in science teaching, have devised tests aimed directly at the proficiency goals of laboratory instruction, and have come up with results of a more meaningful sort (7).

It is admittedly no easy matter to define all the proficiency goals in terms of student performance. One can flounder a long time over the types of performance that form the components of creative thinking, for instance, or skill in evaluative judgment. The result is that nobody has yet been able to produce a completely satisfactory and universally applicable method for assessing achievement in these areas. On the other hand, there have been some interesting attacks on the problem, and possibly in the course of time it may be solved (8, 10, 11). A giant step toward the solution will be made when teachers now uttering pious sentiments on the subject will get down to cases and try to define what they are really looking for when they speak of such things as "creative power" and "sensitivity to values."

Finally, there are the attitudinal goals—those educational objectives which are often blithely called the "intangibles." Everybody applauds them, but few teachers seem to know what to do about them. How does one define such goals as love of music or sense of social responsibility or enthusiasm for abstract ideas in such a way that they can be recognized when seen? What is it that a student does to demonstrate that he likes good literature? We have our dodges on matters of this sort: We count the books a student takes out of the library; we measure the amount of spare time he gives to good reading (provided, of course, we allow him any spare time at all); we engage him in conversation and try to judge from the fervor in his voice how far along the scale of appreciation his reading has brought him, or we ask him outright on some sort of rating schedule how well he likes Shakespeare and T. S. Eliot. But we suspect that these devices for uncovering attitudes are based on exceedingly tenuous inferences. Books may be taken out of the library not to be read, but to maintain an impressive-looking bookshelf. The time spent in reading may really be spent only in an effort to avoid reality. Conversational fervor may be only good acting or the effect of one cocktail too many. And a rating schedule can almost always be faked if much depends upon it.

I dislike to be discouraging in this all-important matter of attitudinal goals, but thus far very few operations have been suggested which define them satisfactorily. There are some breaks in the clouds, though. At Pennsylvania State University a group of experimenters has been trying to get a line on student attitudes toward television instruction. One device they have hit upon is to give the students generous samples of both TV instruction and conventional instruction, and then to permit them a genuine choice as to which type they would take for the remainder of the semester (*3*). This is a real operational definition of a specific attitude. It furnishes a fruitful clue for further development in defining attitudes in other areas, the general principle being that one defines attitudes in terms of his decisions that make an actual difference in what an individual will do or not do.

Measurements of Goals

Once the goals of instruction have been clearly set forth by describing the operations students have to perform to attain them, the problem of devising tests and other techniques for assessing academic achievement is at least 75 per cent solved. The reason is that an achievement test is in effect a sample of all the kinds of tasks that a given course of study is striving to get students to master. As such, the tests should in themselves constitute a definition of the goals to be attained. In putting together an appropriate sample of tasks and checking out their adequacy, there are technical matters in which the experienced tester may serve as a guide to the teacher. But, again, the questions of what to include or not to include, what is more important and what is less important, what constitutes a good response and what constitutes a poor response must in the last analysis be the teacher's decision if the test is to measure progress toward the goals *he* has in mind.

On the other hand, as mentioned above, teachers are busy people who are unlikely to find the time they need to do all that really should be done to work out the goals of their own instruction and to devise fully valid measures for assessing achievement. What are some of the practical compromises?

In the first place, although one is unlikely to find any published standardized test that in all respects fits the goals of a particular course or school, one may, by analyzing such tests question by question, possibly find one that comes reasonably close. Looking at a test, question by question, is important not only for determining a test's general suitability, but also for deciding what questions might properly be eliminated in assessing the performance of one's own students. Surprisingly, the notion of adapting a published test by dropping out irrelevant material seldom occurs to people, yet in many circumstances it is an obvious and justifiable procedure.

Standardized tests, when they can be found and adapted, have two important advantages for any program for assessing academic achievement. First, the makers of such tests have usually lavished a great deal of care on the preparation and tryout of each question to make sure that it is unambiguous, that it discriminates sharply between good and poor students, and that it is of the right level of difficulty for the group at which it is aimed. Second, two or more parallel forms of a standardized test are usually available, so that one has at his disposal the means for accomplishing a highly important part of the assessment job, that of measuring the student's performance twice—once at the beginning of the course and once again at the end.

Testing Thinking Ability

Until recently most standardized tests have concentrated rather heavily on the purely informational goals of instruction and have tended to neglect the proficiency goals. In the last few years, however, there has been a marked change in this respect. More and more tests are made up of questions that require the student to perform various mental operations well beyond the simple operation of recalling learned facts. They are getting at problem solving and reasoning processes of many kinds. Consider the following sets of questions drawn from a booklet describing the achievement tests of the College Entrance Examination Board (*1*). If the reader will take the trouble to wrestle with them, I think he will find that they challenge powers of thought well beyond simple memory, though they also require of the student a firm foundation of factual knowledge.

The first set of questions is intended to test the student's appreciation of those factors that must be controlled so that valid conclusions can be drawn from the results of a scientific experiment:

You are to conduct an experiment to determine whether the rate of photosynthesis in aquatic plants is affected by the addition of small amounts of carbon dioxide to the water in which the plants are growing. You have available all of the equipment and material generally found in a well-equipped science laboratory plus several well-rooted Elodea plants which are growing in a battery jar. It is evident that the plants are healthy because they are giving off bubbles of oxygen.

1. If the addition of carbon dioxide were to have an effect upon aquatic plants, almost immediately after bubbling the gas through the water you would expect to observe a noticeable change in the
   (A) growth of the plants
   (B) temperature of the plants
   (C) coloring of the plant leaves
   (D) rate of bubble production by the plant
   (E) amount of oxygen consumed by leaf respiration

2. If a carbon dioxide generator were not available for the experiment, an adequate supply of carbon dioxide might be provided by
   (A) placing a piece of carbon in the water in which the plants are growing
   (B) burning a candle over the battery jar
   (C) adding carbon tetrachloride to the water
   (D) pumping air into the water
   (E) blowing through a glass tube into the water

3. Which of the following materials would be *least* useful in identifying the escaping gas as oxygen?
   (A) A collection bottle (B) Glass tubing (C) A glass plate (D) Splints
   (E) Matches

4. Which of the following materials could be used to provide a source of carbon dioxide for this experiment?
   (A) Distilled water and carbon
   (B) Zince and carbonic acid
   (C) Limestone and hydrochloric acid
   (D) Limewater and carbon
   (E) Sodium hydroxide and carbon

5. The addition of carbon dioxide could have no observable effect upon the rate of bubbling by the Elodea plants if you had
   (A) previously turned off the light
   (B) no means of regulating the carbon dioxide flow
   (C) no means of regulating the room temperature
   (D) available water temperature
   (E) no cover on the battery jar

6. Before you could conclude whether or not the rate of photosynthesis in aquatic plants in general is affected by the addition of small amounts of carbon dioxide to the surrounding water, you would have to repeat the experiment using
   (A) all the materials of the original experiment
   (B) an entirely different set of materials
   (C) other aquatic plants
   (D) other Elodea plants
   (E) some terrestrial plants

The following set of questions attempts to test the student's knowledge and understanding of United States foreign policy:

SPEAKER I: I don't think the United States has any business getting involved in the affairs of other nations, through foreign aid or any thing else. We have prospered without aid from other countries. Why can't other nations do the same?

SPEAKER II: But we can't afford not to aid other nations. A foreign-aid program offers us a great opportunity to increase our prestige and we should take advantage of it. A nation which ignores other nations will not be regarded as important.

SPEAKER III: Maybe, but let's not forget the fact that foreign aid is also an investment in our own future. If we don't help other free nations, we can't expect to stay free ourselves.

SPEAKER IV: Let's be practical about this. If other nations are too weak to stand on their own two feet, we should help them, yes, but let's remember that when they become dependent on us we must also subordinate them to us. We can only justify foreign aid if we're going to protect our investment.

SPEAKER V: You're all so cold-blooded about this! It isn't a matter of practicality, but of moral obligation to aid other countries. If we could only renounce war, think of the money and material which would be available for constructive work.

1. A humanitarian point of view is best represented by Speaker (A) I (B) II (C) III (D) IV (E) V
2. Since the close of World War II, the United States has mainly justified its foreign-aid policy by arguments such as that advanced by Speaker (A) I (B) II (C) III (D) IV (E) V
3. Which speaker represents a point of view historically associated with the midwestern United States?
   (A) I (B) II (C) III (D) IV (E) V
4. Speaker IV would probably have approved of the
   1. Platt Amendment
   2. Roosevelt Corollary to the Monroe Doctrine
   3. Good Neighbor policy
   (A) 3 only
   (B) 1 and 2 only
   (C) 1 and 3 only
   (D) 2 and 3 only
   (E) 1, 2, and 3

Despite the progress that may have been made in developing standardized tests, one must always bear in mind that they can never do the whole job of assessing academic achievement in a particular situation. In the last analysis, if a teacher wants to measure those aspects of achievement peculiar to his own instruction he must resort to at least some tests of his own making. He can get some good ideas for approaching this enterprise from two books: *Taxonomy of Educational Objectives* (2) and *General Education: Explorations in Evaluation* (5). If one peruses these books looking for new testing ideas rather than faults, one may find much that is helpful in suggesting ways and means of measuring progress toward the goal of more effective thinking.

But the assessment of the student's growth in effective thinking is still not enough. Any teacher with a well-developed conscience is primarily concerned that his students shall acquire increasing maturity in their attitudes, that is, a more grown-up and informed approach to life and learning. The assessment of this aspect of achievement requires ingenuity and a willingness to experiment with tests that might be regarded as "off-beat."

Testing Maturity

Two such instruments may be mentioned as examples. One, called *The Facts About Science* (9), looks on the surface like an ordinary factual test aimed at seeing how much the student knows about scientists and the sorts of things they do. Actually, however, the pay-off response to each of the scored questions represents a false stereotype of the scientist or his work, e.g., "A scientist has no sense of humor." The test has been used to see to what extent high school courses in science influence students away from these false stereotypes. The same approach could be taken to get at student attitudes toward many other social institutions and enterprises.

Another instrument carries the title, *Sizing Up Your School Subjects* (6). It focuses on students' attitudes toward their current academic work and is especially designed for use in educational experiments where a given subject is being taught by two or more methods. Through an indirect approach, which almost certainly guarantees that the student will not fake his responses, it provides the means for comparing different courses or different methods of instruction in the same course with respect to the reactions of students to ten aspects of the material or the teaching. (E.g., What course is best at holding the student's attention? What course is regarded by the student as most valuable to him?) With a little imagination, the technique can be elaborated to cover the attitudes of students toward almost any feature of the academic work in which they are engaged.

Alternative Devices

One of the things that is holding back the development of new and better methods of assessing academic achievement, especially in the area of attitudes, is the tendency to think almost exclusively in terms of paper-and-pencil tests, particularly multiple-choice tests. Multiple-choice tests are useful up to a point. They can do more than most people realize in tapping a student's higher mental processes, and all the possibilities of multiple-choice questions have not yet been fully explored. Nevertheless, the multiple-choice test has, by its very nature, certain severe limitations. So do other forms of written tests, including essay tests.

To break out of this restricted mode of thinking we ought to consider how to exploit the possibilities in the so-called situational tests which psychologists have been working on in recent years. To what extent can such tests be adapted to the measurement of the "intangibles" of academic achievement? Situational tests are still highly experimental and full of technical problems, but they may well be the answer to the question of how to evaluate many of the subtle aspects of human behavior that can never be reached satisfactorily by paper-and-pencil devices.

One effort to apply a situational test in the classroom setting can be found in *The Russell Sage Social Relations Test* (4). On the surface, this is a test of the ability of a group of students to solve cooperatively a series of construction problems. It does in fact give a reasonably good measure of the group's effectiveness in this situation. If properly administered, however, it also yields information about other important aspects of group behavior: how well the students have learned to work together, how they respond to group control, how well they develop among themselves an efficient group organization, how they react on one another, and so on.

This sort of technique, and others like it, should eventually bring us closer to a truly adequate assessment of how students are attaining the attitudinal goals of instruction. Indeed, such techniques can do more. They can dramatize the importance of the goals by demonstrating how far we are falling short of achieving them. The development and application of good situational tests are expensive and time-consuming. Nevertheless, if we really wish to know what is happening to students in our classrooms, we are going to have to give up the notion that we can find out by relying on the "quick-and-dirty" tests that come cheap.

Assessment Is Central

Education these days has become a major concern of national policy. It is in consequence the center of a good deal of bitter controversy, and the issues being debated (segregation, the source of school support, teachers' salaries, federal or local control, "standards") are so overriding that the question of how to assess student achievement seems by comparison to be of minor technical importance. Actually, it ought to be regarded as of central importance to the whole educational enterprise. Until we can reduce our vast ignorance of what is actually happening to the minds and hearts of students in the classrooms, until we can point up the goals of education in terms of what we want students to *do* physically, mentally, spiritually, and until we have better ways of knowing how well we are getting them to do these things, there is hardly much point to all the fuss about the so-called "larger issues." A comprehensive program to develop better methods for assessing achievement in all the classrooms of the country would go a long way toward taking the heat out of the controversies now plaguing us and would furnish the means for replacing the anarchy in education with new vitality and a sense of direction.

References

1. *A description of the College Board Achievement Tests.* Princeton, N. J.: College Entrance Examination Board, 1960.

2. BLOOM, B. S. (Ed.). *Taxonomy of Educational Objectives.* New York, N. Y.: Longmans, Green and Co., 1956.

3. CARPENTER, C. R., and GREENHILL, L. P. *An Investigation of Closed Circuit Television for Teaching University Courses.* University Park, Pa.: The Pennsylvania State University, 1958, p. 77.

4. DAMRIN, D. E. The Russell Sage Social Relations Test: a technique for measuring group problem solving skills in elementary school children. *Journal of Experimental Education,* 1959, *28,* 85–99.

5. DRESSEL, P. L., and MAYHEW, L. B. *General Education: Explorations in Evaluation.* Washington, D. C.: American Council on Education, 1954.

6. DYER, H. S., and FERRIS, A. H. *Sizing Up Your School Subjects,* Princeton, N. J. Educational Testing Service, 1958.

7. KRUGLAK, H., and CARLSON, C. R. Performance tests in physics at the University of Minnesota. *Science Education,* 1953, 37:2, 108–121.

8. MACKINNON, D. W. The highly effective individual. *Teachers College Record,* 1960, *61,* 367–378.

9. STICE, G. *The Facts About Science Tests.* Princeton, N. J.: Educational Testing Service, 1958.

10. TAYLOR, C. W. (Ed.) *Research Conference on the Identification of Creative Scientific Talent.* Salt Lake City, Utah: University of Utah Press, 1956.

11. WILSON, R. C. Improving criteria for complex mental processes. *Proceedings of the 1957 Invitation Conference on Testing Problems.* Princeton, N. J.: Educational Testing Service, 1957.

51. Norms Must Be Relevant *

HAROLD G. SEASHORE, *Test Division, The Psychological Corporation,* AND JAMES H. RICKS, JR., *Test Division, The Psychological Corporation*

THE USUAL purpose of testing is to understand someone better—whether it be a child in school, a patient in a clinic, a youth planning his career, an applicant for a job, an employee being considered for promotion, a soldier being classified for special training, or an older person seeking help in adjusting to retirement. Usually, we wish to make predictions of future behavior. Two things are essential if testing is to contribute to understanding the individual: the test chosen must be *appropriate for the person and the purpose of the testing,* and we must know something about *how others have performed on the test.* Norms provide this second essential. Even if a test is appropriate, reliable, and valid, a score obtained from it is meaningless until it is compared with other scores.

Here we encounter another essential: not only must we have other scores for purposes of comparison, but these other scores—the norms—must be *relevant.* They will be meaningless or even misleading if they are not based on groups of people with whom it is sensible to compare the individuals we are counseling or considering for employment. Seems obvious, doesn't it? But, perhaps because it does seem so obvious, the relevance of norms often receives less attention than the number of cases or the way the norms are expressed.

This is going to be a discussion of relevance—a consideration of whether, and when, norms mean anything. We will assume throughout the rest of this argument that the number of cases in the normative group is large enough to assure stability, and that all the proper statistical requirements have been met. We will not worry about whether the norms are expressed as standard scores, percentiles, ratios, age or grade equivalents, or cut-off scores. The question is what kind of norms (provided they are appropriately computed and expressed and are stable) do we need in order to make intelligent use of somebody's test score.

Norms should yield meaning in terms of the particular purpose for which the testing is done. Because tests are given for a variety of reasons, a variety

* From *Test Service Bulletin* of The Psychological Corporation (May, 1950), No. 39, pp. 16–19. Reprinted by permission.

of kinds of norms is needed. Many of the persons we test should have their scores evaluated by comparison with several reference groups.

Suppose Sue has a score of 152 points on the *General Clerical Test*. She is a senior in a commercial high school finishing the secretarial course. Her advisor, fortunately, not only has available the norms tables in the 1950 edition of the manual for this test but also has accumulated (a) norms in her own school on the past three successive classes of girls finishing in the commercial department, (b) the same information for the secretarial course, and (c) the norms tables or cut-off scores for three local companies which recruit girls from this school. Let us look at Sue's "status" which she, her counselor, and a local employment manager desire to understand better.

1. In comparison with commercial high school senior girls in general, Sue's percentile rank is
   - (a) from the manual 85
   - (b) on local senior norms 75
2. In comparison with commercial high school senior girls finishing secretarial training, Sue's rank is
   - (a) from the manual 75
   - (b) on local norms 60
3. Sue's percentile rank can also be determined
   - (a) on firm X's *all-clerical-applicant* norms 60
   - (b) on firm X's *secretarial* applicant norms 32
4. Firm Y sets a critical score of 130 for all office workers and 150 for stenographic applicants.
5. Firm Z has set 175 points as its minimum score for considering a beginning stenographer.*

We shall not go into detail about how the counselor and employment officer would use these data, since the reader can readily appreciate the richness of interpretation which is made possible by having more than one set of norms. It is clear that a person's score may have many meanings.

Frequently test publishers encounter a desire for *norms based on the "general population."* It is an understandable desire. Testing without a clearly understood purpose in mind may or may not be forgivable; but in fact test users have been known to start with little more than a vague intention to help somebody toward success or to help themselves choose better workers. Having given the *Minnesota Clerical Test* to Bill, who is

---

* It should scarcely need stressing that besides *General Clerical Test* scores other factors (such as her stenographic proficiency) will enter into considering Sue's employability. Maybe Firm Z has to consider that she is a daughter of an important customer!

male, eighteen years old, a recent graduate from high school, and interested in becoming an accountant, they may be confused when faced with the necessity of deciding whether to use norms that compare him with others of his age, or those comparing him with his educational equals, or those representing employed accountants. So, down in the records goes Bill's percentile rank based on the general (or at least the male adult) population—probably the least useful of all the possible ratings that could have been assigned to him.

Historically, the concepts of mental age and intelligence quotient (and the related educational age and educational quotient) were based on an assumption of complete generality of the norms. World War I yielded Alpha and Beta norms on young-enlisted-men-in-general; in later use, the words "young soldier" were frequently read as simply "adult." When we find that Ned has an IQ of 110, we would like to read into that value a comparison of Ned with *all* children—at least with those of his age in our broad American culture. Nowadays, of course, sophisticated test users generally realize that even the best sampling available has failed to represent some groups— regional, racial, socioeconomic, or the like—in their proper proportions.

There are a few situations—primarily clinical ones—in which we really desire to compare Ned and Bill and Sue with children-in-general and Miss Zembro and Mr. Arnold with adults-in-general. The measurement of a person's abilities—particularly over-all general intelligence—in terms of national norms is sometimes desired. For instance, a broad and representative basis for comparison is needed for evaluating children suspected of a mental defect or for estimating reading readiness among kindergarten children. In surveys, national norms may be used to discover the status of a group (say eighth graders in a city) or to judge the educational success of the community in training their youngsters.

However, there is a serious limitation to the use of such national norms in counseling and personnel work. It helps little to know that Sue's score on a clerical test places her at the 63rd percentile on some people-in-general norms. We are not counseling her in general or employing her in general. We need at least the specificity of norms which will permit us to interpret her score in terms of high school graduates and in terms of women only, because the labor market she is entering consists mainly of high school graduates and because we know that she will be competing for a job with women (who, as a group, excel men in most clerical tasks).

Legitimate and illegitimate general norms abound in current test manuals. People-in-general norms are legitimate only if they are based upon careful field studies with appropriate controls of regional, socioeconomic, educational, and other factors—and even then only if the sampling is carefully described so that the test user may be fully aware of its inevitable limitations and deficiencies. The millions entering the armed forces during World War II provided the basis for some fairly good norms on young adult men, though mainly on tests not available to the public. The standardization of the *Wechsler Intelligence Scale for Children* is a recent attempt to secure a representative smaller sample of children aged 5 to 15 for setting up tables of intelligence quotients which may be considered generalized norms for children. The earlier work of Terman's group to set up good national norms on a small, well-chosen sample is well known. In the standardizing of some educational achievement tests, nation-wide samplings of children of each appropriate grade or age and from different types of schools in all parts of the country are sought in an effort to produce norms that are truly general for a given span of grades or ages.

Unfortunately, many alleged general norms reported in test manuals are not backed even by an honest effort to secure representative samples of people-in-general. Even tens or hundreds of thousands of cases can fall woefully short of defining people-in-general. Inspection of test manuals will show (or would show if information about the norms were given completely) that many such massed norms are merely collections of all the scores that opportunity has permitted the author or publisher to gather easily. Lumping together all the samples secured more by chance than by plan makes for impressively large numbers; but while seeming to simplify interpretation, the norms may dim or actually distort the counseling, employment, or diagnostic significance of a score.

With or without a plan, everyone of course obtains data where and how he can. Since the standardization of a test is always dependent on the cooperation of educators, psychologists and personnel men, the foregoing comments are not a plea for the rejection of available samples but for their correct labeling. If a manual shows "general" norms for a vocabulary test based on a sample two-thirds of which consists of women office workers, one can properly raise his testwise eyebrows. There is no reason to accept such norms as a good generalization of adult—or even of employed-adult —vocabulary. It is better to set up norms on the occupationally homogeneous two-thirds of the group and frankly call them norms on female office workers. Adding a few more miscellaneous cases does not make the sample a truly general one.

As a rule, then, in reading a test manual we should reject as treacherous any alleged national or general norms whose generality is not supported by a clear, complete report on the sample of people they represent, or norms which are obviously opportunistic accumulations of samples weighted by their size according to chance rather than logic. *Look for the evidence!*

The dilemma of the test publisher is acute. It is difficult to provide genuinely general norms when these are desirable, and it is impossible to supply all the detailed norms that would be useful.

If the author and the publisher decide that general or national norms are appropriate, they must accept the responsibility of obtaining scores from representative groups and of combining the groups in accordance with a plan that makes sense when compared with census data. No less a responsibility is the reporting in detail of the sources of the data and the rationale of any adjustments that may have been made. If they cannot do this, or choose not to, the limitations of the norms must be properly described. Attempts to hodgepodge handy data into one mass normative table merit severe criticism.

Bpt suppose the publisher and author agree that they have no truly national norms and furthermore do not believe them useful for the test in question. What choices do they then have? The *number* and the *variety* of less-than-general groups are crushing. In theory, norms should be collected for every meaningful subgroup of the population against which any individual's test scores might be compared. Ideally, the *General Clerical Test* (for example) should have tables of norms for many educational levels, experience levels, age levels, fields of clerical work, and for various combinations of these. Furthermore, there should be regional norms, state norms perhaps, local community norms, and finally, specific norms for each firm and school using the test. No one would need all of these but someone would find use for each of them! Eventually it may be hoped that we will even have norms for test scores earned in adolescence by persons grouped according to the job in which they succeeded as adults.

The test user probably never will have at hand all the varieties of norms he really wants and needs. Even the most excellent test manuals do not present enough tables of norms, although those included in the better manuals are well-documented and very useful. What then is the solution of the test author's and publisher's dilemma? How can the test user help himself? By way of summary, let us try to formulate a few principles which can serve as practical guides.

1. *Avoid unjustified "general" norms.* Undocumented, people-in-general norms should not be presented because there is no cogent reason for collecting, publishing or using them.

2. *Define national norms.* So-called national norms on tests should be carefully expressed as generalizations for important and sensemaking subgroups, such as the grade groups on the *Metropolitan Achievement* or the *Differential Aptitude Tests,* or the age groups on the *Wechsler Intelligence Scale for Children.* In the case of national or regional norms especially is it

essential that the sampling procedure be described in sufficient detail for understanding and evaluation by others.

3. *Combine populations with care, and only when the resulting group has definite meaning.* Lumping several groups is as logical, in some instances, as presenting them separately. For example, in the 1950 revision of the *General Clerical Test* Manual all of the samples of *female applicants for office work* were lumped (after being presented separately). The publisher sought data wherever they might be found rather than by plan, but the grouping seemed sensible in order to provide a starting basis for users who have not yet established local norms. As in the case of national norms, it is absolutely essential that the original groups entering such a composite norms table be described and that the reasons which justify combining them be stated plainly. At all times, the distortion that results from merging incongruous data into improperly weighted larger groupings (usually done only in order to make the number of cases look more impressive) should be avoided.

4. *Report all the genuinely useful data available.* Lacking data on the enormous variety of educational, occupational, or clinical groups which would be needed to provide *all* the possible sets of norms, authors and publishers must of course present what data they have available. It would have been unfortunate if failure to cover *all* trades and professions had prevented E. K. Strong, Jr., from providing us with the scoring scales that he was able to develop for his *Vocational Interest Blank.* There is a healthy trend in manuals such as those for the *Bennett Mechanical Comprehension Test Form AA,* the *Wesman Personnel Classification Test,* the *Kuder Preference Record,* and others, to present percentile equivalents or other norms for a dozen or more described groups. Small and ill-defined groups should be omitted from the standardization tables and reported only if they are of very special interest for some reason.

5. *Accumulate and use local and special-group norms.* Local norms should be constructed by the user for appropriate groupings of cases. This is of great importance, both for personnel selection tests used by a firm and for tests used in educational and vocational counseling. It may be necessary to begin by using reasonably appropriate norms published in the test manual, but local norms should be prepared as soon as a hundred or more cases have been accumulated and should be revised from time to time as the testing program continues and additional data become available. While published percentile or standard score norms may provide a temporary starting point, cut-off scores for hiring purposes should be established *only* on the basis of specific local experience and not merely taken from published reports.

6. *Feed local and special norms back to help build the body of knowledge available to test users.* Better norms can be made available in test manuals only if psychologists, educators, counselors, and personnel men accept a responsibility almost as demanding as the responsibility of the author and publisher. Tests are useful to us because of the work that others have already invested in them; we can repay this debt by contributing our own experience to the common treasury of normative and other data. This may be accomplished by articles in professional journals, or simply by sending the data to the publisher for inclusion in revisions of test manuals. If anyone is uncertain as to the appropriate methods of collecting data so that they will be useful to others as well as in his own daily work, The Psychological Corporation on request will gladly suggest recording and reporting methods.

No meaningful information can emerge from testing Sue, Bill, Ned, Miss Zembro or Mr. Arnold unless we can evaluate their raw scores by means of norms which are relevant to our reasons for testing these individuals in the first place. Our better understanding of an individual through tests depends, then, largely upon our having diverse and well-defined sets of norms. Such accumulation of norms is a duty of authors and publishers. And the thousands of test administrators hold a key position in developing these more useful and interpretable bases for comparing test performances.—

INDEX

Index